FUNDAMENTALS OF
MANAGEMENT

SEVENTH EDITION

JAMES H. DONNELLY, JR.

Turner Professor
College of Business and Economics
University of Kentucky

JAMES L. GIBSON

Kincaid Professor
College of Business and Economics
University of Kentucky

JOHN M. IVANCEVICH

Hugh Roy and Lillie Cranz Cullen Chair and
Professor of Organizational Behavior and Management
University of Houston

**BPI
IRWIN**

Homewood, IL 60430
Boston, MA 02116

Associate Publisher   Martin F. Hanifin
Developmental editor   Kama Brockmann
Project editor   Jean Roberts
Production manager   Bette K. Ittersagen
Interior designer   John Rokusek
Cover designer   John Rokusek/Keith J. McPherson
Cover illustration   Cheryl Winser
Artist   Benoit Design
Photo researcher   Judith Lucas
Compositor   Carlisle Communications, Ltd.
Typeface   10/12 Bembo
Printer   Von Hoffmann Press, Inc.

Library of Congress Cataloging-in-Publication Data
Donnelly, James H.
    Fundamentals of management / James H. Donnelly, Jr., James L.
Gibson, John M. Ivancevich.—7th ed.
        p.   cm.
    Includes bibliographical references.
    ISBN 0-256-07846-7
    1. Management.   I. Gibson, James L.   II. Ivancevich, John M.
III. Title.
HD31.D594 1990   89–17645
658—dc20   CIP

Printed in the United States of America
1 2 3 4 5 6 7 8 9 0 VH 7 6 5 4 3 2 1 0

FUNDAMENTALS OF

MANAGEMENT

to
Helene S. Donnelly, Jeanne M. Servais
Dianne Gibson
Anne, Mike, and Pegi Ivancevich

PREFACE

As authors, we are proud to introduce the 20th anniversary edition of *Fundamentals of Management*. On every dimension we continue to be gratified by the recognition of our efforts:

- *Fundamentals of Management* has been identified by management faculty as one of the best management textbooks in the country. It is particularly rewarding for us to know that our book "has changed the way the introductory management course is taught."
- The supplementary resources that accompany our text have been rated the best available.

Apparently, recognition serves as an incentive to each of us to continue to improve our book. *Every revision of* Fundamentals of Management *is a major revision and this edition is no exception.* We believe our constant attention to updating, revising, and restructuring has been an important part of the success of the book. The present edition bears no resemblance to the first; however, the rationale remains the same as for previous editions. Management, we believe, will be practiced best by individuals who have had access to high-quality, challenging management textbooks.

To be effective, a textbook must serve two groups well: (1) those who teach the course and (2) those who take the course.

Pledge to management faculty.   A textbook of high quality will never compromise the integrity of the field it explores. We pledge to provide a text which in every respect is a quality work of management scholarship that we as academicians can be proud of.

Pledge to management students.   A textbook of high quality never loses sight of its ultimate purpose—to help students learn. We pledge to always strive to make our textbook the most contemporary, comprehensive, challenging, readable, and exciting management textbook available in America today.

THE DEVELOPMENT OF THIS EDITION

As with previous editions, developing this edition required extensive market research, interviews with adopters and nonadopters, extensive and comprehensive reviews by a group of commissioned faculty, as well as class testing. The vast amount of information gleaned from this process enabled us to determine which features of the book were most effective and to revise or alter those which needed more work. In addition, a new feature of this edition required photo researchers who worked closely with us to select illustrations that would effectively reinforce the text narrative.

The research resulted in several important changes and additions. The chapter on ethics and social responsibility was moved from Part V to Part I. A new chapter on entrepreneurship was added to Part V. The chapter on international management was completely revised. However, because of the importance of these topics—ethics, entrepreneurship, and the international environment—chapter opening vignettes and chapter inserts were revised to include consideration of these important topics. Whenever possible, these elements now reinforce the relevance of the subject of the chapter to small business or the international environment, or identify an ethical dimension.

In the previous edition we used three "Foundations" sections to introduce the three core sections of the book: managing work and organizations, managing people, and managing production and operations. They served as brief reviews of the historical roots of the particular management problem and/or the literature that first focused on the problem.

In this edition these Foundations sections are much more. Each section has been substantially rewritten to reinforce its relevance to management today. For example, in "Foundations of Managing Work and Organizations," we compare some "principles" of management in 1926 with some from today. Also, we have added a new introductory section for Part V. These sections have been well received by instructors because of the flexibility they provide. They can be used or omitted depending on the needs of the course. Students like them because they provide a sense of where the text has been and is going.

Finally, important new topics have been added that reflect the fluid nature of modern management. As a result, several chapters have been revised to such an extent that they, too, can be considered new.

OUR STANDARDS FOR A HIGH-QUALITY TEXTBOOK

We believe that a high-quality management textbook should possess several key characteristics. It should be comprehensive, systematic, scientific, practical—and exciting.

Comprehensive. This text is comprehensive because it covers the major management topics affecting students, teachers, and practitioners. Research has indicated that our book is being used to cover American Assembly of Collegiate Schools of Business (AACSB) common body of knowledge requirements for both Organizational Behavior/Organization Theory and Production/Operations Management. The materials selected for this book reflect our contacts with teaching colleagues, students, practicing managers, accrediting agencies such as AACSB, and professional societies such as the Academy of Management and the American Management Association.

Systematic. In studying management, a beginning student can easily be overwhelmed by the vast number of concepts, theories, and topics. The systematic approach of *Fundamentals of Management* helps overcome this tendency. In each chapter's subject matter, readers are able to see where they have been, where they are, and where they will be going.

This book is divided into five parts. And each part is structured around three fundamental managerial tasks common to all organizations: managing work and organizations, managing people, and managing production and operations.

Scientific.   *Fundamentals of Management* presents concepts and theories that have been subjected to extensive research. However, our textbook does not attempt to teach social or behavioral science, or operations management. It provides bases for applying to management many relevant contributions from numerous scientific disciplines. In this edition, every chapter has been revised to include the most up-to-date thinking and research.

Practical.   To become an effective manager, a student must learn to analyze management problems and then solve them by applying relevant management theory. *Fundamentals of Management* stresses a practical approach to learning these vital skills. Subject matter is reinforced with descriptions of how actual managers in real organizations have applied the concepts to solve problems. In addition, 69 case applications and experiential exercises bring the chapter material to life in real-world situations.

Exciting.   The practice of management is exciting, and a management textbook should be too. We try to convey this excitement to our readers. Every chapter, except for the opening one, begins with an account of an organization or individual manager facing a particular management problem or real-life situation that will be discussed in the following pages. In addition, each chapter contains at least three contemporary examples of real-world applications of concepts discussed in the chapter. Important points are illustrated and summarized in each chapter.

An Emphasis on Learning

In addition to the features retained and updated from previous editions, several new features that encourage learning have been recently added.

Learning Objectives.   Clear, attainable goals are spelled out at the start of each chapter. In each chapter, the student learns to define, describe, discuss, compare, and identify essential issues affecting modern management.

Management in Action.   To arouse reader interest, we have added all new and more exciting chapter-opening vignettes taken from real-life situations to orient students to concepts and problems discussed in the text.

People in Management.   To demonstrate how managers of leading companies apply management principles in their long-term strategies and everyday management style, we've profiled four managers. These featured profiles appear at the end of the part openers for Parts II, III, IV, and V.

Photographs, Figures, and Tables. Important points are illustrated with well-crafted visuals, including key concepts to reiterate essential material.

Management Focus. A series of all new, timely, real-life examples is drawn from over 60 of America's organizations, large and small. These examples illustrate problems modern managers confront daily, and they appear at exact points in the discussion where the concept or theory is being discussed.

Cases. Throughout the text, cases have either been added and/or updated.

End of Chapter. There are now a total of 42 cases. New ones have been added to this edition, and old ones have been updated and revised. These cases feature familiar organizations and current issues to show practical applications of concepts in the chapters.

End of Part. Comprehensive real-world cases appear at the end of Part II, "Managing Work and Organizations," Part III, "Managing People," and Part IV, "Managing Production and Operations." Analysis of these cases requires comprehension of relevant aspects of the entire part.

End of Text. The book concludes with two issue-oriented integrative cases. The cases tie together all relevant aspects of all chapters.

Summary of Key Points. Every chapter concludes with a concise, point-by-point summary of key topics.

Discussion and Review Questions. Every chapter concludes with relevant questions addressing the major issues explored.

Additional References. Every chapter concludes with additional references to give students initial sources for writing projects. Except for classic works, these references have been totally updated for all chapters and include the latest available work.

Glossary. Every key term in the book is included in an extensive glossary.

Indexes. To help students locate information, the book contains three indexes: a comprehensive name index, a detailed subject index, and a company index that is used to relate concepts to actual firms discussed in the chapters.

Experiential Exercises. Experiential exercises are included at the end of each chapter. We included these learning methods in the previous edition, we received positive reactions to these exercises, and new ones have been added here. They move the material from "seeing" and "listening" to "doing." The understanding of management concepts is greatly enhanced when students can actively join in the learning process. More and more contemporary students seek out courses that include opportunities to learn from experience.

Support for Instructors and Students

We are fortunate to have a complete coordinated and integrated system of support for both teacher and student. As mentioned earlier, the supplementary materials available with *Fundamentals of Management* have been rated the best available. Our goal was to make them even better for the present edition.

Supporting for Instructors

Lecture Resource Manual. We believe that even the most experienced and dedicated teacher will find useful hints and insightful ideas in this unique guide. From a pedagogical perspective, we believe this is the real strength of our instructional support system. We encourage those interested in teaching management to examine this element of the system because we believe there is nothing available that approaches its quality and innovativeness. Over 150 sources were used to develop the material. A special feature of the guide provides a series on two topics that are particularly relevant to management today: Groupthink and Career Issues.

Instructor's Manual. Far more than the traditional instructor's manual, ours is organized to follow each chapter in the text and includes: chapter objectives, chapter synopsis, chapter outline with tips and ideas, suggested films to supplement class discussion, 10 additional end-of-chapter questions along with answers per chapter, exciting "mindbenders" that can be used for class discussion, suggested transparencies, term paper topics, end-of-chapter practical exercises, additional experiential exercises, transparency masters, and suggested class projects and speakers. It is a complete manual in every respect.

Transparencies. A complete set of high-quality, four-color transparencies has been developed specifically for our instructional support system. These transparencies are a separate element in addition to the transparency masters of text illustrations included in the Instructor's Manual, and the additional ones included in the Lecture Resource Manual.

Test Bank. This examination resource contains a wide variety of materials such as true/false, multiple-choice, and essay questions. Items are categorized by type of question.

Automated Test Service. A complete, high-quality testing service is provided.

A Management Experience. This PC-compatible management game is both exciting and challenging. It was designed specifically as an element for *Fundamentals of Management* to provide management students with a truly interactive learning experience.

Support for Students

Study Guide. This innovative supplement is far more than a review for students. It includes articles from *The Wall Street Journal* related to each chapter, experiential exercises, and a reference guide showing how to write to key people in corporations and other organizations. It is truly instructional support for students. Also included is standard fare for such supplements: chapter previews; key terms; chapter outlines; study questions, including true/false, multiple-choice, short answer, and discussion questions. We have found that because of the innovative content of the guide, many instructors use it as an active part of the class rather than as something students use alone to help them prepare for examinations. In fact, many instructors have commented that it is as much a workbook or "practice set" as it is a study guide.

ACKNOWLEDGMENTS

A 20th anniversary is a great opportunity to thank all of those who have contributed in some way to the success of *Fundamentals of Management*. There are scores of adopters who have made important suggestions over the years which have substantially improved the book. In addition, we want to publicly thank and acknowledge the contributions of reviewers of previous editions and of the present edition. Their ideas and suggestions are reflected throughout our book, and they have contributed much to its success.

REVIEWERS OF PREVIOUS EDITIONS

Nick Blanchard
Eastern Michigan University

Mauritz Blonder
Hofstra University

Arthur H. Boisselle
El Paso Community College

Lyle Brenna
El Paso Community College

Sonya Brett
Macomb County Community College

Donald R. Burke
Villanova University

Douglas D. Cantrell
Eastern Michigan University

Bernard C. Dill
Bloomsburg State University

Frank Flaumenhaft
University of New Haven

David Gray
University of Texas at Arlington

Stan Guzell
Youngstown State University

A. Thomas Hollingsworth
University of South Carolina

Milton Holmen
University of Southern California

Fred C. House
Northern Arizona University

W. Dow Hoyt
San Bernadino Valley College

Carolyn Jacobson
Ohio University

Elias Kalman
Baruch College of the City University of New York

Jack Kappeler
Platte Tech Community College

John E. Kinney, Jr.
Chabot College

Eric A. Larson
Onondaga Community College

Wendell H. McCulloch
California State University at Long Beach

John Mee
Indiana University

Robert Miller
Upjohn Research Corporation

Jan Muczyk
Cleveland State University

James R. Necessary
Ball State University

Donald D. Nelson
College of DuPage

M. Gene Newport
University of Alabama in Birmingham

James G. Pesek
Clarion State College

Charles K. Phillips
Stephen F. Austin University

Jon Pierce
University of Minnesota

Lawrence Podell
William Patterson College

William Ryan
Indiana University

Robert L. Trewatha
Southwest Missouri State University

Irwin Weinstock
California State University at Fresno

Martin W. Wensman
Cerritos College

REVIEWERS OF THE PRESENT EDITION

Debra R. Comer
Hofstra University

Deborah F. Crown
University of Colorado—Boulder

Helen Deresky
SUNY—Plattsburgh

Sam Doctors
California State University

Pamela S. Lewis
University of Central Florida

Mary S. Thibodeaux
University of North Texas

John J. Vitton
University of North Dakota

REVIEWERS OF TESTBANK

Charles Flaherty
University of Minnesota

Lindle Hatton
University of Wisconsin—Oshkosh

Our thanks also go to Elizabeth Rubenstein for contributing the "People in Management" profiles.

We owe all of these people a great intellectual debt because they have helped make the last 20 years intellectually fulfilling to each of us. And we believe that together we have provided you with the seventh edition of an educationally rigorous but very readable management textbook.

James H. Donnelly, Jr.
James L. Gibson
John M. Ivancevich

CONTENTS

3

MANAGEMENT IN ACTION:

SOCIAL AND ETHICAL RESPONSIBILITIES OF MANAGEMENT **62**

Cleveland, Ohio: Business to the Rescue 64

PART II   MANAGING WORK AND ORGANIZATIONS

5

8

THE CONTROLLING FUNCTION **222**

MANAGEMENT IN ACTION:

PART III MANAGING PEOPLE

12

13   COMMUNICATION 418

PART IV   MANAGING PRODUCTION AND OPERATIONS

PART V   EMERGING MANAGEMENT ISSUES

22

MANAGEMENT IN ACTION:

FUNDAMENTALS OF
MANAGEMENT

PART

I

MANAGEMENT AND THE MANAGERIAL ENVIRONMENT

1

MANAGERS AND THE STUDY OF MANAGEMENT

LEARNING OBJECTIVES

After completing Chapter 1, you should be able to:

Define
the terms *manager* and *management*.

Describe
the evolution of management as a field of study.

Discuss
why the study of management can be important to almost anyone.

Compare
the three approaches to management.

Identify
the work of management.

Participative management. Quality assurance. Customer service programs. New technology implementation. Just-in-time production systems. Reward programs. Organizational change techniques. All of these approaches have one thing in common: they must be managed. The United States is at a crossroads because of the erosion of its competitiveness. And traditional approaches that worked yesterday or that have not been modified to fit the situation are proving inadequate. Although still having the largest and one of the richest economies, the United States has begun to slip compared to other countries. One reason often cited for the slippage is poor management. If erosion of competitiveness is a problem of management,[1] then managing these and other approaches that we will discuss throughout this book becomes mandatory.

Management is the process undertaken by one or more individuals to coordinate the activities of others to achieve results not achievable by one individual acting alone. Peter Drucker believes that the work of management is to make people productive. To regain our competitive edge in the international arena, society must have managerial competence. Drucker states, "Management, its competence, its integrity and its performance will be decisive both to the United States and to the free world in the decades ahead."[2]

Another view of management is presented in the popular best-seller, *In Search of Excellence,* where Peters and Waterman state:

> There is good news from America. Good management practice today is not resident only in Japan. But, more important, the good news comes from treating people decently and asking them to share, and from producing things that work. . . . Even management's job becomes more fun. Instead of brain games in the sterile ivory tower, it's shaping values and reinforcing through coaching and evangelism in the field—with workers and in support of the cherished product.[3]

Well, who is correct, Drucker or Peters and Waterman? Perhaps both. Drucker's view emphasizes performance, quality, and service. On the other hand, Peters and Waterman emphasize mentorship, a love for managing and working with people; they are glib communicators and "value shapers," lightning rods to get the job done.

There is room for these two and many other views of management. If you learn only one thing as you begin your journey through the subject of management and managing, it is that effective managers do intend to make their employees productive and they also have the ability to inspire people.[4]

WHY STUDY MANAGEMENT?

Learning about management is important for two reasons. First, our society depends on specialized institutions and organizations to provide the goods and services we desire. These organizations are guided and directed by the

[1]Robert Levering, *A Great Place to Work* (New York: Random House, 1988).

[2]Ibid., p. 108.

[3]Tom Peters and Robert H. Waterman, Jr., *In Search of Excellence* (New York: Harper & Row, 1982), p. xxiii.

[4]Anthony P. Carnevale, Leila J. Gainer, and Ann S. Meltzer, *Workplace Basics: The Skills Employers Want* (Alexandria, Va.: American Society for Training and Development, 1989).

To successfully compete in the international arena, or "global village," managers must foster a work environment that encourages worker efficiency, innovativeness, and creativity.

decisions of one or more individuals designated as "managers." It is America's managers who allocate society's resources to various and often competing ends. Managers have the authority and responsibility to build safe or unsafe products, seek war or peace, build or destroy cities, clean up or pollute the environment. Managers establish the conditions under which we are provided jobs, incomes, lifestyles, products, services, protection, health care, and knowledge. It would be very difficult to find anyone who is neither a manager nor affected by the decisions of a manager.

Second, individuals not trained as managers often find themselves in managerial positions. Many individuals presently being trained to be teachers, accountants, musicians, salespersons, artists, physicians, or lawyers will one day earn their living as managers. They will manage schools, accounting firms, orchestras, sales organizations, museums, hospitals, and government agencies. The United States is an organizational society, and its organizations must have managers.

The future success of the United States in the international arena, or "global village," lies in managing productivity, being able to cope with environmental changes, and properly managing the work force.[5] Because it cannot match the wage rates of Mexico, Taiwan, or Malaysia, America must match competitors in the ability to manage and to create a work environment that encourages worker efficiency, innovativeness, and creativity.

THE EVOLUTION OF MANAGEMENT AS A FIELD OF STUDY

Because the growth in the number and size of organizations is relatively new in history, the study of management is relatively new. Many of the first

[5]Martin K. Starr, ed., *Global Competitiveness* (New York: W. W. Norton, 1989).

individuals to study and write about management were practicing managers. They described their own experiences and tried to generalize the principles they believed could be applied in similar situations. Even today, a great deal of what we know about management comes from the autobiographies and memoirs of men and women who are or have been practicing managers.

Now, however, other individuals also are interested in management for scientific reasons. Social and behavioral scientists view the management of organizations as an extremely important social phenomenon worthy of study through scientific inquiry. As scientists, these men and women make no value judgments regarding good or bad management practices. Their objective is to understand and explain the practice of management.

Between the two extremes of management practice and management science are many individuals who have contributed to the study of management. They include engineers, sociologists, psychologists, anthropologists, lawyers, economists, accountants, mathematicians, political scientists, and philosophers.

Such differing perspectives on the same subject cannot be neatly classified. Thus, as a manager, you will have at your disposal many ways of looking at management's tasks. Each may be more useful for some problems than for others. For example, a management theory that emphasizes employee satisfaction may be more helpful in dealing with a problem of high employee turnover than with delays in production. Because there is no single, universally accepted management approach, you should be familiar with the various major theories.

There are three well-established theories of management thought: the **classical approach,** the **behavioral approach,** and the **management science approach.** Although these approaches evolved in historical sequence, later ideas have not always replaced earlier ones. Rather, each new approach has added to the knowledge of the previous ones. At the same time, each approach has continued to develop on its own. And at last, some merging did occur as later theorists attempted to integrate the accumulated knowledge. Two of these attempts to integrate theories—the **systems approach** and the **contingency approach**—will be discussed later in this section.

An interesting lesson of how management history of yesteryear still applies to situations facing managers today involves a book on Attila the Hun, a king who united the Huns, a Mongoloid tribe that invaded the Roman Empire. Ross Perot had recently joined the board of General Motors after GM acquired his Electronic Data Systems for nearly $2.6 billion. To inspire GM's Saturn automobile team, Perot handed out 500 copies of the book about Attila to subordinates.[6] History has portrayed Attila the Hun as "the scourge of God" who ravaged civilized Europe. However, Attila's principles of managing and leading are still of use and are applied today. He was an entrepreneur, diplomat, statesman, motivator, planner, and brilliant strategic implementor. Some of Attila's secrets of successful leadership are:

■ Committed leaders are distinguished by their wisdom, sincerity, authority, and courage.
■ A person can't lead without having the trust and respect of followers.

[6]Wess Roberts, *Leadership Secrets of Attila the Hun* (New York: Warner, 1987).

- You avoid doing stupid things by listening. Listen to your people, to your enemies, and to friends.
- Encourage creativity, freedom of action, and innovation consistent with the goals of the tribe or nation.
- Provide direction to the Huns, never letting them wander aimlessly.
- Never delegate responsibilities that require your direct attention.
- Never reward a Hun for doing less than is expected of him.
- Grant small rewards for light tasks, reserving heaps of booty for dangerous efforts and worthy feats.
- Honor all commitments you make during negotiations.

It's a rare manager who wants to be identified with Attila. But after reading the book, Perot, Robert Crandell [chief executive officer (CEO) of AMR Corporation], Norman Augustine (CEO of Martin Marietta), and James Patterson (CEO of J. Walter Thompson) all found lessons and models for today's manager.[7] The lessons of history are still as powerful today as they were during Attila's reign around 440 A.D. Similarly, the lessons and practices of various approaches to management still have application value and managerial implications, as will be shown throughout the book.

THE CLASSICAL APPROACH: MANAGING WORK AND ORGANIZATIONS

The classical approach was the first attempt to study modern management. Today, it remains a core knowledge area of the modern manager. Management began to be studied seriously at the beginning of this century. Managers were seeking answers to basic, practical questions, such as how to increase the efficiency and productivity of a rapidly expanding work force. The technological insights of engineers became increasingly significant as leaders of business sought to expand the productivity of workers during World War I. These efforts led to an extensive body of knowledge concerning plant design, job design, work methods, and other aspects of the *management of work*.

At about the same time, many small, single-product companies were expanding into large, multiproduct organizations. The individuals who managed these organizations recognized that the *management of organizations* was quite different from the management of work. Thus, men and women began to study the problems of managing large, complex organizations. They viewed management much as it is viewed in this book: as the process of coordinating group effort toward group goals. It was in this period that *planning, organizing,* and *controlling* were identified as the functions that make up the management process. Let us briefly examine each management function.

Planning.   The planning function helps an organization define and meet its objectives. Managers, through their plans, outline what an organization must do to be successful. One example of a par excellence planner is Don McCulloch, the 43-year-old owner of the weight-loss company Nutri/System, Inc.[8] He be-

---

[7]"The Scourge of God," *Success,* March 1989, pp. 52–55.

[8]Christy Marshall, "Turnaround King," *Success,* February 1989, pp. 40–43.

A manager frequently reminds his or her management team of the company's goals and how well those goals are being achieved.

lieves that planning must be simple and repeated again and again. His plan for Nutri/System has five points: (1) take financial control; (2) build enthusiasm with the management team; (3) use innovative marketing; (4) upgrade operations and training procedures; and (5) restructure the system and close down failing operations. The key to planning success is to constantly remind the management team of the company's goals and how well those goals are being achieved.

Organizing.   After establishing objectives and drawing up plans to achieve them, managers must design and develop an organization able to achieve their goals. Organizing means turning plans into action with the help of leadership and motivation.

Less complicated, more productive organizational structures have become the rule. Why? Because again and again in the marketplace, the less complicated firms such as Nucor, Digital Computers, Federal Express, and Honda outperform the more complicated, rigidly organized competition at U.S. Steel, IBM, the U.S. Postal Service, and General Motors. It is now apparent that overly centralized, excessively layered (too many levels of managers), and rigid organizational structures are not always effective or efficient.

Controlling.   A manager must make sure the actual performance of the organization conforms to the performance planned for the organization.

Control will play a major role in the Soviet Union as the Russians use *perestroika* and *glasnost* to turn their economy around. Soviet managers must ensure that quality of production becomes a top priority. They must implement control systems so that better-quality products become available for Soviet citizens and international trade.

The important contributions of the classical approach will be covered in greater detail in Part II of the book.

The management science approach focuses on the technical issues in managing operations.

THE BEHAVIORAL APPROACH: MANAGING PEOPLE

The behavioral approach developed partly because practicing managers found that the ideas of the classical approach did not always achieve total efficiency and workplace harmony. Managers encountered problems because subordinates did not always behave as the classical approach said they were supposed to. Thus, increased interest developed in helping managers become more effective at *managing people*. The behavioral approach uses the concepts of psychology, sociology, anthropology, and other behavioral sciences to assist managers in understanding human behavior in the work environment. The emphasis of the behavioral approach focuses on the interrelationships between people, work, and organizations. It concentrates on such topics as motivation, communications, leadership, and work group formation, which can assist managers with the people aspects of their job.

The important contributions of the behavioral approach will be covered in greater detail in Part III of the book.

THE MANAGEMENT SCIENCE APPROACH: MANAGING PRODUCTION AND OPERATIONS

In one sense, the management science approach is a modern version of the early emphasis on the management of work by the classical approach. Its essential feature is the use of mathematics and statistics as aids in *managing production and operations*. Its management literature focuses on solving technical rather than behavioral problems. It concentrates on concepts and tools useful to managers in solving problems related to what the organization produces. The computer contributed greatly to the growth of this approach, because it can analyze complex production and operations problems in a way not previously possible.

The important contributions of the management science approach will be covered in greater detail in Part IV of the book.

During the last 25 years, there have been attempts to achieve integration of the three approaches to management. One of these attempts, the *systems approach,* stresses that organizations must be viewed as total systems, with each part linked to every other part. Another, the *contingency approach,* stresses that the correctness of a managerial practice is contingent upon how it fits the particular situation in which it is applied. Let us briefly examine each.

The Systems Approach.   The systems approach to management is really a way of thinking about management problems. It views an organization as a group of interrelated parts with a single purpose. The action of one part will influence the others, and managers cannot deal separately with individual parts. In solving problems, managers using the systems approach must view the organization as a dynamic whole and must try to anticipate the intended as well as unintended impacts of their decisions. Such managers do not solve individual problems. Rather, they intervene in a total system of interrelated parts, using the management functions of planning, organizing, and controlling.

The age-old confrontation between production costs and the marketing objective of a broad product line is one example of the interrelated nature of management problems. Each objective conflicts with the other. For production costs to be their lowest, the firm would produce one color and one style. To achieve the marketing objective, several models and several colors would be required but at higher costs. In this situation, a compromise is necessary for the overall system to achieve its objective. The objectives of the individual parts must be compromised to meet the objective of the entire firm.

Using the systems approach, individual managers must adopt a broad perspective of their jobs. With a systems perspective, they can more easily achieve coordination between the objectives of the various parts of the organization and the objectives of the organization as a whole.[9]

Contingency Approach.   The systems approach forces managers to recognize that organizations are systems made up of interdependent parts and that a change in one part will affect other parts. It seeks to identify the characteristics of jobs, people, and organizations, allowing managers to see the interdependence between the various segments of an organization. The basic idea of the contingency approach is that there is no best way to plan, organize, or control. Rather, managers must find different ways to fit different situations. A method highly effective in one situation may not work in other situations. The contingency approach seeks to match different situations with different management methods.

Actually, the idea of contingency, or situational, thinking is not new. An early writer in the classical approach spoke during the 1920s of the "law of the

---

[9]For earlier discussions of the systems approach, see Seymour Tilles, "The Manager's Job—A Systems Approach," *Harvard Business Review,* January–February 1963, pp. 73–81; Fremont E. Kast and James E. Rosenzweig, "General Systems Theory: Applications in Organizations and Management," *Academy of Management Journal,* December 1972, pp. 447–65. For a more recent discussion, see M. Lynne Markus, *Systems in Organizations* (Marshfield, Mass.: Pitman Publishing, 1984).

situation." Mary Parker Follett noted that "different situations require different kinds of knowledge, and the man possessing the knowledge demanded by a certain situation tends in the best managed businesses, other things being equal, to become the leader of the moment."[10]

The contingency approach has grown in popularity over the last two decades because some research has found that, given certain characteristics of a job and certain characteristics of people doing the job, specific management practices tend to work better than others. For example, rigid plans, clearly defined jobs, autocratic leadership, and tight controls have at times resulted in high productivity and satisfied workers. At other times, just the opposite (general plans, loosely defined jobs, democratic leadership, and loose controls) has produced the same results.[11]

If, for instance, productivity needs to be increased, the manager will not automatically assume a new work method is needed (a classical solution) or that a new motivational approach needs to be tried (a behavioral solution). Instead, the manager will study the characteristics of the workers, the nature of the job, and his or her own leadership approach before deciding on a solution.[12]

Managers in the 1990s and beyond must use more of a contingency approach to survive. Reliance on a classical or a behavioral or a management science approach will not be sufficient for tomorrow's organizations. The reasons why the contingency view will become more relevant and prominent are:

1. Increased globalization of enterprise and the need for more government-business alliances to compete internationally.
2. Demands for ethical and social leadership.
3. Changing demographics and skill requirements of the work force.
4. The emergence of new organizational structures that emphasize speed in reacting to environmental changes.
5. Changing needs, preferences, and desires of employees for job security, participation, ownership, and personal fulfillment.

The student of management preparing for the 21st century must learn multiple ways to compete, innovate, create, motivate, and lead. Both the systems approach and the contingency approach can provide valuable insights.

THE WORK OF MANAGEMENT

In introducing the three approaches to management, we have established that all modern managers essentially face three managerial tasks:

---

[10]The many contributions of Mary Parker Follett are collected in Henry C. Metcalf and Lyndall Urwick, eds., *Dynamic Administration* (New York: Harper & Row, 1941).

[11]Henry L. Tosi and John W. Slocum, Jr., "Contingency Theory: Some Suggested Directions," *Journal of Management,* Spring 1984, pp. 9–26; Anna Grandori, "A Prescriptive Contingency View of Organizational Decision Making," *Administrative Science Quarterly,* June 1984, pp. 192–209.

[12]For critiques of the contingency approach, see Justin G. Longenecker and Charles D. Pringle, "The Illusion of Contingency Theory as a General Theory," *Academy of Management Review,* July 1978, pp. 679–82; Harold Koontz, "The Management Theory Jungle Revisited," *Academy of Management Review,* April 1980, pp. 175–87.

1. Managing work and organizations.
2. Managing people.
3. Managing production and operations.

No matter what an organization engages in, its managers will face these three tasks. Thus, managing is more than solving behavioral problems; it is more than solving technical problems; it is more than managing individual work; it is more than planning a department's future. The work of management is all of these. Learning to be a manager requires knowledge and skills relevant to each of these three tasks, which provide a point of departure for the study of management and also provide the structure and organization of this book.

MANAGING WORK AND ORGANIZATIONS

Whether the organization is small or large, private or public, management must make sure the work of the organization gets done and the organization itself is managed. For example, a college dean must make sure the work of the school gets done. Programs must be planned and classes scheduled; students must be advised; classes must be taught; faculty must be hired and evaluated. However, the college as an organization or entity also must be managed. Decisions must be made regarding the organization of the college, the number of departments, the development of job descriptions, and the assignment of tasks and authority. Decisions also must be made regarding changing educational needs and their impact on the present work of the college. Enrollments must be projected, new buildings planned, and funding needs identified. In all kinds of organizations, both the work and the organization itself must be managed.

MANAGING PEOPLE

The popular saying that management is "getting work done through other people," although an oversimplification, underscores the importance of the managerial task of managing people. There are no "peopleless" organizations, so managers must know how to motivate, lead, and communicate, and they must understand interpersonal relations and the behavior of groups of people.

The organizations in our society are far more than instruments for providing each of us with goods and services. They also create the settings in which the majority of us spend our lives. In this respect, they have profound influence on our behavior. We are just becoming aware of some of the psychological effects of this type of involvement.

MANAGING PRODUCTION AND OPERATIONS

Every organization does something. It may manufacture automobiles, cure the ill, educate, protect, govern, or entertain. The process used to produce the organization's output also must be managed. The term **production** focuses on manufacturing technology and on the flow of materials in a manufacturing plant. In fact, the production function in a manufacturing organization is specifically concerned with the activity of producing goods: the design and operation of a system of people, materials, equipment, money, and information to produce a product or group of products.

FIGURE 1–1   The Work of Management

The work of management involves three interrelated tasks: managing work and organizations, managing people, and managing production and operations.

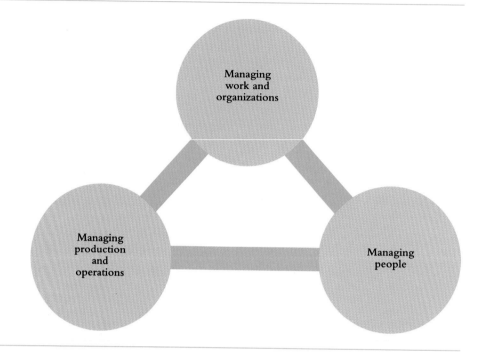

The term **operations** is broader in scope and is used for the production activity in any organization—goods-producing, service-producing, public, private, profit, or nonprofit. Operations management is similar to production management except that it focuses on a wider class of problems. It includes organizations whose technologies may be quite different from those of a manufacturing firm.

Many similarities exist between the flow of materials in a manufacturing firm, the processing of claims in an insurance company, student registration in a college, and the delivery of health care in a hospital. So an important focus of any managerial work is the task of managing operations.

Figure 1–1 illustrates that while each of the three managerial tasks can be discussed separately, they are very much interrelated. The figure also provides us with a framework that we will build upon throughout this book.

Figure 1–2 summarizes the challenges a modern manager faces and the wide knowledge necessary to plan, organize, and control. Managers must rely primarily on information based on the classical approach to manage work and organizations. To manage people, they need behavioral information. To manage operations, they must have a management science perspective.

PLAN FOR THE BOOK

The purpose of this book is to prepare managers—leaders well versed in all traditions of management—for the future. We must all be contingency-

FIGURE 1–2   The Practical Challenges and Required Knowledge of a Modern Manager

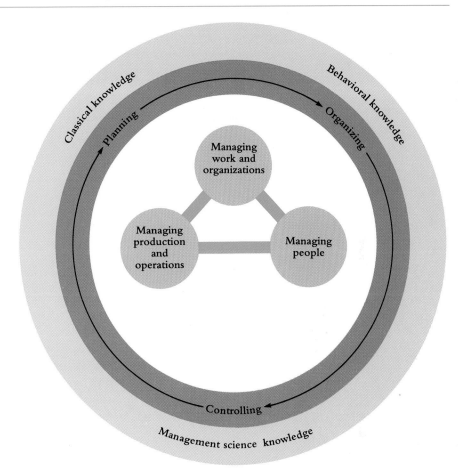

This figure illustrates the management tasks, the management functions, and the three approaches to management.

oriented managers who use, when needed, the appropriate classical, behavioral, and management science concepts, tools, and techniques. Managers must be well grounded in the techniques of planning, organizing, and controlling; they must understand the role of human behavior in organizations; and they must be skilled in the various ways to manage operations. Figure 1–3 illustrates the framework that will be followed in the book.

The three main managerial tasks serve as focal points for the three major sections of this textbook:

■ Part II, "Managing Work and Organizations," contains six chapters devoted to various aspects of the three primary management functions: planning, organizing, and controlling.

■ Part III, "Managing People," concentrates on the behavioral foundations of effective management. This section contains five chapters that discuss such

FIGURE 1–3   Plan for the Book

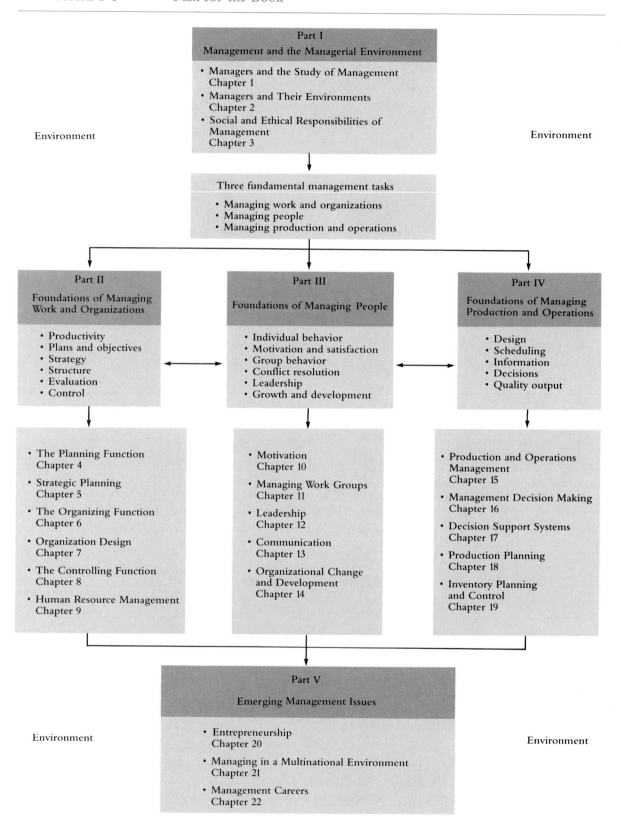

important management topics as motivation, group behavior, leadership, communications, and development of the organization and its members.

- Part IV focuses on the managerial task "Managing Production and Operations." Its five chapters include discussions of production and operations management, decision making, management information systems, and introductory discussions of several tools useful in planning and controlling production and operations.

The book concludes with "Emerging Management Issues," important topics such as management and entrepreneurship, international management, and the career of management.

The remaining two chapters in this introductory section address the environments in which managers must manage and the important contemporary issue of social and ethical responsibilities of management.

SUMMARY OF KEY POINTS

- The United States is at a crossroads in history in that the economic power and position of the nation are being challenged. Management will play a prominent role in the global economic village and competitive markets.

- Management is the process undertaken by one or more individuals to coordinate the activities of others to achieve results not possible by one individual acting alone.

- Three fundamental tasks make up managerial work: managing work and organizations, managing people, and managing production and operations. These three tasks are generally applicable to managers in all types of organizations.

- Management literature offers a variety of viewpoints and emphases. We have sought to introduce some clarity by identifying three mutually supportive approaches to management: classical, which focuses on the task of managing work and organizations; behavioral, focusing on the task

of managing people; and management science, which focuses on the task of managing production and operations.

- Each of the viewpoints and emphases has value. It is, however, important to be more contingency oriented (more flexible, more open minded, more inquisitive) in today's organizations.

- Figure 1–2 outlines the practical challenges and required knowledge of a modern manager. It relates the three management functions of planning, organizing, and controlling to the three fundamental managerial tasks and the three approaches to the study of management. It serves as a summary of this introductory chapter.

- In the study of management, future managers cannot ignore the contributions of any of the three approaches. Each deals with an important task future managers will face. With this in mind, review Figure 1–3, the plan for our book.

DISCUSSION AND REVIEW QUESTIONS

1. Did any management decisions influence you today? Outline and discuss at least one.

2. Why must management be a major force in the global economic village?

3. Some people believe that managers are an important social resource in our nation. Do you agree? Discuss.

4. What is the significance of the fact that our nation is "an organizational society"?

5. What lessons for modern-day managers were practiced by Attila the Hun?

6. Choose any management job with which you are familiar. Outline how the work and organization, people, and operations are managed.

7. What are the important differences between the three approaches to management as you now understand them?

8. Have you ever managed anything—for example, as part of a job or in a social or civic organization? If so, did you perform the management functions of planning, organizing, and controlling without being aware of it? Discuss your managerial experience and relate it to the functions of management.

9. One writer has stated: "People who don't manage are either too young, too old, or found in institu-

tions for the incompetent." What is this writer trying to say? Do you agree? Why?

10. How would a manager in a small manufacturing plant with 100 employees use the contingency approach to make planning decisions, reward decisions, and inventory control decisions?

ADDITIONAL REFERENCES

Aquilar, F. J. *General Managers in Action.* New York: Oxford University Press, 1988.

Cummings, L. L. "The Logics of Management." *Academy of Management Review,* October 1983, pp. 532–36.

Dubno, P. "Attitudes toward Women Executives: A Longitudinal Approach." *Academy of Management Journal,* December 1985, pp. 235–39.

Harvey, J. B. *The Abilene Paradox and Other Meditations on Management.* Lexington, Mass.: Lexington Books, 1988.

Howard, A., and **B. W. Douglas.** *Managerial Lives in Transition: Advancing Age and Changing Times.* New York: Guilford Press, 1989.

Kantrow, A. M. "Why Read Peter Drucker?" *Harvard Business Review,* January–February 1980, pp. 74–82.

Koontz, H. *Toward a Unified Theory of Management.* New York: McGraw-Hill, 1964.

Koprowski, E. J. "Exploring the Meaning of 'Good' Management." *Academy of Management Review,* July 1981, pp. 459–68.

McGill, M. E. *American Business and the Quick Fix.* New York: Henry Holt, 1988.

Maitland, I.; J. Bryson; and **A. Van De Ven.** "Sociologists, Economists, and Opportunism." *Academy of Management Review,* January 1985, pp. 59–65.

Moskowitz, M. *The Global Marketplace.* New York: Macmillan, 1987.

Prein, H. "A Contingency Approach for Conflict Intervention." *Group and Organization Studies,* March 1984, pp. 81–102.

Presthus, R. *The Organizational Society.* New York: Alfred A. Knopf, 1962.

Smith, K. G.; T. R. Mitchell; and **C. E. Summer.** "Top Level Management Priorities in Different Stages of the Organizational Life Cycle." *Academy of Management Journal,* December 1985, pp. 799–820.

Stewart, R. "A Model for Understanding Managerial Jobs and Behavior." *Academy of Management Review,* January 1982, pp. 7–13.

Urwick, L. "That Word 'Organization.'" *Academy of Management Review,* January 1976, pp. 89–91.

Walton, C. C. *Ethos and the Executive.* Englewood Cliffs, N.J.: Prentice-Hall, 1969.

Whitely, W. "Managerial Work Behavior: An Integration of Results from Two Major Approaches." *Academy of Management Journal,* June 1985, pp. 344–62.

Yorks, L., and **D. A. Whitsett.** "Hawthorne, Topeka, and the Issue of Science versus Advocacy." *Academy of Management Review,* January 1985, pp. 59–65.

SELECTED MANAGEMENT AND RELATED PERIODICALS

The vast majority of reports and writings on management is contained in the periodicals listed below. The categories of readings and writings are presented as topical discussion, theory and research, and practical applications. Each source has something of value to read and consider.

Topical Discussion of Management

Academy of Management Review
Business and Society Review
Business Horizons

Business Management
California Management Review
Canadian Manager

Columbia Journal of World Business   *New Management*
Harvard Business Review   *Organizational Dynamics*
Human Resource Management   *P & IM Review*
Interfaces   *Personnel Administrator*
International Management   *Personnel Journal*
Long Range Planning   *Sloan Management Review*
Management International Review   *Strategic Management Journal*
Managerial Planning

Theory and Research on Management

Academy of Management Journal   *Journal of Business*
Administrative Science Quarterly   *Journal of Human Resources*
Advanced Management Journal   *Journal of Management*
Decision Sciences   *Journal of Management Studies*
Group and Organization Studies   *Journal of Systems Management*
Industrial Engineering   *Management Science*
Industrial and Labor Relations Review   *Operations Research*
Information and Management   *Organizational Behavior and Human Decision Processes*
Journal of Applied Behavioral Science   *Personnel Psychology*
Journal of Applied Psychology   *Public Administration Review*

Practical, Anecdotal Applications of Management

Barron's   *Inc.*
Business Week   *Industry Week*
Business Month   *Management Review*
Forbes   *Training and Development Journal*
Fortune   *The Wall Street Journal*

EXPERIENTIAL EXERCISE

ATTITUDES ABOUT BUSINESS ORGANIZATIONS

Purpose

The purpose of this exercise is to identify attitudes that students have about business and various industries.

The Exercise in Class

1. Individually, each student is to complete the surveys about business and various industries (see Exhibits 1 and 2).
2. After individuals complete the surveys, the instructor will form five- to seven-person groups to discuss the individual ratings.

EXHIBIT 1	Survey of Business

In your opinion, have business organizations in general been supportive in each of the following areas? Use the scale below to indicate how supportive you believe business has been, placing the appropriate number in the space after each area of concern.

5—significant support
4—some support
3—undecided
2—little, if any, support
1—no support

Area of concern:

Energy conservation _____
Improving quality of worker's life _____
Controlling environmental pollution _____
Fighting inflation _____
Helping higher education _____
Retraining employees with obsolete skills _____
Developing urban areas _____
Hiring the handicapped _____
Hiring minorities _____
Promoting ethical behavior _____
Technological advancement _____
Rewarding good performance _____
Maintaining fair profit margins _____
A strong government _____

EXHIBIT 2	Survey of Industries

Please provide a rating for the industries listed below. In other words, what are your general impressions of these industries? Why do you feel this way? Use values of 1 to 5 according to the scale below. Place the number you choose for the industry in the appropriate blank space.

5—very good
4—generally good
3—unsure
2—generally poor
1—very poor

Industry:

Automobile	_____	Television	_____
Steel	_____	Aerospace	_____
Tobacco	_____	Health care	_____
Food processing	_____	Education	_____
Banking	_____	Fast food	_____
Publishing	_____	Computer	_____
Religion	_____	Paper	_____
Oil	_____	Insurance	_____
Chemicals	_____	Car repair	_____
Electronics	_____	Prescription drugs	_____
Tire and rubber	_____		

3. Each group will calculate an average group score for each item (adding the individual scores and dividing by the number of individuals in the group to arrive at an average).
4. The average scores will be placed by the group on the board or a flip chart for the class to discuss.

The Learning Message

Differences in student opinions exist. This exercise will display these differences and may also point out why they exist (e.g., backgrounds, pessimism, optimism, values).

2

MANAGERS AND THEIR ENVIRONMENTS

LEARNING OBJECTIVES

After completing Chapter 2, you should be able to:

Define
an organization and its environment in terms of a system.

Describe
the internal environment in which a manager must function.

Discuss
the direct and indirect forces in the external environment, and the challenges they pose for managers.

Compare
the four skills necessary for effective managerial performance.

Identify
the various roles managers must perform.

A Changing Environment and a Changing Industry

Few industries in the United States are as profitable as the $35 billion tobacco industry. A U.S. cigarette maker generally earns 30 percent pretax profit on every pack of cigarettes sold. Today, however, social, political, and legal forces in the industry's external environment are threatening to diminish the industry's sales and profits.

Ever since medical evidence emerged that linked smoking to several serious illnesses, pressure has mounted to make America a smokeless society—an objective that the U.S. surgeon general hopes to achieve by the year 2000. Antismokers are lobbying government to ban smoking in public places, and many states and communities have responded. Congress and state governments are threatening to boost the excise taxes on cigarettes. A growing number of citizens are suing cigarette makers, seeking damages for the deaths of relatives who smoked. Overall, there is a growing social stigma attached to smoking.

Because of these pressures, cigarette consumption has dropped almost 10 percent in the last six years and continues to decline. Tobacco companies have had to respond to a society that increasingly does not want their products. R. J. Reynolds/Nabisco and Philip Morris, the industry's two giants, have responded with a four-part strategy. They are diversifying, buying companies in other industries, to reduce their dependence on cigarette sales. (For example, Philip Morris spent $5.6 billion to purchase General Foods, maker of Oscar Mayer meats, Kool-Aid, and other food products.) The cigarette makers are also boosting cigarette production efficiency, cutting costs by automating their cigarette plants. They are entering international markets, where antismoking pressures are virtually nonexistent. And they are developing tobacco-related products, such as a chewing gum that contains finely ground tobacco, and R. J. Reynolds' ill-fated "smokeless" cigarette.

Whether the cigarette makers' tobacco sales and profits will survive in the United States is unknown. Regardless, the current plight of the tobacco industry is a convincing illustration of the impact of uncontrollable factors in the external environment on an industry.

Source: Adapted from Scott Ticer, "Where There's Smoke, There's Trouble," *Business Week,* January 18, 1988, pp. 88–89; "Big Tobacco's Fortunes Are Withering in the Heat," *Business Week,* July 27, 1987, pp. 47ff.

Many different forces inside and outside an organization influence a manager's performance. So the management functions of planning, organizing, and controlling often must be accomplished under constantly changing conditions. A manager must deal with two environments: the organization's *internal environment,* which usually can be controlled, and the often unpredictable and uncontrollable whims of the outside world, the *external environment.*

THE ORGANIZATION

Organizations vary in purpose and in technology. Schools, hospitals, banks, telephone companies, civic groups, and restaurants are all examples of organizations with differing goals and needs. But they and any other organization have one element in common: managers.

The basic concepts of systems theory can help managers simplify and deal with the complex interactions of internal and external environments.[1] An organization can be viewed as simply one element in a number of elements that depend on each other. The organization takes resources (input) from the larger system (the external environment), processes these resources within its internal environment, and returns them to the outside in changed form (output). Figure 2–1 displays the fundamental elements of the organization as a system.

A business firm has two major inputs: human and nonhuman resources. Human inputs come from the people who work in the firm. They contribute their time and energy to the organization in exchange for wages and other tangible and intangible rewards. Nonhuman resources consist of raw materials and information. These are transformed or used in combination with human resources to provide other resources. A steel mill employs people and blast furnaces, plus other tools and machinery, to transform iron ore into steel and steel products. General Motors takes steel, rubber, plastic, fabrics, and—in combination with people, tools, and equipment—makes automobiles. A university uses resources to teach students, do research, and provide information to society through the educational process. The inputs are students, faculty, and money. A hospital's inputs are its staff, supplies, and patients. The patients are processed through the application of medical knowledge and treatment. The output is patients restored to a level of health consistent with the severity of the disease.

It is the manager who must coordinate the activities of the entire system (organization) or one of the many subsystems (departments) within the organization. For the manager, the systems concept emphasizes that (1) the ultimate survival of the organization depends on its ability to *adapt to the demands of the environment* and (2) in meeting these demands, *the total input-process-output cycle must be the focus of managerial attention.*

THE INTERNAL ENVIRONMENT

This section examines the environment inside the organization in which a manager must function. It identifies the settings where managers work, the

[1]For further discussion, see M. Lynne Markus, *Systems in Organizations* (Marshfield, Mass.: Pitman Publishing, 1984).

FIGURE 2–1   The Organizational Environment as a System

Every organization interacts with a larger system by taking resources and providing outputs.

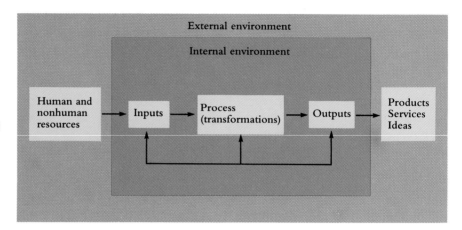

day-to-day activities that utilize much of their time, and some generalized skills necessary to cope with the internal environment. We shall begin by looking at the various *levels* of management, then focus on managerial *skills* and *roles*.

THREE MANAGEMENT LEVELS

Most organizations function on at least three distinct but overlapping levels, each requiring a different managerial focus and emphasis.[2] They include the *operations level,* the *managerial level,* and the *strategic level.* These are illustrated in Figure 2–2.

Operations Level.   We know from Chapter 1 that every organization, whether it produces a physical product or a service, has an operations function.[3] In any organization, therefore, there is an operations level that focuses on performing effectively, whatever it is that the organization produces or does. In the case of a physical product, there is the flow of materials and the supervision of the operations. Colleges must be sure their students are properly processed, registered, scheduled, and taught and their records are maintained. Banks must see that checks are processed and financial transactions are recorded accurately and quickly.

[2]The classic works in this area are Henry Mintzberg, *The Nature of Managerial Work* (New York: Harper & Row, 1973); Henry Mintzberg, "The Manager's Job: Folklore and Fact," *Harvard Business Review,* July–August 1975, pp. 49–61.

[3]For a discussion of technology in service organizations, see Karl Albrecht and Ron Zemke, *Service America* (Homewood, Ill.: Dow Jones-Irwin, 1985); Peter K. Mills and Dennis Moberg, "Perspectives on the Technology of Service Organizations," *Academy of Management Review,* July 1982, pp. 467–78.

FIGURE 2-2   Levels of Management

Three overlapping levels constitute most organizations, each with its own focus and emphasis.

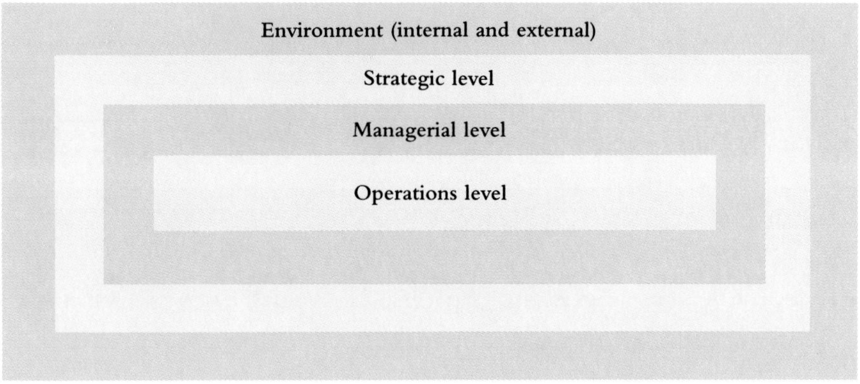

Environment (internal and external)

Strategic level

Managerial level

Operations level

As Figure 2–2 shows, an operations function is at the core of every organization. The managerial task here is to develop the best allocation of resources that will produce the desired output.

Managerial Level.   As an organization increases in size, someone must coordinate the activities at the operations level as well as decide which products or services to produce. These problems are the focus of the managerial level. A dissatisfied student complains to the dean of the college. A sales manager mediates disagreements between customers and salespeople. Production schedules and amounts to be produced must be planned for an automobile manufacturer.

At this level, the managerial task is really twofold: (1) managing the operations function and (2) serving as a liaison between those who produce the product or service and those who use the output. In other words, for the operations level to do its work, a manager must make sure it has the correct materials and also must see that the output gets sold or used.

Strategic Level.   Every organization operates in a broad social environment. As a part of that environment, an organization also is responsible to it. The strategic level must make sure the managerial level operates within the bounds of society. Since the ultimate source of authority in any organization comes from society, the organization must provide goods and services to society in a manner approved by society. Thus, the strategic level determines the long-range objectives and direction for the organization—in other words, how the organization will interact with its environment.[4] The organization also may seek to influence its environment through lobbying efforts, advertising efforts, or educational programs aimed at members of society.

[4]George S. Day, *Analysis for Strategic Marketing Decisions* (St. Paul, Minn.: West Publishing, 1986). Also see Sue Greenfield, Robert C. Winder, and Gregory Williams, "The CEO and the External Environment," *Business Horizons,* November–December 1988, pp. 20–25.

FIGURE 2–3	Managers and the Levels of Management

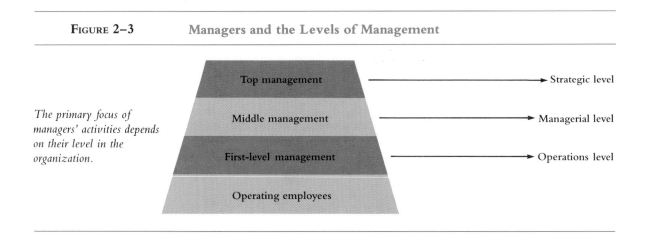

The primary focus of managers' activities depends on their level in the organization.

TYPES OF MANAGERS AND LEVELS OF MANAGEMENT

Understanding the three levels of management can be helpful in determining the primary focus of managers' activities at different levels in an organization. For example, a set of terms widely used in organizations includes **top management, middle management,** and **first-level management.** Figure 2–3 indicates that top management corresponds to the strategic level in Figure 2–2. Middle management corresponds to the managerial level, and first-level management corresponds to the operations level.

While the terms *top, middle,* and *first-level management* may not always correspond exactly to the three levels outlined in Figure 2–2, they do provide an understanding of what managers do at each level. The term *manager* covers all three levels.

The actual terms used to identify managers at various organizational levels differ from organization to organization. Figure 2–4 compares terms typically used in three types of organizations: business, education, and government. But from the chief executive officer (CEO) to the first-level supervisor, all are managers, although the focus of their activities varies.

Generally speaking, the activities of supervisors, chairpersons, and program managers are similar despite the different terms used to identify them. A chairperson of a department in a college could be expected to spend most of the time dealing with the faculty as individuals. Similarly, CEOs, presidents, and cabinet secretaries spend much of their time being concerned about the work that their organization is doing in terms of the expectations of owners, customers, and taxpayers. While we can identify similarities in managerial jobs as a function of their level in the organization, we must recognize that dissimilarities will also exist. These dissimilarities arise from the uniqueness of each organization and the environment in which it exists.[5]

[5]Michael Nash, *Managing Organization Performance* (San Francisco: Jossey-Bass, 1983); Rosemary Stewart, "A Model for Understanding Managerial Jobs and Behavior," *Academy of Management Review,* January 1982, pp. 7–13.

FIGURE 2–4   Managers at Different Organizational Levels in Three
                          Types of Organizations

*Organizations use various
terms to identify managers at
different organizational levels.*

Type of Organization / Level of Management	Business Organization	Educational Institution	Government Organization
Top	Chief executive officer	President	Cabinet secretary
Middle	Superintendent Manager	Vice president Dean	Commissioner Division director
First	Supervisor	Department chairperson	Program manager

SKILLS OF MANAGERS

Certain general skills are needed for effective managerial performance, regardless of the level of the manager in the hierarchy of the organization. However, the mix of skills will differ depending on the level of the manager in the organization. These skills and the necessary mixes are illustrated in Figure 2–5.[6] The figure indicates that there are four basic skills—technical, human, computer, and conceptual—needed by all managers.

Technical skill is the ability to use specific knowledge, techniques, and resources in performing work. Accounting supervisors, engineering directors, or nursing supervisors must have the technical skills of the people they manage in order to perform their management jobs.

Merck & Co., Inc., is one example of the importance of technical skills. Considered by many management experts to be the best-managed company in America, Merck manufactures drugs for medical use. The company's key resource is a top-notch team of scientists. Their technical skills developed a consistent stream of major, productive pharmaceuticals that increased the company's sales by about 20 percent each year during the late 1980s. Merck attracts top talent by paying well and maintaining first-rate lab facilities and a campuslike working environment. Many of its managers possess the same skills: the company's CEO, Roy Vagelos, has a doctorate in medicine.[7]

Managers must accomplish much of their work through other people. For this, *human skill* is essential. A reflection of a manager's leadership abilities, human skill is the ability to work with, communicate with, and understand others.

[6]Technical, human, and conceptual skills were first described in Robert L. Katz, "Skills of an Effective Administrator," *Harvard Business Review,* September–October 1974, pp. 90–102.

[7]See Carol Davenport, "America's Most Admired Corporations," *Fortune,* January 30, 1989, pp. 68ff; Gordon Bock, "Merck's Medicine Man," *Time,* February 22, 1988, pp. 44–45.

FIGURE 2–5   Basic Managerial Skills

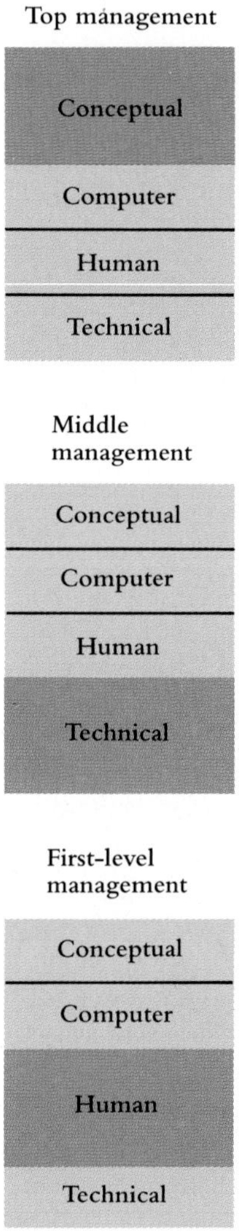

Top management

Conceptual
Computer
Human
Technical

Middle management

Conceptual
Computer
Human
Technical

The mix of managerial skills will vary by organizational level.

First-level management

Conceptual
Computer
Human
Technical

James F. Lincoln, the founder of Lincoln Electric Co., was endowed with considerable human skills. Based near Cleveland, Ohio, with 3,000 employees, Lincoln Electric is the world's leading manufacturer of arc-welding equipment, having 40 percent of the world's market. Lincoln Electric's exceptional success has been attributed to James Lincoln's attitudes toward and relationship with employees. He believed that employees have a basic desire to work productively as members of a company that contributes to society. He believed that pay must be directly linked to performance in order to reward employees for good performance and that a relationship of complete honesty

Management Focus

A Change in Leadership Style

In the early 1980s, CEO Jimmy Treybig managed Tandem Computers with a unique leadership style. At the company's main location in California's "Silicon Valley," Treybig motivated employees by giving inspired speeches about Tandem's future. He stressed hard work and commitment but also flexibility, trust, and communication. No time clocks were installed; few regular meetings with subordinate managers were held. The company's goals were communicated to all employees. Parties were held every Friday afternoon on the company grounds to encourage employees to discuss new ideas. Yoga classes, a swimming pool, and jogging trails were built at Tandem.

In sum, Treybig strived to create a demanding but comfortable work environment. The Tandem environment came to symbolize the new corporate culture of Silicon Valley's upstart computer companies. Profits were high; employee turnover was low. Treybig's "cheerleading" leadership style appeared to work.

However, when the computer industry slumped, so did Tandem's profits. Other problems surfaced: Tandem was suffering from poor cost control, and many managers weren't meeting their objectives. Treybig made the decision to change his leadership style. He implemented a cost cutting program, reassigned many employees, imposed restrictions on corporate-paid travel, and required salaried workers to put in some overtime without pay.

Treybig ended consensus management and established authoritative management. Although he dislikes meetings, weekly staff meetings and quarterly reviews are now the norm. Managers are strictly held to their goals and receive occasionally harsh critiques from the CEO on their performance.

Treybig's style hasn't totally changed. The Friday parties continue, and employees can still scribble their names on the CEO's calendar for a meeting with him. Open communication is still stressed; most of Tandem's 6,200 employees have electronic mail terminals at their desks to communicate with each other. But the emphasis has changed from inspiration to accountability. So far, his changed style seems to fit the bill. Tandem recently reached the $1 billion mark in yearly sales.

Source: Adapted from Brian O'Reilly, "How Jimmy Treybig Turned Tough," *Fortune,* May 25, 1987, pp. 102–4.

and understanding must be maintained between employees and managers. Lincoln incorporated these beliefs into the company's unique compensation system and management practices. His human relations–oriented philosophy is still alive today at Lincoln Electric, some 20 years after his death.[8]

Jimmy Treybig, CEO of Tandem Computers, is also credited with having a unique, human skill–based leadership style. However, as the Management Focus on leadership style notes, this has recently changed.

Managers with *computer skills* understand computers and, in particular, know how to use the computer and software to perform many aspects of their

[8]Harvey Shore, "Mr. Lincoln and His System," *Business Quarterly,* Summer 1986, pp. 10–13; Bruce G. Posner, "Right from the Start," *Inc.,* August 1988, pp. 95–96.

jobs. Computer skill is a valuable managerial asset; in one survey study of 100 personnel directors from America's largest corporations, 7 of every 10 directors believed that computer skills are either important, very important, or essential for advancement in management.[9]

Computer abilities are important because using computers wisely substantially increases a manager's productivity. In minutes, computers can perform tasks in financial analysis, human resource planning, and other areas that otherwise take hours, even days, to complete. The computer is an especially helpful tool for decision making. It instantly places at a manager's fingertips a vast array of information in a flexible and usable form. Software enables managers to manipulate the data and perform "what if" scenarios, looking at the projected impact of different decision alternatives.

Computers also save valuable time in such tasks as reading mail and preparing for and conducting management meetings. Xerox, for example, has saved much time and money by using electronic scanners to input incoming mail for its executives into the computer. Executives now read their mail from their computer monitors. To prepare its 20 division chiefs for the company's annual strategic planning review, Xerox once produced thick and hefty briefing books that, it admits, few of the executives read completely before the meeting. Now, all review documents have been shortened, standardized, and computerized and are read by each executive on his or her computer screen before the meeting. The result: The planning meeting now focuses on issues, not on wading through basic facts. In sum, computer skills are essential to make full use of the considerable advantages that computers provide management.[10]

Conceptual skill is the ability to see the big picture, the complexities of the overall organization and how the various parts fit together. Managers with conceptual skills understand all activities and interests of the organization and how they interrelate.

Jack Welch, CEO of General Electric, is widely recognized as having superior conceptual skills. He used those skills in crafting a new General Electric. Welch eliminated 100,000 jobs (over one fourth of GE's total) and sold billions of dollars worth of GE businesses, taking the company out of the housewares and television industries and into high-tech manufacturing, broadcasting, and other higher-risk and more profitable industries. Welch is now applying conceptual skills in entering new international markets and in eliminating GE's bureaucracy.[11] In another example, company chairman Konosuke Matsushita used considerable conceptual skill in developing a comprehensive, 250-year plan at Matsushita, a Japanese electronics manufacturer and a top GE competitor.[12]

All four of these managerial skills are essential for effective performance. Computer skill is equally important at all levels of management, but Figure 2–5 indicates that the relative importance of the other three skills to a specific

---

[9]"Trying to Climb the Corporate Ladder? Without Basic Computer Skills, You Risk Falling Off, Survey Reports," *Pr Newswire,* January 20, 1988.

[10]Jeremy Main, "At Last, Software CEOs Can Use," *Fortune,* March 13, 1989, pp. 77ff; "How Computers Remake the Manager's Job," *Business Week,* April 25, 1983, pp. 68ff.

[11]Stratford P. Sherman, "The Mind of Jack Welch," *Fortune,* March 27, 1989, pp. 39ff.

[12]Walter Kiechel III, "How Executives Think" *Fortune,* February 4, 1985, pp. 127–28.

manager depends on his or her level in the organization. Technical skill is critical at the lower levels of management. Because they deal with the day-to-day problems in manufacturing and nursing, a production foreman and a nursing supervisor will need more technical skill than the president of a company or a hospital administrator.

On the other hand, the importance of conceptual skill increases as one rises in management. The higher one is in the hierarchy, the more involved one becomes in longer-term decisions that can influence many parts of the organization or the entire organization. Thus, conceptual skill is most critical for top managers.

While human skill is critical at every level in management, it probably is most important at the lowest level. The greatest number of manager–subordinate interactions are likely to occur at this level.

ROLES OF MANAGERS

Managers perform 10 different but closely related roles. These are illustrated in Figure 2–6. The figure shows that the 10 roles can be separated into three different groupings: interpersonal roles, informational roles, and decisional roles.[13]

Interpersonal Roles.   These roles focus on interpersonal relationships. The three roles of figurehead, leader, and liaison result from formal authority. By assuming them, the manager is able to move into the informational roles that in turn lead directly to the decisional roles.

All managerial jobs require some duties that are symbolic or ceremonial in nature. A college dean will hand out diplomas at graduation, a shop supervisor attends the wedding of a subordinate's daughter, the mayor of New York City gives the key to the city to an astronaut. These are examples of the *figurehead role*.

The manager's *leadership role* involves directing and coordinating the activities of subordinates. This may involve staffing (hiring, training, promoting, dismissing) and motivating subordinates. The leadership role also involves controlling—making sure that things are going according to plan.

The *liaison role* gets managers involved in interpersonal relationships outside of their area of command. This may involve contacts both within and outside the organization. Within the organization, managers must interact with numerous other managers and individuals. They must maintain good relations with the managers who send work to the unit as well as those who receive work from the unit. For example, a college dean must interact with individuals all over the campus; a supervisory nurse in an operating room must interact with supervisors of various other groups of nurses; a production supervisor must interact with engineering supervisors and sales managers. Finally, managers often have interactions with important people outside the organization. It is easy to see that the liaison role often can consume much of a manager's time.

The manager
"disseminato
providing to
important bu
information i
not otherwise

[13]These managerial roles were first identified and described in Mintzberg, "The Manager's Job." Also see Jay W. Lorsch, James P. Baughman, James Reece, and Henry Mintzberg, *Understanding Management* (New York: Harper & Row, 1978).

FIGU

Although mai
10 different r
groupings, m
overlap.

are never enough resources to go around; the manager must allocate the scarce resources toward numerous possible ends. Resource allocation, therefore, is one of the most critical of the manager's decisional roles. A first-line supervisor must decide whether an overtime schedule should be established or whether part-time workers should be hired. A college dean must decide, based on available faculty, which courses to offer next semester. The president of the United States must decide whether to allocate more to defense and less to social programs, or vice versa.

In the *negotiator role,* managers must bargain with other units and individuals to obtain advantages for their own units. The negotiations may be over work, performance, objectives, resources, or anything influencing the unit. A sales manager may negotiate with the production department over a special order for a large customer; a first-line supervisor may negotiate for new typewriters; a top manager may negotiate with a labor union representative.

Management Level and Management Roles. A manager's level in the organization influences which managerial roles are emphasized. Obviously, top managers spend much more time in the figurehead role than first-line supervisors do. The liaison roles of top and middle managers involve individuals and groups outside the organization, while the liaison role at the first-line level is outside the unit but inside the organization. Top managers monitor the environment for changes that can influence the entire organization. Middle managers monitor the environment for changes likely to influence the particular function that they manage (for example, marketing). And the first-line supervisor is concerned about what will influence his or her unit. However, while both the amount of time in the various roles and the activities performed in each role may differ, all managers perform interpersonal, informational, and decisional roles.

THE EXTERNAL ENVIRONMENT

Individuals often limit their perspective of an organization to the elements and activities that exist *within* the organization: the employees, managers, equipment, tools, procedures, and other elements that combine to create the organization's product or service. However, this perspective is sorely limited. A complete picture of any organization must include its *external environment,* the large arena that exists outside the organization and comprises many varied forces that impact the organization's structure, processes, and performance. These forces may be *direct,* exerting an immediate and direct influence on the organization, or they may be *indirect,* influencing the climate in which the organization operates (and becoming direct forces under some conditions).

To some degree, these direct and indirect forces are unpredictable and uncontrollable. And they are usually quite powerful, exerting a significant effect on the organization's performance and well-being. For an organization to succeed, its managers must recognize these external forces, comprehend their interrelationships, and understand their real and potential impacts on the organization. Above all, managers must manage the organization (and, in some cases, the environment) to minimize the environmental forces' negative effects and maximize their positive impacts on the organization.

FIGURE 2–7   Direct Forces in the Organization's External Environment

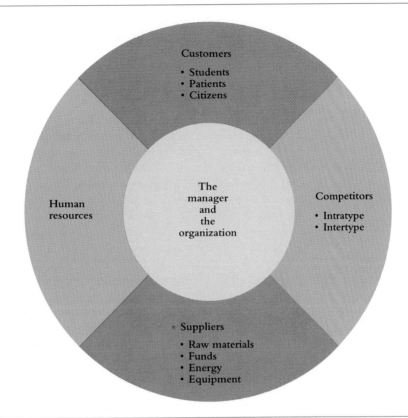

Direct forces have an immediate impact on the organization.

DIRECT FORCES

The major direct forces of an organization's external environment are the customers that the organization must satisfy, the competitors with whom the organization must effectively compete for customers, the suppliers that provide the organization with essential resources, and human resources—people in the external environment from whom the organization must draw an effectively performing work force. Figure 2–7 illustrates these direct forces.

Customers.   Customers purchase an organization's products or services. They may be individuals, such as a freelance writer who buys an IBM® PS/2® personal computer for her writing work. Individual customers differ in many characteristics such as age, education, income, and lifestyle. Customers may also be organizations. IBM, for example, powers its PS/2 computers with microprocessors it buys from Intel Corp. Organizational customers differ in their requirements for service, quality, and delivery times.

Of all the direct forces, customers are perhaps the most vital to organizations. After all, their decision to buy or not buy a firm's output directly determines the company's sales revenues and ultimately its survival. Consider, for example, the highly fickle preferences of listeners of rock music. When customers tired of disco in the late 1970s, their no-buy decisions spelled crisis for Columbia Records and other music companies whose revenues relied heavily on disco artists. Conversely, the advent of the Yuppies in the early 1980s spawned major revenues for many companies. With incomes averaging $51,000 a year, these young urban professionals (3.5 million of them) provided skyrocketing sales for manufacturers of BMW automobiles, high-priced women's fashions, champagne, sailboats, running shoes, and other expensive, status-oriented products.[14] Beyond directly affecting a company's sales, customers also impact the characteristics of a company's product or service: its quality, features, sales price, and even point of sale.

Organizations typically respond to customer forces in the external environment by taking two actions. First, they conduct *customer research* that focuses on both present and potential customers. Organizations seek to identify their present customers' degree of satisfaction with their products and services and to discover any changing preferences.

For example, at Lands' End, the mail-order catalog company, telephone operators make meticulous notes of all comments made by customers; these comments are summarized each month in a written report provided to all managers. Before launching its 1988 Cadillac models, General Motors spent three years with five groups, each consisting of 500 buyers of Cadillacs and other car models. Cadillac surveyed the participants' likes and dislikes concerning the current Cadillac models. They then placed the customers behind the wheels of prototype Cadillac models. While the customers tried the steering wheel, seats, seat belts, and dashboard buttons, GM engineers sat in the back seat, taking notes. Domino's Pizza gleans customer opinion in another way. Each year, it pays 10,000 "mystery customers" $60 each to buy 12 pizzas from each of the company's 5,000 outlets during the year and to evaluate the quality of the pizza and service.[15]

Many organizations emphasize current-customer research because it is commonly recognized that, done effectively, keeping a current customer incurs about one fifth the expense of finding a new one.[16] The failure to detect customers' changing preferences is also quite costly. For example, Nike lost its market leadership in athletic shoes during the mid-1980s partly because it failed to recognize and react to the customers' growing preference for style over performance. However, Nike has since rebounded because it foresaw and reacted to the fickle market's return to preferring performance over style. Nike and Reebok are now battling shoe-to-shoe for market dominance.[17] Avon Products likewise suffered a major decline in cosmetic sales before it realized

[14]See Faye Rice, "Yuppie Spending Gets Serious," *Fortune,* March 27, 1989, pp. 147–49.

[15]Susan Caminiti, "A Mail-Order Romance: Lands' End Courts Unseen Customers," *Fortune,* March 13, 1989, pp. 44–45; Susan Caminiti, "Getting Customers to Love You," *Fortune,* March 13, 1989, pp. 38ff.

[16]Joel Dreyfuss, "Victories in the Quality Crusade," *Fortune,* October 10, 1988, pp. 80ff.

[17]See Barbara Buell, "Nike Catches Up with the Trendy Frontrunner," *Business Week,* October 24, 1988, p. 88; Gretchen Morgenson, "Has the Runner Stumbled?" *Forbes,* September 19, 1988, pp. 118–19.

the problem: many customers had left home to work full-time in the office. When Avon called, no one was home.[18]

Customer research also focuses on potential buyers. Organizations study changes in demographics and other factors to identify groups of possible buyers. Since the late 1980s, for example, more companies have begun to target elderly Americans, given that by the year 2000 over 15 percent of the population will be over 65 years of age.[19] Suffering from a "grandmother" image, Timex Inc. searched for a sizable group of potential buyers to boost its lagging watch sales and found one: athletes and sports-minded individuals.[20]

Organizations use research findings in their second response to customer forces: *providing a product or service that meets preferences* of present and potential customers. Lands' End bases all new products on customer comments, which ensures that every new product has a ready and waiting customer base. The designs of GM's 1988 Cadillac DeVille and Fleetwood models were greatly influenced by its customer research; 1988 Cadillac sales increased 36 percent over sales during 1987. Avon Products followed its customers—into the workplace, selling directly at the office, and into department stores, where it has launched a line of perfume. Timex successfully targeted its newfound market with a line of low-priced watches that sport features specifically designed for aerobics enthusiasts, skiers, runners, and sailors. Timex has since regained its leadership position in the $1.5 billion U.S. watch market. In many cases, responding successfully to customer preferences means effectively handling customer complaints, which is discussed in the Management Focus on transforming complainers.

Beyond these specific examples, U.S. companies nationwide are responding to a major change in customer preferences: a new desire for increased quality in the products and services they buy. Overall, companies are placing greater emphasis on quality, whether it be in speed of service (Lands' End, for example, ships over 90 percent of all orders within 24 hours) or in the features of a product. This focus on improving quality will be discussed further in chapters throughout this book.

Competitors.   Competitors are an organization's opponents, the companies against which the organization competes for customers and needed resources (e.g., employees, raw materials, even other organizations) in the external environment. An organization's *intratype competitors* are companies that produce the same or similar products/services as the organization. General Motors and Ford Motor Co., American and United Air Lines, Philip Morris (maker of Marlboro and Merit cigarettes) and R. J. Reynolds Tobacco (maker of the Winston brand) are intratype competitors that vie for customers. Harvard University and Yale University are also intratype competitors that pursue top-notch students and compete to recruit exceptional faculty.

---

[18]See Kathleen Deveny, "Can Avon Get Wall Street to Answer the Door?" *Business Week,* March 20, 1989, pp. 123–24; Walecia Konrad, "For Avon, Rodeo Drive Is No Easy Street," *Business Week,* December 28, 1987, p. 78.

[19]For a perspective of how the "aging of America" will affect U.S. businesses and their products and services, see Curtis Hartman, "Redesigning America," *Inc.,* June 1988, pp. 58ff.

[20]Christie Brown, "Sweat Chic," *Forbes,* September 5, 1988, pp. 96, 101.

MANAGEMENT FOCUS

Transforming Complainers into Loyal Customers

A growing number of companies are allocating more effort and money to handling customer complaints quickly and effectively. Why? Dissatisfied customers can ravage a company's reputation, given that consumers tell twice as many people about unpleasant experiences as about good ones (according to research). And the effects of an excellent customer complaint–handling program (in terms of greater customer satisfaction, loyalty, and sales) more than pays for the program's costs. In the banking industry, for example, an effective program that costs $1 million to maintain can produce as much as $2.7 million in financial returns, according to research.

This recognized link between complaint handling and profits has spurred many companies to launch complaint-handling programs that involve generous refund policies, intensive staff training, and toll-free 800 numbers. For example:

- At London's Heathrow Airport, British Airways maintains Video Point booths, where dissatisfied customers can stand before a camera and videotape their complaints. Customer service managers review the tapes and respond to every complaint.
- Hechinger Co., a hardware and home-garden equipment retailer in Maryland, accepts returned goods even when they've obviously been damaged by customers. If a customer is really upset, Hechinger sends a dozen roses.
- Coca-Cola has maintained its 1–800-GET-COKE complaint line since 1983, when it realized that only 1 of every 50 displeased customers bothers to complain (the other 49 simply switch to another soft drink). Coca-Cola publicizes the line to encourage feedback. It got plenty of that in 1985, when the company dropped its original formula and launched New Coke. In the weeks that followed, from 400 to 12,000 Coke drinkers called each day, complained, and asked for the old Coke. When Coca-Cola obliged, 18,000 people called, most simply to say thanks.
- General Electric maintains what many observers believe is the state-of-the-art 800-number customer unit, located in Louisville, Kentucky. There, phone operators sit at computer terminals and draw upon a huge central databank that contains 750,000 answers to questions concerning the company's 8,500 different products. GE handles 3 million calls each year, and 95 percent of the callers are satisfied with the unit's service.

Source: Adapted from Patricia Sellers, "How to Handle Customers' Gripes," *Fortune*, October 24, 1988, pp. 88ff.

Intertype competitors are distinctly different and competing organizations. For example, banks such as Chase-Manhattan compete against Sears Roebuck & Co. for savings customers. The Detroit Pistons, San Francisco 49ers, California Angels, and other professional athletic teams continually compete against universities for talented high school athletes. Hewlett-Packard and Microsoft Corp. compete against the U.S. armed forces for talented computer software programmers. And in the acquisitions arena, different businesses compete to buy valued companies. Such competition occurred when, for example, Eastman Kodak Co., largely a camera and film manufacturer, outbid a Swiss pharmaceuticals maker and acquired Sterling Drug Inc.

Organizations focus most of their competitive efforts on customers. In this regard, competition can be viewed as a dynamic, ongoing process of moves

TABLE 2–1	Ten Duels in the U.S. Marketplace

Industry	Competitors*
Credit cards	Visa International versus American Express.
Overnight delivery	Federal Express versus United Parcel Service.
Fast food	McDonald's versus Burger King.
Candy bars	Mars (Snickers) versus Hershey Foods (Reese's Peanut Butter Cup).
Personal computers	IBM versus Apple.
Beer	Anheuser-Busch versus Miller Beer.
Retail stores	Sears Roebuck versus K mart.
Car rental services	Hertz versus Avis.
Motorcycles	Honda versus Yamaha.
Stereo receivers	Pioneer versus Sony.

*Based on 1988 data. For each industry, the first- and second-ranked, different competitors are shown.

and countermoves. For example, in the market for word-processing software, competitor A "moves" by launching a new, attention-getting promotional campaign that touts its product's quality. Competitor B "countermoves" by lowering the sales price on its top-selling product and promoting the price cut. Competitor C makes two moves: the company slashes the price on its best word-processing product and introduces a new, more advanced software product that places the products of both competitors A and B at a distinct disadvantage. Both have a problem and must effectively "countermove," or respond.

These dynamics of moves and countermoves can occur on many fronts and can be fast-paced and difficult to predict. When this occurs, competition is intense, as it is in the soft drink industry, where Coca-Cola and PepsiCo compete for market leadership. Each company continually moves and countermoves on a number of fronts—including new product development, distribution, price, and advertising/promotion. In other industries (especially those regulated by the government), the moves and countermoves are less frequent, more stable, and more predictable (e.g., the utilities industry). Table 2–1 shows 10 industries in which competition, especially between the top two businesses, is especially fierce.

To succeed, an organization must make effective moves and countermoves, ones that maintain or advance the company's position in the marketplace and that cannot be easily nullified by competitors' responses. Doing so requires a thorough grasp of the relevant forces in the environment, especially competition. An organization comes to understand its competitors by performing an ongoing *competitor analysis*. It reviews and evaluates information from many sources (the media, its suppliers, wholesalers, and associates) to obtain a solid understanding of a competitor's objectives, strategies, and competitive advantages (e.g., a strong distribution network) and weaknesses (e.g., a typically slow response to competitors' moves). A thorough competitor analysis enables an organization to better anticipate a competitor's moves and countermoves.[21]

[21]For an excellent discussion of competitor analysis, see Arthur A. Thompson, Jr., and A. J. Strickland III, *Strategic Management: Concepts and Cases* (Plano, Tex.: Business Publications, 1987), chap. 3.

MANAGEMENT FOCUS

The Power of Speed

Honda Motor Co. once took five years to design and develop a new car. Honda now does it in three years. Brunswick, the sporting goods manufacturer, once averaged three weeks to manufacture an order of fishing reels; the order is now shipped in one week. Motorola once spent three weeks manufacturing an order of electronic pagers, a task the company now does in two hours.

According to surveys, many companies are setting speed in operations and management (technically termed "time-based strategy") as a top corporate priority because it can provide powerful competitive advantages. Speed increases sales because customers want their products or services now. Speed reduces production costs because quickly making and delivering a product reduces the need to keep an inventory of the finished product on hand. And in some industries, speedy product development is much more profitable. In the computer industry, for example, researchers have found that a product that is within budget but launched six months late will earn one-third less profits than an on-time product that is 50 percent over budget.

Companies that have successfully accelerated the speed of their operations emphasize that success does not mean simply doing the same things the same way, only faster. People and equipment burn out. Instead, once an ambitious goal is set for, say, making circuit breaker boxes, the company must "start from scratch," analyzing all aspects of production to find new ways of producing the boxes more quickly without sacrificing quality. When General Electric decided to produce the breaker boxes in three days instead of its customary three weeks, the company's analysis resulted in consolidating all production

In this regard, a growing number of companies are establishing competitor intelligence teams typically staffed by two to five employees who are assigned to obtain specific information about a competitor. Top management uses the information in making critical decisions such as whether to enter new markets.

In the mid-1980s, for example, Marriott Corp. was deliberating whether to enter the economy hotel market. It assigned a team of six employees to obtain competitor intelligence on all major budget hotel chains. The team spent several months traveling nationwide, checking into the hotels (two adjoining rooms). Once in the rooms, the team took note of the decor, brands of soap, shampoo, and towels and checked the quality of the bedding, the room's soundproofness, and front desk service. The team provided Marriott's management with a detailed profile of competitors' strengths and weaknesses. Using the information, Marriott entered the economy market with Fairfield Inns, a budget hotel with better-than-competitor quality in most respects. Fairfield Inns maintains an occupancy rate 10 percent above the industry average.

After failing with a wine cooler in the mid-1980s, Coors wanted to reassess the situation before reentering that market. It gave the company's competitor intelligence team the assignment of identifying the profit margins of Gallo

into one plant instead of its six box plants, computerizing engineering tasks, and eliminating first-line supervisors and quality inspectors. Production employees, organized into teams, now handle those tasks effectively and more quickly.

Speedy companies also advocate reducing the number of times a product or service must be approved by someone before it is shipped. Zealous adherence to deadlines is also a must, and establishing employee teams is recommended. AT&T credits its specially developed teams of engineers, manufacturers, and marketers for cutting its development time for a 1988 phone from two years to one. The teams made every decision concerning the phone's internal design, appearance, and price. The result: a phone that was developed more quickly at lower cost and with higher quality.

Teaching employees to value speed is also important. Honda Motor Co. does so by participating in Formula One auto racing each year with cars powered by Honda engines. Every young Honda engineer does a stint at the racetrack as a member of the Formula One team. Honda believes the experience teaches engineers how to make fast, effective decisions. At Domino's Pizza, the importance of speed is communicated in the company's regional division competitions, where the outlet with the best pizza and fastest delivery wins. Pizza makers also study films of Domino's speediest pizza artists at work.

Source: Adapted from Brian Dumaine, "How Managers Can Succeed through Speed," *Fortune*, February 13, 1989, pp. 54–59.

Winery, the competitor to beat. The team bought Gallo's coolers and chemically analyzed their contents to determine the wine and flavorings used. They then obtained the prices of the ingredients from suppliers. The team's verdict: Gallo's profit margins were high, and Coors could not compete on price. Coors stayed out of the wine cooler market.[22]

Overall, organizations strive to establish and protect competitive advantages, particularly strengths that bolster the company's competitive power. As the Management Focus discusses, a growing number of companies are embracing the competitive advantage of speed—creating, producing, managing, and responding as quickly as possible.

Suppliers.   All organizations require resources—funds, energy, equipment, services, and materials—to produce a product or service that succeeds in the marketplace. Suppliers are organizations that provide these resources. Their outputs are the buyer organization's inputs—and therefore can significantly affect the quality, cost, and timeliness of the buyer's product or service. A

[22]Brian Dumaine, "Corporate Spies Snoop to Conquer," *Fortune,* November 7, 1988, pp. 68ff.

buyer organization is vulnerable to several potential supplier problems, such as low materials quality or a supplier's financial crisis or labor strike that prevents the buyer from receiving essential materials. One major problem Reebok faced in 1987 was labor unrest in Korea that prevented the company from filling its retailers' orders.

Because of these potential problems, many organizations reduce their dependence on any one source by spreading their purchases of raw materials and other needed resources across several suppliers. They make sure that the materials they need are standardized and thus can be made by many suppliers. Some companies have gone further, becoming their own suppliers by *backward vertical integration.* These companies manufacture at least some of the raw materials needed to produce the final product or service. This strategy is costly to implement, but it offers the advantages of greater control over materials cost, quality, and delivery. Indeed, one reason Coors could not compete with Gallo in the wine cooler market was that Gallo has backward vertical integration: it makes its own grapes and bottle labels, which lowers its overall production costs.

However, a growing number of companies in some industries are opting for "single sourcing," relying on one supplier for particular parts and materials. At Ford and General Motors, over 98 percent of the purchased materials and parts are single sourced. All steering wheels for a particular model, for example, are provided by one supplier. Companies who are single sourcing are willing to risk greater dependence for the higher materials quality they believe the strategy provides. With fewer suppliers, a company can work more easily with a vendor to boost materials quality. With a guaranteed larger volume of purchases, a supplier is more willing to invest in the production equipment that boosts materials quality. Single sourcing also provides greater consistency in materials, and it affords more flexible production scheduling because, with fewer suppliers, a buyer can more easily coordinate production schedules.[23]

Human Resources.   Human resources are the vast resource of people in the external environment from which an organization obtains its employees. People are perhaps an organization's most precious internal resource because they are the organization's lifeblood. They provide the knowledge, skills, and drive that create, maintain, and advance organizations. To be successful, an organization must attract and keep individuals it needs to achieve its objectives and to thrive.

According to researchers of the U.S. labor force, three recently emerged trends concerning human resources pose major challenges for management:

A more diverse work force.   In the U.S. workplace in times past, the vast majority of employees were white males. However, the workplace is changing. As shown in Figure 2–8, white males will be only 8 percent of all new entrants into the labor force through the year 2000. Women will constitute about two thirds of all new employees; about 92 percent of new employees will be black, Hispanic, or Asian.[24]

---

[23]John H. Sheridan, "Betting on a Single Source," *Industry Week,* February 1, 1988, pp. 31ff.

[24]Mark L. Goldstein, "Tomorrow's Work Force Today," *Industry Week,* August 15, 1988, pp. 41–43.

FIGURE 2–8   Additions to the U.S. Work Force, 1986–2000

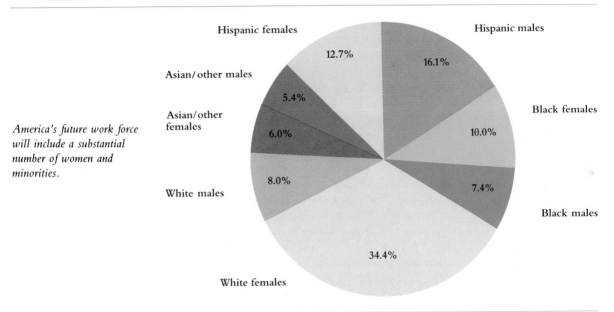

America's future work force will include a substantial number of women and minorities.

Source: "Tomorrow's Workforce Today," *Industry Week,* August 15, 1988, p. 42. Used with permission
Data from Bureau of Labor Statistics.

This changing face of America's work force presents management with an important challenge: how to effectively manage a workplace that is richly diverse in terms of race, ethnic background, and gender. People from widely differing cultures and backgrounds bring different values, beliefs, preferences, and norms of behavior to the workplace. These substantial differences breed conflict among employees and managers unless they work to understand, appreciate, and accommodate these differences. One example: At Intel Corp., a conflict arose between American and Israeli employees at corporate headquarters. The American employees were frustrated by the Israelis' seemingly endless questions and objections. Tension developed between the two groups, which disrupted work. However, the conflict ended when the Americans realized that Israelis view disagreements as a natural, even "fun" part of work. Common understanding resolved the problem.[25]

Across the United States, companies are beginning to address the issue of workplace diversity. Avon Products, for example, maintains "networks" of black, Hispanic, and Asian employees who canvass their constituencies and discuss conflicts they've identified as based on cultural and ethnic differences. Among the problems they've addressed: resentment among Hispanic employees who are criticized for speaking Spanish on the job, and frustration among Asians who resent the stereotype that Asians are technicians and not leaders.[26]

[25]Julie Solomon, "Firms Address Workers' Cultural Variety," *The Wall Street Journal,* February 10, 1989, p. B1.

[26]Ibid.

A growing number of undereducated employees.   An increasing number of young and future employees lack the basic knowledge and skills needed to maintain productive jobs. Some statistics provide evidence of this problem: About 1 million U.S. high school students drop out each year; the dropout rate is about 50 percent in the inner cities. Of those who do graduate, about 25 percent are functionally illiterate, able to read at only the eighth-grade level. Illiteracy rates approach 40 percent among minority students. And among students from 13 countries, American high school seniors rank last in biology, 11th in chemistry, and 9th in physics.[27]

This continuing trend of undereducated employees makes establishing and maintaining a qualified work force a real management challenge. This challenge is critical, given that U.S. businesses are competing internationally against companies in countries such as Japan and Korea, where employees are highly educated. U.S. businesses are responding in two ways: investing more funds in employee training programs and forming alliances with U.S. public education systems to boost the quality of education. These efforts are discussed in more detail in Chapter 3.[28]

An aging population.   Today, over 49 percent of the population is under age 35; by 2000, less than 39 percent will be under 35. In sum, there will be fewer younger employees to replace the older employees who retire. At the same time, more older employees are retiring sooner. In 1970, for example, 83 percent of all men from 55 to 64 years of age were employed; in 1986, only 67.3 percent were employed.[29]

These changing demographics present management with two challenges: find ways to keep older, experienced employees in the work force, and retrain older workers such as those who enter an organization to start a second career. To date, retention strategies have included allowing older employees to work fewer hours and redesigning jobs to accommodate older workers. For example, Builders Emporium, a chain of 121 home centers in California, recruited and retrained older workers when it redesigned salesclerk jobs, eliminating all heavy lifting and emphasizing salesmanship in advertisements.[30]

INDIRECT FORCES

The indirect forces of the external environment can affect managers in at least two ways. First, outside organizations can have a direct influence on an organization or an indirect influence through a direct force. For example, a consumer activist group may lobby for certain causes, such as equal credit opportunities for women or product safety. Local media may apply pressure to keep open a plant that management planned to close. Legislation may force

---

[27]Nancy J. Perry, "Saving the Schools: How Business Can Help," *Fortune,* November 7, 1988, pp. 42ff.

[28]For an excellent report on the undereducation issue, see "Needed: Human Capital," *Business Week,* September 19, 1988, pp. 100ff.

[29]Anthony Ramirez, "Making Better Use of Older Workers," *Fortune,* January 30, 1989, pp. 179ff.

[30]Ibid.

managers to alter the way they report certain information concerning hiring practices.

Second, certain indirect forces can influence the climate in which the organization must function. For example, the economy may expand or decline, requiring responses from management. New technological break-throughs may alter the entire way an organization does business. Imagine, for example, the impact digital watches had on traditional watch manufacturers or the effect of compact discs and cassette tapes on the manufacture of long-playing records. In 10 years, the records' share of the recorded music market declined from over 90 percent to less than 20 percent. The following discussion addresses some of the most important indirect forces in the external environment.

Technological.   Technological forces are developments in technology in the external environment that can impact an organization in two ways. Technological developments can influence an organization's use of knowledge and techniques in producing a product or service and in performing other work (e.g., financial analysis, clerical tasks) of the organization. For example, ultrasound equipment that provides a picture of a patient's heart is an important part of the technology used in diagnosing cardiac diseases; and the advent of laser scanners at cash registers in grocery stores has quickly become a primary element of the technology used in checking a customer's purchases. Second, technological developments also affect the characteristics of an organization's products or services, such as the power of a computer system or the clarity and brightness of a color TV's picture.

Technological forces require that management keep abreast of the latest developments and, where possible, incorporate advancements to maintain the organization's competitiveness. This challenge is made more difficult by the quickening pace of technological change. Consider, for example the projected technological changes listed in Table 2–2. According to experts, these major advancements will occur within the next 10 years. Moreover, the speed of change is expected to continue to accelerate in the 21st century.

A frantic pace of technological change can produce problems for organizations, even those on the cutting edge of technology. Consider, for example, IBM's current dilemma. Technological advancements have so quickly and substantially increased the power and capacity of personal computers that desktop PCs are fast replacing large, mainframe computers in many companies. IBM's problem: It depends on mainframe sales for 60 percent of its profits.[31]

Organizations attempt to keep up with technological change through close contacts with research and development organizations, research scientists, and other individuals involved in technological developments. Companies also update the skills and knowledge of their employees who are responsible for the technology of the organization's work and output. For example, some companies require their engineers to attend technical seminars to keep up-to-date. Many engineering and hi-tech firms allow their technical people to

[31]See Michael W. Miller and Paul B. Carroll, "Akers's Drive to Mend IBM Is Shaking Up Its Vaunted Traditions," *The Wall Street Journal,* **November** 11, 1988, pp. 1, 4.

TABLE 2-2	Some Technological Advances Expected by the Year 2000

Fully computerized automobiles: Equipped with a message screen (which reminds the driver of upcoming appointments), navigation system (which maps, on a color video screen, the quickest route to the driver's destination), and collision avoidance (computerized front and rear radar systems that warn of an impending crash and automatically tighten seat belts, and that alert the driver to oncoming cars).

Miniature computers: Shirt pocket–sized, that respond to handwritten and spoken questions and commands.

Underseas mining and farming.

Electronic books: Open up to display text on two facing screens. One will contain up to 200 books and novels.

Regenerated organs: The ability to regrow human organs instead of replacing them with transplants.

Supercomputers: With the ability to make over 4 trillion calculations per second (about 1,000 times more powerful than today's supercomputers).

Multipurpose telephones: Containing a large, color video screen for picture-phone conversations, and having the ability to send and receive messages and documents and to function as a computer.

Sources: Gene Bylinsky, "Technology in the Year 2000," *Fortune,* July 18, 1988, pp. 92ff; William J. Hampton, "Smart Cars," *Business Week,* June 13, 1988, pp. 68ff.

take sabbaticals—a several-month leave from the company, with pay—to upgrade their skills.[32]

Competitor intelligence teams can provide insight into developments in a competitor's work technology. Xerox Corp., for example, has learned much about the technology its Japanese competitors use in copiers by purchasing their copiers, dissassembling them, and studying the machines' parts and structural designs.[33]

Large companies with substantial resources develop their own technology in production and products or services. Currently, General Motors is conducting a unique experiment with its $52 million Saginaw Vanguard facility, likely the world's most futuristic factory. There the production of front-wheel–drive axles is totally automated. A few engineers and technicians sit at computer terminals in the plant's "command room" and control the lasers, robots, computerized assembly lines, and driverless, automatically guided vehicles that make the axles. GM is experimenting with this futuristic technology to determine whether it is quality and cost effective.[34] Federal Express played a role in developing the computerized technology that has given the company a

[32]Edmund L. Toomey and Joan M. Connor, "Employee Sabbaticals: Who Benefits and Why," *Personnel,* April 1988, pp. 81–84.

[33]See William F. Glavin, "Competitive Benchmarking—A Technique Utilized by Xerox Corp. to Revitalize Itself to a Modern Competitive Position," *Review of Business,* Winter 1984, pp. 9–12; Frances Gaither Tucker, Seymour M. Zivan, and Robert C. Camp, "How to Measure Yourself against the Best," *Harvard Business Review,* January–February 1987, pp. 8–10.

[34]William J. Hampton, "GM Bets an Arm and a Leg on a People-Free Plant," *Business Week,* September 12, 1988, pp. 72–73.

winning competitive edge in overnight delivery. In an instant, Federal Express can locate any package at every step of its journey from initial pickup to final delivery. Technology also enables Federal Express to come when you call, while chief competitor United Parcel Service must maintain a strict pickup schedule.[35] UPS's response: It is fast implementing the kind of technology that has given Federal Express the competitive advantage.[36]

Economic.   Economic forces are changes in the state of America's economy, which is reflected by such indicators as inflation rates, gross national product, unemployment rates, the value of the U.S. dollar, interest rates, and the size of the U.S. budget and trade deficits.

Changes in the economy pose both opportunities and problems for managers. In times of continual moderate growth, many organizations enjoy a growing demand for output, and funds are more easily available for plant expansion and other investments. However, when the economy shifts downward (as in a recession), demand plummets, unemployment rises, and profits shrink. In times of severe recession, as in the early 1980s, the survival of organizations in many industries (e.g., construction and related industries) is threatened.

Organizations must continually monitor changes in the chief economic indicators to minimize threats and capitalize on opportunities. Some organizations utilize projections of future economic conditions in making such decisions as whether to expand plant facilities or enter new markets. However, leading economists often differ in their economic projections; many organizations are therefore skeptical about economic forecasting.

Political, Legal, and Regulatory.   Numerous laws and a multitude of authorities characterize the political, legal, and regulatory forces in the external environment that have an indirect but strong influence on the organization and the climate in which it operates. For example, legislation by federal and state governments affects the wages and taxes that an organization pays, the rights of employees, and the organization's liabilities for harm done to customers by its products. Federal regulatory agencies influence an organization's hiring and promotion of women and minorities (the Equal Employment Opportunity Commission), its workplace safety (the Occupational Safety and Health Administration), the levels of pollutants its factories can release (Environmental Protection Agency), and the establishment and activities of unions in its workplace (the National Labor Relations Board).[37] More recent laws and judicial decisions have banned the use of polygraphs for employment decisions

---

[35]See Larry Reibstein, "Federal Express Faces Challenges to Its Grip on Overnight Delivery," *The Wall Street Journal*, January 8, 1988, pp. 1, 8; Kenneth Labich, "Big Changes at Big Brown," *Fortune*, January 18, 1988, pp. 56ff.

[36]For an excellent discussion of the nature of technological change in high-tech industries and its impact on management, see Gareth Morgan, "Drastic Changes for Management," *Business Month*, March 1989, pp. 67–70.

[37]Few federal regulatory agencies have been more severely criticized than OSHA. For an excellent overview of the criticisms and calls for reform, see Michael A. Verespej, "Time to Reform OSHA," *Industry Week*, January 2, 1989, pp. 46–48.

Political, legal, and regulatory forces in the external environment have an indirect but strong influence on the organization.

and restricted an organization's right to fire and its options in testing employees for drug use.

Political, legal, and regulatory forces can act as both constraint and opportunity. For example, while some organizations view antipollution laws as constraints, these laws have stimulated the growth of the pollution control industry. When the government has acted to combat inflation, those actions have constrained builders of single-unit houses, but spurred growth for apartment builders. Though some organizations oppose the government's tariffs on foreign goods imported into the United States, some organizations have clearly benefited. For example, in the early 1980s, motorcycle maker Harley-Davidson approached bankruptcy, battered by the higher-quality and lower-priced Japanese bikes imported by Honda, Yamaha, and Kawasaki. At Harley-Davidson's request, the U.S. government in 1983 boosted the import tariffs on the Japanese bikes from 4.4 percent to over 49 percent, which eliminated the Japanese's price advantage and gave Harley-Davidson five years to boost product quality and production efficiency. The company is now highly competitive.[38]

Most observers believe that government involvement in organizations will continue, given that people continue to call upon government to protect the

[38]See Mehran Sepehri, "Manufacturing Revitalization at Harley-Davidson Motor Co.," *Industrial Engineering,* August 1987, pp. 87–90; Michael Kolbenschlag, "Harley-Davidson Takes Lessons from Arch-Rivals' Handbook," *International Management,* February 1985, pp. 46–48.

consumer, preserve the environment, and push for an end to discrimination in employment, education, and housing. Consequently, many organizations monitor governmental and legislative developments to ensure their own compliance with the law. In some areas, specialists are hired to monitor and ensure compliance—for example, with affirmative action and labor relations regulations in the area of personnel. Some organizations actively attempt to influence the government by making contributions to political candidates and by lobbying state and federal legislators. Although professional political lobbyists often represent the interests of organizational clients, in recent years a growing number of companies have been utilizing their own employees to lead the company's lobbying efforts.[39]

Cultural and Social.   Cultural and social forces are changes in our social and cultural system that can affect an organization's actions and the demand for its products or services. Every nation has a social and cultural system comprising certain beliefs and values. The American culture and social system, for example, promotes the values of individuality, equality, and free enterprise.

Over time, issues emerge and changes occur that can affect organizations. In the 1970s, for example, the ecology movement had a major impact on legislation and numerous industries. More recently, environmental interest groups have lobbied for legislation to further limit industries' emissions of fossil fuels (gas, coal, and oil) that intensify the greenhouse effect—a phenomenon that could produce disastrous changes in the world's climate.[40] America's growing emphasis on good health has led food companies to lower the cholesterol content of their products. And the social shift toward moderation in drinking (along with the efforts of Mothers Against Drunk Drivers) is largely responsible for the continuing decline of sales in the liquor industry over the last eight years.[41]

Organizations should monitor developments in the social and cultural system. However, many do not, and thus they often underestimate the impact of social and cultural forces. As a result, these forces very often become a direct rather than indirect force, especially if society's expectations are unmet. The topic of organizational social responsibility is discussed further in Chapter 3.[42]

International.   For most U.S. organizations, the external environment (customers, competitors, human resources, and suppliers) is contained within the boundaries of the United States. However, international forces apply when an organization relies on a foreign supplier for resources or competes with international competitors within the United States. The importance of international forces grows considerably when an organization decides to internationalize and expand its products or services (and sometimes manufacturing

---

[39]See John M. Barry, "The New Breed of Lobbyist," *Dun's Business Month,* April 1988, pp. 44ff.

[40]Michael D. Lemonick, "Feeling the Heat," *Time,* January 2, 1989, pp. 36–39.

[41]Peter Bordeaux, "New Forces Are Challenging U.S. Spirits Industry," *Nation's Restaurant News,* December 12, 1988, pp. F9ff.

[42]Ralph Nader, "Reforming Corporate Governance," *California Management Review,* Summer 1984, pp. 126–32.

FIGURE 2–9   Direct and Indirect Forces of the
Organization's External Environment

An organization's, and therefore a manager's, external environment consists of both direct and indirect forces.

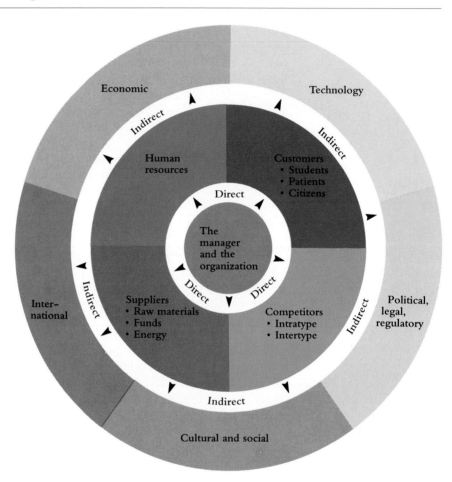

operations) into an international market. Venturing abroad, a company confronts an entirely new set of circumstances and environmental forces. Consumer preferences may differ. Pricing and promotional strategies may be very unfamiliar. Governmental policies in the international market may bear little resemblance to those of the U.S. government. And the cultural and social systems in the international market may contrast sharply with America's system of values and beliefs. Once an organization internationalizes, these international elements become direct rather than indirect forces.

Overall, the decision to do business in other countries presents a significant set of challenges to an organization, because management must learn to operate in an environment where many of the rules of business are very different from those that succeed in the United States. However, an increasing number of companies are entering international markets, generally for two reasons. First, a business might pursue internationalization because of weakening opportunities at home. Product demand may have declined, legislative regulation may have become too burdensome, or economic conditions may be weak. Second, the company may be drawn overseas by outstanding opportunities to market its products or services in other nations while continuing to do business at home. Such businesses as Kentucky Fried Chicken, McDonald's, and Apple Computer are thriving both internationally and domestically.

Whether competition from abroad, opportunities abroad, or dependency on foreign resources is involved, international forces will increase in importance in the next decade. Many experts predict that it is only a matter of time before most U.S. businesses will operate in an international environment. For this reason, we have devoted one chapter (21) to this topic.

MANAGEMENT AND THE EXTERNAL ENVIRONMENT

Figure 2–9 illustrates the direct and indirect forces in the external environment, summarizing our discussion of the organization's external environment. It shows the many forces that influence organizational performance. In every case, a major challenge to management is to identify and understand these forces, anticipate and adapt to those beyond its control, and influence those within its control.

SUMMARY OF KEY POINTS

- In systems theory, the organization is viewed as one of a number of elements that depend on each other. An organization takes resources (inputs) from the larger system (the environment), processes these resources, and returns them in changed form (output). Figure 2–1 presents the organization as a system.

- For the manager, the system concept emphasizes that *(a)* the ultimate survival of the organization depends on its ability to adapt to the demands of the environment and *(b)* in meeting these demands, the total sequence of input-process-output must be the focus of managerial attention.

- Most organizations function on at least three distinct but overlapping levels. The *operations level* focuses on effective performance, whether the organization produces something or performs a service; the task at this level is to develop the best allocation of resources in order to produce the desired output. The *managerial level* focuses on coordinating the activities at the operations level and serves as a liaison between those who produce the product or service and those who use the output. The *strategic level* determines the long-range objectives and direc-

tion of the organization—that is, how the organization will interact with the environment.

- The terms *top, middle,* and *first-level* managers are closely associated with the strategic, managerial, and operations levels. Together (see Figure 2–3), they are useful in understanding the different activities of managers.

- Certain skills are required for effective managerial performance. Technical skill, human skill, computer skill, and conceptual skill are all necessary management skills. However, as Figure 2–5 indicates, a different mix is required, depending on the level of management in the organization.

- Managers at all levels perform a variety of tasks. Specifically, they perform 10 different but closely related roles. The 10 roles can be separated into three different groupings: *interpersonal roles* (figurehead, leader, liaison), *decisional roles* (entrepreneur, disturbance handler, resource allocator, negotiator), and *informational roles* (monitor, disseminator, spokesperson).

- A manager's external environment consists of direct and indirect forces. Direct forces provide an immediate and direct impact on the organization. Indirect forces influence the climate in which the manager functions and often have the potential of becoming direct forces.

■   Direct forces include the organization's customers, competitors, suppliers, and human resources. Indirect forces include technology; the economy; political, legal, and regulatory forces; cultural and social forces; and international forces. For an organization to succeed, its management must recognize these forces, understand their real and potential impacts, and manage the organization to minimize their negative and maximize their positive influences on the organization.

DISCUSSION AND REVIEW QUESTIONS

1.   In your own words, describe an organization as a system. Do you believe this approach is useful? Why?

2.   Describe your management class, using the concept of a system. Must your instructor adapt the management class to the demands of the environment? Can you describe your management class, using the input-process-output cycle?

3.   If you were trying to identify top managers at the school you attend, what titles would you look for? If you had to identify them based on what they do, what would you look for?

4.   Discuss technical, human, computer, and conceptual skills in relation to a college instructor. What, in your opinion, would be a good mix?

5.   In your opinion, can human and conceptual skills be taught, or are they inherent?

6.   Describe an encounter you recently had with a manager. It could be in a business, school, hospital, or governmental organization. What managerial role or roles was the person performing?

7.   As the chapter notes, the direct forces in the external environment pose many challenges to organizations. Which challenge, in your view, is the most difficult for managers? Explain.

8.   Some observers assert that the importance of each of the various forces in the external environment differs across types of industries. Do you agree? Discuss.

9.   "Anyone can manage; all it takes is common sense." What is your opinion of this statement?

10. Some management observers assert that Mintzberg's typology of 10 managerial roles is incomplete. What other roles do managers assume?

ADDITIONAL REFERENCES

Bowen, D. E.; C. Siehl; and **B. Schneider.** "A Framework for Analyzing Customer Service Orientations in Manufacturing." *Academy of Management Review,* January 1989, pp. 75–95.

Bower, J. L., and **T. M. Hout.** "Fast-Cycle Capability and Competitive Power." *Harvard Business Review,* November–December 1988, pp. 110–18.

Burack, E. H. "A Strategic Planning and Operational Agenda for Human Resources." *Human Resource Planning* 11, no. 2 (1988), pp. 63–68.

Child, J. "Information Technology, Organization, and Response to Strategic Challenges." *California Management Review,* Fall 1987, pp. 33–50.

Duffey, J. "Competitiveness and Human Resources." *California Management Review,* Spring 1988, pp. 92–100.

Hallett, J. J. "Training and Education: The Competitive Edge." *Personnel Administrator,* September 1988, pp. 24–32.

Hamel, G.; Y. L. Doz; and **C. K. Prahalad.** "Collaborate with Your Competitors—and Win." *Harvard Business Review,* January–February 1989, pp. 133–39.

Keats, B. W., and **M. A. Hitt.** "A Causal Model of Linkages among Environmental Dimensions, Macro Organizational Characteristics, and Performance." *Academy of Management Journal,* September 1988, pp. 570–98.

Kirpe, D. L., and **D. S. Rice.** "Fast Forward—Styles of California Management." *Harvard Business Review,* January–February 1988, pp. 74–85.

Kulczycky, M. "Intelligence from the Marketplace." *Savings Institutions,* January 1989, pp. 62–70.

Kumpe, T., and **Bolwijn.** "The New Case for Vertical Integration." *Harvard Business Review,* March–April 1988, pp. 75–81.

Lucas, R. "Political-Cultural Analysis of Organizations." *Academy of Management Review,* January 1987, pp. 144–56.

Mintzberg, H. *Mintzberg on Management.* New York: Free Press, 1988.

Naisbitt, J. *Megatrends: Ten New Directions Tranforming Our Lives.* New York: Warner, 1982.

Pavett, C., and **A. Lau.** "Managerial Work: The Influence of Hierarchical Level and Functional Specialty." *Academy of Management Journal,* March 1983, pp. 170–77.

Peters, T. *Thriving on Chaos: Handbook for a Management Revolution.* New York: Alfred A. Knopf, 1987.

Porter, M. E. *Competitive Advantage.* New York: Free Press, 1985.

Pritchett, P. *After the Merger: Managing the Shockwaves.* Homewood, Ill.: Dow Jones-Irwin, 1985.

Sayles, L. *Leadership: What Effective Managers Really Do . . . and How They Do It.* Englewood Cliffs, N.J.: Prentice-Hall, 1979.

Stalk, G., Jr. "Time—The Next Source of Competitive Advantage." *Harvard Business Review,* July–August 1988, pp. 41–51.

CASE 2–1   Turnaround at Top Gun

The Tactical Air Command (TAC) is a large unit of the U.S. Air Force charged with protecting U.S. interests in the skies throughout the world. TAC employs over 115,000 individuals in more than 150 worldwide installations. With 3,800 aircraft, its fleet of planes is easily twice as large as all U.S. airlines combined.

In the late 1970s, TAC was in trouble. Half of its planes were not battle ready; well over 200 planes were "hangar queens"—unusable for at least three weeks because needed spare parts were not available or maintenance checkups could not be carried out. More important, poor maintenance of the planes had boosted the rate of accidents and deaths. Many pilots weren't receiving the air time needed to stay sharp. Morale was low. TAC's best pilots and maintenance/technician personnel were leaving the U.S. Air Force in considerable numbers.

In 1978, TAC received a new commander, General W. L. (Bill) Creech. A 30-year air force veteran, Creech's task was to turn around the now embarrassingly mediocre command.

Creech began by tackling the problem in plane maintenance. The procedures for maintaining or repairing planes at that time were bureaucratic and slow. Because of centralized management, it often took several days to obtain a part and to make a simple repair. Quality was also a problem because often the less experienced maintenance workers repaired the planes. As a result, more than 80 percent of the planes needing repair were not fixed in an average eight-hour shift.

Delays meant that planes sat idle. In 1969 on average, a plan flew 23 "sorties" (practice and training flights) each year; in 1978, the number was down to 11. With planes waiting in line in hangars, pilots missed their training flights. And when planes were flown, they often weren't repaired or maintained.

To address this problem, Creech restructured TAC. The new operating unit became the squadron (24 planes) instead of the much larger wing unit. Instead of keeping the centralized maintenance group that worked on all planes in an installation, Creech established squadron maintenance crews staffed by technicians from the various maintenance specialties. Each crew worked on its own squadron's planes. The crews, including their office-bound sergeant, also moved directly to the flight lines.

Creech's strategy had an impressive impact on morale. Maintenance crews began sporting their squadron's patches on their fatigues and caps. Crew

Source: Adapted from Jay Finegan, "Four-Star Management," *Inc.,* January 1987, pp. 42ff.

members, especially the crew chief, developed an identity with their squadron's planes; many of the chiefs were young, in their early 20s. Once given relatively little managerial responsibility, they were now in charge of $27 million jets. Crew discipline tightened up as the chiefs held their technicians strictly accountable.

The squadron's pilots took notice of the crew's commitment, and a camaraderie developed between pilot and crew. To further promote this commitment, Creech allowed each squadron to paint its colors on its planes—a previously prohibited practice. Competition between squadrons emerged on pilot performance and maintenance quality. Creech established a yearly awards banquet for each wing unit, where trophies were awarded to the year's top maintenance and supply specialists.

Creech's next step was to improve the planning and scheduling of sorties. This task had traditionally been done by officers at wing headquarters. Creech changed that. Each TAC squadron was given a sortie objective; the squadron set its own schedules as long as the goal was met. To boost crew motivation, Creech established a bonus: if a squadron achieved its monthly objective early, everyone in the squadron received an extra three-day weekend. The squadrons responded. Each year, a squadron earns about 10 extra three-day weekends.

Creech made other changes. He simplified the spare parts system, which was very cumbersome (ordering and receiving a part required 243 entries on 13 different forms and 16 hours of administrative work). Creech computerized the spare parts system and purchased minicomputers for the squadron crews. With the computerized system, crews could order parts at their computer terminal in an instant; the part suppliers at the supply station could almost as quickly fill the order. A walk to the supply store normally obtained a part in minutes.

Believing that a high-quality operation should also look high quality, Creech ordered a thorough housecleaning of every TAC facility. All the facilities received a new coat of paint, and many living and working quarters were renovated.

Creech encountered much resistance in implementing his turnaround strategy, in part because he decentralized TAC. He moved decision-making authority to the lower levels of the organization. Resistance understandably came from many officers at the higher levels who felt their authority had been diminished.

Eventually, however, the results of the general's efforts won converts. TAC doubled the number of sorties flown each day. Now, on any day, 85 percent of TAC's planes are mission ready. Only a few hangar queens are grounded. Accident rates have been substantially reduced; few accidents occur because of maintenance problems. And fewer of the best pilots and crew members are leaving TAC.

Perhaps the most impressive aspect of TAC's turnaround: These achievements were accomplished with no additional funding, personnel, or planes. The Pentagon is now implementing General Creech's ideas in several other military installations.

Questions for Analysis

1. In your opinion, what managerial skills (technical, human, computer, and conceptual) did Bill Creech utilize most in accomplishing the turnaround at TAC?

2. Describe the external environment in which Bill Creech and TAC operate. What direct and indirect forces most affect TAC? Discuss.
3. What managerial roles were most important in performing the turnaround task?

CASE 2–2   Management 101 at PepsiCo

As Chapter 2 notes, Coca-Cola and PepsiCo are battling head-to-head for leadership in the soft drink industry. So far, Coca-Cola is winning. However, PepsiCo is gaining steadily, and management experts view it as the better-managed company overall. In fact, PepsiCo emerged in 1989 as one of the 10 best-managed companies in America, according to *Fortune*'s prestigious annual survey of corporate reputations. Many analysts agree that the soft drink producer's chief resource is its exceptionally skilled and dedicated corps of managers.

PepsiCo's high-quality management is at least partly the result of an exceptionally comprehensive management development program, which is designed to "take eagles and teach them to fly in formation," in the words of CEO Wayne Calloway. The program applies a formula for developing managers that includes several ingredients. First, PepsiCo begins by hiring a particular type of future manager—called a "Pepsi Pretty" in the company's lingo. These individuals have attended strong business schools and have talent, exceptional drive and ambition, and a hefty ego.

Once hired, new managers are given challenging performance goals and are expected to work long hours—putting in 60 hours a week including working Saturdays and Sundays is typical for managers throughout the organization. They are also given much responsibility at a young age because PepsiCo believes that managers acquire skills by continually being tested in many different ways. For example, soon after he joined the company, 24-year-old Peter McNally was given full responsibility for a $500 million segment of the snack business of Frito-Lay, a major division of PepsiCo. McNally's assignment was to boost the sales of the 1-ounce, single-serving bags of Frito's potato and taco chips. McNally's idea: market larger, 2-ounce bags for teenagers with big appetites. His idea has helped boost Frito-Lay's sales by 15 percent each year since 1985. At 30, McNally is now vice president of marketing services for PepsiCo's Taco Bell chain.

While they assume substantial responsibilities, PepsiCo's young managers are encouraged to make decisions and make them quickly. Committees and committee meetings are scorned (PepsiCo believes they kill good ideas), as are files and memos (which, if written, cannot exceed one page). Managers are also encouraged to take risks, as long as they are calculated. If a manager does so and fails, his or her career doesn't suffer. For example, PepsiCo's president Craig Weatherup once made a $3 billion goof when, at age 30, he took charge of PepsiCo operations in Japan. Weatherup introduced Diet Pepsi in Japan, and the product flopped. The problem Weatherup hadn't foreseen: The Japanese

Source: Adapted from Brian Dumaine, "Those Highflying PepsiCo Managers," *Fortune,* April 10, 1989, pp. 78ff.

associate the word diet with medicine. PepsiCo's top management's comment to Weatherup: Be more careful next time, but keep taking risks.

PepsiCo's managers work in an exceptionally competitive environment. Open, hotly verbal confrontations between disagreeing managers are frequent. People with reserved, introverted personalities aren't a part of PepsiCo's formula. Each manager's work is also closely evaluated in annual performance evaluation reviews. During the review, the manager discusses performance with his or her boss. If the manager has met assigned goals, the goals for next year are usually increased. If goals were not met, the manager is given one, sometimes two years to meet them. If goals remain unachieved, the manager is let go. Each year, every manager's human skills are evaluated by subordinates, who provide written, confidential appraisals. Each manager receives the evaluations and is counseled when problems arise.

Each winter, PepsiCo's 550 upper-level managers are reviewed and placed in one of four categories. Managers in the bottom category are let go. Those in the top group are promoted. Those in the middle group are placed in one of two categories: those who need more special training or time on the job and those who are promotable but no openings are presently available. This review of upper-level managers is designed to constantly evaluate management careers and to promote continually improved performance.

Overall, PepsiCo's management development program stresses achievement, competitiveness, self-confidence, and risk taking. Those who succeed receive substantial rewards. PepsiCo pays very well (top middle-level managers can earn from $96,000 to $144,000 yearly, excluding perks and benefits). Those top 550 managers also fly first-class and stay at luxury hotels while on business, receive a new company car every two years, and can earn an annual bonus ranging from 25 to 90 percent of salary. It's a tough life at PepsiCo, but the rewards can be plenty.

Questions for Analysis

1. In your opinion, what are the strengths and weaknesses of PepsiCo's approach to management development?
2. PepsiCo's internal environment is intensely competitive and hard driving. Besides its benefits, do you see any shortcomings with this type of climate?
3. In your view, what managerial skills are needed to compete effectively in the soft drink industry?

Experiential Exercise

Profile of an External Environment

Purpose

To enhance students' understanding of the importance, dynamics, and challenges of the external environments in which organizations operate.

The Exercise in Class

The instructor will divide the class into teams, each comprising three to four members. Each team will complete the following steps:

1. Select a company that interests your team and that is well reported in the business literature (several companies discussed in this chapter are excellent in this regard). Then, for your company, identify two direct forces and two indirect forces in the external environment that are strongly influencing the company's well-being.
2. Go to the library and research the company, focusing on these four forces. For each force, obtain from your research a thorough understanding of:
   a. The specific force. (For example, who are the organization's critical competitors and what are their strategies? What social trends and government regulations are influencing the company?)
   b. The current impact of that force on the company.
   c. The company's present strategy for dealing with the force.
3. Prepare a written profile of the company's four external forces that includes the points researched in step 2. Also be sure to include your team's predictions concerning how each force will challenge the company in the future and how the company should respond.

The Learning Message

This exercise should clearly illustrate that the forces in the external environment are very dynamic, at times unpredictable, and that their challenges and impacts vary across different organizations in different industries.

3

SOCIAL AND ETHICAL RESPONSIBILITIES OF MANAGEMENT

LEARNING OBJECTIVES

After completing Chapter 3, you should be able to:

Define
social responsibility in terms that reflect your view of the role of corporations in society.

Describe
the manner in which managers' ethics affect their decisions regarding social responsibility.

Discuss
the purpose, process, and pitfalls of establishing an effective code of ethics.

Compare
arguments for and against a specific corporate action, based on your own ethical standards.

Identify
the various actions managers are taking to ensure that their organizations are ethical.

Cleveland, Ohio: Business to the Rescue

In the early 1980s, Cleveland was a city in deep trouble. Years of industrial decline and poor labor-management relations had produced an 11.4 percent unemployment rate by 1983. The crime rate was spiraling, and the city's environment was very polluted (its oily Cuyahoga River had caught fire years earlier). Incompetent government had placed the city of Cleveland financially in default, the only major U.S. city to default since the Great Depression. Scores of companies were leaving Cleveland, including the Fortune 500–sized Diamond Shamrock Corp.

However, a group of Cleveland chief executive officers (CEOs) pooled their efforts and resources to bring the city back to life. The group (later organized as Cleveland Tomorrow, consisting of the CEOs of Cleveland's top 50 companies):

- Studied, at the mayor's request, the city government's operations and proposed 650 ways to boost efficiency. The mayor implemented about 500 ideas, which have saved the city over $200 million.
- Created the Work in Northeast Ohio Council, staffed by union and management leaders, to go into organizations to teach new management techniques that emphasize labor-management partnerships, product quality, and productivity.
- Mobilized Cleveland-area colleges and universities to help Cleveland businesses modernize their manufacturing technologies and boost product quality.
- Established a $30 million venture capital fund to finance the creation of new businesses, and helped to engineer the renovation of downtown Cleveland.
- Provided $2.5 million to help purchase and renovate homes to sell to poor citizens on a lease-purchase plan.
- Offered hiring preference to Cleveland high school graduates to keep Cleveland children in school.

These efforts and those of other Cleveland businesses are impressive examples of the positive impact that corporate social responsibility can have on a troubled community. Cleveland's unemployment now stands at 5.5 percent, and the number of new businesses is fast increasing. Companies are no longer leaving Cleveland.

Source: Myron Magnet, "How Business Bosses Saved a Sick City," *Fortune*, March 29, 1989, pp. 106ff.

The terms *social responsibility, business ethics,* and *management ethics* appear frequently in popular and technical literature. Every day, newspapers report incidents involving businesses that some people would call socially irresponsible and unethical. Yet, other individuals and groups might consider the actions to be quite proper, from both a social and ethical standpoint.

One of the purposes of this chapter is to provide bases for understanding the meanings and implications of social responsibility and ethics. To accomplish this purpose, we will review (1) society's expectations for corporate and managerial behavior and (2) changing business ethics. The social context in which corporate and managerial decisions and actions occur is dynamic and complex. Thus, to understand the meanings of social responsibility and business ethics is to recognize that they change with time and circumstance.[1]

Another purpose of this chapter is to provide guidelines by which managers can determine socially and ethically responsible behavior. Managers must be cognizant of their own responsibilities for instilling acceptable ethical standards throughout their organizations.[2] They must also be cognizant of the necessity to create organizational procedures and policies that encourage disclosure of unethical behavior.[3] The standard of business and managerial behavior for what is minimally responsible and ethical is that which is legal. Legality must be the recognized threshold of all managerial and organizational action.

THE MEANINGS OF SOCIAL RESPONSIBILITY

A recent review of the literature identifies no less than nine meanings for social responsibility.[4] These nine meanings can be classified in three general categories: **social obligation, social reaction,** and **social responsiveness.**[5]

SOCIAL RESPONSIBILITY AS SOCIAL OBLIGATION

According to this view, a corporation engages in socially responsible behavior when it pursues a profit within the constraints of law as imposed by society. Because society supports business by allowing it to exist, business is *obligated* to repay society for that right by making profits. Thus, legal behavior in pursuit of profit is socially responsible behavior, and *any behavior not legal or not in pursuit of profit is socially irresponsible.*

[1]Ronald L. Crawford and Harold A. Gram, "Social Responsibility as Interorganizational Transaction," *Academy of Management Review,* October 1978, p. 880.

[2]George Strother, "The Moral Codes of Executives: A Watergate-Inspired Look at Barnard's Theory of Executive Responsibility," *Academy of Management Review,* April 1976, pp. 13–22; Len Peach, "Managing Corporate Citizenship," *Personnel Management,* July 1985, pp. 32–35.

[3]L. D. Alexander and W. F. Matthews, "The Ten Commandments of Corporate Social Responsibility," *Business and Society Review,* Summer 1984, pp. 62–66; Robert Boulanger and Donald Wayland, "Ethical Management: A Growing Corporate Responsibility," *CA Magazine,* March 1985, pp. 54–59.

[4]Archie B. Carroll, "A Three-Dimensional Conceptual Model of Corporate Performance," *Academy of Management Review,* October 1979, pp. 497–505.

[5]Suggested by S. Prakash Sethi, "A Conceptual Framework for Environmental Analysis of Social Issues and Evaluation of Business Response Patterns," *Academy of Management Review,* January 1979, pp. 63–74.

This view is associated with economist Milton Friedman and others who believe that society creates business firms to pursue special and specialized purposes—producing goods and services—and that to engage in other pursuits exaggerates the legitimate place of business in society.[6] As Friedman stated: "There is one and only one social responsibility of business—to use its resources and engage in activities designed to increase its profits so long as it stays within the rules of the game, which is to say, engages in open and free competition without deception or fraud."[7]

Proponents of social responsibility as social obligation offer four primary arguments in support of their view. First, they assert, businesses are accountable to their shareholders, the owners of the corporation. Thus, management's sole responsibility is to serve the shareholders' interests by managing the company to produce profits from which the shareholders benefit.

Second, socially responsible activities such as social improvement programs should be determined by law, by public policy, and by the actions and contributions of private individuals. As representatives of the people, the government (via legislation and allocation of tax revenues) is best equipped to determine the nature of social improvements and to realize those improvements in society. Businesses contribute in this regard by paying taxes to the government, which rightfully determines how they should be spent.

Third, if management allocates profits to social improvement activities, it is abusing its authority. As Friedman notes, these actions amount to taxation without representation. Management is taxing the shareholders by taking their profits and spending them on activities that have no immediate profitable return to the company.[8] And management is doing so without input from shareholders. Because managers are not elected public officials, they are also taking actions that affect society without being accountable to society. Further, this type of non-profit-seeking activity may be both unwise and unworkable because managers are not trained to make noneconomic decisions.[9]

Fourth, these actions by management may work to the disadvantage of society. In this sense, the financial costs of social activities may over time cause the price of the company's goods and services to increase, and customers would pay the bill. Managers have acted in a manner contrary to the interest of the customers and ultimately the shareholders.

Although many people disagree with this meaning, *social responsibility* can refer to behavior directed exclusively (but legally) toward the pursuit of profit. A manager can, with some justification, state that he has discharged his obligation to society by creating goods and services in exchange for profit within the limits defined by law.

---

[6]Milton Friedman, *Capitalism and Freedom* (Chicago: University of Chicago Press, 1962).

[7]Milton Friedman, "The Social Responsibility of Business Is to Increase Its Profits," *New York Times Magazine,* September 1970, pp. 33, 122–26.

[8]Ibid.

[9]Henry Mintzberg, "The Case for Corporate Social Responsibility," *Journal of Business Strategy,* Fall 1983, p. 5.

Management

A New Partnership

In the mid-1980s, many U.S. businesses came to an alarming realization: America's work force was becoming increasingly undereducated. One startling statistic: About one fourth of all American adults lacked the basic reading, writing, and math abilities to function effectively in a job. Today, one of every four teenagers never graduates from high school; one of every four who do graduate has the equivalent of an eighth-grade education.

Businesses have responded to this growing "literacy gap" by pouring money into training programs that teach their employees basic reading and other skills. In its plants, for example, Ford Motor Co. has established 50 learning centers, where over 8,500 Ford workers have received basic skills training. And Domino's Pizza spends about $50,000 each year on a reading program for employees.

However, other business efforts are extending beyond the boundaries of the workplace. A growing number of businesses are establishing new partnerships with city and county school systems to boost the quality of education, from the kindergarten through high school level. For their part, businesses are contributing equipment, teacher training, literacy volunteers, paid work-study programs, and money.

American society, business
society's major problems a
Second, contrary to the
trained to deal with societa
that companies "are perhap:
in a capitalist society."[18] The
alleviating major social prob
that business's involvement
the social obligation view p

[18]H. Gordon Fitch, "Achieving
Review, January 1976, p. 45.

Stew Leonard's in Norwalk, Connecticut, gets more than 36,000 suggestions from customers each year. Every customer who leaves a suggestion gets a phone call from the store within 48 hours.

Social Responsibility as Social Reaction

A second meaning of social responsibility is behavior that is in reaction to "currently prevailing social norms, values, and performance expectations."[10] This pervasive view emphasizes that society has expectations for business and corporate behavior that go beyond the provision of goods and services. At minimum, business must be accountable for the ecological, environmental, and social costs incurred by its actions; at maximum, business must react and contribute to solving society's problems (even those that cannot be directly attributed to business).[11]

A somewhat restrictive interpretation of social responsibility as social reaction is that it involves only voluntary actions. This interpretation seeks to separate corporate actions that are *required* by economic or legal imperative and those that are initiated by voluntary, altruistic motives.[12] Thus, this more narrow view would imply that a corporation that pursues only socially obligated behavior is not socially responsible, because such behavior is required, not voluntary.

A leading spokesman for the view that social responsibility goes beyond the law, Keith Davis, states: "A firm is not being socially responsible if it merely complies with the minimum requirements of the law. . . . Social responsibility

[10]Sethi, "A Conceptual Framework," p. 66.

[11]Ibid.

[12]H. Manne and H. C. Wallich, *The Modern Corporation and Social Responsibility* (Washington, D.C.: American Enterprise Institute for Public Policy Research, 1972), as noted in Carroll, "A Three-Dimensional Conceptual Model," p. 498.

goes one step further. It [soc:
obligation beyond the requir
obligation in reaction to pr
publicity would not be social

Whether the firm's action:
pretation of the social reacti
actions that go beyond the l
expectations of specific grou
sumerists, and the like.[14] Bec
legal minimums, firms can de
reaction, however, is conside

The essence of this view (
Demands are made of them
responsible when they react,
these demands. This meanin
responsibility should refer to

SOCIAL RESPONSIBILITY /

According to this view, s(
preventive rather than reactive
become widely used in recen
obligation and social reaction.[1
include taking stands on pub]
group, anticipating future nee
and communicating with the
socially desirable legislation.

A socially responsive co
problems. Progressive manag
and resources to every probl
ment and small business jo!
providing quality education
responsiveness, as profiled in

The social responsiveness
bility. It places managers and
far removed from the traditic
means and ends. Advocates
approach to social responsit
reaction perspective for three

First, business's economic
from the social activities a
business does (such as openii
line) has distinct social conse(

[13]Keith Davis, "The Case for a!
Academy of Management Journal, Jun

[14]Crawford and Gram, "Social

[15]Sethi, "A Conceptual Framew

[16]Peter Arlow and Martin J. Ga!
Economic Performance," *Academy (*

[17]Mintzberg, "The Case," p. 12

Virtually everything a business does, for instance, launching a new line of children's toys, has social consequences.

business's support of social causes, and companies' efforts are likely to receive substantial approval from consumers, the press, and the public.[19]

A CONTINUUM OF SOCIAL RESPONSIBILITY

The three general meanings of social responsibility can be depicted as a continuum. As shown in Figure 3–1, at one extreme is social obligation: business behavior that reflects the firm's economic and legal responsibilities. Occupying the middle position is social reaction: behavior that is demanded by groups having a direct stake in the organization's actions. The farthest extreme, social responsiveness, is anticipatory, proactive, and preventive behavior.

In practice, a corporation can choose to be anywhere along the continuum. To be socially reactive implies the firm's acceptance of social obligation as well. Similarly, to be socially responsive requires both social obligation and social reaction behavior. In a sense, the three meanings refer to different degrees of departure from the usual economic expectations and performance of business firms.

SPECIFIC SOCIALLY RESPONSIBLE ACTIVITIES

So far, the discussion has revolved around *abstract* concepts of social responsibility. However, an organization translates its particular abstract concept of social responsibility into concrete expressions via specific, deliberate activities.

[19]Leonard Silk, "The New (Improved) Creed of Social Responsibility," *Business Month,* November 1988, p. 110.

FIGURE 3–1	A Continuum of Social Responsibility

The continuum formed by the three classes of socially responsible behavior ranges from an emphasis on profit making to an emphasis on social and economic concerns.

Type of behavior:	Socially obligated	Socially reactive	Socially responsive
Primary emphasis:	The organization's economic and legal responsibilities	The organization's economic, legal, and social responsibilities	The organization's economic, legal, social, and citizenship responsibilities

Socially responsible activities can be classified in different ways. One such classification provides eight categories of socially responsible actions. A business can take socially responsible actions in terms of its *product line* by manufacturing a safe, reliable, and high-quality product and in its *marketing practices* by, for example, being truthful and complete in its product advertising. Socially responsible activities in *employee education and training* can include effectively preparing employees to perform jobs well and retraining rather than laying off employees when new technology is implemented. Concerning *environmental control*, a business may be socially responsible by implementing production technology that reduces the amount of pollutants produced by manufacturing processes.

Actions in *employee relations, benefits, and satisfaction with work* can include providing benefits that accommodate important but unfulfilled employee needs such as providing an on-site day care facility for parent employees. In the area of *employment and advancement of minorities or women*, businesses may choose to be socially responsible by focusing efforts on hiring and professionally developing minorities. Efforts to provide a clean, safe, and comfortable working environment are socially responsible activities in the realm of *employee safety and health*.

Some businesses, especially large corporations, focus socially responsible efforts in the area of *corporate philanthropy*, by making donations to universities, arts and cultural foundations, the underprivileged, community development projects, and other groups and causes in society. Today, corporations provide about 11 percent of all financial philanthropic contributions made in the United States.[20] However, growth in corporate giving has tapered off since 1986. Faced with intensifying competition and the need to cut costs and restructure, many companies have found it difficult to justify their philanthropic activities to their employees and shareholders.[21] Companies are also becoming more interested in making contributions that result in more profits. This concern has fueled the popularity of "cause-related marketing," which is profiled in the Management Focus on "Profits and Philanthropy."

Another way to classify socially responsible actions is to identify the *beneficiaries* of each action. As the discussion above indicates, the organization's *customers* benefit in some instances; in others, the *employees* benefit. Beyond employees and customers are definable interest groups, such as racial and

[20]Stanley J. Modic, "Movers and Shakers," *Industry Week,* January 18, 1988, pp. 47ff.

[21]Meg Cox, "Corporate Giving Is Flat, and Future Looks Bleaker," *The Wall Street Journal,* October 17, 1988, p. B1.

MANAGEMENT FOCUS

Profits and Philanthropy: Should They Mix?

In 1983, American Express coined the term *cause-related marketing* when it launched a promotional campaign that pledged to donate a penny to the restoration of the Statue of Liberty every time a consumer used the American Express card. Since then, cause-related marketing has become a very popular strategy for corporate giving. The concept is simple: For each purchase of a product, a business gives a portion of the income to a nonprofit organization (usually a charity). Or the company may simply provide a contribution to a charity in return for publicizing the charity in the company's product ads and promotional displays. (Big-name causes can generate sales.)

By all accounts, a growing number of charities are turning to cause-related marketing to boost corporate giving. For example, Big Brothers/ Big Sisters depends on that philanthropic strategy for about 20 percent of its national budget. The American Red Cross plans to obtain $10 million via cause-related marketing by 1993, which amounts to 40 percent of its national disaster relief budget. The March of Dimes received $150,000 from Campbell Soup Co., its 1988 walkathon sponsor.

However, some observers criticize the strategy, citing that its growing popularity may undermine the independence of philanthropy, possibly leading to a time when companies give only with strings attached. They also assert that cause-related marketing favors only well-known and noncontroversial charities, neglecting equally worthy but lesser-known causes. For example, MasterCard's recent campaign to raise $3 million in three months was for six charities selected partly on the results of a consumer popularity poll. Since its Statue of Liberty campaign, American Express has not launched a nationwide cause-related marketing effort, because the company hasn't found a cause it believes will generate significant enthusiasm.

Cause-related marketing provides charities with publicity and donations, and companies with a positive public image and, sometimes, sales. Despite its critics, it is a trend on the rise.

Source: Adapted from Zachary Schiller, "Doing Well by Doing Good," *Business Week*, December 5, 1988, pp. 53ff.

---

ethnic groups, women's groups, and governmental agencies. In a sense, these groups are other organizations that transact business with the corporation. The focus of these transactions is not exchange of economic goods and services but exchange of concessions based upon relative power. In addition to customers, employees, and interest groups, there are ill-defined beneficiaries such as future generations, society at large, and the common good. Activities such as assistance to the arts are directed to these beneficiaries. For simplicity, two general classes of beneficiaries can be identified: *internal* and *external*.

INTERNAL BENEFICIARIES

Three groups of internal beneficiaries are apparent: *customers, employees,* and *shareholders* (owners). Each of these groups has an immediate and often conflicting stake in the organization. Corporate activities in response to each group can be classified as obligatory, reactive, or responsive.

Responsibilities to Customers.   Much of what is said about the responsibility of business toward its customers is critical.[22] A particular target of criticism has been the business organization's responsibilities regarding the product and marketing.

One social obligation of business relates to product characteristics: quality, safety, packaging, and performance. The relative importance of these characteristics varies among products over time. Even within one industry, the relative importance shifts. For example, the publication of Ralph Nader's *Unsafe at Any Speed* in 1965 raised the issue of automobile safety.

The safety issue reached its highest point in public awareness in the 1970s, when Ford Motor Co. paid approximately $500 million in liability damages related to accidental deaths and injuries to drivers and passengers of defective Ford Pinto automobiles. The public was incensed when a Ford internal memo leaked out that contained a cost-benefit analysis of repairing versus not repairing the defective cars.[23] According to the memo, repairing the defective cars (at $11 per car) would cost Ford $137 million. If the defective cars were not recalled and repaired, the memo stated, 180 burn deaths would likely occur and would cost $200,000 each (this cost estimate is probably based on estimated insurance payments). The memo further stated that 180 burn injuries would likely occur and would cost $67,000 each. According to the memo, not repairing the cars would cost Ford about $49 million to compensate for death and injury. Ford Motor Co. did not recall the cars.[24]

The success of Japanese automobiles rests largely on their superior quality. American consumers believe that Japanese cars are of better quality than American cars, and they express this judgment in their buying decisions. The response of American auto manufacturers has been to implement quality control programs and to publicize those programs in advertisements.

The issue of social responsibility toward customers is relatively fixed at one extreme (as in instances where specific legal directives define product safety) and quite fluid at the other (as in instances where there are general expectations regarding price-quality relationships). Many firms choose to meet their responsibilities to customers by responding promptly to complaints, by providing complete and accurate product information, and by implementing advertising programs that are completely truthful regarding product performance.

Responsibilities to Employees.   Management's responsibilities to employees can be minimally discharged by meeting the legal requirements that relate to employee-employer relationships. Such laws address issues associated with the physical conditions of work (particularly the safety and health issues), wage and hour provisions, unions and unionization, and the like. The thrust of these laws is to encourage management to create safe and productive workplaces within which employees' basic civil rights are not compromised. In addition to these responsibilities, the modern corporate practice of providing

---

[22]The following discussion is based on Frederick D. Sturdivant, *Business and Society: A Managerial Approach*, 3rd ed. (Homewood, Ill.: Richard D. Irwin, 1985), pp. 288–303.

[23]Mark Dowie, "Two Million Firetraps on Wheels," *Business and Society Review*, Fall 1977, pp. 67–72.

[24]Ibid., p. 69.

fringe benefits—retirement funds, health and hospitalization insurance, and accident insurance—has extended the range of socially obligated activity. In some instances, these practices are in response to concerted employee pressure, typically through union activity.

A company may assume other socially responsible activities, such as providing comprehensive employee training, career development, and counseling, and establishing employee assistance programs (EAPs) to help employees with drug and alcohol problems. Today, over 9,000 U.S. businesses, including more than 30 percent of the Fortune 500 companies, have established EAPs.[25]

More companies are realizing that employees are experiencing greater difficulties in meeting the responsibilities of job and family. The growing incidence of two-career couples with children and the longer life span of the elderly mean that more employees need assistance in caring for their children and parents. Companies are responding in several ways. One in 10 U.S. businesses currently provides some type of child care assistance, ranging from financial assistance and referral services to actual day care facilities on the company premises.[26]

A small but growing number of businesses are providing some form of assistance for elderly care. In 1987, IBM launched the first nationwide elder-care referral service for its employees after learning that over 30 percent of its work force cares for elderly relatives. Over 4,000 of IBM's 237,000 employees and 33,000 retirees called for help during the service's first month of activity.[27] Experts predict that in the coming 20 years, leave programs for family care, more flexible work hours, and subsidies for the education of employees and their children will become common employee benefits. [28]

These socially responsible efforts are socially reactive in nature if they are responses to pressures from employees or external parties. The efforts are socially responsive if the organization proactively initiates these activities in the absence of any substantial pressure. However, it is important to note that, like many socially responsible actions, activities taken in the interest of employees can also benefit the organization. For example, several companies that have proactively established day care centers report substantial improvement in attendance and productivity among participating employees.[29]

Responsibility to Shareholders. Management has a responsibility to disclose fully and accurately to shareholders its use of corporate resources and the results of those uses. The law guarantees shareholders the right to financial information and establishes minimums of public disclosure. The fundamental right of a shareholder is not to be guaranteed a profit but to be guaranteed information on which a prudent investment decision can be based. The

[25]"Battling the Enemy Within," *Time,* March 17, 1986, pp. 52ff.

[26]Janice Castro, "Home Is Where the Heart Is," *Time,* October 3, 1988, p. 48.

[27]Ibid.

[28]Julie Solomon, "The Future Look of Employee Benefits," *The Wall Street Journal,* September 7, 1988, p. 21.

[29]Fern Schumer Chapman, "Executive Guilt: Who's Taking Care of the Children?" *Fortune,* February 16, 1987, pp. 30–37.

ultimate action that a shareholder can take is to sell the stock and cease to have an ownership interest.[30]

Many individuals would argue that management's first responsibility is to the shareholder. In fact, those persons would contend that any managerial action that goes beyond socially obligated behavior to the benefit of any group other than shareholders is a violation of management's (and therefore social) responsibility. At the same time, there is evidence that firms that aggressively pursue socially responsive behavior are more profitable than those that do not. The evidence to support this position is controversial because there is little agreement on how social responsibility can be measured and how it should be related to performance measures such as profit and stock prices, the interests of shareholders. Two published reviews suggest that if there is a relationship between socially responsible behavior and corporate performance, it is one that must be taken on faith.[31]

The internal beneficiaries of corporate actions are the focus of much of management's socially obligated behavior. In their relations with customers, employees, and shareholders, managers are most likely to be judged socially responsible. The relationships between the corporation and its internal beneficiaries are so circumscribed by law, regulation, and custom that the corporation is bound to act out of legal obligation. To do so involves no particular accomplishment for the corporation. But to fail to act legally, whether intentionally or not, can lead to all sorts of legal and social condemnation of the corporation and its management. Therefore, corporations have greater opportunities to be socially reactive and responsive in matters involving external beneficiaries.

EXTERNAL BENEFICIARIES

The external beneficiaries of corporate behavior are of two types, *specific* and *general*. Both types benefit from the organization's actions, even though they may have no direct or apparent stake in it.

Specific External Beneficiaries. Modern societies consist of diverse interest groups working to further the well-being of their members. These groups represent rather well-defined populations of individuals seeking to redress historical grievances: minorities and ethnics, women, the handicapped, and the aged. They pursue their interests by bringing political and popular opinion to bear on corporate actions. Some groups are able to have laws implemented that force corporations to support their efforts. For example, equal employment opportunity and affirmative action legislation creates corporate obligations to recruit, hire, and develop women and members of

[30]Howard R. Bloch and Thomas J. Lareau, "Should We Invest in 'Socially Irresponsible' Firms?" *Journal of Portfolio Management,* Summer 1985, pp. 27–31.

[31]Kenneth E. Aupperle, Archie B. Carroll, and John D. Hatfield, "An Empirical Examination of the Relationship between Corporate Social Responsibility and Profitability," *Academy of Management Journal,* June 1985, pp. 446–63; Arieh A. Ullman, "Data in Search of Theory: A Critical Examination of the Relationships among Social Performance, Social Disclosure, and Economic Performance of U.S. Firms," *Academy of Management Review,* July 1985, pp. 540–57.

minority and ethnic groups. The fundamental contention of these groups is that they have been discriminated against in the past and that corporations have been an important cause of that discrimination. Thus, a larger burden of responsibility must be borne by corporations to erase the vestiges of historical discrimination and to create a new environment of equal access to employment opportunities and economic advancement.

Corporate actions involving specific external beneficiaries can be obligatory, reactive, or responsive. Obligatory actions are in response to antidiscrimination laws and regulations. The corporation can be judged both socially and legally irresponsible if it violates these laws. But beyond minimal compliance, a corporation has considerable latitude in the rigor with which it pursues affirmative action programs. How rapidly it fills its managerial ranks with minorities and women is largely a matter of discretion, so long as good faith can be demonstrated. A corporation can be deemed socially reactive if it goes beyond the letter of the law in implementing affirmative action. Socially responsive behavior not only seeks solutions to the immediate problems but attempts to go to the very heart of the causes. Such behavior could include doing business with minority-owned businesses, creating programs to train the hard-core unemployed, and initiating career development programs for women. When such efforts are not prompted by law or pressure, they are clearly socially responsive in nature.

The most important characteristic of these actions—whether they be obligatory, reactive, or responsive—is that the economic, social, and political well-being of a specific group of individuals is enhanced through the corporation's efforts.

General External Beneficiaries. Programs involving general external beneficiaries often are considered socially responsible because they elicit corporate efforts to solve or prevent general social problems. Companies have launched efforts to solve or prevent environmental or ecological problems such as water, air, and noise pollution, and waste and radiation disposal. Actions by Johnson Wax Company in the mid-1970s provide an example of activity in this area. When the first scientific research was published concerning the destructive impact of fluorocarbons on the atmosphere's ozone layer, Johnson Wax immediately withdrew all of its fluorocarbon products worldwide, years before the FDA banned fluorocarbon use. Company officials report that they initially lost business and angered some manufacturers; however, the organization chose to act quickly because it believed the product withdrawal was in society's best interests.[32]

Other organizations have acted to upgrade education, the arts, and community health through gifts and donations of executive time. For example, New York Life is one of a growing number of companies that are donating funds for AIDS research and public education programs. New York Life donated over $1 million to fund an AIDS public information advertising campaign in New York and sponsored a fund-raising benefit that raised $2 million for AIDS research.[33]

[32]Tad Tuleja, *Beyond the Bottom Line* (New York: Facts on File Publications, 1985), p. 78.

[33]Milton R. Moskowitz, "Company Performance Roundup," *Business and Society Review,* 1987, p. 69.

Some organizations have launched efforts to improve the quality of governmental management through leaves of absence for executives to take government positions. Other organizations have contributed to philanthropic causes such as United Way to help upgrade the quality of community life. Companies have also made contributions to overall community development. One notable example is the "Minnesota 5 Percent Club," a group of 45 companies. Each member donates at least 5 percent of its taxable profits to the development of the twin cities, Minneapolis–St. Paul.[34]

Corporations have considerable freedom in this area of social responsibility. They can choose which specific problems to become involved with—or they can choose not to become involved at all. But business leaders recognize the growing importance of issues such as the condition of the environment. For example: "In recent industrial history, few public policy issues have had the social, political, and economic impact that this one [health, safety, and the environment] is having on many companies."[35]

CHANGING EXPECTATIONS FOR CORPORATE PERFORMANCE

No thoughtful person can question the responsibility of a corporation to act within the law. Society expects no less of an individual citizen. But people disagree over other corporate responsibilities—those described in the previous section as socially reactive and socially responsive behavior. Does a corporation have any responsibility to support the arts, rebuild inner-city housing, or make charitable contributions? Some people argue that corporations have been legally required to bear a disproportionate share of the cost of correcting historical discrimination in employment and damage to the environment. Yet the prevailing mood is that large organizations, particularly corporations, are not only *capable* of contributing to social progress beyond that of producing safe and reliable goods and services but are *responsible* for doing so. This attitude did not suddenly appear. It is simply a contemporary expression of the dynamic and evolutionary relationship between society and its institutions.

THE HISTORICAL EVOLUTION OF EXPECTATIONS

One scholar has observed that the relationship between organizations and society has changed in the aftermath of three business crises.[36]

The Crisis of 1870. The industrialization of America and the incorporation of its business occurred during the pre– and post–Civil War eras; the great impetus for the development of corporate power was the mobilization required by the Civil War. During the 1860s, the "captains of industry"— John D. Rockefeller, J. Pierpont Morgan, Jay Gould, and Andrew Carnegie— were creating the great railroad, steel, coal, sugar, tobacco, and oil corpora-

---

[34]James O'Toole, *Vanguard Management: Redesigning the Corporate Future* (Garden City, N.Y.: Doubleday Publishing, 1985), p. 359.

[35]Francis W. Steckmest, *Corporate Performance: The Key to Public Trust* (New York: McGraw-Hill, 1982), p. 109.

[36]Stahrl W. Edmunds, "Unifying Concepts in Social Responsibility," *Academy of Management Review,* January 1977, pp. 38–42.

tions. In comparison to smaller, more traditional proprietorships and partnerships, these corporations had tremendous power—for good and for evil. The abuse of this power, in the form of kickbacks, discriminatory pricing, lockouts, and the manipulation of commodity prices, led to a public outcry for legal action. Consequently, Congress enacted various laws related to rate regulation, fair-trade practices, and labor. The landmark legislation was the Sherman Act of 1890.

The Crisis of 1930.   The passage of the Sherman Act did not reverse the trend toward larger and larger business organizations because the underlying forces were irreversible. Business organizations tended then, as today, to equate growth with profitability—the bigger, the better. Three merger movements occurred between 1870 and 1930 (1870, 1890, and 1920).[37] The effect of these mergers was to create even larger yet legal corporate entities, which enabled the country to mobilize and fight successfully a world war. By 1914, the production of goods and services in the United States was *more than a third of the world's total industrial output.*[38]

The Roaring Twenties was aptly named. More and more people were sharing the fruits of America's industrial development. Thus, the circle of beneficiaries of corporate action widened beyond a small group of owners. Many Americans owned shares of stock. Even more Americans worked for big business. And even more Americans were daily affected by the actions of corporations.

The Great Depression brought an abrupt halt to the euphoric attitude that unchecked business could bring prosperity to all. To the contrary, the blame for the Great Depression was placed squarely on business. In a sense, the country felt that business had betrayed the country's faith. As a result, the power of government to regulate and monitor business practice increased sharply through the efforts of President Roosevelt and supporters of his New Deal reforms. Government action cemented a relationship between corporations and society that placed responsibility on business for fair treatment of customers, employees, stockholders, suppliers, and other groups in society having a *direct stake* in the corporation's actions. Much of contemporary corporate legal responsibility (obligatory responsibility) can be traced to the crisis of 1930.

The era following the 1930 crisis also marked the beginning of society's expectations for socially reactive behavior. After World War II, which was a watershed historical event, business regained the country's confidence as a provider of industrial goods. Employment soared, savings accounts swelled, and, when the war ended, corporations converted to production of consumer goods. The country put behind it the experience, if not the memory, of the Depression. Thus, society turned again to the corporation as a singular source of "the good life," but the definition of the good life was beginning to change.

The Crisis of 1970.   The closer one gets to contemporary history, the more unreliable hindsight becomes. Whether this crisis began in 1970 or 1960,[39] the

[37]Ibid., p. 40.

[38]Sturdivant, *Business and Society,* p. 102.

[39]Thomas J. Zenisek, "Corporate Social Responsibility: A Conceptualization Based on Organizational Literature," *Academy of Management Review,* July 1979, pp. 359–68, suggests

By 1914, the production of goods and services in the United States was more than a third of the world's total industrial output. Pictured here is the Minneapolis Heat Regulator Company, around 1924.

fact remains that society now expects more of its corporations than it did in 1930 and much more than in 1870. But how much more? And specifically for what? The answers to these questions are now being hammered out in political debates, shaped by public relations efforts, and argued in public forums.

The background of the 1970 crisis was an uninterrupted 20-year period during which two economies came into being. One economy, the *public economy,* is run by the government. It regularly intervenes in business practice, redistributes income through taxation and entitlement programs, and regulates labeling, packaging, advertising, and many other business factors. According to some estimates, the public economy makes up one fourth of the national social system.[40] The second economy, the *private economy,* makes up the remaining three fourths. Of this portion, the 500 largest firms account for two thirds of all manufacturing. These two economies confront and accommodate each other. Each has power over the other, and each represents different yet compatible interests.

But in the 1960s and 1970s, the business/government-as-usual relationship was challenged. New ideas—such as consumerism, feminism, environmentalism, and ecology—grew out of the social unrest fed by the unpopular Vietnam War and fanned by the Watergate scandal. As a result, new demands were made on business that went far beyond social obligations as defined by law.

THE CONTEMPORARY EXPECTATION FOR CORPORATE SOCIAL RESPONSIVENESS

The crisis of 1970 reinforced the attitude that corporations must react to problems created by their own actions. But more important, the crisis initiated the idea that corporations should be proactive, that they should be responsive

that 1960 marks the beginning of contemporary dialogue regarding the role of corporations in society.

[40]Edmunds, "Unifying Concepts," p. 40.

to a wide range of social problems because they have the expertise and power to do so. The current debate on the social responsibility of business is not concerned with obligatory behavior: business must be law abiding. The debate is seldom stated in terms of reactive behavior: business should be responsible for its actions. Rather, the debate has to do with socially responsive behavior.

MANAGERIAL ETHICS

The word **ethics,** as commonly understood, refers to principles of behavior that distinguish between good, bad, right, and wrong.[41] The purpose of ethics, or a code of ethics, is to enable individuals to make choices among alternative behaviors. The importance of ethics increases in proportion to the *consequences* of the outcome of a behavior. As an individual's actions become more consequential for others, the ethics of that individual become more important.

The role and state of ethics in American businesses have become a growing concern among managers and the public. Several factors have contributed to this concern. First, scandals involving unethical activities by several major corporations (e.g., General Electric, E. F. Hutton, General Dynamics) have been widely publicized.[42] Over the past decade, two thirds of the Fortune 500 companies have been involved in illegal behavior.[43] Studies also indicate that many managers feel pressured by their employers to commit ethically questionable acts. In one study of 1,500 top, middle, and first-level managers, more than 40 percent of the respondents reported they had compromised their personal principles to meet an organizational demand.[44] Other recent surveys have found that many managers—on average about 75 percent of those polled—feel pressured to compromise their ethical values to meet corporate objectives.[45] These developments have led many individuals and managers to believe that the level of ethics in business has declined over the last decade.[46]

Second, business ethics have become a topic of concern because businesses are realizing that ethical misconduct by management can be extremely costly for the company and for society as a whole. E. F. Hutton and General Electric, for example, each paid several million dollars in criminal penalties and fines for

[41]Verne E. Henderson, "The Ethical Side of Enterprise," *Sloan Management Review,* Summer 1982, p. 38.

[42]For example, see Larue T. Hosmer, *The Ethics of Management* (Homewood, Ill.: Richard D. Irwin, 1987), pp. 151–52; Larue T. Hosmer, "The Institutionalization of Unethical Behavior," *Journal of Business Ethics,* 1987, pp. 439–47.

[43]This finding is the conclusion of Professor Amitai Etzioni, as reported by Saul Gellerman in "Why 'Good' Managers Make Bad Ethical Choices," *Harvard Business Review,* July–August 1986, p. 85.

[44]Barry Z. Posner and Warren H. Schmidt, "Ethics in American Companies: A Managerial Perspective," *Journal of Business Ethics,* 1987, pp. 383–91.

[45]Beth Brody, "Ethics 101: Can the Good Guys Win?" *U.S. News & World Report,* April 13, 1987, p. 54.

[46]See Roger Ricklefs, "Executives and General Public Say Ethical Behavior Is Declining in U.S.," *The Wall Street Journal,* November 1, 1983, pp. 23ff; Roger Ricklefs, "Public Gives Executives Low Marks for Honesty and Ethical Standards," *The Wall Street Journal,* November 2, 1983, pp. 29ff; Stanley J. Modic, "Are They Ethical?" *Industry Week,* February 1, 1988, p. 20.

their managers' misconduct. Beech-Nut has yet to recover from the damage done to its reputation due to selling tainted apple juice.

Third, both managers and the public are realizing that the dynamics of ethics in management decision making are an often complex and challenging phenomenon: determining what is and isn't ethical is often difficult to do. In some situations, the task is easy. We know, for example, that accepting bribes from a supplier is clearly unethical, as is falsifying records or dishonest advertising in promoting a product. However, the ethics of a business situation often are more complex. Every day, managers face ethical questions that have no easy answers. What for example, is a "fair" profit? What is a "just" price for a product? How "honest" should a company be with the press?

Because the ethics of a business situation are often complex, managers sometimes differ in their views of what actions are ethical. Currently, several ethical issues are being debated in the business environment. For example, managers are grappling with the ethics of employee surveillance (monitoring their computer work and telephones to measure employee productivity) and of testing employees for drug use and AIDS.[47] One upcoming ethical controversy in the U.S. business community is the projected future use of genetic testing by employers. This issue is discussed in the Management Focus on that topic.

Because the ethics of managerial decision making are often complex and managers often disagree on what constitutes an ethical decision, two subjects are particularly relevant: (1) the basis that the individual manager can use for determining which alternative to choose in a decision-making situation and (2) what organizations can do to ensure that managers follow ethical standards in their decision making. These two topics are addressed in the following section.

ETHICAL STANDARDS

Managers must reconcile competing values in making decisions. They make decisions that have consequences for (1) themselves, (2) the organization that employs them, and (3) the society in which they and the organization exist. For example, managers can be called upon to make decisions that can be good for them but bad for the organization and society.

Philosophers, logicians, and theologians have studied ethical issues. Their ideas provide guidelines, but only guidelines, for making value-laden decisions. Figure 3–2 depicts a simplified model of ethical behavior with three different bases for developing ethical guidelines.[48]

Maximum personal benefits (egoism), depicted on the vertical axis, can be the sole basis for decision making. A completely selfish individual would always do what is personally beneficial. An extreme view of this ethical approach is that individuals should always seek that which is pleasurable; and conversely, one should avoid pain. Managers driven by egoism would evaluate alternative actions in terms of personal benefit—salary, prestige, power, or whatever they consider valuable. If the action also proves beneficial to the organization and

---

[47]John Hoerr, "Privacy," *Business Week,* March 28, 1988, pp. 61ff.

[48]The discussion that follows is based on Grover Starling, *The Changing Environment of Business* (Boston: Kent Publishing, 1980), pp. 252–58.

MANAGEMENT FOCUS

The Ethics of Genetic Screening

Medical science has recently made much progress in estimating an individual's susceptibility to certain diseases by studying genetic makeup. Today, a person's predisposition to heart disease, certain cancers, Alzheimer's disease, sickle cell anemia, and many other illnesses can be determined by studying the genetic makeup present in a tissue or blood sample.

This advancement is stirring an ethical debate in the business community concerning the use of genetic tests in the workplace. Testing proponents assert that employees should be tested in businesses where they are exposed to chemicals and other potential hazards in the workplace. The tests would enable a business to identify individuals who are highly susceptible to illnesses related to potentially hazardous exposures and to prohibit those workers from jobs involving such exposure. This move would reduce a high-risk employee's chances of illness and lower the company's health costs.

However, many observers oppose genetic screening. They argue that the tests are an invasion of privacy and would be used by businesses as a basis for denying employment and for dismissals. If the tests are allowed, opponents assert, all companies would use the tests, not just businesses where employees are exposed to potential hazards. Many companies would deny employment or would not promote those determined as high risks for illnesses such as Huntington's disease or Alzheimer's disease. These illnesses occur in later years and are not occupation related.

Today, the use of genetic screening is so controversial that few companies will admit to conducting research into developing specific genetic tests for potential work-related illnesses. In 1980, Du Pont was much criticized for testing black employees for sickle cell anemia, a test that the company now performs only upon the employee's request. Presently, no laws exist concerning an employer's right to conduct genetic screening, nor have tests been developed for widespread use. However, progress in test development is quickening. It is only a matter of time before the issue of genetic testing in the workplace becomes as timely and as hotly debated as drug testing is today.

Source: Adapted from John Hoerr, "Privacy," *Business Week,* March 28, 1988, pp. 61–65, 66; Allan L. Otten, "Price of Progress: Efforts to Predict Genetic Ills Pose Medical Dilemmas," *The Wall Street Journal,* September 14, 1987, p. 23.

---

society, all is well and good. But these other benefits are incidental and not the primary intent of the manager.

Maximum social benefits (altruism), depicted on the horizontal axis, can also be the sole consideration in decision making. An altruistic individual will select courses of action that provide maximum social benefit. A manager who follows this ethical guideline would measure right and wrong as the "greatest happiness to the greatest number." As a practical matter, decisions based on only altruistic concerns are particularly difficult to make. For example, altruism provides no means for judging the relative benefits to individuals, unless one is willing to assume that each has the same interest in and benefit from a decision.

Obligation to a formal principle is shown between the extremes of egoism and altruism. Egoism contends that an act is good if the individual benefits from it. Altruism contends that an act is good if society benefits from it. The criteria

FIGURE 3–2	An Ethical Framework

Ethical behavior involves choosing what is good for the individual—egoism—and what is good for society—altruism—with possible formal principles.

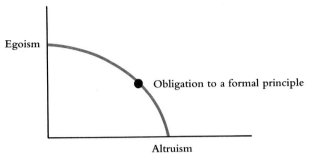

Source: Based on Grover Starling, *The Changing Environment of Business* (Boston: Kent Publishing, 1980), p. 255.

for both ethical guidelines are consequences. In contrast to them, the ethic of adhering to a formal principle is based on the idea that *the rightness or wrongness of an act depends on principle, not consequences.*

Those who adhere to principle in judging their actions could, for example, follow the Golden Rule: "Do unto others what you would have others do unto you." Or they may decide that each action should be judged by the **categorical imperative:** "Act as if the maxim of your action were to become a general law binding on everyone."

But the idea that actions can be judged by one particular principle is unacceptable to many individuals. Some prefer a *pluralistic* approach that would contain several principles arranged in a hierarchy of importance. For example, one writer proposes that managers can be guided in decision making by adhering to the following principles: (1) Place the interests of society before the interests of the organization. (2) Place the interests of the organization before managers' private interests. (3) Reveal the truth in all instances of organizational and personal involvement.[49] These three principles provide guidelines but not answers. The manager must determine the relative benefits to society, company, and self. The determination of benefits and beneficiaries is seldom simple accounting. But the advantage of a pluralistic approach to ethical decision making is that the decision maker, *with intentions to do right,* has the basis for evaluating decisions.

THE ORGANIZATION'S ROLE IN ETHICAL BEHAVIOR

The approaches to developing guidelines for ethical behavior have so far focused on the individual manager. Many observers assert that the organization should play a major role in ensuring that its managers act ethically in managing the firm. The organization's participation is understandable, given that the organization is ultimately responsible for the consequences of the decisions that its managers make.

[49]Robert W. Austin, "Code of Conduct for Executives," *Harvard Business Review,* September–October 1961, p. 53, as cited in Sturdivant, *Business and Society,* p. 147.

Although a company is ultimately responsible, surprisingly few organizations have traditionally provided managers with specific guidelines concerning ethics in decision making. However, given the increasing concern about ethics in organizations, a growing number of companies are attempting to provide guidance for their managers.[50]

At the core of many corporate efforts is the development of a corporate *code of ethics* (often called a *code of conduct*). Typically established by top management, a code usually consists of a written statement of a company's values, beliefs, and norms of ethical behavior.[51] Johnson & Johnson Co.'s "credo," one example of a corporate code of ethics, is shown in Figure 3–3. Like many codes, J&J's credo specifies its values and beliefs concerning its relationships and responsibilities toward its different constituents (i.e., customers, employees, community, and shareholders). The credo also states Johnson & Johnson's objectives concerning each constituency and norms of behavior such as "supporting good works and charities" and "encouraging civic improvements."

Ideally, a code of ethics should provide employees with direction in dealing with ethical dilemmas, clarify the organization's position regarding areas of ethical uncertainty, and achieve and maintain overall ongoing conduct that the organization views as ethical and proper.[52] However, codes often do not achieve these purposes; indeed, many are surprisingly ineffective. For example, a recent study found that organizations with ethics codes were more often found in violation of federal regulations than were organizations with no established codes.[53]

Codes can be ineffective for several reasons. Many ethics codes tend to be legalistic, focusing more on explaining the strict legalities and illegalities of doing business than on tackling the more difficult and complex question of ethics and values.[54] Many codes also tend to focus on conflicts of interest and infractions that employees commit against the company that affect profits, rather than on infractions committed by the company that affect the community and other constituencies.[55] In a review of ethics codes at over 200 Fortune 500 companies, researchers found that over three fourths of the codes addressed neither the company's role in the community nor at least one of the following topics: consumer relations, product safety, or environmental safety.[56]

Many codes fail because they simply are not proactively implemented or enforced. According to recent studies, fewer than 20 percent of companies with codes have an ethics committee to oversee and enforce the code; less than

---

[50]John A. Byrne, "Businesses Are Signing Up for Ethics 101," *Business Week,* February 15, 1988, pp. 56–57.

[51]Earl A. Molander, "A Paradigm for Design, Promulgation, and Enforcement of Ethical Codes," *Journal of Business Ethics,* 1987, pp. 619–31.

[52]Fred Luthans, Richard M. Hodgetts, and Kenneth R. Thompson, *Social Issues in Business* (New York: Macmillan, 1984), pp. 97–105.

[53]Rick Wartzman, "Nature or Nurture? Study Blames Ethical Lapses on Corporate Goals," *The Wall Street Journal,* October 9, 1987, p. 21.

[54]Ibid. See also Donald Robin, Michael Giallourakis, Fred R. David, and Thomas E. Moritz, "A Different Look at Codes of Ethics," *Business Horizons,* January–February 1989, pp. 66–73.

[55]William C. Frederick, "The Culprit Is Culture (An Ethics Roundtable)," *Management Review,* August 1988, pp. 48–50.

[56]Wartzman, "Nature of Nurture?" p. 21.

FIGURE 3–3	Johnson & Johnson's Code of Ethics

Our Credo

We believe our first responsibility is to the doctors, nurses and patients,
to mothers and all others who use our products and services.
In meeting their needs everything we do must be of high quality.
We must constantly strive to reduce our costs
in order to maintain reasonable prices.
Customers' orders must be serviced promptly and accurately.
Our suppliers and distributors must have an opportunity
to make a fair profit.

We are responsible to our employees,
the men and women who work with us throughout the world.
Everyone must be considered as an individual.
We must respect their dignity and recognize their merit.
They must have a sense of security in their jobs.
Compensation must be fair and adequate,
and working conditions clean, orderly and safe.
Employees must feel free to make suggestions and complaints.
There must be equal opportunity for employment, development
and advancement for those qualified.
We must provide competent management,
and their actions must be just and ethical.

We are responsible to the communities in which we live and work
and to the world community as well.
We must be good citizens — support good works and charities
and bear our fair share of taxes.
We must encourage civic improvements and better health and education.
We must maintain in good order
the property we are privileged to use,
protecting the environment and natural resources.

Our final responsibility is to our stockholders.
Business must make a sound profit.
We must experiment with new ideas.
Research must be carried on, innovative programs developed
and mistakes paid for.
New equipment must be purchased, new facilities provided
and new products launched.
Reserves must be created to provide for adverse times.
When we operate according to these principles,
the stockholders should realize a fair return.

Johnson & Johnson

Used with permission of Johnson & Johnson Co.

10 percent of the companies have an official to help employees deal with ethical issues; and fewer than 1 percent of the companies have published procedures to deal with code violations. As a result, the codes lie dormant and ultimately serve little more than a public relations purpose.[57]

However, organizations have achieved effective, "living" codes of ethics, typically by following a multistep implementation strategy. They first trans-

[57]Thomas J. Murray, "Ethics Programs: Just a Pretty Face?" *Business Month,* September 1987, pp. 30ff.

late values and beliefs into specific ethical standards of behavior. Some standards may exist in the code itself; often even more specific standards for particular situations are developed. For example, a specific behavioral standard for Johnson & Johnson's credo objective of high product quality may be immediately reporting to management any evidence of concerns that a product is below the company's quality standards.[58]

These more specific standards may be incorporated as a supplemental part of the ethics code. In this regard, Cummins Engine Company provides its employees with *Cummins Practices,* a set of policies that details rules of conduct for a wide range of business situations, including questionable payments, supplier selection, employee participation in political campaigns, and gifts. Each situation is fully discussed and includes the employee's relevant responsibilities and a list of individuals to contact if the employee needs further guidance.[59] The code and standards are communicated to employees in written form and often in sessions with management. At John Deere, the company's code is present in the "Green Bulletin," a green loose-leaf booklet kept on every manager's desk.[60]

Besides translating the code into behavior standards, companies with effective ethics codes have determined the actions to be taken when code violations occur, communicated the penalties to employees, and implemented the penalties to ensure code compliance. Xerox Corporation, for example, has dismissed employees for violations that are serious (taking bribes) and relatively insignificant (petty cheating on expense accounts). Chemical Bank has likewise fired employees for violating the code, even when such violations were not unlawful. In both cases, actions were taken to communicate the company's commitment to the code and the importance of maintaining ethical behavior.[61]

Many organizations also periodically conduct ethics seminars to keep employees sensitive to the place of ethics in the company and to help them develop skills in handling ethical dilemmas. At Allied Corp., for example, managers who participate in the company's ethics seminars submit case studies of ethical problems they've experienced on the job. The cases are then presented anonymously and discussed by participants.[62] At Chemical Bank, the company's corporate social policy department provides an ethics course based on ethics cases written by the department and founded on interviews with a cross section of Chemical Bank managers. The cases represent the most common and perplexing ethics problems encountered on the job, and the training focuses on providing managers with analytical tools and approaches to think through the problems and find solutions.[63]

Many companies with effective ethics programs emphasize the importance of setting realistic performance objectives for subordinates.[64] Setting unrea-

---

[58]Luthans, et al., *Social Issues in Business,* p. 104.

[59]Oliver F. Williams, "Business Ethics: A Trojan Horse?" *California Management Review,* Summer 1982, pp. 14–23.

[60]O'Toole, *Vanguard Management,* p. 52.

[61]Byrne, "Businesses Are Signing Up for Ethics 101," p. 57.

[62]David Freudberg, "Ministering to the Corporation," *Across the Board,* November 1984, pp. 14ff.

[63]Rita Kay Meyer, "Chemical's Executive Training Emphasizes Ethics," *American Banker,* June 17, 1988, p. 16.

[64]Archie B. Carroll, *Business and Society: Managing Corporate Social Performance* (Boston: Little, Brown, 1981), pp. 78–79.

FIGURE 3–4   The Corporation's Social Responsibility and Managerial Ethics

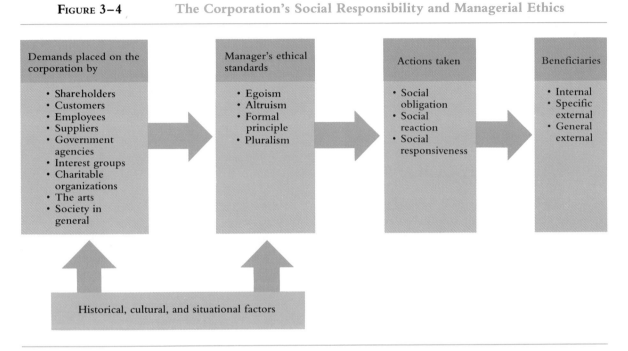

In the final analysis, managerial ethics determine a corporation's socially responsive actions.

sonable goals promotes the use of unethical behavior to achieve those objectives (e.g., cutting corners, making ethical compromises), especially when the performance goals are tightly linked to rewards.

Establishing the position of ethics advocate is another often recommended action.[65] The ethics advocate is normally a top-level executive who, in a sense, serves as the organization's full-time ethical conscience. The advocate evaluates the organization's actions from an ethical perspective and vigorously and openly questions the ethical implications of proposed plans of action. At some companies, the ethics advocate also serves as an ombudsman, someone to whom employees can, with guaranteed anonymity, report ethics violations they have witnessed or express ethical concerns. In many cases, the advocate/ombudsman is an outsider (such as a retired executive), which ensures independence from management and builds credibility with employees.[66]

ETHICS AND SOCIAL RESPONSIVENESS

The relationship between a manager's ethical standards and social responsiveness should be apparent. Ethics serve as bases for assessing the "rightness" of potential actions. In a sense, ethical standards are filters that screen actions according to relative rightness. The ideas that have been developed in our

[65]Ibid., p. 85.

[66]Murray, "Ethics Programs," p. 30. Also see Michael Brody, "Listen to Your Whistleblower: Smart Managers Find Out about Nasty Problems before the Story Shows Up on the 11 O'clock News," *Fortune,* November 24, 1986, pp. 77–78.

discussion of social responsibility, expectations for corporate behavior, and ethics can be integrated as shown in Figure 3–4 (p. 87). Here the corporation is seen as a *means* for achieving the *ends* of various claimants. Social responsibility involves deciding *what* means and *whose* ends are right and good. Ultimately, it is the task of corporate managers to decide the relative rightness of each demand; and ethical standards are the bases for their decisions.

SUMMARY OF KEY POINTS

- The term *social responsibility* is popularly used to prescribe and proscribe corporate activity, yet the meaning of social responsibility has many variations. Therefore, it is imperative to define the term when discussing the issue. The various meanings can be sorted into three categories: social obligation, social reaction, and social responsiveness.

- Social obligation means that business is socially responsible when it meets its primary obligation: to pursue a profit for owners within the law. Conversely a business is socially irresponsible when it pursues activities not related to improving the economic well-being of owners.

- Social reaction means that business is socially responsible when it reacts to prevailing social norms, values, and expectations. The business must sense, understand, and react to what society articulates as representing its expectations. These expectations change with time and place; but in modern times, society has expected business to go beyond its socially obligated behavior of profit seeking as prescribed by law.

- Social responsiveness includes obligatory and reactive behavior but also requires that corporations be proactive and take action to prevent social problems. This meaning places considerable emphasis on the corporation's obligations above and beyond what is legal and expected.

- The activities through which corporations meet their social responsibilities range from producing safe, reliable, quality products to supporting the arts; from providing safe and healthful working conditions to assisting minority enterprises. Each of these activities benefits some group, often to the disadvantage of some other group. Managers must make choices among various interests both inside and outside the corporation.

- The beneficiaries of corporate action are either internal or external. Internal beneficiaries include customers, owners, and employees. External beneficiaries include groups representing minorities, women, the handicapped, and the aged.

- The contemporary demands placed on corporations are the result of an evolutionary process. In earlier times, when corporations were relatively insignificant, society expected them to meet their social obligations. As corporations became larger and more pervasive, society's expectations shifted toward social reaction and responsive corporate behavior.

- Managers are the referees of competing demands on corporate resources. Their ethical standards—criteria for rightness and goodness—filter these demands and determine which will be satisfied. Ethical standards are influenced by the principles of maximum personal benefits (egoism), maximum social benefits (altruism), and obligation to a formal principle.

- Managers and the public are increasingly concerned about ethics in U.S. business because many believe that ethics have declined in the last decade, the costs of unethical conduct by management are often high, and the dynamics of ethics in management are complex and challenging.

- Some organizations are responding to these concerns by developing ethics codes, establishing training seminars in ethics for employees, and creating the position of ethics advocate/ombudsman.

Discussion and Review Questions

1. Explain why corporations have "social responsibilities." How does society express its expectations for corporate behavior?

2. Is it possible for a corporate executive to be both personally unethical and professionally ethical? Which are more demanding: the ethics of personal life or the ethics of professional life?

3. Which of the three meanings of social responsibility reflects your opinion? Explain.

4. Identify organizations in recent events whose actions you believe to be notable expressions of social responsibility.

5. What are the basic arguments for and against each of the three meanings of social responsibility?

6. To which beneficiaries of corporate behavior is management primarily responsible? Explain your answer. Does your answer reflect *your* ethical standards?

7. Explain how a manager's ethics affect decisions regarding social responsibility.

8. One manager's comment: "Ethics codes don't work, because a manager's ethics and values are the product of years of upbringing and experiences. No written document can affect those ethics and values." Do you agree? Explain.

9. In your opinion, what is the greatest challenge in developing an ethical environment within a business?

10. What guidelines do you use in resolving ethical dilemmas you encounter?

Additional References

Barry, V. E. *Moral Issues in Business*. Belmont, Calif.: Wadsworth, 1986.

Beauchamp, T. L. *Ethical Theory and Business*. Englewood Cliffs, N.J.: Prentice-Hall, 1988.

Becker, H., and **D. J. Fritzsche.** "Business Ethics: Cross-Cultural Comparison of Managers' Attitudes." *Journal of Business Ethics,* May 1987, pp. 289–95.

Chrisman, J. J., and **R. W. Archer.** "Small Business Social Responsibility: Some Perceptions and Insights." *American Journal of Small Business,* Fall 1984, pp. 46–58.

Dierkes, M., and **A. B. Antal.** "Whither Corporate Social Reporting: Is It Time to Legislate?" *California Management Review,* Spring 1986, pp. 106–21.

Epstein, E. M. "The Corporate Social Policy Process: Beyond Business Ethics, Corporate Social Responsibility, and Corporate Social Responsiveness." *California Management Review,* Spring 1987, pp. 99–114.

Freeman, R. E. *Corporate Strategy and the Search for Ethics*. Englewood Cliffs, N.J.: Prentice-Hall, 1988.

Fry, L. W.; G. D. Keim; and **R. E. Meiners.** "Corporate Contributions: Altruistic or For-Profit?" *Academy of Management Journal,* March 1982, pp. 94–106.

George, R. J. "The Challenge of Preparing Ethically Responsible Managers: Closing the Rhetoric-Reality Gap." *Journal of Business Ethics,* September 1988, pp. 715–20.

Hosmer, L. T. "Adding Ethics to the Business Curriculum." *Business Horizons,* July–August 1988, pp. 9–15.

Jones, T. M., and **F. H. Gautschi.** "Will the Ethics of Business Change? A Survey of Future Executives." *Journal of Business Ethics,* April 1988, pp. 231–48.

Logan, J. E.; S. P. Logan; and **J. M. E. Mille.** "Corporate Social Responsibility." *Business and Economic Review,* January 1985, pp. 25–27.

Parmerlee, M. A.; J. P. Near; and **T. C. Jensen.** "Correlates of Whistleblowers' Perceptions of Organizational Retaliation." *Administrative Science Quarterly,* March 1982, pp. 17–34.

Paul, K. *Business Environment and Business Ethics: The Social, Moral, and Political Dimensions of Management*. Cambridge, Mass.: Ballinger, 1987.

Preston, L. E., ed. *Research in Corporate Social Performance and Policy*. Greenwich, Conn.: JAI Press, 1981.

Sethi, S. P. "The Inhuman Error: Lessons from Bhopal." *New Management,* Summer 1985, pp. 40–44.

Seymour, S. "The Case of the Willful Whistle-Blower." *Harvard Business Review,* January–February 1988, pp. 103–19.

Shea, G. F. *Practical Ethics*. New York: American Management Association, 1988.

Sweezy, P. M.; J. K. Galbraith; S. J. Tolchin; and **R. S. Browne.** "Can Socially Responsible Societies Compete Economically?" *Business and Society Review.* Winter 1985, pp. 11–14.

Vitell, S. J., and **T. A. Festervand.** "Business Ethics: Conflicts, Practices and Beliefs of Industrial Executives." *Journal of Business Ethics,* February 1987, pp. 111–22.

CASE 3–1   Building Ethics at General Dynamics

For years, General Dynamics Corporation enjoyed a productive relationship with the federal government as the nation's largest defense contractor. However, through much of the 1970s and early 1980s, General Dynamics came under heavy fire for allegedly overcharging the government. At one point, the Pentagon froze all payments to the company to retrieve almost $250 million paid in overcharge billings, according to a federal investigative agency. Criminal charges were filed against General Dynamics by the Justice Department.

Most observers asserted that something was clearly wrong in the ways of doing business at General Dynamics. Company officials agreed, and top management set about building a strong sense of ethical conduct at the company via several steps:

A Written Code of Conduct.   The core of the company's efforts is a 20-page publication that provides guidelines for ethical conduct in business situations and decision making. The "blue book" describes employee's responsibilities for maintaining the company's stipulated ethical standards and states the penalties for violating those standards. The book also specifies individuals with whom employees can discuss problems or questions concerning the application of the company's code. Importantly, the code contains a "squeal clause" that protects employees who identify individuals who are violating the ethical standards.

About 103,000 employees of General Dynamic received a copy of the blue book in sessions with their supervisors. In the sessions, the standards were discussed along with how to apply them in different on-the-job situations. Employees were also asked to sign an acknowledgment card stipulating that they understood the code of conduct and that the code is company policy. Most workers signed the cards although not required to. However, reading the blue book and signing an acknowledgment card is a prerequisite of employment for job applicants.

Ethics Training.   General Dynamics conducted ethics awareness seminars for all employees. The workshop's format included a film concerning the company's values, exercises about ways to resolve ethical dilemmas encountered on the job, and information and discussion about the company's overall ethics program. Seminars for upper-level managers included participation in case studies of ethics.

Ethics Program Directors.   Throughout the corporation, about 40 employees serve as ethics program directors. They answer employees' questions about the company's code and counsel employees on how to handle particular ethics dilemmas. Each director reports directly to the respective subsidiary president.

Source: Adapted from William H. Wagel, "A New Focus on Business Ethics at General Dynamics," *Personnel*, August 1987, pp. 4–8.

Program Structure.   General Dynamic's overall ethics program is coordinated by a full-time corporate ethics director. He works with the company's ethics steering committee, which is composed of the directors of the major functional departments of the company. The committee provides overall direction for the program and for policy development. The company's board of directors also maintains a committee on corporate social responsibility that reviews and approves ethics policy for General Dynamics. Members of this committee are all directors from outside the company.

Ethics Hot Line.   General Dynamics has established 30 hot lines throughout the company and a toll-free number for calling corporate headquarters. Ethics program directors operate the hot lines. In one year of the hot line's operation, over 3,600 calls were received. Over two thirds were requests for information or counsel in handling ethical dilemmas; the remaining contacts concerned reports of potential misconduct. In that year, General Dynamics imposed more than 100 sanctions for misconduct. The sanctions ranged from warning to dismissal and referral for criminal prosecution.

Has the ethics program worked? After conducting a companywide survey and an internal audit on the program, management thinks that the company has achieved a greater awareness of the importance and role of ethics in everyday work at General Dynamics.

QUESTIONS FOR ANALYSIS

1. Evaluate the ethics program at General Dynamics. What are the program's strong points? What changes could be made to make the program more effective?
2. Some observers assert that including a "squeal clause" in a company's code of ethics promotes employee spying on peers, which is unethical. Do you agree? Discuss.
3. Although most employees signed the acknowledgment card, some did not. In your opinion, why would some people refuse to sign? Are these reasons legitimate?

CASE 3–2   The Training Debate

In a number of companies, an interesting ethics debate is emerging concerning management training. The issue: Does management have the right to put employees through training that is physically or psychologically uncomfortable, training that in some cases seeks to alter their fundamental beliefs?

The source of this debate is a growing number of highly unconventional management training programs offered by outside training organizations.

Source: Adapted from Jeremy Main, "Trying to Bend Managers' Minds," *Fortune,* November 23, 1987, pp. 95ff; Martha Brannigan, "Employers' 'New Age' Training Programs Lead to Lawsuits over Workers' Rights," *The Wall Street Journal,* January 9, 1989, p. B1.

Though still a minority in a large training industry, these unusual programs are gaining in popularity. For example:

At a ranch near Sante Fe, New Mexico, managers from Hewlett-Packard, GM, Dow Chemical, and many other organizations attend the Pecos Learning Center, run by the Wilson Learning Corp. There the managers go through a series of exhilarating physical tasks such as launching themselves off a cliff, climbing up telephone poles, and traveling on the "zip line," a cord stretched in midair from one to the other side of the Pecos Valley. The managers travel the line by hanging onto a pulley. The exercises are safe; a safety harness protects each participant.

The camp's activities are designed to bond executives together. Camp officials say that overcoming physical fear is exhilarating and relaxes managers so they can talk about their work and lives. Many participants are pleased with their camp experience. However, some participants have questioned the training. Although the exercises are voluntary, they say they felt pressured to do things they found frightening. They also believed the personal discussions were intrusive.

Another form of training is provided by the MSIA (pronounced messiah) that is run by the Mystical Traveler Consciousness organization. It offers three courses entitled Insight I, II, and III. Courses I and II are "intensive-growth experiences"; course III teaches the mystical principles of the organization's leader.

The Church of Scientology has established two subsidiaries that provide training and consulting services for companies. The content of one of its programs was recently the core of a dispute involving Loretta Garrett, a former head of the sales department of Megaplex, a phone-answering service in Atlanta. At the urging of her boss, Ms. Garrett attended a Church of Scientology course. According to Ms. Garrett, the course focused in part on the principles of Scientology. She was urged to "admit guilt because sales were poor" and to get "past the analytical brain to clear the inner brain, where the poor sales were caused."

Ms. Garrett declined her boss's request that she have her personality "audited" at the local Scientology mission. She quit; her boss told her she was fired. Ms. Garrett has since filed a complaint with the Equal Employment Opportunity Commission.

In another dispute, eight former employees of DeKalb Farmers Market of Atlanta, Georgia, have sued the company, alleging that they were fired or pressured to resign after refusing to attend "human potential" training sessions. The company's management asked the employees to attend the sessions, which were held outside of work. The employees claim that the training sessions, along with other programs introduced at work, clash with their religious beliefs and amount to psychological programming and conditioning. The employees are suing to obtain back pay and damages due to psychological trauma, which they claim they suffered. They are also asking the court to prohibit Farmers Market from forcing other employees to attend the training programs. The company denies the charges.

Perhaps the most publicized incident of employee rebellion against unconventional training occurred at Pacific Bell, a subsidiary of Pacific Telesis. Top management hired associates of Charles Krone, a prominent corporate trainer, to help develop a new culture for the company. Krone's associates worked two years at Pacific Bell to implement principles designed to condition people to "rethink the way they think," to find new ways to solve problems. Resentment among the work force grew. At the request of the California Public Utilities Commission, another consulting group surveyed the work force. Results indicated that employees were angry over the principles and over the implied threat that those who didn't adopt the principles would not advance in the company. Employees also were angry over the practice of "facilitators" attending meetings as "thought police" to ensure that the employees were following the Krone principles. The commission also discovered that the Krone program cost $40 million. The program was suspended; Pacific Bell's president took an early retirement.

QUESTIONS FOR ANALYSIS

1. As a manager who supports unconventional training, what would be your arguments concerning the ethics of providing such training for your employees?
2. As a manager who opposes unconventional training, provide a response to the arguments that you developed for question 1.
3. Which position would you personally take? Explain.

EXPERIENTIAL EXERCISE

ETHICAL DILEMMAS

Purpose

This activity is designed to illustrate the complexity of ethical decision making and how people can differ in their views of what is and is not ethical behavior.

The Exercise in Class

Presented below are four situations often encountered in the workplace that raise ethical issues. Read each scenario and place yourself in the position of the respective decision maker. What would you do?

The Roundabout Raise. When Joe asks for a raise, his boss praises his work but says the company's rigid budget won't allow any further merit raises for the time being. Instead, the boss suggests that the company "won't look too closely at your expense accounts for a while." Should Joe take this as authorization to pad his expense account on the grounds that he is simply getting the same money he deserves through a different route, or should he not take this roundabout "raise"?

Your decision:

The Faked Degree.   Bill has done a sound job for more than a year. The boss learns that Bill got the job by claiming to have a college degree, although he actually never graduated. Should his boss dismiss him for submitting a fraudulent résumé or overlook the false claim because Bill has otherwise proved to be a conscientious and honorable worker, and making an issue of the degree might ruin Bill's career?

Your decision:

Sneaking Phone Calls.   Helen discovers that a fellow employee regularly makes about $100 a month worth of personal long-distance telephone calls from an office telephone. Should Helen report the employee to the company or disregard the calls on the grounds that many people make personal calls at the office?

Your decision:

Cover–Up Temptation.   Bill discovers that the chemical plant he manages is creating slightly more water pollution in a nearby lake than is legally permitted. Revealing the problem will bring considerable unfavorable publicity to the plant, hurt the lakeside town's resort business, and create a scare in the community. Solving the problem will cost the company well over $100,000. It is unlikely that outsiders will discover the problem. The violation poses no danger whatever to people. At most, it will endanger a small number of fish. Should Bill reveal the problem despite the cost to his company or consider the problem as little more than a technicality and disregard it?

Your decision:

1.   Write your decision for each scenario on a sheet of paper.
2.   After everyone has completed step 1, your instructor will discuss the class responses to each situation. The instructor will also provide you with the general responses of about 1,500 adults and 400 middle managers who completed the exercise as a part of a *Wall Street Journal*/Gallup poll on ethics in America.
3.   Compare your responses to those of the general public and the executives. What factors account for any differences between your responses and their decisions?

The Learning Message

This exercise demonstrates the complexities of ethical considerations in decision making and the sources of the complexities: (1) individuals' differing perspectives concerning what is ethical, (2) their differing interpretations and assessments of situations, and (3) their differing goals, needs, and values.

PART
II

MANAGING WORK AND ORGANIZATIONS

FOUNDATIONS OF MANAGING WORK AND
ORGANIZATIONS

FOUNDATIONS OF MANAGING WORK AND ORGANIZATIONS

As the 20th century began, some managers wanting to improve the practice of management began to put their ideas in writing. These managers were particularly concerned with two issues: (1) increasing the productivity of individuals performing *work* and (2) increasing the productivity of *organizations* within which work is performed. Directing their attention to finding ways to manage work and organizations so that higher levels of output would be produced at lower costs, they created a body of management literature that became known as the classical approach.

The approach is "classical" because the issues and problems associated with attaining high levels of productivity have enduring importance regardless of time and place. They are as important today as they were 90 years ago. In fact, because of today's international competition, some would argue they are more important. The classical writers' ideas for improving productivity are widely practiced in every modern organization, whether public or private, business or nonbusiness, profit or nonprofit. The classical approach to management stresses the importance of analyzing the nature of the work to be done and then applying rational principles to plan, organize, and control the work.

This approach to managing reflects the way all modern managers would like to think of themselves. Yet, when the idea of applying objective analysis to management problems first developed almost a century ago, its implications were new and profound, attracting much popular attention.

The emphasis on rational analysis and the application of scientific rigor to facts and information about productivity led to use of the term *scientific management* to describe the earliest attempts to manage the work of individuals. The first supporters of scientific management were practicing engineers and managers who believed and then demonstrated that work could be done more efficiently and thus more productively. Believing that the most efficient—the "best"—way to do a job could be determined through analysis of data, they urged managers to study the actual performance of work and to collect objective data on their observations.

While scientific management ideas were developing, classical organization theory began to evolve. Developers of that theory believed that organizations are the settings within which individuals perform jobs—that the organization is a collection of individual jobs—so the organization should also be designed and managed according to principles and practices that stress efficiency and productivity.

The combination of ideas from scientific management's concern for productive work and classical organization theory's concern for efficient organizations creates an important body of management knowledge, classical management thought.[1] Managers must know and apply this knowledge in

[1]This discussion is consistent with Daniel A. Wren, *The Evolution of Management Thought* (New York: John Wiley & Sons, 1979).

order to survive both domestic and international competition for resources and products. Today's managers and organizations that make headlines about their high performance stress the importance of rational planning, organizing, and controlling the work of individuals and the organization in which the work takes place. But this recognition of the importance of managing did not develop overnight; it took many years to overcome existing management ways.

The effort to learn and practice better ways to manage work and organizations continues even as you read this book. How to best manage work and organizations effectively is the enduring, classical problem of management. The events of the 1980s underscore the importance of managing work and organizations. The upheavals at General Motors, General Electric, and IBM were initiated by efforts to better manage work and organizations to attain higher levels of productivity and quality in response to foreign competitors.

The popular explanation for Japanese business success is that the Japanese know and practice better ways to manage work and organizations. In fact, they practice many of the same techniques first discussed in the scientific management and classical organization theory literature.

THE MANAGEMENT OF WORK

In modern manufacturing, the first-level manager is concerned with the day-to-day routine of coordinating the work of specialized labor. Each specialized worker does a job according to a set of rules and procedures designed to ensure efficient completion of the job. The rules and procedures resulted from analysis of the technical and human requirements of the job and of its relationship to other jobs. Job analysis is an important technique for modern managers. For example, the success of McDonald's can be traced to the careful analysis of each and every job in a McDonald's restaurant.

To appreciate fully the importance of scientific management as a philosophy and practice, you must understand its major contributions.[2] These contributions were in the areas of work management, work simplification, work scheduling, and efficiency.

PRINCIPLES OF WORK MANAGEMENT

As a supervisor at the Philadelphia Midvale Steel Company in the late 1800s, Frederick W. Taylor became interested in ways to improve lathe work. He began gathering facts and applying an objective analysis that was to typify his entire career.[3] He studied the work of individual lathe workers to discover exactly how they performed their jobs; he identified each aspect of each job and measured everything measurable. His goal was to provide the lathe

[2]For a discussion of the historical setting and ideology of scientific management, see Samuel Haber, *Efficiency and Uplift* (Chicago: University of Chicago Press, 1964).

[3]Lyndall Urwick, *The Golden Book of Management* (London: Newman Neame, 1956), pp. 72–79, outlines Taylor's career and personal life. Also see Lyndall Urwick and E. F. L. Brech, *The Making of Scientific Management* (London: Sir Isaac Pitman & Sons, 1951).

operator with scientifically based, objective standards that would define *a fair day's work*.

Taylor's efforts culminated in four principles for managing work:

1. For each element of a man's work, develop a science that replaces the old rule-of-thumb method.
2. Scientifically select, train, teach, and develop the worker. (In the past, workers chose their own work and trained themselves as best they could.)
3. Cooperate with the workers to ensure that all of the work is done in accordance with the science that has been developed.
4. Recognize that there is almost an equal division of work and responsibility between management and workers. Managers take over all work for which they are better fitted than the workers. (In the past, almost all of the work and the greater part of the responsibility were thrown upon the workers.)[4]

These four principles became the basic guidelines for managing the work of individuals.

Taylor was the first individual to study work in a serious manner.[5] His experiments with stopwatch studies and work methods inspired others to undertake similar studies in other industries. One result of the efforts of those who followed was the discovery of ways to simplify work.

PRINCIPLES OF WORK SIMPLIFICATION

Frank and Lillian Gilbreth, a husband and wife team, combined their talents to produce important breakthroughs in work simplification. An untrained but insightful engineer, Frank Gilbreth was an apprentice bricklayer in his first job. His observations of skilled bricklayers' motions convinced him that many of their body movements (bending, reaching, stooping, troweling) could be combined or eliminated. Bricklaying could be simplified, and production could be increased. By combining and eliminating body movements and increasing the number of bricks laid in a given time period, resources (bricklayer's time) are reduced, and output (bricks laid) is increased. The result is an increase in labor productivity.

Gilbreth's analysis of the sequence and path of basic body movements enabled him to reduce the number of motions required to lay brick from 18 to 4½. Bricklayers who used Gilbreth's method increased their production by 200 percent. Economy in the use of human energy, combined with technological improvements such as an adjustable stand to eliminate stooping for the brick and a mortar of proper consistency to eliminate "tapping," resulted in a science of the craft of masonry.[6] Gilbreth's work was quite compatible and consistent with that of Taylor's, since each sought the "one best way" to do a job.

[4]Frederick W. Taylor, *Principles of Scientific Management* (New York: Harper & Row, 1911), pp. 36–37.

[5]Edwin A. Locke, "The Ideas of Frederick W. Taylor," *Academy of Management Journal*, January 1982, pp. 41–24, reviews Taylor's influence on contemporary management and concludes that it is substantial and pervasive.

[6]Claude S. George, Jr., *The History of Management Thought* (Englewood Cliffs, N.J.: Prentice-Hall, 1968), p. 97.

PRINCIPLES OF WORK SCHEDULING

A close associate of Taylor was a young graduate engineer, Henry L. Gantt. Like Taylor and the Gilbreths, Gantt was concerned with problems of productivity at the shop-floor level. Gantt's major contribution to scientific management is a chart showing the relationship between work planned and completed on one axis and time elapsed on the other. The *Gantt Chart* is still used in industry as a method for scheduling work.

While Taylor and the Gilbreths focused on the workers, Gantt believed that the way managers did their work could be improved and made more productive. He believed that expertise should be the sole criterion for the exercise of authority and that managers have the moral obligation to make decisions by scientific methods, not by opinion. Thus Gantt broadened the scope of scientific management by including the work of managers as appropriate for analysis.

PRINCIPLES OF EFFICIENCY

The public became aware of Harrington Emerson in 1910, when he testified as an expert witness before the Interstate Commerce Commission that the railroads could save $1 million per day by using the methods and philosophy of scientific management.

Emerson's ideas are embodied in a set of principles that define the manner in which the efficient use of resources is to be accomplished. His principles encompass the basic elements of the scientific management approach. In summary, they state that a manager should (1) use scientific, objective, and factual analyses; (2) define the aims of the undertaking; (3) relate each part to the whole; (4) provide standardized procedures and methods; and (5) reward individuals for successful execution of the task.

Emerson's contributions go beyond his principles of efficiency. He also recognized the positive lessons to be learned from the military's use of formalized staff and advisory positions. In his capacity as one of the first management consultants, he proposed the creation of an organization whose activities would be defined by clear statements of goals and purposes.[7]

The significant and lasting contributions of scientific management, however, have been the identification of management's responsibilities for managing work. According to the classical approach, management is responsible for:

- *Planning* the work by predetermining the expected quantity and quality of output for each job.
- *Organizing* the work by specifying the appropriate ways and means to perform each task.
- *Controlling* the work by (*a*) selecting and training qualified individuals, (*b*) overseeing the actual job performance, and (*c*) verifying that actual quantity and quality of output meet expectations.

At the work level, the responsibilities of management were defined in terms of functions: planning, organizing, and controlling. Let us now review the classical approach to managing organizations.

---

[7]William F. Muhs, "Worker Participation in the Progressive Era: An Assessment by Harrington Emerson," *Academy of Management Review,* January 1982, p. 101.

THE MANAGEMENT OF ORGANIZATIONS

Practicing managers were the first contributors to the literature on classical organization theory. They brought their practical experiences to bear on the problem of coordinating large-scale organizations.

The two lasting contributions of classical organization theory are (1) the principles of management and (2) the principles of organization. Through the application of these principles, supporters of the theory argued, managers can manage *organizations* on the same basis that they manage *work*.

PRINCIPLES OF MANAGEMENT

Many early writers sought to define the principles of management. Chief among them was a Frenchman named Henri Fayol,[8] manager of a large coal company, who sought to discover principles of management that determine the "soundness and good working order" of the firm. Fayol was not seeking fixed rules of conduct; rather, he sought guidelines to thinking. Deciding on the appropriateness of a principle for a particular situation was, in his view, the "art" of management. Fayol believed that any number of principles might exist, but he described only those he most frequently applied in his own experience.

Fayol's chief desire was to elevate the status of management practice by supplying a framework for analysis. His framework included a statement of management functions and principles of managing organizations.

Management Functions.   Fayol identified five functions in which managers must engage:

1. *Planning:* The manager should make the best possible forecast of events that may affect the firm and should draw up plans to guide future decisions.

2. *Organizing:*   This managerial function determines the appropriate machines, material, and human mix necessary to accomplish the planned courses of action.

3. *Commanding:*   To be successful, the manager should set a good example and thoroughly know the personnel and the agreements made between personnel and the firm. Managers should have direct, two-way communication with subordinates. Furthermore, managers should continually evaluate the organizational structure and subordinates. They should not hesitate to change the structure if they consider it faulty or to fire subordinates who are incompetent.

4. *Coordinating:*   Includes activities that bind together all individual efforts and direct them toward a common objective.

5. *Controlling:*   This means ensuring that actual activities are consistent with plans.

[8]Henry Fayol, *General and Industrial Management,* trans. J. A. Conbrough (Geneva: International Management Institute, 1929). All subsequent references in this text are to the more widely available translation by Constance Storrs (London: Sir Isaac Pitman & Sons, 1949).

TABLE 1	Some Principles of Management, circa 1929

1. *Division of labor.* Work should be divided and subdivided into the smallest feasible elements, to take advantage of gains from specialization.

2. *Parity of authority and responsibility.* Each jobholder should be delegated sufficient authority to carry out assigned job responsibilities.

3. *Discipline.* Employees should obey whatever clearly stated agreements exist between them and the organization; managers should fairly sanction all instances of breached discipline.

4. *Unity of command.* Employees should receive orders from and be accountable to only one superior.

5. *Unity of direction.* Activities that have the same purpose should be grouped together and operate under the same plan.

6. *Subordination of individual to general interests.* The interests of the organization take precedence over the interests of the individual.

7. *Fair remuneration.* Pay should be based on achievement of assigned job objectives.

8. *Centralization.* Authority should be delegated in proportion to responsibility.

9. *Scalar chain.* An unbroken chain of command should exist through which all directives and communications flow.

10. *Order.* Each job should be defined so that the jobholder clearly understands it and its relationship to other jobs.

11. *Equity.* Established rules and agreements should be enforced fairly.

12. *Stability of personnel.* Employees should be encouraged to establish loyalty to the organization and to make a long-term commitment.

13. *Initiative.* Employees should be encouraged to exercise independent judgment within the bounds of their delegated authority and defined jobs.

14. *Esprit de corps.* Employees should be encouraged to define their interests with those of the organization and thereby achieve unity of effort.

These five functions describe the job of managers in organizations. Until the time of the classical organization theorists, the work of managers had been as much ignored as the work of blue-collar workers. Fayol and other practicing managers sought to define the work of managers in terms of categories of activities, or functions, that they themselves had performed in their management careers.

Fayol's Principles. Fayol proposed 14 principles to guide the thinking of managers in resolving problems. These principles are presented in Table 1.

The principles do not answer questions of "how much," but Fayol did not suggest that they would relieve management from the responsibility for determining what he called "the appropriate balance." Indeed, he emphasized time and again that the moral character of the managers determines the quality of their decisions.

Table 2 presents some current, 1990 principles of management. It illustrates that, like Fayol in 1929, modern managers also try to discover principles to guide their thinking, based on their experience. Interestingly, many of the principles are similar to Fayol's.

TABLE 2	Some Principles of Management, circa 1990

1. *Be loyal to employees.* The one critical element of management is loyalty to employees in all matters. [June Collier-Mason, president/chief executive officer (CEO), National Industries]

2. *Accept responsibility.* To be successful in management, you must be not only willing but *eager* to accept responsibility. (Stanley Pace, chairman/CEO, General Dynamics)

3. *Communicate.* Open communication up, down, and across the organization is the most important ingredient for success. (Jerry Benefield, president/CEO, Nissan U.S.A.)

4. *Create the right environment.* Create the environment and atmosphere in which each and every person can contribute to the maximum of his or her capability. (William Weisz, vice chairman/former CEO, Motorola)

5. *Share and treat.* Make sure those who produce share in the results, and treat others as you'd like to be treated. (Ewing Kauffman, chairman/founder, Marion Laboratories)

6. *Keep up with change.* The competitive environment, the technological environment, and the social issues inside a company are changing more rapidly than ever, and management is going to have to keep up with that rate of change. (J. Tracy O'Rourke, president, Allen-Bradley)

7. *Keep employees happy.* If you had to put your finger on the most important thing that will ensure success, I think it would have to be how to deal with your people. (Joseph Canion, president/CEO, Compaq Computer Corporation)

8. *Be a team player.* My advice is to be a team player and to concentrate on getting an agreement throughout your operation as to what needs to be accomplished. (Joe Henson, president/CEO, Prime Computer)

9. *Listen.* You have to listen—to what you're hearing from customers out in the field, from your distributors, from the people on the shop floor, from your general management. (Abraham Krasnoff, vice chairman/CEO, Pall Corporation)

10. *Follow the golden rule.* Follow the golden rule of ethics in business. There are no shortcuts. (Robert Mercer, chairman/CEO, Goodyear Tire and Rubber)

11. *Maintain integrity and trust.* Integrity and trust are the most important part of management. Otherwise, everything collapses. (Gerald Mitchell, chairman/CEO, Dana Corporation)

12. *Follow the fundamentals.* Follow these very carefully: quality, cost, service, product development, control of resources, proper hiring. Apply these fundamentals—and it doesn't make any difference whether you're building a dustpan or a semiconductor. (Stanley Gault, chairman/CEO, Rubbermaid)

13. *Develop a vision.* Great managers are people who develop a clear vision of what they want their business to be. (Jack Welch, chairman, General Electric)

14. *Totally commit to excellent work.* Always do more than you must to just get by. (Fred A. Manske, Jr., senior vice president–International, Federal Express)

Sources: Fred A. Manske, *Secrets of Effective Leadership—A Practical Guide to Success* (Germantown, Tenn.: Leadership Education and Development, 1987); James Brahm, "Tips from the Top," *Industry Week,* July 4, 1988, pp. 30–37; "Privileged Information," *Boardroom Reports,* November 1, 1988, p. 1.

PRINCIPLES OF ORGANIZATION

In 1931, James D. Mooney and Alan C. Reiley authored *Onward Industry,* which was revised in 1947 by Mooney and titled *The Principles of Organization.*[9] This book is a vital part of the literature of classical management thought. It complements Fayol's work and adds a new dimension.

[9]James D. Mooney, *The Principles of Organization* (New York: Harper & Row, 1947).

Mooney viewed management as the technique, or art, of directing and inspiring other people. Organization, on the other hand, is the technique of relating specific duties or functions in a coordinated whole. The primary purpose of management, according to Mooney, is to devise an appropriate organization.

Mooney's personal experience led him to believe that natural laws of organizing existed, and it was these natural laws, or principles, that he sought to discover through logic. The principles of organization, according to Mooney, are:

1. *Coordination:* Coordination is the primary reason for organizing. Since organizations are natural outgrowths of specialization and division of labor, their purpose must be to achieve coordinated performance of all the jobs within the organization.

2. *Authority:* The first essential activity of authority is the definition of each managerial job in terms of its duties and responsibilities. The creation of managerial jobs results in the creation of a chain of command, or hierarchy, in which each successive job up the chain has greater authority than the one below it.

3. *Leadership:* The delegation of authority is guided by the principle of leadership, which (in Mooney's terms) is the personification of authority. Through delegation, leaders confer authority on subordinates, and so on down the chain.

4. *Specialization:* Regardless of the type of organization, the necessity exists (as Fayol, Taylor, and other classical writers had observed) for people to do different jobs at different times.

CONCLUSION

As its first and foremost contribution, the classical approach identified management as a distinct element of organized society. The classical writers believed that management—like law, medicine, and other professions—should be practiced according to principles that managers can learn. Moreover, they argued, these principles can be discovered by the application of scientific methods. Manual tasks, as Taylor pointed out, could be studied and subsequently managed by applying the basic laws of physiology and physics.[10] Mooney showed that the organizing function can be analyzed by applying the fundamentals of logic.

The identification of the planning, organizing, and controlling functions provided a basis for training managers. Many management textbooks, including this one, describe and illustrate these functions. The manner in which management functions are presented and explained often differs, depending on the particular point of view of the author. Yet, any listing of management functions acknowledges that managers are concerned with *what* the organization is to be doing, *how* it is to be done, and *whether* it is achieved.

Business firms, hospitals, universities, and government agencies recognize the need to perform these functions. Planning offices, organizational-analysis

[10]Daniel Nelson, *Frederick W. Taylor and the Rise of Scientific Management* (Madison: University of Wisconsin Press, 1980).

units, and quality control sections can be found in many large organizations. Smaller organizations implement these functions in more general, nonspecialized ways, primarily through the efforts of top management.

The contributions of the classical approach go beyond the important work of identifying the management field and its functions and principles. Many modern management techniques are direct outgrowths of its endeavors. For example, time and motion analysis, work simplification, incentive wage systems, production scheduling, personnel testing, and budgeting are modern management techniques derived directly from the classical approach. The classical approach emphasizes the *rational, logical,* and *integrated* nature of management's responsibilities.

PEOPLE IN MANAGEMENT

Jack Welch

John F. (Jack) Welch, Jr., became CEO of General Electric in 1981 at 45, the youngest person ever to hold this powerful position at GE. In his eight years as leader of the world's 10th-largest industrial corporation, Welch has radically restructured the organization. He has bought and sold over 100 product lines and reduced employment by 100,000 jobs.

GE's revenues have grown 48 percent since Welch took over the top spot. He moved GE out of old, standby businesses, such as housewares and TVs, into broadcasting, investment banking, high-tech manufacturing, and other riskier, more profitable ventures.

Fiercely competitive, Welch believes that the world marketplace will increasingly be dominated by fewer, more formidable players, and that GE must achieve competitive advantages that allow it to rank first or second in every market it serves. Under his leadership, 12 of GE's 14 units are market leaders, both at home and abroad.

Welch began his career with GE as an engineer in their plastics division in Pittsfield, Massachusetts. At the time, GE had no markets and virtually no sales. When he moved to GE's Fairfield, Connecticut, headquarters 17 years later, Welch had achieved major revenues for the plastics business. He had also acquired a reputation as an innovative, if somewhat ruthless, manager.

Welch went to GE headquarters as a senior vice president for consumer affairs. Four years later, he became GE's new CEO. During his tenure as CEO he trimmed the corporate staff from 1,700 to just over 1,000, allowing business heads to report to one of the four members of the executive office. The managers of operating units now use their time finding ways to beat the competition rather than doing paperwork. Welch charges each manager with the task of "developing a vision." Often, this means removing bureaucratic barriers to give individual employees more responsibility.

Before Welch, GE employees expected lifetime employment. Welch offered a combination of incentives in the form of frequent, large bonuses and a work environment designed to enhance workers' skills so that they can find another job if GE no longer needs them.

Another Welch innovation is an intensive management training program designed to develop leaders, not just managers. At GE's training facility in Crotonville-on-Hudson, New York, more than 5,000 people, including every new manager and college recruit, go through training each year to help build corporate loyalty and learn how to work on teams and delegate more authority.

Welch's focus on leadership is seen by some as the wave of the future. "The evidence that leadership is so much more important today is overwhelming," says Harvard business school's John Kotter. "Once again, GE is ahead of the pack."

Source: Peter Petre, "The Man Who Brought GE to Life," *Fortune*, January 5, 1987, pp. 76–77; Stratford P. Sherman, "Inside the Mind of Jack Welch," *Fortune*, March 27, 1989, pp. 38–50; Russell Mitchell with Judith H. Dobrzynski, "Jack Welch: How Good a Manager?" *Business Week*, December 14, 1987, pp. 92–103.

4

THE PLANNING FUNCTION

LEARNING OBJECTIVES

After completing Chapter 4, you should be able to:

Define
the planning function in terms of managerial responsibilities and decisions.

Describe
the planning function in terms of its four principal elements.

Discuss
why the planning function must begin with the determination of objectives.

Compare
arguments for and against the alternative means for implementing a plan.

Identify
the most useful forecasting technique for a particular set of circumstances.

What Can a Small Business Learn from McDonald's?

At a time when other fast-food chains are hurting, McDonald's continues to perform. Recently, it achieved its usual 15 percent increase in sales and profits for the year, finishing the 91st consecutive quarter of increased earnings and sales. In addition, it increased the average profit margin on its restaurants to 17.8 percent despite a 12 percent increase in beef prices. Finally, it topped $1.5 million in average sales for each of its stores for the first time and opened its 10,000th restaurant. With performances like this, McDonald's must be considered an outstanding consumer products firm like Procter & Gamble, General Mills, and Coca-Cola.

But what, if anything, can a small business learn from McDonald's? Looking at the fast-food king's road to success, every small business can learn four important lessons from McDonald's:

1. *Be flexible when things change.* When McDonald's experienced extraordinary growth in the 1970s, some entrepreneurial franchisees disliked the power of the corporation's regional managers. The company changed its policies and gave individual franchisees more opportunities to communicate with top executives. This change enabled the company to respond quickly to local conditions in the 1980s.

2. *Grow from within.* Because of its rapid growth, the company offers great opportunities for employees to rise through the ranks. These people know the business well and have been trained in all of its policies and systems. This policy of promotion from within has resulted in McDonald's being run with more consistency than any of its competitors.

3. *Pay attention to detail.* McDonald's does new things very carefully, often slower than competitors. But when it goes national with any new product, every detail has been perfected. Because of this attention to detail, a product failure is highly unlikely.

4. *Identify problems early.* Aware of the growing shortage of teenage workers, the company was the first to actively recruit older workers and offer employees points that can be traded in for college tuition.

You will see in this chapter that the basic elements of the management function of planning are important for both large and small businesses. Many small businesses fail because management fails to plan.

Source: "McDonald's Profit Jumps 18% on Sales Gains," *USA Today*, April 22, 1988, p. 3B; "The McDonald's Mystique," *Fortune*, July 4, 1988, pp. 112, 196; "Lessons from McDonald's," *Boardroom Reports*, January 1989, pp. 5–6.

Managers have a primary responsibility for planning. In fact, some managers see planning as the primary management function and think that organizing and controlling are secondary. Whatever its relative importance to other management functions, planning is essential if organizations are to achieve effective levels of performance.[1] The ability or inability of a firm to adapt to change is often linked directly to its planning system.

THE FOCUS OF PLANNING

Planning focuses on the future: what is to be accomplished and how. In essence, *the planning function includes those managerial activities that determine objectives for the future and the appropriate means for achieving those objectives.* The outcome of the planning function is a plan, a written document that specifies the courses of action the firm will take.

THE ELEMENTS OF PLANNING

The planning function requires managers to make decisions about four fundamental elements of plans: objectives, actions, resources, and implementation.

Objectives specify future conditions that a manager hopes to achieve. For example, the statement "The firm's objective is to achieve a 12 percent rate of return on investment by the end of 1990" refers to a condition (12 percent rate of return) that the manager hopes to achieve at a specific time in the future (by the end of 1990).

Actions are the means, or specific activities, planned to achieve the objectives. A course of action intended to result in a 12 percent return might be to engage in a product development effort aimed at introducing five new products in 1990.

Resources are constraints on the course of action. For example: "The total cost to be incurred in the development of five new products must not exceed $10 million." A plan should specify the kinds and amounts of resources required, as well as the potential sources and allocations of those resources. Specifying resource constraints also involves *budgeting*—identifying the sources and levels of resources that can be committed to the courses of action.

Finally, a plan must include ways and means to implement the intended actions. *Implementation* involves the assignment and direction of personnel to carry out the plan.

Establishing objectives and choosing courses of action also require *forecasting* the future. A manager cannot plan without giving consideration to future events and factors that could affect what will be possible to accomplish.

Although the four elements of the planning function are discussed separately, they are in fact related. As will be seen, objectives must be set according to what is possible, given the forecasts of the future and the budgeting of resources. Moreover, availability of resources can be affected by the very actions management is planning. In the above example, if a 12 percent return is not achieved, $10 million may not be available, because shareholders,

[1]See Arthur C. Beck and Ellis D. Hillman, *Positive Management Practices: Bringing Out the Best in Organizations and People* (San Francisco: Jossey-Bass, 1986).

FIGURE 4–1 The Planning Function

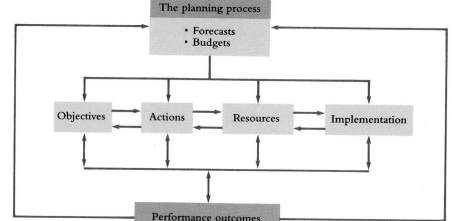

The planning function is a set of related steps by which management determines what is to be done and how it will be done.

---

bondholders, or other sources of capital will not invest the funds. Then, other action may not be feasible.

In some organizations, planning is the combined effort of managers and other personnel. In other organizations, planning is done by the top management group. In still others, it is done by one individual. And, as the Management Focus "Call Rambo" indicates, in some companies it is done by a very interesting type of manager.

Planning activities can range from complex, formal procedures to simple and informal ones. Although the *form* of planning activities varies from organization to organization, the *substance* is the same. Plans and planning always involve objectives, actions, resources, and implementation directed toward improving an organization's performance in the future. Figure 4–1 outlines the planning function.

THE IMPORTANCE OF PLANNING

Planning can occur at all levels in an organization. A production manager who identifies standard output and directs subordinates in using standard procedures is engaged in planning. Sales managers who define sales quotas and assign salespersons to particular territories are engaged in planning. In both instances, these managers determine objectives (standard output, sales quotas), actions (standard procedures, assignment to territories), and resources (production workers, salespersons).

The fact that most managers plan in some form is ample evidence of its importance in management. But we can identify some rather specific benefits.[2]

---

[2]Arthur A. Thompson, Jr., and A. J. Strickland III, *Strategic Management: Concepts and Cases,* 4th ed. (Homewood, Ill.: Richard D. Irwin, 1987), chaps. 1 and 2.

MANAGEMENT FOCUS

Call Rambo!

The 1980s was a decade of rapidly changing financial markets, tough foreign competition, and exciting new technologies that created a dynamic era of change for most American firms. For many, this era was one of opportunity, hard work, and success. For others, however, it was an extremely painful period.

Some people believe that many American managers, trained in less volatile times, were not equipped to develop their company plans in such a rapidly changing environment. They were used to managing in relatively stable and predictable environments. In a world of stable markets and stable technology, managers could assume that the future would look like the present because the present looked like the past. When things changed in the 1980s, many managers could not adapt, and their companies needed help.

What does a company do when it finds itself in such a situation? One increasingly used strategy is to call in a "turnaround specialist." These individuals specialize in saving companies that

have stumbled. They have been referred to as a "Lone Ranger" breed of manager and the "Green Berets" of corporate management. Before agreeing to join a firm, a turnaround specialist demands, as a condition of employment, total freedom to act and to act quickly. And while many of these rescuers achieve great results, one might wonder why the old managers could not do earlier what the turnaround specialists did later on.

One key to success for all turnaround specialists is that they approach the challenge with a new plan that is "their" plan. They approach their jobs without the sentimental attachments to old ways of doing things, to people, or to methods. They often eliminate favorite projects of the past and discard ailing parts of the business. They establish new objectives to guide the company toward the vision they see.

Source: Reported in "The Green Berets of Corporate Management," *Business Week*, September 21, 1987, pp. 110–14.

COORDINATING EFFORTS

Management exists because the work of individuals and groups in organizations must be coordinated, and planning is one important technique for achieving coordinated effort. An effective plan specifies objectives both for the total organization and for each part of the organization. By working toward planned objectives, the behavior of each part will contribute to and be compatible with goals for the entire organization.

PREPARING FOR CHANGE

An effective plan of action, as McDonald's experience has shown, allows room for change. The longer the time between completion of a plan and accomplishment of an objective, the greater the necessity to include contingency plans. Yet, if management has considered the potential effect of the change, it can be better prepared to deal with it. History provides some vivid examples of what can result from failure to prepare for change. The collapse of many banks, savings and loans, and airlines in the last few years is due in large part to those industries' managements' lack of preparedness.

DEVELOPING PERFORMANCE STANDARDS

Plans define expected behaviors; and in management terms, expected behaviors are performance standards. As plans are implemented throughout an organization, the objectives and course of action assigned to each individual and group are the bases for standards, which can be used to assess actual performance. In some instances, the objectives provide the standards: A manager's performance can be assessed in terms of how close his or her unit comes to accomplishing its objective. In other instances, the courses of action are the standards: A production worker can be held accountable for doing a job in the prescribed manner. Through planning, management derives a rational, objective basis for developing performance standards. Without planning, performance standards are likely to be nonrational and subjective.

DEVELOPING MANAGERS

The act of planning involves high levels of intellectual activity. Those who plan must be able to deal with abstract and uncertain ideas and information. Planners must think systematically about the present and the future. Through planning, the *future* state of the organization can be improved if its managers take an *active* role in moving the organization toward that future. Planning, then, implies that managers should be *proactive* and *make* things happen rather than *reactive* and *let* things happen. Through the act of planning, managers not only develop their ability to think futuristically but, to the extent that their plans are effective, their motivation to plan is reinforced. Also, the *act* of planning sharpens managers' ability to think as they consider abstract ideas and possibilities for the future.[3] Thus, both the result and the act of planning benefit both the organization and its managers.[4]

SETTING OBJECTIVES AND PRIORITIES

The planning function begins with the determination of future objectives, and these objectives must satisfy the expectations of many and often conflicting groups in the organization's environment. Whether the organization is a business, university, or government agency, the environment supplies the resources that sustain it. In exchange for these resources, the organization must supply the environment with goods and services at an acceptable price and quality. The increasing interdependence between organizations and their environments has caused corporate managers to turn more and more to formal planning techniques.[5] Moreover, the evidence is clear that organiza-

---

[3]Dale P. McConkey, "Planning for Uncertainty," *Business Horizons,* January–February 1987, pp. 40–45.

[4]Bernard Taylor, "Corporate Planning for the 1990s: The New Frontiers," *Long Range Planning,* December 1986, pp. 13–18.

[5]See Milton Moskowitz, "Lessons from the Best Companies to Work For," *California Management Review,* Winter 1985, pp. 42–47.

An effective plan should take into account the needs of the entire organization as well as the needs of each part of or individual in that organization.

tions using formal approaches to planning are more profitable than those that do not.[6]

Management initiates planning to determine the *priority* and *timing* of objectives. In addition, management must also resolve *conflict* between objectives and provide *measurement* of objectives so that results can be evaluated.[7]

PRIORITY OF OBJECTIVES

The phrase "priority of objectives" implies that at a given time, accomplishing one objective is more important than accomplishing others. For example, to a firm having difficulty meeting payrolls and due dates on accounts, the objective of maintaining a minimum cash balance may be more important than achieving minimum profitability. Priority of objectives also reflects the relative importance of certain objectives regardless of time. For example, survival of the organization is a necessary condition for the realization of all other objectives.

Managers always face alternative objectives that must be evaluated and ranked, and they must establish priorities if they want to allocate resources in a rational way. Managers of nonbusiness organizations are particularly concerned with the ranking of seemingly interdependent objectives.[8] For example, a university president must determine the relative importance of teaching, research, and community service. Because determining objectives and priorities is a judgmental decision, it is a difficult process.

[6]Ibid. Also see V. Ramanujan and N. Vankatramen, "Planning and Performance: A New Look at an Old Problem, *Business Horizons,* May–June 1987, pp. 19–25.

[7]Max D. Richards, *Setting Strategic Goals and Objectives,* 2nd ed. (St. Paul, Minn.: West Publishing, 1986).

[8]See Peter P. Pekar, "Setting Goals in the Non-Profit Environment," *Managerial Planning,* March–April 1982, pp. 43–46, for a discussion of objective setting in nonprofit organizations.

Time Frame of Objectives

Time dimensions imply that an organization's activities are guided by different objectives, depending on the duration of the action that is being planned. Managers usually identify short-run, intermediate, and long-run objectives. Short-run objectives can be accomplished in less than a year; intermediate objectives require one to five years; and long-run objectives extend beyond five years. The relationship between priority and timing is quite close, since long-run objectives are those that must be accomplished to ensure the long-term survival of the organization.

The time dimension is reflected in the practice many organizations have of developing different plans for different periods of time. The long-run objective of a business firm could be stated in terms of a desired rate of return on capital, with intermediate and short-run plans stated in terms of objectives that must be accomplished to realize the ultimate goal. Management is then in a position to know the effectiveness of each year's activities in terms of achieving not only short-run but also long-run objectives.

In some instances, short-run objectives and long-run objectives may appear to be conflicting. Many observers of contemporary business management argue that the emphasis on short-run profitability detracts from efforts to make commitments to such long-run objectives as improving productivity or growth.

In recent years, the increasing pace of environmental change has prompted many organizations to adopt *strategic planning,* which focuses on the definition of long-term objectives and strategies to achieve those objectives. This is in contrast with *functional,* or *operational, planning,* which is done in the individual units within the organization and focuses on more intermediate objectives and problems. Because of its growing importance, strategic planning will be the focus of Chapter 5.

Conflicts among Objectives

At any point in time, shareholders (owners), employees (including unions), customers, suppliers, creditors, and government agencies are all concerned with the operation of the firm. The process of setting objectives must not overlook these interest groups, and plans must incorporate and integrate their interests.[9] The form and weight to be given to any particular interest group illustrates precisely the nature of management's dilemma. Yet management's responsibility is to make these kinds of judgments. Some of the most common planning trade-offs faced by managers in business organizations are:

1. Short-term profits versus long-term growth.
2. Profit margin versus competitive position.
3. Direct sales effort versus development effort.
4. Greater penetration of present markets versus developing new markets.
5. Achieving long-term growth through related businesses versus achieving it through unrelated businesses.

[9]John E. Prescott, "Environments as Moderators of the Relationship between Strategy and Performance," *Academy of Management Journal,* June 1986, pp. 329–46.

6. Profit objectives versus nonprofit objectives (that is, social responsibilities).
7. Growth versus stability.
8. Low-risk environment versus high-risk environment.

Management must consider the expectations of the diverse groups on whom the firm's ultimate success depends. For example, present and potential customers hold ultimate power over the firm. If they are not happy with the price and quality of the firm's product, they withdraw their support (stop buying), and the firm fails because of lack of funds. Suppliers can disrupt the flow of materials to express disagreement with the firm's activities. Government agencies have the power to enforce the firm's compliance with regulations. The existence of these interest groups and their power to affect the objectives of the firm must be recognized by managers. A business firm will exist only as long as it satisfies the larger society.[10] The Management Focus describes how one famous manager balanced company and personal objectives.

Studies of objectives that business managers have set for their organizations confirm the difficulty of balancing the concerns of interest groups. These studies also suggest that the more successful firms consistently emphasize profit-seeking activities that maximize the stockholders' wealth. This is not to say that successful firms seek only profit-oriented objectives but rather that such objectives are dominant.

Evidently, such firms are managed by persons who value pragmatic, dynamic, and achievement-oriented behavior.[11] At the same time, these persons recognize that businesses have an increasing responsibility to do what is best for society.[12] The interrelationship of the manager's values, society's needs, and organizational objectives has been aptly summarized: *"What to make, what to charge, and how to market the wares* are questions that embrace moral as well as economic questions. The answers are conditioned by the personal value system of the decision maker and the institutional values which affect the relationships of the individual to the community."[13]

MEASUREMENT OF OBJECTIVES

Objectives must be understandable and acceptable to those who will help to achieve them. In fact, many people believe that specific, measurable objectives increase the performance of both employees and organizations and that difficult objectives, if accepted by employees, result in better performance than

[10]D. Quinn Mills, "Planning with People in Mind," *Harvard Business Review,* July–August 1985, pp. 97–105.

[11]C. Don Burnett, Dennis P. Yeskey, and David Richardson, "New Roles for Corporate Planners in the 1980s," *Journal of Business Strategy,* Spring 1984, pp. 64–68.

[12]For relevant discussions of these and related management problems, see M. J. Gimpl and S. R. Daken, "Management and Magic," *California Management Review,* Fall 1984, pp. 125–36; R. T. Pascale, "The Paradox of Corporate Culture: Reconciling Ourselves to Socialization," *California Management Review,* Winter 1985, pp. 26–41.

[13]Clarence C. Walton, *Ethos and the Executive* (Englewood Cliffs, N.J.: Prentice-Hall, 1969), p. 192.

MANAGEMENT FOCUS

Company Objectives versus Personal Objectives: Learning from the "Bear"

An important management task is to inform and orient employees about company objectives, a far more complicated task than just passing along information. Psychologist Alan Loy McGinnes believes managers could benefit from a method used by Paul "Bear" Bryant, the legendary University of Alabama football coach.

Before the start of each season, Bryant asked every member of the team to write down personal goals for the year. He would then read each one. Then and only then did Bryant design a set of objectives for the team. McGinnes believes that when he asked each player for his goals, Bryant was conveying a threefold message: (1) I care about you and what you want. (2) You should be thinking ahead. (3) We are building a team in which we are hoping everyone can pursue his goals, and I am going to incorporate into our general plan as many ways as possible for you to reach them.

McGinnis also believes there may have been another reason Bryant and his players put their goals in writing: once people have committed themselves to objectives, a number of psychological influences begin to take effect which greatly increase the odds that they will achieve their goals.

Source: Adapted from Alan Loy McGinnis, *Bringing Out the Best in People: How to Enjoy Helping Others to Excel* (Minneapolis: Augsburg Publishing House, 1988).

do easier objectives. In practice, effective managerial performance requires establishing objectives in every area that contributes to overall organizational performance. Management expert Peter Drucker has stated that objectives should be established in at least eight areas of organizational performance: (1) market standing, (2) innovations, (3) productivity, (4) physical and financial resources, (5) profitability, (6) manager performance and responsibility, (7) worker performance and attitude, and (8) social responsibility.[14] This classification in no way implies relative importance, nor is it the only classification system available.

Drucker has observed that "the real difficulty lies indeed not in determining what objectives we need, but in deciding how to set them."[15] This involves determining *what* should be measured in each area and *how* it should be measured. Immediately, one can recognize the difficulty of measuring performance in certain areas. For example, how can a manager measure employee attitudes and social responsibility? The more abstract the objective, the more difficult it is to measure performance.[16]

[14]Peter Drucker, *The Practice of Management* (New York: Harper & Row, 1954); re-emphasized in Peter Drucker, *Management: Tasks, Responsibilities, Practices* (New York: Harper & Row, 1974). For recent work by this renowned management writer, see *Managing in Turbulent Times* (New York: Harper & Row, 1980); *Innovation and Entrepreneurship* (New York: Harper & Row, 1985).

[15]Drucker, *The Practice of Management,* p. 64.

[16]George S. Odiorne, "Measuring the Unmeasurable: Setting Standards for Management Performance," *Business Horizons,* July–August 1987, pp. 69–75.

Nevertheless, effective planning requires measurement of objectives. A variety of measurements exist to quantify objectives in the eight areas that Drucker suggests.

Profitability Objectives.   These include the ratios of (1) profits to sales, (2) profits to total assets, and (3) profits to capital (net worth). The tendency in recent years has been to emphasize the ratio of profits to sales as an important measure of profitability. Both quantities in this ratio are taken from the income statement, which management generally regards as a better test of performance than the balance sheet.

However, other managers believe that the true test of profitability must combine the income statement and the balance sheet. These managers, therefore, would use either the profit-to-total-asset ratio or the profit-to-net-worth ratio. Which of these two measures is preferred depends on whether the *source* of capital is an important consideration. The profit-to-total-asset ratio measures management's use of all resources, regardless of origin (that is, creditors or owners). The profit-to-net-worth ratio measures how management used the owner's contribution.

The measures are not mutually exclusive. All three ratios can be used as profitability objectives because each measures and therefore evaluates different yet important aspects of profitability.

The purposes of profit are to measure efficiency, recover one cost element of being in business (return on invested capital), and provide funds for future expansion and innovation. The minimum profitability is that which ensures the continuous stream of capital into the organization, given the inherent risks of the industry in which the organization operates.

Marketing Objectives.   These measure performance relating to products, markets, distribution, and customer service objectives. They focus on the prospects for long-run profitability. Thus, well-managed organizations measure performance in such areas as market share, sales volume, number of outlets carrying the product, and number of new products developed.

Productivity Objectives.   Productivity is measured with ratios of output to input. Other factors being equal, the higher the ratio, the more efficient is the use of inputs.

Drucker has long proposed that the *ratios of value added to sales and to profit* are the superior measures of productivity.[17] He believes that a business's objective should be to increase these ratios and that departments in the firm should be evaluated on the basis of these increases. The argument for value added is that it measures the increase in value of the purchased materials due to the combined efforts of the firm, since value added is equal to the difference between the purchase price and the market value of materials and supplies. In this way, the efficiency of the firm's efforts is measured directly. This measure of productivity also could be used for comparisons among the individual departments in the firm.

Physical and Financial Objectives.   These measures reflect the firm's capacity to acquire resources sufficient to achieve its objectives. Measurement

---

[17]Drucker, *The Practice of Management*, pp. 71–73.

TABLE 4–1	Selected Measures of Objectives

Objective	Possible Measures
Profitability	1. Ratio of profit to sales.
	2. Ratio of profit to total assets.
	3. Ratio of profit to capital.
Marketing	1. Market share.
	2. Sales volume.
	3. Rate of new product development.
	4. Number of outlets.
Productivity	1. Ratio of output to labor costs.
	2. Ratio of output to capital costs.
	3. Ratio of value added to sales.
	4. Ratio of value added to profit.
Physical and financial	1. Current ratio.
	2. Working capital turnover.
	3. Ratio of debt to equity.
	4. Accounts receivable turnover.
	5. Inventory turnover.

Management must decide what measures to use to indicate whether objectives are being achieved.

of physical and financial objectives is comparatively easy since numerous accounting measures can be used. Liquidity measures such as the current ratio, working capital turnover, acid-test ratio, debt-to-equity ratio, and accounts receivable and inventory turnover can be used in establishing objectives and evaluating performance in financial planning.

Other Objectives.   Objectives for profitability, market standing, productivity, and physical and financial resources are amenable to measurement. Objectives for innovation, employee attitudes, manager behavior, and social responsibility are, however, not so easily identifiable or measurable in concrete terms. This is important because, without measurement, any subsequent evaluation will be inconclusive. For example, a vaguely stated objective such as "to become more socially responsible" will be virtually impossible to evaluate, whether or not it is accomplished. Selected measures of objectives are summarized in Table 4–1.

AN EXAMPLE OF OBJECTIVES IN PLANNING

Stating objectives clearly is a critical element of planning.[18] Our discussion of objective setting is summarized in Table 4–2, which is based on an organization's actual experience in establishing objectives. This organization established seven objectives that management ranked in the order of priority shown in the table.

Clear objectives can be converted into specific targets and actions. Note that management also stated each objective in Table 4–2 in more specific secondary

---

[18]See Edwin A. Locke and Gary P. Latham, *Goal Setting: A Motivational Technique that Works!* (Englewood Cliffs, N.J.: Prentice-Hall, 1984), for a related discussion and additional examples.

TABLE 4–2	The Development of Objectives		

	Objective	Possible Secondary Objectives	Possible Indicators
	1. Achieve a 15 percent return on investment.	*a.* Earn maximum return on idle funds.	Interest income.
	2. Maintain a 40 percent share of the market.	*a.* Retain 75 percent of old customers. *b.* Obtain 25 percent of first-time customers.	Percent replacement purchases. Percent initial purchases.
	3. Develop middle managers for executive positions.	*a.* Develop a merit review system by year-end. *b.* Select 10 managers to attend industry-sponsored executive school.	Report submitted on November 1. Number selected by January 1.
Management can subdivide some objectives and develop fairly specific indicators of achievement.	4. Help to ensure that clean air is maintained in all geographical areas in which the firm has plant locations.	*a.* Reduce air pollution by 15 percent.	By April 1, pollutants to be 125 pounds/hour measured at stack by electrostatic.
	5. Provide working conditions that constantly exceed industrywide safety levels.	*a.* Automate loading process in plant B. *b.* Reduce in-plant injuries by 10 percent by year-end.	Installation to be 50 percent complete by January 1. Ratio of labor days lost to total labor days.
	6. Manufacture all products as efficiently as possible.	*a.* Increase productivity by 5 percent through installation of new punching machine.	Installed by August 1. Ratio of output to total labor hours.
	7. Maintain and improve employee satisfaction to levels consistent with those in our own and similar industries.	*a.* Improve employee satisfaction levels in all functional areas by 15 percent by year-end.	Ratio of quits to total employees. Attitude survey questionnaires administered to all employees.

objectives, which can become objectives for individual departments. For example, the secondary objective associated with objective 1 can serve as a financial management objective; those associated with objective 2 can be marketing objectives; and those associated with objective 3 can be the goals of the personnel department.

COURSES OF ACTION

Actions, the second element of the planning function, are the catalyst that can determine success or failure in meeting objectives. Planned courses of action are called *strategies* and *tactics,* usually differentiated by the scope and magnitude of the action. Whatever the name, a planned action is directed toward changing a future condition—that is, achieving an objective. For example, if an objective is to increase productivity from five units of output per labor hour to six units per labor hour, a course of action has to be identified and implemented.

In some instances, managers simply do not know what action to take. When President Kennedy stated as a national objective the placing of an American on the moon by 1970, no one knew exactly what action was necessary to accomplish that objective. In other instances, numerous alternative courses of action may be possible. For example, productivity increases can be achieved through a variety of means, including improved technology, employee training, management training, reward systems, and improved working conditions. In such cases, managers must select the least costly but most effective alternative. Often, several possible courses of action will exist for top managers who are planning for the total organization. As the plan becomes more localized to a simple unit in the organization, the number of alternatives tends to become smaller yet more familiar.

The important point is that courses of action and objectives are causally related: the objective is caused to occur by the courses of action. The intellectual effort required in planning involves knowing not only *what* alternatives will accomplish an objective but also *which* one is most efficient. In some instances, managers can test the effects of a course of action by forecasting. Forecasting is *the process of using past and current information to predict future events*.

A typical objective in business planning is to maintain or increase sales volume. Sales volume is a primary source of liquid resources (e.g., cash, accounts receivable, and notes receivable), which managers can use to finance the firm's activities. Courses of action that affect sales include price changes, marketing and sales activities, and new product development. Factors beyond the control of management also affect sales. Such external factors include the price of competing and substitute products, competitors' marketing/sales activities, and general economic conditions (expansion, recession, inflation). Although managers cannot control many of the factors that determine sales volume, forecasting remains a valuable managerial tool.[19]

FORECASTING SALES VOLUME

Four methods currently are used to forecast future events. Here they are presented in the context of forecasting sales volume, although the methods generally are applicable to forecasting other events.

1. *Hunches.* Estimates of future sales can be based on past sales data, comments by salespersons and customers, and instinctive reaction to the "general state of affairs." This approach is relatively cheap and usually effective in firms whose market is stable or at least changing at a predictable rate.

2. *Market survey.* Estimates of future sales can be based on the opinions customers express to the organization's salespeople. More sophisticated statistical sampling techniques yield more refined information; the forecaster can specify both the range of projected sales and the degree of confidence in the estimates.

[19]S. Makridakis, S. Wheelwright, and V. McGee, *Forecasting Methods and Applications* (New York: John Wiley & Sons, 1982).

Tracking past and current sales volume is often a significant part of forecasting future events.

3. *Time-series analysis.* Estimates of future sales can be based on the relationship between sales and time. The movement of sales over time is affected by at least three types of factors: seasonal, cyclical, and trend. This means that a firm's sales can vary in response to seasonal factors, to cycles common to business activity generally, and to trends of long duration. The management of a brewery knows that peak sales occur during the summer months. But it also is aware of the cyclical nature of beer consumption, as beer drinkers shift to liquor when their incomes increase and shift back when their incomes decline. For long-term planning, the manager also must know something about the trend in beer consumption. Consumer preferences change with time and with the introduction of new products.

4. *Econometric models.* These allow a forecaster to evaluate the impact of a number of variables on sales. Even though these techniques are the most sophisticated of the methods, they offer no hope for the elimination of *all* uncertainty; management judgment is still needed. The econometric approach begins with the identification of those variables that affect the sales of the firm's products. Among the obvious variables are price, competing products, and complementary products. Variables such as the age of existing stocks of the goods, availability of credit, and consumer tastes are less obvious. Measurements of these variables are obtained for previous years and matched with sales of the product for the same years.

No perfect method exists for forecasting future sales. Hunches, market surveys, time-series analysis, and econometric models provide estimates that may or may not be reasonable, and they can be no better than the information that goes into them. As technological breakthroughs in information processing occur, we can expect sales forecasts to become more accurate and consequently be better guides for planning. At present, however, forecasting requires a great deal of managerial judgment.

RESOURCES

The third phase of the planning function is budgeting resources for each important plan. The sales forecast presumes that a firm has a product to sell, so managers must first utilize resources to acquire or produce that product. And just as managers use forecasts to approximate income from sales, they must also forecast the future availability of major resources, including people, raw materials, energy, and money.[20] Techniques for forecasting resources are the same as those employed to forecast sales: hunches, market surveys, time-series analysis, and econometric models. The only difference is that the manager is seeking to know the quantities and prices of goods that can be purchased rather than those to be sold.

The sales forecast, whether for 1 or for 10 years, predicts the firm's level of activity. At the same time, the prediction is conditioned by the availability of resources, by economic and social events beyond the control of management, and by the predetermined objectives. Given an adequate supply of resources, the manager's next task is *the allocation of resources necessary to implement a plan*. The principal technique management uses in this phase of the planning function is the *budget*.

A very close relationship exists between budgeting as a planning technique and budgeting as a control technique.[21] But this section is concerned only with the preparation of budgets as a part of planning, prior to operations. However, after the organization has been engaged in activities for a time, actual results are compared with the budgeted (planned) results and may lead to corrective action. This, as we shall see later, is the management function of controlling.[22]

The complexity of the budget phase is shown in Figure 4–2. The sales forecast plays a key role, as is evident in the placement of the sales budget; all other budgets are related to it either directly or indirectly. The production budget, for example, must specify the materials, labor, and other manufacturing expenses required to support the projected sales level. Similarly, the marketing expense budget details the costs associated with the level of sales activity projected for each product in each sales region. Administrative expenses also must be related to the predicted sales volume. The projected sales and expenses are combined in the financial budgets, which consist of pro forma financial statements, inventory budgets, and the capital additions budget.

Forecast data are based on assumptions about the future. If these assumptions prove wrong, the budgets are inadequate. So the usefulness of financial budgets depends mainly on the degree to which they are flexible to changes in conditions. Two principal means exist to provide flexibility: variable budgeting and moving budgeting.

Variable budgeting provides for the possibility that actual output deviates from planned output. It recognizes that certain costs are related to output

[20]Arthur A. Thompson, Jr., "Strategies for Increasing Cost Businesses," *Academy of Management Proceedings,* August 1982, pp. 17–21.

[21]Neil Churchill, "Budgeting Choice: Planning vs. Control," *Harvard Business Review,* July–August 1984, pp. 150–64.

[22]Robert N. Anthony, John Deardon, and Norman Bedford, *Management Control Systems,* 5th ed. (Homewood, Ill.: Richard D. Irwin, 1984), pp. 12–13.

FIGURE 4–2   The Budgeting Process

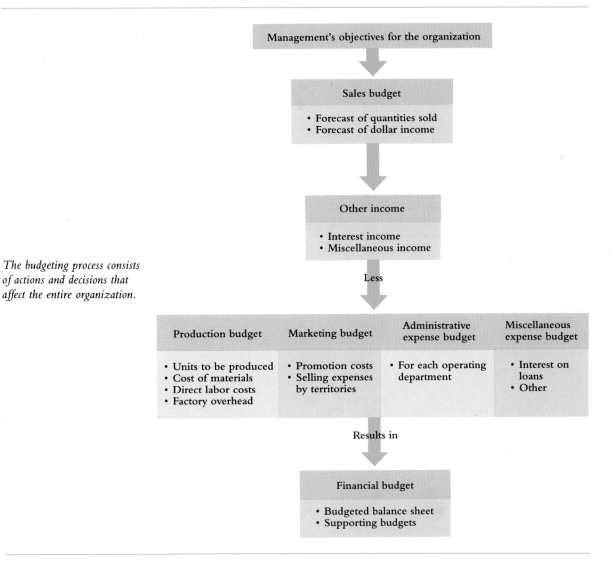

The budgeting process consists of actions and decisions that affect the entire organization.

(variable costs), while others are unrelated to output (fixed costs). Thus, if actual output is 20 percent less than planned output, it does not follow that actual profit will be 20 percent less than that planned. Rather, the actual profit will vary, depending on the complex relationship between costs and output. Table 4–3 shows a variable budget that allows for output variations. It demonstrates the behavior of costs and profits as output varies.

To be complete, variable budgeting requires adjustments in all supporting budgets. The production, marketing, and administrative budgets must likewise allow for the impact of output variation.

Moving budgeting is the preparation of a budget for a fixed period (say, one year), with periodic updating at fixed intervals (such as one month). For

TABLE 4–3	Hypothetical Variable Budget			
Output (units)	1,000	1,200	1,400	1,600
Sales (at $5.00 per unit)	$5,000	$6,000	$7,000	$8,000
Variable costs (at $3.00 per unit)	3,000	3,600	4,200	4,800
Fixed costs	1,000	1,000	1,000	1,000
Total costs	4,000	4,600	5,200	5,800
Planned profit	$1,000	$1,400	$1,800	$2,200

A variable budget recognizes that planned profit and total costs do not vary proportionately with sales.

example, a budget is prepared in December for the next 12 months, January through December. At the end of January, the budget is revised and projected for the next 12 months, February through January. In this manner, the most recent information is included in the budgeting process. Premises and assumptions constantly are being revised as management learns from experience.

Moving budgets have the advantage of systematic reexamination; they have the disadvantage of being costly to maintain. Although budgets are important instruments for implementing the objectives of the firm, they must be viewed in perspective as one item on a long list of demands for a manager's time.

IMPLEMENTATION OF PLANS

All the planning in the world will not help an organization realize objectives if plans cannot be implemented. (Implementation of plans involves resources and actions, as shown in Figure 4–1.) In some instances, the manager can personally take all the necessary steps to apply resources in planned actions to achieve objectives. But in most cases, the manager must implement plans through *other people,* motivating them to accept and carry out the plan. *Authority, persuasion,* and *policy* are the manager's means of implementing plans.

AUTHORITY

Authority is a legitimate form of power in the sense that it accompanies the position, not the person. That is, the nature of authority in organizations is the right to make decisions and to expect compliance to these decisions. Thus, a manager can reasonably expect subordinates to carry out a plan so long as it does not require illegal, immoral, or unethical behavior. Authority is often sufficient to implement relatively simple plans that involve no significant change in the status quo. But a complex and comprehensive plan can seldom be implemented through authority alone.

PERSUASION

Persuasion, another important rule, is a process of selling a plan to those who must implement it, communicating relevant information so individuals understand all implications. In this sense, persuasion requires convincing

Effective implementation includes persuading the organization to accept the plan and communicating all relevant information about the plan.

others to base acceptance of the plan on its merits rather than on the authority of the manager.

This process does present a hazard. What happens if the plan is not implemented after all persuasive efforts have been exhausted? If the plan is crucial and must be implemented, management must resort to authority. Consequently, a manager who has failed once at the use of persuasion must limit use of the technique in the future. Individuals who were the objects of unsuccessful attempts at persuasion and who thought they had the choice of accepting or rejecting a plan would be skeptical of future persuasive efforts.[23] The Management Focus presents a positive technique that some managers have used to gain employee support in implementing plans.

POLICY

When plans are intended to be long-term or permanent fixtures in an organization, management develops policies to implement them. **Policies** usually are written statements that reflect the basic objectives of the plan and provide guidelines for selecting actions to achieve those objectives. Once plans have been accepted by employers who must carry them out, policies become important management tools for implementing them. Effective policies have these characteristics:

1. *Flexibility.*   A policy must strike a reasonable balance between stability and flexibility. Conditions change, and policies must change accordingly. On the other hand, some degree of stability must prevail if order and a sense of direction are to be maintained. No rigid guidelines exist to specify the exact degree of flexibility; only managerial judgment can determine the appropriate balance.

[23]See Toyohiro Kono, "Japanese Management Philosophy: Can It Be Exported?" *Long Range Planning,* Fall 1982, pp. 90–102, for a different look at this problem.

MANAGEMENT FOCUS

Some Managers Use Visions of Greatness to Help Implement Their Plan

All of the bank presidents had left the room after an intensive group interview in which most of the discussion had centered on the problem and difficulties of eliciting people's best efforts in implementing and executing strategy. One executive had remained behind, however, to show us something he had in his wallet. It was a folded 3 by 5 index card on which he had typed: "We will become the best bank in the state for medium-sized businesses by 1992."

Another time, we were visiting a bank branch when the newly appointed branch manager, a former student, called us into her office. After talking over old times, she opened the top drawer of her desk. Taped to the bottom of the drawer was the following statement: "The service we provide the customers of our branch will be demonstrably better than any branch of any bank in the city."

Exactly what is a vision of greatness? It is at least two things:

- A clear image or picture of what you want your business or department to be.
- A focus on what you want to achieve—not necessarily how it will be achieved.

This clear image of what you want is then used to organize and instruct every step toward its achievement. (Note that the above two visions of greatness qualify on each dimension.)

There seems to be unanimous belief in the motivational power of a vision of greatness, similar to athletes mentally rehearsing every move of their performance. When we asked the bank president what purpose his index card served, he replied, "It tells me and everyone else in the bank why we get up and come to work in the morning." Commenting on her vision of service, the branch manager told us: "The only reward most bank employees get for their efforts is that the bank makes more money. I believe people want to commit to something bigger, at least I do."

Source: Adapted from James H. Donnelly, Jr., "Visions of Greatness Can Be a Powerful Motivator," *American Banker,* November 17, 1988, p. 4.

---

2. *Comprehensiveness.* If plans are to be followed, a policy must be comprehensive enough to cover any contingency. The scope of the policy depends on the scope of action controlled by the policy itself. If the policy is directed toward very narrow ranges of activity—for example, hiring policies—it need not be as comprehensive as a policy concerned with say, public relations.

3. *Coordination.* A policy must provide for coordination of the various subunits whose actions are interrelated. Without coordinated direction provided by policies, each subunit is tempted to pursue its own objectives. The ultimate test of any subunit's activity should be its relationship to the policy statement.

4. *Ethics.* A policy must conform to society's prevailing codes of ethical behavior. The increasingly complex and interdependent nature of contempo-

rary society has resulted in a great number of problems involving ethical dilemmas. And as we saw in the previous chapter, the manager is ultimately responsible for the resolution of issues that involve ethical principles.

5.   *Clarity.*   A policy must be written clearly and logically. It must specify the intended aim of the action it governs, define the appropriate methods and action, and delineate the limits of freedom of action permitted to those who are to be guided by it.

The ultimate test of the effectiveness of a policy is whether or not the intended objective is attained. Policies must be subjected to reexamination on a continual basis. If a policy does not lead to the objective, it should be revised.

KEY PLANNING ISSUES

We have seen that planning, a fundamental activity of managers, can cover any time span from the short to the long run. We also have surveyed some of the most important forecasting and budgeting techniques. These do not cover the entire range of problems and issues associated with planning.[24] Our discussion has, however, underscored the fact that planning is the essence of management; all other managerial functions stem from planning.

How does a manager begin the planning process? Many professionals agree that much of the task consists of asking the appropriate questions. Table 4–4 suggests the basic ones. Other, more specific questions might well be asked, but the fundamental questions are appropriate regardless of the type and size of the organization.

SUMMARY OF KEY POINTS

■ The planning function includes those managerial activities that result in predetermined courses of action. Planning necessarily focuses on the future, and management's responsibility is to prepare the organization for the future.

■ Planning requires managers to make decisions about objectives, actions, resources, and implementation. These four factors are essential to effective planning.

■ Through planning, management coordinates efforts, prepares for change, develops performance standards, and manages development.

■ Objectives are statements of future conditions that, if realized, are deemed satisfactory or optimal by the planner. All sets of objectives have three characteristics: priority, timing, and mea-

surement. How management responds to priority, timing, and measurement issues in setting objectives reflects individual values and economic considerations.

■ To be useful in planning, objectives should be stated in measurable terms and should relate to significant organizational performance determinants. In particular, objectives should be set for profitability, marketing, productivity, physical and financial resources, innovation, manager behavior, employee attitudes, and social responsibility.

■ Courses of action to achieve objectives must be specified. The terms *strategies* and *tactics* refer to planned courses of action. An important part of specifying courses of action is that of forecasting

[24]Peter Mills, *Managing Service Industries* (Cambridge, Mass.: Ballinger, 1986), discusses the problems of managing organizations whose product is human performance and not a tangible product.

TABLE 4–4   Key Managerial Planning Issues

	Planning Element	Key Managerial Decisions
	Objectives	1. What objectives will be sought?
		2. What is the relative importance of each objective?
		3. What are the relationships among the objectives?
		4. When should each objective be achieved?
		5. How can each objective be measured?
		6. What person or organizational unit should be accountable for achieving the objective?
	Actions	1. What important actions bear on the successful achievement of objectives?
		2. What information exists regarding each action?
Asking the right questions for each element of the plan is critical.		3. What is the appropriate technique for forecasting the future state of each important action?
		4. What person or organizational unit should be accountable for the action?
	Resources	1. What resources should be included in the plan?
		2. What are the interrelationships among the various resources?
		3. What budgeting technique should be used?
		4. Which person or organizational unit should be accountable for the preparation of the budget?
	Implementation	1. Can the plan be implemented through authority or persuasion?
		2. What policy statements are necessary to implement the overall plan?
		3. To what extent are the policy statements comprehensive, flexible, coordinative, ethical, and clearly written?
		4. Who or what organizational units would be affected by the policy statements?

---

future demand for the organization's output and future availability of resources.

▪ Resource requirements of a plan must be forecast and specified by budgets. Management can select the type of budget that best suits the planning needs of the organization.

▪ The fourth part of planning is implementation, a phase that deals with the fact that plans usually are carried out by other people.

▪ The three approaches to implementation are authority, persuasion, and policy. Approaches can be used individually or in combination.

▪ Implementation by policy has the advantage of continuously reinforcing the plan for those who must implement it. Effective policies are those that produce the planned course of action.

DISCUSSION AND REVIEW QUESTIONS

1. What is the basis for saying that planning is the essential management function? Discuss.

2. A manager is overheard saying, "Plan? I never have time to plan. I live from day to day just trying to survive." Comment.

3. Is it accurate to say that since it involves value judgments, planning is the implementation of the manager's value system? Why?

4. In the university environment, three primary areas for setting objectives are teaching, research, and public service. Discuss potential conflicts that a professor might encounter between these objectives.

5. Describe potential conflicts between the objectives of a production department and the objectives of a marketing department in a business.

6. Is it true that the planning function is only as good as the underlying forecasts? Explain.

7. How would you measure the results of policies designed to meet a firm's social requirements?

8. Consult your school's catalog. Select any school policy statement and evaluate it based on the criteria for a good policy statement that were discussed in this chapter. What is your conclusion?

9. Explain why planning systems should be revised.

10. Discuss the issues that management would take into account when determining whether to use authority or persuasion to implement a plan.

ADDITIONAL REFERENCES

Ackoff, L. R. *A Concept of Corporate Planning.* New York: John Wiley & Sons, 1970.

Allen, L. A. "Managerial Planning: Back to the Basics." *Management Review,* April 1981, pp. 15–20.

Barton, S. L., and **P. Gordon.** "Corporate Strategy: Useful Perspective for the Study of Capital Structure." *Academy of Management Review,* October 1985, pp. 67–75.

Buzzell, R. D., and **M. Chussil.** "Managing for Tomorrow." *Sloan Management Review,* Summer 1985, pp. 3–13.

Christopher, W. F. "Is the Annual Planning Cycle Really Necessary?" *Management Review,* August 1981, pp. 38–42.

Galbraith, J., and **R. Kazanjian.** *Strategy Implementation: Structure, Systems, and Process.* St. Paul, Minn.: West Publishing, 1986.

Kantrow, A. M. "Why Read Peter Drucker?" *Harvard Business Review,* January–February 1980, pp. 74–82.

Lachman, R. "Public and Private Sector Differences: CEOs' Perceptions of Their Role Environments." *Academy of Management Journal,* September 1985, pp. 671–79.

Prescott, J. E. "Environments as Moderators of the Relationship between Strategy and Performance." *Academy of Management Journal,* June 1986, pp. 329–46.

Shim, J. K., and **R. McGlade.** "Current Trends in the use of Corporate Planning Models." *Journal of Systems Management,* September 1984, pp. 24–31.

Teece, D. J. "Economic Analysis and Strategic Management." *California Management Review,* Spring 1984, pp. 87–110.

Valenta, J. R. "Planning-Budgeting Balance." *Managerial Planning,* May–June 1982, pp. 16–18.

Wheelen, T. L., and **J. D. Hunger.** "Using the Strategic Audit." *SAM Advanced Management Journal,* Winter 1987, pp. 4–12.

Wyman, J. "Technological Myopia: The Need to Think Strategically about Technology." *Sloan Management Review,* Summer 1985, pp. 59–64.

CASE 4–1   IBM's Approach to Planning

In the mid-1980s, International Business Machines Corp. made headline news by announcing that it would invest $350 million in its Lexington, Kentucky, plant. The Lexington plant manufactures typewriters, keyboards, and printers and employs 4,200 people. IBM is the largest private employer in the city, and city officials welcomed the firm's commitment to the plant's future.

IBM's investment in automated manufacturing methods was but one aspect of the company's plan for the 1980s. According to published reports, IBM's plan was based on four primary objectives: (1) achieve low-cost production through investment in automated manufacturing facilities; (2) achieve low-cost distribution by selling small computers and office products through independent distributors, mail orders, catalogs, and company-owned retail stores; (3) position the organization and its products to attack the marketplace, segment by segment; and (4) pursue growth and profit opportunities in every area of the computer business from mainframes to home computers. These four objects reflected IBM's transformation to a high-volume, mass market business from a one-at-a-time, custom-built, custom-marketed operation.

IBM's plan for the 1980s and its steps to implement that plan resulted from a sophisticated planning system that enables IBM to react to changes in technology and the marketplace. IBM *expects* change and attempts to stay abreast of it by requiring both line managers and staff specialists to "scan the environment." When they detect a change in technology, competitors' actions, government policy, or economic activity, they alert the management, and a plan of action is initiated. IBM's planning system has two separate, yet interrelated types of plans: program plans and period plans.

Program planning involves efforts to develop a new product, improve an existing product, or improve the performance of a unit within the organization. A program plan usually has a single objective to be accomplished in a brief time span—for example, the decision to upgrade the productivity of the Lexington typewriter plant. When program planning is directed toward product development and improvement, planners first determine customer requirements for information and information processing, then translate those needs into products. If the product is one that IBM has never attempted to produce, planners will depend on the marketing staff for specifications of the customer's needs.

IBM relies on information obtained from its own econometric model to forecast demand for its products as well as to forecast the U.S. economy. Other sources of forecast data are (1) analysis of growth and replacement patterns for existing and new products, (2) historical information, (3) interviews and questionnaire data obtained from customers, and (4) analysis of backlog for existing products. Demand and economic forecasts are combined for projection of future product demand, and projections are translated into product targets and plans of action.

Period planning involves the total organization and each unit within the organization. Each unit may have several program plans in various stages of implementation, but only one period plan is in effect at any one moment. The period plan has two components: (1) a long-range corporate plan and (2) short-range unit plans.

The *long-range corporate plan* covers a five-year period. It results from considerable interaction between line, field, and corporate staff under the direction of the Corporate Management Committee (CMC). The plan specifies corporate and operating-unit profit targets, which then are implemented by specifying corporate and unit strategies that reflect best estimates of economic conditions, competitors' moves, and product development. The corporate plan is the master plan, the basis for action taken throughout the corporation during the five-year period. Four basic objectives—low-cost production, low-cost distribution, product positioning, and wide-spectrum competitive effort—were included in IBM's corporate plan for the decade.

Short-range unit plans cover two years and are based on the corporate's plan. Each unit prepares a plan that focuses on budget and implementation issues. The unit's responsibility is to achieve its assigned target by taking appropriate action within the parameters of its operation. (The Office Products Division, for instance, had to pursue action that reduced production costs. Investing in automated equipment was appropriate action to take to achieve the corporate objective.) Each unit submits its plan to the CMC, where it is reviewed for compatibility with the corporate plan. When approved, the unit proceeds with implementation.

QUESTIONS FOR ANALYSIS

1. Evaluate IBM's approach to planning in terms of the four fundamental parts of plans.
2. In what ways does IBM attempt to react to environmental changes in its planning system?
3. Some critics say that IBM moved too slowly into the personal computer market. If that criticism is valid, could the fault lie with IBM's planning system? Explain.

CASE 4–2   Problem Identification in a Consumer Products Firm

The top management of a large consumer products company is preparing for its annual planning session. Typically, at these sessions, management identifies the company's significant problems, sets priorities, and provides guidelines and policies for the preparation of detailed plans.

The seven functional departments of the company are production, personnel, sales, staff development and training, finance, legal counsel, and engineering. Each of these functions contains subunits and operates on annual plans that have developed from the annual planning sessions. Managers of each of the functional departments have been instructed, in advance of the session, to define the single significant problem facing the company from the perspective of that function. From those enumerated by the functional managers, top managers will devise a set of company problems ranked in order of priority. The problems to be presented for discussion are summarized in the following paragraphs.

Excessive downtime of machine-paced operations is the major concern of the production manager; downtime has increased by 20 percent over the previous year. The problem is blamed on the need for more intensive preventive maintenance to stay within quality control tolerances imposed by new, more restrictive state consumer protection laws.

The manager of the personnel department perceives things differently, seeing the major company problem as the excessive number of grievances that have gone to the departmental level for arbitration. The personnel manager indicates that settlement of grievances at that level is usually inappropriate and reflects the inability of first-line managers to deal with problems.

The sales manager says that the major problem is the spiraling cost of product distribution. The company's distribution system is based on regional warehouses linked to production facilities by a fleet of trucks. The rising cost of fuel is driving up the delivered cost of products and disrupting delivery schedules—all of which indicates the necessity for increasing the delivered price to customers already disgruntled by previous price increases.

The manager of staff development and training cites the inability of first-line supervisors to deal effectively with their subordinates as the firm's major problem. The problem has grown out of the company's affirmative response to equal opportunity laws that require employment of persons formerly considered marginal. For the most part, these new employees have required intensive skill training and close supervision; moreover, they tend to be sensitive to criticism. The problem has resulted in significant expenditures to train supervisors to manage with greater sensitivity.

For the finance department, the company's primary goal must be to reduce reliance on short-term debt to meet current obligations. The financial manager has observed that the company's cash flow is seriously unbalanced, the major cause being the company's liberal credit terms and subsequently unpredictable collections from customers.

The chief legal officer says the company must either meet the recently legislated air quality standards or be brought under injunction. The company's principal source of power is coal. The air quality standards required the removal of air pollutants through the use of filter mechanisms, but at heavy expense to the company.

The engineering department's manager considers the company's most significant problem to be the high number of engineers who have left for better-paying jobs with other companies. He states that salaries must be upgraded or the company will face a continued drain of engineering talent.

QUESTIONS FOR ANALYSIS

1. In what order of priority would you place these problems?
2. Is there any basis for interrelating the problems, or is each a separate, unrelated problem? Explain.
3. Once problems are identified, what information is needed for subsequent planning decisions?

EXPERIENTIAL EXERCISE

USING THE ELEMENTS OF PLANNING IN YOUR OWN LIFE

Purpose

The purpose of this exercise is to apply the elements of planning to your own life.

The Exercise in Class

Every person in the class should apply the four major elements of planning to a personal situation and answer the following questions:

1. What one important *objective* would you like to achieve in the next six months? It may be a personal objective pertaining to weight loss, exercise, caloric intake, diet, grade point average, major purchase, or personal relationship. Or it may be a professional objective such as a promotion, pay raise, or income level. Make sure you adhere to such criteria as time frame and measurement, discussed in the chapter.
2. What specific *actions* (strategies and tactics) do you intend to undertake to achieve your objective?
3. What *resources* will be required for you to achieve your objective? Remember to also include nonmonetary resources such as time, effort, and other people.
4. How do you intend to *implement* the actions you have decided to take to achieve your objectives?

The instructor will randomly select members of the class to present their plans. Other members of the class should make sure the presenters have adhered to the basic elements of planning discussed in the chapter.

The Learning Message

The purpose of the elements of planning is to provide a blueprint for management action. This exercise should illustrate the benefits of formal planning (for individuals as well as for organizations).

5

STRATEGIC PLANNING

LEARNING OBJECTIVES

After completing Chapter 5, you should be able to:

Define
strategic planning in terms of the direction it gives to the entire organization.

Describe
how the mission and strategies of an organization should mesh.

Discuss
why strategic planning has grown in importance in recent years.

Compare
organizational objectives and operational objectives.

Identify
appropriate strategies for each business type identified in a portfolio matrix.

Procter & Gamble: Changing Strategy with Changing Times

We are familiar with many of Procter & Gamble's products. For decades, that company has been a leader in the market for low-priced, repetitively purchased consumable products. Products such as Pringles, Folgers, Right Guard, Tide, Ivory Flakes, and Jif are almost household words.

But what about Vicks Vaporub, Norwich Aspirin, Pepto-Bismol, and Metamucil? During the mid-1980s, all of these products became part of P&G's product line. Through a combination of developing its own new products and acquiring other companies, the company was clearly changing its strategy.

It is safe to say that, like the rest of the country, P&G went on a health kick. Over those years, the company spent almost $2 billion to acquire several producers of health-related products. In fact, P&G now claims to be the largest U.S. provider of over-the-counter remedies. Also, P&G is about to introduce products that could alter American diets and health, including a fat substitute. Clearly the company is focusing on health.

Why is P&G on a health kick? The answer, of course, is that it is a part of the company's strategic plan. As insurance companies and the government try to keep health care costs from rising, consumers are buying more and more over-the-counter drug remedies. Companies are making health claims for products from cereal to chewing gum. Finally, the population is aging, and as the fitness craze demonstrates, interest in health is higher than ever. As P&G's president John Pepper has said, "People are going to be older, but they're not going to want to feel older."

Defining and redefining the purpose and direction of a business is vital. It is one of the critical responsibilities of management, whether the business is large or small. Because change is a permanent part of every manager's world, strategic planning is an important managerial skill. This chapter will describe how managers develop strategic plans.

Source: "P&G Taps More Products via Drug Buy,"
Advertising Age, November 11, 1985, p. 10; "P&G Builds Up Its
Drug Business," *Business Week*, November 1985, p. 52; "Procter & Gamble Goes on a Health Kick," *Business Week*, June 29, 1987, pp. 90–92.

The preceding chapter examined the four phases of planning and introduced important planning terminology. However, before a production manager, marketing manager, and personnel manager can develop plans for their individual departments, a larger plan—a blueprint—for the entire organization must be developed. Otherwise, on what would the individual departments' plans be based?

In other words, for the various planning activities, there is a larger framework that we would like to consider in this chapter. A large business organization usually has several business divisions and several product lines within each division (such as General Electric or Philip Morris). Before any planning can be done by individual divisions or departments, a plan must be developed for the entire organization. Then, objectives and strategies established at the top level provide the planning context for each of the divisions and departments. Divisional and departmental managers can develop their plans within the constraints developed at the higher levels.[1]

THE GROWTH OF STRATEGIC PLANNING

Many of today's most successful business organizations continue to survive because many years ago they offered the right product at the right time; the same can be said for nonprofit and government organizations. Many critical decisions of the past were made without the benefit of strategic thinking or planning. Whether these decisions were based on wisdom or luck is not important. They resulted in momentum that has carried these organizations to where they are today. However, present-day managers increasingly recognize that wisdom and intuition alone are not sufficient to guide the destinies of large organizations in today's ever changing world. These managers are turning to strategic planning.

In earlier, less dynamic periods in our society, the planning systems utilized by most organizations extrapolated current-year sales and environmental trends for 5 and 10 years. Based on these, they made plant, product, and investment decisions. In most instances, the decisions were fairly accurate because the factors influencing sales were more predictable and the environment was more stable.

In the years after World War II, many of the factors on which earlier planners counted could no longer be taken for granted. Uncertainty, instability, and changing environments became the rule rather than the exception. Managers faced increased inflation and increased foreign competition, technological obsolescence, and changing market and population characteristics.

Because changes are occurring so rapidly, there is increased pressure on top management to respond. In order to respond more accurately, on a more timely basis, and with a strategy or course of action in mind, managers are increasingly turning to the use of strategic planning.[2] **Strategic planning** is a

---

[1]John H. Grant and William R. King, *The Logic of Strategic Planning* (Boston: Little, Brown, 1982), chap. 1.

[2]Jane E. Dutton and Susan E. Jackson, "Categorizing Strategic Issues: Links to Organizational Action," *Academy of Management Review*, January 1987, pp. 76–90; Jane E. Dutton and Edward Ottensmeyer, "Strategic Issue Management Systems: Forms, Functions, Contexts," *Academy of Management Review*, April 1987, pp. 355–65.

process that involves the review of market conditions; customer needs; competitive strengths and weaknesses; sociopolitical, legal, and economic conditions; technological developments; and the availability of resources that lead to the specific opportunities or threats facing the organization.[3] In practice, *the development of strategic plans involves taking information from the environment and deciding on an organizational mission and on objectives, strategies, and a portfolio plan.* The strategic planning process is depicted in Figure 5–1.

As indicated, to develop a unity of purpose across the organization, the strategic planning process must be tied to objectives and goals at all levels of management. At Matsushita Corporation, for example, department managers provide three plans every six months: (1) a five-year plan that incorporates technological and environmental changes, (2) a two-year plan that translates strategies into new products, and (3) a six-month operating plan, developed by department managers, that addresses monthly projections for production, sales, profits, inventories, quality control, and personnel requirements.

THE STRATEGIC PLANNING PROCESS

The output of the strategic planning process is a strategic plan. Figure 5–1 shows the four components to such plans: mission, objectives, strategies, and portfolio plan. Let us examine each one.[4]

ORGANIZATIONAL MISSION

The organization's environment supplies the resources that sustain the organization, whether it is a business, a college or university, or a government agency. In exchange for these resources, the organization must supply the environment with goods and services at an acceptable price and quality. In other words, every organization exists to accomplish something in the larger environment, and that purpose or mission usually is clear at the start. As time passes, however, the organization expands, the environment changes, and managerial personnel change. And one or more things are likely to occur. First, the original purpose may become irrelevant as the organization expands into new products, new markets, and even new industries. Second, the original mission may remain relevant, but some managers begin to lose interest in it. Finally, changes in the environment may make the original mission inappropriate. The result of any or all of these three conditions is a "drifting" organization, without a clear mission or purpose to guide critical decisions.[5] When this occurs, management must renew the search for purpose or restate the original purpose.

[3]See Henry Mintzberg, "The Strategy Concept I: Five Ps for Strategy," *California Management Review,* Fall 1987, pp. 11–24; Henry Mintzberg, "The Strategy Concept II: Another Look at Why Organizations Need Strategies," *California Management Review,* Fall 1987, pp. 25–32.

[4]David K. Hurst, "Why Strategic Management Is Bankrupt," *Organizational Dynamics,* Autumn 1986, pp. 4–27, critiques the conventional strategic management model.

[5]Jerome H. Want, "Corporate Mission: The Intangible Contribution to Performance," *Management Review,* August 1986, pp. 46–50.

FIGURE 5–1   The Strategic Planning Process

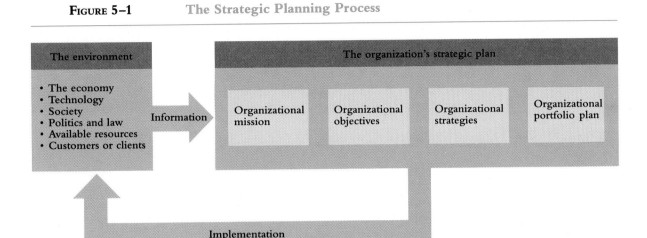

Strategic planning emphasizes the impact of the environment on the organization.

The mission statement should be a long-run vision of what the organization is trying to become—the unique aim that differentiates it from similar organizations. The basic questions that must be answered are "What is our business?" and "What should it be?"[6] The need is not for a stated purpose (e.g., "to produce the highest-quality products at the lowest possible price") that would enable shareholders and managers to feel good or to promote public relations. Rather, the need is for a stated **mission** that provides direction and significance to all members of the organization, regardless of their level.

Developing a Statement: Key Elements. In developing a mission statement, management must take into account three key elements: the organization's history, its distinctive competencies, and its environment.[7]

1. *History.* Every organization, large or small, profit or nonprofit, has a history of objectives, accomplishments, mistakes, and policies. In formulating a mission, the critical characteristics and events of the past must be considered. It would not make sense for McDonald's to become a chain of gourmet restaurants or for Yale University to become a community college, even if such moves were opportunities for growth in the future.

2. *Distinctive competencies.* While an organization may be able to do many things, it should seek to do what it can do best. Distinctive competencies are the things that an organization does well—so well, in fact, that they offer an advantage over similar organizations. Procter & Gamble probably could enter the oil business, but such a decision certainly would not take advantage of its major distinctive competence: knowledge of the market for low-priced, repetitively purchased consumer products. No matter how appealing an

[6]Peter Drucker, *Management: Tasks, Responsibilities, Practices* (New York: Harper & Row, 1974), chap. 7.

[7]Philip Kotler, *Marketing Management: Analysis, Planning, and Control,* 6th ed. (Englewood Cliffs, N.J.: Prentice-Hall, 1986), chap. 2.

opportunity may be, the organization must have the competencies to capitalize on it. An opportunity without the competence to exploit it is not really an opportunity for the organization.[8] It is an illusion.

3.   *Environment.*   The organization's environment dictates the opportunities, constraints, and threats that must be identified before a mission statement is developed.[9] For example, technological developments in the communications field (e.g., long-range picture transmission, closed-circuit television, and the television phone) may have a negative impact on business travel and certainly should be considered in the mission statement of a large motel chain and an airline.

Characteristics of a Mission Statement.   Needless to say, writing a useful and effective mission statement is extremely difficult. It is not unlikely for an organization to spend a year or two developing a useful mission. When completed, an effective mission statement will focus on *markets rather than products;* it will also be *achievable, motivating,* and *specific.*[10]

1.   *Market rather than product focus:* The customers or clients of an organization are critical in determining its mission. Traditionally, many organizations defined their business in terms of what they made ("our business is glass") and, in many cases, named the organization after the product or products (e.g., National Cash Register, Harbor View Savings and Loan Association). Often such an organization has found that when products and technologies become obsolete, its mission is no longer relevant and its name may no longer describe what it does. Thus, a more enduring way of defining the mission is needed. In recent years, a key feature of mission statements has been an *external* rather than *internal* focus. In other words, the mission statement should focus on the broad class of needs that the organization is seeking to satisfy (external focus), not on the physical product or service that the organization is offering at present (internal focus). This has been clearly stated by Peter Drucker:

> A business is not defined by the company's name, statutes, or articles of incorporation. It is defined by the want the customer satisfies when he buys a product or service. To satisfy the customer is the mission and purpose of every business. The question "What is our business?" can, therefore, be answered only by looking at the business from the outside, from the point of view of customer and market.[11]

[8]For a study of the relationship between distinctive corporate competencies and firm performance in 185 industrial firms, see M. A. Hitt and R. D. Ireland, "Corporate Distinctive Competence, Strategy and Performance," *Strategic Management Journal,* July–September 1985, pp. 273–93.

[9]See C. Smart and I. Vertinsky, "Strategy and the Environment: A Study of Corporate Responses to Crises," *Strategic Management Journal,* April–June 1984, pp. 199–214. This study of the largest U.S. and Canadian companies examines the relationship between a firm's external environment and its supply of strategic responses to cope with crises. For a different view of the environment, see L. Smircich and C. Stubbart, "Strategic Management in an Enacted World," *Academy of Management Review,* October 1985, pp. 724–36.

[10]Drucker, *Management,* pp. 77–89; Kotler, *Marketing Management,* chap. 2.

[11]Drucker, *Management,* p. 79.

While Drucker was referring to business organizations, the same necessity exists for both nonprofit and government organizations.[12] They need to state the mission in terms of serving a particular group of clients or customers and/or meeting a particular class of need.

2. *Achievable:* While the mission statement should "stretch" the organization toward more effective performance, it should at the same time be realistic and achievable. In other words, it should open a vision of new opportunities but should not lead the organization into unrealistic ventures far beyond its competencies. Examples would be a pen manufacturer stating it is in the communications business or an antique car restorer viewing its mission in terms of transportation.

3. *Motivational:* One of the side (but very important) benefits of a well-defined mission is the guidance it provides employees and managers working either in geographically dispersed units or on independent tasks. A well-defined mission provides a shared sense of purpose *outside* of the various activities taking place within the organization. Therefore, end results (sales, patients cared for, reduction in violent crimes) can be viewed as the product of careful pursuit and accomplishment of the mission, not as the mission itself.

4. *Specific:* As we mentioned earlier, public relations should not be the primary purpose of a statement of mission, which must be specific and provide direction and guidelines for management's choices between alternative courses of action. In other words, "to produce the highest-quality products at the lowest possible cost" sounds very good, but it does not provide direction for management.

Table 5–1 presents actual mission statements of various types of organizations. While some have been abbreviated, each clearly illustrates its purpose as defined by management. Review each one with respect to the four criteria just discussed.[13]

The questions related to the mission statement need to be asked and answered at the inception of an organization and whenever it is experiencing serious problems. However, a successful organization should also ask them from time to time.[14] The reason for this should be clear: Because of the ever changing environment, even the most successful definition of purpose will sooner or later become obsolete. Thus, the process of periodically addressing the issue will force management to anticipate the impact of environmental changes on the organization's mission, objectives, markets, and products.

While the idea of a mission statement is important in large organizations, the Management Focus indicates that it is just as important for managers in small companies.

---

[12]See Paul C. Nutt, "A Strategic Planning Network for Nonprofit Organizations," *Strategic Management Journal,* January–March 1984, pp. 57–76; Peter Smith Ring and James L. Perry, "Strategic Management in Public and Private Organizations: Implications of Distinctive Contexts and Constraints," *Academy of Management Review,* April 1985, pp. 276–86.

[13]Practical ideas for developing a mission statement can be found in Mark Frohman and Perry Pascarella, "How to Write a Purpose Statement," *Industry Week,* March 23, 1987, pp. 31–34; John A. Pearce II and Fred David, "Corporate Mission Statements: The Bottom Line," *Academy of Management Executive,* May 1987, pp. 109–15.

[14]Drucker, *Management,* p. 87.

TABLE 5–1   Actual Mission Statements

A mission statement reflects the role the organization plays in its environment.

Organization	Mission
1. Office equipment manufacturer	We are in the business of problem solving. Our business is to help solve administrative, scientific, and human problems.
2. Credit union	To produce a selected range of quality services to organizations and individuals to fulfill their continuing financial needs.
3. Large conglomerate	Translating new technologies into commercially salable products.
4. Consumer products paper company	The development and marketing of inedible products for food stores.
5. State department of health	Administering all provisions of law relating to public health laws and regulations of the state board of health, supervising and assisting county and regional boards and departments of health, and doing all other things reasonably necessary to protect and improve the health of the people.
6. Appliance manufacturer	A willingness to invest in any area of suitable profit and growth potential in which the organization has or can acquire the capabilities.

Finally, the mission statements of many organizations will also include major policies they plan to follow in the pursuit of their missions. Such policies establish the ground rules for the organization in its relationships with government, customers or clients, suppliers, distributors, and creditors. An example of such a document is shown in Table 5–2.

ORGANIZATIONAL OBJECTIVES

In the previous chapter, we saw that a critical phase of planning is the determination of future outcomes. These desired future outcomes are objectives. Organizational objectives are the end points of an organization's mission and are what it seeks through the ongoing, long-run operations of the organization. The organizational mission is defined into a finer set of specific and achievable organizational objectives.

As with the statement of mission, organizational objectives are more than good intentions. In fact, if formulated properly, they will:

1. Be capable of being converted into specific actions.
2. Provide direction: serve as a starting point for more specific and detailed objectives at lower levels in the organization. Each manager will then know how his or her objectives relate to those at higher levels.
3. Establish long-run priorities for the organization.
4. Facilitate management control, because they serve as standards for evaluating overall organizational performance.

Organizational objectives are necessary in any and all areas that may influence the performance and long-run survival of the organization. These

---

MANAGEMENT FOCUS

Can Mission Statements Be Useful in Smaller Companies?

The idea of having a "mission" is a trendy concept in corporate America. No doubt they are valuable. They proclaim the corporate purpose and give everyone a clear idea of what the company is supposed to do. Sometimes, it is stated in 10 words or less. But it forces executives to think about their purpose, their competition, and the boundaries of their business. Because of the importance of strategic planning in large organizations, at least 80 percent of the Fortune 500 companies have mission statements.

But what about small organizations or entrepreneurial ventures? Organizations that are not spread out all over the country or the world? Those that have fewer than 500 employees. Can these smaller companies benefit from a mission statement?

Unfortunately, owners of small businesses will usually not have a mission statement or will develop one only in a time of crisis. In small firms where the entire management team can communicate during lunch, everyone often assumes all is well until the roof caves in. More and more, however, well-managed small businesses are developing statements of mission. Here are questions they ask in formulating their mission statement:

1. Do we have a long-term view of the company's future?
2. Can we define the company's business? ("What products do we make? What markets do we serve?")
3. Does our mission statement motivate key employees and shareholders?
4. What image do we want to convey? Stable and conservative? Fast moving and aggressive?
5. What are our company's values?

Source: Mark B. Roman, "The Mission: Setting Your Vision in Words Is the Critical Executive Act," *Success*, June 1987, pp. 54–55.

TABLE 5–2   A Mission Statement that Includes Organizational Policies

Mission and policy statements express an organization's highest standards.

It is the basic purpose of this organization, in all of its decisions and actions, to attain and maintain the following:

1. A continuous, high level of profits, which places it in the top bracket of industry in its rate of return on invested capital.
2. Steady growth in profits and sales volume, and investment at rates exceeding those of the national economy as a whole.
3. Equitable distribution of the fruits of continuously increasing productivity of management, capital, and labor among shareholders, employees, and the public.
4. Design, production, and marketing, on a worldwide basis, of products and services that are useful and beneficial to its customers, to society, and to mankind.
5. Continuous responsiveness to the needs of its customers and of the public, creating a current product line that is "first in performance" and a steady flow of product improvements, new products, and new services that increase customer satisfaction.
6. A vital, dynamic product line, by continuous addition of new products and businesses and prompt termination of old products and businesses when their economic worth, as measured by their profit performance, becomes substandard.
7. The highest ethical standards in the conduct of all its affairs.
8. An environment in which all employees are enabled, encouraged, and stimulated to perform continuously at their highest potential of output and creativity and to attain the highest possible level of job satisfaction in the spirit of the Westinghouse Creed.

	TABLE 5–3	Sample Organizational Objectives: Manufacturing Firm

	Area of Performance	**Possible Objective**
	1. Market standing	To make our brands number one in their field in terms of market share.
	2. Innovations	To be a leader in introducing new products by spending no less than 7 percent of sales for research and development.
	3. Productivity	To manufacture all products efficiently, as measured by the productivity of the work force.
Specific objectives are needed for all areas of an organization to work toward realizing the mission.	4. Physical and financial resources	To protect and maintain all resources— equipment, buildings, inventory, and funds.
	5. Profitability	To achieve an annual rate of return on investment of at least 15 percent.
	6. Manager performance and responsibility	To identify critical areas of management depth and succession.
	7. Worker performance and attitude	To maintain levels of employee satisfaction consistent with our own and similar industries.
	8. Social responsibility	To respond appropriately whenever possible to societal expectations and environment needs.

were identified in the previous chapter as market standing, innovations, productivity, physical and financial resources, profitability, manager performance and responsibility, worker performance and attitude, and social responsibility.

The above areas of objectives are by no means exhaustive; an organization may very well have additional ones. The important point is that management must translate the organizational mission into specific objectives that will support the realization of the mission. Table 5–3 presents some examples of organizational objectives. Note that they are broad statements that serve as guides and that they are of a continuing nature. They specify the end points of an organization's mission and the results that it seeks in the long run, both externally and internally. Most important, however, the objectives in Table 5–3 are all capable of being converted into specific targets and actions for *operational plans* at lower levels in the organization.

ORGANIZATIONAL STRATEGIES

When an organization has formulated its mission and developed its objectives, it knows where it wants to go. The next management task is to develop a "grand design" to get there.[15] This grand design comprises the organiza-

[15]Ellen Earl Chaffee, "The Models of Strategy," *Academy of Management Review,* January 1985, pp. 89–98.

MANAGEMENT FOCUS

A Major Shift in Strategy at Sears

In 1989, Americans saw the most radical change in the 102-year history of Sears Roebuck & Co. The company reduced prices throughout its stores and catalogs as part of a market penetration strategy aimed at winning back its customers. Sears, once a part of most of our lives, had for many become an often ignored, aging relative.

Although Sears does not admit it has become a "discounter," its new strategy is clearly aimed at discounters such as K mart and Wal-Mart. And don't count Sears out. Three of 4 Americans shop at Sears, and 60 million of us have credit cards. (That number could increase even further if the retailer begins accepting Visa and MasterCard.) Sears' penetration strategy has at least four parts:

1. *Lower prices.* Prices will be as low as or lower than the competition who sells the same item.
2. *Immediate sales.* The company would hold the strongest promotional program in its history to kick off the new strategy.
3. *Superstores.* It would expand its appliance and consumer electronics "superstores"—entire stores devoted to a single product area, with a big choice of brand names. Apparel superstores are also being planned.
4. *Expansion.* The company plans to open 200 more stores by 1991.

Source: Andrea Stone, "Sears Shift: Discounting Is Its Future," *USA Today,* November 1, 1988, p. 1A; Andrea Stone, "Retailer Goes Back to Basics," *USA Today,* November 1, 1988, p. 1B; Francine Schwadel and Michael J. McCarthy, "New Sears Strategy on Display in Wichita," *The Wall Street Journal,* November 17, 1988, p. B1.

---

tional strategies. The role of strategy in corporate planning is to identify the general approaches that the organization will utilize to achieve its organizational objectives.[16] Strategy involves the choice of major directions the organization will take in pursuing its objectives.[17] The Management Focus presents the basic components of a major shift in direction for Sears Roebuck, one of America's largest retailers.

Organizations achieve objectives in two ways: by better managing what the organization is presently doing and/or by finding new things to do. In choosing either or both of these paths, management must decide whether to concentrate on present customers, to seek new ones, or both. Figure 5–2 presents the available strategic choices. Known as a product-market matrix, it shows the strategic alternatives available to an organization for achieving its objectives. It indicates that an organization can grow in a variety of ways by concentrating on present or new products and on present or new customers.

---

[16]Michael Goold and Andrew Campbell, "Many Best Ways to Make Strategy," *Harvard Business Review,* November–December 1987, pp. 67–73.

[17]Ari Ginsberg, "Operationalizing Organizational Strategy: Toward an Integrated Framework," *Academy of Management Review,* July 1984, pp. 548–57.

FIGURE 5–2

FIGURE 5–2   Product-Market Matrix

An organization's basic strategy involves decisions about products and markets and about the directions in which it chooses to grow.

Markets \ Products	Present Products	New Products
Present Customers	Market penetration	Product development
New Customers	Market development	Diversification

Market Penetration Strategies.   These strategies focus on improving the position of the organization's present products with its present customers. For example:

1. A snack products company concentrates on getting its present customers to purchase more of its products.
2. A charity seeks ways to increase contributions from present supporters.
3. A bank concentrates on getting present depositors to use additional services.

Such a strategy may involve devising a marketing plan to encourage present customers to purchase more of the product or a production plan to produce the present product more efficiently. In other words, it concentrates on improving the efficiency of various functional departments in the organization.

Market Development Strategies.   Following this strategy, an organization would seek to find new customers for its present products. For example:

1. A manufacturer of industrial products may decide to promote its products in the consumer market.
2. A governmental social service agency may seek out individuals and families who have never utilized the agencies' services.
3. A manufacturer of children's hair care products may decide to enter the adult market because of the declining birthrate.

Product Development Strategies.   In choosing either of the remaining two strategies, the organization in effect seeks new things to do. With this particular strategy, the new products developed would be directed to present customers. For example:

1. A cigarette manufacturer may decide to offer a low-tar cigarette.
2. A social service agency may offer additional services to present client families.
3. A college or university may develop graduate courses for minority students.

Diversification.   An organization diversifies when it seeks new products for customers it is not serving at present.[18] For example:

---

[18]See Jeffrey L. Kerr, "Diversification Strategies and Managerial Rewards: An Empirical Study," *Academy of Management Journal,* March 1985, pp. 155–79, for a study of the

Market penetration strategies encourage present customers to purchase more of a product. Market development strategies seek new customers for present products.

1. A discount store purchases a savings and loan association.
2. A cigarette manufacturer diversifies into real estate development.
3. A college or university establishes a corporation to find commercial uses for the results of faculty research efforts.

On what basis does an organization choose one (or all) strategies? The answer lies in the organization's mission and its distinctive competencies. (This underscores the critical role the mission statement plays in the direction, or directions, the organization takes.) Management will select those strategies that capitalize on the organization's distinctive competencies and are consistent with its mission.[19] In the Management Focus, one company has decided to pursue market development strategies worldwide. And it is doing this by capitalizing on a distinctive competence.

ORGANIZATIONAL PORTFOLIO PLAN

The final phase of the strategic planning process is the formulation of the organizational portfolio plan. In reality, most organizations at a particular time are a portfolio of businesses. For example, an appliance manufacturer may have several product lines (e.g., televisions, washers and dryers, refrigerators, stereos), as well as two divisions (consumer appliances and industrial appliances). A college or university will have numerous schools (e.g., education,

relationship between diversification and the design of managerial reward systems in 20 large industrial firms. Also see Paulette Dubofsky and P. Varadarajan, "Diversification and Measures of Performance: Additional Empirical Evidence," *Academy of Management Journal,* September 1987, pp. 597–606.

[19]N. Venkatramen and J. C. Camillus, "Exploring the Concept of 'Fit' in Strategic Management," *Academy of Management Review,* July 1984, pp. 513–25; Henry Mintzberg and J. A. Waters, "Of Strategies, Deliberate and Emergent," *Strategic Management Journal,* July–September 1985, pp. 257–72.

MANAGEMENT FOCUS

The British Don't Vacuum Their Carpets. They "Hoover" Them!

Many Americans have heard the name Hoover associated with vacuum cleaners. Hoover vacuum cleaners have been around for decades in America and have an excellent reputation for quality and dependability. But is the Hoover brand name valuable overseas? As a matter of fact, people in London do not vacuum their carpets, they hoover them.

Now this famous name belongs to Maytag, which recently bought the vacuum cleaner's maker for $1 billion. Maytag is following the lead of other companies that have taken a global approach to the appliance business and are pursuing market development strategies worldwide: Whirlpool has an option to buy a recently formed joint venture to sell appliances outside the United States, and Electrolux recently purchased the company that owns the Tappan line of appliances.

Last but not least, General Electric Co. recently bought 50 percent of the $1 billion European appliance business of Great Britain's General Electric Company.

What all of this means is that in one 12-month period, the major appliance manufacturers have all gone global with strategic alliances that will enable them to wage worldwide price wars. They all are also preparing for 1992, when Europe will lower the trade barriers between the European countries. But only one of them will have the name Hoover.

Source: "Maytag Scoops Up Hoover," *Business Week,* November 7, 1988, p. 44; "Why GE Took a European Bride," *Business Week,* January 30, 1989, pp. 28–29; "Can Maytag Clean Up around the World?" *Business Week,* January 30, 1989, pp. 86–87.

---

business, law, architecture) and several programs within each school. The YMCA has hotels, camps, spas, and schools. Some widely diversified organizations such as Philip Morris are in numerous unrelated businesses, such as cigarettes, land development, paper products, and breweries.

Managing such groups of businesses is made a little easier if resources and cash are plentiful and each group is experiencing growth and profits. Unfortunately, providing larger and larger budgets each year to all businesses is no longer feasible. Many are not experiencing growth, and profits and/or resources (financial and nonfinancial) are becoming more and more scarce. In such a situation, choices must be made. Management must decide which businesses to build, maintain, or eliminate or which new businesses to add. Some method is needed to help management make the choices. One of the best known and widely used methods to accomplish this is the *business portfolio matrix* developed by the Boston Consulting Group.[20]

---

[20]There are other portfolio models; each has its supporters and detractors. The one presented here, while among the most popular, is also not without critics. The important point is the concept of viewing an organization as a "portfolio" of businesses or activities, each competing for resources. The interested reader should consult Richard G. Hammermesh and Roderick E. White, "Manage beyond Portfolio Analysis," *Harvard Business Review,* January–February 1984, pp. 103–9; J. A. Seeger, "Revising the Images of BCG's Growth/Share Matrix," *Strategic Management Journal,* January–March 1984, pp. 93–97.

FIGURE 5–3   **Business Portfolio Matrix**

Each SBU can be classified according to projected market growth rate and estimated market share.

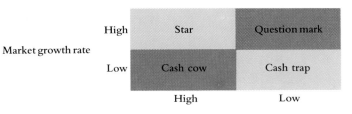

The Business Portfolio Matrix. The first step in this approach is to identify each division, product line, and so forth, that can be considered a business. When identified, these are referred to as **strategic business units** (SBUs). Each SBU:

1. Has a distinct mission.
2. Has its own competitors.
3. Is a single business or a collection of related businesses.
4. Can be planned for independent of the other businesses of the total organization.

Thus, depending on the type of organization, an SBU could be a single product, product line, division, college department of accounting, or state mental health agency. Once the managers have identified and classified all of the SBUs, they need some method of determining how resources should be allocated among the various SBUs. This is the important contribution of the Boston Consulting Group's approach.

Using this approach, the organization would classify all of its SBUs in the business portfolio matrix. (An example is shown in Figure 5–3.) The matrix's basic purpose is to assist management in deciding how much resource support should be budgeted to each SBU.

The business portfolio matrix illustrates two business indicators of great strategic importance. The vertical indicator, *market growth rate,* refers to the annual rate of growth of the market in which the product, division, or department is located. For example, the number of individuals of college age is declining, and the impact on enrollments has been felt. However, enrollments in some fields of study have been increasing. Thus, certain departments in a college would have different market growth rates.

The horizontal indicator, *relative market share,* illustrates an SBU's market share compared to that of the most successful competition. This indicator ranges from high to low relative share of the market. As illustrated, four classifications of SBUs can be identified:

1. *Stars.* An SBU that has a high share of a high-growth market is considered a star. Examples might include an electronics firm with a high share of the compact disc player market or a university with an outstanding, nationally recognized master's degree program in business administration (enrollments in most business schools are growing, in contrast to declining

enrollments across most university departments). Obviously, stars need a great deal of financial resources because of their rapid growth. When growth slows they become cash cows and become important generators of cash for the organization.[21]

2. *Cash cows.* An SBU that has a high share of a low-growth market is labeled a cash cow. A bank with a large share of passbook savings depositors in a community that is not growing and a state university with the largest number of elementary education majors in the state would be examples of such SBUs. They produce a great amount of cash for the organization but, since the market is not growing, do not require a great amount of financial resources for growth and expansion. As a result, the cash they generate can be used by the organization to satisfy current debt and to support SBUs in need of cash.

3. *Question marks.* When an SBU has a low share of a high-growth market, the organization must decide whether to spend more financial resources to build it into a star, or to phase it down or eliminate it altogether. Elimination was the decision made by General Electric with its computer business and line of vacuum cleaners. Many times, such SBUs require high amounts of resources just to maintain their share, let alone increase it.

4. *Cash traps.* When an SBU has a low share of a low-growth market, it may generate enough cash to maintain itself, or it may drain money from other SBUs. The only certainty is that cash traps are not great sources of cash. A men's cosmetics firm that still sells a traditional oily liquid hair tonic or the Slavic language department in a college or university might be examples of cash traps. Cash traps are sometimes referred to as "dogs."

Strategic Choices.   Thus, depending on whether the SBUs are products, product lines, entire divisions, or departments, an organization may have one star, three cash cows, two question marks, and two cash traps. After classifying each SBU according to the business portfolio matrix, management must then decide which of the four alternative strategies should be pursued for each:

1. *Build.* If an organization has an SBU that it believes has the potential to be a star (probably a question mark at present), this would be an appropriate objective. Thus, the organization may even decide to give up short-term profits in order to provide the necessary financial resources to achieve this objective.

2. *Hold.* If an SBU is a very successful cash cow, a key objective would certainly be to hold or preserve the market share so that the organization can take advantage of the very positive cash flow.

3. *Harvest.* This objective is appropriate for all SBUs except those classified as stars. The basic objective is to increase the short-term cash return without too much concern for the long-run impact. It is especially worthwhile when more cash is needed for a cash cow whose long-run prospects are not good because of a low market growth rate.

4. *Divest.* Getting rid of SBUs with low shares of low-growth markets is often appropriate. Question marks and cash traps are particularly suited for this objective.

---

[21]See David A. Aaker and George S. Day, "The Perils of High Growth Markets," *Strategic Management Journal,* October–December 1985, pp. 24–32.

SBUs will change position in the business portfolio matrix. As time passes, question marks may become stars, stars may become cash cows, and cash cows may become cash traps.[22] In fact, one SBU can move through each category as the market growth rate declines. How quickly these changes occur is influenced by the technology and competitiveness of the industry. This underscores the importance and usefulness of viewing an organization in terms of SBUs, and the necessity of constantly seeking new ventures as well as managing existing ones.[23]

STRATEGIC PLANNING: USING THE PROCESS

Strategic planning provides direction for an organization's mission, objectives, and strategies, facilitating the development of plans for each of the organization's functional areas.[24] A completed strategic plan guides each area in the direction the organization wishes to go and allows each area to develop objectives, strategies, and programs consistent with those goals.[25] The relationship between strategic planning and operational planning is an important concern of managers.

RELATING THE STRATEGIC PLAN AND OPERATIONAL PLANS

Most managers in an organization will not directly develop the organization's strategic plan. However, they may be involved in this process in two important ways: (1) They usually influence the strategic planning process by providing information and suggestions relating to their particular areas of responsibility. (2) They must be completely aware of what the process of strategic planning involves as well as the results, because everything their respective departments do, the objectives they establish for the areas of responsibility, should all be derived from the strategic plan.

In well-managed organizations, therefore, a direct relationship exists between strategic planning and the planning done by managers at all levels.[26] The focus of the planning and the time perspectives will, of course, differ. Figure 5–4 illustrates the relationship between the strategic plan and operational plans. It indicates very clearly that all plans should be derived from the strategic plan while at the same time contributing to the achievement of the strategic plan.

---

[22]Gareth R. Jones and John E. Butler, "Costs, Revenue, and Business-Level Strategy," *Academy of Management Review,* April 1988, pp. 202–13.

[23]For a related discussion that focuses on small businesses, see Gerald d'Amboise and Marie Muldowney, "Management Theory for Small Business: Attempts and Requirements," *Academy of Management Review,* April 1988, pp. 226–40.

[24]James J. Chrisman, Charles W. Hofer, and William R. Boulton, "Toward a System for Classifying Business Strategies," *Academy of Management Review,* July 1988, pp. 413–28.

[25]For interesting support of this view, see Ed Bukszar and Terry Connolly, "Hindsight Bias and Strategic Choice: Some Problems in Learning from Experience," *Academy of Management Journal,* September 1988, pp. 628–41.

[26]G. David Wallace, "America's Leanest and Meanest," *Business Week,* October 5, 1987, pp. 78–84.

FIGURE 5–4   Relationship between the Organization's Strategic Plan and Operational Plans

---

At the same time that the strategic plan provides direction for individual departments' plans, they are contributing to the success of the strategic plan.

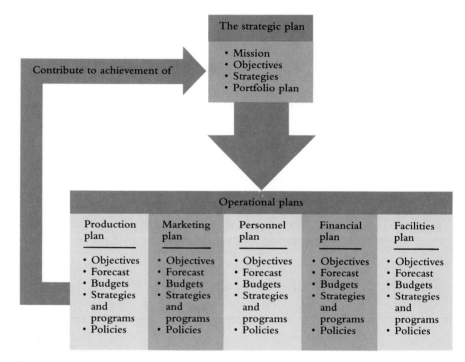

RELATING ORGANIZATIONAL OBJECTIVES AND STRATEGIES TO OPERATIONAL OBJECTIVES AND STRATEGIES

If done properly, planning will result in a clearly defined blueprint for management action *at all levels* in the organization.[27] Figure 5–5 illustrates the *hierarchy of objectives and strategies,* using only one objective from the strategic plan and two strategies from the strategic plan. In the figure, all objectives are related to other objectives at higher and lower levels in the organization. We have illustrated only four possible operational objectives. Obviously, many others could be developed, but our purpose is that the reader clearly understand how objectives and strategies from the strategic plan for the entire organization (above the dotted line) relate to objectives and strategies that are part of operational plans for individual departments (below the dotted line). As we move from the top of the organization toward lower levels (in terms of who does the planning), we increase the detail and specificity of the objectives, and we decrease the time span. However, although the scope, time span, and issues confronted by operational plans differ, they are all derived from those in the strategic plan.[28]

[27]Frederick W. Gluck, "A Fresh Look at Strategic Management," *Journal of Business Strategy,* Fall 1985, pp. 4–19.

[28]While developing strategy is important, implementing it is also critically important. For excellent works devoted entirely to implementation, see Paul J. Stonich, *Implementing Strategy:*

FIGURE 5–5   The Hierarchy of Objectives and Strategies in the Organization

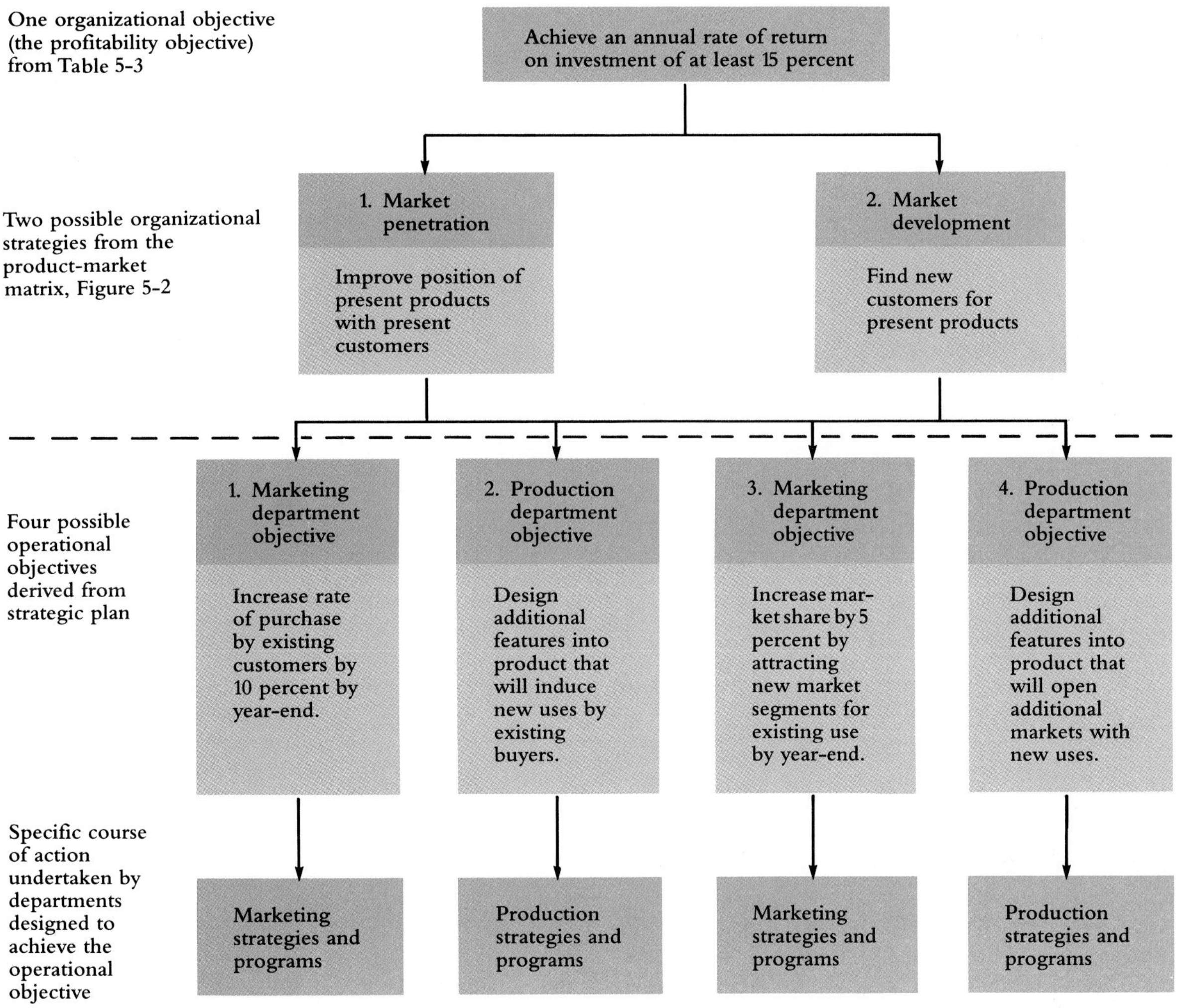

One organizational objective (the profitability objective) from Table 5-3

Two possible organizational strategies from the product-market matrix, Figure 5-2

Four possible operational objectives derived from strategic plan

Specific course of action undertaken by departments designed to achieve the operational objective

Achieve an annual rate of return on investment of at least 15 percent

1. Market penetration

Improve position of present products with present customers

2. Market development

Find new customers for present products

1. Marketing department objective

Increase rate of purchase by existing customers by 10 percent by year-end.

2. Production department objective

Design additional features into product that will induce new uses by existing buyers.

3. Marketing department objective

Increase market share by 5 percent by attracting new market segments for existing use by year-end.

4. Production department objective

Design additional features into product that will open additional markets with new uses.

Marketing strategies and programs

Production strategies and programs

Marketing strategies and programs

Production strategies and programs

If planning is effective, the objectives of individual departments will contribute to the achievement of overall objectives.

SUMMARY OF KEY POINTS

■ Strategic planning involves the total organization in that it specifies the organization's relation to its environment in terms of mission, objectives, strategies, and portfolio plan. The importance of strategic planning has increased as organizations seek more rational responses to environmental change and uncertainty.

■ The organization's mission specifies the organization's basic purpose, its reason for being. The mission statement should take into account the

Making Strategy Happen (Cambridge, Mass.: Ballinger, 1982); Jay Galbraith and Robert K. Kazanjian, *Strategy Implementation: Structure, Systems and Process,* 2nd ed. (St. Paul, Minn.: West Publishing, 1986).

- organization's history, distinctive competencies, and environment.
- To be useful, the mission statement should focus on markets rather than products and should be achievable, motivational, and specific.
- Organizational objectives are derived from the mission. They are guideposts for assessing the degree of movement toward achieving the mission. They are the bases for establishing operational objectives for the subunits and departments of the organization.
- Organizational strategies are the broad approaches the organization takes to achieve its objectives. Business firms can follow four basic strategies: market penetration, market development, product development, and diversification.

The strategies selected by the organization must not only contribute to the achievement of objectives but also be compatible with the mission.

- Organizational portfolios present the relative strength of each strategic business unit and the relative growth rate of the industry in which the business competes. The portfolio analysis suggests corporate strategies based on the positioning of strategic business units in the portfolio matrix.
- The corporate objectives an strategies contained in the strategic plan are converted into operational objectives and strategies. Through strategic planning, organizations can achieve unity and continuity of action.

DISCUSSION AND REVIEW QUESTIONS

1. Discuss this statement: "In well-managed organizations, operational planning must be based on a strategic plan."

2. Explain why you agree or disagree with the following statements:
   a. Planning is the easiest where environmental change is minimal.
   b. Planning is most valuable where environmental change is great.

3. "All managers plan in one way or another." Evaluate this statement.

4. Hospital costs are soaring, leading to daily room rates of $300 or more in some hospitals. Other hospitals are experiencing underutilization, particularly in the maternity and pediatrics sections. Some experts predict that 1,400 hospitals will close in the next 10 years. Could strategic planning be of any assistance to a hospital? Discuss.

5. Are you familiar with any organizations whose missions became obsolete or irrelevant? What happened to the organization? Discuss.

6. This chapter states that an effective mission statement will focus on markets rather than products and be achievable, motivating, and specific. Select three of the actual mission statements presented in Table 5–1 and evaluate them based on these criteria.

7. What is the relationship between organizational mission, organizational objectives, and organizational strategies?

8. Could your college or university make any use of the product-market matrix (Figure 5–2) in its long-range planning? Discuss.

9. Most colleges, universities, hospitals, and churches are facing financial problems. Could any of these organizations make use of the business portfolio plan approach developed by the Boston Consulting Group? Explain.

10. If planning is done properly, how will the operational plans developed by different units of an organization be related to the strategic plan? Explain.

ADDITIONAL REFERENCES

Chanin, M. N., and **H. J. Shapiro**. "Dialectical Inquiry in Strategic Planning: Extending the Boundaries." *Academy of Management Review,* October 1985, pp. 663–75.

David, F. R. "Computer Assisted Strategic Planning in Small Businesses." *Journal of Systems Management,* July 1985, pp. 24–33.

Dutton, J. E., and **E. Ottensmeyer**. "Strategic Issue Management Systems: Forms, Functions, and Contexts." *Academy of Management Review*, April 1987, pp. 355–65.

Ghemawat, P. "Building Strategy on the Experience Curve." *Harvard Business Review,* March–April 1985, pp. 143–49.

Haspeslagh, P. "Portfolio Planning: Use and Limits." *Harvard Business Review,* January–February 1982, pp. 58–73.

Hoskisson, R. E. "Multidivisional Structure and Performance: The Contingency of Diversification Strategy." *Academy of Management Journal,* December 1987, pp. 625–44.

Linneman, R. A., and **H. E. Klein.** "Using Scenarios in Strategic Decision Making." *Business Horizons,* January–February 1985, pp. 64–74.

Miller, D. "Relating Porter's Business Strategies to Environment and Structure: Analysis and Performance Implications." *Academy of Management Journal,* June 1988, pp. 280–308.

Miller, H. J., and **H. L. Smith.** "Retrenchment Strategies and Tactics for Healthcare Executives." *Hospital and Health Service Administration,* May–June 1985, pp. 31–43.

Milliken, F. J. "Three Types of Perceived Uncertainty about the Environment: State, Effect, and Response Uncertainty." *Academy of Management Review,* October 1986, pp. 801–14.

Nagel, A. "Strategy Formulation in the Smaller Firm." *Long Range Planning,* August 1981, pp. 115–20.

Rosenberg, L., and **C. D. Schewe.** "Strategic Planning: Fulfilling the Promise." *Business Horizons,* July–August 1987, pp. 54–63.

"Who's Excellent Now?" *Business Week,* November 5, 1984, pp. 76–88.

CASE 5–1   Citibank's Diversification Strategy

Citibank, a subsidiary of Citicorp, was facing heavy competition in its traditional lines of business. Savings banks, savings and loan associations, credit unions, and brokerage houses were competing effectively with banks by moving into such typical banking activities as interest-bearing checking accounts and by offering higher interest rates for deposits. Because of the squeeze on profit, the bank had to consider other sources of earnings.

Citibank decided to enter the computer services industry, using its considerable expertise and experience in data processing. It identified three distinct business units to be developed.

1. *Systems.* The bank combines its own programs and software with someone else's hardware and markets the system to end-users.
2. *Remote computing.* The bank sells time on its own computers to outside customers.
3. *Software.* The bank sells its software packages to other firms with similar applications.

These three businesses were mutually supportive but were aimed at different customer needs.

The foundation for the move into computer services began in the early 1970s, when Citicorp decided to streamline its own data processing capability. The program moved away from reliance on a central mainframe computer to small minicomputers that could be located near the spot where processing was required. The program encountered numerous problems. But when it was finally going, the effect was to enable one person to handle work that previously would have taken six people.

Many of the products that Citibank now markets were developed as a result of the streamlining program. These products enable other banks to streamline their own "back office" processing and turn a potential cost center into a potential profit center. Citibank not only sells the system but also offers continuing educational and consultative support services. This capability distinguishes Citibank from other suppliers of computer services.

Citicorp's entry into computer services has met considerable opposition from both banking and computer service competitors. Banking competitors believe that Citicorp's data processing relationships with other banks put it in a better position to acquire them. This concern is particularly telling if laws regulating interstate banking are changed so that banks can branch across state lines. Computer service competitors charge that Citicorp is violating the National Bank Act and the Bank Holding Company Act. These acts limit banks and their holding companies from offering services unrelated to their basic banking business.

Other observers note that some customers might well purchase Citibank's computer services with the expectation that their loan applications would receive more favorable treatment. The bank is in the position of playing two different roles but is able to combine the two roles and thereby confuse the customer. For example, Citibank might "persuade" the customer that it should subscribe to the bank's computer services.

Despite these criticisms, Citibank is now well entrenched in the computer services industry. To reverse its decision to enter the industry would involve a complete overhaul of the long-term corporate strategy.

QUESTIONS FOR ANALYSIS

1. What environmental forces caused Citicorp to move into the computer service industry?
2. Is the computer service business consistent with Citicorp's mission? With its distinctive competence?
3. Where would Citicorp's computer service business show up on a portfolio matrix? Explain.

CASE 5–2 Strategic Planning at the Family Store

In 1894, John Jacobi opened a small dry-goods store in a small mountain town in a southeastern state. In addition, he traveled by wagon to larger communities in the state to sell his clothing and other dry goods. By 1916, Jacobi's Dry Goods Store had outgrown its small quarters, moved to a larger facility, and expanded its line to become what would be known today as a small department store. Since the store carried almost everything a typical family would need, John decided to change the name of the store to the Family Store. This he thought was a better description of what the store sold and, in addition, was better for promotional purposes. However, he still traveled the state (in a small truck by this time) to sell to other stores.

EXHIBIT 1	Trends Impacting Retailing Businesses

1. The nation's economy will continue to grow despite a slight recession at the end of the 80s.
2. The post–World War II baby boom generation will be into middle age.
3. Real wages will grow.
4. Family incomes will grow, and the number of employed wives will increase, especially among college-educated women.
5. As "cocooning" (spending more time at home) becomes a trend, the demand for home-oriented products and services will expand more rapidly than the demand for products and services consumed by individuals.
6. Women's earnings will represent a much higher proportion of total personal income.
7. Mature couples (over age 55) will control 75 percent of the nation's assets.

Despite the depression in the late 1930s, the Family Store and John Jacobi continued to thrive because of their good service, wide selection, and reasonable prices; business was so good that by 1936 there were seven stores located throughout the state. John had expanded the business to 12 stores before he passed away in 1952 at the age of 81 and management of the organization was turned over to the oldest son John, Jr. Because of the growing economy, the business continued to thrive during the 1950s and into the 1960s, mainly because of its excellent reputation and little competition from national chains in the rural state.

In the mid-70s, however, business started to decline as some large shopping malls were built throughout the state and regional department store chains entered the state. This, coupled with the entrance of several discount chains (e.g., K mart) into the state, caused sales to decline in many of the Family Stores located in large communities. John's response to these environmental changes was to open five Family Discount Stores in the more populated regions of the state. Thus, as the 70s came to a close, 12 Family Stores and 5 Family Discount Stores were operating in the state.

In 1988, as he reviewed the organization's performance for 1987, it became painfully evident to John that something needed to be done regarding the direction of the organization. With the exception of two, all Family Stores had slowly declining sales each year from 1983 to 1987; the other two had experienced declines during the last three years. The Family Discount Stores unfortunately had not done much better. None of the five had ever achieved the levels of sales and profits originally expected, and two actually lost money during the last two years. On his desk, John had a copy of a list of several social and economic trends that were expected to influence retail businesses in the next decade. These are shown in Exhibit 1.

The way John saw it, it was time to make some critical long-range decisions regarding the organization. For example: Should they concentrate on smaller communities where regional and national chains do not have outlets? Should they compete aggressively with the chains and, if so, on what basis? Should they seek for their organization a unique direction, distinct from any other? What kind of organization is the Family Store?

"Who says we have to be a retailer?" John thought as he left the office. "I can see it now: the Family Record Store, the Family Bookstore, the Family Inn Motel. Who am I kidding? We are a chain of department stores. Maybe we have outworn our purpose and should just sell out to some national chain. Maybe I'm going crazy?"

QUESTIONS FOR ANALYSIS

1. Why is Jacobi facing these problems? Were they inevitable? Discuss in detail.
2. Assume you are hired as a consultant by Jacobi. What, if anything, could you do to help him?

EXPERIENTIAL EXERCISE

THE IMPORTANCE OF THE PLANNING FUNCTION

Purpose

The purpose of this exercise, which requires some out-of-class homework to prepare the answers, is to emphasize the importance of planning in organizations in various industries.

The Exercise in Class

1. Every person in the class should be assigned the same organization from the list below and answer the following questions:
   a. What events in this organization's environment should be considered in developing a strategic plan for the successful achievement of objectives?
   b. How likely are important events to occur? That is, what is the probability of an event (e.g., energy shortage, shortage of qualified job candidates, increase or decrease in demand, increase or decrease in competition)?
   c. How can managerial planning improve the organization's chances of surviving the occurrence of positive and/or negative events cited in your answer to b.
   The organizations for the exercise:

General Motors	Taco Tico	Wells Fargo Bank
Standard Brands	Pacific Stereo	Revlon
Walt Disney	Levi Strauss	Honeywell
General Mills	Sears Roebuck	Volvo

2. After each student completes the first part of the exercise, the instructor will form groups of four to six students. Each group will be assigned a different one of the remaining organizations.

3. Your group should answer questions *a*, *b*, and *c* and report your answers to the class.

The Learning Message

This exercise will show that some organizations need planning more than others because of the events they must deal with in the environment.

6

THE ORGANIZING FUNCTION

LEARNING OBJECTIVES

After completing Chapter 6, you should be able to:

Define
the organizing function in terms of required management decisions.

Describe
the effects of the span of control on the manager and the organization.

Discuss
the relationships between the planning and organizing functions.

Compare
two organizations, using the dimensions of structure as the bases for the comparison.

Identify
the ways to describe differences among jobs.

Marine Midland Bank's Revised Organization

Marine Midland Bank is one of the largest banks in the United States, its growth largely the result of a series of acquisitions of local and regional banks in upstate New York. But even with its relatively large size, Marine Midland has lagged behind its competition in profitability. It has had little success in attracting the kinds of customers that improve profitability: large corporations and wealthy individuals. Prior to 1980, Marine Midland was organized on a regional basis. The organization structure was the result of the acquisition program that had helped the bank prosper. The acquired banks were left largely intact as operating entities, resulting in considerable duplication of specialized and costly activities.

Marine has embarked on a campaign to become more profitable by a combination of personnel, strategic, and organizational changes. The group planning Marine's future believed that its organizational structure would have to be changed if its personnel and strategic changes were to be successful. The group believed that the regional structure was inconsistent with its strategic decision to concentrate on the most profitable banking functions. Consequently, the bank reorganized along functional lines.

The planning group eventually settled on seven main functional categories: retail banking, corporate banking, international banking, trust banking, financial market services, commercial middle-market banking (serving customers with sales of $1 million to $125 million), and commercial asset-based financing (mortgages and equipment leases). The new structure facilitates the development and implementation of corporationwide strategy and policy. For example, Marine has set a minimum trust fund level and charges a fee for servicing small savings accounts. It also has centralized such activities as data processing and accounting. The emphasis on banking functions and customers is reinforced by the organization structure. The anticipated outcome is increased profitability, made possible in part by a more rational organizational structure.

Although there are many complex sources of profitability and productivity, the importance of organization structure cannot be overemphasized. The issue that Marine Midland's management faced is a compelling one in all organizations: What organization structure is best suited to the business? Throughout the history of management practice, managers have struggled with this complicated issue. Let us begin our discussion of the organization function by identifying its purpose.

The purpose of the **organizing function** is to coordinate effort through the design of a structure of task and authority relationships.[1] The two key concepts are design and structure. Design implies that managers make a conscious effort to predetermine the way in which work is done by employees; structure refers to relatively stable relationships and aspects of the organization. **Organizational structure** is considered by many to be "the anatomy of the organization, providing a foundation within which the organization functions."[2] Thus, the structure of an organization, similar to the anatomy of a living organism, can be viewed as a framework. The idea of structure as a framework "focuses on the differentiation of positions, formulation of rules and procedures, and prescriptions of authority."[3] The purpose of structure is to regulate, or at least reduce the uncertainty about, the behavior of individual employees.[4]

The organizing function is the process of breaking down the overall task into individual assignments and then bringing those assignments together in units, or departments, and delegating authority to a unit, or department, manager. Thus, we can describe the organizing function in terms of dividing tasks into jobs, departmentalizing jobs, and delegating authority.[5]

Dividing tasks involves determining the scope and content of individual jobs, which are the building blocks of organization. But to be manageable, jobs must be recombined into departments. *Departmentalization* involves determining (1) the basis by which individual jobs will be recombined into departments and (2) the optimal number of jobs assigned in a department. Finally, *delegating authority* involves distributing the right to make decisions among jobs, particularly managerial jobs.

Depending on the decisions of managers regarding division of tasks, departmentalizing jobs, and delegating authority, organizational structures can vary considerably. As we shall see, tasks can be more or less specialized, jobs can be grouped into departments in different ways, and authority can be centralized or decentralized. As described in this chapter's Management in Action, Marine Midland Bank changed its organization structure by redefining

---

[1]George P. Huber and Reuben R. McDaniel, "The Decision-Making Paradigm of Organizational Design," *Management Science,* May 1986, p. 573.

[2]Dan R. Dalton, William D. Todor, Michael J. Spendolini, Gordon J. Fielding, and Lyman W. Porter, "Organization Structure and Performance: A Critical Review," *Academy of Management Review,* January 1980, p. 49.

[3]Stewart Ranson, Bob Hinings, and Royston Greenwood, "The Structuring of Organizational Structures," *Administrative Science Quarterly,* March 1980, p. 2.

[4]Danny Miller, "The Genesis of Configuration," *Academy of Management Review,* October 1987, pp. 691–93.

[5]Hugh C. Willmott, "The Structuring of Organizational Structures: A Note," *Administrative Science Quarterly,* September 1981, pp. 470–74.

Division of tasks, departmentalization, and delegation of authority will vary considerably depending on an organization's overall structure and the decisions of individual managers.

jobs and reorganizing departments. Thus, an organization's structure can be altered if management decides to do so. Modern management is based on the principle that there is no one best structure; rather, the appropriate structure varies from situation to situation. The challenge to management is to design a structure appropriate to the organization.[6]

In this chapter, attention is paid to the three important parts of all organization structures: jobs, departments, and authority. The next chapter will examine the issues associated with designing the appropriate framework.

Dividing Tasks

The most important consideration in dividing tasks is *specialization of labor.* The gains derived from specialization of labor can be calculated in purely economic terms.[7] Figure 6–1 shows this relationship. As the job is divided into ever smaller elements, additional output is obtained, but more people and capital must be employed to do the smaller jobs. At some point, the costs of specialization (labor and capital) begin to outweigh the increased efficiency of specialization (output), and the cost per unit of output begins to rise.

The problem of determining the appropriate degree of specialization becomes more difficult as the task becomes more abstract.[8] For example, managerial work is more abstract than blue-collar work. Blue-collar work is repetitive, involves definite sequences of actions, and produces tangible

[6]Ronald A. Heiner, "Imperfect Decisions in Organizations: Toward a Theory of Internal Structures," *Journal of Economic Behavior and Organization,* January 1988, pp. 25–44.

[7]Richard E. Kopelman, *Managing Productivity in Organizations: A Practical, People-Oriented Perspective* (New York: McGraw-Hill, 1986).

[8]Louis E. Davis and James C. Taylor, eds., *Design of Jobs* (Santa Monica, Calif.: Goodyear Publishing, 1979).

FIGURE 6–1	The Economics of Specialization

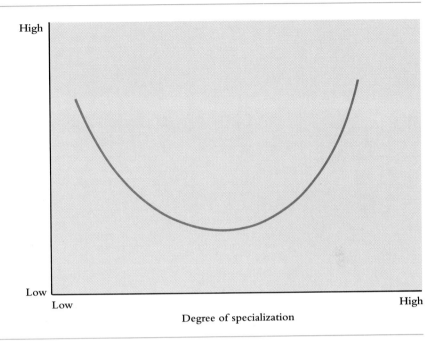

There are limits to the gains realized from specialization of labor.

products. Managers, on the other hand, do not produce tangible products that can be weighed or measured in some way. They seldom use tools or equipment; they get their work done by communicating, thinking, and acting.

The classical approach attempted to determine the best application of specialization of labor to blue-collar jobs. According to the classical writers, the work of lathe operators, assemblers, ironworkers, bricklayers, and similar occupations can be broken down into separable and discrete hand, eye, and body movements. These movements are shown in Table 6–1.

Through the application of **motion studies** and **time studies**, the manager can identify for each job the preferred basic movements: those that minimize effort but result in the completion of the assigned tasks. A typist, for example, must reach for blank paper (transport empty), take hold of the blank paper (grasp), hand carry the blank paper to the typewriter (transport loaded), arrange the blank paper in the typewriter (position), and type the required message (use). The design of the typist job would attempt to increase the output (typed messages) by (1) simplifying the job requirements to the fewest possible movements and (2) eliminating unnecessary movements. The typist would then need to be trained to perform the job using the relatively fewer preferred basic movements.

Thus, individual jobs can be defined in terms of the required movements. But there are other ways to describe jobs—in terms of depth and range, for example. **Job depth** refers to the relative freedom that the jobholder has in performing assigned tasks. Ordinarily, the depth of a job increases as one moves up in the levels of the organization. The job of the chief executive would have more depth than the job of an assembly-line worker. But

TABLE 6–1	Basic Movements of Manual Work

Movement	Objective
1. Grasp	To: Gain control of an object.
2. Position	Line up, orient, or change position of a part.
3. Pre-position	Line up part or tool for use in another place.
4. Use	Apply tool.
5. Assemble	Assemble parts or objects.
6. Disassemble	Separate objects.
7. Release load	Release a part or object.
8. Transport empty	Reach for something.
9. Transport loaded	Change location of an object.
10. Search	Seek to find an object.
11. Select	Locate an object from a group of objects.
12. Hold	Hold object in fixed position and location.
13. Unavoidable delay	Wait for other body member or machine as a part of the work movement.
14. Avoidable delay	Wait for other body member or machine not a part of the work movement.
15. Rest for fatigue	Remain idle as a part of the cycle to overcome fatigue.
16. Plan	Determine course of action.
17. Inspect	Determine quality of item.

The movements of manual work can be identified for any task if that task can be observed.

differences may also exist in job depth among persons at the same level. For example, a maintenance person has considerably more job depth than does a lathe worker, even though the two jobs are usually at the same level in an organization. The maintenance employee typically can select the methods to be used in maintaining and repairing equipment. By contrast, the lathe worker has little discretion in the selection of work methods.

Job range refers to the length of time of the job cycle; the more often the job is repeated in a given time period, the more limited is its range. We can expect to find differences in job range among jobs at the same level and at different levels in the organization. Generally, the more specialized a job, the narrower its range. Thus, depth and range reflect two outcomes of specialization: (1) relative freedom of choice in selecting the means to do a job and (2) relative "size" of the job. Highly specialized jobs would have relatively little depth and range.[9]

In recent years, there has been growing interest in defining jobs in terms of the perceptions of those who perform them. The individuals who have pioneered this perspective believe that jobs can be described in terms of five **core job dimensions**:[10]

1. *Variety.* Individuals can perceive their jobs to have variety. They usually are engaged in work requiring them to perform many different

[9]Donald J. Campbell, "Task Complexity: A Review and Analysis," *Academy of Management Review,* January 1988, pp. 40–52.

[10]J. Richard Hackman, Greg Oldham, Robert Janson, and Kenneth Purdy, "A New Strategy for Job Enrichment," *California Management Review,* Summer 1975, pp. 57–71; J. Richard Hackman and Greg Oldham, "Development of the Job Diagnostic Survey," *Journal of Applied Psychology,* April 1975, pp. 159–70.

operations and procedures. People who have highly specialized jobs usually perceive little variety in their jobs.

2. *Task identity.*   The perception of task identity depends on whether the individual job results in a complete piece of work. Generally, highly specialized jobs produce perceptions of reduced task identity.

3. *Task significance.*   Individuals have perceptions of the relative significance of their jobs to other people.[11] The perception of task significance is inversely related to specialization.

4. *Autonomy.*   The perception of autonomy reflects the individual's sense of personal control over key aspects of the job. The perception of autonomy is directly related to job depth.

5. *Feedback.*   The perception of feedback reflects the amount of information that the individual obtains upon completing the task. Feedback is usually provided by supervisors. In some instances, feedback is a result of doing the work.[12]

Jobs can be designed to provide high levels of any or all of the important job characteristics. Many smaller organizations have devised ways to increase employees' perceptions of these core dimensions, as illustrated in the Management Focus on job design.

Whether one thinks in terms of job movements, job depth and range, or job dimensions, it is evident that jobs differ. But how? And how different should they be? These questions are fundamental and far from simple. The following section provides some guidelines in determining the degree and kind of those differences.

DEPARTMENTALIZING JOBS

Once the total task of the organization is divided into individual jobs, the jobs must be combined into groups, or departments. Departmentalizing jobs involves two considerations: (1) bases for classifying jobs into departments and (2) the size of each department.[13]

DEPARTMENTAL BASES

The managerial problems associated with departmentalization are directly related to the degree that individual jobs have been specialized. That is, the number of ways to group jobs increases with the number of different (specialized) jobs. Thus, the owner-manager of a small-town men's clothing

[11]James W. Dean and Daniel J. Brass, "Social Interaction and the Perception of Job Characteristics in an Organization," *Human Relations*, June 1985, pp. 571–82.

[12]Eugene F. Stone and Hal G. Gueuthal, "An Empirical Derivation of the Dimensions along which Characteristics of Jobs Are Perceived," *Academy of Management Journal*, June 1985, pp. 376–96, identifies Arthur N. Turner and Paul R. Lawrence, *Industrial Jobs and the Worker: An Investigation of Response to Task Attributes* (Cambridge, Mass.: Harvard University Press, 1965), to be the source of contemporary measures of perceived job characteristics.

[13]Mariann Jelinek, "Organization Structure: The Basic Conformations," in *Organization by Design*, ed. Mariann Jelinek, Joseph A. Litterer, and Raymond E. Miles (Plano, Tex.: Business Publications, 1981), pp. 293–302.

MANAGEMENT FOCUS

Job Design in a Small Manufacturer

Rohm & Haas Bayport was founded in 1981 to produce specialty chemicals. The plant is located in LaPorte, Texas, and its 67 employees play active roles in management because their jobs are designed with that activity in mind. The company's philosophy is to provide autonomy and responsibility in each individual's job and consequently to enable employees to feel a sense of ownership of key decisions and actions. Every person in the organization is trained to be and to act like a manager. The 46 process technicians and 15 engineers and chemists report to one of the two manufacturing unit managers, who in turn report to the executive team.

Working in teams of four to seven people, the technicians make operating decisions among themselves. The company has no shift foremen or line supervisors in the usual sense of these positions; technicians are expected to be self-managed. Team members rotate jobs with other team members every 4 to 12 weeks to provide task variety and cross-training. They are also trained to do routine maintenance and repairs of their equipment and not to depend on a separate maintenance unit for that support. Finally, employees evaluate each other's performance and interview applicants for positions. The company's idea is to give individuals nearly complete control of the conditions that govern work pace and quality. And according to company spokespersons, the job designs at Rohm & Haas Bayport contribute to individual performance.

Source: Don Nichols, "Taking Participative Management to the Limit," *Management Review*, August 1987, pp. 28–32.

store employing three persons has little difficulty determining the way jobs should be grouped, as compared to the management of Sears Roebuck & Co.

In general, the bases for grouping jobs fall into two major categories: (1) *outputs* and (2) *internal operations*. These two general categories of bases for departmentalization are discussed below.[14]

Output-Oriented Bases. The three commonly used output-oriented bases are product, customer, and geographic.

1. *Product departmentalization* involves grouping together all activities necessary to manufacture a product or product line. Such groupings permit the utilization of the specialized skills of those people involved with a particular product or product line. An example of this type of departmentalization is presented in a partial organization chart, Figure 6–2A.

2. *Customer departmentalization* is grouping activities on the basis of customers served.[15] For example, a company may have two sales departments

[14]Luther Gulick, "Notes on the Theory of Organization," in *Papers on the Science of Administration*, ed. Luther Gulick and Lyndall Urwick (New York: Columbia University, 1947), pp. 15–30.

[15]Richard B. Chase and David A. Tansik, "The Customer Contact Model for Organization Design," *Management Science*, September 1983, pp. 1037–50.

FIGURE 6–2	Output-Oriented Departmentalization

A. Product lines

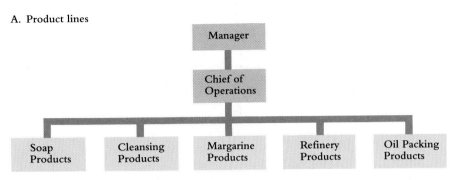

Each of the five product departments produces and sells a specific product.

B. Customer lines

Output-oriented departments can be based on products, customers, or locations.

Each of the two customer departments meets the product and service needs of a specific group of customers.

C. Geographic lines

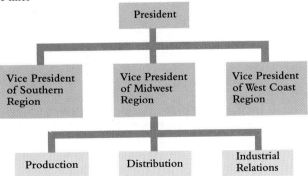

Each of the three regional departments produces and sells products in the assigned geographic area.

FIGURE 6–3	Departmentalization Based on Internal Operations

A. Functional lines

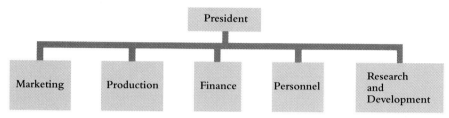

Internal operations–oriented departments can be based on functions of the organization or technical processes.

Each of the five functional departments carries out its assigned part of the total business.

B. Process lines

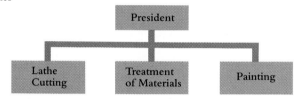

Each of the three process departments carries out its assigned part of the total production process.

that deal with two major groups of customers. One department may service the general public, while the other may be designed to provide goods to an industrial group of customers. The development of customer-oriented service is greatly enhanced through the use of customer departmentalization (shown in Figure 6–2B).[16]

3. *Geographical departmentalization* is grouping activities according to physical, or spatial, location. As described in the Management in Action, Marine Midland Bank was organized by geographic location prior to reorganization. This departmental basis was a convenient choice, given the growth strategy of the bank. Figure 6–2C illustrates geographical departmentalization.

The first classification for grouping work—that is, product, customer, and geography—is oriented toward factors that are external to the actual operations of the firm. For example, the customer is a factor "out there" in the market. The geographical territory is also out there, as is the distribution of the product.

Internal Operations–Oriented Bases.   Two bases for grouping jobs in this category are *function* and *process*.

1. *Functional departmentalization* is used when organizations are designed on the basis of the operations performed by a unit. For example, in a food

[16]Frank Cornish, "Building a Customer-Oriented Organization," *Long Range Planning,* June 1988, pp. 105–7.

TABLE 6–2	Comparison of Department Bases in Four Organizational Settings

	Organizational Settings				
The meanings of function, process, product, and customer vary with the type of organization.	**Basis**	**Business**	**Hospital**	**University**	**Public Health**
	Function	Manufacturing	Surgery	Teaching	Engineering
	Process	Assembly	Diagnosis	Evaluation	Inspector
	Product	Truck	Patient care	Degree	Safe drinking water
	Customer	Military	Children	Graduate student	Residential

processing firm, all activities involved in recruiting and selecting management trainees might be assigned to the personnel department, all marketing activities to the marketing department, and all activities concerned with the actual production of goods would be grouped in the production department. The functional organization design is used extensively in manufacturing firms. But it is also applicable in banking: Marine Midland Bank reorganized along functional departmental bases. Figure 6–3A illustrates the design.

2. *Process departmentalization* groups jobs according to technical operations. For example, the manufacture of a product may include cutting the materials on a lathe, heat-treating the materials, and, finally, painting the product. The same type of technical division of work may be found in a business administration department's office at a college. A number of typists may be assigned specific duties to perform: one types manuscripts, another is concerned with correspondence, and the third handles the telephone and the typing of classroom materials. In Figure 6–3B, the division of work along process lines is presented.

The bases for departmentalization are generally identifiable in any organizational setting. In Table 6–2, four bases are identified in four organizational settings. There we see, for example, that the equivalents to the Pontiac Division of General Motors (product bases) are patient care in hospitals, degrees in universities, and safe drinking water in a public health agency. The only basis not shown is geographic, which becomes relevant only if the organization is dispersed, with offices and facilities in different locations.

Multiple Departmental Bases. Large corporations use different bases at different levels. For example, corporations such as General Motors and General Electric use product as the basis for departmentalizing at the highest level. Each product department, usually termed a *division,* will have all the resources to act as an independent business unit. The departmental basis at the next level down is typically function. In Figure 6–4, the vice president of product B has three functional departments: marketing, production, and personnel. The next level is departmentalized by geography (West Coast and East Coast reporting to marketing), process (manufacturing and finishing reporting to production), and clientele (managerial-related and nonmanagerial-related reporting to personnel). Thus, at each level, different bases can exist both among and within departments.

FIGURE 6—4   Organizational Design Using Mixed Departmentalization

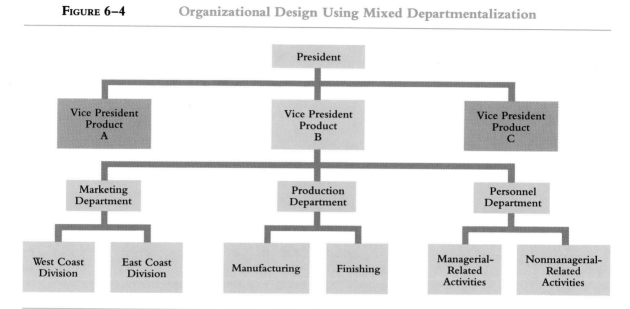

At different levels in the large organization, different bases are used for departmentalization.

Selecting Appropriate Departmental Bases. The principle of departmentalization specifies the guidelines to be followed in grouping activities, but the basis actually chosen is a matter of balancing advantages and disadvantages. For example, departmentalizing on the basis of customers or products has the advantage of bringing together under the control of a single manager all the resources necessary to make the product and/or service for the customers. Additionally, the specification of objectives is considerably easier when the emphasis is on the final product. Yet, at the same time, the ease of objective identification and measurement can encourage the individual departments to pursue their own objectives at the expense of company objectives. A second disadvantage of product/customer departmentalization is that the task of coordinating the activities tends to be more complex. Reporting to the unit manager are the managers of the various functions (production, marketing, and personnel, for example), whose diverse but interdependent activities must be coordinated.

Departmentalization based on internal operations (function and process departments) also has advantages and disadvantages. The primary advantage is that such departments are based on specific skills and training, and activities assigned to the department emphasize the skills that individual members bring to the job.[17] Also, because of the similarity of the subordinates' tasks, coordination of activities in process departments is considerably less complex than in the product department. At the same time, process departments' disadvantages must be recognized, principally the difficulty of providing job depth for the managers of such groups. Since process departmentalization

[17]Peggy Leatt and Rodney Schneck, "Criteria for Grouping Nursing Subunits in Hospitals," *Academy of Management Journal,* March 1984, pp. 150–64.

involves breaking up a natural work flow and assigning parts of this flow to different departments, each departmental manager must coordinate the task with those of other departmental managers. As Figure 6–3B indicates, the president must necessarily limit the freedom of the managers of each of the three process departments in order to coordinate their activities.

The relative advantages of the alternative departmentalization bases can be evaluated in terms of three criteria:[18]

1. Which approach (basis) permits the maximum use of special technical knowledge?
2. Which provides the most efficient utilization of machinery and equipment?
3. Which provides the best hope of obtaining the required control and coordination?

These three criteria, taken together, identify the important issues in determining departmental bases. When the managers of Marine Midland Bank reviewed these three issues, they concluded that functional departmentalization was more advantageous than geographical departmentalization. Accordingly, the bank changed its structure to incorporate the functional basis.

DEPARTMENTAL SIZE

Departmental bases determine the composition of the jobs assigned in a particular department. The second decision regarding departments is to determine the number of jobs assigned to a particular department. This decision involves determining the departmental size.

The size of a department as determined by the number of subordinates who report to a supervisor has two important implications.[19] First, this **span of control** is influential in determining the complexity of individual managers' jobs; all things equal, managing 6 persons is easier than managing 10. Second, the span of control determines the shape, or configuration, of the organization: the fewer the number of people reporting to a supervisor, the larger the number of managers required.[20]

Span of Control and Managerial Work. An early writer demonstrated that as the number of subordinates reporting to a manager increases arithmetically, the number of potential relationships between the manager and the subordinates increases geometrically.[21]

---

[18]Arthur H. Walker and Jay W. Lorsch, "Organizational Choice: Product versus Function," in *Studies in Organization Design,* ed. Jay W. Lorsch and Paul R. Lawrence (Homewood, Ill.: Richard D. Irwin and Dorsey Press, 1970), p. 39.

[19]Lawrence B. Chonko, "The Relationship of Span of Control to Sales Representative's Experienced Role Conflict and Role Ambiguity," *Academy of Management Journal,* June 1982, pp. 452–56; David D. Van Fleet, "Span of Management Research and Issues," *Academy of Management Journal,* September 1983, pp. 546–52.

[20]William G. Ouchi and John B. Dowling, "Defining the Span of Control," *Administrative Science Quarterly,* September 1974, pp. 357–65.

[21]A. V. Graicunas, "Relationships in Organization," in *Papers on the Science of Administration,* ed. Luther Gulick and Lyndall Urwick (New York: Columbia University, 1947), pp. 183–87.

The manager can relate directly to each individual subordinate (direct single) or to each possible group of subordinates (direct group). It is also possible for subordinates to relate to each other (cross). For example, a manager (M) is assigned two subordinates (A and B). The total number of relationships is six: two *direct single relationships* (M to A; M to B); two *direct group relationships* (M to A/B; M to B/A); and two *cross-relationships* (A to B; B to A). But if only one more subordinate (C) is assigned to the manager, the total number of potential relationships increases from 6 to 18: 3 direct single, 9 direct group, and 6 cross-relationships.

The recognition that potential managerial effectiveness is limited as the number of subordinates increases has led others to propose definite limits on the span of control. For example, Ralph Davis distinguished between two categories of span of control, an executive span and an operative span.[22] Executive span refers to the middle and top management positions in an organization. For managers at these levels, span of control should vary from three to nine, depending on the nature of the managers' jobs and responsibilities and the rate of growth of the company, among other factors. Operative span applies to the lowest level of management. Davis proposed that the operative span can be effective with as many as 30 subordinates.

Another writer, Lyndall Urwick, contended that managers should have a limited span of control because a limit exists as to the number of other people or objects to which a person can attend at the same time.[23] Urwick recognized that although a manager with 10 subordinates has 5,210 potential relationships, the actual relationships may be far fewer. However, even if only a portion of the potential 5,210 relationships actually occurred in a day, a manager would be unable to deal with all of them. Based on his interpretation of span of control and the potential relationships, Urwick proposed that the ideal span for top management is 4 but that at other supervisory levels the number may be 8 to 12.

Span of Control and Organizational Shape.   The span of control has important implications for the shape of an organization. For example, assume that a company has 48 nonmanagers and the span of control is 8. There would be six supervisors each. This type of structure is illustrated in Figure 6–5A, where there are three levels of management: president, senior supervisor, and supervisor.

If the same number of workers (48) was supervised by two superiors, an organization with only two managerial levels could be structured. The organizational design resulting from widening the span of control to 24 is presented in Figure 6–5B. By increasing the span of control from 8 to 24, one level of management and six managerial positions are eliminated from the organization.

The relatively flat organization that results from wide spans of control shortens the communication channel from top to bottom. It also fosters more general supervision since, as noted earlier, managers with a wide span of control will not be able to devote as much time to each individual employee.

[22]Ralph C. Davis, *Fundamentals of Top Management* (New York: Harper & Row, 1951).

[23]Lyndall Urwick, "The Manager's Span of Control," *Harvard Business Review,* May–June 1956, pp. 39–47.

A. Narrow span of control

B. Wide span of control

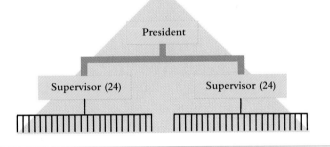

The shape of the organization changes as the average span of control changes.

In contrast, narrow spans of control foster close supervision but at the cost of lengthened communication channels and increased cost of supervision. The cost of excessive supervision does not go unnoticed in organizations experiencing economic hardship. The American auto industry in recent years has sought means to reduce cost, increase productivity, and be more competitive by reducing the number of managers and, as a result, the number of management levels.

Thus, decisions about span of control are far from trivial. As we have seen, the number of people reporting to a manager has direct implications for both the manager and the organization itself. As is the case in most important managerial decisions, no formula specifies the optimal span of control. At best, managers can utilize the following guidelines:

1. The more competent the manager and subordinates, the wider the span of control can be.
2. The fewer nonmanagerial responsibilities assigned to the manager, the wider the span of control can be.

3. The more similar the jobs being supervised, the wider the span of control can be.
4. The more routine the jobs and the overall work of the department, the wider the span of control can be.
5. The closer the physical proximity of the jobs, the wider the span of control can be.

Spans of control can therefore be different for managers at the same level. A manager with demonstrated competence can, for example, manage more jobs than an inexperienced one. Or managers with similar competence can have different spans of control, depending on the nature of the jobs they manage. Thus, the factors that bear on the optimal span of control relate to (1) characteristics of the manager and (2) characteristics of the jobs to be managed.[24]

DELEGATING AUTHORITY

The process of dividing tasks into jobs and departmentalizing the jobs into groups creates a framework for accomplishing the organization's work. Among the jobs that result from departmentalization are managerial jobs. The third consideration is how to delegate authority to each managerial job.

Authority is generally defined as the legally or organizationally sanctioned right to make a decision without approval by a higher-ranking manager. The issue of delegating authority involves balancing the advantages and disadvantages of decentralization of authority and has implications for the creation of a chain of command and the use of staff personnel. The usual practical concern is the extent to which authority will be delegated downward (i.e., decentralized).

PROS AND CONS OF DECENTRALIZATION

Although the exact degree of **decentralization** cannot be precisely specified, relative advantages and disadvantages can be identified.

Advantages. The first advantage of decentralized authority is that it encourages managers to develop their decision-making ability, essential training for promotion into positions of greater authority and responsibility. In the decentralized environment, they will have to adapt to and deal with difficult decisions. They need to become generalists and know something about the numerous job-related factors that must be coped with, often on a daily basis.

Such responsibilities lead directly into the second advantage of decentralized authority: its competitive climate. Managers must prove themselves if they are to advance. In a decentralized structure, they can be readily compared with their peers on the basis of actual decision-making performance. And being

[24]Robert D. Dewar and Donald P. Simet, "A Level-Specific Prediction of Spans of Control Examining the Effects of Size, Technology, and Specialization," *Academy of Management Journal,* March 1981, pp. 5–24.

evaluated on such criteria rather than on personality motivates managers to contribute and perform. In the end, decentralized authority can lead to a more satisfied group of managers because advancement can be directly related to results.

The third advantage of decentralization is that managers are able to exercise more autonomy and this increased job depth satisfies their desire to participate in problem solving. This freedom is assumed to lead to managerial creativity and ingenuity, which contribute to the flexibility and profitability of the organization.

Disadvantages.   Decentralization also has some readily identified disadvantages. As with the advantages, we will cover only the most important ones here.

First, decentralization of authority usually requires more intensive and expensive management training. The initial cost of training is high because managers must often be retrained to make decisions once made at higher levels. Even if additional training is not necessary, the cost will increase because the organization needs to employ more highly skilled, and therefore more expensive, individuals to handle the increased responsibilities.

A second disadvantage is that decentralization requires more sophisticated planning and reporting methods. Delegating the right to make a decision without approval requires establishing methods to measure overall accountability for the use of that authority. Even though the authority is delegated, upper management cannot delegate its responsibility for achieving the organization's mission and objectives. Therefore, upper management must implement more extensive planning and reporting procedures when authority is decentralized. Consequently, the flow of information to upper management will increase.

A third disadvantage applies primarily to instances of change from centralized to decentralized authority. Such a change requires top managers to delegate a portion of their decision-making authority to middle and first-level managers. In some instances, top management may be unwilling or unable to delegate further. These managers may equate authority with power and therefore view delegation as undermining their power and influence in the organization. These attitudes, often highly resistant to change, can limit if not defeat any effort to decentralize.

The relative advantages and disadvantages of decentralization also reflect the stage of business development. For example, a rapidly growing firm often can benefit from decentralization. The Management Focus on decentralization describes just such a circumstance.

CHAIN OF COMMAND

The issue of delegation of authority is also linked to considerations other than centralization/decentralization. One is the matter of **chain of command**.

The chain-of-command relationship is a series of superior-subordinate relationships. Starting at the top of the organization with the president and progressing down to the unskilled employee, the managerial chain of com-

MANAGEMENT FOCUS

VW Obtains Employee Loyalty through Decentralization

Volkswagen's growth from a one-model company located in Wolfsburg, West Germany, to a multinational automaker challenged its management. VW's management must be constantly alert to cost and quality control opportunities because of its heavy reliance on foreign markets. In these markets, VW's cars must compete directly with Japanese cars, which have long had the edge in both cost and quality, and American cars, which are quickly regaining their reputation for reliability and economy. Opportunities to lower production costs and improve quality often mean automation and modernization, which can eliminate the jobs of production workers. So VW's challenge was to find ways to retain one of its important strengths: employee loyalty and commitment.

VW's management recognized that its high-tech policy ran the danger of inciting its workers to retaliation in the form of strikes and walkouts. Similar circumstances had produced precisely those results in other European countries and in the United States. How to avoid those unhappy and costly outcomes was the issue to be confronted.

The opportunity to share and to take responsibility for important decisions is a key job characteristic. Into the job of each production worker, VW's management now builds the expectation that the jobholder will share with management the responsibility for important decisions. In part, the practice is mandated by a German law that requires all major firms to give half the votes on their supervisory boards to labor representatives. But the law only provides the opportunity to involve employees in decision making. VW has taken the concept further than many other companies. The automaker has integrated the practice of sharing power throughout the organization, making responsibility for decision making an element of job performance for managers and workers alike. Through this practice, the company has developed and maintained a stable and loyal work force despite pressures arising from growth and competition.

Source: Dennis Phillips, "How VW Builds Worker Loyalty Worldwide," *Management Review*, June 1987, pp. 37–40.

mand is a hierarchy of jobs differentiated by authority. Figure 6–6 depicts the chain of command in a hypothetical managerial hierarchy.

The chain of command is the formal channel that determines authority, responsibility, and communications. Because of the complexity of these relationships, no individual should ordinarily be subject to the direct command of more than one superior. Receiving commands from two or more superiors is likely to bring about confusion and frustration.

Managers must provide for an unbroken chain of command from top to bottom. At the same time, they must recognize the need to provide for bypassing the chain when conditions warrant. A subordinate should be empowered to communicate directly with a peer outside the chain, for example, provided that the appropriate superiors approve beforehand the circumstances that permit the crossovers. Figure 6–7 shows a bridge between F and G that D and E have approved. Under special circumstances, F and G may communicate directly without going through channels, yet neither would

FIGURE 6–6   Chain of Command

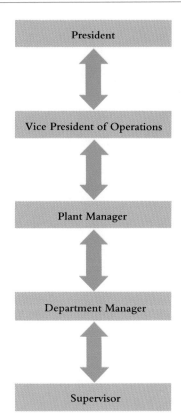

The chain of command is the channel through which the organization routes orders, directives, and other communications.

FIGURE 6–7   Fayol's Bridge

A chain of command can be broken with prior approval of the manager(s) bypassed in the communication.

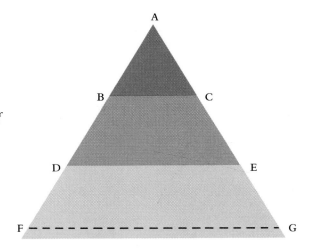

The managerial chain of command is a hierarchy of jobs differentiated by authority.

be accountable to anyone but his or her immediate superior—in this case, D and E, respectively.

Staff Personnel

Delegation of authority also has implications for the way staff personnel are used. An important point in examining organization structure is to distinguish between line and staff. Many different definitions of line and staff can be found in the management literature. Perhaps the most concise and least confusing definition is one that defines line as deriving from operational activities in a direct sense—creating, financing, and distributing a good or service—while staff is viewed as an advisory and facilitative function for the line. The crux of this viewpoint is the degree to which the particular function contributes directly to the attainment of organizational objectives: The **line functions** contribute directly to accomplishing the firm's objectives, while **staff functions** facilitate the accomplishment of the major organizational objectives in an indirect manner. Figure 6–8 illustrates a line-and-staff organizational design.

Using the criterion that the line function contributes directly to the firm's objectives would lead to the conclusion that the marketing and production departments perform activities directly related to the attainment of a most important organizational objective: placing an acceptable product on the market. The activities of the managers of environmental control and engineering are advisory in nature. That is, they are helpful in enabling the firm to produce and market its product but do not directly contribute to the process. Thus they are considered to be staff departments in this particular firm.

The concept of the unbroken chain of command quite clearly defines the appropriate role of the staff specialist in the organization: advising and providing information but having no authority over the work of a particular

FIGURE 6–8   Example of Line-and-Staff Structure

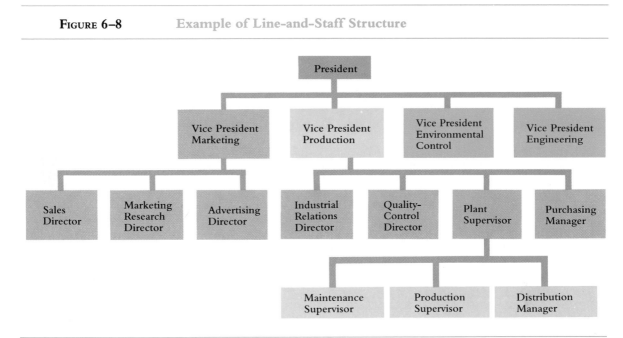

Managers create staff units to assist line units in doing the work of the organization.

line manager's subordinates. To place a subordinate under the jurisdiction of a staff official as well as a line manager would violate and weaken the chain of command. Thus, how authority is delegated has implications not only for who makes what decisions but also for whom one communicates with, whom one directs and is directed by, and where one is located in a hierarchy of authority.

DIMENSIONS OF ORGANIZATION STRUCTURE

The effects of division of tasks, departmentalization, and delegation of authority are "policies and activities occurring within organizations that prescribe or restrict behavior of organizational members."[25] To describe these policies and activities, many different terms have been used by those who research and theorize about organization structure. These terms, the dimensions of structure, enable us to compare organization structures and identify similarities and differences.[26] In recent years, it has become customary to use three dimensions: *complexity, formalization,* and *centralization.*

COMPLEXITY

Complexity is defined as the number of different occupational titles or different functional activities pursued within an organization. Thus, an

[25]Dalton et al., "Organization Structure," p. 57

[26]Richard S. Blackburn, "Dimensions of Structure: A Review and Reappraisal," *Academy of Management Review,* January 1982, pp. 59–66.

organization that has production, marketing, and finance departments reporting to top management would be more complex than one that has only production and marketing. Task specialization that divides work at the same level of an organization determines *horizontal complexity.* Organization structures differ in the degree to which they are horizontally complex.[27]

A second way to view complexity in organizations is in terms of the number of managerial levels—that is, the number of different positions in the chain of command. This type of specialization is called *vertical complexity.* The positions in the chain of command reflect specialization of the managerial functions of planning, organizing, and controlling. Thus, even as organizations can be more or less complex horizontally, so they can also be more or less complex vertically.

The managerial implications of horizontal and vertical complexity are straightforward: it is easier to manage similarities than differences. Accordingly, the more complex an organization or unit, the more difficult are the managerial jobs. Complex organizations are difficult to manage because of the dissimilarities in both the tasks of the units and the jobs of individuals.[28] But the cost of increased complexity can be offset by the increased productivity that results from specialization.

FORMALIZATION

Formalization refers to the extent to which job expectations, rules, procedures, policies, and other sources that describe expected behavior exist in written form.[29] A term sometimes used to describe this dimension is *standardization,* although that term most often refers to written statements that define the exact procedures and methods that a jobholder will use to accomplish a job outcome.

Organizations differ in degree of formalization. Generally speaking, complexity and formalization are correlated: An organization that is highly complex will also be highly formalized, because complexity often results when tasks have well-established methods for accomplishing recognizable and measurable outcomes. In such circumstances, it is practical to put the preferred methods and outcomes into writing so as to reduce the possibility of incorrect or inappropriate behavior. Simple and routine production and administrative tasks lend themselves to extensive formalization; complicated and nonroutine scientific and research tasks are not amenable to formalization.

CENTRALIZATION

As noted earlier, centralization refers to the distribution of decision-making authority throughout the organization.[30] Other terms often used to refer to the

[27]Richard L. Daft and Patricia J. Bradshaw, "The Process of Horizontal Differentiation: Two Models," *Administrative Science Quarterly,* September 1980, pp. 441–56.

[28]Greg R. Oldham and J. Richard Hackman, "Relationship between Organizational Structure and Employee Reactions: Comparing Alternative Frameworks," *Administrative Science Quarterly,* March 1981, pp. 66–83.

[29]James P. Walsh and Robert D. Dewar, "Formalization and the Organizational Life-Cycle," *Journal of Management Studies,* May 1987, pp. 215–32.

[30]Dennis S. Mileti, Doug A. Timmer, and David F. Gillespie, "Intra and Interorganizational Determinants of Decentralization," *Pacific Sociological Review,* April 1982, pp. 163–83, provides

idea include *autonomy* and *participation*. As a practical matter, it is relatively more difficult to identify the degree of centralization than the degree of complexity or formalization. In a sense, everyone in an organization makes decisions. Even the lowliest laborer can decide where to place the shovel to remove dirt from the ditch. And to complicate matters further, decisions often are the result of groups and consultation with other individuals.[31]

The extremes of centralization are identifiable. At one extreme is an organization in which all decisions are made by one individual, the top manager. At the other extreme is an organization in which all decisions are made by all members of the organization. Because decision making is a primary source of power in organizations, political terms are often used to describe the two extremes: "all decisions, one individual" is autocratic; "all decisions, all individuals" is democratic. These terms are value laden and not very useful to describe work organizations, despite the tendency to use them.

In actuality, organizations lie between the extremes; they are more or less centralized but never absolutely centralized or decentralized.[32] The relevant consideration is to ascertain the locus of authority for deciding the objectives of the organization. All other decisions are subordinate to the decision regarding what the organization is seeking to accomplish. To the extent that that decision is widely shared, the organization is less centralized.[33]

Recall that Marine Midland settled this issue by centralizing decisions in the functional units, thus reducing the autonomy of the regional units. In terms of the three dimensions of organizational structure, Marine Midland was more complex and centralized, and probably more formalized, following its reorganization.

As this chapter has indicated, organization structures differ in the extent to which they are complex, formalized, and centralized. These differences reflect decisions that managers make regarding division of tasks, departmentalization bases and sizes, and delegation of authority. But the important thing to understand is not so much that organization structures are different but rather *why* they are different. Specifically, how can managers know that a highly complex, formalized, centralized structure is preferable to an alternative form. That knowledge is the subject of the next chapter.

SUMMARY OF KEY POINTS

■ The organization function involves designing or redesigning a structure of task and authority relationships to achieve coordinated effort. The organizing function includes all managerial activities required to specify the means to accomplish the work of individuals, groups, and organizations.

evidence to suggest the importance of territorial departmentalization in decentralized organizations.

[31]Peter H. Grinyear and Masoud Yasai-Ardekani, "Dimensions of Organizational Structure: A Critical Replication," *Academy of Management Journal,* September 1980, pp. 405–21, discusses formalization in relation to centralization.

[32]Henry Tosi, *Theories of Organization* (New York: John Wiley & Sons, 1984).

[33]Eric J. Walton, "The Comparison of Measures of Organization Structure," *Academy of Management Review,* January 1981, pp. 155–60.

■ The three key decisions of the organizing function are (*a*) the appropriate division of tasks, (*b*) the appropriate basis and size of departments, and (*c*) the appropriate degree of delegated authority. The organization structure takes on a specific form, depending on management's response to each of these decisions.

■ Dividing tasks involves determining the depth and range of each job. Although the principle of specialization of labor indicates that economic gains can be derived from specialized (low depth and range) jobs, at some point the gains of specialization are less than its costs. The managerial decision is to identify the optimal level of specialization for each general class of jobs.

■ Departmentalizing jobs involves recombining jobs into departments according to some basis and of some size. The bases for departments include product, customer, and geographic (external bases) and functional and process (internal bases). The selection of appropriate departmental bases for each level in the organization requires managers to balance the advantages and disadvantages of each basis.

■ The size of departments (the span of control) has managerial and organizational implications. The managerial implications are that as the manager becomes responsible for more and more subordinates, the number of potential relationships increases at an exponential rate. The manager is less and less able to give attention to each subordinate and to each possible group of subordinates. The organization implications are that as the span of control decreases, the number of managerial levels increases: the chain of command through which directives and communications flow lengthens.

■ Delegating authority involves determining how much decision-making latitude should be given to each managerial job. The decision involves determining the appropriate authority commensurate with the responsibility of the job. In practical terms, delegating authority involves balancing the advantages and disadvantages of decentralization.

■ Delegating authority creates a chain of command—a graded chain of jobs that vary by degrees of decision-making authority. Generally, the chain of command should be the official channel for all management directives and communications. Moreover, it should be "unbroken" from top to bottom in the sense that each individual reports to one and only one boss.

■ The three organizing parts—jobs, departments, and authority—can be combined in a variety of structural configurations. That is to say, differences in organization structures are the result of differences in the three parts: jobs can be more or less specialized; departments can be more or less homogeneous; authority can be more or less centralized.

■ Differences in organization structures can be described by noting differences in the dimensions of structure. It has become customary to use three dimensions to describe differences in structure: complexity, formalism, and centralization.

■ Complexity refers to degree of specialization; formalism refers to degree of written rules, procedures, and policies; centralization refers to degree of delegation of authority. Although there are unusual cases, the usual situation is for organizations to tend to be either complex, formal, and centralized or simple, informal, and decentralized. These two extremes are the basic models of organization design.

Discussion and Review Questions

1. What general objectives do managers attempt to achieve through the organizing function? How do they know whether the objectives are in fact achieved?

2. Describe an organization to which you belong, in terms of division of tasks, departmentalization, and delegation of authority.

3. Identify the bases for departmentalization in the college where you are enrolled. What alternative bases could be used? And what would be the relative advantages of each alternative?

4. List some of the symptoms of problems that could be caused by a malfunctioning organization structure.

5. What are the appropriate terms to use in describing individual jobs? Should depth and range be the terms used? Or should variety, task identity, task significance, autonomy, and feedback be used?

6. Explain the difference between potential and actual relationships between a manager and subordinates. Which is the more relevant concept to use when deciding the appropriate span of control?

7. Obtain information regarding the spans of control of the chairpersons in the college you attend.

Chances are, no two will have the same span of control. What accounts for these differences? Should the differences exist?

8. Using the same set of chairpersons studied above, determine the degree of decentralization of authority by documenting the decisions that each can make without checking first with the dean (or other appropriate official). Then determine whether some have more or less authority in comparison to their peers. What accounts for differences in authority among chairpersons.

9. Explain how the idea of an unbroken chain of command is created by the process of delegating authority.

10. Can all the causes of line-staff conflict be eliminated by explicit definition of authority and responsibility? Explain.

ADDITIONAL REFERENCES

Allen, R. W., and **L. W. Porter.** *Organizational Influence Processes.* Glenview, Ill.: Scott Foresman, 1983.

Blau, G. J., and **R. Katerberg.** "Toward Enhancing Research with the Social Information Processing Approach to Task Design." *Academy of Management Review,* October 1982, pp. 543–50.

Carlisle, K. E. *Analyzing Jobs and Tasks.* Englewood Cliffs, N.J.: Educational Technology Publications, 1986.

Cellar, D. F.; M. C. Kernan; and **G. V. Barrett.** "Conventional Wisdom and Ratings of Job Characteristics: Can Observers Be Objective?" *Journal of Management,* 1985, pp. 131–38.

Donaldson, L. "Organization Design and the Life-Cycle of Products." *Journal of Management Studies,* 1985, pp. 25–37.

Gomez-Mejia, L. R.; R. C. Page; and **W. W. Turnow.** "A Comparison of the Practical Utility of Traditional, Statistical, and Hybrid Job Evaluation Approaches." *Academy of Management Journal,* December 1982, pp. 790–809.

Hedge, A. "The Open-Plan Office: A Systematic Investigation of Employee Reactions to Their Work Environment." *Environment and Behavior,* September 1982, pp. 519–42.

Hutton, M., and **R. Collins.** "Job Design: Australian Practice and Prospects." *Practising Manager,* April 1983, pp. 11–15.

Kolodny, H. F., and **B. Dresner.** "Linking Arrangements and New Work Designs." *Organizational Dynamics,* Winter 1986, pp. 33–51.

Kuhn, A., and **R. D. Beam.** *The Logic of Organization.* San Francisco: Jossey-Bass, 1982.

Mecham, R. C. "Quantitative Job Evaluation Using the Position Analysis Questionnaire." *Personnel Administrator,* 1983, pp. 82–88, 124.

Mintzberg, H. *Structure in Fives: Designing Effective Organizations.* Englewood Cliffs, N.J.: Prentice-Hall, 1983.

Montagno, R. V. "The Effects of Comparison Others and Prior Experience on Responses to Task Design." *Academy of Management Journal,* June 1985, pp. 491–98.

Muchnik, M. A. "Integrated Task Management." *Production and Inventory Management,* 1984, pp. 44–55.

Nystrom, P. C., and **W. H. Starbuck.** *Handbook of Organizational Design,* vols. 1 and 2. New York: Oxford University Press, 1983.

Oliver, J. E. "When Is Job Redesign Necessary?" *Manage,* 1984, pp. 14–17.

Perkins, D. N. T.; V. F. Nieva; and **E. E. Lawler III.** *Managing Creation: The Challenge of Building a New Organization.* New York: John Wiley & Sons, 1983.

Telem, M. "The Process of Organization Structures." *Journal of Management Studies,* 1985, pp. 38–52.

Wall, T. "What's New in Job Design?" *Personnel Management,* 1984, pp. 28–29.

Weisbord, M. R. "Participative Work Design: A Personal Odyssey." *Organizational Dynamics,* Winter 1985, pp. 4–20.

CASE 6–1   Organization Structure of Saxe Realty Company

Saxe Realty Company, Inc., located in the San Francisco Bay area, was founded in 1938 by Jules and Marion Saxe. For most of its history, the company was a single-office agency run by its founders. But over time, the company grew in size and sales revenue, which increased from $1 million in 1973 to over $10 million in 1979. Rather than a single office, the company had six branches located in the San Francisco and Marin County area.

The firm grew for many reasons. An important reason was the founders' ability to do certain things very well. They knew how to select locations, time moves, and design offices. They recruited and hired people with above-average ability and trained them to be effective salespersons. The rewards of growth were enjoyed by the Saxe family and employees of their firm.

But with growth came problems stemming from the mismatch between the firm's organization structure, management practices, and the requirements of a large firm compared to a small one. In the early days, Saxe Realty could handle its business matters in simple and informal ways. After all, it was a family corporation, and family members ran it as a family, not as a business.

Some of the problems that surfaced with growth included the absence of clearly defined roles and areas of responsibility. People were in jobs because of family relationships rather than skills. Important decisions were made by relatively few people, who often did not have knowledge of all available information. The firm, moreover, had no strategic plan. It responded and reacted to opportunities rather than being proactive. In a sense, the firm's success had simply outgrown its organization.

Saxe consequently had to make many changes in its operations and organization structure, the overriding goal being to move Saxe away from an entrepreneurial-style firm to a professionally managed one. The change itself involved a process of preparation and implementation. Significant changes do not just come about; they must be planned and managed. But only the end results of the change are of interest here.

The organization structure that Saxe adopted relies on geography as the basis for departmentalization. There is a central office, and the branch offices report to it. Geographic departmentalization encourages decentralization, one of the outcomes sought by Saxe's top management. Branch managers are responsible for the day-to-day activities of their offices. The central office maintains overall direction through planning and controlling processes. For example, all branch offices participate in the annual planning process, during which objectives for each branch are developed. These objectives are then the targets and the responsibility of branch managers.

Saxe's top management developed formal discretions for all key positions, defining the responsibilities of each job with special attention to avoiding overlap and duplication of effort. The company's experience during its entrepreneurial stage was that things were often left undone because everyone assumed that someone else was doing them. In other instances, several people would assume responsibility for a task when it required the attention of only one person. A key consideration in the new organization structure was to define explicitly and formally the work expected from each individual job.

The new structure provides for reporting channels from each branch associate to the chief executive officer. The chain of command is the channel for progress reports on planned objectives, financial and sales reports, and other informational needs. In comparison to the previous organization, the chain of command is much more explicit and formal. Individuals are encouraged to go through channels.

The entire change at Saxe has been both extensive and time consuming. Nearly every aspect of the firm's operations has been affected. And the changes took two years or more to fully implement.

QUESTIONS FOR ANALYSIS

1. Draw an organization chart that depicts the structure being implemented at Saxe.
2. What alternative structures could Saxe have implemented, and what would be the advantages of each in comparison to the one Saxe did implement?
3. What are the relationships between the planning function and the organization function as depicted in the Saxe case?

CASE 6–2   Restructuring at Motorola

Competitive pressures from home and abroad have forced many business firms to consider ways to cut costs and eliminate waste. At the same time that firms sought ways to cut costs, they were also looking for ways to increase the flow of innovative ideas. Many firms responded to these twin challenges in the 1980s by reducing the levels of management and increasing the spans of control. These flatter structures reduced costs by eliminating managerial jobs (and salaries) and increased the flow of ideas by giving individuals more authority to make decisions. Many reports of the positive results of such restructuring efforts filled the popular press.

Some well-known corporate names were associated with this movement. Ford Motor Co., for example, acknowledged that its 12 layers of management should be reduced and brought more in line with Toyota's and Xerox Corporation's reduction in middle management. Even those firms with records of efficient operations announced that they were attempting to do better by reducing the number of managers in their organizations. Dana Corporation, an acknowledged efficiency leader, announced its intention to reduce its five levels of management to four.

These stories came to the attention of top management of Motorola, Inc., which instructed the company's human resource (HR) professionals to evaluate potential gains through flattening the structure. Motorola's top management was particularly concerned with how any efforts to reduce managerial personnel would affect the company's long-standing commitment to certain values. The company enjoyed the reputation of treating employees with

Source: Based on Phil Nienstedt and Richard Wintermantel, "Motorola Restructures to Improve Productivity," *Management Review,* January 1987, pp. 47–49.

respect and dignity, including protecting employees who had served the company well in the past. Any effort to restructure to eliminate managerial jobs would have to be consistent with the company's reputation. Top management was also concerned with how managers themselves would respond to efforts to reduce managerial jobs. Wouldn't they see such efforts as threats, particularly if it meant reducing personnel in their own departments?

Instructed by Motorola to consider appropriate solutions to the problems associated with excess management, professionals in the human resource department devised a strategy for cutting costs while adhering to "people first" values. Their strategy consisted of five steps involving the managers and HR professionals in joint activities:

Step 1: Data gathering. Each top manager drew an organization chart showing every reporting relationship down to the direct-labor level. These hand-drawn charts were to show what really went on in the unit, as distinct from what was supposed to go on.

Step 2: Analysis. HR professionals analyzed the charts and identified issues for discussion with the managers. They indicated instances of too many managerial levels, too narrow spans of control, and overlapping responsibilities.

Step 3: Discussion. The analyses done by the HR professionals were presented to managers for discussion. The managers were given opportunities to explain and clarify the relationships shown on the charts.

Step 4: Goals negotiation. As discussions between managers and HR staff revealed problems, managers were asked to propose solutions. In those instances when managers disagreed with the staff, they were challenged to present their own analyses and solutions.

Step 5: Implementation and tracking. As the changes in organization structure were implemented, the resultant cost savings were documented. The sources of these savings were salaries of managers not replaced upon retirement or transfer. A second source of savings was the replacement of a manager with a nonmanager at a lower salary.

Thus, through elimination of some jobs and redefinition of others, Motorola succeeded in its efforts to reduce costs by restructuring its organization. The restructuring has caused Motorola's managers to constantly ask themselves whether they each can effectively direct one more employee. They ask: "If I manage five, why not six?" The dollar results of the restructuring were impressive, with savings in excess of $4.3 million in the first year. Other results included improved vertical communications, more effective managerial selection and training, and greater participation in decision making by all employees.

QUESTIONS FOR ANALYSIS

1. Should all organizations such as Motorola determine the appropriate number of managers and then devise ways to reach that number? What is the likelihood that everyone in the organization will agree on a particular number?
2. Would you have gone about the process the way Motorola did? Why?
3. How would reducing the number of management layers affect other structural factors such as division of labor, departmentalization, and delegation of authority?

EXPERIENTIAL EXERCISE

DESIGNING THE NEW VENTURE

Purpose

The purpose of this exercise is to provide students with first-hand experience in organizing a new business venture.

The Exercise in Class

Scenario.   A few years ago, George Ballas got so frustrated trying to keep his lawn neatly trimmed around the roots of oak trees that he developed what is now called the Weed Eater. The original Weed Eater was made from a popcorn can that had holes in it and was threaded with nylon fishing line. Weed Eater sales in 1972 totaled $568,000; but by 1978, sales were in excess of $100 million. There are now 20 or so similar devices on the market.

Two brothers from Pittsburgh, George and Jim Gammons, are starting a new venture called Lawn Trimmers, Inc. They are attempting to sell trimmers that do not wear out for over 2,000 trimming applications. The Weed Eater and similar products often have breaks in the nylon lines that require the user to turn off the trimmer and readjust the line. The Gammons have developed a new type of cutting fabric that is not physically harmful and cuts for over 2,000 applications.

In order to sell the Lawn Trimmers, the Gammons brothers will have to market their products through retail establishments. They will make the products in their shop in Pittsburgh and ship them to the retail establishments. The profits will come entirely from the sales of the Lawn Trimmers to retail establishments. The price of the product is already set, and it appears that there will be sufficient market demand to sell at least 6,000 Lawn Trimmers annually.

Activity.   The instructor will set up teams of five to eight students to serve as organizational design experts who will provide the Gammons brothers with the best structure for their new venture. Each group should:

1. Establish a design that would be feasible for the Gammons at this stage in their venture.
2. Select a spokesperson to make a short presentation of the group's organizational design for the Gammons.

The class should compare the various designs and discuss why there are similarities and differences in what is presented.

The Learning Message

This exercise will show that organizational design necessitates making assumptions about the market, competition, labor resources, scheduling, and profit margins, to name just a few areas. There is no one best design that should be regarded as a final answer.

7

ORGANIZATION DESIGN

LEARNING OBJECTIVES

After completing Chapter 7, you should be able to:

Define
organization design in terms of the universalistic and contingency viewpoints.

Describe
the implications of technology, environmental uncertainty, and strategy for the design of organization structure.

Discuss
the fundamental differences between classical and neoclassical organization design.

Compare
the alternative arguments that conclude that there is no "one best" organization design.

Identify
criticisms of the universalistic viewpoint by those who support the contingency viewpoint.

Organizing for Innovation at Raytheon

Raytheon Company depends on innovation for survival. The company competes in the highly technical and volatile electronics-based product industry. In this environment, the development of new products and new technology becomes crucial to the firm's very survival, and it is imperative to design an organization that facilitates new product development. As do other firms, Raytheon uses research and development (R&D) units as an organizational form but supplements them with a centralized, corporate-level New Products Center (NPC).

The New Products Center is a 35-person group located at corporate headquarters in Burlington, Massachusetts. Since its formation in 1969, it has helped develop 39 products that have become mainstays in the firm's product line. The NPC stands alone and works with all the divisions and subsidiaries of the company, including those R&D units that are parts of the divisions and subsidiaries.

The company also uses external consultants and internal and external ventures groups to initiate and sustain innovation. But the NPC plays a special role in this configuration, because it views the entire organization as both a source of clients and a source of resources. It serves as a way to cross functional and divisional boundaries so as to tap all the skills and abilities in Raytheon. All the expertise in all the divisional R&D groups can be made available to the NPC for product development.

The NPC's primary goal is to develop profitable products; new products are worthless if they do not generate profits. Thus, the bottom-line criterion for evaluating NPC's performance is its contribution to profit. Its basic operating procedure is to develop the first functioning model of a new product, which can then be turned over to the appropriate product or business center. If successful, the product will extend the product line and will be manufactured with existing facilities and distributed through existing channels.

The director of the center reports to Raytheon's chief executive officer, thus emphasizing the support of top management for the center's importance. Raytheon's experience with its NPC indicates that other firms could adopt this approach to organizing for innovation.

George Freedman, "Raytheon's New Products Development Center," *Management Review,* December 1987, pp. 40–45.

Managers who must design or redesign the structures of organizations confront a difficult issue. They must choose from among alternatives that have no clear-cut criteria for choice. In deciding on a particular approach to organizing its product development effort, Raytheon's management had to consider various approaches that differed in many ways. The organization design decision is inherently difficult even when the design decision is concerned with only part of the organization.

Contemporary management theory provides some general guidelines managers can use when designing organizations. These guidelines are themselves contradictory and contain assumptions that managers must recognize when they decide on a particular design.[1] In this chapter, we review the present state of knowledge regarding the design of organizations. Our purpose is to provide bases for making choices among organization design alternatives.

We can divide contemporary thinking into two categories of opinion. One category is based on the premise that there is "one best way" to design an organization, regardless of the situation. The body of opinion that supports this premise is termed the **universalistic approach.** The second category of opinion states that the best way to organize depends on the situation. This category is termed the **contingency approach.** Within each of these two categories are differences of opinion as to what precisely is the "one best way" and what factors in the situation must be taken into account.

UNIVERSALISTIC APPROACH

Proponents of the universalistic approach propose two different organizational designs: the *classical design* and the *neoclassical design.*

CLASSICAL ORGANIZATION DESIGN

The characteristics of classical organization design include high complexity, high formalization, and high centralization. The arguments that support classical design have been very influential in the development of modern management theory.

The writers of the scientific management and classical approaches to management made forceful cases for the superiority of classical organization design over any alternative design. They reasoned that classical design is a natural extension of specialization of labor to the organizational level.

Organization structures with high levels of complexity, formalization, and centralization reflect the assumption that *the design of jobs determines the design of organizations.* Figure 7–1 diagrams this assumption and its consequence.

The use of classical designs was widespread during the late 1800s, when industrialization of Western civilization was at its height. A primary social and managerial concern was efficient use of resources with maximum production. Out of these times, two different yet compatible sets of ideas emerged. One set

---

[1]Ralph H. Kilmann, Louis R. Pondy, and Dennis P. Slevin, "Directions of Research on Organization Design," in *The Management of Organization Design: Research and Methodology,* ed. Ralph H. Kilmann, Louis R. Pondy, and Dennis P. Slevin (New York: Elsevier–North Holland, 1976), p. 1.

FIGURE 7–1	Classical Design Assumptions

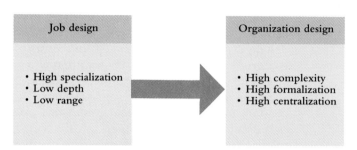

Classical design theory assumes that job design is the principal determinant of organization design.

Job design

- High specialization
- Low depth
- Low range

Organization design

- High complexity
- High formalization
- High centralization

has come to be associated with bureaucracy as an ideal type of organization. The other set is associated with the classical school.

Bureaucratic Approach.   **Bureaucracy** refers to the form of organization first described in the literature of public administration as government by bureaus—that is, unelected civil servants. However, it is more frequently associated with negative consequences of large organizations, such as red tape, unexplained delays, and general frustration. But its more important meaning is to describe an organization design that is "superior to any other form in precision, in stability, in the stringency of its discipline, and in its reliability. It thus makes possible a high degree of calculability of results for the heads of the organization and for those acting in relation to it."[2]

The characteristics of the "ideal" bureaucracy are:

1. It has a clear division of labor, with each job well defined, understood, and routine.
2. Each manager has a clearly defined relationship with other managers and subordinates that follows a formal hierarchy.
3. Specific rules, policies, and procedures guide behaviors of employees in relation to each other and to clients.
4. Impersonal application of rules, policies, discipline, and rewards minimizes the possibility of favoritism.
5. Managers use rigid and equitable criteria to screen and select from among candidates for jobs in the organization.

The desired effect of the ideal type is to de-emphasize the idiosyncrasies of human behavior and to emphasize the predictability of machines and mechanical behavior.

As summarized by Max Weber, the bureaucratic design compares to other designs "as does the machine with nonmechanical modes of production."[3] Weber based this conclusion on extensive analyses of the Prussian civil service

[2]Max Weber, *The Theory of Social and Economic Organization,* trans. A. M. Henderson and Talcott Parsons (New York: Oxford University Press, 1947), p. 334.

[3]Max Weber, *From Max Weber: Essays in Sociology,* trans. H. H. Gerth and C. W. Mills (New York: Oxford University Press, 1946), p. 214.

The term bureaucracy *was originally used to refer to government by bureaus, that is, by unelected civil servants.*

and military organizations. He believed that the advantages of bureaucracy were applicable in any context, whether government, military, or business.

Classical Approach.   The classical approach to organization design proposes that the design of organization structures (that is, the process of design) should be guided by certain *principles of organization*.[4] Thus, managers who are guided by these principles would design a certain type of organization structure: a classical design.

Classical design's most important principles of organization are:

1. *Specialization of labor.* Work should be divided and subdivided to the highest possible degree consistent with economic efficiency.
2. *Unity of direction.* Jobs should be grouped according to function or process; that is, like jobs should be grouped.
3. *Centralization of authority.* Accountability for the use of authority is retained at the executive, or top management, level.
4. *Authority and responsibility.* A jobholder must have authority commensurate with job responsibility.
5. *Unity of command.* Each jobholder should report to one, and only one, superior.

The application of these principles results in highly specialized jobs, departments based on function, narrow spans of control, and centralized authority. Such organizations tend to be relatively "tall," with several layers of management through which communications and directions must pass. Taken together, bureaucratic and classical design theories describe the essential features of the classical organizational design.

[4]See Henri Fayol, *General and Industrial Management,* trans. C. Storrs (London: Sir Isaac Pitman & Sons, 1949), pp. 19–42, for the original statement of classical principles.

The five classical principles of organization are comparable to the five characteristics of the ideal type. Regardless of whether a manager follows the classical principles or the bureaucratic characteristics, the results will be the same. The organization structure will emphasize specialization of labor and centralized authority.

NEOCLASSICAL ORGANIZATION DESIGN

In a historical sense, neoclassical organization design is a reaction to classical design. Its characteristics include low complexity, low formalization, and low centralization. These characteristics describe organization structures in which jobs are relatively unspecialized, departments contain a heterogeneous mix of jobs, spans of control are wide, and authority is decentralized. Thus, neoclassical design can be viewed as the opposite of classical design.

Arguments supporting neoclassical design are based on two criticisms of classical design: (1) classical design is inherently flawed and (2) classical design is irrelevant in contemporary societies. Figure 7–2 outlines the neoclassical approach to organization design.

Classical Design's Inherent Flaws.   The inherent flaws of classical organization design were first noted in the famous Hawthorne studies, a series of experiments carried out at the Western Electric plant in Cicero, Illinois.[5] These studies were the basis for the contention that high specialization of labor and centralized authority underestimate the complexity of employees. Rather than being a passive and inert being dumbly performing assigned tasks, the employee is a unique, multifaceted person who seeks more than monetary rewards from work. The researchers at the Hawthorne plant found that workers were members of friendship groups that defined the level of output considered fair and equitable. These groups seemed to exert far greater influence on employees than their managers did, even though the groups had no authority to back up their influence.

Subsequent studies supported the conclusions of the Hawthorne studies. For example, one study focused on the relationship of rules and procedures to job behavior.[6] The study found instances where the effect of rules was to cause employees to follow them in robot-like fashion and to be unable to cope with instances not covered by the rules. The rules encouraged conforming rather than problem-solving behavior. A later study supported the idea that the primary effect of rules was to define minimal rather than optimal levels of behavior.[7]

Other writers take the position that neoclassical organization design is more compatible with the needs of individuals and that classical designs create inherent conflict. Chris Argyris, for example, believes that organizations designed according to classical and bureaucratic principles suppress the devel-

---

[5]Fritz J. Roethlisberger and W. H. Dickson, *Management and the Worker* (Cambridge, Mass.: Harvard University Press, 1939.)

[6]Robert K. Merton, "Bureaucratic Structure and Personality," *Social Forces* 18 (1940), pp. 560–68.

[7]Alvin W. Gouldner, *Patterns of Industrial Bureaucracy* (New York: Free Press, 1954).

FIGURE 7–2	Neoclassical Design Assumptions

Neoclassical design theory assumes that individual differences and situational characteristics are the principal determinants of organization design.

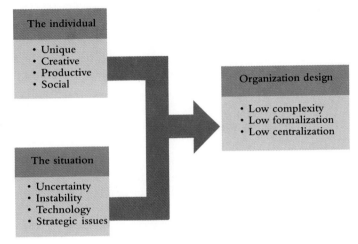

opment and growth of employees.[8] The use of rules and hierarchy to dominate subordinates can cause them to become passive, dependent, and noncreative. Such conditions are not congruent with the human needs for autonomy, self-expression, accomplishment, and advancement. Consequently, the organization forfeits a considerable portion of its human resources.

Contemporary Irrelevance of Classical Design. A considerable body of evidence supports the idea that classically designed organizations are not compatible with contemporary society. As noted earlier, classical designs gained in popularity during the early periods of industrialization and economic development (the late 1800s and early 1900s). That period of relative stable and predictable change gave way to one of instability and uncertainty. Today, advanced technology in communications, transportation, manufacturing processes, and medicine creates the need for organizations to be *adaptable* and *flexible* so that new ways of doing work can be quickly utilized.

A leading advocate of neoclassical design is Rensis Likert.[9] After considerable study, he proposed that in contemporary society neoclassical organizations utilize human and technical resources more fully than classical ones. Neoclassical theory emphasizes the importance of decentralized authority and nondirective, participative management behavior. Relatively wide spans of control and heterogeneous departments facilitate the interaction of multiple and diverse points of view. Consequently, as circumstance and technology

[8]Chris Argyris, *Personality and Organization* (New York: Harper & Row, 1975); more recently, Guy Benveniste, *Professionalizing the Organization: Reducing Bureaucracy to Enhance Effectiveness* (San Francisco: Jossey-Bass, 1987).

[9]Rensis Likert, *New Patterns of Management* (New York: McGraw-Hill, 1961); Rensis Likert, *The Human Organization* (New York: McGraw-Hill, 1967).

change, the organization is able to respond because of the diverse perspectives that can be brought to bear on any issue or problem it confronts.

The most ardent proponents of neoclassical design believe that even if the organization exists in a relatively stable environment, the neoclassical way is best. They contend that individuals have fuller and more satisfying worklives in neoclassical organizations, that neoclassical design is universally applicable, and that it is the best way to organize in modern society. They believe that neoclassical design is therefore superior to classical design.

CONTINGENCY APPROACH

An alternative point of view is that either classical or neoclassical can be the best way to organize, depending on the nature of such underlying factors as the organization's strategy, environment, and technology. The contingency approach to organization design is based on the idea that different organization designs serve different purposes. Classical organizations are more efficient and productive but less adaptive and flexible than neoclassical organizations. A particular organization—whether a business firm, government agency, hospital, university, or one unit within an organization—should be structured on the basis of whether it must be relatively (1) efficient and productive or (2) adaptive and flexible. The critical issue is to determine the circumstances that create the need to be one or the other type of organization.

Those who have contributed to the ideas of contingency design have suggested a number of circumstances, or variables, that influence the design decision. Among these variables are age of the organization, size of the organization, form of ownership, technology, environmental uncertainty, strategic choice, member (employee) needs, and current fashion.[10] There is evidence that older organizations, those that have been around awhile, are more complex, formalized, and centralized than younger ones. Also, researchers have noted the tendency of large organizations to be designed more along classical than neoclassical lines. No attempt will be made here to discuss each of these variables. Rather, we will analyze the three with the most apparent implications for management: technology, environment, and strategic choice.

TECHNOLOGY

Technology can be narrowly defined as "the manufacturing, as distinct from administrative or distributive, processes employed by manufacturing firms to convert inputs into outputs."[11] Alternately, it can be broadly defined as "the types and patterns of activity, equipment and material, and knowledge

---

[10]W. Alan Randolph and Gregory G. Dess, "The Congruence Perspective of Organization Design: A Conceptual Model and Multivariate Research Approach," *Academy of Management Review,* January 1984, pp. 114–27.

[11]Charles Perrow, "A Framework for the Comparative Analysis of Organizations," *American Sociological Review,* April 1967, p. 195. See Michael Withey, Richard L. Daft, and William H. Cooper, "Measures of Perrow's Work-Unit Technology: An Empirical Assessment and a New Scale," *Academy of Management Journal,* March 1983, pp. 45–63.

FIGURE 7–3	Technology and Organization Design

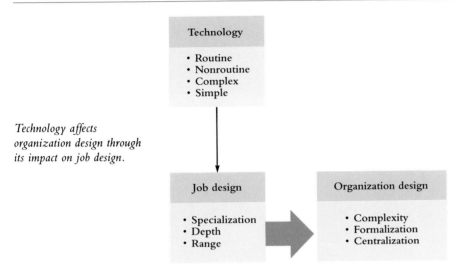

Technology affects organization design through its impact on job design.

or experience used to perform tasks."[12] Either way, it is obvious that performing any kind of work—whether making cars, shoes, or computers or serving clients, patients, customers, or students—involves technology. The technology can be machines or it can be knowledge.

The role of technology as a contingency variable is shown in Figure 7–3. There we see that technology affects the design of jobs, which in turn affects the design of organizations. The organization design, then, is contingent upon the state of technology that management incorporates in the design of individual jobs.

Interest in the relationship between technology and structure was stimulated by the studies of Joan Woodward.[13] In one study, Woodward classified technologies as unit, mass, or process production. *Unit production* referred to production to meet a customer's specific order. Here the product is developed after an order is received. The manufacture of custom-made shirts is an example of unit production technology. *Mass production* refers to the production of large quantities, such as on an assembly line. Zenith Corporation uses mass production technology to make television picture tubes. *Process production* refers to producing materials or goods on the basis of weight or volume. Processing 3 million barrels of oil or producing vats of paint at Sherwin-Williams are examples of process production.

Woodward found a strong relationship between performance and both organizational design and technology. The highest-performing organizations

[12]Denise M. Rousseau, "Assessment of Technology in Organizations: Closed versus Open Systems Approaches," *Academy of Management Review,* October 1979, p. 531.

[13]Joan Woodward, *Industrial Organization: Theory and Practice* (London: Oxford University Press, 1965). A recent study based on Woodward's research is reported in Frank M. Hull and Paul D. Collins, "High-Technology Batch Production: Woodward's Missing Type," *Academy of Management Journal,* December 1987, pp. 786–97.

Mass production at GM is now highly automated, as illustrated here by the use of robot welders.

with unit and process technologies had neoclassical characteristics. However, the highest-performing organizations with mass production technologies had the characteristics of classical structures. These findings are summarized in Figures 7–4 and 7–5.

The effects of unit and process manufacturing technology are jobs with low specialization, high depth, and high range. These jobs are best organized in a structure with relatively low complexity, formalization, and centralization. The rationale is that employees must have considerable latitude, discretion, and freedom of choice in the use of such technologies. Mass production, on the

FIGURE 7–4   Unit and Process Technology and Organization Design

Complex technologies such as unit and process manufacturing methods require complex jobs that must be managed through neoclassical organization designs.

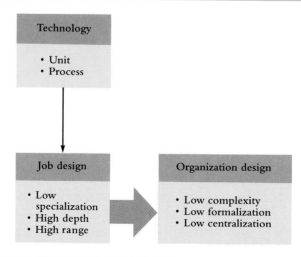

Technology
• Unit
• Process

Job design
• Low specialization
• High depth
• High range

Organization design
• Low complexity
• Low formalization
• Low centralization

FIGURE 7–5   Mass Production Technology and Organization Design

Simple technologies such as mass production manufacturing methods require relatively simple jobs that can be managed through classical organization designs.

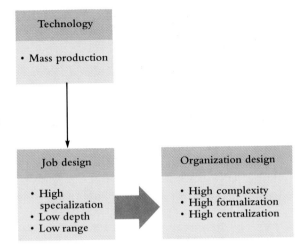

other hand, requires no such latitude on the part of employees, and accordingly a classical organization design fits the situation.

Woodward's findings are evidence that managers must consider the effects of technology on organization design. She encouraged managers to consider the role technology plays in influencing work behavior and to recognize that appropriate design decisions require consideration of technological complexities.[14] Woodward's research has resulted in three principles that suggest how technology influences organizational design:

1. The more complex the technology—going from a unit system to a more process system—the greater the number of managerial personnel and levels of management.
2. The more complex the technology, the larger the number of clerical and administrative personnel.
3. The span of control of first-line managers increases from unit production systems to mass production systems and then decreases from mass production systems to process production systems.

The successful firms in each technology category seem to employ the design characteristics suggested by the three principles. The idea that an organization design must be compatible with the technology it uses to achieve optimal performance is termed organization "fit." An effective organization fits its technological requirements, as suggested by the Management Focus on Honeywell's structure.

Woodward's research stimulated a great number of follow-up studies. Using various definitions and measurements, these studies have examined the

---

[14]Nancy M. Carter, "Computerization as a Predominate Technology: Its Influence on the Structure of Newspaper Organizations," *Academy of Management Journal,* June 1984, pp. 247–70.

MANAGEMENT FOCUS

Honeywell's Neoclassical Structure

In 1985, Honeywell, Inc.'s Armament Systems Division opened a new Defense Systems Group (DSG) plant in Joliet, Illinois. The organizational design of the plant has many of the features of neoclassical design theory that permit the company to cope with the demands of complex technology. A major characteristic of the plant is the relatively wide range and depth given to jobs. All employees participate in policy formulation and goal setting. There are no time clocks and no status hierarchy. Jobs are loosely defined, and employees are encouraged to take on any task they are competent to complete. Information and communications flow through-

out the organization to ensure that individuals are involved fully in the plant's activities and decisions. Many task groups exist that involve individuals from across specialties. In some instances, quality circles are used; in other instances, task forces and committees are used. The exact form of Honeywell's interpretation of neoclassical design varies from plant to plant and from unit to unit within each plant, but the Joliet plant design was a milestone in the company's experience with that approach.

Source: Rosabeth Moss Kanter and John D. Buck, "Reorganizing Part of Honeywell: From Strategy to Structure," *Organizational Dynamics*, Winter 1985, pp. 4–25.

relationship between technology and structure in a variety of settings.[15] As should be expected, the research findings are inconsistent. It is intuitively appealing to expect that routine technology (e.g., mass production techniques) is most efficiently used in organizations adhering to classical design. Likewise, nonroutine technology (e.g., unit and process techniques) should be compatible with neoclassical design. Yet, to demonstrate the validity of what seems obvious is often difficult, both in research and in practice.

The problem of verifying the exact relationship has been complicated by inconsistency in (1) definition and measurement of the two key concepts—technology and structure—and (2) selection of the level of analysis—individual, group, and organizational. Details of these rather technical issues are beyond the scope of this discussion. But it is important to acknowledge the conclusions drawn from a recent survey of the literature on technology structure. According to Fry's extensive review, routine technology (e.g., mass production, assembly lines) is associated with classical design, while nonroutine technology (unit, small batch, and process) is associated with neoclassical design.[16]

ENVIRONMENT

Every organization must operate within an environment. Competitors, suppliers, customers, creditors, and the government make demands on the

[15]Patricia L. Nemetz and Louis W. Fry, "Flexible Manufacturing Organizations: Implications for Strategy Formulation and Organization Design," *Academy of Management Review*, October 1988, pp. 627–38.

[16]Louis W. Fry, "Technology-Structure Research: Three Critical Issues," *Academy of Management Journal*, September 1982, pp. 532–52.

organization. And any of these external forces can have an effect on the organization's design.

The environment can be *stable;* that is, there is little unpredictable change. In a stable environment, customer tastes remain relatively unchanged. New technology is rare, and the need for innovative research to stay ahead of competition is minimal. For example, little has changed in the environments affecting the manufacturers of accordions, zippers, and book covers.

Another type of environment is referred to as *changing.* Changes in the competition's strategy and in market demands, advertising, personnel practices, and technology are rather frequent and somewhat expected. Automobile manufacturers operate in such a changing environment.

A *turbulent* environment exists when changes are unexpected and unpredictable. New competitive strategies, new laws, and new technology can create a turbulent condition. Electronics firms such as IBM, Hewlett-Packard, and Honeywell face unexpected environmental forces.

Matching an organizational design to the environment requires accurate managerial assessment of the environmental forces. Are they stable, changing, or turbulent? A group interested in organizational design studied 20 English and Scottish firms. Through analysis of interview responses, the researchers concluded that two types of organizational systems existed:[17] *Mechanistic* structures had the same characteristics as classical designs; *organic* structures were characteristic of neoclassical designs.

After completing its study, the group concluded that classical structures were optimal in stable environments and neoclassical structures were most suited to turbulent environments. The relationships between environmental characteristics and organizational designs are shown in Figure 7–6. Organizations in stable, placid environments do not confront unexpected events that employees must deal with. Consequently, jobs can be designed to include minimal depth and range and maximum specialization. But changing, turbulent environments create unexpected events and circumstances that cannot be anticipated. Jobs must be designed to give the employees considerable range and depth. The compatible organization design for such jobs is one with low complexity, formalism, and centralization: neoclassical design.

Following the lead of the English study group, an American team studied 10 companies in three industries: plastics, consumer foods, and standardized containers. The team was concerned with how to design departments in organizations faced with distinct environments.[18] Unlike other analysts of organization design, these researchers believed that the organization design decision could be made less complicated if managers consider it in terms of parts of the organization.

Designing Organizational Subunits.   The American team proposed that organizations should be designed with an emphasis on the different subunits, or departments, of the organization. Those departments facing

[17]Tom Burns and G. M. Stalker, *The Management of Innovation* (London: Tavistock Publications, 1961).

[18]Paul R. Lawrence and Jay W. Lorsch, *Organization and Environment* (Homewood, Ill.: Richard D. Irwin, 1967).

FIGURE 7–6   Environmental Characteristics and Organization Design

*Characteristics of the
organization's environment
can affect its design.*

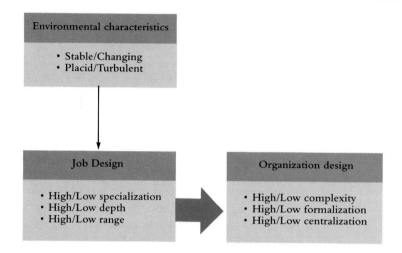

highly uncertain and turbulent environments should follow neoclassical design prescriptions; they should be relatively unspecialized, informal, and decentralized. On the other hand, a department facing certain and predictable environments should follow classical design ideas and be specialized, formalized, and centralized. The contingency viewpoint is reflected in the researchers' conclusion that "the internal functioning of organizations must be consistent with the organization task, technology, or external environment, and the needs of its members if the organization is to be effective."[19]

Environmental characteristics such as uncertainty, change, turbulence, and volatility affect the design of organizational subunits by defining the characteristics of the jobs.[20] The managerial implications of this effect include having a diverse range of organizational designs among departments within the same organization.

For example, a manufacturing firm typically must deal with three critical subenvironments; one is the *market* for its products. This subenvironment is the source of pressure to compete for customers through pricing, promotion, product development, and other marketing activities. The market subenvironment can vary from highly uncertain to highly certain. The degree of certainty will be influenced by (1) the reliability of available information on customer preferences and competitors' actions and (2) the rate of change in those preferences and actions. A relatively certain market subenvironment is one for which reliable information exists regarding stable customer preferences

[19]Ian C. MacMillan and Patricia E. Jones, "Designing Organizations to Compete," *Journal of Business Strategy,* Spring 1984, pp. 11–26; Balaji S. Chakravarthy and Peter Lorange, "Managing Strategic Adaptations: Options in Administrative System Design," *Interfaces,* January–February 1984, pp. 34–46.

[20]J. David Sherman and Howard L. Smith, "The Influence of Organizational Structure on Intrinsic versus Extrinsic Motivation," *Academy of Management Journal,* December 1984, pp. 877–84.

and competitors' actions. An uncertain market subenvironment would be the opposite: unreliable information and changing preferences and actions. Firms in plastics and computer manufacturing face relatively uncertain market subenvironments. Public utilities and container manufacturers face relatively certain market environments.

The environmental contingency model specifies that the organization design of departments must fit the demands of the department's subenvironment. Accordingly, the organization design of the marketing departments facing uncertain environments would take on characteristics of the neoclassical approach. Those facing certain environments would organize according to the classical approach. Thus, there is no best way to organize a marketing department.

Most manufacturing firms face two other important subenvironments. The *technical-economic* subenvironment includes the external sources of information and resources required in the production of the firm's product. This subenvironment can be certain or uncertain, depending on knowledge and rates of change in the technology of production and on the sources, types, and supplies of human, physical, and natural resources. Production departments must be organized to reflect the state of this subenvironment.

The third subenvironment is the *scientific* knowledge that firms use in their research and development departments. Research and development units are typically closer to neoclassical structures than any other department because of the relatively high degree of uncertainty in the scientific subenvironment compared to market and technical-economic subenvironments. After all, the fundamental characteristic of research is to reveal the unknown. But in some industries, the scientific subenvironment can be relatively stable and certain. For example, the container industry's scientific subenvironment is far less uncertain than the personal computer industry's.

The process of designing organization structure on a department by department basis can result in considerable design diversity within the same organization. The environmental perspective emphasizes fitting departments to subenvironments and then designing methods to coordinate the departments toward organizational objectives. The methods can range from strict applications of rules and procedures to the use of cross-departmental groups and individuals.

An organization with departments predominantly designed along classical lines could achieve interdepartmental coordination through rules, procedures, and policy. But an organization made up of departments designed according to neoclassical guidelines could achieve coordinated effort only through cross-departmental teams and individuals. Although we usually think of organizational subunits as different departments under the same roof, it is also possible to think of them as different offices in different countries. With this interpretation, we can understand Unilever's approach to organizing its international operations, as described in the Management Focus.

Unilever and other American corporations that compete abroad have reached the understanding that differences among countries and groups of countries mean differences in organization designs. In this context, the organizational design issue comes down to matching country and organizational differences.

MANAGEMENT FOCUS

Unilever Designs Its International Operations

Unilever has successfully competed in international markets by recognizing that the organizational structures of its international units must be designed to fit national differences. But the firm also understands that in some instances groups of nations have much in common, and units in these countries are organized in much the same manner. The key issue is to determine which national units should be organized as stand-alone, decentralized units with full capability to respond to local conditions and opportunities. Those units would be designed quite differently from those that draw on centralized support and staff functions. As a result of the understanding that each country presents different environmental demands, Unilever has abandoned the idea that each of its international units should be organized in the same manner.

Source: Christopher A. Bartlett and Sumantra Ghoshal, "Managing across Borders: New Organizational Responses," *Sloan Management Review*, Fall 1987, pp. 43–53.

Matrix Organization Design.   Organizations facing environmental uncertainty often cope with its demands by using a **matrix organization design.** In practical terms, the matrix design combines functional and product departmental bases.[21] American Cyanamid, Avco, Carborundum, Caterpillar Tractor, Hughes Aircraft, ITT, Monsanto Chemical, National Cash Register, Prudential Insurance, TRW, and Texas Instruments are only a few of the users of matrix design. Public sector users include public health and social service agencies.[22] Although the exact definition of matrix organization is not well established, most typically it is seen as a balanced compromise between functional and product organization, between departmentalization by process and by purpose.[23]

A matrix design, usually a classical organization design that adopts some of the features of a neoclassical design, is found in organizations that need both high efficiency and high responsiveness to environmental changes. It is often found in technical organizations in which technical, engineering, scientific, and other specialists are grouped together to work on special, complex projects.[24] The project may be either long run or short run, and needed specialists are borrowed from various departments of the organization. The critical point is that a rapid response to a changed circumstance is required.

---

[21]Jay R. Galbraith and Robert K. Kazanjian, "Organizing to Implement Strategies of Diversity and Globalization: The Role of Matrix Organizations," *Human Resource Management*, Spring 1986, pp. 37–54; Diane Krusko and Robert R. Cangemi, "The Utilization of Project Management in the Pharmaceutical Industry," *Journal of the Society of Research Administrators*, Summer 1987, pp. 17–24.

[22]Kenneth Knight, "Matrix Organization: A Review," *Journal of Management Studies*, May 1976, p. 111.

[23]Ibid., p. 114.

[24]Paul R. Lawrence, Harvey F. Kolodny, and Stanley M. Davis, "The Human Side of the Matrix," *Organizational Dynamics*, September 1977, p. 47.

FIGURE 7–7   Matrix Organization Design

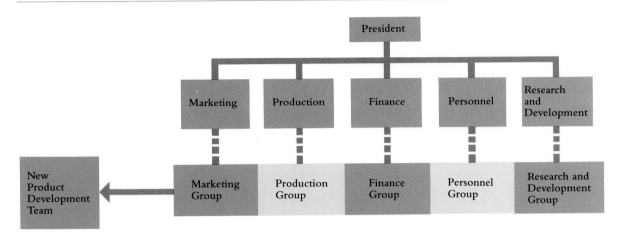

Matrix organization design can provide some of the advantages of both the classical and neoclassical designs but without some of the disadvantages.

Figure 7–7 illustrates a matrix organization.[25] Let us assume that the organization has just found out that its competition has introduced a new product far superior to the company's products. Management considers it critical that the firm respond as soon as possible with a similar or better product; otherwise, the firm could suffer irreversible adverse consequences. It has formed a new-product development team whose sole responsibility is to develop this product quickly. In Figure 7–7, the organization has changed a traditional organizational structure into a matrix organization to facilitate completion of the critical new product. A manager has been appointed to head the project and has provided necessary skilled personnel from each functional area to complete the job. The manager has authority over team personnel and is accountable for their performance.

In many cases, the personnel return to their respective functional units when a project is completed. Some organizations, especially those in highly technical industries, may have several project teams working on different tasks.

In a matrix organization, it is possible for an individual to have two managers. However, proponents believe that a matrix provides the organization with the flexibility to work on critical projects. Matrix organization brings together the specialized talent that is often necessary to complete a project. It preserves the strengths of the classical design while adding the advantages of the neoclassical design.

Organizations of all kinds implemented matrix structures during the 1970s. Yet, by the 1980s, reports circulated in the business literature that these same firms were abandoning it. Texas Instruments, Medtronic, and Xerox had been prominent proponents but were reported to be phasing out matrix. The most damaging criticism of matrix structures was that they stifled the very activity that they were to encourage: product and service development. The creation of

[25]The following discussion is based on Knight, "Matrix Organization."

dual reporting, authority, and evaluation systems and channels also required the creation of considerable paperwork and controls to maintain accountability. However, the only evidence that matrix organizations are ineffective was anecdotal, and no informed analysis has been available until recently.

A recently publicized study sought to document the extent to which matrix organizations had failed to live up to their promise.[26] Concentrating on firms that relied on product development for survival, researchers sent questionnaires to over 500 managers involved in the development of new products and services in the pharmaceutical, aerospace, computer and data processing, telecommunications, and medical instruments industries. Over three fourths of the respondents indicated that their companies had used matrix organization for product development projects, and 89 percent of the users stated that they would probably or definitely use matrix again. Those who responded that they would not use it again said it was because project and functional leaders were unable to coordinate their interrelated activities. But the vast majority of respondents believed that matrix structures are effective, particularly when the project leader is given sufficient authority to complete the job, including authority over all assigned functional personnel. Thus, in contrast to anecdotal information, this evidence indicates the enduring popularity of matrix structures.

STRATEGIC CHOICE

As noted in our discussion of the planning function, strategy involves the selection of missions and objectives and appropriate courses of action to achieve these objectives. Logically, several courses of action could be identified for any given objective, and for each alternative strategy an alternative organization design exists. Thus, the specific organization design should follow from a specified strategy.[27]

Generic Strategies. One influential writer in the field of corporate strategy states that corporations can adopt one of three general, or generic, strategies: cost leadership, differentiation, and focus.[28]

Cost leadership implies that the firm will outstrip its competition by being the low-cost producer. It will build efficiently scaled facilities, pursue cost control policies, avoid marginal customers, and generally be cost conscious in all areas of the business. In other words, the firm will emphasize efficiency and productivity. With lower costs, the firm can afford lower prices. And with lower prices, it can generate larger sales volumes. Two firms that have achieved notable success by striving for cost leadership are Briggs & Stratton and Lincoln Electric.

The organization design that facilitates overall cost leadership must be one that encourages efficiency and productivity. Classical design, with its emphasis on complexity, formalization, and centralization, fits this strategy.

[26]Erik W. Larson and David H. Gobeli, "Matrix Management: Contradictions and Insights," *California Management Review,* Summer 1987, pp. 126–38.

[27]Thomas J. Peters, "Strategy Follows Structure: Developing Distinctive Skills," *California Management Review,* Spring 1984, pp. 17–25.

[28]Michael E. Porter, *Competitive Strategy* (New York: Free Press, 1980), pp. 34–46.

Differentiation involves the firm in creating products that are perceived to be unique. The perception of uniqueness (differentiation) can be based on a variety of factors such as brand image, product features, customer service, and a dealer network. To be effective, differentiation requires creativity, basic research skill, strong marketing, and a reputation for quality. Firms such as Mercedes, Jenn-Air, Coleman, and Caterpillar have successfully pursued that strategy. Differentiation strategy does not imply that cost control is ignored, only that it is not the primary strategic consideration.

The emphasis on differentiation requires flexible response to changing customer preferences and perceptions. Organization designs that facilitate differentiation tend toward neoclassical characteristics, which encourage the freedom of action required for the differentiation strategy.

Focus, the third general strategy, involves achieving either cost leadership or differentiation or both in a particular segment of the market. Rather than competing throughout the market, the firm focuses on one segment. For example, Porter Paint attempts to serve the needs of the professional painter rather than the do-it-yourself customer. Thus, focus strategy implies a trade-off between market share and profitability. The compatible organization design implies a mix of both classical and neoclassical characteristics, because the firm can attempt both cost leadership and differentiation aimed at its segment.

Growth Strategies.   The contemporary impetus for the idea that structure should reflect strategy is the work of Alfred Chandler.[29] After studying the history of 70 of America's largest firms, Chandler concluded that organization structures follow the growth strategies of firms. He also found that growth strategies tend to follow a certain pattern. In their initial stage, firms are typically plants, sales offices, or warehouses in a single industry, at a single location, performing a single function such as manufacturing, sales, or warehousing. But they grow if successful, and their growth follows a fairly standard path through four stages:

1. *Volume expansion.* Firms manufacture, sell, or distribute more of their product or service to existing customers.
2. *Geographic expansion.* Firms continue to do what they have been doing but in a larger geographic area by means of field units.
3. *Vertical integration.* Firms either buy or create other functions. For example, manufacturers integrate backward by acquiring or creating sources of supply; they integrate forward by acquiring or creating sales and distribution functions.
4. *Product diversification.* Firms become involved in new industries through merger, acquisition, or creation (product development).

As a firm moves through each stage, it must change its organization structure. Figure 7–8 depicts the relationships suggested between growth strategy and organizational design.

---

[29]Alfred D. Chandler, *Strategy and Structure* (Cambridge, Mass.: MIT Press, 1962). Robert E. Hoskisson, "Multidivisional Structure and Performance: The Contingency of Diversification Strategy," *Academy of Management Journal,* December 1987, pp. 625–44, reports a recent study of the relationship between strategy and structure.

Figure 7–8   Strategic Choices and Organization Design

The growth strategy that managers choose requires an organization design appropriate to carry out that strategy.

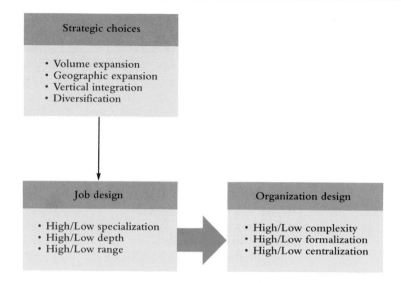

Initially, classical design is appropriate because volume expansion of a single product or service in a single industry stresses low unit cost (efficiency) and maximum resource utilization (production), with relatively low concern for response to change and uncertainty. But as the firm moves through the steps of geographic expansion and ultimately to product diversification, it becomes increasingly concerned about adaptability and flexibility, because it faces diverse and complex environments. Thus, the organization structures of highly diversified firms are characterized by product-based divisions and departments, decentralized authority, and relatively wide spans of control.

Many organizations, large and small, face the issue of managing growth without stifling the sources of the growth. For example, Apogee Enterprise, a leading manufacturer of glass, windows, and curtain walling, has annual sales in excess of $300 million, 150 profit centers, 13 operating units, and 4 divisions. The company manages this complex organization with a headquarters staff of only 11 people. Its philosophy and practice emphasize decentralization and the delegation of authority. Each division and operating unit handles its own staff functions such as marketing, public relations, legal affairs, and human resources. The idea is to develop in profit center managers the attitudes that they are managing their own businesses and that they should act independent of headquarters.[30]

Recent studies bear out the increasing use of a divisional organization form by companies that have diversified into related and unrelated products. One study of Fortune 500 firms found a steady movement toward product-based,

[30]Anthony J. Rutigliano, "Apogee Lets Managers Grow Their Own Businesses," *Management Review,* September 1987, pp. 28–33; Marlene C. Piturro, "Decentralizing: Rebuilding the Corporation," *Management Review,* August 1988, pp. 31–34.

divisional forms of organization.[31] But there is some question whether such divisional structures always follow neoclassical design principles.[32] There is no doubt that organizations such as Philip Morris, which consists of divisions producing and marketing products as diverse as beer, cigarettes, and soft drinks, are more complex than General Motors, whose divisions produce and market different makes of trucks and automobiles.[33]

The idea that organization design should change to reflect the organization's strategic choice implies a growth-oriented strategy and that managers will know the need for changing the structure.[34] This orientation to change and knowing, called a *process approach* to organization design, places its emphasis on how and why an organization moves from one design to another.[35] Implicit in the strategic choice approach is the assumption that managers know that they should alter the organization design as they change the firm's strategy from volume expansion to product diversification.

But the same could be said for other approaches to organization design. Both the technology and the environment approaches assume that managers can know what design to use in a particular situation. The simpler "one best way" approaches also recognize the importance of competent managers. Nevertheless, the proponents of contingency approaches often present their ideas without giving explicit attention to the role of the organization's management, particularly the psychological traits of managers.

Managerial decision making plays a key role in organizational design.[36] In fact, much that has been said in this chapter can be summarized in the idea that structure follows technology, environmental demands, and strategy. Maximum performance is achieved when structure fits the relevant contingencies. Managerial strategy involves the choice of what products and services the organization will supply to specific customers and markets. Thus, a manager who decides to supply a single product to a specific set of customers can be expected to design a far simpler organizational structure than a manager of a highly diversified company serving multiple markets with multiple products and services.

Organizational design remains an important issue in the management of organizational behavior and effectiveness. As the 1990s begin, the issue has become even more important. Strategies that have been successful in the past are proving ineffectual in the face of new international competition, techno-

---

[31]Richard P. Rumelt, *Strategy, Structure, and Economic Performance* (Cambridge, Mass.: Division of Research, Graduate School of Business Administration, Harvard University, 1974).

[32]Peter H. Grinyer and Masoud Yasai-Ardekani, "Dimensions of Organizational Structure: A Critical Replication," *Academy of Management Journal,* September 1980, pp. 405–21.

[33]Charles W. L. Hill and Robert E. Hoskisson, "Strategy and Structure in the Multiplant Firm," *Academy of Management Review,* April 1987, pp. 331–41.

[34]Gregory G. Dess and Nancy K. Origer, "Environment, Structure, and Consensus in Strategy Formulation: A Conceptual Formulation," *Academy of Management Review,* April 1987, pp. 313–30.

[35]Danny Miller, Cornelia Droge, and Jean-Marie Toulouse, "Strategic Process and Content as Moderators between Organizational Context and Structure," *Academy of Management Journal,* September 1988, pp. 544–69.

[36]James W. Frederickson, "The Strategic Decision Process and Organizational Structure," *Academy of Management Review,* April 1986, pp. 280–97.

logical change, and shifting patterns of industrial development. As organizations experiment with new strategies, they will be forced to experiment with new organizational designs. And these designs will more closely resemble neoclassical than classical designs.[37]

SUMMARY OF KEY POINTS

- Designing or redesigning an organization involves choosing from among a number of alternatives. These alternative designs can be classified as either universalistic or contingency.

- Universalistic designs are based on the assumption that there is one best way to organize, regardless of the situation. The best way can be either a classical design (complexity, formalism, and centralization) or neoclassical (simplicity, informalism, and decentralization).

- Classical design, with its high degree of specialization (complexity), written rules and policies (formalism), and low delegation of authority (centralization), emphasizes maximum production and efficiency.

- Neoclassical design, with its low degree of specialization (simplicity), unwritten but implicit rules and policies (informalism), and high delegation of authority (decentralization), emphasizes maximum flexibility, adaptability, and employee satisfaction.

- The alternative to the universalistic approach is the contingency approach. Contingency designs are based on the assumption that the best way to organize depends on the situation or setting. The best design can tend toward either the classical or the neoclassical.

- The contingency approach is more widely accepted in contemporary management theory and practice. However, there is little consensus among its proponents as to what specific factor or set of factors determines which organization design is preferable.

- One factor many believe to be important is technology. According to this view, firms using either job order or process technology will be more effective and productive if their designs tend toward neoclassical characteristics. Firms using mass production technology will benefit from classical characteristics.

- A second factor often linked to organization design is environmental uncertainty. This body of opinion notes that organizations facing uncertain environments require flexibility and adaptability to survive and therefore should use neoclassical designs. In contrast, firms facing certain environments must seek high levels of production and efficiency; thus, classical design is appropriate.

- The environmental contingency approach encourages managers to design the total organization in terms of departmental structures. According to this perspective, the organization's environment actually consists of subenvironments, and the organization must design departments to deal with the demands and conditions inherent to those subenvironments.

- A final influential contingency factor is strategic choice. According to this perspective, a firm's organization design should correspond to the requirements of its overall strategy. Cost leadership strategy, for example, calls for classical design; production differentiation and/or diversification require neoclassical design.

[37]Tom Peters, "Restoring American Competitiveness: Looking for New Models of Organizations," *Academy of Management Executive,* May 1988, pp. 103–9.

DISCUSSION AND REVIEW QUESTIONS

1. Contrast the main arguments of universalistic and contingency approaches to organization design. Which of the two approaches is easier to implement in practice? Explain.

2. Contrast the main features of classical and neoclassical organization designs.

3. Compare what you believe to be the popular meaning of the term *bureaucracy* with the meaning in management literature. Why do *bureaucracy* and *bureaucratic* have negative connotations?

4. Explain why an organization with classical design characteristics is likely to be more efficient and productive but less flexible and adaptable than an organization with neoclassical design characteristics.

5. Compare two organizations that you know either through employment or membership. Describe them in terms of classical and neoclassical design characteristics. What explains the differences you find in the two organizations?

6. What are the bases for the opinion that technology is an important contingency variable? Do you believe

that technology is the primary factor to be considered when management designs a structure? Explain.

7. What are the relevant subenvironments of business firms? Of hospitals? Of universities? What subunits, or departments, exist in typical business firms, hospitals, and universities to deal with those subenvironments?

8. What are the bases for the opinion that environmental uncertainty is an important contingency variable? Do you believe that environmental uncertainty is the primary factor to be considered when management designs a structure? Explain.

9. What are the bases for the opinion that strategy is an important contingency variable? Do you believe that strategy is the primary factor to be considered when management designs a structure? Explain.

10. Develop an explanation of the important contingency variables that would integrate the technology, environmental, and strategic choice points of view.

ADDITIONAL REFERENCES

Barley, S. R. "Technology as an Occasion for Structuring: Evidence from Observations of CT Scanners and the Social Order of Radiology Departments." *Administrative Science Quarterly,* March 1986, pp. 78–108.

Birnbaum, P. H., and **Gilbert Y. Y. Wong.** "Organizational Structure of Multinational Banks in Hong Kong from a Culture-Free Prespective." *Administrative Science Quarterly,* June 1985, pp. 262–77.

Bozeman, B., and **M. Crow.** "Organization Theory and State Government Structures: Are There Lessons Worth Learning?" *State Government,* 1986, pp. 144–51.

Daniels, J. D.; R. A. Pitts; and **M. J. Tretter.** "Strategy and Structure of U.S. Multinationals: An Exploratory Study." *Academy of Management Journal,* June 1984, pp. 292–307.

Dess, G. G., and **D. W. Beard.** "Dimensions of Organizational Task Environments." *Administrative Science Quarterly,* March 1984, pp. 52–73.

Donaldson, L. "Organization Design and the Life-Cycle of Products." *Journal of Management Studies,* 1985, pp. 25–37.

Ettlie, J. E. *Taking Charge of Manufacturing: How Companies Are Combining Technological and Organizational*

Innovation to Compete Successfully. San Francisco: Jossey-Bass, 1988.

Jelinek, M., and **M. C. Burstein.** "The Production Administrative Structure: A Paradigm for Strategic Fit." *Academy of Management Review,* April 1982, pp. 242–51.

Keats, B. A., and **M. A. Hitt.** "A Causal Model of Linkages among Environmental Dimensions, Macro-Organizational Characteristics and Performance." *Academy of Management Journal,* September 1988, pp. 570–98.

Kralewski, J. E.; L. Pitt; and **D. Shatin.** "Structural Characteristics of Medical Group Practices." *Administrative Science Quarterly,* March 1985, pp. 34–45.

Larsson, R., and **D. E. Bowen.** "Organization and Customer: Managing Design and Coordination of Services." *Academy of Management Review,* April 1989, pp. 213–33.

Lawler, E. E., III. "Substitutes for Hierarchy." *Organizational Dynamics,* Summer 1988, pp. 4–15.

Mansfield, R. *Company Strategy and Organizational Design.* New York: St. Martin's Press, 1986.

Mills, P. K., and **D. J. Moberg.** "Perspectives on the Technology of Service Organizations." *Academy of Management Review,* July 1982, pp. 467–78.

Pearce, J. A., II, and **F. R. David.** "A Social Network Approach to Organization Design—Performance." *Academy of Management Review,* July 1983, pp. 436–44.

Routamaa, V. "Organizational Structuring: An Empirical Analysis of the Relationships and Dimensions of Structures in Certain Finnish Companies." *Journal of Management Studies,* 1985, pp. 498–22.

Schoorman, F. D., and **B. Schneider.** *Facilitating Work Effectiveness.* Lexington, Mass.: Lexington Books, 1988.

CASE 7–1   Organization Design of B. F. Goodrich's R&D

The research and development (R&D) effort at B. F. Goodrich is vital for the long-run survival of the firm, just as it is in most industrial organizations. B. F. Goodrich believes that the traditional role of R&D, to develop *new* products and processes, is changing to one of protecting and improving the *current* products and lines of business. R&D effort is directed toward cutting product costs, improving productivity, and responding to safety, health, and environmental problems.

The orientation away from "blue-sky" research to "applied" research requires the research, scientific, and technical personnel in R&D units to be very much involved in the company. To obtain such commitment and involvement, B. F. Goodrich has adopted a number of organization design practices intended to provide a maximally productive internal organization for R&D and to ensure that R&D is properly integrated with the remainder of the organization.

The organization design of R&D units stresses the development of explicit objectives for each unit and for each individual. Once the objectives are developed, individuals have considerable freedom to select how they will achieve those objectives. The job design provides considerable depth and range for scientists to pursue objectives, using the research and technical methods they desire.

A second organization design feature is open communication channels, both upward and downward. Managers and subordinates alike discuss issues and problems prior to selecting a solution. These channels stress informal discussions that are issue directed. The units confront and resolve many nagging personnel and procedural problems before they become major issues. B. F. Goodrich believes that open communications are essential for maintaining the creative environment necessary for fruitful R&D work.

The relationship between R&D and other corporate units also must be designed. The company refers to these relationships as "interfaces" and is strongly concerned about designing organizational practices that reduce conflict between R&D and other units. For example, conflict exists between R&D and manufacturing. One cause of the conflict is the purposes of the two units. Manufacturing's primary objective is to establish a production line that produces continuously a product with specified quality and quantity. Once that line is in place and fine-tuned, manufacturing personnel resist efforts to change it. But it is the purpose of R&D to do precisely that: to change the line when a technical breakthrough is developed. Changing the line to adopt a potentially unsuccessful technology is bound to cause disruption, and manufacturing managers will resist R&D efforts.

To understand B. F. Goodrich's approach to integrating R&D into the line organization, one must understand its overall structure. The company consists of three groups: the Chemical Group, an Engineered Systems Group, and the Tire Group. In addition, there are corporate staff units, including a corporate R&D unit. The company's first integrative practice is to appoint a senior vice president for operations in each of these groups. Reporting to this official are managers of production, manufacturing services, technical, and quality control units. Thus, within each group, there is *one* executive responsible for all production-related issues, including the application of new manufacturing methods developed by research efforts.

The second practice involves the reporting relationship of R&D staff. For example, tire development engineers at the plant level *and* tire research personnel at the corporate-level units all report to the vice president for tire R&D (who in turn reports to the senior vice president for tire operations). This organization design practice focuses all research and development activities for tires under one manager. The arrangement not only accelerates the adoption of new technology but avoids some of the conflict between tire research and tire development as well. The former is concerned with developing prototypes of new tire design; the latter is responsible for getting them into production.

QUESTIONS FOR ANALYSIS

1. Which approach to organization design does B. F. Goodrich seem to be following in managing its R&D effort? Explain.
2. What other organizational units are likely to have conflicting objectives, and how can organization design practices minimize these conflicts?
3. What alternative design practices could B. F. Goodrich consider?

CASE 7–2   Federal Express Strives for a Lean Organization

Federal Express specializes in transporting high-priority business goods and documents throughout the United States and abroad. It employs 42,000 individuals and operates facilities in more than 300 U.S. cities and 15 foreign cities. The company has stated that one of its key strategic objectives is to maintain a lean organization structure. This objective reflects Chief Executive Officer Frederick W. Smith's concern that an organization can get out of control in a fast-growth environment such as the one in which Federal Express competes. The responsibility for maintaining the lean organization is delegated to all line managers, who receive support from the organization's planning department, located in the personnel division. To develop strategies that

Source: William H. Wagel, "Keeping the Organization Lean at Federal Express," *Personnel*, March 1987, pp. 4–12.

would achieve the objective, it was necessary to first define exactly what was meant by the term *lean organization*.

After an extensive review of managerial literature, the planning department manager found that the concept usually included three dimensions: the number of managerial levels, the span of control, and certain work force statistics that related the number of managers to types of nonmanagerial employees. When these dimensions are applied to Federal Express, it is found that the maximum number of managerial levels is five. The manager of corporate planning believes that five levels of management are well within the limits implied by lean organization. The average span of control for all managers in Federal Express is 1:12. The average span is calculated by dividing the number of nonmanagement employees by the number of managers and 12 is the quotient. But since it is an average, managers in the company may have more or less than 12. The planning department manager believes the span of control is consistent with a lean organization. The manager also believes that its work force statistics are consistent and cites as evidence its 2:1 staff officers per $1 million in sales compared to an average of 5 for other service organizations.

Federal Express management believes that it has established the correct definition of a lean organization. The many studies undertaken by the corporate planning department indicate that the organization has achieved and maintained just such an organization structure despite the pressures of growth to add staff and managers. As it looks to the future, management wants to be sure that its policies perpetuate and reinforce the objective of remaining a lean organization.

The challenge to maintain a lean organization is formidable in a growth-oriented firm. Federal Express responded to that challenge by implementing a number of techniques and practices. Some of these include:

1. The company developed an awareness campaign consisting of presentations at staff meetings, articles in the employee newsletter, and the creation of a logo featuring a belt-tightening organization.
2. It communicates with other, like-minded firms to share information on policies and techniques that worked for them in efforts to keep a lean organization.
3. Federal Express has created performance evaluation systems that reward both managerial and nonmanagerial employees for ideas that contribute to a lean organization.
4. The company has implemented a process for reviewing all requests for additional staff and managerial positions. The process involves a stringent and detailed analysis of all alternatives to an additional position, including combining tasks, technology, and external contracting.

In addition to these proven practices, Federal Express is considering other, somewhat nontraditional techniques:

1. The company is examining the applicability of self-managed work groups that together would do many of the first-line managerial tasks, such as scheduling, training, and performance appraisal. One potential effect of self-managed work groups is even wider spans of control because fewer managers are required.

2. Group incentives are being evaluated as a way to make bonuses available to members of high-performing groups. Since the bonus would be paid to the group and distributed on a per-person basis, this technique would encourage groups to forgo hiring additional personnel because that would dilute each individual's share.
3. The company is turning to scientific management practices to discover sources of productivity increases in the work flow processes. Work simplification has the effect of reducing the demand for additional employees.
4. The company is considering staffing short-term functions in new departments by hiring temporary employees with the understanding that the employee will be reassigned at a definite future date. Through this variation of sunset laws, all new positions in new departments must be justified.

Federal Express balances its commitment to a lean organization against its commitment to avoiding layoffs. Thus, the effort to achieve the objective of a lean organization must be ongoing and constant, with every personnel action seen as an opportunity to further that end.

QUESTIONS FOR ANALYSIS

1. What do you think of Federal Express's interpretation of the term *lean organization?* Does it seem that the company is practicing a modern-day version of managing by principles of organization? Explain.
2. What are some of the potential outcomes associated with downsizing an organization? Are all these outcomes good for Federal Express?
3. What technological, environmental, and strategic factors influenced Federal Express's decision?

EXPERIENTIAL EXERCISE

ORGANIZATIONAL DESIGN IN THE CAMPUS SETTING

Purpose

This exercise enables students to use certain theories of organization design to describe the organizational design of units that make up their college or university.

The Exercise in Class

The instructor will divide the class into groups of 8 to 10 students. Each group will:

1. Select a particular organizational unit found on campus. The unit can be an academic department, division, or college. Or it can be an administrative, maintenance, or athletic unit. Your group should select the unit for which it can obtain the greatest amount of information.

2. Select one of the contingency theories of organization design discussed in the text (technology, environmental uncertainty, and strategic choice).

3. Use the theory to describe and analyze the unit's organizational design. Emphasize the points of difference between what the theory predicts and what actually exists. Also suggest reasons for the differences.

4. Present the group's analysis to the class, examining the extent to which the organizational structure contributes to or distracts from the unit's effectiveness.

The Learning Message

This exercise is very effective at reinforcing students' understanding of the purposes, strengths, and limitations of theory in the context of management.

8

THE CONTROLLING FUNCTION

LEARNING OBJECTIVES

After completing Chapter 8, you should be able to:

Define
the controlling function in terms of the three features of effective control.

Describe
representative standards, information, and corrective action for general methods

Discuss
the bases for distinguishing among preliminary, concurrent, and feedback control methods.

Compare
the control techniques designed to maintain quality of inputs and those designed to maintain quality of outputs.

Identify
the different standards that can be used to assess potential profitability of capital investments.

Japan's Approach to Quality Is Really
an American Approach

Japan, in the years following World War II, had a worldwide reputation for producing shoddy goods. In 1950, a group of Japanese leaders invited Dr. W. Edwards Deming, a statistician with the U.S. Department of Agriculture, to teach Japanese managers and engineers how to improve their product quality. Deming accepted the invitation, and he lectured in Japan for years, teaching his approach to quality control. His message: Establish quality as a top corporate objective. Approach quality control not by inspection at the end of the production line but by building quality into the manufacturing process. Make quality everyone's responsibility. Japan listened to Dr. Deming.

Today, many consider Deming to be the father of Japan's quality achievements. After years of obscurity in the United States, the 85-year-old quality control expert is in high demand. Campbell Soup, General Motors, the U.S. government, and many other organizations now gladly pay $10,000 per day for his services and to learn his approach to quality control.

Statistical process quality control is at the core of Deming's approach. In this approach, quality is built into the manufacturing process by studying each point in the process, identifying problem areas, and then correcting them one by one. The approach requires sophisticated statistical analysis.

Whether Deming's methods are used or not, the management function of control is a critical one. All effective management control has three parts: standards, information, and corrective action. This chapter reviews a number of management control methods in terms of these three parts.

Source: Adapted from Barbara Ross, "W. Edwards Deming: Shogun of Quality Control,"
Magazine for Financial Executives, February 1986, pp. 25–31; Jeremy Main, "Under the Spell of Quality Gurus,"
Fortune, August 18, 1986, pp. 31ff.

The third management function, the **controlling function**, includes *all activities the manager undertakes in attempting to ensure that actual results conform to planned results.*[1] In this chapter, the controlling function is presented in terms of three primary topics. First, we describe the conditions that determine the effectiveness of the controlling function. Managerial control is effective when *standards* can be established for the variables that are to be controlled, when *information* is available to measure the established standards, and when managers can take *corrective action* whenever the variable deviates from its desired state, or standard. Second, we will provide a basis for classifying and understanding managerial control procedures. This classification scheme is then used to discuss the third topic: managerial control procedures. Managers utilize a number of control procedures, and these *practical* applications are emphasized in this chapter.

Standards are derived from—and have many characteristics of—objectives. Standards are targets. To be effective, they must be stated clearly and related logically to the objectives of the unit. Standards are the criteria against which future, current, or past actions are compared. They are measured in a variety of ways, including physical, monetary, quantitative, and qualitative terms. The various forms that standards can take will be made clear in subsequent discussions of control methods.

Managers must provide information that reports actual performance and permits comparison of the performance against standards. Such information is most easily acquired for activities that produce specific and concrete results; for example, production and sales activities have results that are easily identifiable and for which information is readily obtainable. The performance of legal departments, research and development (R&D) departments, and human resource departments, however, is quite difficult to control because the outcomes of such activities are hard to measure.

Managerial actions to correct deviations depend on the discovery of the need for action and the ability to implement the desired action.[2] People responsible for taking corrective steps must know that they are indeed responsible and that they have the assigned authority to take action. Unless managers' job and position descriptions include specific statements clearly delineating these two requirements, the control function will fall short of its objective.

In many organizations, responsibility and authority for corrective action often are ambiguous.[3] Numerous organizations consist of so many interdependent units that corrective action often must be taken by individuals who lack the delegated authority but who must nonetheless influence others to accept solutions.

In summary, the control function involves the implementation of methods that provide answers to three basic questions: What are the planned and

---

[1]For other definitions of management control, see Kenneth A. Merchant, *Control in Business Organizations* (Marshfield, Mass.: Pitman Publishing, 1985); Robert J. Mockler, *The Management Control Process* (Englewood Cliffs, N.J.: Prentice-Hall, 1972).

[2]Richard L. Daft and Norman B. Macintosh, "The Nature and Use of Formal Control Systems for Management Control and Strategy Implementation," *Journal of Management*, Spring 1984, pp. 43–66.

[3]Michel Lebas and Jane Weigenstein, "Management Control: The Role of Rules, Markets, and Culture," *Journal of Management Studies*, May 1986, pp. 259–72.

MANAGEMENT FOCUS

Same Plan but Tighter Controls for Sharper Image

The Sharper Image Corporation is a marketer of adult toys, which it sells through catalogs and in over 60 stores. Just a few years ago, the company's growth was outstanding. Unfortunately, 1988 profits were off about 20 percent. The problem seems to be twofold—one part strategy, the other part management controls.

On the strategy issue, competitors (including department stores) have been copying the company's strategy with some success, the result being that Sharper Image no longer enjoys the clear lead it used to. However, the company has no plans to change its strategy. Some experts laugh at such items as a $3,800 suit of armor that the company sells. However, management states that such items are only novelties to get people into the store. The company's real money makers are such basics as briefcases, cordless phones, and radios.

On the issue of tighter controls, however, management does agree that change is required. The founder can no longer do everything himself, and the company needs stronger financial management, which is not his strength. The declines in 1988 were greater than expected. Margins fell because of unfavorable exchange rates on items purchased from the Far East and because of overreliance on low-margin electronic gear. "We were overconfident and loose in our controls," the founder admitted.

Source: Adapted from "The Sharper Image May Need to Refocus," *Business Week*, November 21, 1988, p. 84.

expected results? By what means can the actual results be compared to planned results? What corrective action is appropriate from which authorized person? The Management Focus on the Sharper Image Corporation provides an excellent example of the relationship between the management functions of planning and control.

THREE TYPES OF CONTROL

Figure 8–1 describes the three types of managerial control, which are based on the focus of the control.[4] They are preliminary control, concurrent control, and feedback control.

Preliminary control focuses on preventing deviations in the quality and quantity of resources used in the organization. Human resources must meet the job requirements as defined by the organization: Employees must have the physical and intellectual capabilities to perform assigned tasks.[5] The materials

[4]In this section, we identify feedback control as a separate type. Many students will recognize that feedback also can be viewed as part of the broader concept of control insofar as it refers to the information reported to the manager. Also see Peter Lorange, M. F. S. Morton, and S. Goshal, *Strategic Control* (St. Paul, Minn.: West Publishing, 1985).

[5]Preliminary control of human resources is one element of personnel management. See John M. Ivancevich and William Glueck, *Foundations of Personnel*, 4th ed. (Homewood, Ill. Richard D. Irwin, 1989).

FIGURE 8–1   The Controlling Function

Control methods focus on specific elements of the system, either inputs, processes, or outputs.

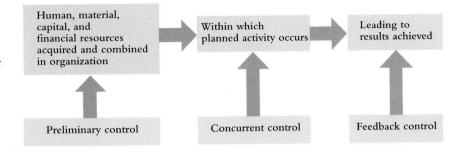

must meet acceptable levels of quality and must be available at the proper time and place. In addition, capital must be on hand to ensure an adequate supply of plant and equipment. Finally, financial resources must be available in the right amounts and at the right times. Methods that enable management to implement preliminary control are described later in this chapter.

Concurrent control monitors ongoing operations to ensure that objectives are pursued. The standards guiding ongoing activity are derived from job descriptions and from policies resulting from the planning function. Concurrent control is implemented primarily by the supervisory activities of managers. Through personal, on-the-spot observation, they determine whether the work of others is proceeding in the manner defined by policies and

Flight controllers in Houston witness the landing of the space shuttle Discovery, ensuring that actual results conform to planned results.

FIGURE 8–2   Simple Feedback Control System

Feedback control systems are self-correcting.

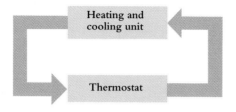

---

procedures.[6] Delegation of authority provides managers with the power to use financial and nonfinancial incentives to affect concurrent control.

Feedback control methods focus on end results. Corrective action is directed at improving either the resource acquisition process or the actual operations. This type of control derives its name from the fact that *historical* results guide *future* actions. An illustration of feedback control (see Figure 8–2) is a thermostat, which automatically regulates the temperature of a room. Since the thermostat maintains the preset temperature by constantly monitoring the actual temperature, future results (temperature) are directly and continually determined by historical results (again, temperature). The feedback methods employed in business include budgets, standard costs, financial statements, quality control, and performance evaluation.

In the three types of control, examine the *focus* of corrective action. As shown in Figure 8–3, preliminary control methods are based on information that measures some attribute or characteristic of resources; the focus of corrective action is in turn directed at the resources. That is, the variable measured is the variable acted upon. Similarly, concurrent control methods are based on information related to some activity, and activity is then acted upon. However, the focus of corrective action associated with feedback control is not that which is measured—results. Rather, resources and activity are acted upon.[7]

This distinction between preliminary, concurrent, and feedback control permits classification of some of the more widely used control techniques, as shown in Table 8–1. The 10 techniques are presented in the remainder of this chapter, and the emphasis will be on standards, information, and corrective action as appropriate for each technique.[8]

PRELIMINARY CONTROL

Preliminary control procedures include all managerial efforts to increase the probability that actual results will compare favorably with planned results.

[6]Lawrence L. Steinmetz and H. Ralph Todd, Jr., *First-Line Management*, 3rd ed. (Homewood, Ill.: Richard D. Irwin, 1986).

[7]Stephen G. Green and M. Ann Welsh, "Cybernetics and Dependence: Reframing the Control Concept," *Academy of Management Review*, April 1988, pp. 287–301.

[8]See Kiyoshi Suzaki, *The New Manufacturing Challenge: Techniques for Continuous Improvement* (New York: Free Press, 1987). The theme of this work is that control is an ongoing and continuing process.

FIGURE 8–3   The Three Types of Control as Distinguished by Focus of Corrective Action

The focus of corrective action may not always be the variable that is measured.

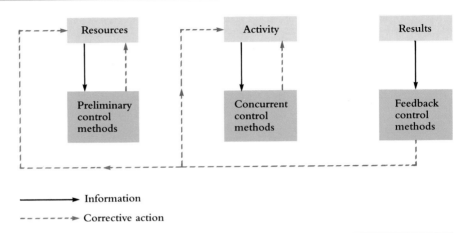

From this perspective, policies are important means for implementing preliminary control, since policies are guidelines for future action. Yet, it is vital to distinguish between *setting* policies and *implementing* them.[9] Setting policy is included in the planning function, whereas implementing policy is a part of the control function.[10] Similarly, job descriptions are aspects of the control function, since they predetermine the activity of the jobholder.[11] At the same time, however, it is necessary to distinguish between *defining* and *staffing* the task structure. Defining jobs is part of the organizing function; staffing them is part of the controlling function.

HUMAN RESOURCES: SELECTION AND STAFFING

The organizing function defines the job requirements and predetermines the skill requirements of the jobholders. These requirements vary in degree of specificity, depending on the nature of the task. At the shop level, the skill requirements can be specified in terms of physical attributes and manual dexterity. On the other hand, the job requirements of management and staff personnel are more difficult to define in terms of concrete measurements.[12]

Preliminary control is achieved through procedures that include the selection and placement of managerial and nonmanagerial personnel.[13] We should

[9]Peter Lorange and Declan Murphy, "Considerations in Implementing Strategic Control," *Journal of Business Strategy*, Spring 1984, pp. 27–35.

[10]George Schreyogg and Horst Steinman, "Strategic Control: A New Perspective," *Academy of Management Review*, January 1987, pp. 91–103.

[11]See Luis R. Gomez-Mejia, Henry Tosi, and Timothy Hinkin, "Managerial Control, Performance, and Executive Compensation," *Academy of Management Journal*, March 1987, pp. 51–170.

[12]For a related discussion, see Richard E. Walton, "From Control to Commitment in the Workplace," *Harvard Business Review*, March–April 1985, pp. 76–84.

[13]Ivancevich and Glueck, *Foundations of Personnel*, 4th ed., chap. 2.

	Types of Control	Control Techniques
	Preliminary	Selection and placement.
		Staffing.
		Materials inspection.
Managers have many control techniques available by which to take corrective action.		Capital budgeting.
		Financial budgeting.
	Concurrent	Direction.
	Feedback	Financial statement analysis.
		Standard cost analysis.
		Quality control procedures.
		Employee performance evaluation.

TABLE 8–1   Control Types and Techniques

distinguish between procedures designed to obtain qualified subordinate managers (staffing) and those designed to obtain qualified nonmanagers and operatives (selection and placement). Although basic procedures and objectives are essentially the same, the distinction is important because managerial competence is a fundamental determinant of the organization's success.

Candidates for positions must be recruited from inside or outside the firm, and the most promising applicants must be selected from the list of contenders, based on the matching of an applicant's skills and personal characteristics to the job requirements. The successful candidate must be trained in methods and procedures appropriate for the job. Most organizations have elaborate procedures for providing training on a continual basis. The Management Focus indicates that careful attention to preliminary control of human resources is also important to service companies such as airlines, hotels, financial institutions, and health care organizations.

MATERIALS

The raw material that is converted into a finished product must conform to standards of quality.[14] At the same time, a sufficient inventory must be maintained to ensure a continuous flow to meet customer demands. The techniques of inventory control are discussed in a later chapter; at this point, we are only concerned with the quality of incoming materials.

In recent years, numerous methods to control the quality of materials have been devised that use statistical sampling—inspection of samples rather than of the entire lot. These methods are less costly in terms of inspection time, but there is the risk of accepting defective material if the sample does not happen to contain any of the defectives.

A complete discussion of statistical sampling is beyond the scope of this book, but the essence of the procedure can be explained easily. Suppose, for example, that management sets a standard 3 percent level of defective items as

---

[14]At this point, note that quality is important in services as well as products. Later in the chapter, we will discuss service quality.

MANAGEMENT FOCUS

Top Service Winners Rely Heavily on Preliminary Control Methods

To answer the question "Who provides the best service in the United States?" *Fortune* magazine reviewed the quality ratings given to service companies by consumer and other groups. They found some answers: L. L. Bean was judged tops among catalog merchants, American Airlines offers the best airline service, and Liz Claiborne provides the best sales service for retailers in the clothing industry. *Fortune* also found that service winners share the same formula for service success. Interestingly, the formula relies heavily on the preliminary control of human resources. The winners:

1. Selectively recruit and keep good people.
2. Thoroughly train employees in quality service.
3. Motivate and reward quality performance.
4. Aggressively monitor quality performance.

Source: Adapted from Bro Uttal, "Companies that Serve You Best," *Fortune*, December 7, 1987, pp. 98ff.

a maximum that it will accept from the supplier. The material is inspected by selecting a random sample and calculating the percentage of defective items in that sample. The decision that must then be made, based on the sample, is whether to accept or reject the entire order or to take another sample. Errors can be made in sampling, so that a lot is accepted when it contains more than 3 percent defectives or is rejected when it contains less than 3 percent defectives. The control system constructed will be based on a careful balancing of the relative costs of these two types of errors.[15]

The preliminary control of materials illustrates a control system that is quite routine. The standard is easily measured, and information (the sample) is readily available. The question of whether to accept or reject materials recurs frequently, and decisions must be made on a fairly regular basis. The decision to accept or reject (or take another sample) is based on straightforward instructions; given the sample results, the decision is automatic. The inspector's instructions may read: "If sample defectives are equal to or less than 3 percent, accept the lot; if sample defectives are equal to or more than 5 percent, reject the lot; if sample defectives are between 3 and 5 percent, take another sample." If a second sample is required, the inspector's actions will be determined by another set of instructions.

CAPITAL

The acquisition of capital reflects the need to replace existing equipment or to expand the firm's productive capacity. Capital acquisitions are controlled by

[15]See Joel G. Siegel and Matthew S. Rubin, "Corporate Planning and Control through Variance Analysis," *Managerial Planning*, September–October 1984, pp. 33–36, for a related discussion.

establishing criteria of potential profitability that must be met before the proposal is authorized. Such acquisitions ordinarily are included in the *capital budget*, an intermediate and long-run planning document that details the alternative sources and uses of funds. Managerial decisions that involve the commitment of present funds in exchange for future funds are termed *investment decisions*. The methods that serve to screen investment proposals are based on economic analysis.

In this section, a number of widely used methods will be discussed. Each involves formulating a standard that must be met in order to accept the prospective capital acquisition.

The Payback Method.   The simplest and apparently most widely used method is the payback method. This method calculates the number of years needed for the proposed capital acquisition to repay its original cost out of future cash earnings. For example, a manager is considering a machine that will reduce labor costs by $4,000 per year for each of the four years of its estimated life. The cost of the machine is $8,000, and the tax rate is 50 percent. The additional after-tax cash inflow from which the machine's cost must be paid is calculated as follows:

Additional cash inflow before taxes (labor cost savings)		$4,000
Less: Additional taxes		
Additional income	$4,000	
Depreciation ($8,000 ÷ 4)	2,000	
Additional taxable income	2,000	
Tax rate	.5	
Additional tax payment		1,000
Additional cash inflow after taxes		$3,000

The payback period can be calculated as follows:

$$\frac{\$8,000}{\$3,000} = 2.67 \text{ years}$$

The proposed machine will repay its original cost in two and two-thirds years; if the standard requires a payback of three years or less, the machine would be an appropriate investment.

The payback method suffers many limitations as a standard for evaluating capital resources. It does not produce a measurement of profitability. More important, it does not take into account the time value of money; that is, it does not recognize that a dollar today is worth more than a dollar at a future date. Other methods include these important considerations.

Rate of Return on Investment.   One alternative measure of profitability, consistent with methods ordinarily employed in accounting, is the simple rate of return. Using the above example, the calculation would be as follows:

Additional gross income		$4,000
Less: Depreciation ($8,000 ÷ 4)	$2,000	
Taxes	1,000	
Total additional expenses		3,000
Additional net income after taxes		$1,000

The rate of return is the ratio of additional net income to the original cost:

$$\frac{\$1,000}{\$8,000} = 12.5 \text{ percent}$$

The calculated rate of return would then be compared to some standard of minimum acceptability, and the decision to accept or reject would depend on that comparison. The measurement of the simple rate of return has the advantage of being easily understood. It has the disadvantage, however, of not including the time value of money. The discounted rate of return method overcomes this deficiency.

Discounted Rate of Return.   The discounted rate of return is a measurement of profitability that takes into account the time value of money. Similar to the payback method, only cash inflows and outflows are considered. The method is widely used because it is considered the "correct" method for calculating the rate of return. Based on the above example:

$$\$8,000 = \frac{\$3,000}{(1+r)} + \frac{\$3,000}{(1+r)^2} + \frac{\$3,000}{(1+r)^3} + \frac{\$3,000}{(1+r)^4}$$

$$r = 18\%$$

The discounted rate of return (r) is 18 percent, which is interpreted to mean that an $8,000 investment repaying $3,000 in cash at the end of each of four years yields a return of 18 percent.

The rationale of the method can be understood by thinking of $3,000 inflows as cash payments received by the firm. In exchange for each of these four payments of $3,000, the firm must pay $8,000. The rate of return, 18 percent, is the factor equating cash inflows and present cash outflow.[16]

---

[16]The time value of money is explicitly considered in the method in the following way. If we remember that 18 percent is the rate of return and that there are four distinct and separate future receipts of $3,000, we can see that $8,000 is the *present value* of the future proceeds.

$2,542 = Present value of $3,000 to be received in 1 year, or $2,542 × 1.18 = $3,000
 2,155 = Present value of $3,000 to be received in 2 years, or $2,155 × (1.18)^2 = $3,000
 1,826 = Present value of $3,000 to be received in 3 years, or $1,826 × (1.18)^3 = $3,000
 1,547 = Present value of $3,000 to be received in 4 years, or $1,547 × (1.18)^4 = $3,000
$8,070 = Total present value; error due to rounding.

FINANCIAL RESOURCES

Adequate financial resources must be available to ensure payment of obligations arising from current operations. Materials must be purchased, wages paid, interest charges and due dates met. The principal means of controlling the availability and cost of financial resources is budgeting—particularly cash and working-capital budgets.

These budgets anticipate the ebb and flow of business activity when materials are purchased, finished goods are produced and inventoried, goods are sold, and cash is received.[17] This operating cycle results in a problem of *timing* the availability of cash to meet the obligations. The simple relationship between cash and inventory is shown in Figure 8–4. When inventories of finished goods increase, the supply of cash decreases as materials, labor, and other expenses are incurred and paid. As inventory is depleted through sales, cash increases. Preliminary control of cash requires that cash be available during the period of inventory buildup and be used wisely during periods of abundance. This requires the careful consideration of alternative sources of short-term financing during inventory buildup and alternative short-run investment opportunities during periods of inventory depletion.

To aid in the process, managers use certain financial ratios. For example, the control standard may be stated in terms of the current ratio (the ratio of current assets to current liabilities), and a minimum and a maximum are set. The minimum ratio could be set at 2:1 and the maximum at 3:1, which would recognize the cost of both too little and too much investment in liquid assets. The control would be in terms of corrective action taken when the actual current ratio deviates from the standard. Other financial ratios contributing to control of financial resources include the acid-test ratio, inventory turnover, and average collection period. These ratios are discussed in greater detail in the section on feedback control methods.

CONCURRENT CONTROL

Concurrent control consists primarily of actions of supervisors who direct the work of their subordinates. **Direction** refers to the acts of managers when they undertake (1) to instruct subordinates in proper methods and procedures and (2) to oversee subordinates' work to ensure that it is done properly.

Direction follows the formal chain of command, since the responsibility of each superior is to interpret for subordinates the orders received from higher levels. The relative importance of direction depends almost entirely on the nature of the tasks performed by subordinates. The supervisor of an assembly line that produces a component part requiring relatively simple manual operations may seldom engage in direction. On the other hand, the manager of a new product research unit must devote considerable time to direction. Research work is inherently more complex and varied than manual work. So it requires more interpretation and instruction.

[17]Frank Collins, Paul Munter, and Don W. Finn, "The Budgeting Games People Play," *Accounting Review*, January 1987, pp. 29–49.

FIGURE 8–4   Simple Relationship between Cash and Inventory

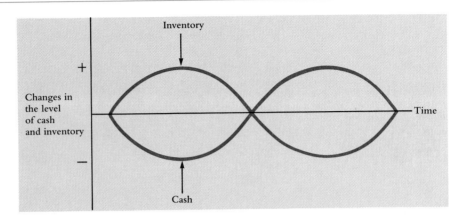

Understanding cash flows and how they relate to inventory is a critical management skill.

Directing is the primary function of the first-line supervisor, but every manager in an organization engages at some time in directing employees. The direction given is guided by the stated goals and policies of the organization as determined in the planning function. As a manager moves up the hierarchy, the relative importance of directing diminishes as other functions become relatively more important. For example, the chief executive officer will devote considerably more time to the planning and organizing functions.

The scope and content of the direction phase vary according to the nature of work being supervised, as noted above.[18] Also, a number of other factors determine differences in the form of direction. For example, since direction is basically the process of personal communications, the amount and clarity of information are important factors. Subordinates must receive sufficient information to carry out the task and must understand the information that they receive. On the other hand, too much information and too much detail can be damaging. The manager's mode and tone of expression also greatly influence the effectiveness of direction.

The tests of effective direction are related to the characteristics of effective communication. To be effective, a directive must be reasonable, understandable, appropriately worded, and consistent with the overall goals of the organization. Whether these criteria are met is not the manager's decision to make. Rather, it is the subordinate who decides. Many managers have assumed that their directives were straightforward and to the point, only to discover that their subordinates failed to understand or to accept them as legitimate.

The process of direction includes not only the manner in which directives are communicated but also the mannerisms of the person who directs. Whether the supervisor is autocratic or democratic, permissive or directive, considerate or inconsiderate, influences the effectiveness of direction as a

---

[18]For an excellent discussion of problems in managing professional employees, see Joseph A. Raelin, "The Basis for the Professional's Resistance to Managerial Control," *Human Resource Management,* Summer 1985, pp. 147–75.

Feedback control methods focus on historical outcomes as the bases for correcting future actions.

concurrent control technique.[19] A later chapter delves deeply into leadership behavior and how it influences the performance of individuals and groups.

Direction involves day-to-day oversight of the subordinates' work. As deviations from standards are identified, managers take immediate corrective action through demonstration and coaching their subordinates to perform assigned tasks appropriately.

FEEDBACK CONTROL

The distinguishing feature of feedback control methods is a focus on *historical* outcomes as the bases of correcting *future* actions. For example, the financial statements of a firm are used to evaluate the acceptability of historical results and to determine the desirability of making changes in future resource acquisitions or operational activities. In this section are outlined four feedback control methods widely used in business: financial statement analysis, standard cost analysis, quality control, and employee performance evaluation. Our discussion of these four examples will demonstrate the general features of feedback control techniques.

FINANCIAL STATEMENT ANALYSIS

A firm's accounting system is a principal source of information from which managers can evaluate historical results. Periodically, the manager receives a set of financial statements that usually includes a balance sheet, an income statement, and a sources-and-uses-of-funds statement. These statements summarize and classify the effects of transactions in terms of assets, liabilities, equity,

[19]Barry Waldon, "The Human Side of Control," *Supervisory Management*, June 1985, pp. 34–39.

revenues, and expenses—the principal components of the firm's financial structure.[20]

A detailed analysis of the financial statements' information enables management to determine the adequacy of the firm's earning power and its ability to meet current and long-term obligations. Managers must have measures of and standards for profitability, liquidity, and solvency. Whether a manager prefers the rate of return on sales, on owner's equity, on total assets, or a combination of all three, it is important to establish a meaningful norm—one that is appropriate to the particular firm, given its industry and stage of growth. An inadequate rate of return will negatively affect the firm's ability to attract funds for expansion, particularly if a downward trend over time is evident.

The measures of liquidity reflect the firm's ability to meet current obligations as they become due.[21] The widest known and most often used measure is the current ratio: the ratio of current assets to current liabilities. The standard of acceptability depends on the particular firm's operating characteristics. Bases for comparison are available from trade associations that publish industry averages. A tougher test of liquidity is the acid-test ratio, which relates only cash and near-cash items (current assets excluding inventories and prepaid expenses) to current liabilities.

The relationship between current assets and current liabilities is an important one. Equally important is the *composition* of current assets. Two measures that indicate composition and rely on information found in both the balance sheet and income statement are the accounts receivable turnover and the inventory turnover. The accounts receivable turnover is the ratio of credit sales to average accounts receivable. The higher the turnover, the more rapid the conversion of accounts receivable to cash. A low turnover would indicate a time lag in the collection of receivables, which in turn could strain the firm's ability to meet its own obligations. The appropriate corrective action might be a tightening of credit standards or a more vigorous effort to collect outstanding accounts. The inventory turnover also facilitates the analysis of appropriate balances in current assets. It is calculated as the ratio of cost of goods sold to average inventory. A high ratio could indicate a dangerously low inventory balance in relation to sales, with the possibility of missed sales or a production slowdown. Conversely, a low ratio might indicate an overinvestment in inventory to the exclusion of other, more profitable assets. Whatever the case, the appropriate ratio must be established by the manager, based on the firm's experience within its industry and market.

Another financial measure is solvency, the ability of the firm to meet its long-term obligations—its fixed commitments. The solvency measure reflects the claims of creditors and owners on the assets of the firm. An appropriate balance must be maintained—a balance that protects the interests of the owners yet does not ignore the advantages of long-term debt as a source of funds. A commonly used measure of solvency is the ratio of net income before interest and taxes to interest expense. This indicates the margin of safety; ordinarily, a

---

[20]See Burton A. Kolb and Richard DeMong, *Principles of Financial Management,* 2nd ed. (Homewood, Ill.: Richard D. Irwin, 1988); Diane Harrington and Brent D. Wilson, *Corporate Financial Analysis,* 2nd ed. (Homewood, Ill.: Richard D. Irwin, 1986).

[21]Avi Rushinek and Sara F. Rushinek, "Using Financial Ratios to Predict Insolvency," *Journal of Business Research,* February 1987, pp. 74–77.

high ratio is preferred. However, a very high ratio combined with a low debt-to-equity ratio could indicate that management has not taken advantage of debt as a source of funds. The appropriate balance between debt and equity depends on many factors. But as a general rule, the proportion of debt should vary directly with the stability of the firm's earnings.

The ratios discussed above are only suggestive of the great number and variety of methods used to evaluate the financial results of the firm. (Accounting as a tool of analysis in management has a long history.[22]) The point here is that financial statement analysis as a part of the management process is clearly a feedback control method.

Standard Cost Analysis

Standard cost accounting systems are considered a major contribution of the scientific management era. A standard cost system provides information that enables management to compare actual costs with predetermined (standard) costs. Management then can take appropriate corrective action or assign to others the authority to take action. The first use of standard costing was to control manufacturing costs. But in recent years, standard costing has also been applied to selling, general, and administrative expenses.[23] Here we discuss standard manufacturing costs.

The three elements of manufacturing costs are direct labor, direct materials, and overhead. For each of these, an estimate must be made of cost per unit of output. For example, the direct labor cost per unit of output consists of the standard usage of labor and the standard price of labor. The standard usage derives from time studies that fix the expected output per labor hour; the standard price of labor will be fixed by the salary schedule appropriate for the kind of work necessary to produce the output. A similar determination is made for direct materials. Thus, the standard labor and standard materials costs might be as follows:

Standard labor usage per unit	2 hours
Standard wage rate per hour	$ 5.00
Standard labor cost (2 × $5.00)	$10.00
Standard material usage per unit	6 pounds
Standard material price per pound	$ .30
Standard material cost (6 × $ .30)	$ 1.80

The accounting system enables the manager to compare incurred costs and standard costs. If during the period covered by the report, for example, 200 units of output were produced, the standard labor cost is $2,000 (200 × $10.00), and the standard material is $360 (200 × $1.80). If the actual payroll cost for that same time period was $2,400 and the actual material cost was $400, there was an *unfavorable labor variance* of $400 and an *unfavorable material variance* of $40. Management must determine the reasons for the variances and decide what corrective action is appropriate.

[22]A. C. Littleton, *Accounting Evolution to 1900* (New York: Russell & Russell, 1966).

[23]See Ralph H. Garrison, *Managerial Accounting: Concepts for Planning, Control, Decision Making,* 5th ed. (Homewood, Ill.: Richard D. Irwin, 1988).

Assuming that the standards are correct, the manager must analyze the variance and fix the responsibility for restoring the balance between standard and actual costs. It is obvious that if actual labor costs exceed standard labor costs, the reason for the difference is found in labor usage and labor wage rates. Either actual labor usage exceeded standard labor usage or actual wage rates exceeded standard wage rates, or some combination of both. Suppose that, in this example, the accountant reports the actual payroll consisted of 450 actual hours at an average wage rate of $3.33. The questions management must resolve are now narrowed to two: What happened during the period to cause output per labor hour to go down (to produce 200 units of output should require 400 labor hours)? And why was the average wage rate more than the standard wage rate? The answers to these questions are found in the resources and activity stages of the cycle (see Figure 8–3).

Similar analyses are made to discover the causes for the unfavorable material variance. The first step is discovering the relationship between actual and standard usage and between actual and standard price. As with the labor, the manager may find actual material usage exceeded that specified by standard and/or the actual price exceeded the standard price. Once the cause is isolated, the analysis must proceed to fix responsibility for corrective action.

The analysis of manufacturing-overhead variance is considerably more complicated than that for labor and material.[24] However, it is still necessary to isolate the causes through comparisons with standards and budgets. The Management Focus presents competitive benchmarking, a cost analysis technique Xerox Corporation has used successfully in improving product quality. The technique is based on the analysis of competitive products.

QUALITY CONTROL ANALYSIS

Quality control uses information regarding attributes and characteristics of output to ascertain whether the manufacturing process is "in control" (i.e., producing acceptable output). To make this determination, the manager must specify the crucial product characteristic. It may be weight, length, consistency, or defects. A major development in the last 10 years or so has been the emergence of concern for product quality, perhaps due mostly to the influx of Japanese imports with a reputation for quality.[25] American business managers have responded by instituting quality-improvement programs.

Management must often be concerned with consistent *quantity* as well as quality.[26] For example, a peanut butter manufacturer must maintain a minimum quantity of 12 ounces of peanut in each container. The company could weigh each container when it is filled—that is, 100 percent of the output could

---

[24]The reader can consult any text in cost accounting and management accounting for discussions of standard cost analysis. We also recommend Robert S. Kaplan, "One Cost System Isn't Enough," *Harvard Business Review*, January–February 1988, pp. 63–70.

[25]Several excellent works are available on quality control and approaches to quality improvement. Especially noteworthy are W. Edwards Deming, *Quality, Productivity, and Competitive Position* (Cambridge, Mass.: MIT Press, 1982); A.V. Feigenbaum, *Total Quality Control* (New York: McGraw-Hill, 1983); Richard J. Schonberger, *World Class Manufacturing: The Lessons of Simplicity Applied* (New York: Free Press, 1986), pp. 123–43.

[26]See David A. Garvin, "Competing on the Eight Dimensions of Quality," *Harvard Business Review*, November–December 1987, pp. 101–9.

MANAGEMENT FOCUS

Competitive Benchmarking in Cost Analysis

In 1980, Xerox Corporation suddenly found that the Japanese had more than a 40 percent cost advantage in copiers and that its own market share in copiers had severely declined. When David Kearns assumed the CEO position in 1982, Xerox faced a critical challenge: regain its lost market share.

The new CEO launched the "Leadership through Quality" program to boost product quality and reduce manufacturing costs. One important element of the program is a technique known as competitive benchmarking.

Competitive benchmarking is a cost analysis technique used to obtain important information on competitor costs and to set tougher standards for cost control. In the technique, Xerox targets a competitor who is clearly producing copiers at a lower cost. Xerox purchases one of the copiers, and product analysts take the copier apart,

piece by piece, in the Xerox lab. Their objective is to determine the cost of designing and producing each part. In doing so, Xerox can estimate a competitor's total production cost as their new standard for cost control.

Xerox has also applied competitive benchmarking to other types of costs. For example, Xerox analysts pinpointed Kodak's handling and distribution costs by purchasing a number of Kodak copiers and then tracing where they were shipped from and examining how the copiers were packed.

Source: David Kearns, "Changing a Corporate Culture: Leadership through Quality," in *Handbook for Creative and Innovative Managers*, ed. R. L. Kuhn (New York: McGraw Hill, 1988); Irving J. DeToro, "Strategic Planning for Quality at Xerox," *Quality Progress*, April 1987, pp. 16–20; France Gaither Tucker, Seymour M. Zivan, and Robert C. Camp, "How to Measure Yourself against the Best," *Harvard Business Review*, January–February 1987, pp. 8–10.

---

be inspected. An alternative is to inspect samples of output to make inferences about the process, based on the sample information. This latter approach is termed *statistical quality control*. This method makes use of statistical sampling theory; and since the amount of time devoted to inspection is reduced, the cost of inspection also is reduced. Moreover, the acceptable standard of 12 ounces is achieved.

EMPLOYEE PERFORMANCE EVALUATION

No doubt, the most important and difficult feedback control technique is performance evaluation. It is so important because people are the most crucial resource in any organization. As is so often said, "People make the difference."[27] Evaluating people is difficult because the standards for performance are seldom objective and straightforward; many managerial and nonmanagerial jobs do not produce outputs that can be counted, weighed, and evaluated in objective terms. Because of the importance of employee performance evaluation, the next chapter will present an in-depth discussion of the topic.

---

[27]This important but often overlooked point is forcefully made in Tom Peters, *Thriving on Chaos* (New York: Alfred A. Knopf, 1987).

The discussion of the controlling function is conveniently summarized in Table 8–2. There the techniques are compared in terms of standards, information, and corrective action relevant for each one. The table also brings into focus the relationship between the planning function as a source of standards and the organizing function as a source of information. The overriding managerial responsibility is to integrate the three functions into a coherent management process that enables the organization to achieve the levels of performance expected by the individuals and groups that sustain it.

TABLE 8–2   Summary of the Controlling Function

Effective control techniques must have standards, information, and corrective action.

Technique	Standards	Information	Corrective Action
1. Job description	Job specifications—skills, experience, education bearing on job success.	Test scores, credentials, background data.	Hire/no hire; remedial training.
2. Selection	Job specifications—skills, experience, education bearing on job success.	Test scores, credentials, background data.	Place/no place; remedial training.
3. Materials inspection	Percent of number defective within tolerance limits.	Sampling of inputs.	Accept, reject, or retest.
4. Capital budgeting	Simple rate of return; payback period; discounted rate of return.	Projected cost, revenue, and engineering data.	Accept, reject.
5. Financial budgeting	Requirements arising out of the forecasting step of planning.	Projected cost, revenue, and engineering data.	Accept, reject; revise.
6. Direction	Required job behavior in terms of end results.	Plans and job specifications.	Change plans and/or job specifications; train, fire people.
7. Financial statement analysis	Relevant data found in trade, banking, and rule-of-thumb sources.	Balance sheet, income statement.	Revise inputs; revise direction.
8. Standard cost analysis	Standard times/usage from engineering studies.	Cost accounting system.	Revise inputs; revise direction.
9. Quality control	Percent or number defective consistent with marketing strategy.	Sampling procedures.	Revise inputs; revise direction.
10. Employee performance evaluation	Job-related performance criteria.	Managerial observations; self-reports.	Retrain, replace personnel; change assigned jobs.

MANAGEMENT CONTROL AND THE CRITICAL ISSUE OF QUALITY

In this chapter, we have seen that preliminary, concurrent, and feedback control methods are important contributors to product and service quality. What this means is that controlling quality is important throughout the product or service production process. As product and service quality become key international competitive issues, this view of quality control as a journey rather than a destination has increased. It marks a change in the way many managers think.

During the past two decades, management thinking about the relationship between quality and productivity has drastically changed.[28] Historically, quality has been viewed largely as a controlling activity that takes place somewhere near the end of the production process, an after-the-fact measurement of production success. As such, efforts to ensure quality increase the costs associated with making available that good or service. For that reason, quality and productivity have been viewed as conflicting; one is increased at the expense of the other. This assumption has clearly hindered quality improvement in many companies.

Over the years, more and more managers have come to realize that quality is not something that is measured at or near the end of the production process but rather is an essential "ingredient" of the product or service being produced. As such, quality is an overall approach to doing business and becomes the concern of all members of the organization. When quality comes to be viewed this way, the following conditions prevail:

- The number of defects decreases, which causes output to increase.
- Making it right the first time reduces many of the rejects and much of the rework.
- Making employees responsible for quality eliminates the need for inspection.

These conditions also apply to service quality, whether the service is performed for the customer or for some other department in the same organization. The ultimate result is that quality is viewed as reducing rather than increasing costs.

IBM, Caterpillar, Michelin, Procter & Gamble, and Ford Motor Co. are some of the many companies that now use this concept of quality in their overall strategy. You may recognize it as similar to the one discussed in the chapter-opening Management in Action as crucial to Japan's success. The fact is, they are similar. Dr. Deming, the now world-renowned consultant credited with helping to make Japan's products world class, believes that improvement of quality transfers waste of labor hours and of machine time into the manufacture of good products and good service. Management in some Japanese companies observed 40 years ago that improvement of quality

---

[28]Everette E. Adam, Jr., James C. Hershauer, and William A. Ruch, *Productivity and Quality* (Englewood Cliffs, N.J.: Prentice-Hall, 1981).

FIGURE 8–5   How Improved Quality Increases Productivity
(the Deming Chain Reaction)

Improvements in quality can also result in improvements in productivity.

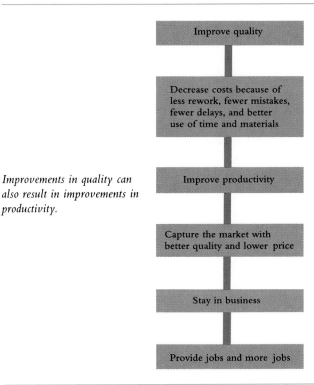

naturally and inevitably leads to improvements in productivity. Once management in Japan adopted the chain reaction illustrated in Figure 8–5, quality became everyone's aim.[29]

SUMMARY OF KEY POINTS

- The controlling function includes activities undertaken by managers to ensure that actual results conform to planned results. The controlling function logically follows the planning and organizing functions.

- The three necessary requirements for effective control are predetermined standards, information, and corrective action.

- Three types of control can be identified that are based on the focus of corrective action. Preliminary control focuses on inputs; concurrent control focuses on ongoing operations; feedback control focuses on inputs and ongoing operations.

- The controlling function is highly developed in management practice. A great number of meth-

[29]Summarized from W. Edwards Deming, *Out of the Crises* (Cambridge, Mass.: MIT Center for Advanced Engineering Study, 1986). For some interesting examples of quality improvement efforts by U.S. businesses, see Otis Port, "The Push for Quality," *Business Week,* June 8, 1987, pp. 130ff.

ods and systems allow managers to attain high levels of performance in the controlling function.

■ Preliminary control methods require standards of acceptable quality and quantity of inputs, such as material, financial, capital, and human resources. Information permitting managers to determine whether resources meet standards allows for corrective action.

■ Concurrent control methods require standards of acceptable behavior, activity, and execution of ongoing operations. The primary source of information for concurrent control is supervisors' observations; the corrective action is directed toward improving the quality and quantity of resources and improving the operations.

■ Feedback control methods require standards of acceptable quality and quantity of outputs. The information must reflect the desired characteristics of the output. But unlike preliminary and concurrent control, the focus of corrective action is not that for which the standard is set—output. Rather, managers take corrective action to improve inputs and operations.

■ Quality is not something that is controlled at or near the end of the production process. It should be viewed as an essential ingredient of the product or service being produced.

DISCUSSION AND REVIEW QUESTIONS

1. Some management experts say that the term *control* should not be used in the management literature. These experts argue that control implies some loss of freedom and individuality and that such implications should be avoided. Do you agree with these experts? What is your reasoning?

2. Illustrate the relationship between goals, policies, and standards in the context of an organization of which you are a member.

3. Why are preliminary and concurrent control procedures so widely used in universities, hospitals, governmental agencies, and other nonmarket institutions?

4. The term *cybernetics* was coined by system theorists such as Norbert Wiener. Research this term and relate it to the chapter discussion of feedback control procedures.

5. Some management writers have argued that the creation of organization structures is basically a form of the controlling function and not a separate managerial function. Respond to this argument.

6. A number of standards have been discussed as measures of investment profitability. These measures include the payback period, the rate of return, and the discounted rate of return. If only one measure is "correct," why do others exist in management practice?

7. Financial managers state the financial ratios are similar to other statistical data in that they can be used, or misused, to prove a point. How can the nonfinancial expert, such as a plant superintendent, know whether the financial expert is misusing such ratios to press for a certain point of view in an executive decision?

8. Under what circumstances would the use of feedback control procedures be inappropriate?

9. The concept of "responsibility accounting" has received much attention in the accounting literature. Research this concept in terms of its relationship to the chapter discussion of necessary conditions for effective managerial control.

10. "Performance evaluation would be a simple task if it weren't for the fact that people are involved." Comment on this statement.

11. Directing is a crucial aspect of control; and information received (the perceived performance of subordinates) and information sent (orders and instructions) are key elements of directing. What abilities and traits do you believe are associated with effective directing?

ADDITIONAL REFERENCES

Chow, C. W., and **W. S. Waller.** "Management Accounting and Organizational Control." *Management Accounting,* April 1982, pp. 36–41.

Ferry, M. J. "Quality Assurance." *Journal of Information Management,* Winter 1985, pp. 25–27.

Gray, H. J. "A New Synthesis—Blending Control with Creativity." *Management World,* October 1984, p. 1.

Jaeger, A. M., and **R. B. Baliga.** "Control Systems and Strategic Adaptation: Lessons from the Japanese Experience." *Strategic Management Journal*, April–June 1985, pp. 115–34.

Jeffrey, N. "Preparing for the Worst: Firms Set Up Plans to Help Deal with Corporate Crises." *The Wall Street Journal*, December 7, 1987, p. 23.

King, Carol A. "Service Quality Assurance Is Different." *Quality Progress*, June 1985, pp. 14–18.

Logan, G. M. "Loyalty and a Sense of Purpose." *California Management Review*, Fall 1984, pp. 149–56.

Muczyk, J. P., and **R. E. Hastings.** "In Defense of Enlightened Hardball Management." *Business Horizons*, July–August 1985, pp. 23–29.

Murr, D. W.; P. Munter; and **D. W. Finn.** "The Budgeting Games People Play." *Accounting Review*, January 1987, pp. 29–49.

Symonds, W. C. "How Corporations Are Learning to Prepare for the Worst." *Business Week*, December 23, 1985, p. 76.

Worthy, F. S. "Accounting Bores You? Wake Up." *Fortune*, October 12, 1987, pp. 43–53.

Zimmerman, C. D. "Quality: Key to Service Productivity." *Quality Progress*, June 1985, pp.. 32–35.

CASE 8–1   Controlling the Quality of Customer Service at American Express

The Card Division of American Express recognizes how important it is to develop and maintain high quality in customer service. Customer service is related not only to customer goodwill but to profits as well. The company estimates that it gains 33 cents of extra sales revenue for each day earlier a card is mailed to a customer. On an annual basis, that 33 cents per day per card turns into $1.4 million in net profit. Getting new and replaced cards into the hands of customers in a timely manner is an important aspect of customer service quality. But when American Express began to delve more deeply, it discovered considerable ambiguity surrounding the concept.

The decision to control the quality of customer service reflected the importance of the concept. But the initiative had to be provided by a key manager. Ruth C. Finley, a regional vice president of the Card Division, was the prime mover behind the effort. She stated: "For some time, we had been dissatisfied with the traditional approach for evaluating customer service. Reports to management were biased because they seldom included customers who had problems but did not complain, or those who were only marginally satisfied with the company's service." She believed that the true measure of customer service must be based on the perceptions of cardholders and service establishments and that standards must reflect those perceptions.

The decision to base customer service quality on the perceptions of those who receive the service meant a major overhaul in the firm's control procedures. The company began by determining what customers expected from American Express. Analyses of letters of complaint indicated three important attributes of customer service: timeliness, accuracy, and responsiveness. Cardholders expected bills to be received on time, address changes processed quickly, and complaints acted upon.

Once customer expectations were identified, the company's quality assurance staff began to develop standards for the delivery of customer service. Eventually, the staff indicated more than 180 standards to measure customer quality. These standards reflected acceptable performance of service elements such as processing applications, issuing cards, responding to billing inquiries, and authorizing charges on accounts. The standards were based on customers' expectations of what constituted timely, accurate, and responsive service.

Other factors also were considered. In addition to customers' perceptions, the performance standards reflected competitive, capability, and economic factors. For example, some standards are imposed by *competition*; others are influenced by the organization's current processing *capability*; while yet other standards must reflect the *economic* trade-off potential. As each of these factors was considered, the appropriate standards began to take shape, and the program was implemented.

The program had impact. The time required to process personal card applications was reduced from 35 days to 15 days, the time required to replace cards from 15 days to 2 days, the time needed to respond to customer inquiries from 16 days to 10 days. The profit potential of these improvements was quite large. For example, the reduction in the delivery time for new and replaced cards yielded an estimated additional revenue of $17.5 million. Also, when cards were received in a timely manner, the customer did not have to use a competitor's card.

The revenue and profit potential of the quality control program had side benefits. The program focused the attention of the entire company on customer expectations. Departments prided themselves on their record of rendering customer service. Moreover, employee morale increased because every employee has a stake in and makes contributions to improving customer service. Each employee now feels more a part of the company and representative of the company when serving customers.

The success of the program in controlling customer service in the card division stimulated similar efforts in other company divisions. The company's Travel and Travelers Cheque Division began to implement a similar procedure. American Express is convinced that standards can be set for any quantity that is vital to profitability, regardless of the ambiguity and subjectiveness of the quantity itself.

QUESTIONS FOR ANALYSIS

1. Is the American Express program for controlling the quality of customer service a form of preliminary, concurrent, or feedback control?
2. Identify the three elements of effective control in the American Express program.
3. For what reasons should American Express set standards at the "economically feasible" level rather than at the highest possible level?

CASE 8–2   Developing a New Product

The plant manager of a major electronics manufacturer called a meeting with his immediate subordinates to decide whether to go into full-scale production and marketing of a new product, a miniature thermostat. The miniature thermostat MT had been in the developmental process for the past

EXHIBIT 1	Cost Accounting Data for the MT

	Actual Costs	Standard Costs
Direct labor	5.9¢	5.2¢
Direct material	34.0	19.4
Manufacturing overhead (438 percent of standard direct labor)	22.8	22.8
Total manufacturing cost	62.7	47.4
Spoilage (10 percent)	6.3	4.7
Selling and administrative costs (40 percent of direct labor and overhead)	11.5	11.2
Total cost per MT	80.5	63.3
Required price to achieve 14 percent markup in selling price	93.6¢	73.6¢

three years, and the manager believed that it was time to make a decision. The meeting was to be attended by the marketing manager, the production superintendent, the purchasing manager, and the plant cost accountant. The plant manager instructed each official to bring appropriate information and be prepared to make a final decision regarding the MT.

Prior to the meeting, the plant manager noted the following facts concerning the MT:

1. Developmental efforts had been undertaken two years ago in response to the introduction of a similar product by a major competitor.
2. Initial manufacturing studies had indicated that much of the technology and know-how to produce the MT already existed in the plant and its work force.
3. A prototype model had been approved by Underwriter's Laboratory.
4. A pilot production line had been designed and installed. Several thousand thermostats already had been produced and tested.
5. Market projections indicated that the trend toward miniaturization of components such as thermostats was likely to continue.
6. The competitor who had introduced the product was successfully marketing it at a unit price of 80 cents.
7. The cost estimates derived by the cost accountant over the past two years consistently indicated that the firm could not meet the competitor's price and at the same time follow its policy of marking up all products 14 percent to the selling price.

Because of the plant manager's concern for the cost of the MT, the cost accountant was asked to brief the group at the outset of its meeting. The accountant's data are shown in Exhibit 1.

The accountant noted that the firm would not be able to manufacture and sell the MT for less than 80.5 cents each, given present actual costs. In fact, to meet their markup objective would require a selling price of approximately 94 cents each, impossible since the competitor was selling the same product for 80 cents. She explained that if the MT could be manufactured at standard costs, the product could compete successfully with the competitor's thermostat.

The marketing manager stated that the MT was an important product and that it was critical for the firm to have an entry in the market. He maintained that in a few years, the MT would be used by all major customers; he also stated that competition already had moved into the area with a strong sales program. He added that he personally did not place too much reliance on the cost estimates, because the plant had so little experience with full-scale production of the MT.

The manufacturing superintendent stated that he was working with engineers to develop a new method of welding contacts and that if the technique proved successful, direct labor cost would be reduced significantly. This would have a cumulative effect on cost, since overhead, spoilage, and selling and administrative expenses are based on direct labor. He also believed that with a little more experience, the workers could reach standard times on the assembly operations. He stated that much progress in this direction had been made in the past four weeks.

The purchasing manager stated that material costs were high because the plant did not procure materials in sufficient quantity. She stated that with full-scale production, material costs should reduce to standard.

Questions for Analysis

1. If you were the plant manager, what would be your decision regarding the MT?
2. If you decided to manufacture the MT, would your decision indicate that the standard of 14 percent markup is not valid?

Experiential Exercise

Paper Plane Corporation

Purpose

To work on a task that requires planning, organizing, and controlling.

The Exercise in Class

Unlimited groups of six participants each are used in this exercise. These groups may be directed simultaneously in the same room. Approximately a full class period is needed to complete the exercise. Each person should have assembly instructions (Exhibit 1) and a summary sheet (Exhibit 2) plus ample stacks of paper (8 ½ by 11 inches). The physical setting should be a room large enough so individual groups of six can work without interference from other groups. A work area should be provided for each group.

EXHIBIT 1   **Instructions for Aircraft Assembly**

Instructions for aircraft assembly

Step 1: Take a sheet of
paper and fold it
in half, then open it
back up.

Step 2: Fold upper corners
in the middle.

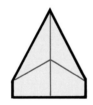

Step 3: Fold the corners to
the middle again.

Step 4: Fold in half.

Step 5: Fold both wings down.

Step 6: Fold tail fins up.

Completed aircraft

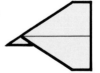

EXHIBIT 2	Summary Sheet

Round 1:

Bid: _____ aircraft @ $20,000.00 per aircraft

= _____

Results: _____ aircraft @ $20,000.00 per
aircraft = _____

Less: $300,000.00 overhead

_____ × $3,000 cost of raw materials

_____ × $25,000 penalty

Profit: _____

Round 2:

Bid: _____ aircraft @ $20,000.00 per aircraft

= _____

Results: _____ aircraft @ $20,000.00 per
aircraft = _____

Less: $300,000.00 overhead

_____ × $3,000 cost of raw materials

_____ × $25,000 penalty

Profit: _____

Round 3:

Bid: _____ aircraft @ $20,000.00 per aircraft

= _____

Results: _____ aircraft @ $20,000.00 per
aircraft = _____

Less: $300,000.00 overhead

_____ × $30,000 cost of raw materials

_____ × $25,000 penalty

Profit: _____

The participants are doing an exercise in production methodology. Each group must work independent of the other groups. The objective is to make paper airplanes in the most profitable manner possible.

Scenario.   Your group is the complete work force for Paper Plane Corporation. Established in 1943, Paper Plane has led the market in paper plane production. Presently under new management, the company is contracting to make aircraft for the U.S. Air Force. You must establish a plan and organization to produce these aircraft. You must make your contract with the air force under the following conditions:

a.   The air force will pay $20,000 per airplane.
b.   The aircraft must pass a strict inspection.
c.   A penalty of $25,000 per airplane will be imposed for failure to meet the production requirements.
d.   Labor and other overhead will be computed at $300,000.
e.   Cost of materials will be $3,000 per bid plane. If you bid for 10 but make only 8, you must pay the cost of materials for those you failed to make or that did not pass inspection.

Activity.   The summary sheet will be used to record the activities of the groups in each round of the exercise. Rounds are timed events utilizing competition among the groups:

1. Your group should choose a manager and an inspector, and the remaining participants will be employees.
2. The facilitator will give the signal to start each 10-minute round, during which your group will act out the above scenario.
3. After the first round, your group should report its production and profits to the entire class, explaining the manner in which you planned, organized, and controlled for the production of the paper airplanes.
4. This same procedure is followed for as many rounds as there is time.

The Learning Message

This exercise is an application of the planning, organizing, and controlling management functions. It will illustrate how these functions, if applied, can improve the end result or performance.

9

HUMAN RESOURCE MANAGEMENT

LEARNING OBJECTIVES

After completing Chapter 9, you should be able to:

Define
human resource management (HRM).

Describe
the activities conducted by various divisions of a human resource department: employment, training and development, wage and salary management, and employee benefits and services.

Discuss
the view that HRM is both a staff function and a line responsibility.

Compare
HRM activities in large and small business organizations.

Identify
the roles that government plays in each phase

Now There Is Global Competition for Good Employees

Everyone knows there is global competition among companies for customers. But did you know that there is now a world market for talented people?

Many companies compete for high-quality employees, who are getting harder to find. The result is that some companies are beginning to look worldwide when trying to fill key positions, especially technical positions.

The chief executive officer (CEO) of Interactive Business Systems Inc., a data-processing consulting firm in Oak Brook, Illinois, found himself having to turn away business because his company was short of people to handle it. So about two years ago, he began placing ads in British computer magazines. An employee from South Africa put out the word there. To the CEO's surprise, top-notch candidates started getting in touch. Initial telephone interviews revealed that they were very eager to expand their technical expertise and were looking for opportunities to learn.

To date, Interactive Business Systems has brought more than a dozen workers from South Africa. The company plans to recruit next in Canada. While it takes a little effort, the CEO says it is worth it: "There's a talent pool of good people with a good work ethic out there."

Tomorrow's college graduates vying for the best positions will be competing with more than their fellow classmates. They will be in competition with talented and motivated people from all over the world.

Managing work and organizations is accomplished through the use of the skills and talents of people. People are the source of all productive effort, and organizational performance depends on individual performance. In this chapter, we apply the elements of the controlling function to human resources.

Source: Reported in "Recruiting over There," *Inc.*, March 1988, p. 112.

To meet the challenges of managing, managers must understand the potential of human resources and then secure, retain, and develop these resources. This is the foundation of what is called human resource management (HRM).

The management of any organizational unit or department—marketing, finance, accounting, production—involves the accomplishment of objectives through use of the skills and talents of people. Thus, HRM is considered both a line management responsibility and a staff function.[1]

In organizations of any size, human resources must be recruited, compensated, developed, and motivated.[2] The small organization typically cannot afford to have a separate HRM (sometimes called personnel or industrial relations) department that continually follows the progress of individuals and reviews the accomplishment of goals.[3] Instead, each manager is responsible for using the skills and talents of employees. Larger firms usually have an HRM department that can be a source of help to line managers. In either case, much of the work in recruitment, compensation, and performance appraisal must be finalized and implemented by managers. How important is human resource management? The conclusion of the Management Focus on successful versus effective managers may surprise you.

HUMAN RESOURCE MANAGEMENT FUNCTION

The HRM program at General Mills serves the needs of that organization and facilitates the accomplishment of its objectives. But without modifications, their program would probably not be well suited for Burger King or Eli Lilly. Each company develops its own HRM program after considering such factors as size, types of skills needed, number of employees required, unionization, clients and customers, financial position, and geographic location.[4]

Successful HRM programs also require cooperation from managers, because it is the managers who must interpret and implement policies and procedures. Line managers must translate into action what an HRM department provides. Without managerial support at the top, middle, and lower levels, HRM programs cannot succeed. Therefore, it is important that managers clearly understand how to mesh their responsibilities with those of the HRM department.[5]

---

[1]John M. Ivancevich and William F. Glueck, *Foundations of Personnel,* 4th ed. (Homewood, Ill.: Richard D. Irwin, 1989), p. 7.

[2]R. Wayne Mondy, Robert W. Noe, and Robert E. Edwards, "What the Staffing Function Entails," *Personnel,* April 1986, pp. 55–58.

[3]See Brian D. Steffy and Steven D. Maurer, "Conceptualizing and Measuring the Economic Effectiveness of Human Resource Activities," *Academy of Management Review,* April 1988, pp. 271–86.

[4]"Human Resource Managers Aren't Corporate Nobodies Any More," *Business Week,* December 2, 1985, pp. 58–59; Cynthia A. Lengnick-Hall and Mark L. Lengnick-Hall, "Strategic Human Resources Management: A Review of the Literature," *Academy of Management Review,* July 1988, pp. 454–70.

[5]Raymond E. Miles and Charles C. Snow, "Designing Strategic Human Resource Systems," *Organizational Dynamics,* Summer 1984, pp. 36–52.

MANAGEMENT FOCUS

The Difference between Successful Managers and Effective Managers

Are successful managers different from effective managers? The authors of the book *Real Managers* believe there are some important differences. They define successful managers as those who have moved up the hierarchy quickly. Effective managers are defined as those who have achieved high levels of quality and quantity of work in their departments while, at the same time, generating high levels of satisfaction and commitment among employees. The difference? Effective managers (those who get the job done) spend more time in routine communication and human resource management.

Source: Fred Luthans, Richard M. Hodgetts, and Stuart A. Rosenkrantz, *Real Managers* (Cambridge, Mass.: Ballinger, 1988).

Human resource management can be defined as the process of accomplishing organizational objectives by acquiring, retaining, terminating, developing, and properly using the human resources in an organization. Accomplishing objectives is a major part of any form of management. Unless objectives are regularly accomplished, the organization ceases to exist.

The *acquisition* of skilled, talented, and motivated employees is an important part of HRM. The acquisition phase involves recruiting, screening, selecting, and properly placing personnel. *Retaining* competent individuals is important to any organization. If qualified individuals regularly leave a company, it becomes continually necessary to seek new personnel, which costs money and time. The opposite of retention is, of course, *termination,* an unpleasant part of any manager's job. Employees occasionally must be terminated for breaking rules, failing to perform adequately, or job cutbacks. Procedures for terminations usually are specified by an HRM staff expert or are covered in a labor contract.

Developing personnel involves training, educating, appraising, and generally preparing personnel for present or future jobs. These activities are important for the economic and psychological growth of employees. The need for personal growth cannot be satisfied in an organization that does not have an active development program.

The *proper use of people* involves understanding both individual and organizational needs so that the full potential of human resources can be utilized. This part of human resource management suggests that it is important to match individuals over time to shifts in organizational and human needs.

HRM in larger organizations such as Alcoa, Bausch & Lomb, Polaroid, and Marriott is performed in a staff department like the one shown in Figure 9–1. Remember, however, that each company organizes its department according to its own set of needs and objectives.

FIGURE 9–1   Example of a Personnel/Human Resource Management Department

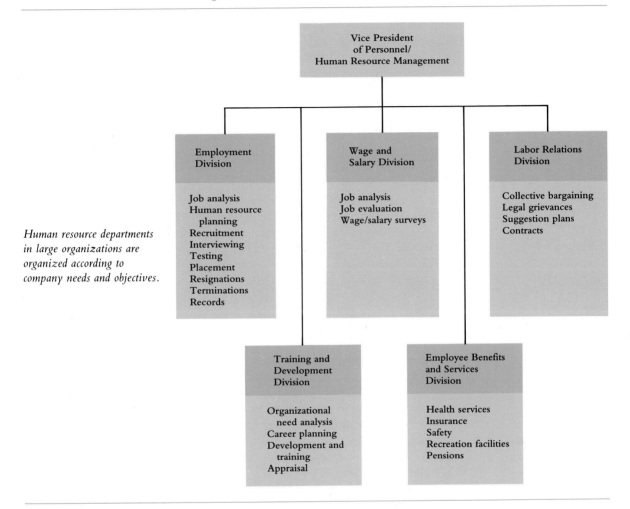

Human resource departments in large organizations are organized according to company needs and objectives.

THE EMPLOYMENT DIVISION

An organization can only be as effective as the people who operate the office, store, plant, or equipment. Thus, acquiring the necessary qualified people is the first phase of any HRM program. This phase is carried out by the employment division.[6] Recruitment, selection, placement, and other activities of the employment division stem from the human resource plans established by managers throughout the organization.[7]

[6]M. Beer, B. Spector, P. R. Lawrence, D. Q. Mills, and R. Walton, *Managing Human Assets* (New York: Free Press, 1982), p. 12.

[7]Judy D. Olian and Sara L. Rynes, "Organizational Staffing: Integrating Practice with Strategy," *Industrial Relations,* Spring 1984, pp. 170–93.

Human resource planning involves estimating the size and makeup of the future work force. This process helps the organization acquire the right numbers and kinds of people when they are needed. Experience indicates that the longer the period predicted, the less accurate the prediction. Other complicating factors include changes in economic conditions, fluctuations in the labor supply, and changes in the political environment.[8]

Both formal and informal approaches to human resource planning are used. For example, some organizations use mathematical projections. Data are collected on such topics as the supply of resources, labor market composition, demand for products, and competitive wage and salary programs. From these data and previous records, statistical procedures are used to make predictions. Of course, unpredictable events can alter past trends, but somewhat reliable forecasts can be made.[9]

Suppose that the president of Lifter, Inc. didn't know that the company would receive contracts from Boeing, Ford, and Republic Steel. In this case, the firm has to do the best it can to meet the increased demand for its products; the president is faced with not having enough people to do the work to fulfill the contracts.

Estimating from experience is a more informal forecasting procedure.[10] For example, simply asking department managers for opinions about future human resource needs is an informal forecasting procedure. Some managers are confident in planning, whereas others are reluctant to offer an opinion or are just not reliable forecasters.

The J. C. Penney Company, a large retail merchandiser, plans its human resource needs from information supplied by each retail store. Penney's develops five-year, consumer demand projections for each position in the organization. Personnel needs in management are supplied primarily through promotion, because experienced employees have low turnover and clearly defined career paths. The company recruits recent college graduates for lower-level managerial and staff positions. All J. C. Penney managerial employees are called associates to give them a stronger sense of commitment to the organization, and each employee is evaluated on potential for being promoted. These evaluations give the company a readily available, company-wide inventory of human resources. A computer is used to match present and anticipated vacancies with available associates.

RECRUITMENT

The primary objective of **recruitment,** an essential step in staffing an organization, is to attract the best-qualified applicants to fill vacancies.[11]

[8]For excellent discussions of human resource planning, see James M. Walker, "Moving Closer to the Top," *Personnel Administrator,* December 1986, pp. 52–57, 117; John A. Hooper, Ralph F. Catalanello, and Patrick L. Murry, "Shoring Up the Weakest Link," *Personnel Administrator,* April 1987, pp. 49–55, 134.

[9]For a discussion of some nontraditional sources of new employees, see Gloria Glucksteen and Donald C. Z. Ramer, "The Alternative Employment Marketplace," *Personnel Administrator,* February 1988, pp. 100–104.

[10]Gary Dessler, *Personnel Management* (Reston, Va.: Reston Publishing, 1984), p. 120.

[11]Margaret Magmus, "Is Your Recruitment All It Can Be?" *Personnel Journal,* February 1987, pp. 54–63.

The primary objective of recruitment is to attract the best-qualified applicants to fill vacancies.

However, even before acquiring applicants, it is necessary to understand clearly the job that needs to be filled. The methods and procedures used to acquire an understanding about jobs are called **job analysis.**[12] Through job analysis, managers decide what kind of people to hire.

Sources of Job Information.   Job analysis is the process of determining the tasks that make up a job and the skills, abilities, and responsibilities an employee needs to successfully accomplish that job. Numerous methods are used to collect and classify job analysis information. Interviews, surveys, self-reports, and expert-observer rating scales are some of the more popular job analysis data collection procedures. The facts about a job are found in a **job description** and a **job specification.** A comparison of these is shown in Figure 9–2.

An efficient job analysis program provides information that is used by every unit within the human resource management department. For example, to recruit and select effectively, qualified personnel must be matched with job requirements. Complete job information is provided by the description and the specification. Another example involves the establishment of proper rates of pay. If equitable pay systems are to be developed, it is necessary to have a complete job description. An example of a job description is provided in Figure 9–3.

Two widely used systematic job analysis approaches are functional job analysis (FJA) and the position analysis questionnaire (PAQ).[13]

[12]Sidney Gael, *Job Analysis* (San Francisco: Jossey-Bass, 1983), p. 35.

[13]Marc J. Wallace, Jr., N. Fredric Crandall, and Charles H. Fay, *Administering Human Resources* (New York: Random House, 1982), pp. 187–97.

FIGURE 9–2   Sources of Job Information

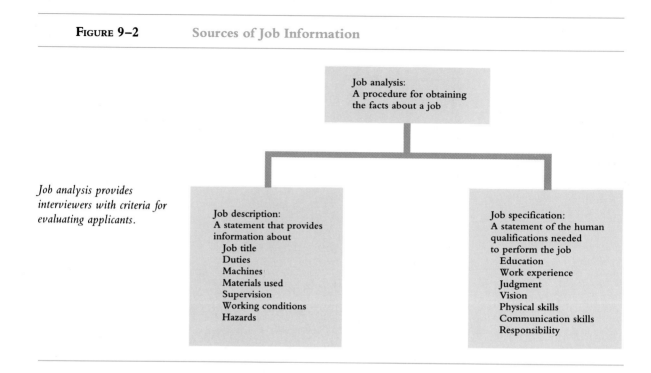

Job analysis provides interviewers with criteria for evaluating applicants.

Functional job analysis focuses on four dimensions of an individual job:

1. What the worker does in relation to data, people, and jobs.
2. What methods and techniques the worker uses.
3. What machines, tools, and equipment the worker uses.
4. What materials, products, subject matter, or services the worker produces.

The first three dimensions relate to job *activities,* and the fourth relates to job *outcomes.* FJA provides a description of jobs that can be the basis for classifying them according to any one of the four dimensions. It can also be the basis for defining standards of performance. For example, managers can prescribe what an individual should do with what methods and machines to produce a standard level of output. FJA is the most widely used systematic job analysis method[14] and is the basis for the most extensive listing of occupational titles.[15]

The **position analysis questionnaire** focuses on the actual behavior of the individual in the performance of the job. PAQ has been the object of considerable attention by experts who believe that position analysis must take into account not only job-oriented dimensions but also worker-oriented dimensions.[16] A PAQ analysis attempts to identify six dimensions:

[14]Ibid., p. 196.

[15]U.S. Department of Labor, *Dictionary of Occupational Titles,* 4th ed. (Washington, D.C.: U.S. Government Printing Office, 1977).

[16]E. J. McCormick, P. R. Jeanneret, and R. C. Mecham, "A Study of Job Characteristics and Job Dimensions as Based on the Position Analysis Questionnaire (PAQ)," *Journal of Applied Psychology,* August 1972, pp. 347–68.

FIGURE 9–3   Sample Job Description

Job: New-Products Manager
       Victoreen Electronics (plant)
       Palos Park, Illinois

The new-products manager reports directly to the vice president of product planning.

The new-products manager plans, organizes, and directs the development and testing of electronic products manufactured for industrial customers of the organization.

Responsibility Domain

A. Plans from worksheet to final production all electronic products requested by the vice president of product planning.
B. Establishes appropriate project teams to carry out plans within time and budget constraints.
C. Provides managerial guidance and counseling to project team leaders on all phases of the project.
D. Develops adequate quality testing for all newly developed products.
E. Prepares cost-benefit analysis on each project assigned.

Supervision Domain

A job description provides information about a job's duties, technology, conditions, and hazards.

Project leaders (3)   Accountant/economist (1)
Operational engineers (15)   Drafter (1)
Process technicians (3)   Secretary (1)
Apprentice operational engineers (3)

Coordination Domain

■ Coordinates activities with each new-products manager through preparation of prework planning document.
■ Coordinates with purchasing department in arranging for the purchase of necessary materials to complete projects.
■ Coordinates with personnel department in arranging for proper recruiting, selection, training and development, and compensation of employees within the supervision domain.

Job description completed   _____
                                                                                                                Date

Prepared by job analyst   _____
                                                                                                                Signature

Accepted by vice president of product planning   _____
                                                                                                                Signature

Filed by vice president of personnel   _____
                                                                                                                Signature

1. Information sources critical to job performance.
2. Information processing and decision making critical to job performance.
3. Physical activity and dexterity required by the job.
4. Interpersonal relationships required by the job.
5. Physical working conditions and the reactions of individuals to those conditions.
6. Other job characteristics, such as work schedule and work responsibility.

PAQ and FJA overlap considerably. Each attempts to identify work activities and outcomes. But PAQ includes the additional consideration of the employee's psychological responses to the job demands and context. Thus, PAQ attempts to acknowledge that job performance is a combination of job dimensions and human characteristics. It enables managers to set standards and obtain information about the individual, the performance of work, and the results of work.

Performing accurate job analysis is for many jobs a complex task. For example, the job of managing is difficult to analyze. Planning, organizing, and controlling involve abstract thinking and decision making. And these activities are difficult to quantify. However, if performance appraisals are to be meaningful, fair, and comprehensive for the manager's job or any job, a systematic job analysis that results in the identification of standards is essential.

Legal Aspects of Recruiting.   Individuals responsible for recruiting are faced with many legal requirements. For example, a certain percentage of minority group members and women must now be recruited for positions that have seldom been filled by these people. These requirements are enforced by laws administered by the Equal Employment Opportunity Commission (EEOC).[17] Through Title VII of the Civil Rights Act of 1964 and the Equal Employment Opportunity Act of 1972, the federal government attempts to provide equal opportunities for employment without regard to race, religion, age, creed, sex, national origin, or disability.[18] These laws have broad coverage and apply to any activity, business, or industry in which a labor dispute would hinder commerce. The laws also cover state and local governments, government agencies, and agencies of the District of Columbia.

Some of the specific provisions of the Equal Employment Opportunity Act of 1972 are:

- It is unlawful for an employer to fail or refuse to hire, to discharge, or otherwise to discriminate against any individual with respect to compensation, conditions, or privileges of employment because of race, color, religion, sex, age, or national origin. This applies to applicants for employment as well as current employees.
- Employers may not limit, segregate, or classify employees in any way that would deprive them of employment opportunities because of race, color, age, religion, sex, or national origin.
- The EEOC has the power to file action in a federal district court if it is unable to eliminate alleged unlawful employment practices by the informal methods of conference, conciliation, and persuasion.
- Employment tests may be used if the employer can prove that they are related to the job or promotion sought by the individual. Tests should be validated for each company.
- No discriminatory statements may be included in any advertisements for job opportunities.

---

[17]See Ann Weaver Hart, "Intent vs. Effect: Title VII Case Law that Could Affect You: Part I," *Personnel Journal,* March 1984, pp. 31–47; Ann Weaver Hart, "Intent vs. Effect: Title VII Case Law that Could Affect You: Part II," *Personnel Journal,* April 1984, pp. 50–58.

[18]Kenneth Sovereign, *Personnel Law* (Reston, Va.: Reston Publishing, 1984).

The EEOC attempted at first to encourage employers to follow the guidelines of the law. Now the EEOC is more aggressive and asks employers to prepare **affirmative action programs.**[19] The employer must spell out how the company plans to increase the number of minority and female employees. If EEOC investigators do not like the distribution of employees, they can propose adjustments. The employer may then state why these adjustments can or cannot be made.

Even if the EEOC does not get involved with an employer, an individual who feels that discrimination is taking place may sue. The number of complaints of job discrimination increased from 8,800 in 1966 to over 80,000 in 1988.[20]

Airline hiring practices have been the subject of two important court decisions on recruitment. One held that female gender is not a bona fide occupational qualification for the job of cabin flight attendant. Another held that an airline's policy that stewardesses must be single is unlawful. No other female employees were subject to the policy, and there was no formal policy restricting employment to single male stewards. Another court ruled it illegal to fire a female employee because she is pregnant and unmarried. A sex discrimination case against a New York law firm was settled, before a court ruling, when it agreed to recruit, hire, and promote women attorneys on the same basis as men.

The legal procedures regarding equal employment opportunities and recruitment are important to employers. Organizations have to adjust to and work with these laws. Although adjustments are sometimes difficult, they seem to be a better alternative than becoming involved in long and costly court battles. Providing equal opportunities to all qualified job applicants makes sense both legally and morally. The vast majority of managers in organizations believe that all citizens have a right to any job they can perform reasonably well after a sufficient amount of training.

Recruiting Actions.   If the needed human resources are not available from within the company, outside sources must be tapped. A well-known firm, such as General Mills, will have a file on previous applicants. Even though such applicants were not hired, they frequently maintain an interest in working for a company with a good reputation and image. By careful screening of these files, some good applicants can be added to the pool of candidates.

Advertising in newspapers, trade journals, and magazines is a means to secure new applications.[21] When a company lists a post office box number and does not provide the company name, this is called a *blind advertisement*. Blind ads are used to eliminate the necessity of contacting every applicant, since some will be unqualified.

One of the most important sources for recruiting first-level managers is the college campus. Many colleges and universities have placement centers that work with company recruiters. The applicants read advertisements and information provided by the companies and then are interviewed. The most

[19]Paul S. Greenlaw, "Affirmative Action or Reverse Discrimination," *Personnel Journal*, September 1985, pp. 84–86.

[20]Correspondence and discussions with EEOC, Washington, D.C., January 1989.

[21]Allan Halcrow, "Anatomy of a Recruitment Ad," *Personnel Journal*, August 1985, pp. 64–65.

Management Focus

The Ethics of Recruiting: The Courtship Phenomenon

The job offer sounded like it was made for her. So Lynda McDermott left her job at an accounting firm and became executive vice president of a consulting firm. According to her new boss, she would play a major role in attracting new business.

Eleven months later, Lynda quit. Her boss, she says, had relegated her to administrative duties. "He's a wonderful salesperson," Lynda stated with some bitterness.

As Lynda sees it, she was the victim of a job bait-and-switch. Promised a certain kind of work as an applicant, the new employee soon realizes that the job is something quite different, leading to frustration, broken promises, and poor performance.

Making promises that can't be kept is called the "courtship phenomenon." Recruiters paint the best picture they can about the job and their firm. These inflated claims can backfire and should not be made. What recruiters must do is be perfectly honest, make no promises that can't be kept, and let the applicant talk to recent hires. Every job has some shortcomings, and these need to be communicated clearly before a person accepts or rejects a job offer.

Source: Adapted from Larry Reibstein, "Crushed Hopes: When a New Job Proves to Be Something Different," *The Wall Street Journal*, June 10, 1987, p. 25.

promising students are invited to visit the company, where other interviews are conducted.

In locating experienced employees, organizations can use private employment agencies, executive search firms, or state employment agencies. Some are no-fee agencies, which means that employers pay the fee (if there is one) instead of the applicant. An organization is not obligated to hire any person referred by an agency, but the agency is usually informed when the right person is found.

Recruiting includes an ethical dimension that must also be considered. Some firms tend to hype a job or to mislead applicants, especially when there is a shortage of available talent. This type of behavior often backfires. And as the Management Focus on recruiting ethics suggests, legal consequences may ensue as well.

EMPLOYEE SELECTION AND PLACEMENT

The selection and placement of personnel begin with a need for human resources and are also heavily influenced by legal requirements. Discriminatory practices in recruiting, testing, and job offerings are illegal, as stated in the Civil Rights Act of 1964 and the Equal Employment Opportunity Act of 1972. The selection process is a series of steps that starts with the initial screening and ends with the orientation of newly hired employees. Figure 9–4 is a flow diagram showing each step in the process.

Preliminary Interview.   This screening, used to weed out unqualified applicants, is often the first personal contact an applicant has with a company.

FIGURE 9–4   Steps in the Selection Process

The selection process requires inputs from the organization as well as the applicant.

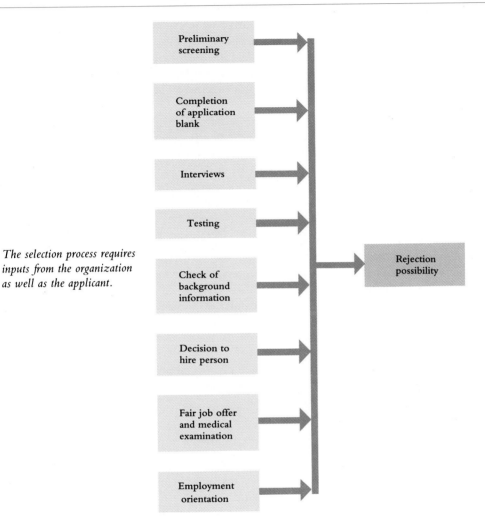

Application.   The applicant who passes the preliminary screening usually completes an application blank. The application blank is used to obtain information that can help in reaching an employment decision. It is important that the questions on the blank be able, at least in a general sense, to predict job success. The appropriate questions are usually developed after a careful job analysis is completed.

Interviews.   Interviews are used throughout the selection process, but there are three basic interviewing steps.[22] First, interviewers must acquaint themselves with the job analysis. Second, they must analyze the information on

[22]William L. Donoghy, *The Interview: Skills and Applications* (Glenview, Ill.: Scott, Foresman, 1984), p. 18.

application blanks. Third, interviewers need to ask questions that will elicit information that can add to what is included on the application blank. While performing these three interviewing steps, the interviewer must be courteous, create a favorable atmosphere, and provide the applicants with information and a positive image of the organization.[23]

Not all interviewers portray a positive image of themselves or their company. Anyone who has ever interviewed for a job will recognize some of the interviewers described in the Management Focus.

Testing.   For years, selection tests have been used to screen applicants.[24] Widespread use started during World War II, when the Army Alpha test was used to measure intelligence. Installation of a sound testing program is costly and time-consuming, and it must be done by experts. Just because a test has been useful for selecting sales personnel in one company is no reason to believe that it will be just as useful in another company.

The advantages of a testing program include:

- *Improved accuracy in selecting employees.* Individuals differ in skills, intelligence, motivation, interests, and goals. If these differences can be measured and if they are related to job success, then performance can be predicted to some extent by test scores.
- *An objective means of judging.* Applicants answer the same questions under the same test conditions, so one applicant's score can be compared to the scores of other applicants.
- *Information for present employee needs.* Tests given to present employees can provide information about training, development, or counseling needs. Thus, tests can objectively uncover needs.

Despite these advantages, tests have become controversial in recent years. Important legal rulings and fair-employment codes have resulted in strict procedures for developing tests. The following criticisms have been directed at testing programs:[25]

- *Tests are not infallible.* Tests may reveal what people can do but not what they will do.
- *Tests are given too much weight.* Tests cannot measure everything about a person. They can never be a complete substitute for judgment.
- *Tests discriminate against minorities.* Ethnic minorities, such as blacks and Mexican-Americans, may score lower than whites on certain paper-and-pencil tests. Title VII, Equal Employment Opportunity, of the Civil Rights Act of 1964 prohibits employment practices that artificially discriminate against individuals on the basis of test scores.[26]

Despite the problems, controversies, and costs involved, tests are widely used. Testing is a part of the employment process, one of the tools that can

---

[23]Richard A. Fear, *The Evaluation Interview* (New York: McGraw-Hill, 1984), p. 78.

[24]Anne Anastasi, *Psychological Testing* (New York: Macmillan, 1982), p. 12.

[25]G. Stephen Taylor, "Personality Tests for Potential Employees: More Harm than Good," *Personnel Journal,* January 1988, pp. 60–64.

[26]Dale Yoder and Paul D. Standoher, "Testing and EEO: Getting Down to Cases," *Personnel Administrator,* February 1984, pp. 67–76.

MANAGEMENT FOCUS

Beware of These Interviewers

Interviewers are critical to any organization's success because they are closely involved in staffing. Some interviewers' weaknesses can result in poor hiring decisions. Be particularly aware of:

1. *Cloners.* They look for themselves in job applicants. They particularly like applicants from the same college or with the same training.
2. *Promisers.* Every candidate that leaves the interview believes he or she will be offered the job.
3. *Interlocutors.* They like to argue with applicants. A lot like lawyers, they see every interview as a challenge and try to trap the applicant.
4. *Worriers.* They hire only mediocre applicants because they feel threatened by the best applicants.

5. *Conspirators.* They look for the most subservient applicants. Basically, they hate people.
6. *Inferiors.* These readily admit they know nothing about the job for which they are interviewing candidates.
7. *Donors.* Because they really like people and would love to offer everyone the job, they can't say no.
8. *Talkers.* Because they love to hear themselves talk, they hire applicants who listen well.
9. *Listeners.* They fail to ask probing questions and expect the applicant to do all the talking.
10. *Postponers.* These find it difficult to make a choice between candidates, and they often end up losing the better ones.

Source: Based on an interview with Robert Half, president of Robert Half International, and reported in *Boardroom Reports,* December 1988, p. 2.

help the manager make selection decisions. In summary, test results provide some usable information, but they do not provide a total picture of how well the person will perform.[27]

Steps in the Hiring Decision.   After the preliminary steps—screening, evaluating the application form, interviewing, and testing—the company may consider making an offer. If so, a *background check* is often done to verify information, usually by letter, by telephone, or in person. One important group of references consulted is previous employers; the company tries to gather facts about the applicant's previous record of job performance. Under the Fair Credit and Reporting Act (1971), the prospective employer is required to secure the applicant's permission before checking references.

When the reference check yields favorable information and the *decision to hire* is made, the line manager and the human resource department representative meet to decide what the offer will be. The *job offer* is usually made contingent on successful completion of a *physical examination*. The objective is to screen out people whose physical deficiencies might be expensive liabilities and to place people on jobs they are physically able to handle. The *orientation* of a new

[27]Cristina G. Banks and Loriann Roberson, "Performance Appraisers as Test Developers," *Academy of Management Review,* January 1985, pp. 128–42.

employee is fully discussed in the next section. But it is part of the selection process in that, as Figure 9–4 shows, rejection is still possible if the orientation is not successfully accomplished.

Training and Development

Training and development programs include numerous activities that inform employees of policies and procedures, educate them in job skills, and develop them for future advancement. The importance of training and development to the organization cannot be overemphasized.[28] Through recruitment and placement, good employees can be brought into the company, but they need orientation and continual education and development so that their needs can be met and the objectives of the organization can be achieved simultaneously.[29]

Training Programs

Training is a continual process of helping employees perform at a high level from the first day they start to work. It may occur at the place of work or at a special training facility, but it should always be supervised by experts in the educational process.[30]

To be effective, a training program must accomplish a number of goals. First, it must be based on organizational and individual needs. Training for training's sake is not the aim. Second, the training objectives should spell out what problems will be solved. Third, all training should be based on sound theories of learning; this is a major reason that training and management development are not tasks for amateurs. Finally, training must be evaluated to determine whether a training program is working.[31]

1. *Locating needs.* Before a training program can be developed, problem areas must be pinpointed. Organizations can use a number of techniques to identify problems, including reviewing safety records, absenteeism data, job descriptions, and attitude surveys to see what employees think about their jobs, bosses, and the company.

2. *Setting objectives.* Once training needs have been identified, objectives need to be stated in writing. These objectives provide a framework for the program. The objectives need to be meaningful and challenging. Objectives usually fall under two major categories: skills and knowledge. Skill objectives focus on developing physical abilities; knowledge objectives are concerned with understanding, attitudes, and concepts.

3. *Conducting programs.* A variety of methods are available for attaining skill and knowledge objectives. Such factors as cost, available time, number of

---

[28]Joseph P. Kahn and Susan Buchsbaum, "The Training Imperative," *Inc.*, March 1986, pp. 119–20.

[29] David F. Jones, "Developing a New Employee Orientation Program," *Personnel Journal*, March 1984, pp. 86–87.

[30]Chris Lea, "Where the Training Dollars Go," *Training*, October 1987, pp. 51–56.

[31]Elaine I. Berke, "Keeping Newly Trained Supervisors from Going Back to Old Ways," *Management Review*, February 1984, pp. 14–16.

persons to be trained, background of trainees, and skill of the trainees determine the method used. Some of the more widely used are:

- *On-the-job training.* A supervisor or other worker may show a new employee how to perform the job.
- *Vestibule training.* This term describes training in a classroom or away from the actual work area.
- *Classroom training.* Numerous classroom methods are used by business organizations. The lecture, or formal presentation, is one method. Another, a conference or small discussion group, gets the student more involved than the lecture method.

DEVELOPMENTAL METHODS

Training is generally associated with operating employees; development is associated with managerial personnel. **Management development** refers to the process of educating and developing selected personnel so that they have the knowledge and skills needed to manage in future positions. The process starts with the selection of a qualified individual and continues through that individual's career.[32]

The objectives of management development are to ensure the long-run success of the organization, to furnish competent replacements, to create an efficient team that works well together, and to enable each manager to use his or her full potential. Management development may also be necessary because of high executive turnover, a shortage of management talent, and our society's emphasis on lifelong education and development.

Employees can acquire the knowledge and skills necessary to become successful managers in two main ways.[33] One is through formal development programs; the other involves on-the-job development. On-the-job programs include:

- *Understudy programs.* A person works as a subordinate partner with a boss so that eventually he or she can assume the full responsibilities and duties of the job.
- *Job rotation.* Managers are transferred from job to job on a systematic basis. The assignment on each job generally lasts about six months.
- *Coaching.* A supervisor teaches job knowledge and skills to a subordinate. The supervisor instructs, directs, coaches, and evaluates the subordinate.

These on-the-job development plans emphasize actual job experience. They are used to increase the manager's skill, knowledge, and confidence. The Center for Creative Leadership believes that managers must also develop "mental toughness." The importance of this characteristic is described in the Management Focus.

Formal management development programs are often conducted by training units within organizations or by consultants in universities and specialized training facilities around the country. In the very large corporations (e.g., General Electric, Westinghouse, AT&T), full-time training units conduct

[32]Jeffrey A. Sonnenfeld and Maury A. Peiperl, "Staffing Policy as a Strategic Response: A Typology of Career Systems," *Academy of Management Review,* October 1988, pp. 588–600.

[33]Paul Petre, "Games that Teach You to Manage," *Fortune,* October 29, 1984, pp. 65–72.

MANAGEMENT FOCUS

Developing Mental Toughness on the Job

The Center for Creative Leadership is a non-profit research and educational institution in Greensboro, North Carolina. It was formed to improve the practice of management. Two of the centers researchers are Morgan McCall, Jr., and Michael Lombardo. In one of their most important studies, *The Lessons of Experience,* they found that career success in management requires, above all else, mental toughness. As managers progress, they learn lessons, accumulate experience, and change. Managers who are mentally tough do not allow setbacks, mistakes, or failures to permanently damage their confidence and self-esteem. McCall and Lombardo

believe that as managers progress through their careers, they become like forged steel. Each stage makes them harder and more flexible. The researchers identify six stages:

1. *First supervisory job.* The manager discovers the people side of management. He or she comes face to face with the realization that technical skills will not be enough: To succeed as a manager you must get things done through other people.
2. *Project and task force assignments.* The manager's perspective changes from that of an expert in some field to that of a manager who must motivate people from a variety of fields. He

regular management development courses. For example, one major course offered at General Electric, the Advanced Management Course, is designed for the four highest levels of management. It is conducted over a period of 13 weeks, and its content includes strategic planning, economics, social issues, and management principles.

PERFORMANCE APPRAISAL

Performance appraisal involves the formal evaluation of an individual's job performance. It includes feedback to the individual and determination of

Very large corporations regularly conduct management development courses for managerial personnel.

or she begins to appreciate the need for skills in selling, persuasion, and discovering what others are thinking.

3. *Line to staff switches.* The manager begins to understand the importance and impact of the corporate culture. When there is no right answer or objective criterion on which to act, the manager begins to value his or her own views and loses any self-doubts.

4. *Starting a project from scratch.* Here the manager learns what is really important and how to organize a team to get a job done. The challenge of creating a staff forces the manager to learn the fine art of selecting, training, and motivating people. This task changes the manager for good.

5. *Fix-it and turnaround assignments.* Here the manager learns how to make difficult decisions that have a human cost and to deal with subordinate performance problems. The manager must balance the needs of employees with the need to cut and rebuild.

6. *A change in scope.* In this stage, the manager makes a mental transition from running the show alone to making sure other managers are developed.

Source: Morgan McCall, Jr., and Michael Lombardo, *The Lessons of Experience* (Greensboro, N.C.: Center for Creative Leadership, 1988).

whether and how the performance can be improved.[34] As a control technique, effective performance appraisal requires standards, information, and corrective action. The *standard* in performance evaluation is prior specification of acceptable levels of job performance. *Information* must be available to measure actual job performance in comparison to standard job performance. Finally, managers must be able to take *corrective action* to restore any imbalance between actual and standard job performance. Recall from the previous chapter that standards, information, and corrective action are the three elements of the management function of control.

Because performance appraisal involves individuals judging the quality and quantity of job performance of other individuals, the process is often emotional; it brings into play ideas and perceptions of fairness and equal treatment. The human element of performance appraisal must be taken into account if it is to serve individual and organizational purposes.[35]

As shown in Figure 9–5, a performance appraisal system has the characteristics of all feedback control methods. Through the system, managers can obtain information related to inputs (employees), activities (job performance), and outputs (outcomes). Corrective action is directed toward changing employees' knowledge and skills, as well as job performance, activities, and behaviors. The effectiveness of a performance appraisal system depends on the quality of the three elements of all control techniques: standards, information, and corrective action.

[34]Evelyn Eichel and Henry E. Bender, *Performance Appraisal: A Study of Current Techniques* (New York: American Management Association, 1984).

[35]Roy W. Regel and Robert W. Hollman, "Gauging Performance Objectively," *Personnel Administrator,* June 1987, pp. 74–78.

FIGURE 9–5   Performance Appraisal

Effective performance appraisal requires effective feedback control.

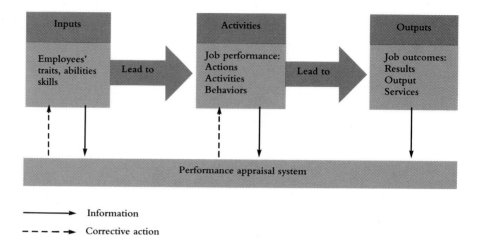

Standards.   The most crucial aspect of performance appraisal is identifying the standard of effective performance. In performance evaluation systems, it is customary to refer to standards as "criteria"—ways of identifying success in an activity.[36] A criterion for a major league pitcher is earned run average; a criterion for a student is the grade earned in a course or the grade point average after one year at college. An important and necessary step in developing a performance appraisal system is the development of criteria that indicate successful performance.

Primary sources of individual job performance criteria are the organization's overall objectives and strategies. It is an important principle that individual performance should contribute to organizational performance. Although this principle seems self-evident, it remains difficult to implement, particularly when organizational objectives change.

Information.   Information enables managers to judge the performance of subordinates. Managers must decide three issues regarding performance information: the source, the schedule, and the method.

Sources of information.   Five possible parties can provide appraisal information: (1) the supervisor or supervisors of the appraisee, (2) the peers, (3) the appraisee, (4) subordinates of the appraisee, and (5) individuals outside the work environment. In most situations, the appraiser is the immediate supervisor of the person rated and should be most familiar with the employee's performance. In addition, many organizations regard performance appraisal as an integral part of the immediate supervisor's job. The supervisor's appraisals usually are reviewed by higher management, thereby reducing the possibility of favoritism and personal bias.

[36]Frank J. Landy and Don A. Trumbo, *Psychology of Work Behavior* (Chicago: Dorsey Press, 1980), p. 99.

Some organizations use group ratings to appraise managerial personnel; members of the group could include superiors, subordinates, and peers. Although some companies use peer appraisal systems, lack of success with this method is not unusual. Peers need mutual cooperation to do their jobs, and performance appraisal undermines the spirit of cooperation.

There is some interest in using self-appraisals.[37] The major claims in support of this approach are that it improves the employee's understanding of job performance, increases the personal commitment of employees because of their participation in the performance appraisal process, and reduces the hostility between superiors and subordinates over ratings. Some employers fear that self-appraisals will be unusually high and not sufficiently critical of current performance.

There is some support for the use of multiple appraisers. The major advantage of using superior, peer, and self-ratings is that this provides a great deal of information about the appraisee. In making decisions about promotion, training/development, and career planning, as much information as possible is needed to suggest the best alternative courses of action for the employee.

Schedule of appraisal.   There is no specific schedule for appraising all types of employees. In general, one formal appraisal a year is provided for long-term employees. Recent hires usually are appraised more frequently than other employees. The time to appraise will depend on the situation and on the intent of the appraisal. If performance appraisals either are too far apart or occur too frequently, the appraisee may not be able to use the feedback to make improvements.

An appraisal program conducted solely for the sake of appraising employees soon will lose impact unless it becomes integrated with the main emphasis of the organization.[38] The performance appraisal program should be considered a continual process that focuses on task accomplishment, personal development, and the organization's objectives.

Appraisal methods.   At one extreme, the most simplistic method of information gathering consists solely of the manager's periodic observations of the subordinate's work behavior. Based on these observations, the manager makes judgments of the subordinate's performance. At the other extreme are complex systems that involve documents, procedures, and reviews. In such formal systems, the manager completes forms documenting the subordinate's performance during the period covered by the appraisal. A number of performance evaluation systems have been developed.

Graphic rating scales. The oldest and most widely used performance evaluation procedure, the graphic-scaling technique, appears in many forms. Generally, the rater is supplied with a printed form, one for each subordinate to be rated. The form contains a number of job performance criteria to rate. The rating scales are distinguished by (1) how the criteria are defined, (2) the degree to which the person interpreting the ratings can tell what response was

[37]Donald J. Campbell and Cynthia Lee, "Self-Appraisal in Performance Evaluation: Development versus Evaluation," *Academy of Management Review,* April 1988, pp. 302–14.

[38]D. Cederbloom, "The Performance Appraisal Interview: A Review, Implications, and Suggestions," *Academy of Management Review,* January 1982, pp. 219–22.

intended by the rater, and (3) how carefully the performance criteria are spelled out for the rater.

Some common rating-scale formats are depicted in Figure 9–6. The first distinguishing feature, the meaning of the possible response categories, usually is handled by the use of "anchor statements." Anchor statements or words are placed at points along a scale. For example, rating scales (a), (b), (c), and (h) in the figure use anchors.

The second distinguishing feature among rating scales is the degree to which the person interpreting the ratings can tell what response is intended. The clarity of the intended response is better with scales (e), (f), and (g) than with the other scales shown. "Quality" of work can be interpreted differently by various raters.

The meaning of a performance criterion must be carefully spelled out for the appraiser. For example, scales (a), (b), (e), and (g) give the rater little help in defining the criterion. Scales (c) and (h) provide the rater with fairly good definitions.

Behaviorally anchored rating scales. Behaviorally anchored rating scales (BARS) are constructed through the use of critical incidents.[39] Once the important areas of performance are identified and defined by employees who know the job, critical-incident statements are used as criteria to discriminate among levels of performance. The form for a BARS usually covers 6 to 10 specifically defined job behaviors, each uniquely described. Each description is based on observable behaviors and is meaningful to the employees being evaluated.

An example of a BARS for engineering competence is presented in Figure 9–7. The criterion is defined for the appraiser; the descriptions defining the particular response categories are easy to interpret. The feedback provided by the BARS is specific and meaningful. For example, if the appraisee is given a 1.50 on this criterion, the individual is provided with the specific performance incident that the appraiser used to make the rating.

Despite the time, cost, and procedural problems of developing and implementing BARS, this system seems to possess some advantages. Specifically, a BARS program could minimize subordinate or appraisee defensiveness toward evaluation. By being involved in the development of BARS, appraisees have input into how they are to be appraised. The BARS development steps could include both superiors and subordinates. In a sense, then, all of the parties involved can contribute to the creation of the evaluation criterion.

Another advantage of using BARS is that the appraisal program concentrates on job-specific and job-relevant behaviors. Many performance appraisal programs are abstract and not meaningful to either the appraised or the appraiser. Thus, when providing feedback to employees, the appraisers must convert the ratings to examples of actual job behavior. There are, in many cases, variances in appraisers' ability to make these conversions from the rating

---

[39]P. C. Smith and L. M. Kendall, "Retranslation of Expectations: An Approach to the Construction of Unambiguous Anchors for Rating Scales," *Journal of Applied Psychology,* April 1963, pp. 149–55.

FIGURE 9–6   Samples of Rating-Scale Formats

Performance criteria must be carefully defined on rating scales.

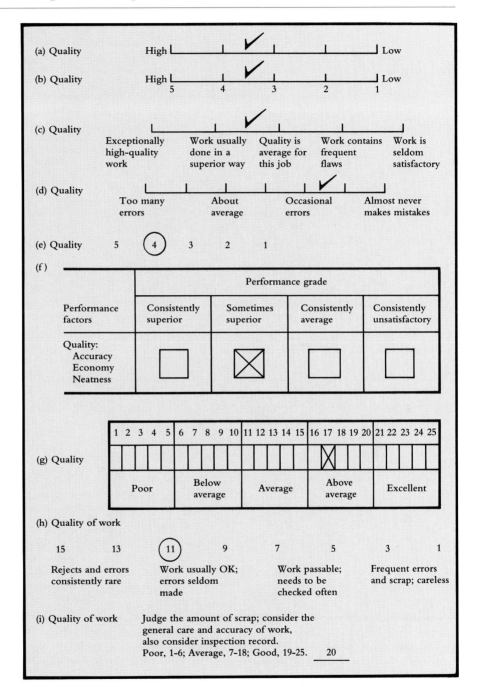

FIGURE 9–7   A BARS Performance Dimension

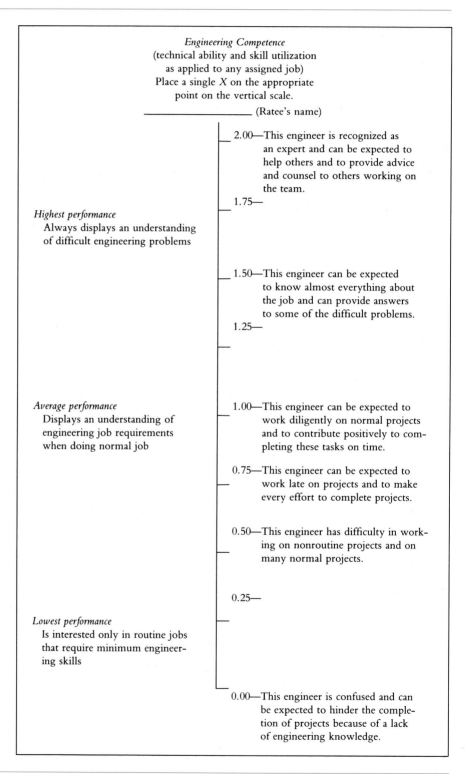

BARS focus on actual behavior to discriminate among levels of performance.

scale to meaningful job behaviors. BARS already contain behaviors that the superior can use in developing the appraisal counseling interview.

Finally, since job-knowledgeable employees participate in the actual development steps, the final rating form is assumed to be reliable and valid and to cover all aspects of the job. (A common problem of many performance appraisal techniques is that they do not evaluate all aspects of a job.) The use of BARS also provides valuable insights for developing training programs. The skills to be developed are specified in terms of actual behavioral incidents rather than abstract or general skills. Trainees could learn expected behaviors and how job performance is evaluated.

WAGE AND SALARY MANAGEMENT

Money is important, both economically and psychologically. Without it, we cannot buy the goods and services that make life comfortable. Money is also equated with status and recognition. For both of these reasons, employees are quite sensitive about the amount of pay they receive and how it compares to what others in the company and in society are earning. We can see, then, how money, or compensation, can strongly affect the motivation of employees. Because of its importance, employee motivation is the subject of an entire chapter later in our book. For now, let us just say that it is important for employees to believe that they are being fairly compensated for the time, effort, and results they provide the employer.[40]

EMPLOYEE COMPENSATION

The most common system by which nonmanagerial employees are compensated is **wages,** which are based on time increments or number of units produced. Nonmanagerial employees traditionally have been paid at an hourly or daily rate, although some are now being paid biweekly or monthly. Employees who are compensated on a weekly or longer schedule are paid **salaries.** Hewlett-Packard is one organization that eliminated the daily rate of pay and now considers all personnel at all levels to be salaried employees.[41]

Wages. Some organizations try to motivate employees to improve performance by paying on the basis of the number of units produced. This is called a piecework system. Piece rates are calculated by dividing the hourly wage for the job by the number of units an average employee is expected to produce an hour. For example, if the rate of pay is $5 per hour and the average employee is expected to produce 25 units per hour, then the piece rate is 20 cents per hour. A worker who produced 40 pieces under this plan would earn $8 for the hour.

A daily rate of pay is easier than a piece rate to understand and use, because time standards and records of the employee's output are not needed. Unions generally prefer the daily rate of pay over systems that involve piecework or incentive payments. This preference is based on the belief that a piecework

[40]George Milkovich and Jerry M. Newman, *Compensation* (Plano, Tex.: Business Publications, Inc., 1984), pp. 269–87.

[41]Edward E. Lawler III, "The New Pay," *New Management,* Summer 1985, pp. 52–59.

system tends to reduce a group orientation. By being paid on the basis of individual effort, a worker can produce at any level he or she wants to. Unions prefer to encourage group solidarity and a united front.

Many factors help determine the wage rate for a nonmanagerial job. Wages for certain jobs are affected by the availability of and demand for qualified personnel, although unions and the government may hinder the effects of supply and demand. Through strike threats and contract agreements, for example, unions can prevent employers from lowering wage rates even when qualified personnel are available.

The existing wage rates in competing companies or in the community also help determine wage scales. Organizations typically conduct wage surveys to assess hourly rates, piecework or other incentive rates, and fringe benefits offered by other organizations. If the wage rates of an organization are too low, it may be unable to attract qualified personnel.

In many organizations, the relative worth of a job and the wage adjustments for it are determined by using **job evaluation** systems. A job is compared with others within the organization or with a scale. Under the ranking method, all jobs are ranked, from highest to lowest, on the basis of skill, difficulty, working conditions, contribution to goods or services, or other characteristics. This is a simple plan but not totally objective. The personalities of the current jobholders often distort rankings. Nor are unions enthusiastic about job evaluation. With such a system, the union negotiator has almost no role to play.

Wage and salary administration, like other areas of HRM, has been the target of various laws. For instance, full-time employees must be paid at least $3.35 per hour. Since the first minimum wage law, enacted in 1938, the rate has risen over 1,000 percent, from 25 cents to $3.35 as of January 1, 1986. In addition, the Fair Labor Standards Act (1938) forbids the employment of minors between 16 and 18 years of age in such hazardous occupations as coal mining, logging, and woodworking. And the Equal Pay Act (1963) forbids employers to pay employees differently on the basis of sex. Women performing the same work as men must receive the same wage or salary. AT&T was required to pay $6.3 million to 6,100 women employees whose pay had suffered because of their sex.[42] The act does not prohibit compensation differences based on seniority, merit, or performance.

Salaries.   Salaried employees are assumed to have more influence over the way they perform their jobs than are employees who are paid wages.[43] But in developing an equitable compensation system for executives, a similar approach is used: Comparisons are made, surveys are conducted, and both the supply and demand of candidates and the job duties and responsibilities are analyzed.

One method developed specifically for evaluating middle and top management positions was initiated by the consulting firm of Hay Associates. First, analysts evaluate each position from information provided in the job description. Three factors are analyzed: job know-how, problem solving, and

---

[42]Michael F. Carter, "Comparable Worth: An Idea Whose Time Has Come?" *Personnel Journal,* October 1981, pp. 792–94.

[43]Paul G. Engel, "Salaried Plants: Panacea for Productivity?" *Industry Week,* January 21, 1985, pp. 39–42.

accountability. Then, through a statistical procedure, the evaluation for the jobs in a particular company are converted to the Hay control standards, a special ranking system. Hay Associates publishes annual surveys showing the compensation practices of a number of companies for similar jobs. All Hay clients use the same evaluation method, so they can compare management salaries.

BENEFITS AND SERVICES

Benefits and services are forms of supplementary compensation. They represent monetary and nonmonetary payments over and above wage and salary rates. Benefits are financial in nature, whereas services are employer-supplied programs, facilities, or activities (such as parks, gymnasiums, housing, transportation) that are considered useful to employees.

If benefits and services are to yield a return to the employer and provide something positive to employees, they must be developed and used systematically. Too often, the so-called fringes are improperly installed. It is important to determine what benefits and services are preferred by employees and what resources are available to meet these preferences, and then to select the best package within the means of the company.[44] The developers of the package also need to consider its ability to accomplish the following goals:

1. *Attract and retain competent personnel.*   Employees and candidates looking at opportunities evaluate the total compensation package—wage/salary plus fringes. A company gains popularity when people in the community see it as having a competitive compensation package.

2. *Satisfy security needs.*   Through a sound program of benefits and services, an organization can satisfy employees' security needs, including retirement income, disability income, death benefits, medical and dental protection, and educational assistance. These needs may be too expensive for employees to provide themselves.

3. *Meet government regulations.*   Federal and state laws require companies to support such benefits as unemployment compensation and survivors' insurance. The states provide unemployment compensation to unemployed people who are seeking employment. These benefits are typically provided for at least 26 weeks.

The benefits and services offered to employees are significant. The average firm pays about 33 percent of its payroll to benefits.

SUMMARY OF KEY POINTS

- Human resource management (HRM) is the process of accomplishing organizational objectives by acquiring, retaining, terminating, developing, and properly using the human resources of an organization.

- The human resource department in a firm (usually a medium-sized or large firm) typically includes areas handling employment, training and development, wage and salary, employee

---

[44]Robert Levering, Milton Moskowitz, and Michael Katz, *The 100 Best Companies to Work For in America* (Reading, Mass.: Addison-Wesley Publishing, 1984), p. 350. Also see Robert Levering, *A Great Place to Work: What Makes Some Employers So Good (and Most So Bad)* (New York: Random House, 1988), chaps. 1 and 2.

benefits and services, and labor relations functions.

- Human resource planning is an important activity that involves estimating the size and makeup of the future work force.

- Job analysis is an important process used in HRM to determine both the tasks that make up the job and the skills, knowledge, and responsibilities an employee needs to successfully accomplish the job.

- The federal government attempts to provide equal opportunities for employment without regard to race, religion, age, creed, sex, national origin, or disability through Title VII of the Civil Rights Act of 1964 and the Equal Employment Opportunity Act of 1972.

- Selection for employment is a process with a number of steps. The steps in the process include preliminary screening, application blank, interviews, testing, background check, the decision to hire, job offer and medical examination, and orientation.

- Training and development programs are used to inform employees of policies and procedures, educate them in job skills, and develop them for future advancement.

- Management development refers to the process of educating and developing selected personnel so that they have the knowledge and skills needed to manage future positions.

- Performance appraisal requires managers to make decisions about how well individuals perform their jobs.

- Performance appraisal requires standards of acceptable job performance. These standards are called criteria, and they measure aspects of the job that are critical to effective job performance.

- Nonmanagerial employees are usually paid wages on the basis of time worked. Managerial employees are usually paid salaries on the basis of a weekly or monthly rate.

- Benefits and services are forms of supplementary compensation. Benefits are financial (e.g., insurance protection); services are programs provided by the employer (e.g., a gymnasium).

DISCUSSION AND REVIEW QUESTIONS

1. Discuss with a small business owner the types of human resource management that the owner engages in. What did you find out?
2. Why are organizations so interested in benefits and services for employees?
3. What is the difference between a job description and a job specification?
4. How active is the government in the HRM activities conducted by an organization?
5. Why is testing such a controversial part of the selection sequence?
6. Why is job analysis such a vital step in the development of any performance appraisal technique or method?
7. An engineer stated, "My job is so complex and dynamic that it is virtually impossible to find criteria for assessing job performance." What do you think about this claim? Why?
8. Why is it costly to develop a behaviorally anchored rating scale?
9. Why is forecasting such an important part of human resource planning?
10. Are equal employment opportunity and affirmative action programs the same concept or activity? Explain.

ADDITIONAL REFERENCES

Baird, L., and **I. Meshoulan**. "Managing Two Fits of Strategic Human Resource Management." *Academy of Management Review,* January 1988, pp. 116–28.

Greenhalgh, L.; A. T. Lawrence; and **R. I. Sutton**. "Determinants of Work Force Reduction Strategies in Declining Organizations." *Academy of Management Review,* April 1988, pp. 241–54.

Lawrence, B. S. "New Wrinkles in the Theory of Age: Demography, Norms, and Performance Ratings." *Academy of Management Journal,* June 1988, pp. 309–37.

Mills, D. Q. "Planning with People in Mind." *Harvard Business Review,* July–August 1985, pp. 97–105.

Popovich, P., and **J. P. Wanous.** "The Realistic Job Preview as a Persuasive Communication." *Academy of Management Review,* April 1982, pp. 570–78.

Rodgers, D. D. "Computer-Aided Interviewing Overcomes First Impressions." *Personnel Journal,* April 1987, pp. 148–52.

Schuster, J. R. "Compensation Plan Design." *Management Review,* May 1985, pp. 21–25.

Shenkar, O., and **Y. Zeira.** "Human Resources Management in International Joint Ventures: Directions for Research." *Academy of Management Review,* July 1987, pp. 546–57.

Stevens, G. E. "Understanding AIDS." *Personnel Administrator,* August 1988, pp. 84–88.

Wanous, J. P. *Organizational Entry: Recruitment, Selection, and Socialization of Newcomers.* Reading, Mass.: Addison-Wesley Publishing, 1980.

CASE 9–1   Southern Bell's Appraisal Program

Recently, Southern Bell Telephone & Telegraph Company (an AT&T operating company) implemented what they call the management development and evaluation plan (MDEP). The specific purposes of MDEP are to help develop skills and job knowledge in the managerial ranks, to provide useful performance-based information for salary decisions, to evaluate a manager's potential for advancement, and to provide feedback to the appraisees. Southern Bell believes that all employees should be provided with a formal appraisal of their job performance.

One of the first steps in Southern Bell's MDEP program is the identification and description of major responsibilities. These responsibilities relate to the job itself, self-development, and affirmative action. From the responsibilities, a program of objectives is set for each appraisee.

To assist appraisers in determining the value of accomplishing these objectives, Southern Bell has identified six factors to use as measurement criteria. These factors are:

1. Difficulty of accomplishment.
2. Amount of supervisor and/or manager support required.
3. Other circumstances outside employee's control that facilitated or inhibited the achievement.
4. Effectiveness of the employee in reducing barriers to future achievements.
5. Employee's efforts to facilitate the achievement of others.
6. Contribution to organizational objectives.

Bell system managers seldom use all six factors for measuring achievements. They have found that the first three factors apply more frequently than do the last three. It is also likely that an appraiser may weigh a certain factor more heavily in a specific situation than at another time. Management believes that the six factors stimulate the appraiser to be more aware of the context of the situation and the total worth of accomplishing the objective.

In the performance appraisal process, feedback provides the information necessary to improve objective-oriented performance and encourages and assists employees to develop and grow to their fullest potential. After the appraiser (usually the immediate supervisor) completes the MDEP ratings, supervisors who work in the same department join together to perform a group review. This group can accept or modify the ratings of the original appraisal.

After completion of the appraisal and the group review, the immediate supervisor and subordinate have a formal feedback and career counseling session. At this meeting, both sets of ratings are reviewed, compared, discussed, and analyzed.

QUESTIONS FOR ANALYSIS

1. Does the use of the six factors as measurement criteria in Southern Bell's MDEP program eliminate the need for appraiser judgment? Why?
2. Why would a group review differ from the ratings given by the appraiser?

CASE 9–2   Goal Setting at Tenneco

Tenneco is a large, diversified company operating in eight major industries. Among the Tenneco companies are J. I. Case, manufacturer and marketer of farm and construction equipment; Newport News Shipbuilding and Dry Dock Company; Walker Manufacturing Company and Monroe Auto Equipment Company, manufacturers of automotive equipment; Packaging Corporation of America, a supplier of paperboard, folding cartons, and corrugated container; Tenneco Oil, producer, refiner, and marketer of petroleum and related products; Tennessee Gas Transmission Company, marketer of a wide range of industrial chemical products; and Tenneco West, which produces and markets agricultural products. Tenneco employs about 85,000 people, of which 15,000 are managers and professionals.

A task force with representatives from each divisional company of Tenneco recommended to the president that a performance planning and evaluation (PP&E) and goal-setting program be implemented. In support of the PP&E program, the president stated:

> If we fail to offer maximum opportunity to any one person in our organization, we are failing in one of our basic management responsibilities. . . . Accordingly, I expect this philosophy and method of management to receive enthusiastic support at all levels within Tenneco.

Simply stated, Tenneco's top management wanted the program to create an atmosphere that encouraged self-motivation and personal satisfaction.

The PP&E program involves the diagnosis of each job by incumbents, who are then expected to broadly define the key responsibilities of their jobs. Next, specific objectives and priorities of these objectives are spelled out, with an emphasis on work performance and personal-development objectives. Many goal-setting programs place primary emphasis only on the work objectives, disregarding development objectives. This is not the case in the PP&E program. A balance between work performance and objectives for personal development is reached through dialogue, transaction, and agreement between the supervisor and each subordinate, in a formal meeting. After one year, the results of the subordinate's actual performance and development progress are measured against stated objectives and priorities. The performance evaluation session focuses on results, with special attention paid to specific plans and accomplishments in personal development.

This special concern about personal development is the most unique feature of the Tenneco PP&E program. The program also has some other important features:

1. Active top management support displayed by participation of senior executives in all phases of PP&E.
2. The use of external evaluations to monitor the impact, if any, of PP&E on the attitudes and performance of participants.
3. The use of data collected by external evaluators to make modifications. Presently, each company is able to develop its own feedback plan. Feedback in the PP&E programs means the use of the evaluator's information, collected and reported to the divisional company management, to make modifications.

The Tenneco PP&E system contains areas in which subjective measures and judgments are used. However, the care exercised in planning, implementing, supporting, and evaluating the PP&E program appears to have had a positive impact on the Tenneco managers' attitudes about goal setting. Tenneco managers seem stimulated and interested in performance and setting goals for personal development. The secret may be that goal setting is used not only to assess performance contributions but also to develop managers for more responsible duties in the future.

QUESTIONS FOR ANALYSIS

1. What advantages were there in using a task force with representatives from each divisional company to develop performance planning and evaluation (PP&E) at Tenneco?
2. Did Tenneco's president seem concerned about the development of people? How did you reach this conclusion?
3. What would be the value of Tenneco's top management supporting the PP&E program?

EXPERIENTIAL EXERCISE

A CONTROL PROCEDURE: YOUR PERSONAL PERFORMANCE APPRAISAL

Purpose

The purpose of this exercise is to apply performance appraisal guidelines to your own activities and objectives.

The Exercise in Class

1. Write a paragraph (150 words or less) describing a successful you. What would make you successful? Select your school, job, family, or personal life as a reference point. In your paragraph, list the outcomes (results) that would mean you were successful (e.g., school—grade point average 3.3, graduating with honors, receiving highest grade on final; job—promotion to next level in two years, receiving recognition, receiving large merit increase).

2. For the reference point (choose one), select five areas of major concern and the measure of success you would use. Determine whether the measures of success are subjective or objective. Do they have a time frame?

Major area of concern	How is success measured?	Subjective/ objective	Time frame yes/no
1. _____ _____	_____ _____	_____	_____
2. _____ _____	_____ _____	_____	_____
3. _____ _____	_____ _____	_____	_____
4. _____ _____	_____ _____	_____	_____
5. _____ _____	_____ _____	_____	_____

3. Develop the major areas of concern into specific personal objectives—one for each major area of concern. Each objective should be one single sentence, clearly stated, with a time period specified. Rank the objectives from the most important to the least important.

    Ranked Objectives

    1. _____
    2. _____
    3. _____
    4. _____
    5. _____

4. The instructor will form groups of three students to share their success stories, measures of success, and objective statements. Are there differences in what are considered success measures, objectives, and priorities?

The Learning Message

Even self-appraisal of performance is a control procedure. It serves to direct individual behavior toward objectives that are meaningful, clear, comprehensive, and challenging. Explicit objectives that are well stated must be carefully worked on. Skill in developing objectives can be improved with practice. Good objectives can be helpful in planning, organizing, and controlling behavior and attitudes.

COMPREHENSIVE CASE PART II:
MANAGING WORK AND ORGANIZATIONS

MIRACLE CORPORATION

INTRODUCTION

Earl E. Brown, president of Miracle Corporation, a large conglomerate with 20 divisions, was surprised to hear the rumor that major problems were developing in his company. This was related to him by a personal friend who is an investment banker. Mr. Brown was dumbfounded, since the annual results just released revealed Miracle's best year ever with regards to sales, profit, asset utilization, and other measures. In consultation with the partner in charge of the audit, Brown decided that Wayne Riddlebarger of the management service division of the CPA firm employed by Miracle should investigate the possible problems and their causes. Excerpts from Riddlebarger's findings are given below.

HISTORY OF MIRACLE CORPORATION

Miracle Corporation was started rather modestly in the late 1920s. During World War II, it experienced a tremendous expansion that has continued at an accelerated pace until now. In the 1950s, the engineers received most of top management's attention. In the early 60s, the greatest influence on policies was exerted by marketing personnel. Most attention and money went to advertising and market research, as these areas were the "in thing" at the time. In the late 60s and early 70s, diversification and expansion received the greatest emphasis by top management. The corporation had to borrow extensively to maintain the growth rate, and the corporate debt became gigantic. During the mid-1970s, the postwar recession hit the industry, along with the double-digit inflation that began in 1973.

These adverse factors increased the cost of doing business considerably, particularly the expense of interest. Also, some of the expansion and diversification schemes proved less than satisfactory. Profit dropped 65 percent from the high of 1971, falling each year after until it reached 2.1 percent in 1975, down from an average of 7.3 percent in 1960. Feeling that costs were out of control, bankers and investors made a number of demands during a stormy meeting. They wanted better controls, higher returns, and a more favorable financial ratio position.

A New Vice President.   Brown hired Patrick Kelly, partner in charge of the audit, as vice president for planning, information, and control. This newly created position was to replace the controller of the company, who was

Source: Prepared by Felix P. Kollaritsch, The Ohio State University. Permission to publish granted by the author.

retiring. Kelly was to be in charge of coordination of planning, operational control, appraising marketing programs, analyzing acquisition opportunities, reporting to top management, and other regular accounting matters. Accepting this position with the provision that he be given a free hand and the support of top management for three years, Kelly was aiming at the following objectives:

1. His highest priority was to cut the costs of doing business. Methods would include evaluation of all projects and, if their returns were far below the expected rate, eliminating them.
2. New investment must provide at least a 20 percent return.
3. The profit margin must be improved.
4. Corporate debts should be reduced as rapidly as possible.

Creating a Climate for Change.   The first year on the job, Kelly did very little but tour all 20 divisions, studying their operations and problems, and promoting his ideas of planning and control to divisional top management. Successful, he quickly moved to develop a reporting system tailor-made for Miracle Corporation. He also hired his own people for the corporate controller's staff and a divisional staff. With the consent of nearly all division managers, the division controllers were now reporting to him. He also created a corporate internal auditing group.

The Planning Process.   Kelly introduced elaborate information-gathering and planning systems and made sure that observance of each detail was strictly enforced.

Division managers were asked to prepare a five-year plan. These plans were approved by the executive committee, composed of President Brown, the executive vice president, and the corporate vice presidents for sales, production, finance, personnel, and planning. (The detailed outline of the corporate command structure is shown in Exhibit 1.) In February of each year, these plans were extended for one year.

From the five-year plans, yearly budgets were prepared by division managers, including details on sales, expense figures, sales price, volume, projections by products, working-capital position, and so on. These budgets were broken down into quarterly budgets. Toward the end of the second month of any quarter, the division managers would meet to update the budget for the next quarter. They were to identify factors that might alter their forecasts.

In order to pinpoint possible problems before they became fact, each division controller had to submit a report at the middle of each month to the vice president of planning, stating whether or not the division could meet its goals as set out in the monthly budget. Kelly called this "anticipatory planning." This was a modification of the original procedure, which called for a monthly meeting of all the division managers for the purpose described above. However, these midmonthly division managers' meetings were resented so much that Kelly had to discontinue them and replace them with the division controllers' midmonth report.

EXHIBIT 1   Miracle Corporation: Organization Chart

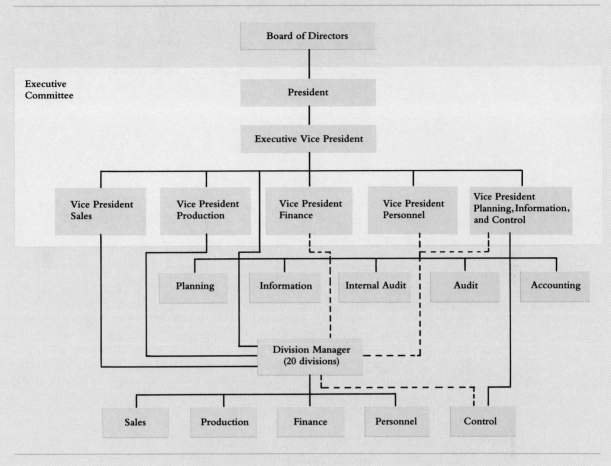

Top Management.   Here are some representative comments that Riddle-barger received from interviews with company executives:

President: "So far at least, the new way has apparently paid off. To our business today, financial and operating controls have become important for success and, most of all, survival."

Executive vice president: "What more can one ask? Our return on equity has improved from 6.7 percent to 10.5 percent since Mr. Kelly joined us. We are making things happen; we don't wait for them to happen."

Vice president, production: "The company has been successful in paring down the inventories considerably because of tighter control. So far, the controls have led to the shutdown of five plants with rates of return not up to our expectations."

Vice president, finance: "Economic conditions and pressures dictate that we get more out of our investment, and now we are. Our working capital position has improved considerably."

Vice president, personnel: "The payroll of the corporation is down from 6,000 in 1973 to 5,000 right now."

Vice president, sales: "The product mix has been upgraded. We dropped about 13 percent of our product lines. We are finally facing up to economic facts and problems."

Vice president, planning (Kelly): "Today, the job of good management involves elaborate monitoring and cross-checking of all kinds of data. I know that some division managers are unhappy, but they must realize that planning and controls are necessary and are here to stay."

Division Managers.

The following are excerpts from some of the most frequently repeated remarks by various division managers:

1. "Political infighting? No more—we have an open war. The result has been that dozens of operating executives have left—and I mean the best of the lot. It takes a month to get an appointment with the executive vice president or the president, and then you can't talk to them without Mr. Kelly being present."

2. "Sure, he has good ideas. I'm sold on them. But whenever he applies controls, they turn out differently from the way they were explained to me. They inhibit our ability to produce and sell."

3. "I think he wants to support some universities. He hired more M.B.A.s for his shop than we have in the total organization. Yes, they have attractive credentials, but very little experience. These whiz kids have ready access to top management. It takes me an eternity to get their ear."

4. "The corporate operating force has grown 20 percent; yet, Mr. Kelly's office has grown 38 percent in the same period. Expenses of his office have increased 82 percent. Those of the operating force, only 39 percent."

5. "These are shortsighted measures. Top management is seeking quick returns at the expense of long-term payoffs. Too many opportunities have slipped by because the payoff comes too late."

6. "We are overstressing mechanistic controls and management tools. Our continued success depends on creativity, and creativity has been put into a straitjacket. His policies raise serious questions about the future growth of this corporation."

7. "We are open to raiding and cannot attract competent managers any more. Five years ago, when my sales manager died in a car accident, 50 well-qualified persons applied for that opening. This year, when our sales manager left because he was fed up, I received five applications. None of them came close to the quality of those 50 of five years ago."

8. "Sure, I was mad at him! When he required a large allowance for overdue accounts receivable, my profit (and with it, my bonus) went down. But we corrected this situation, and he was right. But these controls are requiring more and more of my employees' time and reduce the productivity. Do you want to hear something? I wanted to buy a pencil sharpener; but since it had a motor, it was considered a machine, and I had to fill out a capital asset requisition form. Since I could not document a 20 percent return, there was no sense in forwarding it. If I had bought for a few hundred dollars a real antique handcranked pencil sharpener, I could

have authorized that. Besides, I'm an engineer but was unable to fill out the capital requisition form; I needed my controller to do it. Needless to say, I bought it as an office furnishing."

Questions for Analysis

1. Evaluate Patrick Kelly's overall approach to solving the problems of Miracle Corporation.
2. What potential organizational problems did Kelly set in motion by having the division controllers report directly to him?
3. Evaluate Kelly's four objectives in terms of explicit criteria.
4. What type of organizational structure does Miracle Corporation have (Exhibit 1)? Evaluate whether it "fits" the demands and opportunities of the company's environment and strategy.
5. Why did the division managers resent the midmonthly meetings with Kelly. Explain why the controllers' midmonthly reports are or are not adequate substitutes for these meetings.
6. What performance standards should be used to evaluate Kelly's performance? What performance standards should be used to evaluate division managers' performance?
7. Explain why top management and division managers have quite different opinions about the effects of Kelly's efforts.

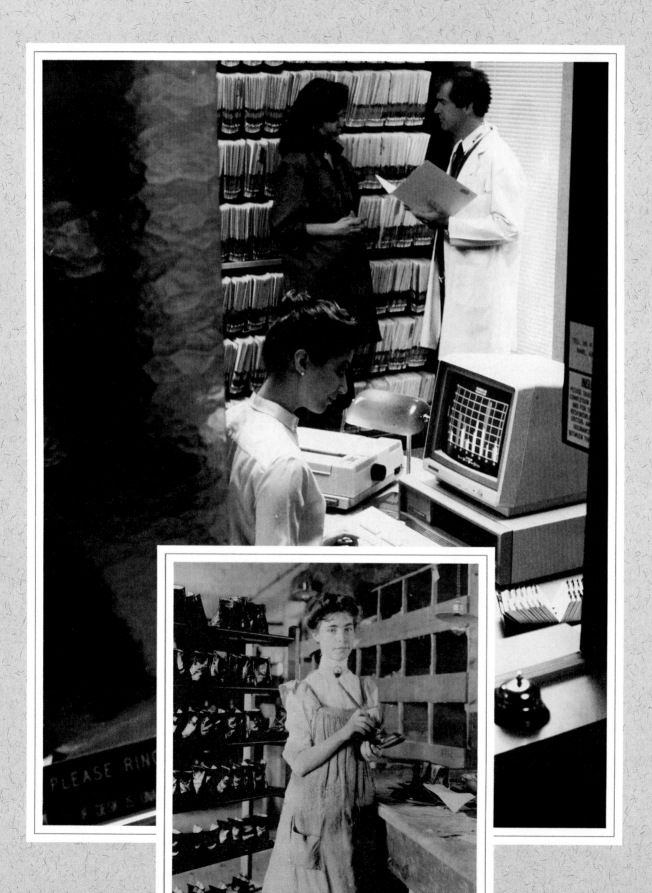

PART

III

MANAGING PEOPLE

FOUNDATIONS OF MANAGING PEOPLE

10
MOTIVATION

11
MANAGING WORK GROUPS

12
LEADERSHIP

13
COMMUNICATION

14
ORGANIZATIONAL CHANGE AND DEVELOPMENT

FOUNDATIONS OF MANAGING PEOPLE

Early approaches to management were built on the notion that if management could properly plan, organize, and control jobs and organizations, productivity would increase. The early approaches also emphasized the technical aspects of work, at the expense of work's personal aspects. Therefore, it is not surprising that theories were developed that challenged some of the early fundamentals. The fundamentals of managing people evolved into two branches with heavy behavioral and humanistic orientations. One branch may be identified as *human relations;* it became popular in the 1940s and early 1950s. The second branch is *behavioral science,* which came into popular use in the early 1950s and today receives much emphasis in the literature on management. Both branches and important characteristics of each are illustrated in Figure 1.

A report prepared by the American Assembly of Collegiate Schools of Business (AACSB), *Management Education and Development: Drift or Thrust into the 21st Century,* pointed out the need for future managers to learn to use people skills.[1] The report emphasizes that successful managers must be able to communicate, make decisions, lead, create a positive motivational environment, and resolve conflicts. In the past, the subject of people management skills has almost been an afterthought in schools and training programs. The AACSB report suggests that more courses and training programs will become available because business and industry want employees to have more than technical and analytical skills. It is in the skills area of people management that managers need to prepare, develop, and study for the 21st century.

THE HUMAN RELATIONS APPROACH

Human relations writers brought to managers' attention the important role played by individuals in determining the success or failure of an organization. Basically accepting the major premises of the classical approach, the human relations approach showed how these premises should be modified in view of differences in individual behavior and the influence of work groups on the individual—and vice versa. Thus, the formulators of human relations theory concentrated on the *social* environment surrounding the job, while classical writers were concerned mainly with the *physical* environment. For the student of management, the human relations movement has produced a wealth of important ideas, research findings, and values about the role of the individual in an organization.

We do not know if the "captains of industry" in the 1990s learned any specific lessons from the Hawthorne studies. But before you read about the

---

[1]Lyman W. Porter and Lawrence E. McKibbon, *Management Education and Development* (New York: McGraw-Hill, 1988).

FIGURE 1   Fundamentals of Managing People: Two Approaches

Human relations approach	Behavioral science approach
• Stimulated by the Hawthorne studies	• Involved in the scientific search for understanding behavior
• Concern for individual dignity	• Use of psychology, sociology, and anthropology to understand behavior
• Concern for developing human potential	• Use of research to gain knowledge
• Concern for social environment	• Acceptance of total person

research, think about Sam Walton, reportedly the richest man in America and the head of the Wal-Mart stores; Fred Smith, who started Federal Express; David Packard, founder of Hewlett-Packard; Mary Ann Keller, Wall Street analyst; and Susan W. Bowen, president of Champion Awards, Inc. These are effective managers who employees claim are trustworthy, are interested in creating a pleasant work environment, and will listen to what employees have to say. Human dignity, individual self-esteem, and relationships are important considerations when effective managers make decisions. Exploitation, manipulation, and insensitivity toward people are not accepted in organizations with people-oriented management.

THE HAWTHORNE STUDIES

In 1924, the National Research Council (NRC) of the National Academy of Sciences decided to study how lighting in the workplace influenced individual efficiency. From 1924 to 1927, the NRC studied this relationship at the Cicero, Illinois, Hawthorne Plant of Western Electric. The initial experiments were so inconclusive that everyone was ready to abandon the whole project.[2] Despite the early results, a team of Harvard University industrial psychologists became involved in the Hawthorne studies. This research team originally set out to study the relationship between productivity and physical working conditions.

Research.   The research at Hawthorne can be grouped in four phases.[3] Each successive phase developed as an attempt on the part of the researchers to answer questions raised by the previous phase. The four stages were:

[2]For a complete account of these studies, see Fritz J. Roethlisberger and W. H. Dickson, *Management and the Worker* (Cambridge, Mass.: Harvard University Press, 1939). Also see a report on a symposium held to celebrate the 50th anniversary of the original Hawthorne studies in Eugene L. Cass and Frederick G. Zimmer, *Man and Work in Society* (New York: Van Nostrand Reinhold, 1975).

[3]Paul R. Lawrence and John A. Seiler, *Organizational Behavior and Administration* (Homewood, Ill.: Richard D. Irwin, 1965), p. 165.

1. Experiments to determine the effects of changes in illumination on productivity.
2. Experiments to determine the effects of changes in hours and other working conditions (for example, rest periods, refreshments) on productivity (the relay assembly test room experiment).
3. Conducting a plantwide interview program to determine worker attitudes and sentiments.
4. Determination and analysis of social organization at work (the bank wiring observation room experiment).

Experiments in illumination.   The researchers divided the participating workers into two separate groups. The *experimental* group was exposed to varying intensities of illumination. Another group, called the *control* group, continued to work under constant intensities of illumination. Surprisingly the researchers found that as they increased the illumination in the experimental group, both groups increased production. When the researchers decreased the intensity, output continued to rise for both groups. Finally, the illumination in the experimental group was reduced to that of moonlight. Then, and only then, was there a significant decline in output. The researchers concluded that illumination in the workplace had little or no effect on the productivity of the two groups. At this point, the research team from Harvard became involved.

Relay assembly test room experiment.   In the second phase of the study, several persons volunteered to work under controlled conditions isolated from the other workers. Several changes were made in the conditions of the job (for example, workplace temperature and refreshments) with little effect on productivity. In another phase, a group of women employees was placed together in an isolated part of the assembly department. The experimental group was given a special group incentive as a wage payment. In this case, output increased for each operator.

Overall, the relay assembly test room experiment was designed to determine the effects of changes in various job conditions on group productivity. The researchers concluded that these factors had little or no effect.

Employee interviews.   After the first two phases, the researchers concluded that their attempt to relate physical conditions of the job to productivity did not produce any significant results. So they postulated that the *human element* in the work environment apparently had a significantly greater impact on productivity than the technical and physical aspects of the job. The researchers summarized this impact as follows:

> In brief, the increase in the output rate of the women in the relay assembly test room could not be related to any change in their physical conditions of work, whether experimentally induced or not. It could, however, be related to what can only be spoken of as the development of an organized social group and a peculiar and effective relation with its supervisors.[4]

[4] Ibid., p. 173.

On the basis of their extensive interview program, the researchers proposed that the work group as a whole determined the production output of individual group members by enforcing an informal norm of what a fair day's work should be.

Bank wiring observation room experiment. To test the premise formulated at the conclusion of the interview program, the researchers conducted a final experiment. The procedure in this part of the study was similar to that used in the relay assembly test room, except that nine males who assembled terminal banks for telephone exchanges were selected.

This experiment focused on the effect of a group piecework incentive pay plan. The assumption was that the workers would seek their own economic interests by maximizing their productivity and that faster workers would pressure the slower ones to improve their efficiency. However, the researchers found that pressure was actually a form of social behavior. In order to be accepted in the work group, the worker had to act in accord with group norms and not be a "rate buster" by overproducing or a "chiseler" by underproducing. The group defined what constituted a day's work, and as soon as they knew that they could reach this output level, they slacked off. This process was more marked among the faster workers than the slower ones.

The researchers concluded that the work group set the fair rates for each of its members. They found no relationship between productivity and intelligence, dexterity, and other skills. They concluded that the wage incentive plan was less important in determining an individual worker's output than was group acceptance and security.

Review and Critique of the Hawthorne Studies. The Hawthorne studies have been criticized by some behavioral scientists because of the lack of scientific objectivity used in arriving at conclusions. Some critics feel that there was bias and preconception on the part of the Harvard researchers. One writer developed a detailed comparison between the conclusions drawn by the researchers and the evidence they presented, and found that their conclusions were almost entirely unsupported.[5]

Although they have been criticized, the Hawthorne studies had a significant impact on management practice, teaching, and research.[6] Obviously, the assumptions of early management writers began to be questioned.[7] Subsequent studies of the behavior of workers confirmed criticisms and led to revised assumptions about human nature.[8] Behavioral scientists began attacking the "dehumanizing" aspects of the scientific management approach and bureaucratic forms of organization; a great number of training programs were undertaken to teach managers how to better understand people and groups in the

[5]Alex Carey, "The Hawthorne Studies: A Radical Criticism," *American Sociological Review,* June 1967, pp. 403–16.

[6]Ibid., p. 403.

[7]Henry A. Landsberger, *Hawthorne Revisited* (Ithaca: New York State School of Industrial and Labor Relations, Cornell University, 1958).

[8]Elton Mayo, *The Social Problems of an Industrial Civilization* (Cambridge, Mass.: Harvard University Press, 1945).

work situation. With this, the pendulum began to swing away from the supposed depersonalized view of classical management to a more personalized (some would say *over*personalized) view. Consequently, the worker, rather than the job or production standards, became the focus.

THE BEHAVIORAL SCIENCE APPROACH

The behavioral science approach to management began to appear in the early 1950s, after the Foundation for Research on Human Behavior was established. The goal and objectives of this organization were to promote and support behavioral science research in business, government, and other types of organizations. The behavioral science approach to the study of management can be defined as:

> The study of observable and verifiable human behavior in organizations, using scientific procedures. It is largely inductive and problem centered, focusing on the issue of human behavior and drawing from any relevant literature, especially in psychology, sociology, and anthropology.[9]

Many things about the classical management and human relations approaches bothered advocates of the behavioral science approach. For example, they recognized that managers did indeed plan, organize, and control. But they believed that viewing management solely in this way led mainly to *descriptions* of what managers do rather than to an *analysis* and *understanding* of what they do. Many also believed that while the "economic man" model of the classical writers was an oversimplification, the "social man" model of the human relations approach likewise was oversimplified. You will see later how the emphasis of the behavioral science approach has shifted more and more to the nature of work itself and the degree to which it can fulfill the human need to use skills and abilities.

Finally, advocates of the behavioral science approach were bothered by the fact that both practitioners and scholars had accepted without scientific validation much of the management theory that preceded them. These advocates wanted to test theory and see what was successful and unsuccessful. Their scientific approach has added greatly to the body of knowledge, since they provided a means of testing the earlier theories. Through their work, some aspects of the classical approach have been modified, while others have withstood the test of scientific validation.

THE BEHAVIORAL SCIENCES

When we use the term *behavioral sciences,* we refer to the disciplines of psychology, sociology, and anthropology.

Psychology is the study of human behavior. The many branches of general psychology have provided concepts and theories useful to the study of management. For example, **social psychology** deals with behavior as it relates to other individuals. It studies how groups and individuals influence and

---

[9]Alan C. Filley, Robert J. House, and Steven Kerr, *Managerial Process and Organizational Behavior* (Glenview, Ill.: Scott, Foresman, 1976), p. 16.

modify each other's behavior. **Organizational psychology** is a relatively new branch dealing with behavior and attitudes within an organizational setting. It studies the effect of the organization on the individual and the individual's effect on the organization.

Books such as Robert Levering's *A Great Place to Work* emphasize how widespread psychology's influence on management has become.[10] The list of companies cited and the use of self-motivation, participation, quality of work life, new organizational designs, team building, job enrichment, and other psychologist-initiated techniques fills 312 pages. Does a manager have to be a psychologist in the 1990s to be effective? Definitely and thankfully not. However, the manager would be better able to work with the changing face and nature of the 1990s work force if she or he remembered some of the lessons taught in "Psychology 101."

Sociology attempts to isolate, define, and describe human behavior in groups. It strives to develop laws and generalizations about human nature, social interaction, culture, and social organization.

One of sociology's major contributions to management thought has been its focus on emergent groups, which often are treated in management literature as the informal components of organizations. Sociologists also have an interest in formal organizations, which they approach as the study of bureaucracy. They focus on bureaucratic behavior as well as the structural relationships in bureaucratic organizations. Sociologists have provided managers with knowledge regarding leader and follower roles and how patterns of power and authority are applied in organizations.

At Johnsonville Foods in Sheboygan, Wisconsin, the application of sociological principles is very easy to spot. Workers in teams, with no identifiable hierarchy above them, do all the hiring, firing, and evaluation.[11] The result is a cohesive workplace, a family spirit, a pleasant environment. Sociologists have for decades been providing insights and ideas about groups. Some old-line firms still close their eyes and don't look at the success stories. Unless more of such firms familiarize themselves with sociological information, they are likely not to survive the 1990s. Teams, partnerships, ownership, and cohesiveness are what more and more employees are asking for today.

Anthropology examines the learned behaviors of people, including all of the social, technical, and family behaviors that are a part of the broad concept known as culture. **Cultural anthropology,** the science devoted to the study of different peoples and cultures of the world, is important to the behavioral sciences because the ways in which individuals behave, the priority of needs they attempt to satisfy, and the means they choose to satisfy them are all functions of culture.

The evidence that economists provide to managers is that people, not machines, are the driving force behind economic development. And as increased numbers of females and foreign-born workers become a major part of the work force in the 1990s, cultural anthropologists inform managers that different people from different backgrounds and cultures will have to be integrated into organizations. To avoid forfeiting economic growth and power to the Japanese, South Koreans, West Germans, French, and others, U.S.

---

[10] Robert Levering, *A Great Place to Work* (New York: Random House, 1988).

[11] Tom Peters, "Tomorrow's Companies," *Economist*, March 4, 1989, pp. 19–22.

managers must scientifically study the human resources available for employment, training, and education.[12] Cultural anthropologists have a wealth of knowledge, insight, and recommendations that managers need to use more and more in the 1990s.

While psychology and sociology have had greater impact in shaping management thought, cultural anthropology has made significant contributions regarding the effect of culture on organizations. In the future, as firms expand their activities overseas, anthropology undoubtedly will also provide managers with valuable insights as they attempt to perform the functions of planning, organizing, and controlling in different cultural environments.

CONCLUSION

The fundamentals of managing people should in no way be viewed separately from the fundamentals of managing work and organizations. Management writers have identified management as a process consisting of the functions of planning, organizing, and controlling and have provided insights into the nature and demands of these tasks. While reading Part III, the question the reader should ask is: How can behavioral science theory and research help managers contribute to the human aspects of the management process?

[12]"Needed: Human Capital," *Business Week*, September 19, 1988, pp. 100–103.

PEOPLE IN MANAGEMENT

Barbara Gardner Proctor

The impressive career of Barbara Gardner Proctor, founder and president of Chicago's Proctor & Gardner Advertising, Inc., has been shaped by a series of "firsts." In 1963 she was the first black in agency advertising in Chicago. In 1970 she was granted the first service loan ever issued by the Small Business Administration, which she transformed into the nation's first full-service advertising agency specializing in marketing to black communities, with a black woman as president. She built that agency into a $12.2-million business whose clients include Kraft Foods and Sears Roebuck.

Proctor started in advertising in the early 1960s as a copywriter for Post-Keyes-Gardner/Chicago. Five years later she joined North Advertising Agency as a copy supervisor. In 1970 she decided to form her own agency.

Proctor has directed the advertising for dozens of accounts, including Gillette, Paper Mate, FTD Florists, and Maybelline. Everything that goes out the door of her office high above the Chicago River is written by her.

Proctor, a no-frills manager, runs her entire company with only 25 full-time and 8 flextime employees. She ignores the once prevalent view that an ad agency must have eight employees for every $1 million of income. Proctor keeps staff size down by billing clients at an hourly rate, for services rendered, rather than based on income generated. Instead of secretaries at Proctor & Gardner, there are support teams. These six-person teams, assigned to all key departments, combine clerical with managerial functions.

Another Proctor innovation is the absence of performance reviews or official promotions. At Proctor & Gardner, people assume more responsibility as they are willing and/or able to do so. When an employee takes on enough additional responsibility to merit a promotion, that person is promoted—without a change in job title.

Proctor meets with Proctor & Gardner's four vice presidents biannually to determine the company's direction and create five-year plans. In 1985, for example, they determined that by 1990 Proctor & Gardner would be an events-marketing company. Thus, instead of focusing their efforts on the eight media, the company now looks around the country for local events, such as festivals and talent shows, to which they can tie their customers' campaigns. Proctor & Gardner supports community based events, and Proctor insists that black vendors be used where possible, thus providing jobs for people who might otherwise be unemployed.

Asked what advice she has for students on how to succeed in business, Proctor said, "Concentrate your energies on developing curiosity, self-discipline, and flexibility. The ability to succeed in the future will require these characteristics as our world continues to demand incisive analysis, concentrated expertise, and rapid adaptation."

Sources: Courtland L. Bovée and William F. Arens, *Contemporary Advertising* (Homewood, Ill.: Richard D. Irwin, 1982), p. 271; personal interview.

10

MOTIVATION

LEARNING OBJECTIVES

After studying Chapter 10, you should be able to:

Define

the meaning of motivation.

Describe

the difference between content and process theories
of motivation.

Discuss

goal directedness as a major factor in each theory
of motivation presented.

Identify

the five core motivational dimensions used in job
enrichment.

Compare

the distinguishing characteristics of the
reinforcement and expectancy theories
of motivation.

Do Computerized Performance Monitors Actually Increase Performance?

As computer information systems become more and more accurate in calculating the amount of work done by an individual employee and as employers implement systems that give the employee more specific feedback, a debate has developed as to whether the feedback is helpful to productivity or is simply computer-aided harassment.

In the following real-life examples, some form of feedback and/or productivity system was instituted either for better control or to increase productivity for the individual:

Location Feedback. Many businesses in highly competitive or technological industries require employees to move from building to building through computer key cards. Originally designed to keep others out, this accurate location information has also been used during monthly reviews to question why an employee spent so much time out of his or her department.

Daily Speed and Accuracy Feedback. In many large insurance companies, computers monitor the productivity of each representative: for instance, the number of checks written in a given day, the amount of time the representative holds a particular claim, the number of phone calls answered, the number of letters sent and received, and the number of customer complaints. Unfortunately, if something is not measured, it is not seen as important.

Continuous Speed and Accuracy Feedback. The Home Shopping Club uses constant feedback to the television "hosts" to show how each product is selling and whether they should change their selling tactic: keep it, drop the price, or switch to a new product.

Feedback, only one of the ways mentioned in this chapter to motivate employees, can be added to many techniques and systems to let the worker know what is expected in the job.

Source: Adapted from Rebecca A. Grant, Christopher A. Higgins, and Richard H. Irving, "Computerizing Performance Monitors: Are They Costing You Customers?" *Sloan Management Review,* Spring 1988, pp. 39–45.

Motivation is concerned with the "why" of human behavior. Why do people do things? Why does Harry have frequent run-ins with the boss? Why does Dianne work so much harder than Jim? Answering such questions is greatly aided by an understanding of human motivation. In this chapter, motivation will be the main focal point because it is important to management for three reasons: First, employees on the job must be motivated to perform at an acceptable level. Second, managers themselves must be motivated to do a good job. Third, employees (managerial and nonmanagerial) must be motivated to join the organization.

WHAT IS MOTIVATION?

Motivation has been defined as "all those inner-striving conditions described as wishes, desires, drives, etc. . . . . It is an inner state that activates or moves."[1] From a manager's perspective, a person who is motivated:

- Works hard.
- Sustains a pace of hard work.
- Has self-directed behavior toward important goals.

Thus, motivation involves effort, persistence, and goals.[2] It involves a person's desire to perform. The actual performance is what managers can evaluate to determine indirectly the person's desire.

When a person's performance is determined to be unsatisfactory, low motivation is often considered the problem. Certainly, in many cases, that is true. However, performance problems are not automatically caused by low levels of motivation. Other factors such as shortage of resources or lack of skills may be the cause of poor performance. It is important not to immediately conclude that performance difficulties are motivation problems.

THE MOTIVATION PROCESS

An unsatisfied need is the starting point in the process of motivation. A deficiency of something within the individual, it is the first link in the chain of events leading to behavior. The unsatisfied need causes tension (physical or psychological) within the individual, leading the individual to engage in some kind of behavior to satisfy the need and thereby reduce the tension. Note in Figure 10–1 that this activity is directed toward a goal. Achieving the goal satisfies the need, and the process of motivation is complete. For example, an achievement-oriented person is driven by the desire to succeed and is motivated by a desire for a promotion and/or accomplishment in order to satisfy the need.

Each year *Fortune* publishes a list of fascinating, exceptional business leaders for the year and a vignette about each.[3] Those stories indicate that goal

---

[1]Bernard Berelson and Gary A. Steiner, *Human Behavior: An Inventory of Scientific Findings* (New York: Harcourt Brace Jovanovich, 1964), p. 239.

[2]Herbert L. Petri, *Motivation: Theory and Research* (Belmont, Calif.: Wadsworth Publishing, 1981), p. 4.

[3]Geoffrey Calvin, "The Year's 25 Most Fascinating Business People," *Fortune*, January 2, 1989, pp. 32–59.

FIGURE 10–1   The Process of Motivation

Motivation starts with an unsatisfied need and drives behavior toward satisfaction.

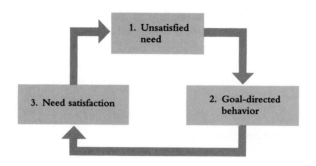

directedness is a common characteristic found in each person. A few of the goal-oriented leaders presented in *Fortune* in 1989 are:

- *Hugh McColl,* chairman of NCNB banking institution, who moved aggressively into Texas and bought the First Republic Bank Corporation. He claims that by the year 2000, Texas will be the number two state in population and Florida will be number four. He wants NCNB to be there, and his goal now is to move faster and bigger into Florida.
- *Jacques Delors,* president of the European Economic Community (EEC) Commission. He has rallied politicians, union leaders, business leaders, and citizens to the idea of a united Europe in 1992. He has stated that his goal is to make Europe (12 countries) in the EEC an economic power on the same level as the United States and Japan.
- *Frances Lear,* who started *Lear's,* a magazine for women over 40. It has been a success. The sole owner and editor, she states that in the year 2000, 46 percent of all American women will be over 40. Her goal is to increase her empire by adding more magazines and to have her own weekly television talk show.

Is everyone goal directed? A lot of people are asking this question. The obvious answer is no. There is however, enough evidence to suggest that most people are goal directed.

UNDERSTANDING MOTIVATION: THE USE OF THEORIES

Many theories of motivation exist that managers can use to improve their understanding of why people behave as they do. None provides a universally accepted explanation of human behavior. People are far too complex. Our purpose in presenting the most popular theories is not to identify the one best approach. Rather, it is to introduce ideas that managers can use to develop their own motivational approach.

The two most discussed groups of theories are content theories and process theories. *Content theories* are concerned with identifying what it is within an

There is significant evidence to suggest that most people are goal-oriented.

individual or the work environment that energizes and sustains behavior.[4] That is, what specific things motivate people?

On the other hand, *process theories* try to explain and describe the process of how behavior is energized, directed, sustained, and finally stopped. Process theories first attempt to define the major variables necessary for explaining choice (e.g., Should I work hard?), effort (e.g., How hard do I need to work?), and persistence (e.g., How long do I have to keep this pace?).

First, two content theories—Maslow's need hierarchy and Herzberg's two-factor theory—will be discussed. Second, two process theories—expectancy and reinforcement—will be introduced. After each theory is explained, we will show how it can be applied by managers.

CONTENT THEORIES OF MOTIVATION

MASLOW'S HIERARCHY OF NEEDS

Maslow's need hierarchy theory has enjoyed widespread acceptance since it was introduced. His theory of motivation stresses two fundamental premises:

---

[4]John P. Campbell, Marvin D. Dunnette, Edward E. Lawler III, and Karl E. Weick, Jr., *Managerial Behavior, Performance and Effectiveness* (New York: McGraw-Hill, 1970), p. 341.

Maslow's hierarchy of needs stresses that man is a "wanting animal" whose needs depend on what he already has.

1. Man is a wanting animal whose needs depend on what he already has. Only needs not yet satisfied can influence behavior. In other words, a satisfied need is not a motivator.

2. Man's needs are arranged in a hierarchy of importance. Once one need is satisfied, another emerges and demands satisfaction.

Maslow hypothesized five levels of needs. These needs are (1) physiological, (2) safety, (3) social, (4) esteem, and (5) self-actualization.[5] He placed them in a framework referred to as the *hierarchy of needs* because of the different levels of importance. This framework is presented in Figure 10–2.

Maslow states that if all of a person's needs are unsatisfied at a particular time, satisfaction of the more predominant needs will be more pressing than the others. Those that come first must be satisfied before a higher-level need comes into play. Let us briefly examine each need level:

1. *Physiological needs.*   This category consists of the human body's primary needs, such as food, water, and sex. Physiological needs will dominate when they are unsatisfied, and no other needs will serve as a basis for motivation. As Maslow states, "A person who is lacking food, safety, love, and esteem probably would hunger for food more strongly than for anything else."[6]

2. *Safety needs.*   When physiological needs are adequately met, the next higher level of needs assumes importance. Safety needs include protection from physical harm, ill health, economic disaster, and the unexpected. From a

---

[5]Less described and hence not as well known are the cognitive and aesthetic needs hypothesized by Maslow. Examples of cognitive needs are the need to know or understand and the manipulation of the environment as the result of curiosity. The aesthetic needs are satisfied by moving from ugliness toward beauty. Maslow did not include them in the formal hierarchy framework. Abraham H. Maslow, *Motivation and Personality* (New York: Harper & Row, 1954), pp. 93–98.

[6]Ibid., p. 82.

FIGURE **10–2**   Maslow's Hierarchy of Needs Theory

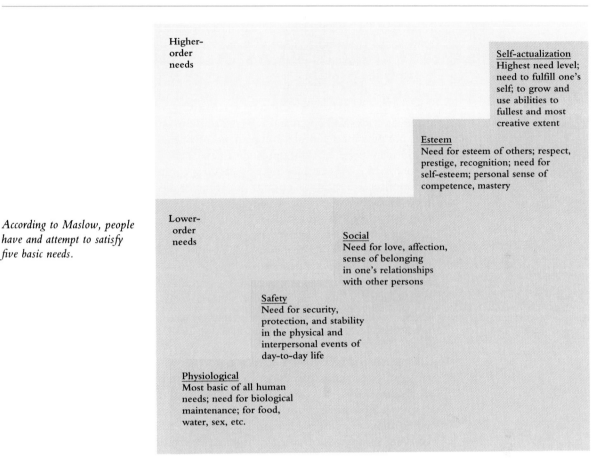

According to Maslow, people have and attempt to satisfy five basic needs.

Higher-order needs

Self-actualization
Highest need level; need to fulfill one's self; to grow and use abilities to fullest and most creative extent

Esteem
Need for esteem of others; respect, prestige, recognition; need for self-esteem; personal sense of competence, mastery

Lower-order needs

Social
Need for love, affection, sense of belonging in one's relationships with other persons

Safety
Need for security, protection, and stability in the physical and interpersonal events of day-to-day life

Physiological
Most basic of all human needs; need for biological maintenance; for food, water, sex, etc.

managerial standpoint, safety needs show up in an employee's attempts to ensure job safety and fringe benefits.

3. *Social needs.* These needs are related to the social nature of people and their need for companionship. Here the hierarchy departs from the physical or quasi-physical needs of the two previous levels. Nonsatisfaction of this level of need may affect the mental health of the individual.

4. *Esteem needs.* The need for both awareness of importance to others (self-esteem) and actual esteem from others is included. Esteem from others must also be felt as warranted and deserved. Satisfaction of these needs leads to a feeling of self-confidence and prestige.

5. *Self-actualization needs.* Maslow defines these needs as the "desire to become more and more what one is, to become everything one is capable of becoming."[7] This means that the individual will realize fully the potentialities of talents and capabilities. Obviously, as the role of an individual varies, so will the external aspects of self-actualization. In other words, whether the person is

[7]Ibid., p. 92.

a college professor, corporate manager, parent, or athlete, the need is to be effective in that particular role. Maslow assumes that satisfaction of the self-actualization needs is possible only after the satisfaction of all other needs. Moreover, he proposes that the satisfaction of the self-actualization needs will tend to increase the strength of those needs. Thus, when people are able to achieve self-actualization, they tend to be motivated by increased opportunities to satisfy that need.[8]

Applying Maslow's Theory in Management.   The need hierarchy theory is widely accepted and referred to by practicing managers. Although it does not provide a complete understanding of human motivation or the means to motivate people, it does provide an excellent starting point for the student of management. The hierarchy is easy to comprehend, has a great deal of commonsense appeal, and points out some of the factors that motivate people in business and other types of organizations. For example, most organizations in industrialized nations such as the United States, Canada, Japan, and West Germany have been extremely successful in satisfying lower-level needs. Through wages or salary, individuals are able to satisfy their and their families' physiological needs. Organizations also help to satisfy security or safety needs through both salary and fringe benefit programs. Finally, they aid in satisfying social needs by allowing interaction and association with others on the job. Some work-related examples that managers can influence under each of the five need categories are presented in Table 10–1.

Criticisms of Maslow's Theory.   Maslow's theory is presented as being universally accepted as accurate. However, people in different firms, positions, or countries differ. Individual differences certainly exist. An accountant in Budapest, Hungary, working for the Hungarian Credit Bank may be concerned about a comfortable work area, a salary to help support her family, and receiving some time off during the summer months. However, an accountant at Chase Manhattan Bank in New York may have extensive self-actualization needs and not be overly concerned with physiological and security needs.

Another criticism of the need hierarchy is that needs overlap and can fit in more than one, even all of the categories. An equitable salary, for example, may satisfy needs in all five categories; the salary received by a person has an impact on many different needs.

It is also stated that Maslow's need hierarchy is static. Needs change over time, in various situations, and when people make comparisons about their satisfaction and the satisfaction of others. A 22-year-old recent college graduate perceives, experiences, and copes with needs differently than a 62-year-old preparing for retirement and leisure activities.

HERZBERG'S TWO-FACTOR THEORY

Another content explanation of motivation was advanced by Frederick Herzberg in 1959. He based his theory on a study of need satisfactions and on

---

[8]Abraham H. Maslow, *Motivation and Personality* (New York: Harper & Row, 1970), p. 81.

TABLE 10–1   Areas of Management Influence in the Five Need Hierarchy Categories

Need Category	Management Influence Areas
Self-actualization	Challenges in job.
	Advancement opportunities.
	Chances for creativity.
	Motivation toward high achievement.
Esteem	Public recognition of good performance.
	Significant job activities.
	Respectful job title.
	Responsibility.
Social	Social interaction opportunities.
	Group stability.
	Encouragement toward cooperation.
Safety	Safe working conditions.
	Job security.
	Fringe benefits.
Physiological	Fair salary.
	Comfortable working conditions.
	Heat, lighting, space, air-conditioning.

Managers can help employees satisfy needs.

the reported motivational effects of these satisfactions on 200 engineers and accountants. The theory is referred to as the two-factor theory of motivation.[9]

In the study of engineers and accountants, Herzberg and his associates asked the subjects to think of times both when they felt especially good and when they felt especially bad about their jobs. Each employee was then asked to describe the conditions that led to these particular feelings. It was found that the employees named different kinds of conditions as causes of each of the feelings. For example, if recognition led to a good feeling about the job, the lack of recognition was seldom indicated as a cause of bad feelings. Based on the study, Herzberg reached two conclusions:

1. Some conditions of a job operate primarily to dissatisfy employees when they are not present. However, the presence of these conditions does not build strong motivation. Herzberg called these **maintenance factors,** since they are necessary to maintain a reasonable level of satisfaction. He also noted that many of these have often been perceived by managers as factors that can motivate subordinates but that they are, in fact, more potent as dissatisfiers when they are absent. He named 10 maintenance factors:

Company policy and administration.
Technical supervision.
Interpersonal relations with supervisor.
Interpersonal relations with peers.
Interpersonal relations with subordinates.
Salary.

[9]See Frederick Herzberg, B. Mausner, and B. Snyderman, *The Motivation to Work* (New York: John Wiley & Sons, 1959).

Job security.
Personal life.
Work conditions.
Status.

2.   Some job conditions build high levels of motivation and job satisfaction. However, if these conditions are not present, they do not prove highly dissatisfying. Herzberg described six of these **motivational factors,** or satisfiers:

Achievement.
Recognition.
Advancement.
The work itself.
The possibility of personal growth.
Responsibility.

In summary, the maintenance factors cause much dissatisfaction when they are not present but do not provide strong motivation when they are present. On the other hand, the factors in the second group lead to strong motivation and satisfaction when they are present but do not cause much dissatisfaction when they are absent. Herzberg's study of engineers and accountants suggested to him that the opposite of satisfaction is not dissatisfaction but simply "no satisfaction." Figure 10–3 compares his view of job satisfaction to a traditional view.

The reader probably has noted that Herzberg's motivational factors are job centered; that is, they relate directly to the job itself, the individual's performance, the job's responsibilities, and the growth and recognition obtained from it. Maintenance factors are peripheral to the job itself and more related to the external environment of work. Another important finding of the study is that when employees are highly motivated, they have a high tolerance for dissatisfaction arising from the maintenance factors. However, the reverse is not true.

The distinction between motivational and maintenance factors is similar to what psychologists have described as *intrinsic* and *extrinsic* motivators. Intrinsic motivators are part of the job and occur when the employee performs the work. The opportunity to perform a job with intrinsic motivational potential is motivating because the work itself is rewarding. Extrinsic motivators are external rewards that have meaning or value after performing the work or away from the workplace. They provide little, if any, satisfaction when the work is being performed. Pay, of course, is a good example of what Herzberg classifies as a maintenance factor and what some psychologists call an extrinsic motivator.

Applying Herzberg's Theory in Management.   Herzberg certainly has extended Maslow's ideas and made them more applicable to the work situation. He has drawn attention to the critical importance, in work motivation, of job-centered factors previously given little attention by behavioral scientists. This insight has resulted in an increased interest in **job enrichment,** an effort to restructure jobs to increase worker satisfaction.

FIGURE 10-3   Contrasting Theories of Satisfaction and Dissatisfaction

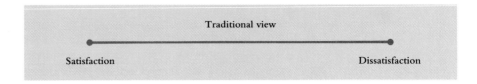

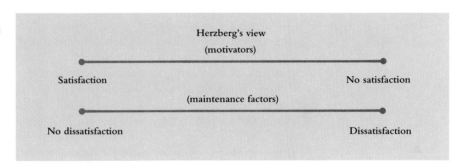

Herzberg's view of satisfaction and dissatisfaction departed from the traditional view.

Herzberg's response to motivation problems is an important one. Traditionally, managers would respond to motivation problems with more money, increased fringe benefits, and improved working conditions. Often, the result of such actions was still no more effort to work harder. Herzberg's theory offers an explanation for this phenomenon. If managers focus only on maintenance factors, motivation will not occur. The motivators must be built into the job to improve motivation.

Criticisms of Herzberg's Theory.   One limitation of Herzberg's original study and conclusions is that the subjects consisted of engineers and accountants. That these individuals were in such positions indicates that they had the motivation to seek advanced education and expected to be rewarded. The same may not hold true for the nonprofessional worker. In fact, some testing of Herzberg's model on blue-collar workers showed that certain factors considered maintenance factors by Herzberg (pay and job security) are considered by blue-collar workers to be motivational factors.[10]

Some critics believe that Herzberg's inference concerning differences between dissatisfiers and motivators cannot be completely accepted and that the differences between stated sources of satisfaction and dissatisfaction in

[10]Michael R. Malinovsky and John R. Barry, "Determinants of Work Attitudes," *Journal of Applied Psychology*, December 1965, pp. 446–51. For a discussion of other alternative interpretations of the two-factor theory and the research support for the various interpretations, see N. King, "Clarification and Evaluation of the Two-Factor Theory of Job Satisfaction," *Psychological Bulletin*, July 1970, pp. 18–31; D. A. Ondrack, "Defense Mechanisms and the Herzberg Theory: An Alternate Test," *Personnel Psychology*, March 1974, pp. 79–89.

Herzberg's study may be the result of defensive processes within those responding. Detractors point out that people are apt to attribute the causes of satisfaction to their own achievements but likely to attribute their dissatisfaction more to obstacles presented by company policies or superiors than to their own deficiencies.[11]

Other critics believe that the two-factor theory is an oversimplification of the true relationship between motivation and dissatisfaction as well as between the sources of job satisfaction and dissatisfaction.[12] Reviews of several studies show that one factor can cause job satisfaction for one person and job dissatisfaction for another.

Herzberg assumes that there is a strong relationship between satisfaction and productivity. But his research only examined satisfaction, not productivity. Other researchers have questioned the conclusion that satisfaction and productivity are highly and positively related.[13]

Since his original work, Herzberg has cited numerous replications of the original study that support his position.[14] These subsequent studies were conducted on professional women, hospital maintenance personnel, agricultural administrators, nurses, food handlers, manufacturing supervisors, engineers, scientists, military officers, managers ready for retirement, teachers, technicians, and assemblers. And some were conducted in other cultural settings: Finland, Hungary, Russia, and Yugoslavia. However, some researchers have used the same research methods employed by Herzberg and obtained results different from what his theory would predict,[15] while several using different methods have also obtained contradictory results.[16]

COMPARING HERZBERG'S AND MASLOW'S MODELS

There is much similarity between Herzberg's and Maslow's models. A close examination of Herzberg's ideas indicates that what he actually is saying is that some employees may have achieved a level of social and economic progress such that the higher-level needs of Maslow (esteem and self-actualization) are the primary motivators. However, they still must satisfy the lower-level needs for the maintenance of their current state. Thus, money might still be a motivator for nonmanagement workers (particularly those at a low wage

[11]See the classic Victor H. Vroom, *Work and Motivation* (New York: John Wiley & Sons, 1964), pp. 128–29.

[12]For one of the earliest criticisms, see R. J. House and L. A. Wigdor, "Herzberg's Dual-Factor Theory of Job Satisfaction and Motivation: A Review of the Evidence and a Criticism," *Personnel Psychology,* Winter 1967, pp. 369–89.

[13]R. J. Caston and R. Braito, "A Specification Issue in Job Satisfaction Research," *Sociological Perspectives,* April 1985, pp. 175–77.

[14]Frederick Herzberg, *Work and the Nature of Man* (Cleveland: World Publishing, 1966). This is a classic work by Herzberg.

[15]An early study is Donald P. Schwab, H. William DeVitt, and Larry L. Cummings, "A Test of the Adequacy of the Two-Factor Theory as a Predictor of Self-Report Performance Effects," *Personnel Psychology,* Summer 1971, pp. 293–303.

[16]Marvin D. Dunnette, John P. Campbell, and Milton D. Hakel, "Factors Contributing to Job Satisfaction and Job Dissatisfaction in Six Occupational Groups," *Organizational Behavior and Human Performance,* May 1967, pp. 143–74; C. L. Hulin and P. A. Smith, "An Empirical Investigation of Two Implications of the Two-Factor Theory of Job Satisfaction," *Journal of Applied Psychology,* October 1967, pp. 396–402.

FIGURE **10-4**   Maslow's and Herzberg's Theories: Similarities*

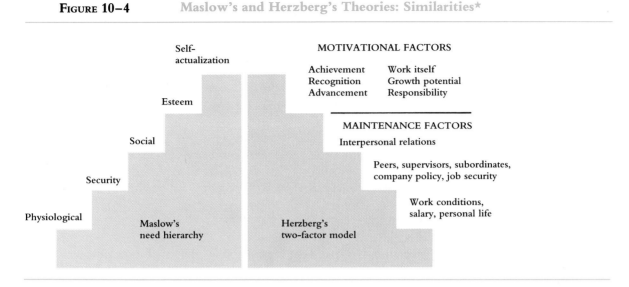

*Also see Keith Davis, *Human Behavior at Work* (New York: McGraw-Hill, 1977), p. 53.
Maslow and Herzberg proposed similar ideas, with different labels.

level) and for some managerial employees. In addition, Herzberg's model adds to Maslow's model because it breaks down the five need levels into two job-oriented categories: maintenance and motivational. Figure 10–4 compares the structure of the two. Table 10–2 compares areas in which they differ.

PROCESS THEORIES OF MOTIVATION

In contrast to the two content theories—Maslow's need hierarchy and Herzberg's two-factor model—expectancy theory and reinforcement theory are process theories. They concentrate on how motivation occurs, that is, how behavior is initiated, directed, sustained, and stopped.

VROOM'S EXPECTANCY THEORY

The expectancy theory of motivation as initially presented in 1964 by psychologist Victor Vroom views motivation as a process governing choices.[17] Vroom suggests that individuals are motivated at work to make choices among different behaviors—for example, intensities of work effort. A person may choose to work at a moderate rate or an accelerated rate. The choice is made by the individual. If a person believes that his or her work effort will be adequately rewarded, there will be motivated effort: a choice will be made to work so that a preferred reward is received. The logic of expectancy motivation is that *individuals will exert work effort to achieve performance that will result in preferred rewards.*

[17]Vroom, *Work and Motivation.*

TABLE 10–2	Maslow's and Herzberg's Theories: Differences		
	Topic	**Maslow's Need Hierarchy**	**Herzberg's Two-Factor Theory**
	1. Relevance	People in society in all types of jobs and in retirement.	Mostly to white-collar and professional employees.
	2. Impact of needs on behavior	All needs can motivate behavior.	Only some intrinsic needs serve as motivators.
	3. Role of financial rewards	Can motivate.	Not a key motivator.
	4. Perspective	Applies to all people and their lives.	Is work centered.
	5. Type of theory	Descriptive (what is).	Prescriptive (what should be).

Maslow and Herzberg have basic differences in five points of comparison.

Three primary variables in the expectancy theory of motivation are choice, expectancy, and preference.[18] *Choice* designates the individual's freedom to select from a number of alternative behaviors. For example, a person's work may be fast or slow, hard or moderate; the employee may stay home or come to work. In some cases, working fast may lead to more pay if compensation is based on the number of units produced. *Expectancy* is the belief that a particular behavior will or will not be successful. It is a subjective probability. Expectancy would be zero if a person believed that it was impossible to produce, say, 50 units a day; it would equal one if a person felt certain of being able to produce 22 units a day. *Preferences,* also referred to by Vroom as valences, are the values a person attaches to various outcomes (rewards or punishment).

Another issue covered in the **expectancy motivation model** is called *instrumentality*—the probability that a person assigns to the performance–outcome link. It is the probability that a particular performance level will lead to a specific outcome.

Figure 10–5 gives a general explanation and a work-oriented example of the expectancy theory. The work-oriented example is presented to show how the theory can be applied. To predict whether a person will select path A or B, you need to examine the interrelationships of the variables in the model. The motivation to work is expressed as:[19]

$$M = E \times I \times P$$

That is, motivation to work (M) results from expectancy (E) times instrumentality (I) times preference (P). Because this is a multiplicative interrelationship, think about the consequences if E, I, or P approaches zero in value.

Suppose that the work example in Figure 10–5 applies to Nan Brewer and her manager Nick. Nick is not sure whether a pay bonus will motivate Nan to perform better. Using the expectancy theory, Nick would predict that Nan's motivation to work hard would be low if:

[18]Ibid.

[19]Because the preference variable is also called valence, the expression may be $M = E \times I \times V$.

FIGURE 10–5   How the Expectancy Theory of Motivation Works

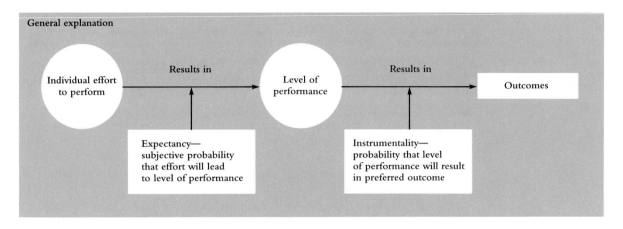

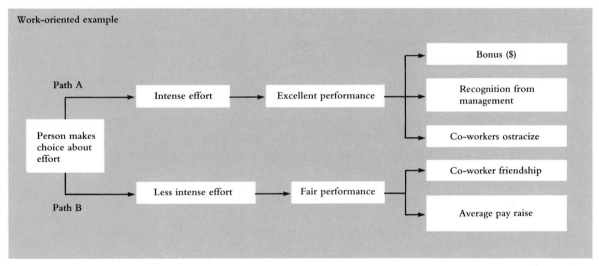

This example of expectancy theory shows how the theory works in a job situation.

1. Expectancy is low: Nan feels that she really can't achieve the bonus level of performance.
2. Instrumentality is low: Nan is uncertain about whether excellent performance will result in the bonus money.
3. Preference is low: Nan doesn't value receiving the bonus.
4. Any combination of 1, 2, or 3.

The expectancy theory of motivation requires a manager such as Nick to know three things when applying the theory: First, what are the person's beliefs about working hard and achieving a particular level of performance (expectancy)? Second, does the person believe that various outcomes (positive or negative) will result from the achievement of the particular level of performance (instrumentality)? And third, how much value does a person assign to outcomes (preferences)?

In one study, 1,000 employees were asked to rank-order 10 work-related factors.[20] If Nick reviewed this type of research, he would have some information how the sex, age, income level, job type, and organizational level influence expectancy and preferences. Not everyone prefers a promotion or job security. Table 10–3 summarizes the results of the study.

Applying the Expectancy Theory in Management.   Managers can influence expectancies by selecting (hiring) individuals with particular skills and abilities, training people to improve their skills and abilities, and providing individuals with the leadership support to achieve a particular level of performance. The manager also can influence instrumentalities by being supportive, realistic, and offering advice. The manager can influence preferences by listening to employee needs, guiding employees to help them accomplish desired outcomes, and providing proper resources to achieve the desired performance.

It is important for managers to understand the vital role of perception in motivation. A person's expectancies, instrumentalities, and valences depend on his or her perceptions. The importance of perceptual differences among workers with similar skill levels is made obvious by the expectancy theory. Different levels of motivation among people with similar skills could be explained in terms of perceptual differences.

Criticisms of Expectancy Theory.   Many critics believe the expectancy theory to be more complex than either Maslow's or Herzberg's theory.[21] There also are problems of measuring and studying the main variables in the model. How should preferences be determined? How should expectancy be determined? However, despite the lack of tested validity, the expectancy model still adds insight into the role that perception plays in choices, expectancy, and preferences.[22]

We might ask each reader: Do you make choices? Do you have expectancies? Do you have reward preferences? Instead of making the expectancy theory a complex approach, the Management Focus offers five straightforward steps to using Vroom's theory.

REINFORCEMENT THEORY

Reinforcement theory is another widely discussed process theory of motivation. Reinforcement theory considers the use of positive or negative

---

[20]K. A. Kovach, "What Motivates Employees? Workers and Supervisors Give Different Answers," *Business Horizons,* September–October 1987, pp. 58–65.

[21]See Victor H. Vroom, "Organizational Choice: A Study of Pre- and Post-Decision Processes," *Organizational Behavior and Human Performance,* August 1966, pp. 212–25; J. R. Galbraith and L. L. Cummings, "An Empirical Investigation of the Motivational Determinants of Task Performance: Interactive Effects between Instrumentality–Valence and Motivation–Ability," *Organizational Behavior and Human Performance,* August 1967, pp. 237–57. For a critical review of field research on expectancy, see D. P. Schwab, "Expectancy Theory Predictions of Employee Performance: A Review of the Theory and Evidence," *Psychological Bulletin,* July 1972, pp. 1–9.

[22]Terence Mitchell, "Expectancy-Value Models in Organizational Psychology," in *Expectancy, Incentive, and Action,* ed. N. Feather (Hillsdale, N.J.: Erlbaum & Associates, 1980).

TABLE 10-3   What Workers Want (ranked by subgroup)*

	Work Factors									
Subgroup	Interesting Work	Full Appreciation of Work Done	Feeling of Being In on Things	Job Security	Good Wages	Promotion and Growth in Organization	Good Working Conditions	Personal Loyalty to Employees	Tactful Discipline	Sympathetic Help with Personal Problems
Sex										
Men	2	1	3	5	4	6	7	8	9	10
Women	2	1	3	4	5	6	7	8	9	10
Age										
Under 30	4	5	6	2	1	3	7	9	8	10
30–41	2	3	4	1	5	6	7	9	10	8
41–50	3	2	1	4	5	8	7	6	9	10
Over 50	1	2	3	7	8	9	4	5	10	6
Income level										
Under $12,000	5	4	6	2	1	3	8	7	10	9
$12,001–18,000	2	3	1	4	5	6	7	8	9	10
$18,001–25,000	1	3	2	4	6	5	7	8	9	10
Over $25,000	1	2	4	3	8	7	6	5	10	9
Job type										
Blue collar										
Unskilled	2	1	5	4	3	6	9	8	7	10
Skilled	1	6	2	3	4	5	7	9	10	8
White collar										
Unskilled	1	3	5	7	6	4	2	9	10	8
Skilled	2	1	4	5	6	3	7	8	9	10
Organizational level: nonsupervisory										
Lower	3	4	5	2	1	6	7	8	9	10
Middle	1	2	3	4	6	5	7	8	9	10
Higher	1	2	3	6	8	5	4	7	10	9

*Ranked from 1 (highest) to 10 (lowest).

Source: Adapted from K. A. Kovach, "What Motivates Employees? Workers and Supervisors Give Different Answers," *Business Horizons,* September–October 1987, p. 61.

Many factors influence employees' individual job-related expectations and preferences.

reinforcers to motivate or create an environment of motivation. This theory of motivation is not concerned with needs or why people make choices. Instead, it focuses on the environment and its consequences for the person. That is, behavior is considered to be environmentally caused. For example, suppose John Lofton, a hard-working employee, is given a $100 bonus for doing a good job. In the future, John continues to work hard, expecting another bonus

MANAGEMENT FOCUS

Five Simple Steps to Using Expectancy Theory

Here are five steps that allow managers to use the power of expectancy in the office.

1. *Define the expectations.* Many managers never sit down with their employees and discuss what is expected by management. They usually assume that the employees know. Many times, however, the reality is quite different. Employees don't want to ask because they would look incompetent or might be embarrassed. Instead, they assume what is expected.

2. *Make the work valuable.* All employees have personal goals that they want to work toward. But different employees may have very different goals. Managers must find out what these goals are so that they can help make the work more valuable.

3. *Make the work doable.* When employees do not reach goals, managers assume the problem is with the employee. However, no one can get excited about a job that is impossible to perform in the expected time. Managers should make realistic assignments; when there is some question about difficulty, they can invest more time in monitoring the performance of employees. In this way, they can see the difficulty of the assignment and adjust the workload before the employee becomes demoralized.

4. *Give regular feedback.* Employees complain that they never hear how they are doing until they make an error. But feedback can perform two functions: criticism and development. As criticism, it should be given quickly and specifically; it should concentrate on the actions in question and not bring up past grievances. For development, it should be given regularly, so that employees can improve their techniques before they invest more time in building bad habits.

5. *Reward employees when they meet expectations.* Money, promotions, developmental training, and awards are external rewards that a company can give to an employee when a job is well done. Many times, however, management does not relate them to performance, which weakens them as motivators. A strong relationship between performance and rewards gives the employee something to work for and can foster internal rewards such as the feeling of a job well done or attainment of some personal goal.

Source: Adapted from Thomas L. Quick, "Expectancy Theory in Five Simple Steps," *Training and Development Journal*, July 1988, pp. 30–32.

payment. Why does John continue to work hard? When John first worked hard, his behavior was reinforced by a $100 bonus. This reinforcement is an environmental consequence of good performance.

The explanation of why John continued to work hard, according to reinforcement theory, centers on Thorndike's law of effect, which states that *behavior that results in a pleasing outcome will likely be repeated; behavior that results in an unpleasant outcome is not likely to be repeated.*[23]

Operant conditioning is a powerful tool used for changing employee behavior. The term *operant conditioning* in the management literature applies to controlling work behavior by manipulating the consequences. It is based on the research work of psychologist B. F. Skinner and is built on two principles:

[23]E. L. Thorndike, *Animal Intelligence* (New York: McGraw-Hill, 1911), p. 244.

(1) Thorndike's law of effect and (2) properly scheduled rewards influence individual behaviors.[24] **Behavior modification** is the contemporary term used to describe techniques for applying the principles of operant conditioning to the control of individual behavior.

Applying Reinforcement Theory in Management.

Suppose you are a manager and your employee Mary Banner is often late with required budget reports. There are four types of reinforcement that you could use. First, you could focus on reinforcing the desired behavior (which, in this example, is preparing budget reports on time). You could use positive or negative reinforcement. **Positive reinforcement** would include rewards such as praise, recognition, or a pay bonus. **Negative reinforcement** also focuses on reinforcing the desired behavior. However, instead of providing a positive reward, the "reward" is that the employee avoids some negative consequence. Thus, Mary would complete the report on time to avoid the negative consequence of being reprimanded by her manager.

Alternatively, the manager might focus on reducing the tardiness of submitting the budget report by use of two other reinforcements: extinction or punishment. Through the use of **extinction** (withholding positive reinforcement), Mary might unlearn her bad habit of submitting late reports. Another method that reduces the frequency of undesired behavior is called **punishment.** In this case, punishment could involve the public reprimand of Mary by the manager for submitting a late report.

Positive and negative reinforcement addresses the issue of having employees learn desired behaviors. On the other hand, unlearning undesired behaviors involves the use of extinction or punishment. Figure 10–6 summarizes the Mary Banner example.

An interesting example of the use of reinforcement theory is the case of Kendall Company in Franklin, Kentucky.[25] As part of the "Gold Coin" program, plant managers carry a $\frac{1}{10}$-ounce gold coin with them that they award to an employee "on the spot" for good ideas. Then the winners' photographs are published in the local paper. Instant recognition is used at Kendall to encourage repetition of the behavior.

In applying positive reinforcement to motivate desired behaviors, managers can use different schedules. A **continuous reinforcement** schedule involves administering a reward each time a desired behavior occurs. For example, every time a budget report is submitted on time, Mary would be rewarded. An **intermittent reinforcement** schedule involves rewarding desired behavior only periodically. According to research results:[26]

1. Continuous reinforcement schedules usually result in the fastest learning.
2. Intermittent reinforcement schedules result in slower learning but stronger retention of what is learned.

---

[24]B. F. Skinner, *Science and Human Behavior* (New York: Macmillan, 1953); B. F. Skinner, *Contingencies of Reinforcement* (New York: Appleton-Century-Crofts, 1969).

[25]"Going for the Gold at Kendall," *Quality Update*, Fall 1988, p. 14.

[26]H. Davis and H. M. Hurwitz, eds., *Operant-Pavlovian Interactions* (Hillsdale, N.J.: Erlbaum & Associates, 1977).

FIGURE 10–6   Reinforcement Options Available to Managers: Illustration

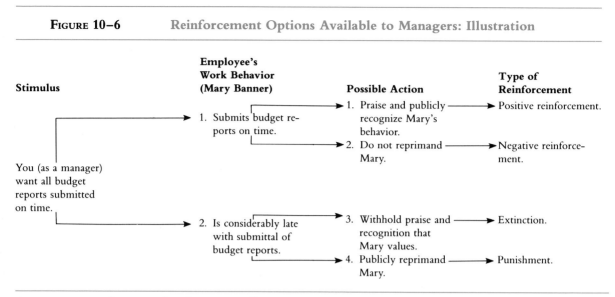

A manager can use four types of reinforcement to affect employees' behavior.

Criticisms of Reinforcement Theory.   Some critics state that the idea of rewarding or reinforcing performance is bribery and that it is used to manipulate one person to fit a manager's concept of the ideal employee.[27] Others argue that motivating employees through behavior modification relies solely on extrinsic rewards such as pay. What about intrinsic rewards, such as feeling the challenge of doing a good job? [28] Other issues of concern include: What reinforcers should be used? For whom? How long will a reinforcer be successful? Can reinforcers be effectively used with employees who are independent, creative, and self-motivated?

It is helpful to keep these criticisms in mind when considering the managerial use of reinforcement theory. They help illustrate some of the problems associated with this approach. Also, a word of caution: Reinforcement theory (like any of the other motivation theories) is not a solution to every motivation problem.

AN INTEGRATING MODEL OF MOTIVATION

All of the motivation theories presented here contain the theme that motivation is goal directed. Although the theories use different terms and appear to be quite different, they are not in conflict with each other. Basically, each looks at some segment of overall motivation or looks at the same aspect of motivation from a slightly different perspective.

[27]H. Waird, "Why Manage Behavior? A Case for Positive Reinforcement?" *Human Resource Management*, Spring 1976, pp. 15–20.

[28]Craig Schneier, "Behavior Modification in Management: Review and Critique," *Academy of Management Journal*, September 1974, pp. 528–48.

FIGURE 10–7   An Integrative Motivational Model (bringing together content and process theories)

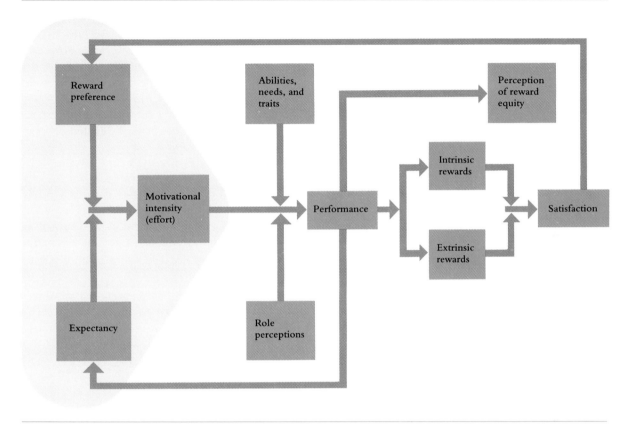

Source: Adapted from Lyman W. Porter and Edward E. Lawler III, *Managerial Attitudes and Performance* (Homewood, Ill.: Richard D. Irwin, 1968), p. 165.

Effective management must combine theories of motivation.

PORTER–LAWLER MODEL

Psychologists Lyman Porter and Edward Lawler offer a model that attempts to integrate ideas, variables, and relationships presented in other explanations of motivation such as the need hierarchy, two-factor theory, expectancy theory, and reinforcement theory.

The Porter–Lawler model is presented in Figure 10–7. It points out the relationship of performance, satisfaction, and rewards and introduces the importance of having individuals performing jobs for which they have the proper skills, abilities, and traits. There also is the issue of performance measurement. Performance must be measured accurately and systematically so that rewards can be distributed equitably. If they are not distributed fairly, expending the necessary effort to do the job will seem senseless to employees. If no meaningful difference in rewards is made between high and low performers, high performers will lose motivational intensity and probably cut back on their performance.

The integrative model uses motivational concepts discussed so far. For example, expectancy theory predicts that an employee will exert intense effort (motivation) if he or she perceives strong relationships between effort and performance, performance and rewards, and rewards and satisfaction. In order for effort to lead to performance, the individual must have a clear understanding of his or her expected role, abilities, needs, and other characteristics. The performance–reward relationship will be strong if the person perceives that intrinsic and extrinsic rewards are equitable. If there is perceived equity (fairness), satisfaction will result. The rewards would be reinforcing and satisfying and would lead to future encouragement of goal-directed behavior.

USING THE MODEL

The Porter-Lawler model and the individual theories discussed in this chapter point out that motivation is a complex process. Managers should consider the types of variables shown in the integrative model. Certainly, it indicates that motivation holds some important keys for understanding performance and satisfaction. A periodic review of the motivation process can be beneficial if managers ask themselves:

1. What are the needs of this subordinate?
2. Can I play a role in helping this subordinate satisfy these needs?
3. Are the rewards that I control and administer contingent on performance? Are they sufficient to induce the type of effort needed to do the job?
4. Does the employee have the skill, traits, behaviors, and experience necessary to perform the job?
5. Am I accurately measuring performance? If not, why not?
6. For how long will the employees continue to be motivated? What must I do to sustain motivation?

MANAGEMENT STRATEGIES FOR INCREASING MOTIVATION

Behavioral scientists have called attention to a number of programs that motivate workers to improve performance. Two programs that have been beneficial to some managers are job enrichment and relating pay to job performance.

JOB ENRICHMENT

The idea of "quality of life" at work has received much attention from practicing managers, government officials, and union leaders.[29] It appears that many workers become increasingly dissatisfied and frustrated by routine, mechanically paced tasks. They react negatively with output restrictions, poor-quality work, absenteeism, high turnover, and pressure for higher

---

[29]A report on a major project is found in Barry A. Macy, "A Progress Report on the Bolivar Quality of Life Project," *Personnel Journal,* August 1979, pp. 527–30, 558–59.

wages, expanded fringe benefits, and greater participation in decisions that directly affect their jobs.

Earlier, we discussed the Herzberg two-factor theory. The practical contribution of Herzberg's theory is a motivational technique known as **job enrichment,** supported by many managers as a solution to the problem of the quality of life at work.[30] As Herzberg describes it, job enrichment:

> seeks to improve both task efficiency and human satisfaction by means of building into people's jobs, quite specifically, greater scope for personal achievement and recognition, more challenging and responsible work, and more opportunity for individual advancement and growth. It is concerned only incidentally with matters such as pay and working conditions, organizational structure, communications and training, important and necessary though these may be in their own right.[31]

Herzberg emphasizes the importance of differentiating between *job enrichment* and **job enlargement.** He views job enrichment as providing the employee with an opportunity to grow psychologically and mature in a job, while job enlargement merely makes a job larger by increasing the number of tasks. Job enrichment, when applied, attempts to make a job motivational.[32] Research has indicated that jobs higher on job enrichment factors result in higher satisfaction and lower boredom and absenteeism than found with other job design techniques. However, research also indicates that enriched jobs require more training time and result in slightly higher anxiety and stress.[33]

Basically, what this means is that job enrichment occurs by increasing a job's range and depth.[34] **Job range** refers to the number of activities performed on the job, while **job depth** refers to the autonomy, responsibility, and discretion or control over the job. Job enrichment means that the range and depth of a job are increased. On the other hand, job enlargement means that a job's range, but not necessarily its depth, is increased.

The Core Dimensions of Jobs. Building on Herzberg's work, Richard Hackman and others have identified five core dimensions that, if present, provide enrichment for jobs.[35] Hackman, after conducting research on many different occupations, concludes that these core dimensions are often **not** found in many managerial and blue-collar jobs. He also states that there are large

---

[30]Frederick Herzberg, "One More Time: How Do You Motivate Employees?" *Harvard Business Review,* January–February 1968, p. 53.

[31]William J. Paul, Jr., Keith B. Robertson, and Frederick Herzberg, "Job Enrichment Pays Off," *Harvard Business Review,* March–April 1969, p. 61.

[32]Michael A. Campion and Paul W. Thayer, "How Do You Design a Job?" *Personnel Journal,* January 1989, pp. 43–46.

[33]Michael A. Campion, "Interdisciplinary Approaches to Job Design," *Journal of Applied Psychology,* August 1988, pp. 467–81.

[34]James L. Gibson, John M. Ivancevich, and James H. Donnelly, Jr., *Organizations: Behavior, Structure, Processes,* 6th ed. (Plano, Tex.: Business Publications, 1988), p. 478.

[35]J. Richard Hackman, Greg Oldham, Robert Janson, and Kenneth Purdy, "A New Strategy for Job Enrichment," *California Management Review,* Summer 1975, pp. 57–71.

individual differences in how employees react to core dimensions. Not all employees want or can benefit from enriched jobs.

1. *Variety.* The first core dimension is variety in the job. Variety allows employees to perform different operations, using several procedures and perhaps different equipment. Jobs that are high in variety often are viewed as challenging because they use all of an employee's skills.

2. *Task identity.* The second core dimension, task identity, allows employees to perform a complete piece of work. Overspecialized jobs tend to create routine job duties that result in a worker performing one part of the entire job. There is a sense of loss or of nonaccomplishment in doing only a part of a job. Thus, broadening the task to provide the worker with a feeling of doing a whole job increases task identity.

3. *Task significance.* The amount of impact that the work being performed has on other people is called task significance. This impact may be within the organization or outside in the community. The feeling of doing something worthwhile is important to many people. For example, an employee may be told by a respected supervisor that she has done an outstanding job that has contributed to the overall success of the department. The task has significance because it is recognized as important for the entire department.

4. *Autonomy.* The fourth core dimension, autonomy, refers to the idea that employees have some control over their job duties and work area. This seems to be an important dimension in stimulating a sense of responsibility. The popular practice of management by objectives is one way of establishing more autonomy, because it provides employees with an opportunity to set work and personal goals.

5. *Feedback.* Feedback, the fifth core dimension, refers to information that workers receive on how well they are performing. People in general have a need to know how they are doing. They need this feedback frequently so that necessary improvements can be made.

Diagnosing Jobs. These five core dimensions are what Hackman and his associates believe need to be modified to accomplish job enrichment. They suggest that organizations can study jobs to determine the quantity and quality of the core dimensions for each job. A procedure developed to analyze the core dimensions is called the job diagnostic survey (JDS).[36]

Profiles of two jobs are presented in Figure 10–8, one a skilled technician, the other an assembly-line position. By use of the JDS, worker opinions, and managerial opinions, a job's core dimensions can be studied and the weak dimensions can be pinpointed. Managerial attention to these problem areas can result in job enrichment. Not all jobs can be enriched in each core dimension. This constraint, however, should not stop managers from attempting to search further for methods to improve the total job or a specific core dimension.

Hackman's diagnostic approach to job enrichment attempts not only to profile jobs but to examine the employee's readiness for enrichment and the special problems that may hinder any job redesign. The employee who does

---

[36]Erwin L. Malone, ''The Non-Linear Systems Experiment in Participative Management,'' *Journal of Business,* January 1975, pp. 52–64.

FIGURE 10–8   Profiles of Core Dimensions for Two Jobs

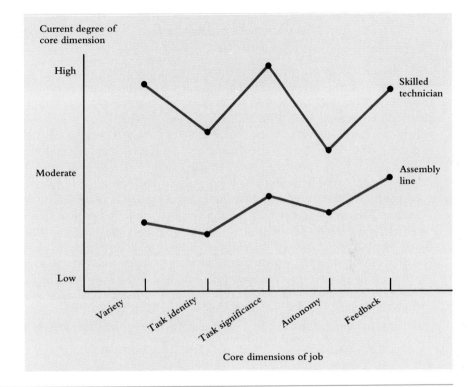

The technician job will be harder to enrich. Why?

not have a need for autonomy and feedback may not respond favorably to job enrichment. Thus, an employee's need strength is an important factor in developing the most appropriate job enrichment strategy.

One special problem of job enrichment that needs to be considered is how the program can be continued after it is started. How far will management go in each core dimension area? What is the limit of autonomy that management is willing to build into the job? If management is reluctant to continually diagnose and modify the job enrichment program, further improvement will be difficult. The management team needs to consider the following questions when reviewing job enrichment:

1. Can the employee accept more responsibility?
2. Can the employee work with more autonomy?
3. Is management able to accept changes in jobs that may result in more worker autonomy and more feedback?

Three arguments for considering and using job enrichment are spelled out in the Management Focus.

Organizational Applications of Job Enrichment. Example 1: Volkswagon (VW) of Wolfsburg, West Germany, lost money in the early

MANAGEMENT FOCUS

Three Arguments for Job Enrichment

Although job design and job enrichment may be defined and explained, it may be difficult to understand why job enrichment is needed and when it is appropriate. Here are three ways that job enrichment can be viewed as a suitable solution for three current trends in business management.

First, factory-type jobs are being exported to developing countries while domestic jobs are becoming more information intensive and service oriented. This means that the historical management techniques such as division of labor and work simplification will not be effective in this country. In information-intensive jobs, developing rules that cover every possible situation is difficult, and judgments have to be made by individual employees. They must be trained to make effective judgments and be given the inde-

pendence to solve their own problems. Giving such autonomy and responsibility to individual employees is an important part of job enrichment.

Second, the education level, skills, personal goals, and socioeconomic demands of today's work environment call for individual control principles, not external control systems. Employees that come to work today are looking for more out of their jobs than did the employees of previous generations. At the same time, companies are requiring more commitment and drive from today's employees. Unlike past generations, simply having a job is not enough. If it doesn't come with a positive social atmosphere and a chance for personal growth, and if it is not in a field of interest to you, you think twice

1980s, after growth and profits ruled the day in the 1970s.[37] VW had to automate and use robots to compete in the marketplace; they also decided to enrich employees' jobs on the assembly line. Job recognition, increased job responsibility, and increased work autonomy were built into jobs. This motivational approach has contributed to increased employee loyalty, reduced absenteeism, and less turnover.

Example 2: An attempt to enrich jobs was built into a General Foods plant.[38] The new plant management established work teams of 7 to 14 employees. Teams were given large amounts of autonomy and frequent feedback. There also was a high degree of variety built into each job. Most routine work was mechanized. The five core dimensions appear to have been provided, to a large extent. Preliminary results indicated that the plant compared favorably to more traditionally operated plants: productivity was greater, and absenteeism and turnover were less. It has since been suggested that the positive results may have occurred because the facility was new, because they began to weaken six years after the plant opened.[39]

[37]Dennis Phillips, "How VW Builds Worker Loyalty Worldwide," *Management Review,* June 1987, pp. 37–40.

[38]Richard E. Walton, "How to Counter Alienation in the Plant," *Harvard Business Review,* November–December 1972, pp. 70–81; Richard E. Walton, "The Diffusion of New Work Structures: Explaining Why Success Didn't Take," *Organizational Dynamics,* Winter 1975, pp. 3–22. Also see Lyman D. Ketchum, "How to Start and Sustain a Work Redesign Program," *National Productivity Review,* Winter 1981–1982, pp. 75–86.

[39]"Stonewalling Unit Democracy," *Business Week,* March 28, 1977, pp. 78, 81–82.

about taking it. Likewise, a company is not impressed with you unless you do extra work on your own time, conform to the corporate culture, and get along with your subordinates and superiors. This complex combination of implied rules and expectations, rather than being suited to a formalistic system, requires a set of principles to which employees can adhere. Job enrichment allows employees to make their own decisions and matches the notion of general guidelines rather than work rules.

Finally, companies are "downsizing," eliminating layers of middle management to cut costs and become more competitive. This allows them to be more flexible but limits their ability to promote their good talent. Where only four levels of managers now exist instead of the previous six, promotions are not obtainable as quickly. However, without promotions, good employees might feel that they are not being rewarded for their work and may quit. Job enrichment can play a very important part in this scenario, because a reward system can be designed to give high performers higher pay and more control, responsibility, and autonomy over their work. Instead of being over their peers, they control more of the activities than their peers do. Although not a promotion per se, such an arrangement enables employees to distinguish themselves from poorer performers.

Source: Adapted from Bernard J. Reilly and Joseph A. DiAngelo, Jr., "A Look at Job Redesign," *Personnel*, February 1988, pp. 61–65.

Example 3: The Non-Linear Systems experiment offers a caution to advocates of job enrichment.[40] The firm manufactured digital electrical measuring instruments. Management replaced an assembly line with teams of 3 to 12 employees having minimal supervision. The teams decided how the instruments would be produced. Work could be rotated and the pace controlled by the team. Each group was also responsible for resolving conflicts and handling disciplinary problems. The first set of findings at Non-Linear revealed increased productivity and morale. Over a period of years, however, productivity and quality began to suffer. The teams were not able to make quick decisions, because there was little structure within the units. The team members became dissatisfied. After approximately four years of experimenting, the firm reverted to its previous managerial practices.

These three experiences suggest that the implementation of job enrichment principles can be successful in some situations but not in others.[41] There also is the question of how long performance improvements can continue, an important issue in the General Foods and Volkswagon examples. Job enrichment should not be viewed as a universally desirable program. Some workers

[40]Malone, "The Non-Linear Systems Experiment in Participative Management."

[41]For more thorough reviews of job enrichment, see Ricky W. Griffin, *Task Design: An Integrative Approach* (Glenview, Ill.: Scott, Foresman, 1982); Randall Dunham, "Job Design," in *Organizational Behavior,* ed. Steven Kerr (Columbus, Ohio: Grid, 1979); Ramon J. Aldag and Arthur P. Brief, *Task Design and Employee Motivation* (Glenview, Ill.: Scott, Foresman, 1979).

and managers cannot operate effectively under job enrichment conditions. Therefore, both worker and managerial reactions need to be considered before implementing job enrichment.

RELATING PAY TO JOB PERFORMANCE

The money that employees receive for working is actually a package made up of pay and various fringe benefits, such as health insurance, vacation pay, life insurance, and sick leave. Each of the content and process theories of motivation suggests that money can have some influence on effort and persistence.

In Maslow's need hierarchy, pay has the potential to satisfy each of the five needs. However, according to Herzberg's two-factor model, pay is a maintenance factor that should not contribute significantly to workers' motivation. Expectancy theory would indicate that since pay can satisfy a variety of needs, it has an attraction. Pay would be a good motivator if workers perceive that good performance is instrumental to obtaining it. Reinforcement theory would view pay as an environmental consequence that could be used to stimulate positive work behaviors.

A number of research studies suggest to managers that a pay plan, in order to motivate, must (1) create a belief that good performance leads to high levels of pay, (2) minimize the negative consequences of good performance, and (3) create conditions so that desired rewards other than pay are seen to be related to good performance.[42] Research findings suggest that many organizations, although they try, do not do a very good job of relating pay to performance in either managerial or nonmanagerial jobs. Surprisingly, in the managerial ranks (where no unions exist), pay is not related to performance. This may mean that pay is not a very powerful motivator or that money is being wasted when offered in hopes that it will motivate better managerial performance.

One survey of personnel practices reported high dissatisfaction with pay programs,[43] which can affect performance and other variables. Figure 10–9 illustrates some of the potentially negative consequences of being dissatisfied with pay. Managers must understand that pay is very important to some people and is a highly valued reward. It can serve to satisfy needs and to increase the motivation intensity of the employee. If a worker's desire for more pay is not satisfied, the consequences could be reduced performance, filing of grievances, interest in going on strike, or even seeking a job elsewhere.

In order to head off pay dissatisfaction problems, a number of organizations have used some innovative plans. A few of these innovative efforts will be briefly introduced.

Money as a Motivator.   Nucor Manufacturing Corporation has a management team that, unlike Herzberg, believes that money is the best motivator. Most Nucor employees are unskilled and semiskilled when they are hired.

---

[42]Good discussions of pay and performance appear in George T. Milkovich and Jerry M. Newman, *Compensation,* 2nd ed. (Plano, Tex.: Business Publications, 1988); Edward E. Lawler III, *Pay and Organizational Effectiveness* (New York: McGraw-Hill, 1971).

[43]Campbell, et al., *Managerial Behavior,* pp. 51–59.

FIGURE 10–9   Consequences of Pay Dissatisfaction

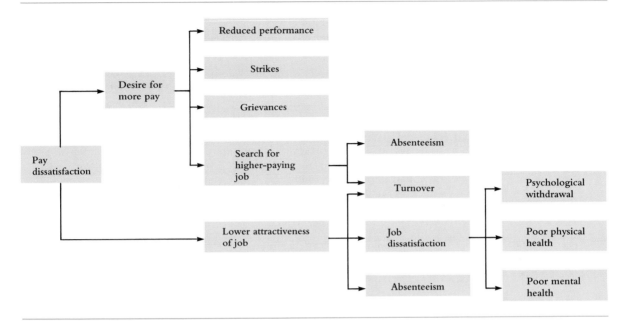

Source: From *Pay and Organizational Effectiveness: A Psychological View* by Edward E. Lawler III. Copyright © 1971 McGraw-Hill Book Company. Used with permission of McGraw-Hill Book Company.

Pay is very important to some employees, and being dissatisfied with pay has negative consequences.

Furthermore, Nucor employees seem to place a high value on job security, which management attempts to provide.

Nucor currently operates five steel joist fabrication plants. The entire corporation has five organizational levels from the president to the operating employee. There are no assistant managers, group managers, or directors. All of Nucor's facilities are in rural areas. These organizational features and plant locations are rather unusual in the steel joist fabrication industry.

The company currently has four incentive compensation programs. The focal point of these programs is groups, not individuals. The incentive systems are for production employees; department heads; secretaries, accounting clerks, accountants, and engineers; and senior officers. The groups range in size from 25 to 30. Approximately 2,500 Nucor employees are under the main program, called the production incentive system.[44]

To a certain extent, Nucor views each of the 25 to 30 groups of production employees as being in business for itself. What workers earn is largely dependent on their performance. There are no bonuses paid when equipment is not operating. The rules for absenteeism at Nucor are simple. There are four grace days per year. Additional days off are approved for military service or jury duty. Anyone not there for other days loses the week's bonus. Additionally, being more than a half-hour late means losing the bonus for the day.

[44]Tom Peters, *Thriving on Chaos* (New York: Alfred A. Knopf, 1987), pp. 335–36.

The production incentive program is only one part of the Nucor system. At the department-head level, the company has an incentive compensation program based on the contribution of the particular department to the company as a whole.

The third incentive plan applies to employees who are neither in a production function nor at the department-manager level: accountants, secretaries, clerks, and so on. The bonus they receive is based on either the division's return on assets or the corporation's return on assets. Every month, each division receives a report showing, on a year-to-year basis, its return on assets. This chart is posted in the employee cafeteria or break area, together with the chart showing the bonus payout.

The fourth Nucor program is for senior officers. They receive no profit sharing, no pension or retirement plans, or other similar executive perks. More than half of each officer's compensation is based directly on company earnings. If the firm is doing well, the executives do well. Their base salaries are set at 70 percent of what an individual in a comparable position with another company would receive.

Nucor does not have a retirement plan that is actuarially based; rather, it has a profit-sharing plan with a deferred trust. Under the plan, 10 percent of the firm's pretax earnings is put into profit sharing annually. Of this amount, 20 percent is set aside to be paid to employees in March of the following year as cash profit sharing. The remainder is put into a trust.

Vesting in the profit-sharing trust is much like that of a retirement plan. An employee is 20 percent vested after a year in profit sharing, with an additional 10 percent vesting each year thereafter.

Another example of incentive at Nucor is the service awards program. Instead of handing out pen and pencil sets, money clips, or gift certificates for seniority, Nucor issues company stock. After five years of service, an employee receives five shares of Nucor stock. Another five years of service and they receive another five shares, and so on.

Salaried Payments.   Companies such as Eaton Corporation, TRW, Dow Chemical, Dana Corporation, and Rockwell International have implemented all-salaried compensation payments for most of their employees.[45] TRW, for instance, now has 20 plants on a salary basis, compared with just 3 a decade ago. An employee relations survey by the Conference Board found that all-salaried compensation systems ranked ahead of flextime, payment-for-knowledge plans, autonomous work teams, and productivity or gain-sharing bonuses among a list of approaches that managers of nonunion groups are encouraged to develop or sustain.

Implementing a salaried system is complex, and eventual improvement in morale and performance depends on a host of variables. Geographic location, the strength of organized labor, and the climate of management-employee relations are important variables. The ideal scenario for management, according to a consultant in New York, is "to move down South and open a new plant in a right-to-work state with weak unions. You don't have a lot of inbred attitudes."

[45]Paul G. Engel, "Salaried Plants: Panacea for Productivity?" *Industry Week,* January 21, 1985, pp. 39–42.

At Dow Chemical, a gradual shift to salary plans over an 18-year period has involved both old and new facilities. However, it should be noted that the Dow shift has resulted in the creation of salaried plants in the firm, more of which are unionized. Whether unions and salaried employees are mutually exclusive entities is an issue that will take more time to analyze.

Paid Personal Leave Plans.   A study of employee behaviors at Rapid City Regional Hospital indicated that approximately 20 percent of the employees were using more than 50 percent of the paid sick leave at the hospital.[46] The existing plan at that time provided full-time employees with:

- Ten vacation days after 1 year of employment, increasing to 15 days after 5 years and 20 days after 10 years.
- Eight fixed holidays.
- One day of sick leave accrued per month to a maximum of 45 days.

The plan, as the study indicated, was being abused by some employees and had become very expensive.

The new paid personal leave program (PPL) was combined with the existing plan; 40 hours of guaranteed sick leave was combined with vacation and holiday hours in a lump-sum account. Since Rapid City Hospital did not have any long-term disability plan, management decided to double the previous maximum accumulation of 45 days to 90 days, put into a separate account called the extended-illness accrual bank (EIAB). EIAB would be accrued on the basis of six days per year.

The PPL plan would mean that an employee with one to four years of service would accrue an annual total of 23 days of paid leave a year; employees with 10 years of service or more would accrue 33 days per year of paid leave. Each employee would have to use at least 75 percent of his or her earned PPL each year. The difference between the 75 percent taken and the total hours earned could be accrued from one year to the next until a maximum of 30 days is reached. Any excessive accrued PPL could be cashed in or transferred to a person's EIAB account if the employee so desired.

The major emphasis of the PPL is that the leave is an earned benefit that employees should use. The employees appear to like having the responsibility for scheduling their time off on the basis of the earned benefits. Surveys indicate that a majority of employees like the plan, view it as rewarding, and understand that time off is an earned benefit. Comments also indicate that morale has been improved because employees believe that they are receiving their fair share of time off.

SUMMARY OF KEY POINTS

- Motivation is an inner state that helps describe the wishes, desires, drives, and needs of individuals.

- Two important content theories of motivation are Maslow's need hierarchy theory and Herzberg's two-factor theory. Maslow arranges

---

[46]James H. Brockman, "Give Employees the Responsibility of Scheduling Their Time Off," *Personnel Journal*, October 1985, pp. 96–102.

five needs in a hierarchy based on different levels of importance. Herzberg presents two sets of job conditions: maintenance and motivational. The maintenance factors are external to the job and cause dissatisfaction when they are not present. The motivational factors are job centered and tend to motivate individuals.

■ The expectancy theory of motivation is a process theory that suggests that individuals are motivated to make choices among different behaviors or intensities of work effort. An individual will exert effort to achieve performance that will result in receiving preferred rewards.

■ The reinforcement theory of motivation, also a process theory, relies on the use of reinforcers

(positive, negative, extinction, punishment) to motivate. It is concerned with the environment and its consequences for the person.

■ Job enrichment seeks to improve both task efficiency and human satisfaction by building into jobs greater range for personal achievement and recognition, more challenging and responsible work, and more opportunity for individual advancement and growth.

■ In order for a pay plan to motivate, it must (1) create a belief that good performance leads to high levels of pay, (2) minimize the negative consequences of good performance, and (3) create conditions so that desired rewards other than pay are seen to be related to good performance.

DISCUSSION AND REVIEW QUESTIONS

1. How is reinforcement theory used by the instructor in the course you are now taking?

2. Why is job enrichment referred to as a motivational approach to job design?

3. The manager of a team of engineers in a manufacturing plant was overheard to say, "I believe that money is the best of all possible motivators. You can say what you please about all that other nonsense; but when it comes right down to it, if you give a guy a raise, you'll motivate him. That's all there is to it." In light of what we have discussed in this chapter, advise this manager.

4. Why would a professional athlete earning over $1 million not be satisfied with this amount of reward for performing? Discuss the concept of satisfaction in terms of perception, as presented in Figure 10–7.

5. Some critics of job enrichment and behavior modification programs state that most of the declared successes are based on faulty measurements or short periods of time. A proper evaluation over a longer period of time would show less positive results with these programs. Comment.

6. Why would a man or woman who has attained vast wealth by, say, his or her early 40s continue for years to work very hard to achieve outstanding job performance?

7. In this chapter, it was emphasized that managers must be familiar with the fundamental needs of people in order to motivate employees successfully.

Select two individuals you know well. Do they differ, in your opinion, with respect to the strength of various needs? Discuss these differences and indicate how they could affect behavior. If you were attempting to motivate those persons, would you use different approaches for each? Why?

8. Can a student's "job" be enriched? Assume that you are to consult with your professor about applying the two-factor motivation model in your class. You are to answer these questions: Can you apply this approach to the classroom? Why? If you can, differentiate between maintenance and motivational factors and develop a list of motivational factors your professor can use to enrich the student's job.

9. Assume that you have just read Vroom's thoughts on how the *goals* of individuals influence their *effort* and how the behavior the individual selects depends on an assessment of the probability that the behavior will successfully lead to the goal. What is your goal in this management course? Is it influencing your effort? Do you suppose another person in your class might have a different goal? Is that person's effort (behavior) different from yours? If your professor was aware of this, could it be of any value?

10. What argument could be made to support the position that some employees consider pay earned to be the most significant intrinsic reward associated with the job?

ADDITIONAL REFERENCES

Arehart-Treichel, J. *Biotypes.* New York: Times Books, 1980.

Arvey, R. D., and **J. M. Ivancevich.** "Punishment in Organizations: A Review, Propositions, and Research Suggestions." *Academy of Management Review,* January 1980, pp. 123–32.

Baird, L. S., and **W. C. Hamner.** "Individual versus System Rewards: Who's Dissatisfied, Why, and What Is Their Likely Response?" *Academy of Management Journal,* December 1979, pp. 783–92.

Brennan, E. J. "Merit Pay: Balance the Old Rich and the New Poor." *Personnel Journal,* May 1985, pp. 82–85.

Brennan, E. J. "The Myth and the Reality of Pay for Performance." *Personnel Journal,* March 1985, pp. 73–75.

Chase, M. "Intel to Cut Salaries up to 10%, Impose 1-Year Freeze." *The Wall Street Journal,* November 18, 1982, p. 24.

Hackman, J. R. "The Design of Work in the 1980s." *Organizational Dynamics,* Summer 1978, pp. 3–17.

Henderson, R. I. "Designing a Reward System for Today's Employee." *Business,* July–September 1982, pp. 2–13.

Herzberg, F. "Herzberg on Motivation for the 1980s." *Industry Week,* 1979, pp. 58–63.

Hills, F. S.; K. D. Scott; S. E. Markham; and **M. J. West.** "Merit Pay: Just or Unjust Desserts." *Personnel Administrator,* September 1987, pp. 53–59.

Kazdin, A. E. *Behavior Modification in Applied Settings.* Homewood, Ill.: Dorsey Press, 1980.

Kerr, J., and **J. W. Slocum, Jr.** "Managing Corporate Culture through Reward Systems." *Academy of Management Executive,* May 1987, pp. 99–107.

Krechel, W., III. "Your New Employment Contract." *Fortune,* July 6, 1987, pp. 109–10.

Landry, F. J., and **W. J. Becker.** "Motivation Theory Reconsidered." In *Research in Organizational Behavior,* ed. L. L. Cummings and B. M. Staw. Greenwich, Conn.: JAI Press, 1987, pp. 24–35.

Lawler, E. E., III. "The New Pay." *New Management,* Summer 1985, pp. 52–59.

Lindroth, J. "Inflation, Taxes and Perks: How Compensation Is Changing." *Personnel Journal,* December 1981, pp. 934–40.

Main, J. "Merchants of Inspiration." *Fortune,* July 6, 1987, pp. 69–74.

Pender, C. C. *Work Motivation.* Glenview, Ill.: Scott, Foresman, 1984.

Petty, M. M.; G. W. McGee; and **J. W. Cavender.** "A Meta-Analysis of the Relationships between Individual Job Satisfaction and Individual Performance." *Academy of Management Review,* October 1984, pp. 712–21.

Posner, B. G. "Right from the Start." *Inc.,* August 1988, pp. 95–96.

Sims, H. P., Jr. "Further Thoughts on Punishment in Organizations." *Academy of Management Review,* January 1980, pp. 133–38.

Steers, R. M., and **L. W. Porter,** eds. *Motivation and Work Behavior,* 3rd ed. New York: McGraw-Hill, 1983.

Stein, J. "Flexible Benefits." *Houston Post,* August 29, 1982, p. 1BB.

Sussman, M., and **R. P. Vecchio.** "A Social Influence Interpretation of Worker Motivation." *Academy of Management Review,* April 1982, pp. 177–86.

"Upsurge in ESOPs." *Dun's Business Month,* February 1983, pp. 76–79.

Zaleznik, A. *The Managerial Mystique: Restoring Leadership in Business.* New York: Harper & Row, 1989.

CASE 10–1   Physical Fitness, Recreation, and Motivation

Organizations have used both monetary and nonmonetary rewards to motivate employees. However, performance, absenteeism, turnover, and loyalty problems still exist and trouble managers. One move to create an atmosphere and working climate conducive to better performance and motivation has been the use of recreational programs:

1. Peoples Jewelry Company has a program that provides discount tickets for amusement parks, hotels, resorts, and cultural events. The company found that after the program started, absenteeism went down 23 percent.
2. Eastman Kodak has a 300,000-square-foot recreational area that includes a putting green, tennis courts, softball diamonds, a gymnasium, physical-fitness rooms, bowling lanes, squash courts, and pistol ranges.
3. Xerox has a $3.5 million recreation center with facilities for swimming, golf, handball, racquetball, soccer, squash, and basketball.
4. Integon Corporation, an insurance company with about 600 employees, hired a professional to run its recreation program, including tennis, racquetball, Christmas parties for adults and children, pizza nights, arts and crafts classes, and subsidized memberships at the local YMCA.

Most recreation programs include families in at least some of their activities. James H. Hoke, president of Practical Management Consultants of Southfield, Michigan, says, "A perceptive recreation director will produce several couples' activities yearly to avoid job jealousy and fantasies about unknown company people that can build resentments at home."

Recreation programs also can be helpful for employees nearing retirement. They can develop interests and hobbies to pursue in retirement, and some retired employees volunteer to help run the recreation programs.

Operating costs for recreation programs vary almost as widely as the programs themselves. While some programs have annual budgets of more than $750,000, others manage on less than $5,000. The average is about $11,000.

Sources of funding for such programs usually include employee dues and special assessments for activities, employer contributions, and frequently the profits from vending machines. Some programs also receive profits from canteens, food service, and company stores. Incorporated employees' associations that operate with such funding usually are approved by the Internal Revenue Service as nonprofit organizations.

There is no question that employees benefit from recreational facilities; management finds them advantageous as well. They make recruiting easier and reduce turnover because happy employees are less likely to quit or be lured away, are absent less, and often are more productive. This makes for more profitable companies whose managers view their recreation programs as sound investments.

QUESTIONS FOR ANALYSIS

1. Would you (do you) participate if the organization you worked for had recreation activities similar to the Xerox, Eastman Kodak, Integon, and Peoples Jewelry programs?
2. How could a recreational program be used as a positive motivator of on-the-job performance?
3. Recreation programs date back to the 1800s. Why has there been a renewed interest in the potential impact of recreation programs on employees?

CASE 10–2   Is Motivation the Root of Postal Inefficiencies?

For many Americans, the post office is an example of what happens when everything is managed wrong. Some critics have claimed that "postal service" is an oxymoron (a phrase that contradicts itself). When Congress proposed a form of socialized medicine, bumper stickers appeared that read, "If you like the postal service, you'll love socialized medicine." Over the years, costs have risen while services were cut back, following a declining trend some experts feel has been happening for decades.

How much of this is a motivation problem? How much time and money could be saved if the workers had a high morale and/or a stake in the success of the operation?

The tasks performed by the majority of the postal workers are very boring. Mail sorters, for instance, sit 12 in a row, one behind another, for 45 minutes at a time and sort letters at a rate of one per second. This means that they have $^6/_{10}$ths of that second to read the ZIP code and the remaining $^4/_{10}$ths to type it into the console. They are only required to be accurate 95 percent of the time, so 1,620 pieces of mail could be misplaced every 45 minutes by each group without anyone getting in trouble.

Rules implemented over the years with the intent of improving productivity are probably doing just the opposite. Many of the tasks that used to be performed by letter carriers have been centralized. Changes of address must be filed through a central mail facility, where operators input the change on the computer that forwards the mail. If a letter carrier notices that someone has moved or the name is misspelled, he or she is not allowed to make a change or give the letter to another carrier. Instead, he or she must reroute the letter back through the system.

Operators on the letter sorting machines are not allowed to make decisions. When they see a Chicago address with a Cleveland ZIP code, they must route it to Cleveland and let a post office make the change and reroute it back.

The postal service has a nearly military style of management. Beyond the uniforms, the post offices are run like shop floors at the turn of the century. Postal regulations fill a book the size of a dictionary and are followed religiously. Some facilities require employees to punch white cards when they go to another part of the building. A facility in Indianapolis built a glass cage for those who were injured on the job. Its purpose was to humiliate the workers that were "fool enough" to injure themselves. The cage was in full view of most of the workers, and the "inmates" were not even allowed to read while in the cage. The local union representative thought that it might have an opposite effect—that workers would not work hard for fear of injuring themselves and being put on display.

Source: Adapted from John B. Judis, "The Postal Service Struggles with Old Problems, New Competition, and the Public," *New York Times Magazine*, September 28, 1988, pp. 21–54.

One reason why there is little change in the system is that about 50 percent of the postal workers are represented by the union. The stereotypical union attitude toward innovative management programs is that the government is trying to undermine the control of the union. Because of this, little chance exists for the kinds of programs that boost productivity and morale, such as cost savings sharing and flexible work shifts.

QUESTIONS FOR ANALYSIS

1. In 1987, the Reagan administration proposed a possible privatization program designed to sell parts of the postal system to private industry. How would this help and/or hurt the accountability (or profitability) of the system?
2. Using Vroom's expectancy theory, explain why the glass room should have worked. Use it to show why it should not work.
3. From the information in this case, determine what level of Maslow's hierarchy of needs the postal system's management seems to be using to motivate employees. What would be a realistic motivation level if you were a postal employee?

EXPERIENTIAL EXERCISE

YOUR JOB PREFERENCES COMPARED TO OTHERS

Purpose

This exercise is designed to identify what makes a job attractive or unattractive to you. Preferences of employees, if known, could be used as information by managers to develop and restructure jobs that are more attractive, rewarding, and generally more fulfilling. It is this type of information that would permit a manager to create a positive motivational atmosphere for subordinates.

The Exercise in Class

1. Think about your present job (if you have one) or the type of job you would like. Decide which of the following job factors is most important to you. Place a 1 in front of it. Then decide which is the second most important to you and place a 2 in front of it. Keep ranking the items in order of importance until the least important job factor is ranked 14. Individuals differ in the order in which these job factors are ranked. What is your present preference?

    _____ Advancement (opportunity for promotion).
    _____ Pay (income received for working).
    _____ Fringe benefits (vacation period, insurance, recreation facilities).
    _____ Schedule (hours worked, starting time).

_____ Location (geographic area: Midwest, South, West, East, South-west).

_____ Supervisor (a fair, influential boss).

_____ Feedback (receiving prompt, meaningful, and accurate feedback on job performance).

_____ Security (steady work, assurance of a future).

_____ Challenge (interesting and stimulating work).

_____ Working conditions (comfortable and clean work area).

_____ Co-workers (colleagues who are friendly, interesting).

_____ The organization (working for a company you are proud of).

_____ Responsibility (having responsibility to complete important job).

_____ Training and development opportunities (the ability to receive training and development in the organization or through external sources).

2. Now rank the job factors as you think other members of your class would rank them. Look around and think how the average person in your class would rank the job factors.

_____ Advancement.

_____ Pay.

_____ Fringe benefits.

_____ Schedule.

_____ Location.

_____ Supervisor.

_____ Feedback.

_____ Security.

_____ Challenge.

_____ Working conditions.

_____ Co-workers.

_____ The organization.

_____ Responsibility.

_____ Training and development opportunities.

3. The instructor will form four- to six-person groups to discuss the _individual_ and _other_ rankings. Each group should calculate averages for both rankings. What does this show? The members of your group should discuss these average scores.

4. The average individual and average other rankings should be placed on the board or flip chart and discussed by the entire class.

The Learning Message

Individuals consider different factors important. Can a manager realistically respond to a wide range of different preferences among subordinates?

11

MANAGING WORK GROUPS

LEARNING OBJECTIVES

After studying Chapter 11, you should be able to:

Define

in a concise manner such terms as *social loafing*, *groupthink*, and *synergy*.

Describe

the conditions under which group decision making is preferred over individual decision making, and vice versa.

Discuss

how cohesiveness can influence a group's overall performance.

Compare

the causes of and solutions to intragroup and intergroup conflict.

Identify

the key reasons why informal groups appear in organizations.

EDGE: A Group Decision–Making Game

One common complaint about group decision-making techniques and systems is the time that they take. Many, such as Delphi, require several iterations while companies wait for answers. Enter EDGE, a group decision-making technique played like a board game in around 40 minutes.

On 3 by 5 cards, each group member prepares at least four suggestions for solving a particular problem. To improve a company's competitive edge (thus the name), suggestions might be "develop a global perspective," "change continually to improve," or "focus on customers' needs."

These cards and others prepared beforehand are shuffled, and three are dealt to each member. Members study the suggestions and arrange them in order of preference. The remaining cards are placed on a side table. Members may quietly discard and pick up as many cards as they like (so long as they have three in their hand) and then exchange at least one card with another player. Thus, they can choose other suggestions over their own.

Teams are formed with no minimum or maximum number. However, only three cards can be held by a group; all others must be discarded by the group.

Each group must then make one transparency or poster depicting the suggestions in the group hand. This forces the group to define rather general statements and transpose them into something specific to the problem at hand or the company. It also helps the members agree on the phrases' meanings. All posters are presented to the rest of the group, and any ambiguities are explained.

Finally, outside judges evaluate the "winners" in terms of internal consistency of the three suggestions, the inclusiveness of the poster, and appropriateness of the visuals.

The goal, as with similar group techniques in this chapter, is to reduce the amount of information that each member must digest, promote objective discussion of the suggestions, and encourage creativity while limiting criticism. In EDGE, bad ideas are discarded without verbal criticism (or abuse). Players can abandon bad ideas painlessly. Forming groups further reduces the number of suggestions and also creates alliances. The posters let the teams explain their ideas.

Source: Adapted from Sivasailam Thiagarajan, "Beyond Brainstorming," *Training and Development Journal,* September 1988, pp. 57–60.

Few managers question the existence of work groups. For years, behavioral scientists have paid special attention to the processes occurring within groups and affecting individuals and organizations. Therefore, any examination of the fundamentals of managing people must provide a framework for understanding the nature of work groups. This chapter will provide (1) a classification of the different types of work groups, (2) the reasons for formation and development of work groups, (3) the characteristics of groups, and (4) the results of group membership.

A work group is a collection of employees (managerial or nonmanagerial) who share certain norms and who strive to satisfy their needs through the attainment of the group goal(s). Students often ask why work groups should be studied in a management text. Many different answers can be provided:

1. The formation of work groups is inevitable. Managers create some work groups to perform work and tasks. Others form to satisfy employees' social needs. Therefore, it is in management's interest to understand what happens within work groups, because they are found throughout the organization.
2. Work groups strongly influence the overall behavior and performance of members. To understand the forces of influence exerted by the group requires a systematic analysis.
3. Group membership can have both positive and negative consequences for the organization. If managers are to avoid the negative consequences, it is in their interest to learn about work groups.

The common thread found in most answers is that groups exist and affect the attitudes and behaviors of employees. Managing a group is a skill managers must learn and practice. Whether one manages a committee, a scout troop, a project team, or a sports team, there are some principles to consider. The Management Focus uses a football example to illustrate managing a group.

Kurt Lewin, a recognized scholar, perhaps explained it best in a classic speech on why groups need to be understood:

> Although the scientific investigations of group work are but a few years old, I don't hesitate to predict that group work—that is, the handling of human beings not as isolated individuals, but in the social setting of groups—will soon be one of the most important theoretical and practical fields. . . . It is easier to affect the personality of 10 people if they can be melted into a group than to affect the personality of any 1 individual separately.[1]

CLASSIFICATION OF GROUPS

Every organization has technical requirements that arise from its objectives. The accomplishment of these objectives requires certain tasks to be performed, and employees are assigned to groups to perform these tasks. In addition, other types of groups form that are not the result of deliberate design.

[1] Alvin Zander, "The Psychology of the Group Process," *Annual Review of Psychology,* 1979, p. 418.

MANAGEMENT FOCUS

If Managers Really Used a Football Model

Probably the most used analogies for managing groups are the military and sports. If the military model is used, managers might want their group to "rally 'round the flag," "regroup and plan the battle," or "dig trenches and lie low." In the sports model, managers might "head for the showers" or "go into a huddle." In this Management Focus, the idea of using sports principles is carried "all the way" and compared to management procedures as they are today.

The sports model used here comes from the "winningest" coach in college football history, the late Paul W. "Bear" Bryant. Using the observations of people around him, we can translate his successful sports system to the business environment, focusing specifically on his training methods.

Bryant's players had the best training they could get. He used observation-based training, with cameras and coaches. If a player did not realize what he was doing wrong with his feet, Bryant would show him a film of how he was doing it. If the player couldn't fix the problem, Bryant would show him an exemplary player doing it right.

At each stage of training, players knew just where they were excelling, where they were having difficulty, and what they needed to improve. There was no hugging on the field if they did well, nor was there finger-pointing and yelling if they did poorly. The players were simply given constant feedback on their performance.

How many businesses use this kind of training? First, it is estimated that fewer than 5

Accordingly, we can identify two broad classes of groups in organizations: formal and informal.

Most employees belong to a group based on their position in the organization. These **formal groups** are the departments, units, and so forth that management forms to do the work of the organization. The demands and processes of the organization lead to the formation of these groups.

On the other hand, whenever employees associate on a fairly continuous basis, they tend to form groups whose activities may be different from those required by the organization. These **informal groups** are natural groupings of people in the work situation in response to social needs. In other words, they do not arise as a result of deliberate design but rather evolve naturally. While this distinction is convenient for our discussion on specific types of groups in organizations later in the chapter, both formal and informal groups exhibit the same general characteristics. Thus, throughout the chapters, the term *work group* will include both formal and informal groups unless otherwise specified.

The influence of informal groups on employee behavior and performance was spelled out in our discussion of the Hawthorne studies in the Part III Foundation. In the bank wiring room portion of the study, a group of workers was observed for approximately three months. The group decided to produce two units a day and to finish the second unit exactly at quitting time. Any group member who tried to speed up the work was ridiculed. These behaviors existed despite the fact that the group had the capability to produce more and despite the existence of what management believed was a good pay incentive plan.

percent of the chief executive officers of Fortune 500 companies have ever witnessed the training in their organizations. Second, if you ask them, most managers will have difficulty telling you what specific effects training has had on job performance. (In fact, many organizations use "days in training" as their measure of training proficiency, which encourages training directors to keep trainees off their job and in a classroom or in front of a video screen as long as possible.) The typical business cannot state with reliability how its training is really helping the organization. Bryant, on the other hand, could easily explain why every film was shot and what every drill was intended to show.

It doesn't seem that businesses could afford Bryant's extensive observation-based training.

But the "winningest" coach earned that title by training consistently winning teams, a goal sought after by organizations and managers alike. Training, of course, is crucial because—to use an old cliché—"the chain is only as strong as its weakest link." Both sports and business teams must rely on *all* their members to "carry the ball" to victory, or success. That being true, can businesses afford *not* to expend the effort and money needed for thorough training?

Source: Adapted from Thomas F. Gilbert and Marilyn B. Gilbert, "The Science of Winning," *Training,* August 1988, pp. 33–40.

The point of the Hawthorne example is not that informal groups are disruptive to managers. Rather, it illustrates the powerful influence that work groups can exert over their members. This influence can be economic, social, psychological, or even physical. Table 11–1 compares some of the main characteristics of formal and informal groups.

FORMATION OF WORK GROUPS

Chapter 10 stated that individuals have a number of needs, most of which are satisfied when interacting with others. Groups form because they sustain and satisfy these needs. There is no single reason why individuals join groups.

PHYSICAL REASONS

In organizations, a typical procedure is to place together workers in similar occupations. For example, in the construction of a home, bricklayers perform their jobs in close proximity to each other. The same situation exists in offices where secretaries are located elbow to elbow.[2] People in close proximity to each other tend to interact and communicate with each other. If workers are not able to do this on a fairly regular basis, group formation is less likely.[3]

[2]William G. Scott and Terence R. Mitchell, *Organization Theory* (Homewood, Ill.: Richard D. Irwin, 1976), p. 171.

[3]Dorwin Cartwright and Ronald Lippitt, "Group Dynamics and the Individual," *International Journal of Group Psychotherapy,* January 1957, p. 88.

TABLE 11-1   Formal and Informal Groups: A Comparison

Formal and informal groups differ in a number of important dimensions.

Dimension	Formal Group	Informal Group
1. Major objectives	Profit, efficiency, service.	Member satisfaction, member security.
2. Origin	Planned by organization.	Spontaneous.
3. Influence on members	Position authority, monetary rewards.	Personality, expertise.
4. Communication	Flows from top down, uses formal channels.	Grapevine, person-to-person, using all channels.
5. Leader	Appointed by organization.	Emerges from group.
6. Interpersonal relations	Established by job and work-flow pattern.	Developed spontaneously.
7. Control	Reliance on threat, use of monetary rewards.	Strong social sanctions.

ECONOMIC REASONS

In some situations, work groups form because individuals believe they can derive more economic benefits from their jobs if they form into groups. For example, individuals working at different stations on an assembly line may be paid on a group incentive basis. Whatever the particular group produces determines the wages for each member. Because of the interest of the workers in their wages, they will interact and communicate with each other. By working as a group instead of as individuals, they may perceive and actually obtain higher economic benefits.

Japan's Auto Alley has pointed out how American employees and Japanese managers have formed alliances and teams for economic reasons.[4] The economic motive has resulted in Mazdas being made in Michigan, Hondas in Ohio, Toyotas in Kentucky, and Nissans in Tennessee. The Japanese managers have trained and motivated American workers to work as a team to turn out cars of quality comparable to the made-in-Japan original. An egalitarian work atmosphere reinforces cooperation, teamwork, and a positive culture in the Japanese-managed plants.

Another example of the economic motive for informal work group formation might be a nonunion organization. The workers form to bring pressure against management for more economic benefits. The group members would have a common interest—increased economic benefits—that would lead to group affiliation.

SOCIOPSYCHOLOGICAL REASONS

Workers in organizations also are motivated to form work groups to satisfy safety, social, esteem, and self-actualization needs.

[4]Louis Kraar, "Japan's Gung-Ho U.S. Car Plants," *Fortune,* January 30, 1989, pp. 97–108.

Safety.   Work groups can protect members from outside pressures, including serving as a buffer from management's demands for better quality and quantity of production, insistance that they punch the clock on time, and recommendations for change in their work area layouts. By being a member of a group, individual employees can become involved in group activities and openly discuss these management demands with fellow workers who usually support their viewpoint. Without the group to lean on when various management demands are made, employees often assume that they stand alone against management and the entire organization. This "aloneness" leads to a degree of insecurity.

Another form of safety need occurs in instances when a new employee is asked to perform a difficult job task over an extended period of time. Not wanting to contact the supervisor continually for help in correctly performing the job, the employee depends largely on the group for help, gaining a form of security need satisfaction. Whether the supervisor believes that continual requests for help by a new employee are signs of inability to perform the job is not the main issue. The important point is how new workers perceive their situation and job security.

Social.   Employees often join work groups because of their need for affiliation. The basis of affiliation ranges from wanting to interact with and enjoy other employees to more complex desires for group support of self-image. A management atmosphere that does not permit interaction and communication suppresses the desire of employees to feel a sense of belonging.

We learned from our discussion of motivation in Chapter 10 that people have social needs. Informal and formal group affiliations permit people to satisfy these needs. The employee who is not able to satisfy social needs is likely to withdraw, become aggressive, and compensate in other ways such as absenteeism or work slowdowns.

Esteem.   Some employees are attracted to a work group because they think they gain prestige by belonging. In an organization, a particular group may be viewed by employees as being a top-notch work group. Consequently, membership among the elite bestows upon the members prestige that is not enjoyed by nonmembers. This prestige is conferred on members by other employees (nonmembers), which often leads to more gratification of the esteem need. And by sharing in the activities of a high-prestige work group, the individual identifies more closely with the group.

Self-Actualization.   The desire of individuals to utilize their skills with maximum efficiency and to grow and develop psychologically on the job is interpreted as the self-actualization need. Employees often believe that rigid job requirements and rules do not enable them to satisfy this need sufficiently. One reaction is to join a work group, which is viewed as a vehicle for communicating among friends about the use of a job-related skill. The jargon utilized and the skill employed are appreciated by the knowledgeable group members, which can lead to a feeling of accomplishment. This feeling and other similar feelings related to a belief that one is creative and skillful can lead to more satisfaction of the self-actualization need.

SPECIFIC TYPES OF GROUPS IN AN ORGANIZATION

Both managers and nonmanagers belong to a number of different groups within the organization. Memberships in multiple groups often overlap.[5] In some instances, individuals are members of a group because of position in the organization. However, through group contacts, they begin to affiliate with some of its members on an informal basis.

To illustrate the point that individuals rarely belong to just one group, look at the case of Joe DiNardo, an electrical engineer who works for American Bridge and Iron in Chicago. Joe is friendly with each worker on his project team (a formal group): a senior mechanical engineer, an industrial designer, a safety specialist, and three technicians. He also regularly discusses project problems with two electrical engineers and the design specialists who work at the Barrington, Illinois, project site. Joe always eats lunch with office accountant Mickey Wright, drafting supervisor Don Spellman, and production analyst Mike Jackson. And every Wednesday he bowls with Mickey, as well as ironworker Mel Perkowski and district manager Mitch Kelso. Each of the groups to which Joe belongs has a different membership. Some of the groups are formal, and some are informal.

Another, more specific way to classify groups is to refer to them as *command, task, interest,* and *friendship groups.*[6] Command and task groups are formal groups because they are defined by the organization structure; interest and friendship groups are not defined by the organization structure and are *informal* groups.

COMMAND GROUPS

The command group is represented in the organization chart as the subordinates who report directly to a given supervisor. The relationship between the department manager and the three supervisors in a machine shop is spelled out in the organization chart. As the span of control of the department manager increases, the command group grows in size.

TASK GROUPS

Employees that work together to complete a project or job are considered a task group. Assume that three office clerks are required for (1) securing a file of an automobile accident claim, (2) checking the accuracy of the claim by contacting persons involved, and (3) typing the claim, securing the required signatures of those involved, and refiling the claim.

These activities create a situation in which three clerks must communicate and coordinate with each other if the file is to be handled properly. Their activities and interactions facilitate the formation of the task group. Joe DiNardo's project team, mentioned previously, can be referred to as a task group.

[5]Rensis Likert, *New Patterns of Management* (New York: McGraw-Hill, 1961), chap. 8.

[6]This is the widely used and insightful framework offered by Leonard R. Sayles, "Research in Industrial Human Relations," *Industrial Relations Research Association* (New York: Harper & Row, 1957), pp. 131–45.

INTEREST GROUPS

Another type of group formation occurs when workers organize to present a united front on a particular issue. This type of group is called an interest group, since the members have joined together to achieve some common objective, such as an equitable pension plan. Its members may or may not be members of the same command or task group.

When the desired objective has been achieved or is thought to be within reach, the interest group might disband. Thus, it typically exists for a shorter period of time than other types of groups.

FRIENDSHIP GROUPS

Because of some common characteristic such as age, ethnic background, political sentiment, interest in sports, or desire to drink coffee in the lounge at 10:30 A.M., employees may form a friendship group. Such groups often extend their interaction and communication to off-the-job activities. For example, they get to know each other in the workplace and then bowl together or take their families on picnics. Mickey Wright and Joe DiNardo ate lunch together and bowled together, thus forming a friendship group.

The membership patterns of interest and friendship groups are not tightly controlled by the organization. However, managerial actions such as laying out a work area, allowing workers to take coffee breaks at a specific time, and demanding a certain level of productivity can influence the interaction and communication patterns of employees, causing certain individuals to affiliate with each other so that interest and friendship groups emerge.

COMMITTEES: SPECIAL KINDS OF GROUPS

Many unkind things have been said about committees: "A camel is a horse designed by a committee"; "A committee is a body that keeps minutes and wastes hours"; and "A committee is a group that works hard at making common sense seem difficult."[7] Despite this, the use of committees in organizations is very common for such purposes as resolving conflict, recommending action, generating ideas, and making decisions.[8]

Behavioral scientists recommend that a committee be kept relatively small, since size affects the quality of a group's decision and the ability of its members to communicate.[9] As size increases, a growing number of members seem to feel threatened and less willing to participate actively, which can increase stress and conflict.

Committee Chairperson.   In most committees, a chairperson is expected to provide direction. Successful committees often have chairpersons who understand group processes and keep the committee moving toward its

[7]Ralph L. Woods, *The Modern Handbook of Humor* (New York: McGraw-Hill, 1967), p. 8.

[8]Rensis Likert and Jane Gibson Likert, *New Ways of Managing Conflict* (New York: McGraw-Hill, 1976), pp. 213–15.

[9]Alan C. Filley, "Committee Management Guidelines from Social Science Research," *California Management Review,* Fall 1970, pp. 13–21.

objectives without becoming constrained by endless debates, conflict, and personality clashes.

A committee chairperson must walk a fine line: A passive one may lose the members' respect. On the other hand, an overly dominating one will not usually acquire the group's acceptance. Without group respect, the chairperson is a leader without a group.

A few managerial guidelines that can aid committee chairpersons are:[10]

1. Listen carefully and with an open mind.
2. Allow each member to voice opinions and do not place your opinions above others.
3. Get everyone involved in the committee's activities.
4. Display an active interest in the purpose of the committee and the ideas of the membership.
5. Help the committee focus on the task at hand and the progress being made.

Committee Members. The image of a committee is that of a group cooperating to reach an objective. But what is found in some committees is negative competition and a general lack of cooperation. Behavioral studies indicate that in cooperative groups, as distinguished from competitive groups, one finds stronger motivation to accomplish the task, more effective communication, more ideas generated, more membership satisfaction, and more group productivity.

These findings suggest that when cooperation prevails, there are generally positive results. Thus, the importance of the chairperson should not be underestimated.

QUALITY CIRCLES: AN ACTION-ORIENTED GROUP APPROACH

Quality circles have taken American and Canadian industry by storm. A study by the New York Stock Exchange showed that 44 percent of all companies with more than 500 employees had quality circle programs.[11] A **quality circle** (QC) is a task group designed for highly participative activity on the part of group members. An organization attempting to introduce and use QCs needs to carefully determine if the existing culture supports, or can be supportive of, a participative approach.[12]

The QC employees and supervisors from the same work area voluntarily meet on a regular basis to study quality control and productivity improvement techniques and to identify and solve work-related problems. Some specific features of quality circles are:

1. Small groups ranging in size from 4 to 15 members. Eight or nine seems to be the most popular size.
2. Members located in the same work area.

---

[10]G. M. Prince, "How to Be a Better Chairman," *Harvard Business Review,* January–February 1969, pp. 98–108.

[11]Edward E. Lawler III and Susan A. Mohrman, "Quality Circles after the Fad," *Harvard Business Review,* January–February 1985, p. 65.

[12]R. Douglas Allen, "Establishing and Sustaining Management Support for Quality Circles," *Business Review,* Summer 1988, pp. 13–15.

3. A work area supervisor who is usually, though not always, the leader of the circle.
4. Voluntary participation.
5. Meetings once every week on company time for one-half to one hour, with pay.
6. Training in the techniques of problem solving (e.g., brainstorming, cause-and-effect analysis, flowcharts).
7. Choice of the problems and projects that members will work on.
8. Circles exist as long as the members wish to meet.

QCs are an American invention that the Japanese used with enthusiasm and have been given credit for pioneering.[13] The Japanese were more supportive of participation approaches in the workplace and consequently have become the biggest adopters of QCs. It is estimated that about one in every eight Japanese employees (over 6 million workers) engages in the QC process.[14]

Structure and Process.   The term *quality circle* refers to both a structure and a process. Its structure is basically the composition of the group, defined by the positions of its members in the wider organization. For example, a group of mechanics, technicians, and assembly-line operators and the first-line supervisor would constitute the quality circle. The circle members are represented on an organization chart as a task or command group. Quality circles typically follow a four-step process to solve problems.

1. Identification of problems and development of solutions.
2. Managerial review of the proposed solution and a decision on whether or not to implement it.
3. Organizational implementation of the solution.
4. Evaluation of the success of the solution by the quality circle and the organization.

These subprocesses in the quality circle process are presented in Figure 11–1.

Quality Circles in U.S. Manufacturing Plants.   In one of only a few scientifically studied QC situations, two electronics manufacturing plants were examined to assess the impact of QCs on satisfaction, performance, and commitment.[15] A field experiment was used to examine one plant using QCs and one plant not using QCs on those three variables. In the QC plant, where participation was voluntary, the volunteers participated in a two-day training program in problem solving.

Participants in both plants were assessed before QCs were implemented and at 6 months, 18 months, and 36 months after implementation of the QCs. The results showed that job satisfaction, commitment, and performance in the QC plant improved gradually up to the 18-month point and then decreased back to the initial levels. Edward Lawler and Susan Mohrman describe a similar cycle of improvement followed by return to initial state, which they called a QC

---

[13]IAQC—International Association of *Quality Circles,* Summer 1987, p. 3.

[14]David Bain, *The Productivity Prescription* (New York: McGraw-Hill, 1982), p. 202.

[15]Ricky W. Griffin, "Consequences of Quality Circles in an Industrial Setting: A Longitudinal Assessment," *Academy of Management Journal,* June 1988, pp. 338–58.

FIGURE 11–1   The Quality Circle Process

Quality circles achieve results in terms of performance improvements and higher morale.

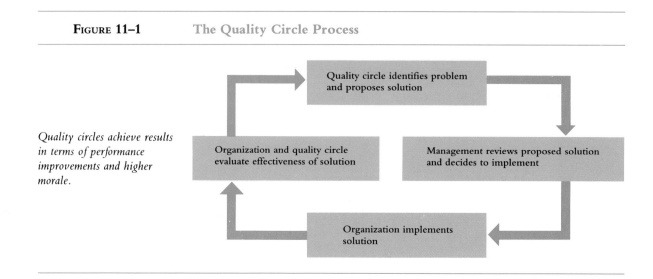

"honeymoon effect."[16] There is a lot of initial excitement, enthusiasm, and self-motivation, which eventually declines and dissipates. Managers need to determine how to sustain the initial bursts of enthusiasm so that increased commitment, satisfaction, and performance can become ingrained in QC culture.

Quality Circles at Toyota.   Toyota Auto Body Company has over 800 quality circles. The firm produces bodies for passenger cars, trucks, and commercial vans, then sells them to Toyota Motor Company. Of the 6,000 employees in the company (three fourths of them blue-collar workers), about 72 percent are participating in quality circles.[17]

Originally, supervisors led the quality circles at Toyota Auto Body, but today senior workers lead many of the groups. Some leaders are elected or serve on a rotation basis. The circles meet after regular hours, and members receive overtime pay at half their regular pay.

To provide technical assistance to quality circles, Toyota Auto Body formed an industrial engineering project team. The team has 45 members, half of whom are engineers and half of whom are shop employees who have received special training.

The company provides two major incentives for participation in quality circles: competition and money. Circles compete regularly for the best solution to the problem and the best presentation at the department level. Each month, the best of these compete against those of other departments for companywide honors. The winner enters regional and national competitions.

As financial incentives, the company pays for quality circle participation. In addition, it pays more for suggestions submitted by quality circles, $272, than

---

[16]Edward E. Lawler III and Susan A. Mohrman, "Quality Circles: After the Honeymoon," *Organizational Dynamics,* Winter 1987, pp. 42–54.

[17]Philip C. Thompson, *Quality Circles* (New York: AMACOM, 1982), pp. 19–26.

it pays for suggestions from individuals, only $227. On the average, 75 percent of all suggestions submitted come from quality circles.

To promote, train, and coordinate quality circle activities, Toyota Auto Body has set up a quality circle general office that coordinates the quality circle activities and is responsible for quality circle training and results. This office, which reports directly to the plant manager, also conducts monthly meetings of quality circle leaders in which information is exchanged, problem-solving topics discussed, and mutual respect and support encouraged.

The total commitment to quality circles by upper management is an important key to the success of the groups at Toyota Auto Body. For 18 years, the quality circles have existed and been involved in changing the organization. The organization views the quality circles as the most important technique for successful management.

The Bottom-Line Score Card.   Advocates of quality circles feel their greatest advantage is that they tap brainpower at all levels of the organization. Participating employees also are able to improve communication and gain a new sense of respect for each other as they work together. The result is that the traditional adversarial "we-they" relationship between the workers and their supervisor is replaced by an attitude of "all of us working together."[18]

Despite an abundance of popular stories about quality circles, some caution is needed. Robert C. Cole, director of the Center for Japan Studies at the University of Michigan, raises the issue of how much the Japanese culture contributes to quality circle success in that country. He states: "The task of evaluating the applicability of Japanese management practices in the United States and judging what are to be the needed adaptations is a Herculean task."[19] He cautions U.S. managers to look closely at and evaluate results over an extended time period—four, five, six years.

Also, what is referred to as "group decline" may emerge over time. That is, the quality circle meets less often, it becomes less productive, and fewer resources are committed to the program; the quality circle limps along because of social satisfaction rather than the group's problem-solving effectiveness. As a result, the commitment to quality circles shrinks, and opponents become more aggressive in resisting the quality circle approach.[20]

Although there are some glowing success reports pointing to positive impact, some managers are learning that quality circles are not able to solve structural deficiencies, poorly designed reward systems, managerial conflict, union-management strife, and other difficulties. Organizations considering the use of quality circles need to examine employee receptivity, costs, expectations, goals, and employee preparedness before leaping into this form of group participation.[21]

---

[18]Michael Le Boeuf, *The Productivity Challenge* (New York: McGraw-Hill, 1982), p. 143.

[19]Ron Zemke, "What's Good for Japan May Not Be Best for You or Your Training Department," *Training/HRD,* October 1981, p. 63.

[20]Lawler and Mohrman, "Quality Circles after the Fad," p. 69.

[21]Gordon W. Meyer and Randall G. Stott, "Quality Circles: Panacea or Pandora's Box?" *Organizational Dynamics,* Spring 1985, pp. 34–50.

DEVELOPMENT OF WORK GROUPS

Task groups, committees, or quality circles go through various stages of development. Initially, a group flounders while searching for an identity and a direction. Later, the group begins to focus on helping each other and supporting the group's goals. Finally, the group is able to utilize fully the skills and abilities of members. These changes occur gradually and are often difficult to recognize.

Groups primarily develop along two main dimensions: member relationships and task and problem-solving activities. The development of work groups is distinctly related to learning—learning to work together, to accept each other, and to trust each other. These phases are referred to as the maturation of a group.[22] Various models of group development are available, such as Schutz's FIRO model, Whitaker's integrative model, and Hill and Gruner's model.[23] However, for ease of managerial application, the use of managerial language, and the incorporation of organizationally relevant dimensions such as relationship development and task and problem-solving activities, the four-phase model is insightful. The four-phase process outlined here clearly points out some characteristics and attitudes inherent in group development.[24]

I. Mutual acceptance: Members of a group are often hampered by their mistrust of each other, the organization, and their superiors. They are fearful that they do not have the necessary training or skill to perform the job or to compete with others. These feelings of insecurity motivate employees to seek out others in the same predicament and to express their feelings openly. After an initial period of uneasiness and learning about the feelings of others, individuals begin to accept each other.

II. Decision making: During this phase, open communication concerning the job is the rule. Problem solving and decision making are undertaken. The workers trust each other's viewpoints and beliefs; they develop strategies to make the job easier and to help each other perform more effectively.

III. Motivation: The group is reaching maturity and the problems of its members are known. Members have accepted that it is better to cooperate than to compete. Thus, the emphasis is on group solidarity.

IV. Control: A group reaching this phase has successfully organized itself, and members are contributing according to their abilities and interests. The group exercises sanctions when control is needed to bring members into line with the group's norms.

As employees develop from a "bunch" to a mature group, they display and acquire personal trust, interactions, and friendships. Figure 11–2 illustrates the

---

[22]Warren G. Bennis and Herbert A. Shepard, "A Theory of Group Development," *Human Relations,* Summer 1963, pp. 415–57.

[23]John P. Wanous, Arnon E. Reichers, and S. D. Malik, "Organizational Socialization and Group Development: Toward an Integrative Perspective," *Academy of Management Review,* October 1984, pp. 670–83.

[24]This discussion of the development of groups is based largely on Bernard Bass, *Organizational Psychology* (Boston: Allyn & Bacon, 1965), pp. 197–98. A number of alterations have been made by the authors. Also see J. Stephen Heiner and Eugene Jacobson, "A Model of Task Group Development in Complex Organizations and a Strategy of Implementation," *Academy of Management Review,* October 1976, pp. 98–111.

FIGURE 11–2	Four Phases of Group Development

Phase	Mutual acceptance (I)	Decision making (II)	Motivation (III)	Control (IV)
Relationships among members	Mistrust Aloofness	Open communication Developing knowledge about members	Cohesiveness Cooperation	Sanctions are communicated Status system is understood
Task and problem-solving functions	Searching for objectives and mission	Problems and roles identified Tasks assigned	Helping each other Sharing information	Abilities and skills fully used Problem solving
Level of maturity	Low			High

Source: Leonard R. Sayles and George Strauss, *Human Behavior in Organizations,* © 1966. Reprinted by permission of Prentice-Hall, Inc., Englewood Cliffs, N.J.

A group matures as it moves through the four phases.

four phases of development.[25] Management needs to determine which phase of development a group is in at any particular point. This is, of course, difficult but important, since it can provide answers about a group's capability.

One example of a mature organization is Herman Miller, Inc., an office furniture manufacturer. The company encourages participation in decision making, open communications, trust, and interaction between managers and nonmanagers.[26] To illustrate why Herman Miller would be called a mature, total organization, consider the case of the assembly-line employee discussing a problem with the chairman, Max De Pree. The employee asked Max, "Don't you know that two production managers were just fired?" A line employee snapping at a chairman! Not only did this happen, but Max agreed to look at the situation. He found that an injustice had been committed, and he corrected the problem. The two well-liked managers were offered their jobs back; the vice president who had fired them was asked to resign.

Max De Pree is committed to building a mature, participatory organization. The credo is dedication to fine furniture design and work group insistence on

[25]Fremont E. Kast and James E. Rosenzweig, *Organization and Management* (New York: McGraw-Hill, 1979), p. 290.

[26]Kenneth Labich, "Hot Company, Warm Culture," *Business Week*, February 27, 1989, pp. 74–78.

The ability to carry out expected roles provides the group with a pattern or arrangement.

top quality. There is also an attempt to share values, ideas, goals; to work as a team; and to respect each person. This is not a dream or rhetoric. It is real and a part of the organization's culture. When employees are hired, there is close checking of a candidate's character and ability to get along with people, to work as a team player.

Another example of an unusual approach to building a mature team is presented in the Management Focus on Ernst Home and Nursery. How the president instilled a team spirit and shaped a culture illustrates what leadership can do in organizations.

CHARACTERISTICS OF WORK GROUPS

The creation of a formal organization structure results in characteristics such as specified relationships between subordinates, superiors, and peers; leaders assigned to positions; communication networks; standards of performance; and a status rank order according to the position an individual is filling. Logically, if an organization is to accomplish its objectives, retain its personnel, and project a favorable image to the public, it must have structure and a favorable work atmosphere (that is, the employees must to some extent enjoy going to work). Work groups have characteristics similar to those of formal organizations and include standards of conduct, communication systems, and reward and sanction mechanisms. These and other characteristics of groups are discussed here.

GROUP STRUCTURE

As a group progresses through each developmental phase, structures emerge. Members begin to take on roles or a set of activities and behavior expected by others. The ability to carry out expected roles provides the group with an arrangement or a pattern for its members. If roles are not carried out according to the expectations of members, it is difficult to maintain a group structure.

MANAGEMENT FOCUS

Remodeling at Ernst Inspired by Teamwork

When Hal Smith, president of Ernst Home and Nursery, asked a team of newly recruited top executives to join him for a climb to the top of 14,000-foot Mount Rainier two years ago, he did not receive an overwhelming response. Only after the trip would they find out that Smith wanted to instill a team spirit among the executives, something that could be transferred to their daily business activities. This type of unusual management style and a drive to make a family out of the company has helped Ernst to climb some impressive mountains of its own.

One of the most inspiring feats was a remodeling program started in January 1988. What made this so special was that all major decisions were made by store-level employees. First, focus groups of customers were interviewed to determine what they liked and disliked about the layout and atmosphere of the stores. Then, one representative from each of the 70 stores was brought into a brand-new store, which was to be a prototype for all the others. This team took the information from the customers and used its collective expertise to remodel the store. The job included color schemes, layout, and choice of displays, gondolas, and fixtures. The store was then arranged and merchandised by the group, right up until the grand opening.

Representatives were then given blueprints of the new layout and sent back to their "home" stores to supervise the remodeling there. Remodeling at each store was done by employees during operating hours, a very nontraditional approach. What this meant was that Ernst did not have to lay off employees during the slow season, because they were able to help with the remodeling. It also created an air of activity in the stores.

When the smoke cleared, Ernst had successfully remodeled 70 stores in less than one year, at a cost that was roughly half what it would have been through a traditional method. Each store now has a home-service expert to help with do-it-yourself projects, a new look, and a team of employees that feel that they own a part of the new design. Compared to climbing Mount Rainier, choosing a color of a sign might seem trivial; but for the employees at Ernst, it was just as great an accomplishment.

Source: Adapted from "Teamwork Inspires Ernst Remodel Program," *Chain Store Age Executive*, August 1988, pp. 96–98.

How the failure to maintain a group structure can have disastrous effects on satisfaction, group morale, and overall effectiveness has been vividly described by researchers who studied Chinese prisoner-of-war camps established during the Korean War.[27] The Chinese separated officers from noncommissioned officers so that a formal hierarchy couldn't be established. Squad leaders were appointed by the Chinese. Often the lowest-ranking enlisted prisoners were selected. All organized activity was prohibited. No emergent leaders were permitted to stay in the group. The Chinese used spies, gossip, and rumor to disrupt group structure and activities. They passed misinformation into the groups, creating an atmosphere of mistrust among squad members. The disruption, instability, and normlessness conditions resulted in little group structure. The prisoners had no view of what roles they were to perform. The

[27]E. P. Schein, J. Schneier, and G. H. Barker, *Coercive Persuasion: A Socio-Psychological Analysis of the Brainwashing of American Prisoners by the Chinese Communists* (New York: W. W. Norton, 1961).

lack of a group structure resulted in poor morale, reduced resistance, and a dampening of the will to attempt escape.

GROUP GOALS

Work groups generally have two sets of goals. The organization's managers set goals for work groups. These *manager-assigned* goals reflect the reason for the group's formation. A second set of goals is the *group goals*.[28]

Within the groups, there are *achievement goals* that serve to provide the group with direction and an end-result target. *Maintenance goals* sustain the group and maintain its existence. Of course, not all members always agree with either the achievement or maintenance goals. On occasion, conflict with group goals is why members drop out and form new groups or join other groups.

As a group develops, the goals become clearer and more meaningful to members. Research indicates that a number of factors increase a person's commitment to the achievement and the maintenance of group goals. Some of these factors are participating in group activities, tying incentives to goal achievement, providing feedback on goal accomplishment, and training group members in the goal-setting process.[29]

At General Motors, group goals and achieving them have become important for job security. In 1986, at GM's Inland Division plant in Livonia, Michigan, workers needed 48 hours, 6 minutes to make the interior portion of a door for a Chevrolet sedan. In 1988, they were able to do it in 12 hours, 7 minutes. The goal for the early 1990s is six minutes total. GM executives and the United Automobile Workers union decided that for the company to become competitive in the international marketplace, worker group goals must be established, communicated, and evaluated. The major incentive for achieving the group goals was stopping the loss of business to foreign competitors who were producing high-quality automobiles in significantly less time than U.S. firms.[30]

LEADERSHIP

As a group attempts to accomplish an objective such as producing a product without a single defect and as individual members get acquainted, one or more of the many group roles become filled. One of the most important is that of the group leader, who emerges from within and is accepted by the informal group. In the formal organization, however, the leader is appointed.

The leaders in formal organizations are followed and obeyed because employees perceive them as possessing power and influence to reward or punish them for not complying with requests. The formal leaders possess the power to regulate the formal rewards of the members of a work group. On the other hand, informal group leaders do not possess this power.

The informal leader typically serves a number of facilitating functions. First, any group of individuals that does not have a plan or some coordination

[28]Jerry C. Wofford, *Organizational Behavior* (Boston: Kent Publishing, 1982), p. 311.

[29]John M. Ivancevich, "Different Goal Setting Treatments and Their Effects on Performance and Job Satisfaction," *Academy of Management Journal*, September 1977, pp. 406–19.

[30]"How the UAW Is Doing Its Part for GM's Parts," *Business Week*, February 13, 1989, p. 78.

becomes an ineffective unit. The individuals are not directed toward the accomplishment of objectives, and this leads to a breakdown in group effectiveness. The leader serves to initiate action and provide direction. If there are differences of opinion on a group-related matter, the leader attempts to settle the differences and move the group toward accomplishing its objectives. Second, some individual must communicate to nonmembers the group's beliefs about policies, the job, the organization, the supervision, and other related matters. In effect, the group leader communicates the values of the group.

A number of research studies have identified the personal characteristics of group leaders, which can be summarized as follows:

1. The leadership role is filled by an individual who possesses attributes the members perceive as being critical for satisfying their needs.
2. The leader embodies the values of the group and is able to perceive these values, organize them into an intelligible philosophy, and verbalize them to nonmembers.[31]
3. The leader is able to receive and decipher communications relevant to the group and effectively communicate important information to group members.[32]

One partner and friend who emerged as a group leader is Joseph "Rod" Canion, president and chief executive officer (CEO) of Compaq Computers of Houston.[33] (Compaq, after only seven years, is one of the three largest U.S. computer manufacturers and challenges IBM's market dominance in personal computers.) Canion, along with two other partners, decided to start a company. They chipped in $1,000 each for seed money to attract venture capital. They worked together, experimented with computers, and came up with the idea of a portable computer built around the PC standard. Canion continued to push for finding venture capitalists (individuals with money to support the idea), and he did. After finding the money, Canion started hiring people. His two partners still met with him and provided ideas, but Canion emerged as the spokesperson, the front person, the communicator of the Compaq story.

When Canion unveiled the Compaq portable, Mitch Kapor, the founder of Lotus® 1–2–3®, was present with his yet unnamed spreadsheet program. Kapor tried his program and, presto, it worked. It was the first demonstration of Compaq's portable and Lotus 1–2–3, which are now both billion-dollar businesses. Compaq, under Canion's leadership, continues to set new standards for the PC industry.

STATUS WITHIN THE GROUP

Managers in an organization are accorded status because of position in the hierarchy. That is, the top management group of the firm has more prestige or status than middle managers in the organization, while middle managers have more prestige or status than lower-level managers. The cornerstone of status

---

[31]Scott and Mitchell, *Organization Theory*, pp. 175–82.

[32]Ibid.

[33]Charles Fuller, "Move Over, Big Blue," *Entrepreneur*, March 1989, pp. 66–72.

in the formal organization is a comparative process. The top-level positions embody more authority, responsibility, power, and influence and are accorded more status. In effect, a status hierarchy emerges, with the top-level positions listed first and the lower-level positions listed last.

In an informal group, a similar type of status system develops for many different reasons. The individuals performing in leadership roles possess prestige because of the role; consequently, they are ranked by group members as being at a particular level of status in the group hierarchy. The seniority of a member is a factor many groups consider to be important. A worker having more seniority is often thought of as "organizationally intelligent," which means knowing how to adapt to the demands of supervisors, subordinates, or peers. This ability to adjust is an important status factor with group members.

The skills of an individual in performing a job are another factor related to status. An individual who is an expert in the technical aspects of the job, managerial or nonmanagerial, is given a high status ranking in some groups. This type of status does not mean that the individual actually utilizes the skill to perform more efficiently but that the group members perceive this skill in the individual.

Norms and Control

Once a group addresses specific task goals, a pattern of behavior begins to emerge. The pattern becomes a regular feature of the group dynamics and is called a **norm,** which is an "attitude, opinion, feeling, or action—shared by two or more people—that guides their behavior."[34] The more an individual complies with norms, the more that person accepts the group's standards of behavior. Work groups utilize norms to bring about job performance acceptable to the group. In the workplace, a number of different production-related norms can exist. For example: (1) don't agree with management in its campaign to change the wage structure; (2) present a united front to the supervisor concerning the displeasure of the group about the firing of Mr. Jones; (3) resist the suggestions of the new college graduate assigned to the group's work area; (4) do not produce above the group leader's level of production; (5) help members of the group to achieve an acceptable production level if they are having difficulty and if you have time; and (6) don't allow the union steward to convince you to vote for his favorite union presidential candidate.

Three specific social processes bring about compliance with group norms: group pressure, group review and enforcement, and the personalization of norms.

Group Pressure. In groups, pressure can be applied to members to conform to group norms. Pressure is excessive when it interferes with the group's goal accomplishment. On the other hand, pressure is inadequate when lack of conformity to group norms is detrimental to a member, the group, or

[34]Robert R. Blake and Jane S. Mouton, "Don't Let Group Norms Stifle Creativity," *Personnel*, August 1985, p. 28.

the organization. Conformity is optimal when it results in cooperation, efficiency, and the accomplishment of group goals.[35]

A number of factors influence the level of conformity in a group. *Task characteristics* such as the nature of a particular job affect conformity. An employee faced with a difficult, unfamiliar, and ambiguous task is more inclined to conform to a group norm.

The *personality* makeup of an individual influences that person's conformity behavior. A person who is deficient in self-esteem is more likely to conform than one who has the opposite personality traits.[36] Also, the more intelligent the individual, the less likely he or she is to conform to group norms.

Group characteristics affect conformity. For example, as size increases, pressures to conform increase. Also, when the majority of a group strongly supports a position, a member is more inclined to conform than when he or she has one or more partners who disagree with the majority view.[37] There is a tendency to conform when the consequence for deviance is social isolation by the group.

An interesting conformity phenomenon has evolved at Borden's Inc. as a tactic to put off would-be corporate takeovers.[38] In the merger/acquisition world, "poison pills" are a well-known antitakeover tactic. The tactic centers on making it easy for the company's existing shareholders to buy stock at a cheap price. Then, when takeover specialists arrive, there is a lot of stock to buy, and the cost of acquisition becomes too high to take over the firm.

At Borden's, the company's top executives have teamed together to form a contract called the "people pills." The top executives all signed three-year contracts. They agreed to resign en masse if any new owner (takeover) fires or changes the responsibilities of any one of them. The agreement says the acquirer must pay the managers $10 million to $30 million, depending on when the offending action occurs, to buy out their contracts if they resign. Each manager is a part of the group conforming to the contractual agreement. The takeover specialist now has to deal with a tightly knit group that has protected itself with the "people pill" defense.

Group Review and Enforcement.   When individuals become members of a group, they quickly become aware of group norms. The group position on such matters as production, absenteeism, and quality of output is communicated. The group members then observe the actions and language of new members to determine whether the group norms are being followed.

If individual members, both old-timers and newcomers, are not complying with generally accepted norms, a number of different approaches may be

---

[35]L. A. Rosenberg, "Conformity as a Function of Confidence in Self and Confidence in Partner," *Human Behavior*, Spring 1963, pp. 131–39.

[36]Ibid.

[37]Solomon E. Asch, "Opinions and Social Pressures," *Scientific American*, November 1955, pp. 31–35.

[38]"First It Was Poison Pills—Now It's People Pills," *Business Week*, January 16, 1989, pp. 33–34.

employed. A "soft" approach would be a discussion between respected leaders and those persons deviating from the norm. If this does not prove effective, more rigid corrective action is used, such as the membership scolding the individual or individuals both privately and publicly. The ultimate type of enforcement would be to ostracize the nonconforming members, which might take the form of not communicating with them.

These are only a few of the numerous strategies to bring deviants into line. Other, more severe techniques, such as sabotaging the nonconformer's performance, have also been utilized. Review and enforcement occur at managerial levels in a form similar to that in nonmanagerial ranks.

Personalization of Norms. The behavioral patterns of people are influenced significantly by their value systems. Their values in turn are influenced by the events occurring around them; values are learned and become personalized. For example, the norm of a work group may encourage group members to treat college graduates and noncollege individuals equally and courteously. This norm may be accepted by the person as morally and ethically correct. Prior to group affiliation, the member may have displayed little interest in a "fair treatment of all" philosophy. However, based on a latent feeling of fairness, the member personalizes this group-learned norm. It becomes a standard of conduct correct from a group and social vantage point.

In some but definitely not in all instances, group pressures, group review and enforcement, and personalization of norms may conflict with organizational objectives such as higher production, improved quality of output, lower absenteeism, and loyalty to the firm. The emphasis here is on the word *some*. It is incorrect to assume that all groups are established to resist the achievement of organizational goals. In fact, some groups are very loyal and committed to the success of their organization.

COHESIVENESS

Cohesiveness is another important group characteristic. **Group cohesiveness** is defined as the attraction of members to the group and the strength of forces on the individual member to remain active in the group and resist leaving it.[39]

All of these characteristics of groups are influenced to some degree by the cohesiveness within the group.[40] For example, the greater the attraction within the group, the more likely it is that the membership will adhere closely to a group norm.

Research findings have allowed those interested in work group cohesiveness to isolate some of the more important factors that affect it. The factors identified in Figure 11–3, examples of some of the variables uncovered in research studies, are representative of the types of conditions that can enhance or reduce cohesiveness of work groups.

---

[39]This definition is based on the group cohesiveness concept presented by Stanley E. Seashore, *Group Cohesiveness in the Industrial Work Group* (Ann Arbor: Institute for Social Research, University of Michigan, 1954).

[40]Leonard R. Sayles and George Strauss, *Human Behavior in Organizations* (Englewood Cliffs, N.J.: Prentice-Hall, 1966), p. 101.

FIGURE 11–3   Some Factors that Influence Group Cohesiveness

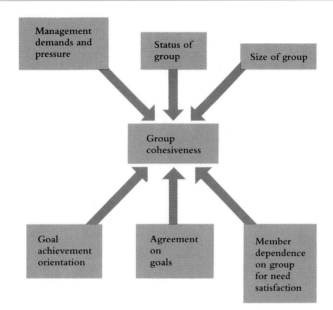

Many factors can promote or hinder cohesiveness in a group.

Ford, after suffering years of decreased sales and shrinking profit margins, instituted what was called the "Team Taurus" approach.[41] Designers, assembly workers, and marketing and finance people were brought together to develop the best car possible. In the usual sequential team approach, designers worked on a design and then "tossed their work over the wall," or passed their work to engineering; the engineers "tossed their work over the wall" to production; and so forth. The "not invented here" (NIH) syndrome took hold. NIH refers to the fact that most people are not likely to accept ideas or recommendations that other people have initiated. Tossing something to the next group meant that a lot of reinventing occurred.

Team Taurus was a large group, but all the voices were heard in the same room. The team came up with a want list of 1,401 items suggested by Ford employees. In an Atlanta setting, drawings and sketches were spread across the wall and on flip charts. This was a contrast to the secrecy often found in the automobile industry. The team was able to incorporate about 80 percent of the want list items. The result of the Team Taurus approach: *Motor Trend* picked the Ford Taurus as the car of the year.[42]

Size.   One important and necessary condition for the existence of a group is that members interact and communicate with each other. If the group is so large that members do not get to know each other, there is little likelihood that the group will become very cohesive. Research studies indicate an inverse

[41]Robert Waterman, *The Renewal Factor* (New York: Bantam Books, 1987), pp. 81–83.

[42]Lynn Adkins, "Such a Grand Design," *Business Month,* December 1987, pp. 30–31.

The degree of group cohesiveness depends on a number of factors, including size, dependence of members on the work group, goal agreement, and achievement.

relationship between size of group and group cohesiveness.[43] Smaller groups coalesce faster than larger groups.

In addition to affecting cohesiveness, a group's size can influence how much effort members apply to a task. A phenomenon called **social loafing** has been identified.[44] This involves the tendency of individuals in a group not to work hard, because there are others around to carry the workload. In cohesive groups, social loafing would not be tolerated once it was identified. Also, there are more opportunities for social loafing in large groups. A person not doing the share of work is often hard to identify. If a group leader is able to point out each member's contribution, it would reduce the tendency to loaf. Social loafing is found not only in the workplace but also within family units, student groups, and volunteer groups.[45]

Why don't people do their share of work? Perhaps if a person sees someone in the group not working hard, there is a tendency to slow down, stop pushing hard, or simply reduce one's effort. Coasting behind others or reducing effort is possible, especially when a group is larger and there are opportunities to become lost in the crowd. In offices or production lines, serving on a large committee, or working in a large department, individuals can become lost; they can engage in social loafing.

[43]Seashore, *Group Cohesiveness*, pp. 90–95. Also see Robert C. Cummins and Donald C. King, "The Interaction of Group Size and Task Structure in an Industrial Organization," *Personnel Psychology*, Spring 1973, pp. 87–94.

[44]S. Latane, S. Harkins, and K. Williams, "Many Hands Make Light the Work: Causes and Consequences of Social Loafing," *Journal of Personality and Social Psychology*, 1979, pp. 822–32.

[45]Robert Albanese and David D. Van Fleet, "Rational Behavior in Groups: The Free-Riding Tendency," *Academy of Management Journal*, April 1985, pp. 244–55.

Dependence of Members on the Work Group.   A group that is able to satisfy a significant portion of an individual's needs will appear attractive to that individual. Group processes such as communication and overall friendship make the group a key factor in the individual's life. Thus, what the group stands for, its norms, and its membership are bonds that relate the individual to the group. The greater the individual's dependence on the group, the stronger will be these bonds of attraction.

Goal Agreement.   Membership agreement on the goals of the group provides the basis for cohesiveness. Inability to agree results in internal conflict, disharmony, and dissatisfaction, which contribute to a lack of focus and direction. Consequently, the accomplishment of achievement and maintenance goals suffers when group cohesiveness declines.[46]

Achievement of Goals.   The attainment of a set of group-established goals (for example, better production than another group) has an influence on members. For example, a work group that attains a highly desired rating for completing a task enhances the value of being a group member; individuals feel a pride in being members of a work group that has performed in such a manner that they are recognized as being superior.

Work groups that have successfully attained preestablished goals are likely to be highly cohesive units, the members tending to be more attracted toward each other because they have worked together in the past and because their efforts have resulted in achieving a desired goal. Thus, success and cohesiveness are interrelated: Success in goal achievement encourages cohesiveness, and cohesive work groups are more likely to attain preestablished goals. It is important to consider that although group cohesiveness can lead to successful achievement of goals, it can prove detrimental when group and organization goals are not congruent.

Status of Group.   In an organizational setting, work groups typically are ranked in a status hierarchy. An intergroup status hierarchy may develop for many different reasons, including the following:

1. One group is rated higher than another in overall performance; this is a measure of success in the organization.
2. To become a member of the group, individuals must display a high level of skill.
3. The work being done by the group is dangerous or financially more rewarding or more challenging than other work.
4. The group is less closely supervised in comparison to other groups.
5. In the past, members of the group have been considered for promotion more often than members of other groups.

These are only some of the criteria that affect the status hierarchy of groups.[47] Generally, the higher a group ranks in the intergroup status hierarchy, the greater its cohesiveness. However, the higher-status groups appear attractive

---

[46]G. H. Graham, "Interpersonal Attraction as a Basis of Informal Organization," *Academy of Management Journal,* December 1971, pp. 483–95.

[47]For a listing of other status criteria, see Sayles and Strauss, *Human Behavior,* p. 102.

only to some nonmembers. Individuals on the outside of the group may not want to become members of a high-status group, because membership then entails close adherence to group norms.

Management Demands and Pressure.   It is certainly true in many organizations that management has a significant impact on group cohesiveness. The members of work groups tend to stick together when they are pressured by superiors to conform to some organizational norm (for example, punching in at 8:00 and not 8:05 A.M., or producing at least five more units of output per day).

The group cohesiveness attributed to managerial demands may be a short-run or long-run phenomenon. A group may be loosely knit (low in cohesiveness), and a company policy statement interpreted as a threat to the job security of group members causes the members of the group to become a more cohesive and unified whole in order to withstand the perceived management threat. In some cases, after the danger is past (that is, the policy statement is rescinded), the group gradually drifts back toward low cohesiveness. In other cases, the cohesiveness may be a longer-lasting phenomenon.

The cohesiveness of a group affects a number of important factors, such as satisfaction and performance. Members of cohesive units usually are more satisfied with their group affiliation than are members of noncohesive groups. This does not mean, however, that cohesive group members are more satisfied with their jobs, their bosses, or the organization.

Cohesive groups are more highly motivated to attain group goals. However, recall from our discussion of goal achievement and cohesiveness that group and organizational goal congruence is an important consideration. Cohesive groups that have high productivity goals and good relationships with management generally will have high productivity. Cohesive groups having poor relationships with management often have low productivity. The preferred condition is a highly cohesive group whose goals align with management expectations and goals.

Intragroup Conflict

Conflict is an everyday occurrence in life. *Conflict results when there are incompatible goals, cognitions, or emotions within or between individuals or groups, that lead to opposition or antagonistic interaction.*[48]

Conflict among members of a group can arise in a variety of ways. In the mutual acceptance and decision-making phases of group development, there are likely to be disagreements over member roles, plans, schedules, and standards. These disagreements can cause the group to be ineffective and fragmented. Coalitions and power centers emerge and create anxiety for the membership. Management needs to be alert for these types of conflicts, especially in the relatively immature group.

Interpersonal conflict among members always is present to some extent. Differences in opinions, attitudes, values, and beliefs create tension. We tend to like people with values, beliefs, and opinions similar to our own. The

[48]Don Hellriegel, John W. Slocum, Jr., and Richard Woodman, *Organizational Behavior* (St. Paul, Minn.: West Publishing, 1989), p. 109.

"personality clash" happens not only between superiors and subordinates but among members of groups. Individuals who are in a state of conflict with other members are also likely to be dissatisfied with the interpersonal features of the group. In addition, the member who is having interpersonal conflicts is likely to withdraw from engaging in most group activities.

Of course, if group performance is affected by intragroup conflict, management has a stake in determining the reasons for the problems. However, before managerial prescriptions are implemented, it is necessary to fully understand the reasons. This requires careful diagnostic work: observation, discussions, and reviews of performance records. Management's intent is not to eliminate intragroup conflict but to minimize it so that individual and organizational goals can be achieved.

INTERGROUP CONFLICT

Management prefers that groups cooperate and work toward the accomplishment of organizational and individual goals. However, conflicts often develop between groups. If the groups are working on tasks that are interdependent (i.e., department A's output flows to department B, and B's output flows to department C), the coordination and effectiveness of working together are crucial managerial issues. The relationships can become antagonistic and so disruptive that the entire flow of production is slowed or even stopped.

As an employee-owned company, Weirton Steel has performed generally better than competitors. The company's owners now want to keep receiving their profit-sharing payments.[49] Management, however, wants the employees to give up some of the payments to keep the company competitive. There is a conflict between the need for strong management and employee desires to keep profit-sharing payments at the rate expected.

Although conflict exists between management and labor at Weirton Steel and in many firms, cooperation is the most desirable result of group interaction. For example, two groups can cooperate because they both oppose the introduction of new equipment. The equipment is being introduced to improve cost control, but the groups working together can make the period of testing the new equipment a bad experience for management.

Determinants of Intergroup Conflict. Conflict develops between groups for many reasons.[50] Some of the more important ones relate to limited resources, communication problems, differences in interests and goals, different perceptions and attitudes, and lack of clarity about responsibilities.

1. *Limited resources.* Groups that possess an abundance of materials, money, and time usually are effective. However, when a number of groups are competing for limited resources, there is a good chance that conflict will result. The competition for the limited equipment dollars, merit-increase money, or new positions can become fierce.

2. *Communication problems.* Groups often become very involved with their own areas of responsibility. Each tends to develop its own vocabulary.

---

[49]"Has Weirton's ESOP Worked Too Well?" *Business Week,* January 23, 1989, pp. 66–68.

[50]Likert and Likert, *New Ways.*

Paying attention to an area of responsibility is a worthy endeavor, but it can result in communication problems. The receiver of information must be considered when a group communicates an idea, proposal, or decision. This often is not the case, and misinformed receivers become irritated and hostile.

3. *Different interests and goals.* A group of young workers may want management to do something about the inadequate promotion system. However, management is being accused by older workers of ignoring improvements in the company pension plan. Management recognizes the two different goals but believes that the pension issue is the more pressing and addresses it. The groups may want management to solve both problems, but this is not currently possible. Thus, one group becomes hostile because it is ignored.

4. *Different perceptions and attitudes.* Individuals perceive differently. The groups to which they belong also can have different perceptions. Groups tend to evaluate in terms of their backgrounds, norms, and experiences. Since each of these can differ, there is likely to be conflict between groups. Most groups tend to overvalue their own worth and position and undervalue the worth and position of other groups.

5. *Lack of clarity.* Job clarity involves knowing what others expect in terms of task accomplishment. In many cases, it is difficult to specify who is responsible for a certain task. This difficulty exists in most organizations. Who is responsible for listing a talented management trainee—the personnel department or the training department? Who is responsible for the increased interest in the product line—marketing, advertising, or research and development? The inability to pinpoint positive and negative contributions causes groups to compete for control over those activities that are recognized.

The causes of conflict just cited are common. Each needs to be managed. The management of intergroup conflict involves determining strategies to minimize such problems.

Conflict Management Strategies. Management's reaction to disruptive intergroup conflict can take many different forms.[51] In a typical sequence of events, management first will try to minimize the conflict indirectly; if this fails, it will become directly involved.

Indirect approaches. Initially, managers often avoid direct approaches to solving conflict between groups. *Avoidance* is easy in the short run, since the causes of conflict are unknown and giving attention to conflict admits that it exists. Unfortunately, avoidance does not always minimize the problem. Matters get worse because nothing seemingly is being done about the problem and the groups become more antagonistic and hostile.

Another indirect strategy is to encourage the groups to meet and discuss their differences and work out a solution without management involvement. This strategy can take the form of bargaining, persuasion, or working on a problem together.

Bargaining involves the groups agreeing about what each will get and give to the other. For example, a group may agree to give another group quick

---

[51]Robert R. Blake and Jane S. Mouton, *Solving Costly Organizational Conflicts* (San Francisco: Jossey-Bass, 1984), pp. 7–10.

turnaround time on the repairs of needed equipment if the other group agrees to bring complaints about the quality of repairs to them before going to management. Bargaining can be successful if both groups are better off (or at least no worse off) after an agreement is reached.

LKAB is a government-owned firm in Sweden that mines iron ore. Management (all except the very top level) and operating employees are members of a variety of unions.[52] A wildcat strike spread to 5,000 employees. After almost two months on strike, the various groups decided to use consolidation and joint bargaining to end the strike. Group meetings and a joint counsel of management and labor met frequently. Ombudsmen were used, but the use of numerous committees from the joint counsel brought the conflict to an end.

Persuasion involves the groups finding common areas of interest. They attempt to find points of agreement and show how these are important to each in attaining organizational goals. Persuasion is possible if clashes between group leaders do not exist.

A problem can be an obstacle to a goal. In order for groups to minimize their conflicts through *problem solving,* they must generally agree on the goal. Then the groups can propose alternative solutions that satisfy the parties involved. For example, one group may want the company to relocate the plant in a suburban area, and the other group may want better working conditions. If both agree that a common goal is to maintain their jobs, then building a new facility in an area that does not have a high tax rate may be a good solution.

Direct approaches.   Management may use *domination* to minimize conflict. It may exercise authority and require that the problem be solved by a specific date. If management uses authority, the groups may unite and resist the domination. Management becomes a common enemy, and they forget their differences in order to deal with their opponent.

Another direct approach is to *remove the key figures* in the conflict. If two individuals are in conflict because of personality differences, this may be a possible alternative. Three problems exist with this approach: First, the figures who are to be removed may be respected leaders of the groups. This could lead to more antagonism and greater conflict. Second, it is difficult to pinpoint accurately whether the individuals in conflict are at odds because of personal animosities or because they represent their groups. Third, removal is not always good, because of a danger that "martyrs" will be created. The causes of the removed leaders will be remembered and fought for even though the persons themselves are gone.

A final, direct strategy to minimize conflict is that of finding *superordinate goals.* These goals are desired by two or more groups but only can be accomplished through cooperation of the groups. Studies have shown that when conflicting groups are faced with the necessity of cooperating in order to accomplish a goal, conflict can be minimized and cooperation increased.[53] For example, a companywide profit-sharing plan may be used to encourage

[52]Olle Hammarstrom, "Joint Worker-Management Consultation: The Case of LKAB Sweden," in *The Quality of Working Life: Cases and Commentary,* ed. Louis E. Davis and Albert B. Cherns (New York: Free Press, 1985), pp. 66–79.

[53]M. Sherif and C. W. Sherif, *Groups in Harmony and Tension* (New York: Harper & Row, 1953).

groups to work together. At the end of the year, a percentage of company profits will be distributed equally to each employee. Conflict between groups can reduce the amount of profits each person receives. Thus, the superordinate goal, generating optimal profits, takes precedence.

End Results: Member Satisfaction and Effective Decisions

Two potential end results, or consequences, of group membership are the satisfaction of members and the reaching of effective group decisions. Behaviorists and managers have, in recent years, increased their efforts to understand the causes of member satisfaction and decision making within groups.

MEMBER SATISFACTION

One survey of 37 studies showed specific relationships between work group member satisfaction and (1) perceived freedom to participate, (2) perceived goal attainment, and (3) status consensus.[54]

Perceived Freedom to Participate. A member's perception of freedom to participate influences need satisfaction. Individuals who perceived themselves as active participators reported themselves more satisfied, while those who perceived their freedom to participate to be insignificant typically were the least satisfied members in a work group.

The freedom-to-participate phenomenon is related to the entire spectrum of economic and sociopsychological needs. For example, the perceived ability to participate may lead individuals to believe that they are valued members of the group. This assumption can lead to the satisfaction of social, esteem, and self-actualization needs.

Perceived Goal Attainment.   A number of studies indicate that a group member's perception of progress toward attaining desired goals is an important factor in satisfaction.[55] Groups that progressed toward the attainment of goals indicated higher levels of member satisfaction, while members of groups not adequately progressing showed a lower satisfaction level.

Status Consensus.   This concept is defined as agreement about the relative status of all group members. Several studies indicate that when the degree of status consensus is high, member satisfaction tends to be high; where status consensus within the group is low, member satisfaction tends to be low. Status consensus is more readily achieved in groups where:

1. The group task specialist is perceived by the membership to be competent.
2. A leader emerges who plays a role that is considered an important group task.

[54]Richard Heslin and Dexter Dunphy, "Three Dimensions of Member Satisfaction in Small Groups," *Human Relations,* May 1964, pp. 99–112.

[55]Clovis R. Shepherd, *Small Groups: Some Sociological Perspectives* (San Francisco: Chandler Publishing, 1964), p. 101.

3. A leadership role emerges and is filled by an individual who concentrates on coordinating and maintaining the activities of the group.

This research suggests that the perceptions of the membership concerning freedom to participate, movement toward goal attainment, and status consensus significantly influence the level of need satisfaction attained by group members. Research also clearly indicates that when an individual member's goals and needs are in conflict with the goals and needs of the overall group, lower levels of membership satisfaction result.

Health and welfare agency employees' degree of satisfaction toward their place of work was the focus of one study.[56] Researchers measured the flow of communication among staff members in formally scheduled meetings as well as informal contacts. The total communication among colleagues was not associated with satisfaction. But the direction of the flow, whether it was up or down the hierarchy or among peers at the same level, was correlated with satisfaction. That is, when most of the informal talk was from subordinates to supervisors, more unfavorable views of the workplace existed. And when most of the informal messages were directed from superiors to subordinates, favorable workplace attitudes were the rule.

GROUP DECISION-MAKING EFFECTIVENESS

A number of research studies have raised the question of whether group decision making is superior, inferior, or equal to individual decision making. Norman Maier, instead of developing an exact answer to the question, discussed assets and liabilities of group decision making.[57]

Group Assets. In a group, there is a greater total of knowledge and information. Thus, decisions that require knowledge should give groups an advantage over individuals. This additional information is helpful in reaching the best decision possible.

Many problems require making decisions that depend on the support of other group members. More members accept a decision when a group solves the problem than when one person solves it. A person reaching a decision must persuade others in the group who may resist being told what the best solution is for the problem. Individuals, by working on the problem, believe that they are more responsible for the solution. This feeling of shared responsibility is satisfying to some people.

A decision made by an individual and to be carried out by others needs to be communicated to those who must execute it. Thus, the individual decision maker must communicate effectively before positive action is taken. The chances for communication breakdowns are reduced when the individuals who must execute the decision have participated in making it. They were involved in reaching the decision and are aware of how it was reached, which improves understanding.

[56]C. B. Bagley, J. Hage, and M. Aiken, "Communication and Satisfaction in Organizations," *Human Relations,* 1975, pp. 611–26.

[57]Norman R. F. Maier, "Assets and Liabilities in Group Problem Solving," *Psychological Review,* July 1967, pp. 239–49.

Group Liabilities.   Making a decision in a group exerts pressure on each member. The desire to be an accepted and cooperative group member tends to silence individual disagreement and favors agreement. If the majority is forceful enough, its decision usually will be accepted regardless of whether the quality is adequate.

In some groups, a dominating individual takes over. This person, because of a strong personality, organizational position, reputation, or status, can dominate the group. None of these traits or characteristics is necessarily related to decision-making skill. And they can inhibit group discussion, reduce creativity among other members, and stop members from making positive contributions.

"Stand taking" may hinder a group in reaching a good solution. Most problems have more than one possible solution, and individual group members may have personal preferences. Sometimes, a member may take a stand on his or her preference and will feel that a defeat means loss of face. Thus, the member becomes more concerned with winning than with finding the best group decision.

Group versus Individual Decision Making.   The logic of using a group instead of an individual to solve a problem or make a decision is based on the premise that "two heads are better than one." This premise rests on the notion of synergy. *Synergy* exists when the whole is greater than the sum of its parts.[58] Social loafing is an example of negative synergy. A project engineering team that uses the talents and skills of each individual is an example of positive synergy.

One method of improving the quality of decision making is the use of team building. The "Team Building" Management Focus illustrates that the method does not always work as a performance enhancement approach.

Work groups generally are superior to individuals in reaching decisions when it is desirable to have a wealth of information that no one person possesses. However, if an expert is present, it is not always advantageous to use a group. Groups also are superior to individuals in most cases when accuracy is important: By taking a number of judgments together and averaging them, random error is reduced. Also, there is the opportunity in a group to critically evaluate judgments so that accuracy improves.

But group decision making has some drawbacks. If a group is dominated by one member or a small coalition, the contributions of other members are sacrificed. Also, members who do not contribute to problem solving and decision making are less inclined to accept the group solution. In fact, the noncontributing members may harm the group's attempts to implement a solution. And there is the issue of time. Group decision making generally requires more time than individual decision making.

Instead of stating that either group or individual decision making is superior, it is better to consider the issues and tasks involved. Complex and large-scale tasks, such as building an airplane, could benefit from group effort because of the magnitude of the job and the physical and mental effort

---

[58]Robert Albanese and David D. Van Fleet, *Organizational Behavior* (Hinsdale, Ill.: Dryden Press, 1983), p. 273.

MANAGEMENT FOCUS

Why Do Team-Building Attempts Fail at the Executive Level?

Team building among executives is designed to improve the quality of decision through better communication, increased creativity, and other synergistic factors. Many times, however, there are problems that limit the effectiveness of the group even to the point that it would be more effective to have no group at all. Top-level teams involving 275 executives in 27 Fortune 500 firms encountered the following problems:

■ The teams considered teamwork "soft" or unbusinesslike.

■ The teams were uncomfortable with "muddling," the process of exploring a full range of alternatives for a particular problem.

■ The teams displayed poor listening skills.

■ The teams demonstrated few "probing skills," the use of questions, short statements, and strategically timed silence to elicit information.

■ The teams were dominated, swayed, and victimized by higher-ranking executives.

■ The teams limited their options, often to two competing ideas, when others were available.

■ The teams were not sure how to cycle their decisions downward to obtain the same commitment the group had.

■ The teams' mission statements were neither complete not functional.

Many of these problems could have been avoided had the team members possessed a better understanding of the purpose of the team, so they could participate accordingly. A majority had not been trained in systematic decision making and did not understand the value of brainstorming techniques in raising the quality of decisions. This resulted in an attitude that feedback was criticism and should be quelled.

If these issues could be addressed, then perhaps the thousands of hours that managers and executives spend in meetings could be more valuable to the participants and productive for the firm.

Source: Adapted from Robert E. Lefton and V. R. Buzzotta, "Teams and Teamwork: A Study of Executive-Level Teams," *National Productivity Review*, Winter 1987–1988, pp. 7–19.

---

required.[59] On the other hand, assembly of an electric generator may be more efficiently completed by an individual, since there are fewer tasks.

It also is important for managers to weigh a few group disadvantages such as (1) group decision making is more time-consuming; (2) intragroup conflicts are likely to occur and must be resolved; (3) there is a possibility of social loafing in groups;[60] and (4) "groupthink."[61] **Groupthink** occurs when group pressures lead to reduced mental efficiency, poor testing of reality, and lax moral judgment. Highly cohesive groups that stress unanimous acceptance of group decisions encourage the onset of groupthink. The groupthink process is presented in Figure 11–4. The diagram shows how a cohesive group plus structural problems in the organization plus a provocative situation combine to

[59] J. R. Campbell, "Individual versus Group Problem Solving in an Industrial Sample," *Journal of Applied Psychology*, April 1968, pp. 205–10.

[60] B. Latane, K. Williams, and S. Harkins, "Social Loafing," *Psychology Today*, October 1979, p. 104; M. N. Dobosh, "Peril of Work within Groups: Social Loafing," *The Wall Street Journal*, March 19, 1981, pp. 1, 27.

[61] Irving L. Janis, *Groupthink* (Boston: Houghton Mifflin, 1983).

FIGURE 11–4   The Groupthink Process

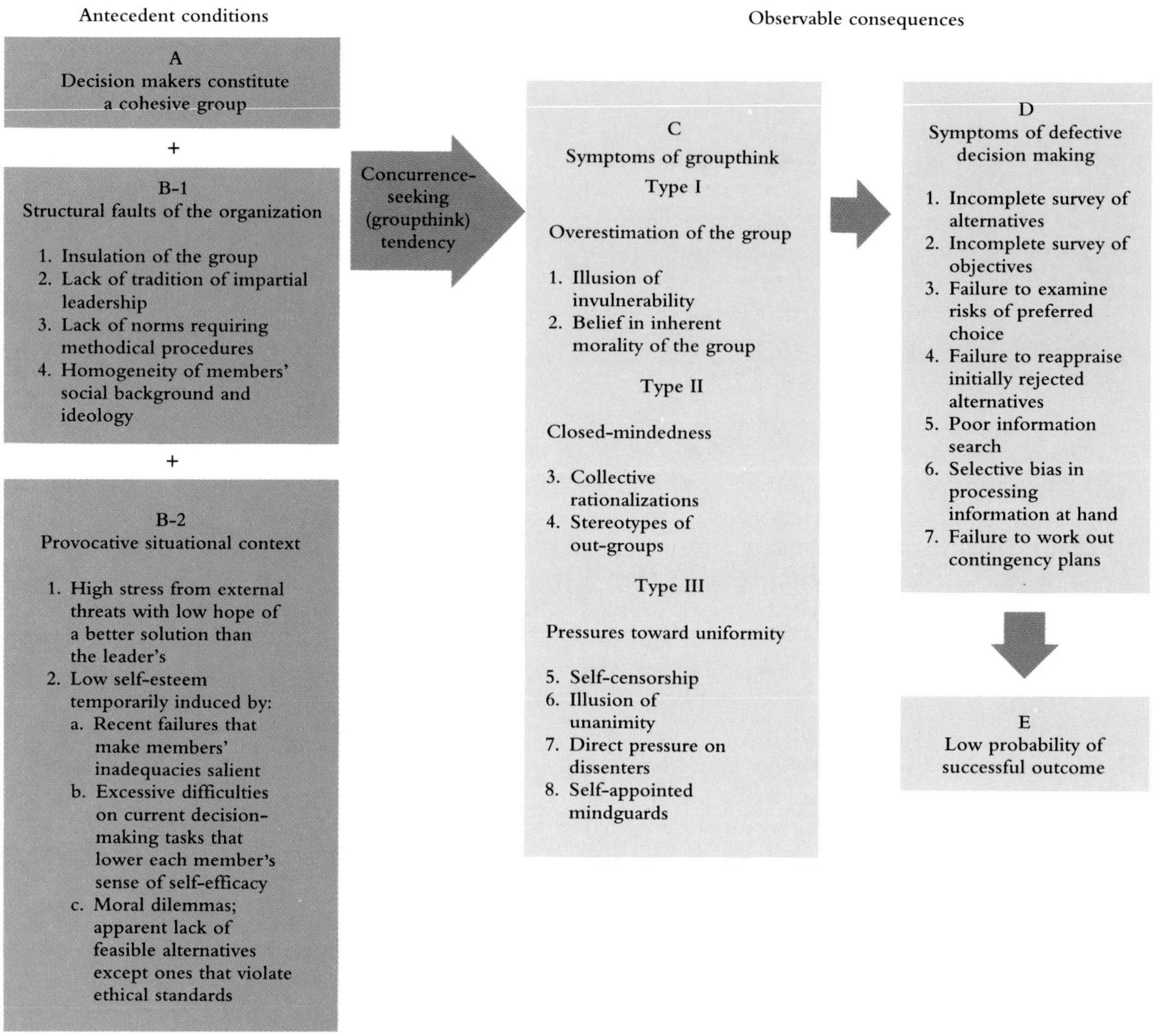

Antecedent conditions

Observable consequences

A
Decision makers constitute a cohesive group

+

B-1
Structural faults of the organization

1. Insulation of the group
2. Lack of tradition of impartial leadership
3. Lack of norms requiring methodical procedures
4. Homogeneity of members' social background and ideology

+

B-2
Provocative situational context

1. High stress from external threats with low hope of a better solution than the leader's
2. Low self-esteem temporarily induced by:
   a. Recent failures that make members' inadequacies salient
   b. Excessive difficulties on current decision-making tasks that lower each member's sense of self-efficacy
   c. Moral dilemmas; apparent lack of feasible alternatives except ones that violate ethical standards

Concurrence-seeking (groupthink) tendency

C
Symptoms of groupthink
Type I

Overestimation of the group

1. Illusion of invulnerability
2. Belief in inherent morality of the group

Type II

Closed-mindedness

3. Collective rationalizations
4. Stereotypes of out-groups

Type III

Pressures toward uniformity

5. Self-censorship
6. Illusion of unanimity
7. Direct pressure on dissenters
8. Self-appointed mindguards

D
Symptoms of defective decision making

1. Incomplete survey of alternatives
2. Incomplete survey of objectives
3. Failure to examine risks of preferred choice
4. Failure to reappraise initially rejected alternatives
5. Poor information search
6. Selective bias in processing information at hand
7. Failure to work out contingency plans

E
Low probability of successful outcome

Source: Irving L. Janis, *Groupthink: Psychological Studies of Policy Decisions and Fiascoes* (Boston: Houghton Mifflin, 1982), p. 244 (also pp. 174–75).

Groupthink results from complications of cohesiveness and leads to defective decision making, jeopardizing the group's success.

produce concurrence seeking, then symptoms of groupthink, then defective decision making, and finally a low probability of success. The symptoms of groupthink are categorized in box C as overestimation of the group, closed-mindedness, and pressures toward uniformity.

What can be done by managers to prevent groupthink? A manager can (1) assign a devil's advocate, (2) appoint a critical evaluator, (3) bring in outside experts to challenge the views of the group, or (4) not permit the group to disband until debate and disagreements are presented.[62]

[62]Ibid.

TABLE 11–2	**Summary of Key Group Characteristics**	

	Characteristics	**Major Point(s)**
	Group goals	Groups typically have two sets of goals: manager-assigned goals and group goals.
	Leadership	In informal groups, leaders emerge from within. In the formal organization, the leader is appointed.
	Status	Status systems develop over time. Seniority, skill, and expertise influence a person's status within the group.
What makes groups tick: another reminder.	Norms	Work groups utilize norms to affect dress, language used, and job performance.
	Cohesiveness	High group cohesiveness aligned with high performance goals is associated with high group performance.
	Intragroup conflict	There is likely to be disagreement among different members because of plans, schedules, and standards.
	Intergroup conflict	A few of the crucial reasons for intergroup conflict are limited resources, different perceptions, different interests, and lack of clear communication channels.

SUMMARY OF KEY POINTS

- Work groups are formed formally and informally in organizations. Groups are extremely important because they influence individual and organizational goals and performance.

- Groups are formed because of physical proximity and the desire to satisfy needs.

- There are numerous and overlapping groups in organizations. Employees are members of multiple groups at the same time. Formal groups include command and task groups. Informal groups include interest and friendship groups.

- Committees are special kinds of task groups. Committees exist to accomplish such purposes as resolving conflict, recommending action, generating ideas, and making decisions.

- Quality circles were invented in the United States but popularized in and exported from Japan. A quality circle is a small group of employees and their supervisor, who voluntarily

meet on a regular basis to study quality control and productivity improvement techniques and to identify and solve work-related problems.

- Groups move through various phases of development to maturity. Development occurs along two dimensions: (1) relationships among members and (2) task and problem solving. The four phases of development are called mutual acceptance, decision making, motivation, and control.

- Group characteristics have a potential impact on how groups function. Their main features are summarized in Table 11–2.

- Groups perform better than individuals in some situations and equal to or worse than individuals in others. Groups usually outperform individuals when complex and large-scale tasks must be completed.

DISCUSSION AND REVIEW QUESTIONS

1. What did Lewin mean when he stated that "it's easier to affect the personality of 10 people if they can be melted into a group than to affect the personality of any 1 individual separately"?

2. How would social loafing be handled within a highly cohesive group?

3. Informal groups exist in organizations and are very **important to their members.** If an organization has a

number of informal groups, is this an indication that the company is being poorly managed? Why or why not?

4. What should a manager know about conducting a committee meeting?

5. How is the concept of group norms and control used by weight reduction clinics and stop-smoking clinics?

6. Explain how work groups' performance norms develop.

7. How would a group's structure influence the members' behavior and attitudes?

8. Explain how synergy in a group can be positive or negative.

9. What is the potential danger of groupthink in an organization such as Compaq?

10. How can one individual dominate the discussion or activities of a group attempting to reach decisions?

ADDITIONAL REFERENCES

Biddle, B. J. *Role Theory: Expectations, Identities, and Behaviors.* New York: Academic Press, 1979.

Hackman, J. R. "The Design of Self-Managing Work Groups," In *Managerial Control and Organizational Democracy,* ed. B. King, S. Streufert, and F. E. Fiedler. Washington, D.C.: Winston and Sons, 1978.

Herzberg, F. "Group Dynamics at the Roundtable." *Industry Week,* November 16, 1981, pp. 39–40.

Klein, S. M. *Workers under Stress: The Impact of Work Pressure on Group Cohesion.* Lexington: University of Kentucky Press, 1971.

Martins, L., and **M. Jacobs.** "Structured Feedback Delivered in Small Groups." *Small Group Behavior,* February 1980, pp. 88–107.

Ohmae, K. "Quality Control Circles: They Work and Don't Work." *The Wall Street Journal,* March 29, 1982, p.19.

Roark, A. E. and **L. Wilkinson.** "Approaches to Conflict Management." *Group and Organization Studies,* December 1979, pp. 440–52.

Shaw, M. E. *Group Dynamics: The Psychology of Small Group Behavior.* New York: McGraw-Hill, 1981.

Shaw, M. E. "An Overview of Small Group Behavior." In *Introduction to Organizational Behavior,* ed. L. L. Cummings and R. B. Dunham. Homewood, Ill.: Richard D. Irwin, 1981, pp. 280–82.

Shea, G. P. "Work Design Committees: The Wave of the Future." *Journal of Applied Management,* March–April 1979, pp. 6–11.

Tervell, R. "How to Keep Quality Circles in Motion." *Business,* January–March 1982, pp. 47–50.

Zander, A. *Motives and Goals in Groups.* New York: Academic Press, 1971.

CASE 11–1   Volvo Uses Teamwork and Gainsharing Effectively

While North American automobile firms are looking to Japan for cost-cutting systems and techniques, Volvo (possibly the grandfather of automobile assembly) continues to add to its long list of innovative manufacturing designs. Over the past 15 years, the Volvo production facilities have championed the following techniques:

■ *Work group–oriented manufacturing:* At Kalmar, teams make many of the scheduling and strategic decisions for their part of the manufacturing process.

■ *Flexitime shifting:* At Köping and nearby Lindesberg, flexible shifts allow convenient schedules for mothers and part-time workers. To achieve this,

Source: Adapted from Pal Bernstein, "The Ultimate in Flexitime: From Sweden, by Way of Volvo," *Personnel,* June 1988, pp. 70–74; Warren Hauck and Timothy L. Ross, "Expanded Teamwork at Volvo through Performance Gainsharing," *Industrial Management,* July–August 1988, pp. 17–20.

the plants offer 12 different variations on weekly shifts ranging from 24 to 40 hours a week.

■ *Performance gainsharing:* Volvo employees can benefit individually from successes in the plant's productivity. When cost-saving methods are introduced or absenteeism is reduced, the employees get a part of the savings.

All of the systems work together to try and offset what has plagued many Swedish companies, absenteeism and turnover. These are notorious problems because Swedes work less than any other nation in the world, only 1,500 hours per year. This is partly due to policies such as mandatory five-week vacations, nine-month maternity leave (which fathers can share), and time off for educational or political activities. What many Swedes call a full-time job, Americans would call a part-time job.

Sweden's currency has been devalued 25 percent since 1981. Raw materials have become more expensive, and increased productivity is the only way that the company can successfully compete. One of the most revolutionary ways that Volvo has achieved this is through its use of work groups.

In classical management, promoted by Frederick Taylor in the early 20th century, work teams were the menace and specialization was the answer. This was because well-rounded artisans could ask for more money than the unskilled laborer. Today, management seemingly has turned 180 degrees in its view of work teams. Quality and commitment have become the goals of Volvo; and to foster them, the employees need to have some kind of ownership of the job. The 125 work teams at Kalmar are responsible for crafting a single section of the manufacturing process. This includes scheduling, techniques, cleanliness of the shop, and quality control. They virtually become their own inspectors. As a result, they become involved with their job and their group members.

In this way, through peer groups, Volvo has created a social force to keep the employees coming to work.

QUESTIONS FOR ANALYSIS

1. How might the work groups combined with the financial incentive work together to involve Volvo employees in their work?
2. Could this system work in America? What barriers do U.S. automobile firms seem to have that are not present in Sweden?
3. What factors would contribute to the development of cohesiveness in groups like those in the Kalmar plant? How would it be different at the Köping plant?

CASE 11–2   Lakeland Police Department

The mission of the Lakeland Police Department is to protect the life and property of the citizens and visitors to the city of Lakeland. Recently, Bob Lukash, chief of police, has been faced with two major problems. First, there is a serious lack of understanding between residents of low-income areas and the police. This problem has generated a number of suggested solutions from politicians, community leaders, and police officers. Second, some embarrassing conflicts are occurring between the Personnel Division and the Training Division. They have become so disruptive that newspaper articles about it are appearing in the *Lakeland Times*. Chief Lukash wants to resolve the problem between the units as soon as possible.

The first problem has led to charges of police brutality and discrimination. The chief is now considering two suggestions for improving understanding between residents and the police:

- To train officers who work in the low-income area in human relations. The rationale is that through training, the officers will become more understanding.
- To form a neighborhood committee consisting of local leaders and a few police officers trained in social problems. The committee would discuss the problems and attempt to find reasonable solutions.

The chief currently is thinking through these two alternatives and will make a decision in a few days.

The second problem involves two divisions in the department. The Training Division is responsible for police training and the investigation of applicants seeking to join the department. The division's training school offers a six-week course for new recruits twice a year. Between 10 and 12 people attend each session. The Personnel Division recruits through interviews, advertisements, and word of mouth. In the past year, the Personnel Division has been accused by the Training Division of not doing a good job in attracting qualified candidates. The Training Division's commanding officer Nick Tandy has met with Chief Lukash twice to voice this complaint. He asked the chief to lean on personnel director Martin Rossano to make him more aggressive in recruiting quality candidates.

Martin Rossano informed the chief that the Training Division has suddenly raised its requirements without notifying the Personnel Division. He believes that this is why good candidates are lacking. The failure to communicate these changes in requirements has resulted in bad feelings between Tandy and Rossano for the past year.

The chief has told both commanding officers that he will not tolerate this type of conflict. The newspapers have had a field day with it, and the chief wants it stopped. He has scheduled a meeting for Monday morning and ordered both officers to attend. Tandy and Rossano also have been told to bring with them a suggested solution to the problem.

QUESTIONS FOR ANALYSIS

1. Which solution do you consider to be the best for improving community-police relations?
2. Why has the conflict between Tandy and Rossano become disruptive?
3. What are some feasible solutions to the conflict between Personnel and Training?

EXPERIENTIAL EXERCISE

GROUP BRAINSTORMING IN ACTION

Purpose

The purpose of this exercise is to provide experience in group brainstorming—to learn to use and pool the ideas, good and bad, of group members.

The Exercise in Class

The rules for the group brainstorming session are:

- Each group member is to contribute at least two ideas. The ideas must be written on a sheet of paper.
- The instructor (or group leader) will write each idea on a chalkboard or flip chart.
- Every idea will be recorded, no matter how unrealistic.
- While ideas are being recorded, there must be NO evaluation by other group members. This is an important part of brainstorming, the freedom to simply "say it like it is" and have no fear of being evaluated.

1. The instructor will form groups of six to eight persons. A group leader, who serves mainly as a recorder of ideas, will be elected. The leader should also contribute ideas.
2. The groups will brainstorm and develop solutions to this problem:

    The midwest region of the United States is becoming known as the "rust bowl" of America. Steelworkers and autoworkers have been losing their jobs. Today, there are only 260,000 steelworkers in the United States, while in 1977 there were 460,000. Most of the job loss has occurred in the "rust bowl" states—Illinois, Michigan, Ohio, Indiana, and Pennsylvania. The dire prediction is that those who have lost their jobs will never again work in steel mills or auto plants. The jobs are lost forever. Assume that this prediction is basically correct. Using a brainstorming method, develop some solutions that labor, management, and government can take to ease the social, emotional, and psychological pain of job-loss victims. What should and can be done?

3. Each group member is to independently develop two solutions for the job-loss problem. After about 20 minutes, begin recording the solutions.
4. Discuss the brainstorming procedure in the group. If it were being done in an organization, what would be the next step to take once brainstorming has been completed?

The Learning Message

This exercise will indicate that it is rather difficult to brainstorm. The technique sounds easy, but it is difficult to accomplish. Group members will find that it is difficult to refrain from evaluating the quality of each idea during the brainstorming.

12

LEADERSHIP

LEARNING OBJECTIVES

After completing Chapter 12, you should be able to:

Define
what is meant by the term *leadership*.

Describe
the difference between the terms *leadership* and *management*.

Discuss
the power bases that leaders can use to influence the work behavior of followers.

Compare
the similarities and differences in the University of Michigan, Ohio State, and Managerial Grid personal-behavioral explanations of leadership.

Identify
important differences among situational theories of leadership.

After Years of Bureaucracy, Can Soviet Managers Be Trained to Be Managerial Leaders?

Until recently, managers in most companies in the Soviet Union were given strict guidelines concerning production quotas, production processes, pricing schedules, and marketing. Because of such control, managers did not have to worry about cutting costs, conserving scarce resources, or showing any type of initiative to uphold productivity or quality. In fact, much of the leadership ability that Western managers are hired for was simply not required of their Soviet counterparts.

Now, under Mikhail Gorbachev, the Soviet government is trying to breathe new life into industries by promoting *khozraschot,* or increased local company control. This is a unilateral transfer of control back to the individual companies in all areas of production, human resource management, and marketing. For the first time, Soviet managers are expected to make their own product mix and volume decisions, purchase raw materials from alternate suppliers, and even hire and fire employees on the basis of market fluctuations and performance criteria.

Success of the plan hinges on whether managers in the 48,000 industrial companies can perform the miracles expected of them. Can managers who lack essential training and experience in areas such as market planning, production management, international finance, and organizational development effectively turn their companies around? They are certainly trying. The government is supporting education abroad, executive education programs, and private management consulting firms in an attempt to foster improved management practices. One such education program is a Western-style school of business called the East-West Management Institute in Budapest, Hungary.

How will Soviet managers pilot the industrial revolution? By doing what they had never been asked to do before, lead. They are now expected to implement systems in their companies to ensure productivity and quality, which in reality is a mandate to change the way their employees view their jobs. They need to be creative and effective in gaining the trust and support of subordinates so that they can pull the industrial sector back on its feet.

In this chapter, the importance of leading will be discussed. When competent managers are deprived of planning for the future and are not allowed to lead their subordinates, they can only concentrate on other functions of management such as organizing and controlling. In this case, the success of the industrial turn-around in the Soviet Union depends on how well the government can introduce leading into the management equation.

Source: Adapted from Thomas H. Naylor, "The Reeducation of Soviet Management," *Across the Board,* February 1988, pp. 28–37.

Interest in the subject of leading others has existed throughout the history of studying human behavior. However, behavioral scientists in the past 40 years have scientifically analyzed leadership in organizational settings, finding that leadership is a complex process that can be explained by various theories and models. And many of the available theories and models are contradictory or overlap.[1]

WHAT IS LEADERSHIP?

Some writers have given the impression that leadership is a synonym for management. This assumption is not correct. Leaders are found not only in the managerial hierarchy but also in informal work groups. The difference between leadership and management has been stated as follows:

> Leadership is a part of management but not all of it. . . . Leadership is the ability to persuade others to seek defined objectives enthusiastically. It is the human factor which binds a group together and motivates it toward goals. Management activities such as planning, organizing, and decision making are dormant cocoons until the leader triggers the power of motivation in people and guides them toward goals.[2]

Figure 12–1 emphasizes graphically that managers are not always effective leaders. Of course, organizations of all sizes prefer to have and attempt to develop managers who also are leaders.

An important feature of the above definition of leadership is that leadership is a process whereby one individual exerts influence over others. Several attempts have been made to clarify and depict the basis upon which a superior might influence a subordinate or a group of subordinates. One of the most concise and insightful approaches is offered by John French and Bertram Raven.[3] They define influence in terms of **power**—the control a person possesses and can exercise on others—and propose five different bases for such power:

1. *Coercive power.* This is power based on fear. A subordinate perceives that failure to comply with the wishes of a superior would lead to punishment (for example, an undesirable work assignment, a reprimand). Coercive power is based on the expectations of individuals that punishment is the consequence for not agreeing with the actions, attitudes, or directives of a superior. In the 1989 strike between Eastern Air Lines president Frank Lorenzo and International Machinist Union president William Winpisinger, both used coercive power: threats, intimidation, anxiety. Of course, a strike, picket lines, Chapter 11 bankruptcy, and more conflict resulted.[4]

[1] Warren Bennis, *Why Leaders Can't Lead* (San Francisco: Jossey-Bass, 1989).

[2] Keith Davis, *Human Relations at Work* (New York: McGraw-Hill, 1967), pp. 96–97.

[3] John R. P. French and Bertram Raven, "The Bases of Social Power," in *Group Dynamics,* 2nd ed., ed. Dorwin Cartwright and Alvin F. Zander (Evanston, Ill.: Row, Peterson, 1960), pp. 607–23.

[4] Amanda Bennett, "Personalizing the Conflict at Eastern Air," *The Wall Street Journal,* March 9, 1989, p. B1.

FIGURE 12–1   The Preferred Leader-Manager Mix

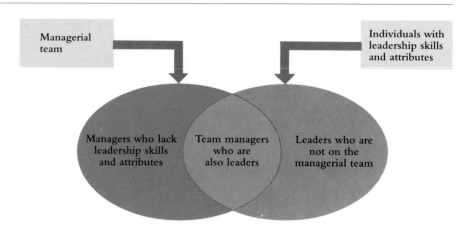

Leaders = Managers only in some cases, since leadership is only one part of management.

2. *Reward power.* This is the opposite of coercive power. A subordinate perceives that compliance with the wishes of a superior will lead to positive rewards. These rewards could be monetary (increases in pay) or nonmonetary (a compliment for a job well done).

3. *Legitimate power.* This type of power comes from the position of a superior in the organizational hierarchy. For example, the president of a corporation possesses more legitimate power than the vice president, and the department manager has more legitimate power than the first-line supervisor.

4. *Expert power.* An individual with this type of power is one with an expertise, special skill, or knowledge. The possession of one or more of these attributes gains the respect and compliance of peers or subordinates. In some cases, individuals with expert power are placed in managerial positions and are expected to lead. This seems to be true in professional sports. Great athletes with skills are assumed to be potential leaders.

5. *Referent power.* This power is based on a follower's identification with a leader. The leader is admired because of one or more personal traits, and the follower can be influenced because of this admiration.

Coercive, reward, and legitimate power are specified primarily by the individual's position in the organization. The first-line supervisor in an organization is at a lower managerial level than the department manager and consequently has significantly less coercive, reward, and legitimate power than does the department manager.

The degree and scope of a manager's referent and expert power are dictated primarily by individual characteristics. Some managers possess specific qualities (for example, skills or attributes) that make them attractive to subordinates. Managers could be considered attractive because of an ability to express themselves clearly or because they appear completely confident in performing the job. Thus, the individual leader controls the referent and expert power

Would this man, Albert Einstein, have been an effective leader?

bases, while the organization controls the coercive, reward, and legitimate power bases.

THE LEADERSHIP JOB: A MUTUAL-SHARING VIEW

Unquestionably, the manager has the legitimate power to influence decisions as granted by the organization. However, influence should be viewed as a mutual exercise. In order to influence, one must be influenced to some degree. That is, the leader must be influenced by followers.

A leader who attempts to influence through coercion or fear will eventually face problems. This is not to say that the leader should be stripped of the right to discipline followers in an equitable manner. It does suggest, however, that the leader should be viewed as approachable, equitable, and considerate. The leader can exert more influence if viewed as being open to influence in some situations.

This mutual-sharing view of leadership has an important message: Influence can be divided or shared and both parties can gain. A leader, by sharing influence with followers, can benefit from establishing better interaction and more respect. The followers can benefit by learning more about the leader. It has been shown that managers and employees in effective organizations perceive themselves as having greater influence. The greater the total influence leaders and followers have in the organization, the better seems to be the performance of the total system.[5]

An example of the mutual-sharing view is what happens at Photocircuits, a division of Kollmorgen Corporation in Glen Cove and Riverhead, New York. Managers have their performance assessed by—and get feedback from—their subordinates.[6] So far, participation has been voluntary. This reverse performance review has become a matter of company policy.

The objective of the reverse performance review is to build a mutual relationship between managers and subordinates. It is designed to encourage them to talk to each other as equals. And some of its original skeptics seem to be changing their tune. Frank Fuggine, vice president of human resources, stated: "I was skeptical when the reverse review was proposed. But it's been a real eye-opener. I learned more about myself. . . . I found people in general were very candid and in most cases welcomed the opportunity. That really surprised me."

LEADER ATTITUDES: IMPORTANT ASSUMPTIONS

Douglas McGregor introduced the idea that the attitudes that managers hold about the nature of people will greatly influence their behavior. A manager who views subordinates as being lazy, uncooperative, and possessing poor work habits will treat them accordingly.[7] Likewise, managers who see their employees as hardworking, cooperative, and possessing positive work habits will treat them in this manner. McGregor referred to this attitude-behavior link as the "self-fulfilling prophecy"

McGregor's views about manager attitudes were presented in terms of assumptions. McGregor distinguished between what he called Theory X and Theory Y managers. Theory X managers behaved according to these assumptions:

- The average employee inherently dislikes work and will avoid it when possible.
- Most employees must be coerced, directed, and closely supervised to get them to put forth the effort to achieve organizational objectives.
- Most employees have little ambition and prefer job security above all other outcomes.
- Most employees avoid taking on responsibilities.

The Theory X manager making these assumptions would use an authoritarian and directive style of leadership.

On the other hand, Theory Y managerial behaviors would be based on the following assumptions and would reflect a less authoritarian leadership style:

---

[5]For two classic studies, see D. C. Pelz, "Influence: A Key to Effective Leadership in the First-Line Supervisor," *Personnel*, 1952, pp. 201–21; M. Rosner et al., "Worker Participation and Influence in Five Countries," *Industrial Relations*, 1973, pp. 200–212.

[6]"Another Perspective of Managers' Performance—from Subordinates," *Management Review*, August 1982, pp. 29, 32, 33.

[7]Douglas McGregor, *The Human Side of Enterprise* (New York: McGraw-Hill, 1960). This is McGregor's original work.

- The expenditure of physical and mental effort in work is as natural as play or rest.
- Most people prefer to exercise self-direction and self-control.
- People learn, when encouraged, to accept and seek responsibilities.
- People are interested in displaying imagination, ingenuity, and creativity to solve organizational problems.

Under a Theory X manager, the employee who is having difficulty meeting standard output levels is seen as lazy, one that needs to be closely supervised. However, the Theory Y manager would view this employee as perhaps needing training, more support, or more autonomy to do the job. The self-fulfilling prophecy of managing and leading others is aptly stated:

> What a manager expects of his subordinates and the way he treats them largely determine their performance and career progress. A unique characteristic of superior managers is their ability to create high performance expectations that subordinates fulfill.[8]

Are you an X, Y, or X and Y person? If you are facing a crisis, what approach do you use? Are you the kind of leader that industry needs in the 1990s and the 21st century? How new leaders are found is discussed in the Management Focus.

Attempts to explain and understand leadership have shown a trend toward integrating various theories of leadership. Instead of creating more theories of leadership behavior, the focus here is upon systematically organizing and categorizing what is already available. There appear to be three broad categories of leadership theories: *trait theories, personal-behavioral theories,* and *situational theories.* Some of the situational theories have borrowed from the trait theories and from various personal-behavioral theories. Therefore, it is best to consider the three categories of theories as having many similarities and some differences.

TRAIT THEORIES OF LEADERSHIP

The identification of various personal traits of leaders as criteria for describing or predicting success has been used for some time. Some executives engaged in recruiting and selecting managers believe that the trait approach is as valid as any other method. However, the comparison of leaders by various physical, personality, and intelligence traits has resulted in little agreement among researchers.

PHYSICAL TRAITS

Some advocates of the trait theory contend that the physical stature of a person affects ability to influence followers. For example, in an early extensive review of 12 leadership investigations, Ralph Stogdill determined that 9 of the studies found leaders to be taller than followers, 2 found them to be shorter, while 1

---

[8]J. Sterling Livingston, "Pygmalion in Management," *Harvard Business Review,* July–August 1969, p. 82.

MANAGEMENT FOCUS

How Do Industry Leaders Find New Leaders?

In a recent survey, 15 of the Fortune "Reputation Study" top 20 companies were asked how they recruited and developed leaders. They all enjoyed fruitful performance appraisal programs, succession-planning processes, and programs to identify potential, but some things distinguished them from the rest. Five such techniques were shared by most of the firms.

First, they agreed that line management should drive the recruiting effort. Although the human resource group took care of most of the coordination and logistical efforts, the companies liked to use the line managers and executives because they were in the best position to know how many and what kind of people will be needed to run the company in the future.

Second, the best firms targeted a select number of schools, treating them like major customers. Hewlett-Packard likes to focus on 30 schools so that they can develop close relationships with the schools, network with the faculties, and donate computer equipment to facilitate research.

Third, many of the firms tried hard to keep their hiring standards high across the entire firm. Some, such as Morgan Guarantee, bring all new recruits to a central training program. In their lengthy New York training program, if any particular office is sacrificing standards, it would show.

Fourth, the firms actually looked for leadership potential in the prospective employees. They felt that unless they concentrated specifically on leadership, they could hire smart technicians with little common sense and weak interpersonal skills.

Finally, the top 15 companies usually felt that if they wanted someone badly, he or she was worth special treatment. A General Mills executive claimed: "When we find someone we really want, we work hard to close the sale. For example, if we meet such people at one of our informal wine and cheese gatherings, we'll immediately send a follow-up letter and invite them to Minneapolis."

Source: Adapted from John P. Kotter, "How Leaders Grow Leaders," *Across the Board,* March 1988, pp. 38–42.

concluded that height was not the most important factor.[9] Other physical traits that have been studied with no conclusive results include weight, physique, and personal appearance.

PERSONALITY

A research study by Edwin Ghiselli reports on several personality factors that are related, in most though not all cases, to effective leadership.[10] He found that leaders who have the drive to act independently and are self-assured (for example, have confidence in their leadership skills) are successful in achieving organizational objectives.

[9]Ralph Stogdill, "Personal Factors Associated with Leadership," *Journal of Applied Psychology,* January 1948, pp. 35–71.

[10]See the classic Edwin E. Ghiselli, "Managerial Talent," *American Psychologist,* October 1963, pp. 631–41.

INTELLIGENCE

After surveying the literature, Stogdill concluded that leadership ability is associated with the judgment and verbal facilities of the leader.[11] Ghiselli also concluded that an individual's intelligence is an accurate predictor of managerial success within a certain range. Above and below this range, the chances of successful prediction significantly decrease.[12] It should be noted, however, that the leader's intelligence should be close to that of the followers. The leader who is too smart or not smart enough may lose the followers' respect.

TRAIT RESEARCH

Ghiselli has studied eight personality traits and five motivational traits:[13]

Personality traits
Intelligence: of a verbal and symbolic nature.
Initiative: the willingness to strike off in new directions.
Supervisory ability: the ability to direct others.
Self-assurance: favorable self-evaluation.
Affinity for the working class.
Decisiveness.
Masculinity/femininity.
Maturity.

Motivational traits
Need for job security.
Need for financial reward.
Need for power over others.
Need for self-actualization.
Need for occupational achievement.

His research on these traits is well respected because of the scientific quality of the work. Table 12–1 summarizes the results of Ghiselli's studies, which suggest the relative importance of the traits. They must be tempered, however, because the traits are not totally independent of each other. There are some interesting pieces of information: First, intelligence and self-actualization are important for success. Second, the concept of power over others is not very important. (This tends to support McGregor's Theory Y orientation.) Third, the supervisory-ability trait basically refers to the ability to use planning, organizing, and controlling to direct subordinates. Finally, masculinity/femininity seems to have little to do with managerial success.

Warren Bennis conducted a study of 90 outstanding leaders and their subordinates. He identified four common traits and competencies that leaders in the 1990s must possess and/or develop:[14]

---

[11]Stogdill, "Personal Factors."

[12]Ghiselli, "Managerial Talent."

[13]Edwin E. Ghiselli, *Explorations in Management Talent* (Santa Monica, Calif.: Goodyear Publishing, 1971).

[14]Warren Bennis, "The 4 Competencies of Leadership," *Training and Development Journal,* August 1984, pp. 15–19.

Table 12–1		The Importance of Personal Traits to Management Success

<table>
<tr><td></td><td>Importance</td><td>Personal Trait</td></tr>
<tr><td rowspan="6">Some personal traits predict leadership success, and some have little predictive power.</td><td>Great</td><td>Supervisory ability.
Occupational achievement.
Intelligence.
Self-actualization.
Self-assurance.
Decisiveness.</td></tr>
<tr><td>Moderate</td><td>Lack of need for security.
Affinity for working class.
Initiative.
Lack of need for high financial reward.
Maturity.</td></tr>
<tr><td>Little</td><td>Masculinity/femininity.</td></tr>
</table>

Source: Adapted from Edwin E. Ghiselli, *Explorations in Management Talent* (Santa Monica, Calif.: Goodyear Publishing, 1971).

- *Management of attention:* The ability to communicate a sense of outcome, goal, or direction that attracts followers.
- *Management of meaning:* The ability to create and communicate meaning with clarity and understanding.
- *Management of trust:* The ability to be reliable and consistent so people can count on them.
- *Management of self:* The ability to know themselves and to use their skills within limits of strengths and weaknesses.

The Bennis research findings suggest that leaders empower their organizations to create a positive work environment. When followers feel good about work, trust the leader, and understand what is expected of them, they become dedicated and committed to performing well.[15] This is what a leader can help create—a dynamic, stimulating work environment.

An example of a creative leader is George W. Jenkins, founder and president of Publix Super Markets, Inc. The employees are excited about working for Publix.[16] Jenkins has instilled pride, sensitivity, and a sharing attitude in them. The founder has created a family environment. Employees are welcomed, feel good about the company, and appreciate commitments from the leader that are kept. Publix has given employees a career, not just a job, in a very competitive business, and employees work hard to repay Jenkin's promises, commitments, reliability, trust, and pride.

Shortcomings

A manager who is confident, independent, and intelligent has a higher probability of succeeding. However, the trait approach has some shortcom-

[15]Warren Bennis and Bert Nanus, *Leaders: The Strategies for Taking Charge* (New York: Harper & Row, 1986).

[16]Robert Levering, *A Great Place to Work* (New York: Random House, 1988), pp. 33–39.

Directive leadership means showing the way to others.

ings. First, except for Ghiselli, trait theorists do not specify the relative importance of various traits. Should an organization attempt to find leaders who are confident or those who act independently? Which should be weighted more? Second, the research evidence is inconsistent. For every study that supports the idea that a particular trait is positively related to improved effectiveness, there seems to be one that shows a negative relationship or no relationship at all. Finally, though large numbers of traits already have been uncovered, the list grows annually, suggesting that still others will be found in the future. The cumbersome listings lead to confusion and disputes and provide little insight into leadership.[17]

The debate about traits is likely to continue. Whether leaders are born or are developed is the topic of the Management Focus. What traits were you born with that can be used in leadership positions?

PERSONAL–BEHAVIORAL THEORIES

Personal-behavioral (P–B) theories contend that leaders may best be classified by personal qualities or behavioral patterns (styles). P–B theories of leadership focus on what the leader does in carrying out the managerial job. Of these, there is no specific style that is universally accepted.

A CONTINUUM OF LEADERSHIP

Robert Tannenbaum and Warren Schmidt propose that managers often have difficulty deciding what type of action is most appropriate for handling a

[17]See Rodman L. Drake, "Leadership: It's a Rare Blend of Traits," *Management Review,* August 1984, pp. 24–26. For another listing that is based on research findings, see Bernard M. Bass, *Stogdill's Handbook of Leadership* (New York: Free Press, 1982), pp. 75–76.

MANAGEMENT FOCUS

Traits: Are Good Salespeople Born or Made?

Stable, self-sufficient, self-confident, goal directed, decisive, intellectually curious, speedy, accurate. These are the traits that a major testing company associates with being a successful salesperson. Most of these attributes can be trained, said over 80 percent of the respondents in a recent survey of over 10,000 sales and marketing executives in 10 industries. However, the same group also knew people that they considered to be "born salespeople."

What seemed to distinguish the born salesperson was an enormous ego and an extroverted personality. Others referred to their ability to exchange pleasantries, or the "gift of gab," claiming that a little personality can go a long way. Even some of the training executives agreed that it was difficult to instill a spirit to win or the interpersonal skills that many children learn on the baseball field or among friends and family.

But these aren't enough. With the ego and other built-in qualities, most felt that salespeople also need a lot of skills to be effective. For instance, they must be able to match their product with the needs of the customer. This comes from knowledge and experience. To be a consultant type of salesperson rather than a relationship type, they might have to come up with individually designed solutions, which requires years of expertise and training.

Another unresolved area was the existence of self-motivated people. Although two thirds of the respondents claimed that there was no such thing as a self-motivated salesperson, there was also a vocal minority. Consultant Stewart Washburn was in the nonbeliever camp, likening motivation to a fire that needs to be set and fanned by management. His idea of the most effective motivator was the field supervisor, one who can coach salespeople. Tony Alessandra, another sales consultant, prefers career interviews as motivators. These are sessions that don't review performance but cover only what the salesperson likes and dislikes about the job and working conditions and covers what his or her goals are for the future. Alessandra claims that you can get a good idea about what is having an impact on your sales force in just a few career interviews.

Others still hold fast to the notion that self-motivation exists and even that certain physical traits can indicate a self-motivated person. San Francisco State University marketing professor Rich Nelson advises that certain groups work harder than others. Divorced women, he says, are hard workers as well as being stable and dedicated. (Keep in mind that there are laws against asking whether someone is divorced.) Dan Heindel, regional sales manager for Alcoa's Sheet and Plate Division in Dallas, is convinced that the best salesperson in the world is the daughter of a successful business executive. "When you talk about inborn tendencies to succeed in sales," Heindel says, "in my experience, no one beats them."

Source: Adapted from Arthur Bragg, "Are Good Salespeople Born or Made?" *Sales and Marketing Management*, September 1988, pp. 74–78.

particular problem.[18] They are not sure whether to make the decision or to delegate the decision-making authority to subordinates.

To provide insight into the meaning of leadership behavior with regard to decision making, Tannenbaum and Schmidt suggest a continuum, presented in

---

[18]Robert Tannenbaum and Warren H. Schmidt, "How to Choose a Leadership Pattern," *Harvard Business Review,* May–June 1973, pp. 162–80.

FIGURE 12–2   Continuum of Leadership Behavior

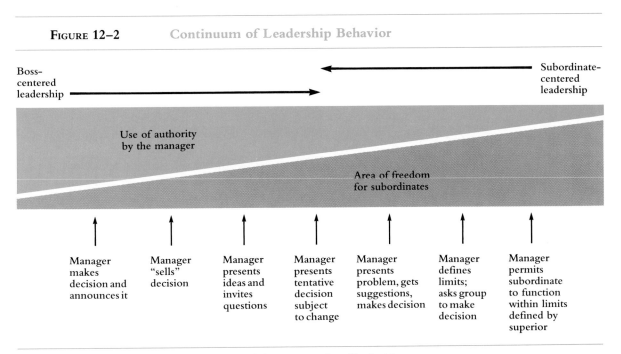

Boss-centered leadership

Subordinate-centered leadership

Use of authority by the manager

Area of freedom for subordinates

| Manager makes decision and announces it | Manager "sells" decision | Manager presents ideas and invites questions | Manager presents tentative decision subject to change | Manager presents problem, gets suggestions, makes decision | Manager defines limits; asks group to make decision | Manager permits subordinate to function within limits defined by superior |

Autocratic to democratic: Relating decision-making behaviors to styles of leadership.

Figure 12–2. Leadership actions are related to the degree of authority used by managers and to the amount of freedom available to the subordinates in reaching decisions. The managerial actions depicted on the left characterize managers who maintain a high degree of control, while those on the right are those of managers who delegate decision-making authority. Along the continuum, there are a number of leadership styles. According to this theory, effective leaders would be those who are adaptable—that is, who can delegate authority effectively because they consider their capabilities, subordinates' capabilities, and objectives to be accomplished. Thus, Tannenbaum and Schmidt imply that leaders should not choose either a strictly "autocratic" or "democratic" style but should be flexible enough to cope with different situations.

JOB-CENTERED/EMPLOYEE-CENTERED LEADERS

From 1947 on, Rensis Likert and a group of social researchers at the University of Michigan conducted studies of leadership.[19] They studied leaders in industry, hospitals, and government, obtaining data from thousands of employees.

After extensive analyses, the leaders studied were classified as job centered or employee centered. The *job-centered leader* structures the jobs of subordinates, closely supervises to see that designated tasks are performed, uses

[19]Rensis Likert, *New Patterns of Management* (New York: McGraw-Hill, 1961). For a discussion of the history of Likert's work, see Rensis Likert, "From Production- and Employee-Centeredness to Systems 1–4," *Journal of Management,* Fall 1979, pp. 147–56.

incentives to spur production, and determines standard rates of production based on procedures such as time study. The *employee-centered leader* focuses attention on the human aspects of subordinates' problems and on building effective work groups with high performance goals. Such a leader specifies objectives, communicates them to subordinates, and gives subordinates considerable freedom to accomplish their jobs.

The University of Michigan research showed that the majority of high-producing groups were led by supervisors who displayed an employee-centered style. In a study of clerical workers, the employee-centered manager was described as a general supervisor and the job-centered manager as a close supervisor. Once again, productivity data clearly indicated that the general type of supervision (employee centered) was more effective than the close supervision style (job centered).

Based on his extensive research, Likert suggested that the type of leadership style significantly influences various performance criteria. Such criteria as productivity, absenteeism, attitudes, turnover, and defective units were found to be more favorable from an organizational standpoint when employee-centered, or general, supervision was utilized. Likert implied that the choice is of the either-or variety—that is, management can be categorized and practiced as employee centered or job centered. His recommendation was to develop employee-centered managers whenever possible.

Two-Dimensional Theory

In 1945, a group of researchers at Ohio State University began extensive investigations of leadership, focusing on the study of leader behavior. Their efforts uncovered many provocative insights and changed the conceptual foundation of leadership research from a trait-based approach to a behavior base.

Perhaps the most publicized aspect of the studies was the isolation of two dimensions of leadership behavior, identified as "consideration" and "initiating structure."[20] These two dimensions were used to describe leadership behavior in organizational settings. The researchers assessed how supervisors think they should behave in leadership roles. They also attempted to ascertain subordinates' perceptions of supervisory behavior. The findings allowed the Ohio State researchers to classify leaders on consideration and initiating-structure dimensions.

Leaders who scored high on the consideration dimension reflected a work atmosphere of mutual trust, respect for subordinates' ideas, and consideration of subordinates' feelings. Such leaders encouraged good superior-subordinate rapport and two-way communication. A low consideration score indicated that leaders were more impersonal in their dealings with subordinates.

---

[20]See any of the following for excellent presentations of the two-dimensional theory: E. A. Fleishman, "The Measurement of Leadership Attitudes in Industry," *Journal of Applied Psychology,* June 1953, pp. 153–58; E. A. Fleishman and D. A. Peters, "Interpersonal Values, Leadership Attitudes and Managerial Success," *Personnel Psychology,* Summer 1962, pp. 127–43; Abraham K. Korman, "Consideration, Initiating Structure, and Organizational Criteria—A Review," *Personnel Psychology,* Winter 1966, pp. 349–61; Chester A. Schreisheim and Barbara J. Bird, "Contributions of the Ohio State Studies to the Field of Leadership," *Journal of Management,* Fall 1979, pp. 135–45.

A high initiating-structure score indicated that leaders structured their roles and those of subordinates toward the attainment of goals. They were actively involved in planning work activities, communicating pertinent information, and scheduling work.

One early research study attempted to compare supervisors having different consideration and initiating-structure scores with various performance measures.[21] The first measure was obtained from proficiency ratings made by plant management. Other measures were unexcused absenteeism, accidents, formally filed grievances, and employee turnover. Indexes for each of these measures were computed for each foreman's work group for an 11-month period.

Supervisors who worked in production divisions were compared to supervisors in nonproduction divisions on consideration scores, initiating-structure scores, and proficiency ratings. In the production divisions, the supervisors who were rated by their superiors as most proficient scored high on structure and low on consideration. In the nonproduction division, the relationships were reversed.

After comparing the leadership scores and proficiency ratings, the researchers compared leadership scores to the other performance measures: unexcused absenteeism, accidents, formally filed grievances, and employee turnover. In general, it was determined that high structure and low consideration were related to more absenteeism, accidents, grievances, and turnover.

A number of studies have supported the general findings cited above, while other research findings present contradictory evidence.[22] Despite these differences, it certainly is true that the Ohio State researchers stimulated the interest of practitioners and researchers in systematically studying leadership.

MANAGERIAL GRID THEORY

Another P–B theory is the Managerial Grid®. Robert Blake and Jane Mouton proposed that leadership style could be plotted on a two-dimensional grid.[23] Individuals are asked questions about their leadership style and, based on the responses, are placed at the appropriate point on the grid. Blake and Mouton use the Managerial Grid as a framework to help managers learn what their leadership style is and to track their movement toward the ideal (9,9) team management style. This grid is presented in Figure 12–3.

Five specific leadership styles are used to highlight different approaches to leading others. Of course, these are only five of the many possible styles of leadership that can be and are utilized.

1,1 *Impoverished:* A minimum effort to accomplish the work is exerted by the leader.

[21]E. A. Fleishman, E. F. Harris, and H. E. Burtt, *Leadership and Supervision in Industry* (Columbus: Bureau of Educational Research, Ohio State University, 1955).

[22]For a number of studies that dispute some of the findings of the Ohio State researchers, see Korman, "Consideration." For more supportive studies, see S. Kerr and Chester A. Schreisheim, "Consideration, Initiating Structure, and Organizational Criteria: An Update of Korman's 1966 Review," *Personnel Psychology,* Winter 1974, pp. 558–68.

[23]Robert R. Blake and Jane S. Mouton, *The Managerial Grid* (Houston: Gulf Publishing, 1964).

FIGURE 12–3   Blake and Mouton's Managerial Grid

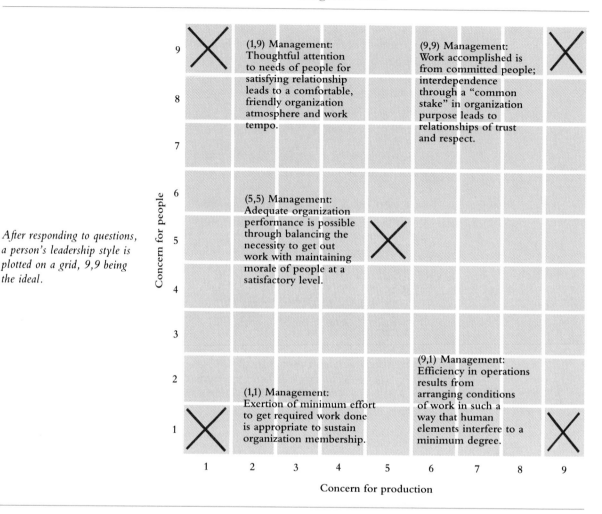

After responding to questions, a person's leadership style is plotted on a grid, 9,9 being the ideal.

(1,9) Management: Thoughtful attention to needs of people for satisfying relationship leads to a comfortable, friendly organization atmosphere and work tempo.

(9,9) Management: Work accomplished is from committed people; interdependence through a "common stake" in organization purpose leads to relationships of trust and respect.

(5,5) Management: Adequate organization performance is possible through balancing the necessity to get out work with maintaining morale of people at a satisfactory level.

(1,1) Management: Exertion of minimum effort to get required work done is appropriate to sustain organization membership.

(9,1) Management: Efficiency in operations results from arranging conditions of work in such a way that human elements interfere to a minimum degree.

Concern for people

Concern for production

Source: Robert R. Blake and Jane S. Mouton, *The Managerial Grid* (Houston: Gulf Publishing, 1964).

9,1 *Task:* The leader concentrates on task efficiency but shows little regard for the development and morale of subordinates.

1,9 *Country club:* The leader focuses on being supportive and considerate of employees. However, task efficiency is not a primary concern of this easygoing style.

5,5 *Middle of the road:* Adequate task efficiency and satisfactory morale are the goals of this style.

9,9 *Team:* The leader facilitates production and morale by coordinating and integrating work-related activities.

Blake and Mouton assume that the leader who is a 9,9 individual would be using the most effective style; however, defining a 9,9 leader for every type of job is very difficult. Blake and Mouton imply that a managerial development program can move leaders *toward* a 9,9 style. They recommend six manage-

TABLE 12–2	Personal–Behavioral Theories of Leadership			
	Theories	**Two Concepts**	**Derivation**	**Theory Development**
	1. Leadership continuum theory	Boss centered Subordinate centered	Opinions of Tannenbaum and Schmidt	By authors' description
The four personal-behavioral theories have similar concepts but use different labels.	2. Supportive theory	Job centered Employee centered	Research at the University of Michigan—Likert	By field research studies
	3. Two-dimensional theory	"Consideration" "Initiating structure"	Research at Ohio State University—Fleishman	By field research studies
	4. Managerial Grid	Concern for people Concern for production	Research by Blake and Mouton	By description and limited research

ment development phases (laboratory seminar groups, team building, inter-group processes, goal setting, goal feedback, and evaluation) to aid the manager in acquiring concern for fellow employees and the expertise to accomplish objectives such as productivity and quality.

The Management Grid is an attitudinal approach that attempts to measure a person's true values, opinions, and feelings. It relates task effectiveness and human satisfaction to a formal managerial development program. This program is unique in that (1) line managers, not academicians or consultants, run the program; (2) a conceptual framework of management (the grid) is utilized; and (3) the entire managerial hierarchy undergoes development, not just one level (for example, first-line supervisors).[24]

SYNOPSIS OF THE PERSONAL-BEHAVIORAL APPROACH

Examination of the various P–B theories presented in this section indicates that similar concepts are discussed but different labels are utilized. For example, the continuum, Likert, the Ohio State researchers, and the Managerial Grid approach each utilize two broadly defined concepts, summarized in Table 12–2.

Each approach in Table 12–2 focuses on two concepts; however, some differences should be emphasized:

1. The continuum theory is based primarily on personal opinions. Although the opinions of the originators are respected, they should be supported with research evidence before much faith can be placed in this particular theory.

2. Likert's supportive theory implies that the most successful leadership style is employee centered. He suggests that we need look no further. However, the critical question is whether the employee-centered style works in all situations. Some studies dispute Likert's claim.

[24]Robert R. Blake and Jane S. Mouton, "Using the Managerial Grid to Ensure MBP," *Organizational Dynamics*, Spring 1974, pp. 50–62.

3.   The Ohio State researchers found that from a production standpoint, the leader with a high initiating-structure score was preferred by the executives of the company. Thus, Likert's claim, or any other claim, that one best leadership approach has been discovered is subject to debate.

4.   Blake and Mouton's Managerial Grid is an intuitively sound proposal. However, only limited research has been reported to test the grid. Also, it is not safe to assume that a 9,9 leader will always be successful. The need is obvious for research testing 9,9 in different settings, with various types of leader-follower situations, and with diverse sets of constraints (e.g., time, monetary resources, technology).

SITUATIONAL THEORIES OF LEADERSHIP

An increasing number of managers are questioning the premise that a particular leadership style is effective in all situations. They believe that a manager behaving as a considerate leader, for example, cannot be assured of effective results in every situation. As noted earlier in this chapter, the Ohio State researchers found that supervisors who scored high on initiating structure were relatively more proficient when managing production rather than nonproduction workers. Thus, evidence exists, even in the literature on personal-behavioral theories, to support the view that effective leadership depends upon the interaction of the situation and the leader's behavior.

The identification of key situational factors and the determination of their relative importance are difficult undertakings. In this section we will review four theories that take into account certain situational factors. They are contingency theory, path–goal theory, leadership-style theory, and tridimensional theory.

CONTINGENCY THEORY

With a considerable body of research evidence behind him, Fred Fiedler developed a dynamic situational, or contingency, theory of leadership.[25] Three important situational dimensions are assumed to influence the leader's effectiveness:

1.   *Leader-member relations:*   The degree of confidence the subordinates have in the leader. It also includes the loyalty shown the leader and the leader's attractiveness.
2.   *Task structure:*   The degree to which the followers' jobs are routine as contrasted with nonroutine.
3.   *Position power:*   The power inherent in the leadership position. It includes the rewards and punishments typically associated with the position, the leader's formal authority (based on ranking in managerial hierarchy), and the support that the leader receives from supervisors and the overall organization.

[25]Fred E. Fiedler, *A Theory of Leadership Effectiveness* (New York: McGraw-Hill, 1967); Fred E. Fiedler and Martin M. Chemers, *Leadership and Effective Management* (Glenview, Ill.: Scott, Foresman, 1975).

Fiedler measures leadership style by evaluating leader responses to what is called a least preferred co-worker (LPC) questionnaire. The leaders who rate their least preferred co-worker in more positive terms (high LPC) are assumed to be people oriented and supportive. Those leaders who give low LPC ratings are more task oriented.

In developing his theory, Fiedler uses the term *situational favorableness,* defined as the degree to which a situation enables a leader to exert influence over the group. In other words, leader-member relations can be either good or poor, task structure can be high or low, and position power can be either strong or weak. The various combinations of these three dimensions can be favorable, moderate, or unfavorable.

According to Fiedler, we should not talk simply about good leaders or poor leaders. He implies that there is no "one best way" to lead. A leader who achieves effectiveness in one situation may or may not be effective in another. The logic is that managers should think about the situation in which a particular leader performs well or badly.

The situational leadership logic is extended in Table 12–3. The examples represent the various combinations of the three dimensions. Furthermore, suggestions on what leadership action to take in the eight situations are indicated.

As suggested by Fiedler in his contingency theory and by Table 12–3, there may be a need to engineer the situation to fit the leader's style. Fiedler offers some pragmatic procedures for improving a leader's relations, task structure, and position power.

1. *Leader-member relations* could be improved by restructuring the leader's group of subordinates to be more compatible in terms of background, education level, technical expertise, or ethnic origin. Note that this would be extremely difficult in a unionized group, since they may assume that this restructuring is a management plan to weaken the union.

2. The *task structure* can be modified in either direction. The task can be made more structured by spelling out the jobs in greater detail. It can be made less structured by providing only general directions for the work that is to be accomplished. Some workers like minimal task structure, while others want detailed and specific task structure.

3. *Position power* can be modified in a number of ways. A leader can be given a higher rank in the organization or more authority to do the job. A memo can be issued indicating the rank change or the authority a leader now possesses. In addition, a leader's reward power can be increased if the organization delegates authority to evaluate the performance of subordinates.

Fiedler's suggestions may not be feasible in every organizational setting. Such factors as unions, technology, time, and costs of changes must be considered. For example, a unionized company that has a highly routine technology and currently is faced with intense competition in new product development may not have the patience, time, and energy to modify the three situational dimensions so that its leaders become more effective.

Interestingly, Fiedler's suggestions do not include leadership training.[26] In fact, he believes that training is not an effective approach, reporting that his

---

[26]Fred E. Fiedler, "The Leadership Game: Matching the Man to the Situation," *Organizational Dynamics,* Winter 1976, pp. 6–16.

TABLE 12–3   Situational Leadership Applied to Eight Situations

Situation	Leader-Member Relations	Task Structure	Position Power	Most Effective Leadership	Reason(s) for Effectiveness
1. First-line supervisor at Ford Motor Co.	Good	High	Strong	Task oriented	Employees respect task expertise, recognize power, and permit supervisor to lead.
2. Chairperson of college department	Good	High	Weak	Task oriented	Faculty member elected because he/she possesses group values. Understands what the group needs to do and pushes for task completion.
3. Sales manager at Procter & Gamble	Good	Low	Strong	Task oriented	Manager has formal authority and power, but salespeople work all over territory. They must have some autonomy because of unstructured nature of job.
4. Committee chairperson	Good	Low	Weak	About equally task and relationship oriented	Chair has little power and must rely on both types of leadership to accomplish job.
5. Middle-level manager at IBM	Poor	High	Strong	Relationship oriented	Manager is not well liked but has power to motivate. Can accomplish more if relationship approach is used.
6. Supervisor at General Mills	Poor	High	Weak	Relationship oriented	Employees know what they're supposed to accomplish. Supervisor is unpopular and has little say-so. More effective to use relationship style instead of creating more hostility.
7. Operating-room nurse supervisor	Poor	Low	Strong	Almost equally task and relationship oriented	Difficult to control unstructured activities through use of power. Because person is unpopular, it is best to use relationship orientation when appropriate and task orientation if necessary.
8. Detective in charge of other detectives working on a case	Poor	Low	Weak	Task oriented	Detective has little power, is not well liked, and case is unstructured. Concentrate on solving the case.

Eight situations and the best leadership style to use for each combination of leader-member relations, task structure, and position power.

own research has shown disappointing results from training. On the average, people with training perform about as well as people with little or no training.

Critics question Fiedler's methodology for measuring LPC, the subjects he used in some of his research (e.g., basketball teams, the Belgian Navy, and students), and the fact that only high and low LPC scores are considered.[27]

[27]An early review article that was critical of the situational, or contingency, model of leadership is George Graen, Kenneth Alvaris, James B. Orris, and Joseph A. Martella, "Contingency Model of Leadership Effectiveness: Antecedent and Evidential Results," *Psychological Bulletin*, October 1970, pp. 285–96.

Despite critics and some glaring shortcomings, Fiedler provided a starting point for situational leadership research.

PATH-GOAL THEORY

A leadership approach that draws heavily on the expectancy theory of motivation is called the path-goal theory.[28] It proposes that the leader is a key individual in bringing about improved subordinate motivation, satisfaction, and performance. The theory suggests that four leadership styles can be and are used:

1. *Directive*. The leader directs, and there is no subordinate participation in decision making.
2. *Supportive*. The leader is friendly and is interested in subordinates as people.
3. *Participative*. The leader asks for, receives, and uses suggestions from subordinates to make decisions.
4. *Achievement oriented*. The leader sets challenging goals for subordinates and shows confidence that they can achieve the goals.

The path-goal theory, unlike Fiedler's theory, suggests that these four styles are used by the *same* leader in different situations.[29]

The important key in this theory is the way the leader affects the "paths" between subordinate behavior and goals. In a sense, the leader is the coach who charts out realistic paths for the team. The leader can affect the paths by:

1. Recognizing and stimulating subordinates' needs for rewards over which the leader has some control.
2. Rewarding goal achievement.
3. Supporting subordinates' efforts to achieve the goals.
4. Helping reduce frustrating barriers to achieving goals.
5. Increasing the opportunities for personal satisfaction for subordinates.

Basically, the leader attempts to help the subordinate find the best path, to set challenging goals, and to remove stressful barriers along the way.

Since the path-goal theory was proposed, there have been a limited number of studies testing its assumptions. One study of 10 different samples of employees found that supportive leadership has its most positive effect on satisfaction for subordinates who work on stressful and frustrating jobs. Another study determined that in three separate organizations, subordinates doing nonroutine job tasks working for achievement-oriented leaders were more confident that their efforts would result in better performance.[30]

---

[28]For two early works, see Martin G. Evans, "The Effect of Supervisory Behavior on the Path-Goal Relationship," *Organizational Behavior and Human Performance,* May 1970, pp. 277–98; Robert J. House, "A Path-Goal Theory of Leader Effectiveness," *Administrative Science Quarterly,* September 1971, pp. 321–38.

[29]Robert J. House and Terence R. Mitchell, "Path-Goal Theory of Leadership," *Journal of Contemporary Business,* Autumn 1974, pp. 81–97.

[30]See Alan C. Filley, Robert J. House, and Steven Kerr, *Managerial Process and Organizational Behavior* (Glenview, Ill.: Scott, Foresman, 1976), pp. 256–60.

LEADERSHIP-STYLE THEORY

Another situational leadership theory is offered by Victor Vroom and Fred Yetton.[31] Their theory attempts to identify the appropriate leadership style for a given set of circumstances, or situations. Five leadership styles are suggested by the Vroom-Yetton theory:

A–I: The leader solves the problem or reaches a decision using available information.

A–II: The leader obtains the information from followers, then decides on the solution to the problem. The leader may or may not inform followers what the problem is in acquiring information from them. The role of followers is to supply information.

C–I: The leader shares the problem with subordinates individually, getting their ideas and suggestions without bringing them together as a group. The leader makes the decision, which may or may not reflect followers' influence.

C–II: The leader shares problems with subordinates as a group, obtaining their ideas and suggestions. The leader then makes a decision that may or may not reflect followers' influence.

G–II: The leader shares a problem with followers as a group. Together the group generates and evaluates alternatives and attempts to reach consensus on a solution. The leader acts as a chairperson. The solution that has the support of the entire group is accepted and implemented.

The letters in the code identify the leadership practice: A stands for autocratic; C stands for consultative; and G stands for group. The appropriate style of leadership (A–I, A–II, C–I, C–II, G–II) depends on seven attributes of the problem situation. The attributes, along with diagnostic questions, are shown in Table 12–4. The leader, if interested in, say, the importance of the quality of a decision (the first problem attribute), could ask himself or herself the diagnostic question: "Is there a quality requirement such that one solution is more likely to be rational than another?"

Vroom and Yetton use a decision tree for determining the best leadership style for a problem situation. Figure 12–4 illustrates how the diagnostic questions are asked from A to G, and where a yes or no answer takes a person along the tree. The person using the decision tree works across it as the questions are answered. In this way, a leader can identify the appropriate situation and leadership style.

The Vroom-Yetton theory is being tested and validated in various settings. One study by Arthur Jago found that managers higher in the management hierarchy tend to use more participative styles than managers lower in the hierarchy.[32] Another study indicated that managers of retail franchises who

---

[31]Victor Vroom and Philip Yetton, *Leadership and Decision Making* (Pittsburgh: University of Pittsburgh Press, 1973). Much of the validation of this model and some of the refinements were initiated by Arthur Jago of the University of Houston.

[32]Arthur G. Jago, "Hierarchical Level Determinants of Participative Leader Behavior" (Ph.D. dissertation, Yale University), *Dissertation Abstracts International* 30 (1977), p. 2921B; Arthur G. Jago and Victor H. Vroom, "An Evaluation of Two Alternatives to the Vroom/Yetton Normative Model," *Academy of Management Journal*, June 1980, pp. 347–55.

TABLE 12-4   Problem Attributes and Diagnostic Questions Developed
by Vroom and Yetton

The Vroom-Yetton theory suggests seven situational factors that the leader needs to consider.

Problem Attributes	Diagnostic Questions
A. The importance of the quality of the decision.	Is there a quality requirement such that one solution is likely to be more rational than another?
B. The extent to which the leader possesses sufficient information/expertise to make a high-quality decision.	Do I have sufficient information to make a high-quality decision?
C. The extent to which the problem is structured.	Is the problem structured?
D. The extent to which acceptance of commitment on the part of subordinates is critical to the effective implementation of the decision.	Is subordinates' acceptance of decision critical to effective implementation?
E. The probability that the leader's autocratic decision will receive acceptance by subordinates.	If I were to make the decision by myself, is it reasonably certain that it would be accepted by my subordinates?
F. The extent to which the subordinates are motivated to attain the organizational goals as represented in the objectives explicit in the statement of the problem.	Do subordinates share the organizational goals to be obtained in solving the problem?
G. The extent to which subordinates are likely to be in conflict over preferred solutions.	Is conflict among subordinates likely in preferred solutions?

more closely conformed to the style identified by the Vroom-Yetton decision tree were more successful and had employees who reported higher amounts of job satisfaction.[33]

TRIDIMENSIONAL LEADER EFFECTIVENESS THEORY

Paul Hersey and Kenneth H. Blanchard (coauthor of *The One Minute Manager*) have identified two leadership behaviors similar to those the Ohio State researchers discovered.[34] The two types of behavior are called task and relationship. *Task behavior* is defined as the extent to which leaders are likely to organize and define the roles of the followers, explain what must be done, and direct the flow of work. *Relationship behavior* is defined as the extent to which leaders are likely to maintain personal relationships with members of their group through being supportive, sensitive, and facilitative.

Since the effectiveness of leaders depends on how their leadership style interrelates with the situation, an effectiveness dimension is added to the task

[33]C. Margerison and R. Glube, "Leadership Decision-Making: An Empirical Test of the Vroom and Yetton Model," *Journal of Management Studies,* February 1979, pp. 45–55.

[34]Paul Hersey and Kenneth H. Blanchard, *Management of Organizational Behavior* (Englewood Cliffs, N.J.: Prentice-Hall, 1988), pp. 116–22.

FIGURE 12–4 The Vroom-Yetton Decision Tree

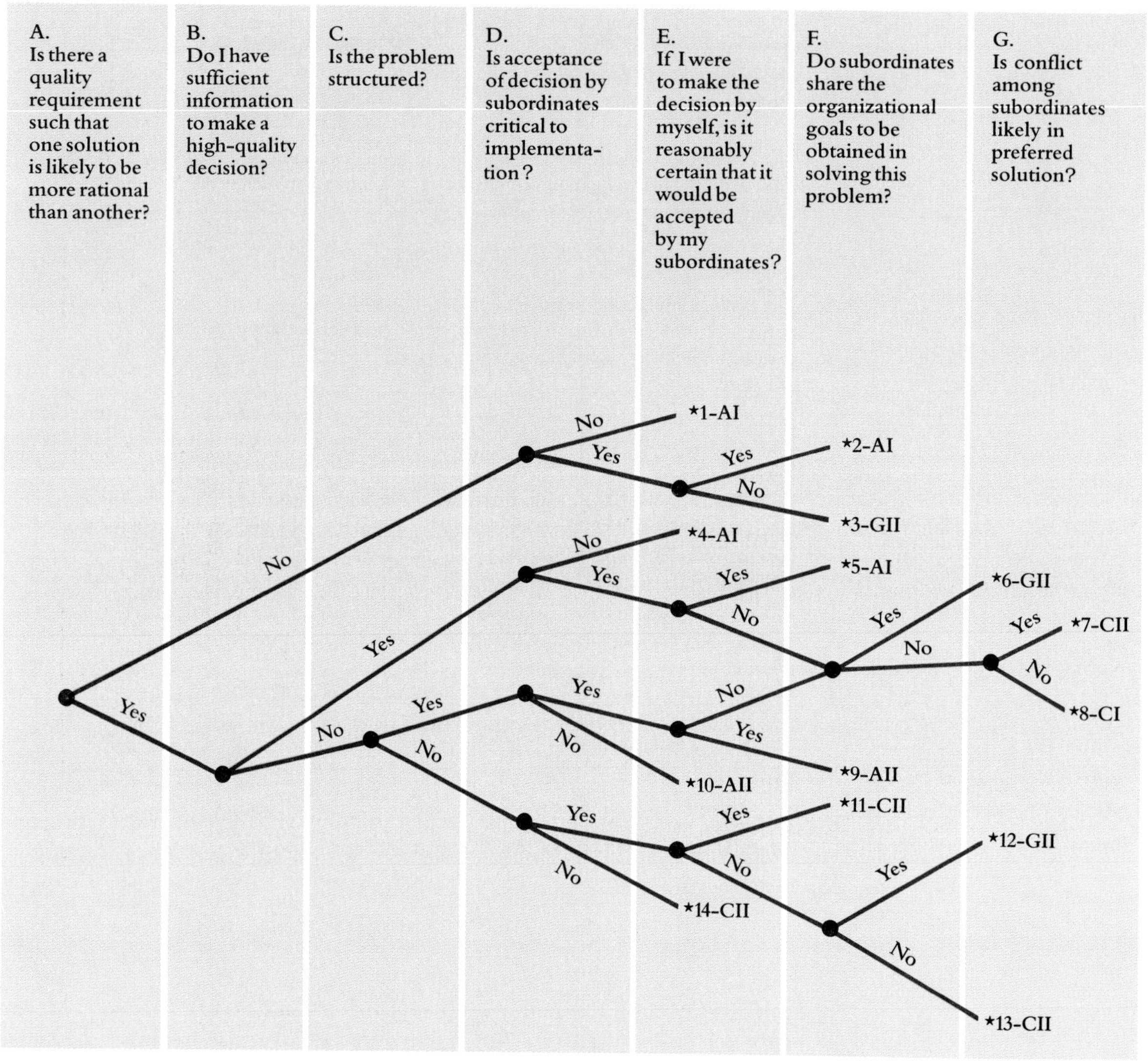
A.
Is there a quality requirement such that one solution is likely to be more rational than another?
B.
Do I have sufficient information to make a high-quality decision?
C.
Is the problem structured?
D.
Is acceptance of decision by subordinates critical to implementa-tion?
E.
If I were to make the decision by myself, is it reasonably certain that it would be accepted by my subordinates?
F.
Do subordinates share the organizational goals to be obtained in solving this problem?
G.
Is conflict among subordinates likely in preferred solution?
*1-AI
*2-AI
*3-GII
*4-AI
*5-AI
*6-GII
*7-CII
*8-CI
*9-AII
*10-AII
*11-CII
*12-GII
*13-CII
*14-CII

The seven situational factors and a decision tree can be used in the selection of a leadership style.

and relationship base. This results, according to Hersey and Blanchard, in the integration of leadership style and situation demands. When the style of a leader is appropriate in a given situation, it is called *effective;* when the style is inappropriate in a given situation, it is called *ineffective.*

Effective and ineffective styles are represented on a continuum, since effectiveness is a matter of degree. Hersey and Blanchard use an effective

FIGURE 12–5   Hersey-Blanchard Tridimensional Leader Effectiveness Model

Whether a leadership style is effective or ineffective will depend on the environment (circumstances) in which the leading will take place.

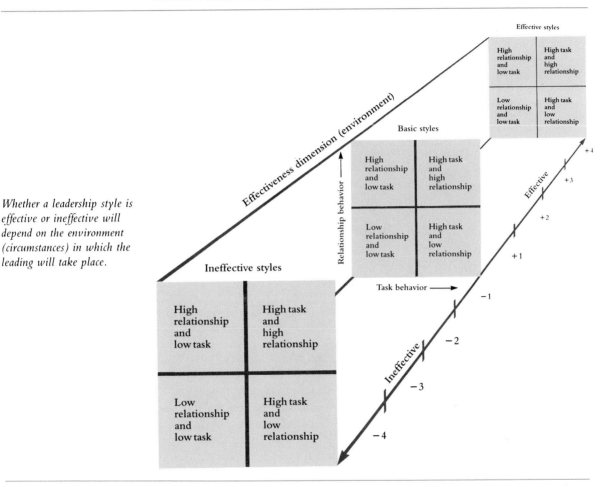

Source: Paul Hersey and Kenneth H. Blanchard, *Management of Organizational Behavior* (Englewood Cliffs, N.J.: Prentice-Hall, 1988), p. 119.

scoring range of +1 to +4 and an ineffective scoring range of −1 to −4. Figure 12–5 illustrates the tridimensional leader effectiveness model.

To determine a leader's preferred style, Hersey and Blanchard use leaders effectiveness and adaptability description (LEAD) questionnaires.[35] First developed for use in training programs, the LEAD-self questionnaire contains 12 leadership situations in which respondents are asked to select from four alternative actions—a high-task/low-relationship behavior, a high-task/high-relationship behavior, a high-relationship/low-task behavior, and a low-relationship/low-task behavior—the style they believe most closely would describe their own behavior in the situation. For example:

[35]Ibid,. pp. 270–75.

Situation	Leader Actions
Your subordinates, usually able to take responsibility, are not responding to your recent redefinition of standards.	A. Allow group involvement in redefining standards but don't push.
	B. Redefine standards and supervise carefully.
	C. Avoid confrontation by pressure.
	D. Incorporate the group recommendations but see that new standards are met.

The LEAD-self yields a self-perception picture of the person's style, style range, and style adaptability. A LEAD-other questionnaire is completed by subordinate(s), superior(s), or associate(s) of the leader(s).

Hersey and Blanchard call specific attention to a leader's range, or flexibility. Each leader differs in the ability to vary his or her style in different situations. Flexible leaders have the potential to be effective in a number of situations. In structured, routine, simple, and established work flow situations, leadership flexibility is not that important (e.g., the labor-intensive General Motor's Maquiladora plants in Juarez, Mexico). However, in unstructured, nonroutine, high environmental change, and fluid work situations, leadership flexibility is at a premium (e.g., the Merck Research and Development laboratory in New Jersey).

The jury is still out on how insightful and valuable the Hersey and Blanchard leader effectiveness model is for managers. To date, a handful of studies have been conducted, and the conclusions reached are rather ambiguous.[36] The popularity of the Hersey and Blanchard explanation and leadership training approach seems to be growing around the world. Bank America, Shell, Tenneco, Caterpillar, IBM, and Xerox are some of the training and assessment users of the tridimensional leader effectiveness model.

Since the magic leadership trait or style was never discovered, researchers and practitioners have turned more to the situational approach. The leader's effectiveness in today's work organization is considered to be influenced significantly by various situational factors identified by Fiedler, Vroom and Yetton, Hersey and Blanchard, and others.

COMPARISON

There certainly are a growing number of situational theories of leadership. However, each approach adds insight into a manager's understanding of leadership. Table 12–5 contains a brief explanation of the three popular leadership theories that stress the importance of situational variables. Although the Fiedler theory has the largest research base and has been around for years, the Vroom-Yetton theory appears to offer the most promise for managerial training. At present, there is not enough evidence available to say how effective training is in applying the Vroom-Yetton theory to managerial problem solving and decision situations.

---

[36]Robert P. Vecchio, "Situational Leadership Theory: An Examination of a Perspective Theory," *Journal of Applied Psychology*, August 1987, pp. 444–51.

TABLE 12-5	Comparison of Popular Situational Theories of Leadership			
Points of Comparison	**Contingency Theory (Fiedler)**	**Path-Goal Theory (House)**	**Vroom-Yetton Theory***	**Hersey-Blanchard Theory**
1. Theme	No best style. Leader success determined by the interaction of environment and leader personality variables.	Most successful leaders are those who increase subordinate motivation by charting out and clarifying paths to effective performance.	Successful leadership style varies with situation. Leader can learn how to recognize requirements of situation and how to fit style to meet these requirements.	Successful leaders adapt their styles to the demands of a situation.
2. Leadership styles (range of choices)	Autocratic or democratic.	Directive to achievement.	Autocratic to participative.	Task behavior to relationship behavior.
3. Research base (number of supportive studies)	Large, in many settings: military, educational, industrial. Some contradictory results.	Moderate to low. Generally supportive.	Low but increasing. Generally supportive.	Low but generally supportive.
4. Application value for managers	Moderate to low: leaders can't generally be trained.	Moderate.	High: leaders can be trained.	Moderate but increasing.

*The contributions of Arthur Jago to the refinement and testing of this model have led some to refer to this approach as the Vroom-Yetton-Jago theory.

Theme, leadership style, research base, and application value are important points of comparison in the four major situational theories of leadership.

SELECTED FACTORS INFLUENCING LEADERSHIP EFFECTIVENESS

We have defined leadership as the ability to persuade others to seek defined objectives enthusiastically. We also have identified three approaches to the study of leadership: trait, personal-behavioral, and situational. The trait and personal-behavioral approaches indicate that effective leadership depends on a number of variables such as intelligence, decisiveness, and style. No one trait or style is best for all situations.

PERCEPTUAL ACCURACY

McGregor indicated how perception plays a role in leadership. Managers who misperceive employees may miss the opportunity to achieve optimal results. If you feel someone is lazy, you tend to treat him or her as a lazy person. Thus, managerial perceptual accuracy is extremely important. It is important in each of the situational models.[37]

[37]Douglas McGregor, "On Visionary Leadership," *New Management*, Winter 1985, pp. 46–52.

What is the analogy between being a parent and being a leader?

Background, Experience, and Personality

The Leader. The leader's background and experience will affect the choice of style. A person who has had success in being relationship oriented probably will continue the use of this style. Likewise, a leader who doesn't trust followers and who has structured the task for years will use a close supervision or autocratic style.

Despite Fiedler's opinion, the majority of leadership researchers believe that what has been used can be altered. That is, a leader who perceives that his or her preferred style is not working well can change it accordingly. Of course, some individuals are so rigid in their preferences and personality makeup that alteration is extremely difficult.

The Follower. Followers are an important factor in the leader's choice of style. As stated earlier, the leadership job is a mutual-sharing process. For example, a leader with technically proficient followers is best advised to be more participative and less autocratic. On the other hand, inexperienced, recent hires with a minimum of work knowledge may prefer a leader who structures the task and is firm. Then an autocratic or job-centered leader works best.

Hersey and Blanchard stress the notion of the follower's maturity. They define *maturity* as the ability and willingness of people to take responsibility for directing their own behavior. The term has two components: job maturity and psychological maturity. *Job maturity* is the knowledge, skills, and experience to perform without close supervision. *Psychological maturity* is the willingness to do the job.

The astute leader attempts to determine the background and maturity of followers, which may signal the style that is most appropriate. In any event, the followers must be given serious consideration in making a judgment about which leadership style can achieve the desired results.

SUPERIOR'S EXPECTATIONS AND STYLE

Superiors are comfortable with and prefer a particular leadership style. A superior who prefers a job-centered, autocratic approach encourages followers to adopt a similar approach. Imitation of the superior's example is a powerful force in shaping leadership styles.

Since superiors possess various power bases, their expectations are important. For example, many firms seek to improve the relationship skills of first-level supervisors and send these managers to an off-the-job training program. Research indicates that during and immediately after these programs, supervisors' relationship skills are improved. However, soon after returning to the job, the learned skills often disappear. Why? A reasonable explanation is that the supervisors' superiors prefer more task-oriented behaviors instead of relationship-oriented behaviors.

TASK UNDERSTANDING

The task of a group or an individual refers to what is to be done on a job. Tasks are imposed by management or self-generated by the employee. A task has physical properties and behavioral features. The physical properties are the stimuli surrounding the job; these stimuli may be a set of instructions from management or the way the employee interprets the job. The behavioral properties are the requirements or kinds of responses expected of a person doing the task.

The task may be very structured, such as the job duties of a worker on an assembly line. The worker is instructed by management what to do with the products being processed. The goal or requirement of this type of job is to produce as many units as possible of good quality.

Other tasks, such as those of a research and development engineer or planning expert, may be unstructured. In these jobs, the goals are not easily defined. Thus, the leader may have to work hard to display "paths" and goals for the employees.

Leaders must be able to assess correctly the tasks their followers are performing. In an unstructured task situation, directive or autocratic leadership may be very inappropriate; the employees need guidelines, freedom to act, and the necessary resources to accomplish the task. Leaders must properly diagnose the tasks of followers so that proper leadership style choices are made. Because of this requirement, a leader must have some technical knowledge of the job and its requirements.

PEER EXPECTATIONS

Leaders form relationships with other leaders. These peer relationships are used to exchange ideas, opinions, experiences, and suggestions. A leader's peers can provide support and encouragement for various leadership behaviors, thus influencing the leader in the future. Often, for example, when peers inform a leader that he was too easy on an uncooperative follower, the leader

FIGURE 12–6   Selected Factors that Influence Leadership Effectiveness

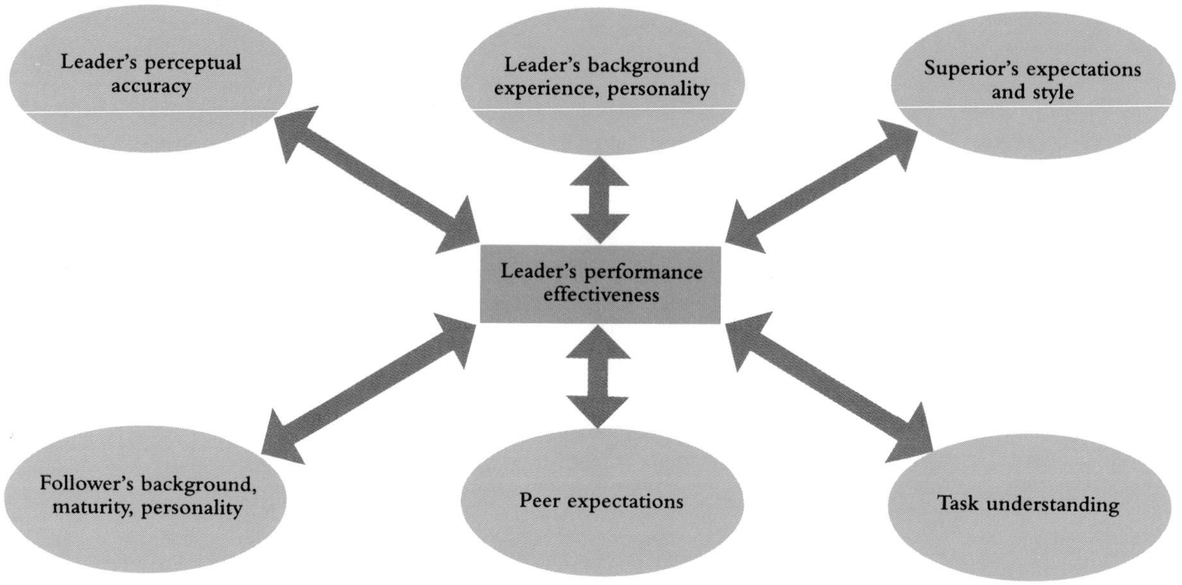

Leaders must diagnose themselves and the total leadership environment in order to effect good leadership.

may respond by becoming very harsh and restrictive. Peers are an important source of comparison and information in making leadership style choices and modifications.

INTEGRATING INFLUENCE FACTORS

Figure 12–6 integrates these six important factors influencing leadership effectiveness. Leadership also influences these factors. Although many other factors that are not presented also influence leadership effectiveness, these six seem to be as important as any and serve to illustrate concisely the reciprocal nature of leadership.

The emphasis in Figure 12–6 is on leaders' ability to diagnose themselves and their total leadership environment. Perhaps if leadership training programs are used, they should stress diagnostic skills. But it should not be concluded that individuals can be trained easily to accurately diagnose work situations and to develop appropriate leadership abilities. This type of training difficulty was summed up by Fiedler:

> Industrial psychologists and personnel men typically view the executive's position as fixed and immutable and the individual as highly plastic and trainable. When we think of improving leadership performance, we generally think first of training the leader. Yet, we know all too well from our experience with psychotherapy, our attempts to rehabilitate prison inmates, drug addicts or juvenile delinquents—not to mention our

difficulties with rearing our own progeny—that our ability to change personality has its limitations.[38]

If leaders are to become skilled at diagnoses and flexible enough to adapt leadership style to the circumstances at hand, patience is essential. The organization must be willing to plan and to fund development programs that are time-consuming. The approach we are suggesting is not applicable in those instances where changing the situation is less costly than changing the leader.

The clear message being received in executive suites around the United States is that America is losing its competitive edge in manufacturing, electronics, steel, and some service industries. There is a consensus that we must dramatically revise many managerial, industrial, and leadership practices to remain competitive in the international arena. Managers and leaders must be part of the rededication to become more competitive. "Made in the U.S.A." often signals poor quality.[39]

American management is at a crossroads in terms of leadership. Managers must be open to new styles of managing, new methods of leadership, and new competitive practices and procedures that are emerging from other countries. In the past, when little competition existed in world markets, American managers tended to ignore how others in the world planned, organized, controlled, and directed work, people, and operations.[40] Ignoring positive examples of leadership makes little sense today. Managing- and leading-as-usual strategies are not going to solve international marketplace, global relationship, and foreign competition problems.

Consumers and clients throughout the world are demanding quality, value, and service. It does not matter if a person lives in the United States, Singapore, Italy, New Zealand, South Korea, Kenya, or Poland.[41] As consumers, we write with Cross, Waterman, Mont Blanc, or Scripto pencils or travel with Samsonite, Gucci, or Vuitton suitcases because of the kind of value we could afford and desire. At the cash register, the country of origin of the product or service is becoming less and less important. The fact that a "British" sneaker by Reebok (now owned by an American firm) was made in Korea is becoming less and less important. Customers care only about quality, price, design, value, and appeal.

Learning how the best international managers perform their jobs needs to be a top priority for improving quality, price, design, value, and appeal of products. A few examples of the "best" firms around the world will reveal some situational leadership principles that could be applied on the job.

Two American Superleaders.   A cursory reading of management writings might suggest that Japan has the answers for leadership; there are enough Japanese leadership success stories to fill books. The Japanese successes have triggered a growing interest in finding effective American leaders. And one

---

[38]Fiedler, *A Theory of Leadership,* p. 247.

[39]Richard D. Lamm, "Crisis: The Uncompetitive Society," in *Global Competitiveness,* ed. Martin K. Starr (New York: W. W. Norton, 1988), p. 14.

[40]Thomas N. Gilmore, *Making a Leadership Change* (San Francisco: Jossey-Bass, 1988).

[41]Keniche Ohmae, "The Global Logic of Strategic Allowances," *Harvard Business Review,* March–April 1989, pp. 143–54.

doesn't have to go very far to locate effective, astute, and powerful American leaders.

Louis Gerstner, now president of RJR Nabisco, was president of American Express (AMEX) from 1985 to 1989. He was a consultant at McKinsey Corporation before joining AMEX.[42] He believes that decentralization, delegation, and employee participation in decision making are the new-generation management techniques. Instead of requiring less leadership, these behaviorally oriented approaches require more. This requires leaders who can create a mission, enthusiasm, and most of all a clear vision. Under Gerstner, AMEX no longer expected cradle-to-grave employees. He wanted individuals to contribute to AMEX but not to feel locked in or obligated to stay when they are not being challenged. He only reviewed salaries once every two years. The annual bonus, which can increase or decrease based on performance, was significant in Gerstner's approach at AMEX.

Richard Mahoney, president of Monsanto, is another of the new breed of American leader. He is dedicated to "firing up" his employees. When he took over, Monsanto's spirit, environment, and return on investment were OK but not outstanding. Copying the Japanese was a fashionable way to turn a company around. Mahoney opted instead for an approach that stressed "ownership" from within. He wanted to convince his employees that he needed their brainpower as much or more than their muscle power. He eliminated layers of foremen, supervisors, and quality inspectors. Plant workers were put in charge. They received financial reports, unheard of prior to Mahoney's push for ownership from within. Now, workers on the line know what their section's profit or loss is at the end of the month.

Mahoney has also instituted team competition. The entire agriculture division in St. Louis had 60 teams vie for the best production plan. The event was billed as the "tournament of champions." Another leader-directed change is to give workers contact with customers.[43] Product design teams listen to customers. The direct contact is refreshing and revealing.

The ownership feeling at Monsanto has been legitimized by Mahoney. He encourages it, rewards it, and practices what he preaches. Self-motivation has become a reality. Getting the best out of workers does not come only with a Japanese approach; it also comes from a Monsanto practice that is working.

A Korean Superleader.   The microwave oven was invented in the United States four decades ago.[44] It became one of the world's best-selling appliances because of the South Koreans. At Samsung, a young engineer named Yun Soo Chu used leadership to show the way. Chu was given the assignment to take the American invention and design it for the world marketplace. He knew he was starting behind American and Japanese producers. However, he felt that Korea's wage workers and a willingness to wait for a payback were his advantages.

[42]"A Work-Out for Corporate America," *Economist*, January 7, 1989, pp. 55–58.

[43]"No Blues on the Mississippi," *Economist*, January 7, 1989, p. 56.

[44]Ira Magaziner and Mark Patinkin, *The Silent War* (New York: Random House, 1989), pp. 21–44.

Chu's plan was to organize a team. In the United States, such a team would be headed by product designers; factory engineers would come second. At Samsung, production is king. So Chu merged his product and factory people so that design was accomplished with manufacturing in mind. Chu analyzed the situation, considered the maturity of his employees, developed a team-oriented plan, and took decisive action. He learned what the world wanted and built an assembly line that could do the job on time. Today, Samsung manufactures 80,000 microwave ovens a week.

Chu and his team were able to produce a high-quality microwave at a cost America's biggest appliance makers such as General Electric (GE) could no longer match (assembly-line labor cost at GE is $8 per hour; at Samsung, 63 cents per hour). Thus, GE has entered into an agreement with Samsung. The Korean firm provides GE with large and medium-size microwave ovens. Samsung has 250 separate models of microwave ovens that it produces for 20 countries. Yun Soo Chu is hard at work, ready to lead Samsung into other foreign markets. Chu has a map of Sweden on his desk. Samsung has opened markets there, and Chu is sending his engineers to Sweden so that they learn what the Swedes want to purchase.

A European Superleader.   Jacques Delors, the French president of the European Economic Community (EEC), is a bold leader who has displayed many important leadership traits. Delors is the architect of the plan to bring Europe together as a major economic force by 1992. His vision, persistence, and decision-making style helped design the 1992 EEC plan.[45]

Delors leads the EEC council, consisting of member states Belgium, Denmark, France, West Germany, Greece, Ireland, Italy, Luxembourg, the Netherlands, Portugal, Spain, and the United Kingdom. The council has developed a 1992 internal market plan that considers technical barriers to free trade across borders, capital markets, services, transportation systems, and legal issues. The 1992 agreement will mean the free movement of people, services, capital, and goods within the EEC. Emphasizing his vision that Europe must be economically strong, Delors has stated that without a powerful Europe, "all television sets in 15 years would be Japanese, all programming American, and all the viewers European." Through his vision and charisma, Delors has instilled European pride. Europeans now believe that they will be the equals of the Americans and the Japanese when competing internationally.

Can one man be responsible for such a change in a continent's self-esteem? He is not the sole reason for Europe's resurgence, but Jacques Delors has shown many of the leadership qualities discussed in this chapter. He is task oriented, experienced, intelligent, and a very decisive decision-maker, and he loves to work with people.

Effective leaders can be found throughout the world. Americans and Japanese do not have a corner on the leadership market. The leaders in 1990 will have to work as situational detectives. That is, they will have to understand themselves, their followers, the task, and goals that must be accomplished.

[45]Tim Dickson, "Delors Leads E.C. toward 1992," *Europe,* January–February 1989, pp. 32–33.

SUMMARY OF KEY POINTS

- Leadership and management are not synonymous terms. Leadership is the ability to persuade others to seek defined objectives enthusiastically.

- Leaders possess five potential power bases to influence followers: coercive, reward, legitimate, expert, and referent.

- McGregor believed that a manager's attitudes and assumptions explain his or her behavior toward followers. These attitudes were categorized as Theory X and Theory Y. The attitude-behavior relationship generates a self-fulfilling prophecy. If a manager assumes a person is a winner, then the manager will treat the person as a winner.

- Numerous attempts to study and understand leadership have been made. Three major approaches are trait, personal-behavioral, and situational.

- Trait theories attempt to discover various traits that describe or predict leadership success. Some of the more important traits are intelligence, self-assurance, and decisiveness.

- Personal-behavioral theories contend that leaders may be classified by personal qualities or behavioral patterns. Continuums of leadership, two-dimensional models, and managerial grids are used to explain leadership in personal-behavioral terms.

- The situational factors that influence leadership are given prominence in Fiedler's contingency theory, the House path-goal theory, the Vroom-Yetton theory, and the Hersey-Blanchard tridimensional theory.

- Leaders exist throughout the world. Some common traits among international leaders seem to be confidence, vision, and decisiveness.

DISCUSSION AND REVIEW QUESTIONS

1. How would a leader assess the maturity of her or his followers?

2. Does the Vroom-Yetton approach to leadership suggest that leaders can or cannot be trained to improve their effectiveness? Explain.

3. What role is the leader expected to play in the path-goal leadership theory?

4. Why is the diagnostic skill of the leader so vital to the situational approach to leadership?

5. Why is decisiveness such a prominent characteristic in international leaders?

6. Explain how the three situational dimensions discussed by Fiedler can be modified in an organization.

7. Which of your personal traits probably influence or will influence the style of leadership you usually use?

8. What other factors not included in Figure 12–6 are important in achievement of leadership effectiveness?

9. Can a leader be trained to use the four traits discovered by Bennis in his research?

10. Why should American leadership techniques not be accepted carte blanche in Canada or Spain?

ADDITIONAL REFERENCES

Bass, B. M. "Leadership: Good, Better, Best." *Organizational Dynamics*, Winter 1985, pp. 26–40.

Bennis, W., and **B. Nanus.** *Leaders' Strategies for Taking Charge.* New York: Harper & Row, 1985.

Blanchard, K. H. *Leadership and the One Minute Manager.* New York: Morrow, 1985.

Blanchard, K. H., and **S. Johnson.** *The One Minute Manager.* New York: Morrow, 1982.

Boyatzis, R. E. *The Competent Manager: A Model for Effective Performance.* New York: John Wiley & Sons, 1982.

Conger, J. A.; R. N. Kanugo; and **Associates.** *Charismatic Leadership.* San Francisco: Jossey-Bass, 1988.

Fiedler, F. E. *New Approaches to Effective Leadership.* New York: John Wiley & Sons, 1987.

Hatakeyama, Y. "The Unsung Hero of Japanese Management: The Middle Manager." *Management Review,* July 1982, p. 33.

Jago, A. G., and **V. H. Vroom.** "Sex Differences in the Incidence and Evaluation of Participative Leader Behavior." *Journal of Applied Psychology,* December 1982, pp. 776–83.

Janis, I. L. *Crucial Decisions.* New York: Free Press, 1989.

Kanter, D. L., and **P. H. Mirvis.** *The Cynical Americans.* San Francisco: Jossey-Bass, 1989.

Kraar, L. "Japan's Gung-Ho U.S. Car Plants." *Fortune,* January 30, 1989, pp. 98–108.

Maccoby, M. *The Leader.* New York: Simon & Schuster, 1981.

McClelland, D. C., and **R. E. Boyatzis.** "Leadership Motive Pattern and Long-Term Success in Management." *Journal of Applied Psychology,* December 1982, pp. 737–43.

Miller, S. S. "Make Your Plant Manager's Job Manageable." *Harvard Business Review,* January–February 1983, pp. 69–74.

Rehder, R. R.; R. W. Hendry; and **M. M. Smith.** "Nummi: The Best of Both Worlds?" *Management Review,* December 1985, pp. 36–41.

Thompson, P. H.; K. L. Kirkham; and **J. Dixon.** "Warning: The Fast Track May Be Hazardous to Organizational Health." *Organizational Dynamics,* Spring 1985, pp. 21–33.

Yukl, G. M. *Leadership in Organizations.* Englewood Cliffs, N.J.: Prentice-Hall, 1981.

CASE 12–1   A Leadership Team at Mennen Company: Will It Work?

Mennen Company is a privately held toiletries manufacturer attempting to make the transition from management by family owners to management by outsiders—professionals. Mennen, for the first time in its 103-year history, is being led by a chairman and chief executive officer, L. Donald Horne, and a president, Harold Danenberg, who have no blood ties to the Mennen family.

The company has been plagued in the past by conflict between the family and top-level professional managers. Three chief operating officers quit or were fired during one eight-year period. Pointing up the sensitivity of what is happening at Mennen, Horne and Danenberg have embarked on an aggressive, growth-oriented strategy that appears to clash with the cautious, take-few-risks management style established under three generations of Mennen chief executive officers. There is another complication to the Horne and Danenberg aggressive-team approach in the presence of G. Jeff Mennen, 41, who has held the job of vice chairman since his father retired.

Based in Morristown, New Jersey, the company was one of the nation's pioneer marketers of consumer packaged goods. It helped break down American male inhibitions about using sweet-smelling aftershave lotions and colognes, and it was the first to sell shaving cream in a tube and talcum in sifter cans. But despite these feats, it was never in the league of Procter & Gamble, Johnson & Johnson, or Colgate-Palmolive. Mennen's profit margins consistently have lagged behind its competitors'. Mennen was satisfied with making a comfortable living and not dominating any market. Family-run companies often have this kind of philosophy of management and success.

In addition to a shortage of new products and a sluggish growth record, Mennen consistently has had sour relations with retailers. Operating inefficiencies, poor promotional efforts, and little shelf display creativity or enthusiasm by Mennen have helped create this situation.

The Horne and Danenberg team has moved in with new products (Hawk and Millionaire men's fragrances), increased the advertising budget by $20 million annually, and introduced jazzier store displays. They also have weeded out some marginal products such as Balm Barr, a women's cocoa-based skin product.

The Horne and Danenberg style of leading Mennen can be described as aggressive, risk taking, and fast moving. These characteristics are much different than the conservative, slow, limited-growth orientation previously used by Mennen's.

QUESTIONS FOR ANALYSIS

1. The Horne and Danenberg leadership style is described as being loved by some and totally hated by others at Mennen—there is no middle ground. In your opinion, why is this the case?
2. Using the Ohio State leadership terminology, how would you describe the Mennen leadership approach prior to the arrival of Horne and Danenberg?

CASE 12–2   The Troubled Hospital Superintendent

Tyler Medical Center consisted of four buildings, had 475 patient beds, and employed 1,850 people. It was known throughout the state as a quality medical institution and a good place for medical researchers and interns to work. The Board of Trustees of the hospital relied heavily on the judgment of the superintendent of the hospital, Don Gloversmen, regarding hospital administration.

Tyler was organized around six functionally defined areas. Each area had a head who reported to Don. The areas were:

1. Medical Services.
2. Nursing Services.
3. Accounting Services.
4. Dietary Services.
5. Plant and Housekeeping Services.
6. Pharmaceutical Services.

Don, as superintendent, was the only person in the hospital who had legitimate power to make decisions concerning administrative matters. He had to handle complaints and requests from administrators in each of the areas. Two that were extremely difficult to work with were Medical Services and Nursing Services.

Don analyzed each of the personnel components of these units:

Medical Services: Medical doctors and laboratory technicians. Included are such individuals as physician in charge of neurology, physician in charge of pediatrics, director of surgery, director of clinical laboratories, and director of anesthesiology. The medical doctors are largely male, while the technicians are split about evenly between male and female.

Nursing Services: Primarily females in charge of providing nursing care at bedside and staffing operating rooms, delivery rooms, and nurseries. The nursing group and staff include approximately 975 employees.

Don communicated in most instances with the administrators in these two service areas. He found that his leadership style of being frank, open, and direct worked better with the Medical Services heads than with the Nursing Service heads. He wanted to be the best superintendent the hospital ever had but found that his approach of being the same kind of leader for all the people he worked with was not effective.

Don reached the conclusion that he was not effective in his relationship with the nursing administrators. They seemed to be hostile toward him and the other functional areas, especially the Medical Service area. In addition, a number of patients had complained about rudeness by the nurses. The strain in his relationship with Nursing Services always seemed to peak at the monthly meeting of nursing administrators.

Each month, the 42 nursing supervisors met with Don. In these sessions, he attempted to ascertain how the nursing area was performing. The nursing administrators complained that no standards for assessing performance were used to determine effectiveness. They also complained that they were being watched closely, while Medical Services never had discussions with the superintendent about performance.

After last month's disruptive and volatile meeting, Don decided to look at the problem. He assumed that there might be a serious flaw in his leadership ability. He also thought about what he had read about the situational approach to leadership.

QUESTIONS FOR ANALYSIS

1. What are some of the causes of Don's problem with the nursing administrators?
2. As a superintendent in Tyler Medical Center, would it be necessary to consider situational leadership theories? Why?
3. What kind of modification in the three situational dimensions—leadership-member relations, task structure, and position power—could aid Don in improving his relationship with Nursing Services?

EXPERIENTIAL EXERCISE

LEADERSHIP SKILLS: SETTING THE TONE FOR PROBLEM SOLVING

Purpose

The purpose of this exercise is to demonstrate an effective approach to problem solving and to indicate the attitudes and skills required of a leader.

The Exercise in Class

Scenario.   The assembly-line job is an arrangement in which a crew of seven, working in a circle, assembles an electronic generator in a manufactur-

EXHIBIT 1   Assembly Work Area: Circle 3

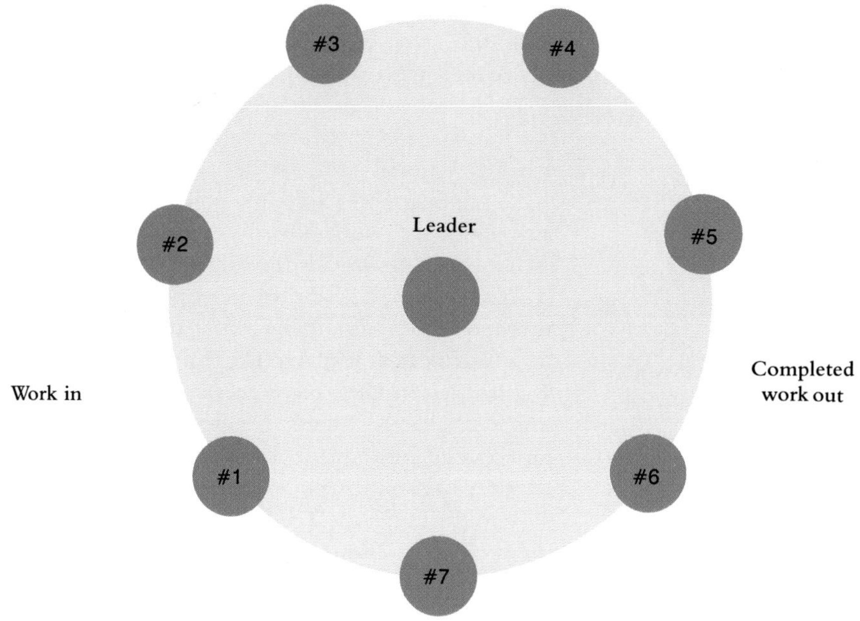

ing plant. Each person does a particular job and sends the unit to the next person, and so forth. There are eight such assembly circles, each one with a supervisor. The average production per day of the circles is as follows:

1. 83	5. 80
2. 78	6. 76
3. 64	7. 60
4. 78	8. 70

The total department production is dependent on the output of the eight assembly circles. The desired total output for the eight circles is 675 units.

The assembly line is simple and requires little formal training. The crew members must be alert, have good finger dexterity and eyesight, and be in good physical condition to keep up with the pace. The materials for each crew member are located in bins right next to the workstation. The stations (1–7) are of equal difficulty, and pay for all crew members is based on hourly rates.

Exhibit 1 illustrates the assembly work area. The assembly-line members work for the leader and report directly to him or her. There seems to be a bottleneck at station 3 of circle 3. The crew member there is 59 years old with 33 years of service. The emphasis on improvement of output has pointed out his or her deficiencies.

Activity.   The above scenario will be acted out by the class. Eight students are needed to play the roles: one supervisor and seven crew members. Role players can be male or female in any combination. Students not participating as role players will serve as observers. Teams of three to four observers should be established as consulting teams. The assembly line should be recreated as closely as possible to the circular arrangement in Exhibit 1.

1. The class should individually read the instructions.
2. The role players should be given their role-play instructions (instructor will have them) and individually read them carefully. Only their roles should be given to them.
3. Observers should read the instructions for observers. The observer-consultants will be asked to come up with a feasible solution.
4. The *crew members,* after reading and learning the role sheets, discuss in front of the class and with the supervisor a solution to the production problem.
5. Observers should watch and listen to the role-play, which should cover about 20 to 25 minutes. The instructor will stop the role-play at a natural stopping point.
6. After the role-play, the observers/consultants and crew and supervisor discuss solutions.
7. The observers should answer questions on the instruction sheets that were issued to them.

The Learning Message

Notice how the supervisor's style and interactions in the first few minutes will determine the quality of the solution. The leader will set the tone and direction for the exercise.

13

COMMUNICATION

LEARNING OBJECTIVES

After completing Chapter 13, you should be able to:

Define
each element in the process of communication.

Describe
communication in organizations.

Discuss
nonverbal communication and its importance
in organizations.

Compare
the situations in which an informal and a formal
channel of communication would be utilized.

Identify
the major reasons why communications
break down.

L'eggs, Godiva Communicate Using Laptop Computers

Imagine a team of distribution route representatives that can keep track of several product lines at once and tell you at the end of the day exactly how many of each line should be on the next day's truck. Also imagine a group of field representatives that can check on the status of a customer's order, quote prices, and have the order at the factory before they leave the client's office. Too good to be true? Sara Lee's L'eggs Division and Campbell Soup's Godiva Chocolatier enjoy this advanced communication and flexibility through the use of high-powered, portable, laptop computers.

At L'eggs, delivery trucks were getting too large, carrying a lot of inventory to each site to handle the unknown potential volume. After reps were given portable computers that could track the inventory needs of the locations, managers could effectively estimate customers' needs on subsequent deliveries. Now L'eggs carries inventory "just in time" rather than "just in case."

At Godiva, laptop PCs mean that their field reps are no longer chained to an office. They can walk into a client's office with up-to-date information and prices; they can review information stored from previous meetings about or with the client; they can handle budgeting, forecasting, and electronic mail from any office, home, or hotel with a telephone jack. For Godiva's reps, this mobility has several advantages: First, they have tools to solve their own problems and have a greater "ownership" over the information they use. Rather than order takers, they are deal-makers. Second, having more up-to-date customer information puts them on the same level as the buyers. Being able to sell the most products while limiting the risk of excess inventory to spoil, they gain confidence in the eyes of the buyer. Third, they feel more important. To Godiva, this is just as important as the productivity benefits. A $5,000 laptop computer gives the representatives status and prestige in the eyes of the customers and an improved outlook about their jobs and their company.

Although L'eggs and Godiva have transferred some power and influence to the inventory and field representatives through the use of portable computers, they have also increased the quality of communication. This allows them to better understand and meet market demands and changes. This innovative approach to organizational communication illustrates the importance of communication.

Source: Adapted from Jon Pepper, "Sweet Success in Sales Automation," *Working Woman*, April 1989. pp. 59–62.

Managing people effectively requires an understanding of several behavioral factors. Communication is surely one of them. Surveys clearly show that communication is one of the most vital skills that workers, managerial and nonmanagerial, need.[1] Managers rarely work with "things" but rather with "information about things." Thus, communication pervades the management functions of planning, organizing, and controlling.

But what is communication? How can we communicate with each other? And how do we know when we have? "Telling isn't teaching, and listening isn't learning." This old adage known to instructors expresses in a few words the essence of poor and ineffective communication. In the context of our discussion, it can be restated as: "Writing isn't communicating, and reading isn't understanding." Why not? There are many reasons for ineffective communication. The one cited most often is that we tend to think in too-simple terms about this very complicated process. To communicate something to someone involves the emotional, psychological, and mental characteristics of both persons, as well as the technical characteristics of the medium used to communicate. The understanding that the teller intended to impart may be far different from what was actually imparted to the listener. Effective communication is so important for the effective management of people that we hope that our discussion of what it is and how it is achieved "communicates" fully its complexity.

THE IMPORTANCE OF COMMUNICATION

The following statements, or ones very similar, are heard on a regular basis in most organizations: "The purchase order has not been sent because you never said it was a rush request." "I really never thought she was serious about resigning." "When the president says as soon as possible, he means now." In these and similar situations, we often hear, "What we have here is a failure to communicate." That statement communicates clearly to everyone, because all of us have faced situations in which the problem was poor communication. Whether it be on a person-to-person basis, nation to nation, in large organizations, or in small groups, breakdowns in communication seem to be pervasive.

Sometimes, the failure to communicate has life-and-death consequences. The explosion of the *Challenger* and the loss of its seven-member crew in 1986 was partly due to a communication problem. The engineers feared the integrity of the O-rings (seals), but this information never got to key NASA officials. And a communication breakdown cost the lives of 100 people when a walkway collapsed in the lobby of the Hyatt Regency Hotel in Kansas City. Subcontractors changed the walkway design without consulting a specification manual. The manual pointed out the load that the walkway could bear.

It is difficult to find an aspect of a manager's job that does not have the potential for communication breakdowns. Problems arise when directives are misunderstood, rumors spread, informal remarks by an executive are misinterpreted or distorted, or casual kidding in a work group leads to anger. Thus,

---

[1]Therese R. Welter, "Readin' and Writin' and . . . ," *Industry Week,* January 16, 1989, pp. 33–34.

the real issue is not whether managers communicate but whether they do it effectively or ineffectively. Everything a manager does or (in many cases) doesn't do communicates something to some person or group. The only question is: With what effect?

What can be communicated and the effect is illustrated by Mellon Bank's recent annual report. It used photos of four successful managers and reports, in sequence, how each spends time at work.[2] One manager is shown at his desk at 7 A.M. reviewing documents, at 5 P.M. meeting with a client, and at 8 P.M. studying more documents. Another senior bank officer is shown starting the day at 7:30 A.M. and going home at 8 P.M. Each of the other two have long, 11-hour days. What was the message? The nine-to-fiver will not succeed at Mellon. The company wanted to communicate that effort at Mellon counts. Would the sequence of photos communicate this to you?

UNDERSTANDING THE PROCESS OF COMMUNICATION

Communication is *the transmission of common understanding through the use of symbols*. The term is derived from the Latin *communis,* meaning "common." In other words, unless a common understanding results from the transmission of symbols (verbal or nonverbal), there is no communication.

Numerous examples of communication in international settings illustrate the importance of understanding. For example, in restaurants in the United States, a waiter is called "Sir" or "Waiter," and customers don't snap their fingers. In Europe, a customer clinks a glass with a spoon to get attention. In Singapore, customers extend their right hand, palm down, and rapidly open and close their fingers.[3]

ELEMENTS OF COMMUNICATION

Figure 13–1 presents our model and the key elements of communication.[4] It identifies the basic elements of communication as the communicator, perception/interpretation, encoding, the message, the channel, decoding, the receiver, feedback, and noise. In simple terms, an individual or group (the communicator) has an idea, message, or understanding to transmit to another individual or group (the receiver). To transmit the idea, the communicator must translate the idea into a meaningful form (encoding) and send the message by verbal, nonverbal, or written means (the channel). The message is received through the senses of the receiver and translated into a form meaningful to the receiver (decoded). With a nod of the head, a facial expression, or some action, the receiver acknowledges whether understanding

---

[2]"Four Portraits with a Message," *The Wall Street Journal,* March 15, 1989, p. B1.

[3]Philip R. Harris and Robert T. Moran, *Managing Cultural Differences* (Houston: Gulf Publishing, 1987), p. 44.

[4]The most widely used contemporary model of the process of communication has evolved mainly from the work of Shannon and Weaver, and Schramm. See Claude Shannon and Warren Weaver, *The Mathematical Theory of Communication* (Urbana: University of Illinois Press, 1948); Wilbur Schramm, "How Communication Works," in *The Process and Effects of Mass Communication,* ed. Wilbur Schramm (Urbana: University of Illinois Press, 1953), pp. 3–76.

FIGURE 13–1   Communication Model with Feedback

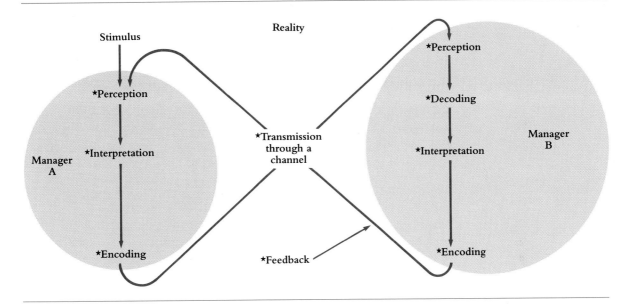

*Noise (and miscommunication) can occur here.

Source: Adapted from Kitty O. Locker, *Business and Administrative Communication* (Homewood, Ill.: Richard D. Irwin, 1989), p. 45.

Communication is a multistep process, with movement in both directions necessary for a successful interchange.

has been achieved (feedback). The intended message can be distorted by the presence of distractions in each element (noise).

Let us examine each element more closely in an organizational setting.

Communicator (Person). Communicators in an organization can be managers, nonmanagers, departments, or the organization itself. Managers communicate with other managers, subordinates, supervisors, clients, customers, and parties outside the organization. Nonmanagers likewise communicate with managers and nonmanagers, clients, customers, and external parties. People in sales departments communicate with people in production departments, and engineering personnel communicate with product design teams. Communications within the organization are important means for coordinating the work of separate departments. And more and more organizations communicate with employees, unions, the public, and government. Each of these communicators has a message, an idea, or information to transmit to someone or some group.

Perception and Interpretation. A person's view or perception of what is being communicated is crucial. Perception is reality to the person. It is how the person views the message. In perceiving, a person often must make an interpretation: What does the communicator mean?

Interpretation played a crucial role when two Boeing 747 jumbo jets collided on the ground in Tenerife in the Canary Islands. The two pilots were given specific instructions from the control tower.[5] The KLM pilot was told to taxi to the end of the runway, turn around, and wait to be cleared but didn't interpret the order to wait as an order he needed to follow. The Pan Am pilot interpreted his order to turn off at the third intersection as meaning the third unblocked intersection. He didn't count the first, blocked ramp, so he was on the main runway when the KLM plane plowed into his plane at 186 miles per hour. The result was a tragedy, costing 576 people their lives. Fatal errors by two experienced pilots were caused by misinterpretation.

Encoding.   Within the communicator, an encoding process must take place that translates the communicator's ideas into a systematic set of symbols expressing the communicator's purpose. The major form of encoding is language. For example, accounting information, sales reports, and computer data are translated into a message. The function of encoding then is to provide a form in which ideas and purposes can be expressed as a message.

Message.   The result of the encoding process is the message—either verbal or nonverbal. Managers have numerous purposes for communicating, such as to have others understand their ideas, to understand the ideas of others, to gain acceptance of themselves or their ideas, and to produce action. The message, then, is what the individual hopes to communicate, and the exact form that the message takes depends to a great extent on the medium used to carry it. Decisions relating to the two are inseparable.[6]

Channel.   The channel is the carrier of the message. Organizations provide information for their members by a variety of means, including face-to-face communication, telephone, group meetings, computers, memos, policy statements, reward systems, production schedules, sales forecasts, and videotapes.

Less obvious, however, are *unintended* messages that can be sent by silence or inaction on a particular issue, as well as decisions about which goals and objectives are *not* to be pursued and which methods are *not* to be utilized.

Nonverbal communication, communication that doesn't use words, is a part of everyday life. A friendly smile, a worried expression, the seating arrangements at a committee meeting, the size and location of an office, the reception area, furniture—all are nonverbal communicators. They indicate a person's power, status, position, or friendliness. The interpretation of nonverbal cues is important. However, nonverbal cues are as easily misinterpreted as verbal messages (words).

Body language is fascinating nonverbal communication. Open body positions include leaning forward with uncrossed arms and legs. Closed, or defensive, body positions include leaning back with arms and legs crossed. Open positions are assumed to suggest acceptance and openness to what is being discussed. Closed positions suggest that people are physically or psychologically uncomfortable.

---

[5]Andrew D. Wolvin and Caroline G. Coakley, *Listening* (Dubuque, Iowa: Wm. C. Brown, 1985), p. 6.

[6]Dale A. Level, "Communication Effectiveness: Method and Situation," *Journal of Business Communication,* Fall 1972, pp. 19–25; Terrence R. Mitchell, *People in Organizations: Understanding Their Behavior* (New York: McGraw-Hill, 1978), p. 214.

Americans see eye contact as a signal, a body language that connotes sincerity, interest, and honesty. In Korea, however, prolonged eye contact is considered rude. Arabs dislike talking to someone wearing dark glasses or while walking side by side; it is considered impolite not to face someone directly. In Muslim countries, women and men are not supposed to have eye contact.[7]

Gestures are a form of body language. In the United States, the thumbs-up sign means good work, nice going, it's OK. In Greece, it is a vulgar insult.[8] The formation of a circle with the thumb and the index finger in the United States means OK. Imagine a manager gesturing this way to a recent French immigrant to the United States working as a technician! In France, this gesture would mean you're worth nothing.

Paul Ekman has conducted extensive research on facial expression.[9] He believes that proper training can allow a manager, for example, to link facial expression and emotion. He has devised a scoring technique called FAST, for facial affect scoring technique. Emotions linked with facial parts in nonverbal communications include:

Fear: Eyes.
Sadness: Brows, forehead, eyes.
Disgust: Nose, cheeks, mouth.
Happiness: Cheeks, mouth, eyes.
Surprise: Any area of face.
Anger: Forehead, brows.

Ekman's research suggests that the left side of the face displays the most emotion. Thus, if one is attempting to use facial expression to assess nonverbal communication, the left side and especially the eyes should be observed.

Decoding.   For the process of communication to be completed, the message must be decoded by the receiver. Decoding is a technical term for the thought processes of the receiver. Thus, it involves interpretation. Receivers interpret (decode) the message in light of their own previous experiences and frames of reference. The closer the decoded message is to the intent of the communicator, the more effective is the communication. In a business organization, if the message that the chief executive receives from the marketing research department includes technical terms known only to marketing researchers, no communication exists. In fact, an often cited complaint in organizations that employ staff specialists is that they frequently cannot communicate. Each staff group (e.g., accountants, personnel, and marketing research) has a unique language and symbols that persons outside the group cannot decode.

Receiver (Person).   Whether there is sound when a tree falls in a deserted forest is a philosophical problem. But whether communication occurs without

[7]Marjorie F. Vargas, *Louder than Words* (Ames: Iowa State University Press, 1986), p. 47.

[8]Paul Ekman, Wallace V. Friesen, and John Bear, "The International Language of Gestures," *Psychology Today,* May 1984, p. 64.

[9]Pauline E. Henderson, "Communication without Words," *Personnel Journal,* January 1989, pp. 22–29.

a receiver is not a philosophical problem. By definition, communication requires a communicator and a receiver. The foregoing discussion of decoding difficulties underlines the importance of taking the receiver into account when a communicator attempts to transmit information. "Telling isn't teaching" if the teacher uses language that the student cannot understand (cannot decode). Engineers cannot expect to communicate to nonengineers if the symbols they use are beyond the receivers' training and ability to comprehend. Effective communication requires the communicator to anticipate the receiver's decoding ability, to know where the receiver "comes from." Effective communication is receiver oriented, not media oriented.

Feedback. *One-way* communication processes do not allow receiver-to-communicator feedback. *Two-way* communication processes provide for such feedback.[10] It is desirable to make provision for feedback in the communication process.[11] It decreases the potential for distortion between the intended message and the received message. A feedback loop provides a channel for receiver response, enabling the communicator to determine whether the message has been received and has produced the intended response. For the manager, communication feedback may come in many ways. In face-to-face situations, *direct* feedback is possible through verbal exchanges as well as through such subtle means as facial expressions that indicate discontent or misunderstanding. In addition, communication breakdowns may be indicated by *indirect* means, such as declines in productivity, poor quality of production, increased absenteeism or turnover, and conflict or a lack of coordination between units.

Noise.   In the framework of communications, noise is any interfering factor that, if present, can distort the intended message. Noise can be present in any element (as noted in Figure 13–1). Later in this chapter, a number of sources of noise are identified, including differing frames of reference, stereotyping, and semantics.

COMMUNICATION IN ORGANIZATIONS

The design of an organization should provide for communication in four distinct directions: downward, upward, horizontal, and diagonal.[12] These four directions establish the framework within which communication takes place in an organization. Examining each of them will enable the manager to better appreciate the barriers to effective organizational communication and the means for overcoming those barriers. Figure 13–2 illustrates the four direc-

[10]The classic experiment comparing one-way and two-way communication is described in Harold J. Leavitt and R. A. H. Mueller, "Some Effects of Feedback on Communications," *Human Relations,* 1951, pp. 401–10. Also see Harold J. Leavitt, *Managerial Psychology* (Chicago: University of Chicago Press, 1978).

[11]See P. H. Lewis, *Organizational Communications: The Essence of Effective Management* (Columbus, Ohio: Grid, 1975), p. 95; D. M. Herold and M. M. Greller, "Feedback: The Definition of a Construct," *Academy of Management Journal,* March 1977, pp. 142–47.

[12]Also see S. B. Bacharach and M. Aiken, "Communication in Administrative Bureaucracies," *Academy of Management Journal,* March 1977, pp. 365–77.

FIGURE 13–2 Communication in Organizations

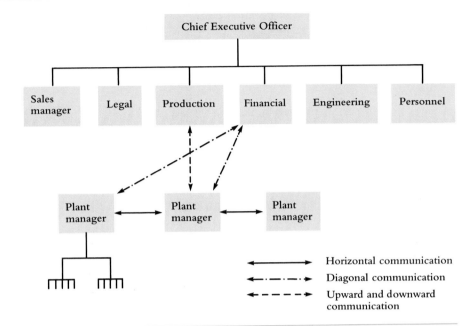

Communication in organizations flows in four distinct directions, and channels must be provided in the design of the organization.

tions in which organizational communication flows. While these are the major communication flows, many others can and do exist.

DOWNWARD COMMUNICATION

Downward communication flows from individuals at higher levels of the hierarchy to those at lower levels. The most common downward communications are job instructions, official memos, policy statements, procedures, manuals, and company publications. Researchers have identified the five most common types of downward organizational communication as job instructions, job rationale, organization policy, procedures and practices, employee performance feedback, and indoctrination of company goals.[13]

In many organizations, downward communication often is both inadequate and inaccurate, as reflected in the often heard statement among organization members that "we have absolutely no idea what's happening." Such complaints are indicative of inadequate downward communication—and the need individuals have for information relevant to their jobs. The absence of job-related information can create unnecessary stress among organization members.[14]

[13]F. M. Jablin, "Superior-Subordinate Communication: The State of the Art," *Psychological Bulletin*, November 1979, pp. 1201–22.

[14]John M. Ivancevich and James H. Donnelly, Jr., "A Study of Role Clarity and Need for Clarity in Three Occupational Groups," *Academy of Management Journal*, March 1974, pp. 28–36.

In large organizations, communicating with employees typically is undertaken by a trained staff of communication experts. The usual function of the staff is to produce a publication aimed at these three purposes: (1) to explain the organization's plans and programs as they are implemented, (2) to answer complaints and criticisms, and (3) to defend the status quo and those who are responsible for it. The medium often selected to accomplish these purposes is a periodic publication, the "house organ." The publication's intended messages are those that present the organization's side of issues. Large organizations are viewed more and more with distrust and suspicion. Although they may not always be successful in convincing the general public that their actions are public minded, it has become increasingly necessary for them to win the support of their employees.

UPWARD COMMUNICATION

A high-performing organization needs effective upward communication as much as it needs effective downward communication. Effective upward communication is difficult to achieve, especially in larger organizations. However, it often is necessary for sound decision making. Widely used upward communication devices include suggestion boxes, group meetings, reports to supervisors, and appeal or grievance procedures. In the absence of these flows, employees find ways to adapt to nonexistent or inadequate upward communication channels.

The practices of ESCO Corporation of Portland, Oregon, reveal the company's commitment to upward communications. Employees in this company who wish to communicate directly with top management—whether to express complaints, suggestions, questions, compliments, or comments— simply dial a listed telephone number and state their views. The calls are recorded, transcribed, and reviewed by ESCO's vice president of industrial relations in charge of personnel. The vice president forwards the transcriptions to the appropriate department managers for reply and action. If callers give their names, they receive a written answer; if they choose to be anonymous, the answers are posted on the bulletin board. Every call is answered, always within 48 hours.

Effective upward communication channels are important because they provide employees with opportunities to have a say. The Egg McMuffin and all its clones originated from an idea generated by a lower-level McDonald's employee.[15] The employee sent the idea upward because he felt that it was a good suggestion that management would use. Upward channels are equally important because top management depends on subordinates for vital information. An example is the dependence of generals on lieutenants and sergeants for tactical information. The outcomes of battles and maneuvers are reported upward. History is replete with instances in which upward communications became distorted, with important consequences.

---

[15]Alan Zaremba, "The Upward Network," *Personnel Journal*, March 1989, pp. 34–39.

MANAGEMENT FOCUS

Communication between Sales and Credit Departments Can Improve a Company's Cash Flow

In this chapter, we stress that communication between departments can help a company's performance. However, two departments that could benefit from such communication—sales and credit—rarely do. Why don't they?

The lack of communication and cooperation between sales and credit exists because in most companies they are set up as adversaries. For example, a car salesperson spends hours talking and test driving with potential buyers in order to get them interested in a particular model. Ultimately, they decide to buy the product, and a price is negotiated. As far as the salesperson is concerned, it is a "done deal." Then the credit manager enters into the picture. He or she decides that the buyers are unworthy of credit, and the sale is lost. The salesperson pleads with the credit manager to reconsider, but the credit manager says, "Customers that can't pay their bills are worse than no customers at all."

What could help in this scenario is increased communication. If the sales department became the eyes and ears of the credit department, the company would come out ahead. First, the salespeople need to know what criteria the credit department uses in evaluating customers. If sales personnel realize that people are certain to be rejected, they can spend much less time on that customer. Salespeople may, in turn, have additional information that the credit department could use in its evaluation. This is especially true in situations where businesses are selling to other businesses. The salespeople who visit the firms are the best source for specialized information, such as marketing strengths, quality of the sales team, and distribution advantages. Having such information, the credit department can make better decisions.

In other types of sales, the sales team is in many cases unaware of problem accounts and continues to call on them for additional sales. Credit departments could relay information on delinquent accounts. With such increased communication, the two departments can better understand that they are not working against each other but are performing two important functions that can run smoother with each other's help.

Source: Adapted from Les Kirschbaum, "It Pays to Work Together," *Business Age*, March 1989, pp. 34–36.

HORIZONTAL COMMUNICATION

Often overlooked in the design of most organizations is provision for the horizontal flow of communication. When the supervisor of the accounting department communicates with the director of marketing concerning advertising budget expenditures, the flow of communication is horizontal. Although vertical (upward and downward) communication flows are the primary considerations in organizational design, effective organizations also need horizontal communication. Horizontal communication—for example, between production and sales in a business organization and between different departments within a hospital—is necessary for the coordination of diverse organizational functions. The Management Focus provides an example of horizontal communication between two departments.

Staff meetings bring together individuals from throughout the organization to discuss common issues.

Diagonal Communication

Although diagonal communication probably is the least used channel of communication in organizations, it is important in situations in which members cannot communicate effectively through other channels. For example, the comptroller of a large organization may wish to conduct a distribution cost analysis, and one part of the analysis may involve having the sales force send a special report directly to the comptroller rather than through the traditional channels in the marketing department. Thus, the flow of communication would be diagonal rather than upward and then horizontal. In this case, the use of a diagonal channel would minimize the time and effort expended by the organization.

INTERPERSONAL COMMUNICATIONS

Communication flows from individual to individual in face-to-face and group settings. Such flows, called "interpersonal communications," vary in form from direct orders to casual expressions. The primary manner in which managers relate to and learn from people in their environment is through interpersonal communication—information the managers receive and transmit. And the way in which managers receive and transmit information depends in part on how they relate to two very important *senders* of information, themselves and others.

Regions of Information

Information is held by oneself and by others, but each of us does not fully have or know that information. The different combinations of knowing and

FIGURE 13–3   Regions of Information Influencing Communication

The four regions of information known and not known by the self and others can be modified by two improvement strategies.

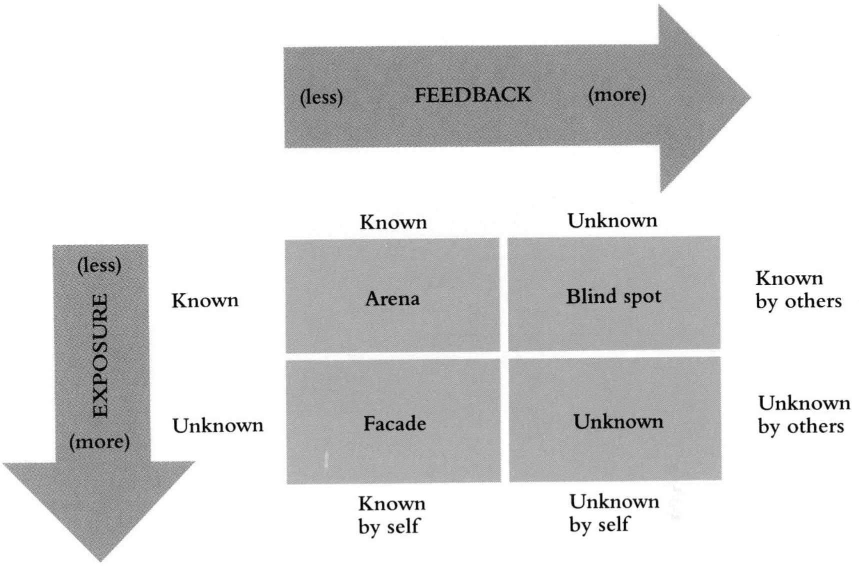

not knowing relevant information are shown in Figure 13–3. The figure identifies four combinations, or regions, of information known and unknown by the self and others.[16]

1. *The arena.* The region most conducive for effective interpersonal relationships and communication is called the arena. In this setting, all the information necessary to carry on effective communication is known to both the communicator (self) and the receivers (others). For a communication attempt to be in the arena region, the parties involved must share identical feelings, data, assumptions, and skills. The arena is the area of common understanding.

2. *The blind spot.* When relevant information is known to others but not to the self, a blind spot results. In this context, one is at a disadvantage when communicating with others, because one cannot know their feelings, sentiments, and perceptions. Consequently, interpersonal relationships and communications suffer. The blind spot presents an interpersonal handicap for the self, since one hardly can understand the behaviors, decisions, or potentials of others without having data on which these are based. Others have the advantage of knowing their own feelings, while the self is unaware of these.

3. *The facade.* When information is known to the self but unknown to others, a person (self) may resort to superficial communications, that is, present a false front, or facade. This situation is particularly damaging when a subordinate "knows" and an immediate supervisor "does not know." The facade, like a blind spot, diminishes the arena and reduces the possibility of effective communication.

[16]The discussion in this section is based on J. Hall, "Communication Revisited," *California Management Review,* Fall 1973, pp. 56–67.

Who is reducing the blind spot and who is reducing the facade?

4. *The unknown.* This region, the unknown, constitutes that portion where the relevant information is not known by the self or by other parties to the relationship: "I don't understand them, and they don't understand me." It is easy to see that under such circumstances, interpersonal communication will be poor. The unknown area often occurs in organizations when individuals in different specialties must coordinate what they do through communications.

IMPROVEMENT STRATEGIES

Figure 13–3 indicates that an individual can improve interpersonal communications by utilizing two strategies, exposure and feedback:

1. *Exposure.* Increasing the arena area by reducing the facade area requires that the individual be open and honest in sharing information with others. The process that the self uses to increase the information known to others is called exposure because it leaves the self in a sometimes vulnerable position. Exposing one's true feelings, "telling it like it is," often involves risks.

2. *Feedback.* When the self does not know or understand, more effective communications can be developed through feedback from those who do know. Thus, the blind spot can be reduced with a corresponding increase in the arena. Of course, whether the use of feedback is possible depends on the individual's willingness to "hear" it and on the willingness of others to give it. Thus, the individual is less able to control the obtaining of feedback than the provision of exposure. Obtaining feedback is dependent on the active cooperation of others, while exposure requires the active behavior of the self and listening of others.

MANAGEMENT STYLES

Interpersonal style refers to *the way in which an individual prefers to relate to others.* The fact that much of the relationships among people involve communication indicates the importance of interpersonal style.

The day-to-day activities of managers place a high value on effective interpersonal communications. Managers provide information (which must be understood); they give commands and instructions (which must be obeyed and learned); and they make efforts to influence and persuade (which must be accepted and acted upon). Thus, the way in which managers communicate, both as senders and receivers, is crucial for obtaining effective performance.

Theoretically managers who desire to communicate effectively can use both exposure and feedback to enlarge the area of common understanding, the arena. As a practical matter, such is not the case. Managers differ in their ability and willingness to use exposure and feedback. At least four different managerial styles can be identified:

1.   *Type A:*   Managers who use neither exposure nor feedback are said to have a Type A style. The unknown region predominates in this style because the manager is unwilling to enlarge the area of his or her own knowledge or the knowledge of others. Such managers exhibit anxiety and hostility and give the appearance of aloofness and coldness toward others. If an organization has a large number of Type A managers in key positions, then we would expect to find poor and ineffective interpersonal communications and a loss of individual creativity. Type A managers often display the characteristics of autocratic leaders.

2.   *Type B:*   Some managers desire a degree of satisfying relationships with their subordinates; but because of their personalities and attitudes, these managers are unable to open up and express their feelings and sentiments. Consequently, they cannot use exposure, and they must rely on feedback. The facade is the predominant feature of interpersonal relationships when managers overuse feedback to the exclusion of exposure. The subordinates likely will distrust such managers, because they realize that these managers are holding back their own ideas and opinions. Type B behavior often is displayed by managers who desire to practice some form of permissive leadership.

3.   *Type C:*   Managers who value their own ideas and opinions but not the ideas and opinions of others will use exposure at the expense of feedback. The consequence of this style is the perpetuation and enlargement of the blind spot. Subordinates soon will realize that such managers are not particularly interested in communicating, only in telling. Consequently, Type C managers usually have subordinates who are hostile, insecure, and resentful. Subordinates soon learn that such managers are mainly interested in maintaining their own sense of importance and prestige.

4.   *Type D:*   The most effective interpersonal communication style is one that uses a balance of exposure and feedback. Managers who are secure in their positions will feel free to expose their own feelings and to obtain feedback from others. To the extent that the manager practices Type D behavior successfully, the arena becomes larger, and communication becomes more effective.

To summarize, the primary force in determining the effectiveness of interpersonal communication is interpersonal style, the attitude of managers toward exposure and feedback. The most effective approach is that of the Type D manager. Type A, B, and C managers resort to behaviors detrimental to the effectiveness of communication and to organizational performance.

WHY COMMUNICATIONS BREAK DOWN

Why do communications break down? On the surface, the answer is relatively easy. We have identified the elements of communication as the communicator, perception/interpretation, encoding, the message, the channel, decoding, the receiver, feedback, and noise. If noise exists in any other element *in any way,* clarity of meaning and understanding will be impaired. A manager has no greater responsibility than to develop effective communications. In this section, we shall discuss some barriers to effective communication: differing frames of reference, selective perception, value judgments, source credibility, semantic problems, filtering, time pressures, and overload. These sources of noise can exist in both organizational and interpersonal communications.

DIFFERING FRAMES OF REFERENCE

Individuals can interpret the same communication differently, depending on their previous experience. The result is variations between the *encoding* and *decoding* processes. When the processes are alike, communication is most effective. When they are different, communication tends to break down. In terms of interpersonal communication, the arena is relatively small when compared to blind spots, facades, and unknown areas. To the extent that individuals have distinctly different frames of reference, effective communication among those individuals will be difficult to achieve.[17]

One result of different frames of reference is that communications become distorted. For example, teenagers have different experiences than do their parents (the oft-cited generation gap?); district sales managers have different perceptions than do salespersons. In an organization, the *jobs* that people perform will create barriers and distortions in communications. For example, a pricing problem will be viewed differently by the marketing manager and by the plant manager. An efficiency problem in a hospital will be viewed by the nursing staff from its frame of reference and its experiences; this may result in interpretations that differ from those of the staff physicians.

Different *levels* in the organization also will have different frames of reference. First-level supervisors have frames of reference that differ in many respects from those of vice presidents, because they are in different positions in the organization's structure. As a result, the needs, values, attitudes, and expectations of these two groups will differ, and this often will produce unintentional distortions of the communications between them. Neither group is wrong or right.

In any situation, individuals will choose that part of their own past experiences that relates to their current experiences and is helpful in forming conclusions and judgments. Unfortunately, such incongruities in encoding and decoding result in barriers to effective communication.

---

[17]For a related study, see J. D. Hatfield and R. C. Huseman, "Perceptual Congruence about Communication as Related to Satisfaction: Moderating Effects of Individual Characteristics," *Academy of Management Journal,* June 1982, pp. 349–58.

SELECTIVE PERCEPTION

Each of us "catalogs" the world in our own way. *Selective perception* occurs when people block out new information, especially if it conflicts with what they believe. Thus, when people receive information, they are apt to hear only those parts that conform to or reaffirm their beliefs. Information that conflicts with preconceived notions either is not processed or is distorted to confirm our preconceptions.

For example, a notice may be sent to all operating departments that costs must be reduced if the organization is to earn a profit. Such a communication may not achieve its desired effect, because it conflicts with the "reality" of the receivers. Operating employees may ignore or be amused by the notice in light of the large salaries, travel allowances, and expense accounts of some managers. Whether these expenditures are justified is irrelevant; what is important is that such preconceptions result in breakdowns in communication.

Finally, selective perception results in **stereotyping.** When an individual has preconceived ideas about other people and refuses to discriminate between individual behaviors, that person is applying selective perception to his relationships with other people. Stereotyping is a barrier to communication, because those who stereotype others use selective perception in their communications and tend to hear only those things that confirm their stereotyped images. For example, some managers stereotype union stewards, some men stereotype successful females, and some women stereotype aggressive men.

POOR LISTENING SKILLS

Listening should consume about half of the time that a superior and subordinate spend together; it doesn't, because one or both persons fail to listen.[18] For example, a meeting between a boss and employee might go something like this: "Boss, I really have a problem finishing the report." "Is that so, Bob? Well, sit down a minute and let me hear about it." However, before Bob can even start his story, the boss begins to cite his current problem. "I've got to do something about the production unit. It is producing at 15 percent below standard rate. I am really on the carpet with the chief." As the boss finishes, he says: "Sorry, Bob, I've got a meeting to attend, so come on back tomorrow and we can get to your problem." Bob leaves completely frustrated, his problem still on his mind and no one to talk to about a solution.

The boss simply failed to listen. He heard what Bob said, but he really wasn't listening. Failing to listen may result from a host of personal habits. We speak at rates of 100 to 200 words a minute, read at two or three times our speaking rate, and think several times faster than we read. As a result, a listener can move through a discussion much faster than can a speaker. Because of the speed involved, we typically develop poor listening habits. Bad listening habits are of particular interest in work settings. For example, if either a manager or a subordinate fails to listen to the other, the objectives of the discussion, feedback session, or job instruction will not be accomplished.

---

[18]William C. Hemstreet and Wayne M. Baty, *Business Communications* (Boston: Kent Publishing, 1984), p. 308.

MANAGEMENT FOCUS

Can I Put You on Hold?

How many times have you sworn that you would never do business with a company because you could never get the information you wanted over the phone? They were rude or insensitive or never transferred you to the right person. In the United States alone, nearly half a billion potential customers reach for the telephone each day, building their image of a company from what they hear on the other end of their telephone.

Companies commit seven deadly telephone sins, each having the power to communicate the wrong impression to the calling customers:

1. *The poisonous greeting.* The tone and manner of the person who answers the phone turn you off immediately. Management specialist Robert F. Roesch says to "avoid sounding cool, detached, uninterested, or tired." By sounding warm and interested and speaking slowly and clearly, you create an impression that you care.

2. *Abandonment.* Surveys show that most people become impatient after 45 seconds. Coming back on the line can help keep the connection alive and curb the impatience. When people are left on hold for long periods of time, even with music, they are distraught by the time you finally talk to them.

3. *Extension football.* You call a company and ask a question, and the receptionist relays you to so-and-so. You recite the request again and are bounced to another person. Everyone has encountered this, and it doesn't take long before you become exasperated. Whoever answers the phone should know the answers or know where to get the information. They can also relay the request before they connect the caller, so that the

VALUE JUDGMENTS

In every communication situation, receivers make value judgments by assigning an overall worth to a message prior to receiving the entire communication. Such value judgments may be based on the receiver's evaluation of the communicator, the receiver's previous experiences with the communicator, or the message's anticipated meaning. Thus, a hospital administrator may pay little attention to a memorandum from a nursing-team leader because "she's always complaining about something." An employee may consider a merit evaluation meeting with the supervisor as "going through the motions," because the employee perceives the supervisor as being concerned about administrative matters to the exclusion of performance.

Many value judgments are based on telephone communications. The Management Focus highlights common telephone "sins" and the judgments that result.

SOURCE CREDIBILITY

Source credibility refers to the trust, confidence, and faith that the receiver has in the words and actions of the communicator. The level of credibility that the receiver assigns to the communicator directly affects how the receiver views and reacts to the words, ideas, and actions of the communicator.

customer need not repeat the whole question to each person he or she is transferred to.

4. *Consummate boredom.* Whether it is Monday morning or Friday afternoon, a company should not want callers feeling that they are wasting the company's time. People that are bored or in bad moods should stay away from the phone.

5. *Picking daisies.* Everyone from the receptionist to the president is guilty of not giving the caller their undivided attention. Callers can sense when people are distracted, so all concentration should be on the caller's wants.

6. *Telephone speech.* This has to do with how humans sound on the phone. Speech consultant Ralph Proodian claims that a tight collar or even a tight belt affects our voices. Bad posture, improper breathing, and tension can

contribute to a loss of clarity in our phone voices, especially in the pronunciation of consonants.

7. *Losing the boss.* Few situations are more irritating for a customer than failing to reach the person they called, especially when no one knows where that person is or when he or she might return. Having employees leave word with the receptionist can alleviate the problem. Even if the return time is not exact, it gives the caller a better idea than a frustrating "I don't know."

If a company relies on the telephone to communicate with its customers, then it must be aware of how its reputation and image are affected by how it treats its telephone customers.

Source: Adapted from Howard Dana Shaw, "Seven Deadly Telephone Sins," *In Business*, January–February 1989, pp. 44–45.

Thus, how subordinates view a communication from their manager is affected by their evaluations of the manager. The degree of credibility they attach to the communication is heavily influenced by their previous experiences with the manager. Hospital medical staff members who view the hospital administrator as less than honest, manipulative, and not to be trusted are apt to assign negative motives to any communication from the administrator. Union leaders who view managers as exploiters, and managers who view union leaders as inherent enemies, are likely to engage in little real communication.

Source credibility played a role in March 1989 when cyanide was found in grapes imported from Chile by the United States. The Food and Drug Administration (FDA) warned consumers against any fruit imported from Chile.[19] The message sent by the FDA to U.S. produce wholesalers and retailers resulted in all Chilean fruit being pulled off the market as a precaution against possible food poisoning. About $25 million of Chilean fruit was destroyed as a result of the first FDA message.[20]

In another incident involving source credibility, nutrition experts issued a message that pesticide residue on fresh fruits (especially apples) put children at

[19]Bruce Ingersoll, "Fruit from Chile under Quarantine to Be Destroyed," *The Wall Street Journal,* March 20, 1989, p. A3.

[20]Bruce Ingersoll, "Cyanide Found in Grapes Sent from Chile," *The Wall Street Journal,* March 14, 1989, p. A3.

increased risk of cancer.[21] The reaction to the message was alarm. Was this an overreaction? The National Defense Council, which issued the warning, is a litigation group, not a scientific organization. Even the council believes that people overreacted. How credible is the council? The U.S. Environmental Protection Agency believes that the council's warning was just that—a warning. However, when the health of children is mentioned, the credibility of the source is usually not the first area of concern.

SEMANTIC PROBLEMS

Communication is the transmission of information and understanding through the use of common symbols. Actually, we cannot transmit understanding. We can only transmit information in the form of words, which are the common symbols. Unfortunately, the same words may mean entirely different things to different people. The understanding is in the receiver, not in the words.

When a plant manager announces that a "budget increase" is necessary for the growth of the plant, the manager may have in mind the necessity for new equipment, an expanded parts inventory, and more personnel. To the existing personnel, however, growth may be perceived as excess funds that can be used for wage and salary increases.

Again, because different groups use words differently, communication often can be impeded. This is especially true with abstract or technical terms and phrases. "Cost-benefit study" would have meaning to persons involved in the administration of the hospital but probably would mean very little to the staff physicians; in fact, it might even carry a negative meaning to the latter. Such concepts as trusts, profits, and Treasury bills may have concrete meaning to bank executives but little or no meaning to bank tellers. Because words mean different things to different people, it is possible for a communicator to speak the same language as a receiver but still not transmit understanding.

In some cultures, saying no is not acceptable. Koreans are taught not to say no. However, Koreans are taught not to take yes literally. Chinese trade negotiators avoid saying no directly. They say it is "possible." In Japan, ways to avoid saying no include silence, counterquestions, changing the subject, or delaying answers.

Occupational, professional, and social groups often develop words and phrases that have meaning only to group members. Such special language can serve many useful purposes. It can provide group members with feelings of belonging, cohesiveness, and (in many cases) self-esteem. It also can facilitate effective communication *within* the group. The use of in-group language can, however, result in severe semantic problems and communication breakdowns when outsiders or other groups are involved. Technical and staff groups often use such language in an organization, not for the purpose of transmitting information and understanding but rather in order to communicate a "mystique" about the group or its function.

[21]Barbara Rosenvicz, "Pesticide Risk from Apples: Who's Right?" *The Wall Street Journal,* March 10, 1989, pp. B1, B3.

FILTERING

Filtering is a common occurrence in upward communication in organizations. It amounts to "manipulating" information so that the information is perceived as positive by the receiver. Subordinates "cover up" unfavorable information in messages to their superiors. The reason for such filtering should be clear. Upward communications carry control information to management. Management makes merit evaluations, grants salary increases, and promotes individuals based on what it receives by way of the upward channel. The temptation to filter is likely to be strong at every level in the organization.

The shape of the organization determines the extent to which information can be filtered. An organizational design with many levels of management (a "tall" organization) will experience more information filtration than will one with fewer levels (a "flat" organization). The reason is fairly simple: the more levels through which upward communications must flow, the greater is the opportunity for each successive layer of management to take out what it does not want the next level to know. An advantage of flat organizational designs is that they minimize the problem of filtration.

TIME PRESSURES

The pressure of time is an important barrier to communication. An obvious problem is that managers do not have the time to communicate frequently with every subordinate. Time pressures can often lead to serious problems. *Short-circuiting* is a failure of the formally prescribed communications system that often results from time pressures. What it means simply is that someone who normally would be included has been left out of the formal channel of communication.

For example, suppose that a salesperson who needs a rush order for a very important customer goes directly to the production manager with the request, since the production manager owes the salesperson a favor. Other members of the sales force get word of this and become upset over this preferential treatment and report it to the sales manager. Obviously, the sales manager would know nothing of the deal, since the sales manager has been short-circuited.

In some cases, going through formal channels is extremely costly or impossible from a practical standpoint. Consider the impact on a hospital patient if a nurse had to report a malfunction in some critical life-support equipment in an intensive care unit to the nursing-team leader, who in turn had to report it to the hospital engineer, who then would instruct a staff engineer to make the repair.

COMMUNICATION OVERLOAD

One of the vital tasks performed by a manager is decision making. One of the necessary ingredients for effective decisions is *information*. The last decade has been described as the Information Era, or the Age of Information. Because of the advances in communication technology, difficulties may arise, not from the absence of information but from excessive information. Managers often are deluged by information and data. As a result, they cannot absorb or adequately respond to all of the messages directed to them. They "screen out" the majority of messages, which in effect means that these messages are never decoded. Thus, the area of organizational communication is one in which more is not always better.[22]

The barriers to communication discussed here, though common, are by no means the only ones that exist. Examining these barriers indicates that they are either *within individuals* (e.g., frame of reference, value judgments) or *within organizations* (e.g., in-group language, filtering). This point is important because *attempts to improve communications must focus on changing people and/or changing the organization structure*.[23]

IMPROVING COMMUNICATION IN ORGANIZATIONS

Managers striving to become better communicators have two separate tasks. First, they must improve their messages—the information they wish to transmit. Second, they must improve their own understanding of what other people are trying to communicate to them. They must become better encoders and decoders; *they must strive not only to be understood but also to understand*. Techniques for improving communication are following up, regulating information flow, utilizing feedback, empathy, simplifying language, listening effectively, and utilizing the grapevine.

FOLLOWING UP

Following up involves assuming that you may have been misunderstood and, whenever possible, attempting to determine whether your intended meaning was actually received. As we have seen, meaning is in the mind of the receiver. An accounting unit leader in a government office forwards notices of openings in other agencies to the accounting staff members. Although this may be understood among longtime employees as a friendly gesture, a new employee might interpret it as a negative evaluation of performance and a suggestion to leave.

REGULATING INFORMATION FLOW

Regulating the flow of communications ensures an optimum flow of information to managers, thereby eliminating the barrier of "communication overload." Both the quality and quantity of communications are controlled. The idea is based on the *exception principle* of management, which states that only significant deviations from policies and procedures should be brought to the attention of managers. In terms of formal communication, then, managers should be communicated with only on matters of exceptions and not for the sake of communication.

[22]Charles A. O'Reilly III, "Individuals and Information Overload in Organizations: Is More Necessarily Better?" *Academy of Management Journal,* December 1980, pp. 684–96.

[23]See Paul M. Muchinsky, "Organizational Communication: Relationships to Organizational Climate and Job Satisfaction," *Academy of Management Journal,* December 1977, pp. 592–607.

TABLE 13–1   Characteristics of Effective and Ineffective Feedback
in Human Resource Management

*Feedback from management is
ineffective if it does not promote
improved employee performance.*

Effective Feedback	Ineffective Feedback
1. Intended to help the employee.	1. Intended to belittle the employee.
2. Specific.	2. General.
3. Descriptive.	3. Judgmental.
4. Useful.	4. Inappropriate.
5. Timely.	5. Untimely.
6. Willingly heard by employee.	6. Makes the employee defensive.
7. Clear.	7. Not understandable.
8. Valid.	8. Inaccurate.

Source: Fred Luthans and Mark J. Martinko, *The Practice of Supervision and Management* (New York: McGraw-Hill, 1979), p. 183.

Certain types of organizational designs are more amenable to this principle than are other types. Certainly, in neoclassical organization, with its emphasis on free-flowing communication, the principle would not apply. However, classical organizations would find the principle useful.

UTILIZING FEEDBACK

Feedback is an important element in effective two-way communication. It provides a channel for receiver response, enabling the communicator to determine whether the message has been received and has produced the intended response.

In face-to-face communication, direct feedback is possible. In downward communication, however, inaccuracies often occur because of insufficient opportunity for feedback from receivers. Thus, a memorandum addressing an important policy statement may be distributed to all employees, but this does not guarantee that communication has occurred. One might expect that feedback in the form of upward communication would be encouraged more in neoclassical organizations, but the mechanisms discussed earlier that can be utilized to encourage upward communication are found in many different organizational designs. A healthy organization needs effective upward communication if its downward communication is to have any chance of being effective. Table 13–1 presents some of the major characteristics of effective and ineffective feedback for employee performance.

EMPATHY

Empathy is the ability to put oneself in the other person's role and to assume the viewpoints and emotions of that person. This involves being receiver oriented rather than communicator oriented. The form of a communication should depend largely on what is known about the receivers. Empathy requires communicators to place themselves in the receivers' positions for the purpose of anticipating how the message is likely to be decoded.

It is vital that a manager understand and appreciate the process of decoding. Decoding involves perceptions, and the message will be filtered through the perceptions of the receiver. For vice presidents to communicate effectively with supervisors, for faculty to communicate effectively with students, and for government administrators to communicate effectively with minority groups, empathy is often an important ingredient. Empathy can reduce many of the barriers to effective communication that have been discussed above. The greater the gap between the experiences and background of the communicator and the receiver, the greater is the effort that must be made to find a common ground of understanding—ground on which there are overlapping fields of experience.

SIMPLIFYING LANGUAGE

Complex language has been identified as a major barrier to effective communication. Students often suffer when their instructors use technical jargon that transforms simple concepts into complex puzzles.

Colleges and universities are not the only places, however, where complex language is used. Government agencies also are known for their often incomprehensible communications. We already have noted instances in which professional people attempt to use their in-group language in communicating with individuals outside their group. Managers must remember that effective communication involves transmitting understanding. If the receiver does not understand, then there has been no communication. In fact, techniques discussed in this section have as their sole purpose the promotion of understanding.

EFFECTIVE LISTENING

Just listening is not enough; one must listen with understanding. Can managers develop listening skills? Numerous pointers for effective listening have been found to be useful in organizational settings. For example, one writer cites "Ten Commandments for Good Listening": stop talking, put the speaker at ease, show the speaker you want to listen, remove distractions, empathize with the speaker, be patient, hold your temper, go easy on argument and criticism, ask questions, and stop talking. Note that "stop talking" is both the first and last commandment.[24]

Such lists of guidelines can be useful for managers. However, more important than these lists is the *decision to listen*. The above guidelines are useless unless the manager makes the conscious decision to listen. The realization that effective communication involves being understood as well as understanding probably is far more important than lists of guidelines. Then and only then can such guidelines become useful.

It is important to remember that inattention is one of the problems that occur in a conversation. To avoid inattention, a person must:

---

[24]Keith Davis, *Human Behavior at Work* (New York: McGraw-Hill, 1985), p. 387.

- Listen carefully for answers to key issues or questions.
- When the conversation is completed, check to determine whether you understand what was communicated.
- Jot down the key points and what the next step or course of action will be.

At work, listening is difficult. Interruptions, the perceptual differences of the communicators, and other events create problems. Listening effectively means that decoding and interpretation have occurred.

UTILIZING THE GRAPEVINE: INFORMAL COMMUNICATION SYSTEMS

The grapevine is an important informal communication channel that exists in all organizations. It basically serves as a bypassing mechanism and often is faster than the formal system it bypasses. In most cases, managers can count on the fact that the grapevine is fast, efficient, and accurate and fulfills people's need to communicate. Because it is flexible and because it usually involves face-to-face communication, the grapevine is capable of transmitting information rapidly. Through the grapevine, the resignation of an executive may become common knowledge long before it has been officially announced.

For management, the grapevine frequently may be an effective means of communication. It is likely to have a stronger impact on receivers because it is face-to-face and allows for feedback. Because it satisfies many psychological needs, the grapevine will always exist. No manager can do away with it. Research indicates that over 75 percent of the information in the grapevine is accurate.[25] Of course, the 25 percent that is distorted can be devastating.

If the grapevine is inevitable, managers should seek to utilize it or at least attempt to assure its accuracy. One way to minimize the undesirable aspects of the grapevine is to improve other forms of communication. If information exists on issues relevant to subordinates, then damaging rumors are less likely to develop.

SUMMARY OF KEY POINTS

- The quality of managerial decisions depends in large part on the quality of information available. Communication is the process of achieving common understanding; for managerial purposes, it is undertaken to achieve an effect.

- If the intended effect is not achieved, communication has not taken place.

- The elements of communication are the communicator, perception/interpretation, encoding, the message, the channel, decoding, the receiver, feedback, and noise. All of these elements must be in harmony if communication is to achieve understanding and effect.

- Nonverbal communication doesn't use words. But nonverbal signals (cues) can be misinterpreted just as easily.

- A crucial factor in determining the effectiveness of communication in organizations is the way in which organizations are structured. Upward, downward, diagonal, and horizontal communication flows are more likely to occur in neoclassical than in classical organization structures.

- The extent to which individuals share understanding depends on their use of feedback and exposure. People differ in this regard, with some preferring feedback and others preferring expo-

[25]Ibid., p. 267.

sure. A balanced use of both is the most effective approach.

■ Numerous barriers exist that contribute to communication breakdowns. Managers must be aware of barriers relevant to their situations. Major barriers are differing frames of reference, selective perception, poor listening skills, value judgments, source credibility, semantic prob-

lems, filtering, time pressures, and communication overload.

■ Improving communication in organizations involves following up, regulating information flow, utilizing feedback, empathy, simplifying language, listening effectively, and utilizing the informal communication system (the grapevine).

DISCUSSION AND REVIEW QUESTIONS

1. During disagreements, we often hear someone say: "That's not what I said." Discuss what this statement means in terms of the elements of communication presented in the chapter.

2. As American corporations hire increasing numbers of immigrants, what role will the assessment of nonverbal communication play in interviewing job candidates?

3. Based on your own experience, which element of communication has most often been the cause of your failures to communicate? What do you believe you can do to improve your communication effectiveness?

4. Are you a Type A, B, C, or D person when you engage in interpersonal communications? Are you

satisfied to be what you think you are? Why? If not, how could you change?

5. Think of your management course in terms of the basic elements of communication. For example: Who is the communicator? What is the message? Who is the receiver? Is effective communication occurring? Why? Identify where, if at all, breakdowns are occurring and why.

6. How can a manager improve his or her credibility as a communicator with subordinates?

7. Describe a situation in which you have been the receiver in a one-way communication process. Can you think of any reasons why some people might prefer it? List them.

ADDITIONAL REFERENCES

Centron, M.; A. Pagano; and **O. Port.** "The Telecommunications Boom." *Management Review,* November 1985, pp. 57–59.

Eisenhart, T. "You're Talking—But Are They Listening?" *Business Marketing,* January 1989, pp. 30–38.

Larson, J. R., Jr. "The Supervisory Feedback Process: A Preliminary Model." *Organizational Behavior and Human Performance,* 1984, pp. 42–76.

Liden, R. C., and **T. R. Mitchell.** "Reactions to Feedback: The Role of Attributions." *Academy of Management Journal,* June 1985, pp. 291–308.

Penley, L. E., and **B. Hawkins.** "Studying Interpersonal Communication in Organizations: A Leadership Application." *Academy of Management Journal,* June 1985, pp. 309–26.

Poole, M. S. "An Information-Task Approach to Organizational Communication." *Academy of Management Journal,* July 1978, pp. 493–504.

Roberts, K. H., and **C. A. O'Reilly III.** "Failures in Upward Communication in Organizations: Three Pos-

sible Culprits." *Academy of Management Journal,* June 1974, pp. 205–15.

Roberts, K. H., and **C. A. O'Reilly III.** "Some Correlates of Communication Roles in Organizations." *Academy of Management Journal,* March 1979, pp. 42–57.

Rockey, E. H. *Communicating in Organizations.* Cambridge, Mass.: Winthrop Publishers, 1977.

Saunders, C. S. "Management Information Systems, Communications and Departmental Power: An Integrative Model." *Academy of Management Review,* July 1981, pp. 431–42.

Thiederman, S. "Overcoming Cultural and Language Barriers." *Personnel Journal,* December 1988, pp. 34–40.

Tubbs, S. L., and **S. Moss.** *Human Communication.* New York: Random House, 1977.

Tushman, M. L. "Impacts of Perceived Environmental Variability on Patterns of Work Related Communications." *Academy of Management Journal,* September 1979, pp. 482–500.

Watson, K. "An Analysis of Communication Patterns: A Method for Discriminating Leader and Subordinate Roles." *Academy of Management Journal,* March 1982, pp. 107–20.

Wiener, N. *The Human Use of Human Beings.* New York: Doubleday Publishing, 1954.

Wyatt, N., and **M. Phillips.** *Studying Organizational Communication: A Case Study of the Farmers Home Administration.* Norwood, N.J.: Ablex, 1988.

Ziegenfuss, J. T., Jr. *Organizational Troubleshooters: Resolving Problems with Customers and Employees.* San Francisco: Jossey-Bass. 1988.

CASE 13–1 "A Can of Worms for McDonald's"

In the summer of 1978, a rumor began circulating in the Southeast that McDonald's was putting red worms in its hamburger meat to boost its protein content. Although the rumor was untrue, it quickly spread from Chattanooga to Atlanta and north to Ohio and Indiana. By the time it reached the northern states, the rumor was clearly cutting into McDonald's sales.

McDonald's was already rumor weary. In the preceding months, the company had finally succeeded in squelching the absurd rumor that Ray Kroc, McDonald's president, was making financial donations to the Church of Satan. Now the company was faced with the challenge of devising a strategy to debunk the worm story.

McDonald's decided to repeat their Satan rumor strategy and deal with the rumor locally. Company officials identified the areas where the rumor was running rampant. In these areas, the company distributed McDonald's materials about its food content and letters from the secretary of agriculture assuring customers that the hamburger served was wholesome, properly identified, and in compliance with standards prescribed by the food safety and quality regulations.

Franchise owners in these areas followed a three-part strategy: First, distribute an illustrated materials kit on McDonald's beef to customers. Second, if this action doesn't work, run local ads on the company's high quality of food. Third, as a last resort, contact the press for coverage on food quality. In working with franchise owners, McDonald's stressed one unbreakable rule: Never mention the word *worm.*

Despite the efforts by franchises in the affected areas, sales plummeted. McDonald's research found that although most consumers believed the rumor was ridiculous, they were beginning to go elsewhere for fast food. Meanwhile, the rumor was catching fire. Over 75 percent of the populations of Atlanta and Cincinnati had heard the rumor; in Atlanta, many believed it was true.

In November, McDonald's decided to go public and attack the rumor nationwide. At a press conference in Atlanta, the company denied it used "protein additives" in its hamburger meat. Shortly thereafter, McDonald's ran a nationwide ad campaign with color photos of its hamburgers and copy stressing its 100 percent U.S. government inspected beef.

A few weeks later, the rumor faded away. However, some observers questioned McDonald's strategy. Some observers asserted that McDonald's should have gone public sooner. Others argued that they should not have gone public at all.

Source: Adapted from Frederick Koenig, *Rumor in the Marketplace* (Dover, Mass: Auburn Publishing, 1985).

Questions for Analysis

1. What are the pros and cons of going public with a rumor and denying it in a nationally publicized press conference?
2. In your opinion, did McDonald's follow the best strategy? What other options could they have chosen?

CASE 13–2   "Do You Know What I Like about You?"

Jim McCabe, only 33, is a successful bloodstock agent in the highly volatile and competitive thoroughbred horse industry. He locates thoroughbred buyers and sellers for his clients, as well as breeding rights for stallions and mares. It is a complicated and risky business. His knowledge of thoroughbred horses and their bloodlines, along with much hard work, has enabled him to achieve success. Educated in the physical sciences (master's degree), he chose the thoroughbred industry because of his love of horses. His firm, which he began alone five years ago, now employs five other agents, three researchers whose task it is to research thoroughbred bloodlines, three secretaries, an office manager, and myself. My title when I was hired four months ago was assistant office manager, but no one ever told me what I was supposed to do. For a part-time job while in college, the pay is good, and I'm learning a great deal about a business I knew nothing about previously. In addition, there is always some kind of excitement around the office.

I stood by the door of McCabe's office. He was on the phone, and before I could knock, he motioned for me to come in and sit down. Every inch of his desk was covered by reports, memos, horse-sale catalogs, telephone messages, and racing results. Other reminders on bits of paper were taped to the wall, and a "to do" list with at least 10 entries on it was taped to the base of the telephone. Evidently these were things that he had "to do" immediately. While talking on the phone, he added another item to this list.

As he continued the phone conversation, he was shaking his head and signing letters at the same time. Finally, he put his hand over the phone and said to me, "This is Robinson in Florida on that two-year-old filly deal. All the tests on her leg are not in yet, but he insists on giving me every detail on the entire test procedure. The guy is going to drive me nuts."

Turning his attention back to the phone he removed his hand and resumed talking. "Right, Robbie, OK . . . Great . . . OK . . . Sure . . . Call me back on that . . . Terrific . . . 'Bye."

He hung up the phone with a sigh of relief and looked at me. "Do you know what I like about you, Tinsley?" I didn't have time to answer, nor did he, because the phone rang again. "Yea . . . Fine . . . Terrific . . . Count me in . . . 'Bye." At this point, his secretary looked in and said, "John Towne of Winthrop Farms is on hold. It sounds urgent."

McCabe shook his head again and went back to the telephone. After a few minutes of conversation, he put his hand over the receiver and called to his secretary. "Get Johnson and Burke in here, fast." Johnson was the office manager, and Burke was an agent. They arrived as he hung up the phone.

"Burke," he said, "you know that deal you put together for the syndication of that three-year-old, Ol' Blue? Well, they don't like it. Put this information into it and tell me what effect the changes will have on us. When you get it finished, bring it to me so I can call Towne back." Burke left.

"Johnson, I want all of the training fees, jockey expenses, and all other expenses on that horse. Don't give them to me by the month like you did last time. I need totals in *all* categories; and for crying out loud, this time break out the 'other' category a little better. I looked real good last week when Towne asked me what the $6,300 in 'other expenses' was for. I want all the information at my fingertips in case we've got to go to war with these people." Johnson left.

"Now, Tinsley, what did you need me for?"

"Just sign this bill of sale," I said. "No reason to spend a lot of time on it. It's for the sale of that yearling you asked me to take care of."

"That's what I like about you, Tinsley," he said as he leaned back in his chair and signed the bill of sale. "When I give you a job, you listen. Then you do it right the first time and tell me when it's done. You don't tell me how you did it, the problems you're having doing it, who you met while doing it, and every other Mickey Mouse detail. If the rest of the people around here had that ability, I might be able to get some work done. I think I got more work done five years ago when I had nobody working for me."

As I left his office, I didn't have time to thank him, because the phone began ringing.

QUESTIONS FOR ANALYSIS

1. What is your impression of McCabe?
2. What is your opinion of his communications to the other employees of the firm?
3. What might be the reasons for his demands on employees?
4. Could this influence the effectiveness of the organization? In what ways?

EXPERIENTIAL EXERCISE

PERCEPTUAL DIFFERENCES

Purpose

To illustrate how people perceive the same situation differently through the process of selective perception.

The Exercise in Class

The instructor will divide the class into groups of four students each. Each group should then complete the following steps:

Source: William V. Haney, *Communication and Interpersonal Relations: Text and Cases* (Homweood, Ill.: Richard D. Irwin, 1979), pp. 250–51.

1. As individuals, complete the following quiz. Do not talk to your group members until everyone in the class has finished.
2. Your instructor will provide the answers to the 15 questions. Score your responses.
3. As a group, discuss your members' responses. Focus your discussion on the following questions:
    a. Why did perceptions differ across members? What factors could account for these differences?
    b. Many people don't perform very well with this quiz. Why? What other factors beyond selective perception can adversely affect performance?

Quiz: *The robbery* The lights in a store had just been turned off by a businessman when a man appeared and demanded money. The owner opened a cash register. The contents of the cash register were scooped up, and the man sped away. A member of the police force was notified promptly.

Answer the following questions about the story by circling T *for true,* F *for false, or* ? *for unknown.*

1. A man appeared after the owner turned off his store lights.   T   F   ?
2. The robber was a man.   T   F   ?
3. The man who appeared did not demand money.   T   F   ?
4. The man who opened the cash register was the owner.   T   F   ?
5. The store owner scooped up the contents of the cash register and ran away.   T   F   ?
6. Someone opened a cash register.   T   F   ?
7. After the man who demanded money scooped up the contents of the cash register, he ran away.   T   F   ?
8. While the cash register contained money, the story does not state how much.   T   F   ?
9. The robber demanded money of the owner.   T   F   ?
10. A businessman had just turned off the lights when a man appeared in the store.   T   F   ?
11. It was broad daylight when the man appeared.   T   F   ?
12. The man who appeared opened the cash register.   T   F   ?
13. No one demanded money.   T   F   ?
14. The story concerns a series of events in which only three persons are referred to: the owner of the store, a man who demanded money, and a member of the police force.   T   F   ?
15. The following events occurred: someone demanded money, a cash register was opened, its contents were scooped up, and a man dashed out of the store.   T   F   ?

A Learning Message

This exercise aptly demonstrates the wide variety of perceptual differences among people when considering a situation where little factual information is provided. The exercise should also indicate that most people selectively perceive the information they are comfortable with in analyzing a situation. Many will also subconsciously fill in gaps of information with assumptions they suppose are facts.

14

Organizational Change and Development

Learning Objectives

After completing Chapter 14, you should be able to:

Define
the term *organization development.*

Describe
a five-step model or framework that displays the organization change process.

Discuss
four major reasons why people resist change.

Compare
specific techniques that are used to bring about structural, people, and technological changes.

Identify
some of the productivity and human resource advantages and disadvantages associated with robotics in work settings.

The Peters Principles of Change

Tom Peters, famous management consultant, sees change as a major threat to large businesses that cannot adapt. He outlines 10 forces that contribute to the demise of the large corporation:

1. *Unprecedented uncertainty.* Today, things are not as stable and predictable as they were 25 years ago, but many companies have refused to address the changes.

2. *Time.* Speed, flexibility, and adaptiveness are becoming prominent competitive forces. The computer-age ability to get instant feedback for quick decision making can help small companies manage uncertainty—and force the rest of the industry to follow suit.

3. *Fractured markets.* Niche marketing is a growing, driving force that challenges most large companies, which have traditionally gained profits through mass production.

4. *Quality, design, and service.* In many cases, U.S. products are inferior in quality and design to imported goods. To reverse this trend, companies must become obsessed with those issues. Serving the customers' needs reliably is also of utmost importance.

5. *Giant firms' behavior.* Major firms have carelessly fumbled away advantages and technologies. The Goliath company of the future cannot afford to lose such advantages and must "think small" in order to maneuver in the market.

6. *Organizational configurations.* Hierarchies may be a thing of the past. With technology-based information systems, computerized networking, and expert systems, companies can function without all those layers of management.

7. *Modifications in economies of scale.* Old ideas of economies of scale are being challenged. Big might be best for access to capital and factor markets, but successful large firms of the future will be collections of smaller firms.

8. *Cooperative networks.* If companies are going to be specialists, they will need to rely more on other companies. In a cooperative network, interdependent firms depend on each other's success and benefit together.

9. *Internationalization for all.* Businesses operating today are, in effect, each other's subcontractors. With the global nature of information and transportation, any national market is any other company's opportunity.

10. *Line workers' job enrichment.* The most critical employees for getting cost-saving information and quality improvement are the line workers. In the future, these workers have to be given more decision-making responsibility.

How will organizations react to such dramatic changes? In this chapter, we will examine these and other forces, evaluate their impact, and examine some alternatives.

Source: Adapted from Tom Peters, "Tomorrow's Companies' New Products, New Markets, New Competition, New Thinking," *Economist,* March 4, 1989.

Organizational change is a pressing problem for modern managers; and in recent years, a great deal of literature has appeared focusing on the need for *planning* for change.[1] Some companies have instituted staff units whose mission is organizational planning.[2] The planning units are specific responses to the need for systematic, formalized procedures to anticipate and implement changes in the structure, technology, and personnel of the organization.

Other companies are changed by specialists, like Don McCulloch, called turnaround experts. McCulloch, a change manager, was head of marketing for Pizza Hut in 1981 during the development and launch of pan pizza, now the chain's top product (it accounts for approximately 70 percent of sales).[3] He helped change the profit picture at C. F. Hathaway, the shirt company. He then turned his talents to change Nutri/System (a weight loss company) from just one of many to a firm in which sales doubled and profit increased tenfold after his second year as owner. McCulloch has a knack for anticipating market changes. He moves fast, acting quickly to change structure, technology, and personnel after carefully studying the situation.

In this chapter, the processes of organizational change and development are discussed. Before beginning, however, we must explain the manner in which we are using the terms *change* and *development*. As even the casual reader of management literature soon must realize, the term *organization development* (OD) involves a variety of meanings and management strategies. In its most restrictive sense, it refers specifically to some form of sensitivity training; in a larger and more encompassing sense, it refers to any systematically planned, programmatic effort to improve the effectiveness of an organization through the application of behavioral science concepts, theories, and approaches. The change effort may focus on the way in which the organization is structured, the behavior of employees, or the technology that is used in getting the work done. Therefore, *OD is a method for facilitating change and development in structures and processes (e.g., relationships, roles), people (e.g., styles, skills), and technology (e.g., more routineness, more challenge).*[4]

The growing realization that organizations can be changed and made more effective through managerial applications of behavioral science knowledge has created a wealth of literature.[5] This chapter presents some of the established ideas from this literature, in the context of practical management. In order to provide a theme, we present the material in terms of a model describing the important factors of the change and development process. For simplicity, we will use the phrase "the management of change" to include the concept of organization development in its broadest sense.

[1]Organizational change is broadly interpreted for purposes of this discussion. Some management students restrict the term to changes in the formal structure, but we will include changes in employee behavior and technology.

[2]Donald L. Kirkpatrick, *How to Manage Change Effectively* (San Francisco: Jossey-Bass, 1985).

[3]Christy Marshall, "Turnaround King," *Business Month,* February 1989, pp. 40–43.

[4]Frank Friedlander and L. Dave Brown, "Organization Development," *Review of Psychology,* 1974.

[5]Michael Beer, *Organization Change and Development* (Santa Monica, Calif.: Goodyear Publishing, 1980); Wendell L. French and Cecil H. Bell, Jr., *Organization Development* (Englewood Cliffs, N.J.: Prentice-Hall, 1978); Edgar Huse, *Organization Development* (St. Paul, Minn.: West Publishing, 1980).

RESISTANCE TO CHANGE

Most organizational change efforts eventually run into some form of employee resistance. Change triggers rational and irrational emotional reaction because of the uncertainty involved.

WHY DO PEOPLE RESIST CHANGE?

Instead of assuming that employees will resist change or act in a particular manner, it is better to consider in a general way the reasons why people resist change. Four common reasons have been found.[6] As you read about each of them, think about your own reasons for resisting change. Do any of the reasons fit you?

Parochial Self-Interest.   One reason some people resist organizational change is the fear of losing something they value. Individuals fear the loss of power, resources, freedom to make decisions, friendships, and prestige. In cases involving fear of loss, individuals think of themselves and what they may have to give up. The fearful individual only has his or her parochial self-interest in mind when resisting change. The organization and the interests of co-workers are not given much priority.

Misunderstanding and Lack of Trust.   When individuals do not fully understand why change is occurring and what its implications are, they will resist change. Misunderstanding about the intent and consequences of organizational change is more likely to occur when trust is lacking between the individual and the person initiating the change. In organizations characterized by high levels of mistrust, misunderstandings will probably accompany any organizational change.

Different Assessments.   Since individuals view change—its intent, potential consequences, and personal impact—differently, there are often different assessments of the situation. Those initiating changes see more positive results because of the change, while those being affected and not initiating the changes see more costs involved with the change. Take, for example, the introduction of robots. Management might view the change to robots as a benefit, while subordinates may consider the robot introduction as a signal that they will lose their jobs.

The initiators of change frequently make two overly broad assumptions: (1) They have all the relevant data and information available to diagnose the situation. (2) Those to be affected by the change also have the same facts. Whatever the circumstances, the initiators and the affected employees often have different data and information. This leads to resistance to change. However, in some cases, the resistance is healthy for the firm, especially in the situation where the affected employees possess more valid data and information.

[6]Four reasons are discussed in John P. Kotter and Leonard A. Schlesinger, "Choosing Strategies for Change," *Harvard Business Review,* March–April 1979, pp. 106–14. Our discussion of resistance to change is based on this article.

Low Tolerance for Change.   People resist change because they fear they will not be able to develop the new skills necessary to perform well. Individuals may understand clearly that change is necessary, but they are emotionally unable to make the transition. For example, this type of resistance is found in offices that are introducing computerized word-processing systems. Some secretaries and even their bosses are resisting these changes that are clearly needed if office productivity is to be improved.

A low tolerance for change also is found in individuals who resist change to save face. Making the necessary adjustments and changes would be, they assume, an open admission that some of their previous behavior, decisions, and attitudes were wrong.

MINIMIZING RESISTANCE TO CHANGE

Resisting change is a human response, and management needs to take steps to minimize such resistance. Minimizing resistance can reduce the time it takes for a change to be accepted or tolerated. Also, the performance of employees can rebound more quickly if resistance is kept at a minimal level.

A number of methods have been useful in minimizing resistance to change. Table 14–1 summarizes six approaches.

1. *Education and communication.*   One of the most common ways to reduce resistance is to communicate and educate before the change occurs. This helps people prepare for the change. Paving the way, showing the logic, and keeping everyone informed helps cut down resistance. The Management Focus explains how education can be used to change a person's mind-set.

2. *Participation and involvement.*   Having those to be affected help design and implement the change helps increase their commitment to the change. If individuals feel their ideas and attitudes are being included in the change effort, they tend to become less resistant and more receptive.

3. *Facilitation and support.*   Being supportive is an important management characteristic when change is implemented. It is especially important for managers to be supportive (e.g., showing concern for subordinates, being a good listener, going to bat for subordinates on an issue that is important) and to help facilitate the change when fear and anxiety are at the heart of resistance.

4. *Negotiation and agreement.*   Reducing resistance can be brought about through negotiation. Discussion and analysis can help managers identify points of negotiation and agreement. Negotiated agreement involves giving something to another party to reduce resistance. For example, getting a person to move to a less desirable work location may require paying him a bonus or increasing his monthly salary. Once this negotiation agreement is reached, others may expect the manager to grant them the same concessions in the future.

5. *Manipulation and co-optation.*   Manipulation involves the use of devious tactics to convince others that a change is in their best interests. Holding back information, playing one person against another, and providing slanted information are examples of manipulation. Co-opting an individual involves giving him or her a major role in the design or implementation of the change.

TABLE 14–1   Methods for Reducing Resistance to Change

Approach	Situational Use	Advantages	Drawbacks
Education + Communication	Where there is a lack of information or inaccurate information and analysis.	Once persuaded, people often will help with the implementation of the change.	Can be very time-consuming if many people are involved.
Participation + Involvement	Where the initiators do not have all the information they need to design the change, and where others have considerable power to resist.	People who participate will be committed to implementing change, and any relevant information they have will be integrated into the change plan.	Can be very time-consuming if participators design an inappropriate change.
Facilitation + Support	Where people are resisting because of adjustment problems.	No other approach works as well with adjustment problems.	Can be time-consuming, expensive, and still fail.
Negotiation + Agreement	Where someone or some group will clearly lose out in a change, and where that group has considerable power to resist.	Sometimes it is a relatively easy way to avoid major resistance.	Can be too expensive in many cases if it alerts others to negotiate for compliance.
Manipulation + Co-optation	Where other tactics will not work or are too expensive.	It can be a relatively quick and inexpensive solution to resistance problems.	Can lead to future problems if people feel manipulated.
Explicit + Implicit coercion	Where speed is essential, and the change initiators possess considerable power.	It is speedy and can overcome any kind of resistance.	Can be risky if it leaves people angry at the initiators.

Source: Reprinted by permission of the *Harvard Business Review*. An exhibit from "Choosing Strategies for Change" by John P. Kotter and Leonard A. Schlesinger, March/April 1979. Copyright © 1979 by the President and Fellows of Harvard College; all rights reserved.

Managers need to carefully analyze the change situation before deciding on an appropriate approach to reducing resistance to change.

The ethical problems associated with manipulation and co-optation are obvious and should preclude the widespread use of these techniques.

6. *Explicit and implicit coercion.* In using explicit and/or implicit coercion, the manager engages in threatening behavior. He or she threatens the employees with job loss, reduced promotion opportunities, poor job assignments, and loss of privileges. The coercion is intended to reduce a person's resistance to the management-initiated change. Coercive behavior can be risky because of the bad feelings and hostility generated.

Each of these six approaches has advantages and drawbacks that need to be carefully considered. Managers can use them in different situations and in various combinations. Use of any of the six approaches depends on a systematic analysis of the particular situation. Often this involves the use of a model, or framework, to help provide guidelines and an overview of the situation.

MANAGEMENT FOCUS

Training Mind-Set Needed for Change

Change is one of the most threatening aspects of a person's job. Early on, employees are taught how to do a particular task and, as they become proficient, are rewarded with bonuses and promotions. They learn how external events can result in certain organizational reactions, and they get a feel for the business. This is their organizational mind-set.

Changing the tasks introduces an element of uncertainty and a modification of the mind-set. Because the mind-set represents the employee's "place" in the company, he or she will resist any alterations. This is why it is so difficult for organizations to implement wholesale changes effectively.

The ability to change mind-sets creates an important competitive advantage for the firm. First, employees facilitate business strategies and allow them to happen. Without the help of lower managers and workers, the company can fall into a SPOTS ("strategic plans on top shelf") trap. A strategic plan that is not implemented is of little value to a company.

Second, people address organizational goals from individual perspectives. If all the employees of an organization can concentrate on the same goals and have the same mind-set, there are no limits to the possible accomplishments. Rather than solving problems through lengthy and potentially damaging political negotiation, individuals can become aligned with the company's goals and can solve coordination problems before they reach the political arena. This shared mind-set can be achieved in many ways. A Honda assembly plant in Marysville, Ohio, requires applicants to write an essay on why working for Honda is consistent with their lifetime goals. This initiates a set of values about working for Honda before the applicants are even hired.

Third, people can help build a capacity for change. Performance evaluation and management systems can shift reward structures to emphasize change. Many times, a company wants to change but does not modify the reward system that is vital to the mind-set of the employees. 3M changed its policy so that a larger percentage of the sales personnel's bonuses was determined by sales of products introduced in the last three years. This resulted in an increased awareness of innovation.

Source: Adapted from David Ulrich and Arthur Yeung, "A Shared Mindset," *Personnel Administrator*, March 1989.

A MODEL FOR MANAGING CHANGE

The management of change can be broken down into subprocesses or steps. A model describing this process is illustrated in Figure 14–1 and consists of five steps linked in a logical sequence. The prospects for initiating successful change and minimizing resistance are enhanced when the manager explicitly and formally goes through each successive step. For this reason, each step and process is discussed in a separate section of this chapter.

The knowledgeable manager is one who recognizes the multiplicity of alternatives and is not predisposed toward one particular approach to the

FIGURE 14–1   The Process of Managing Organizational Change

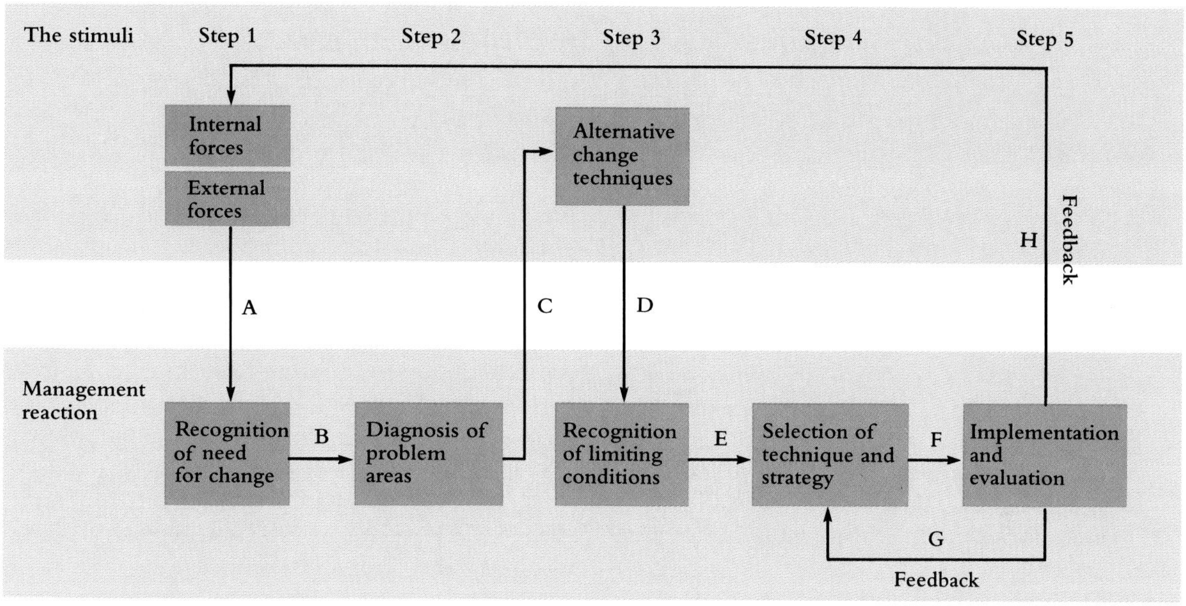

Managers will manage change with greater success by explicitly and formally following each successive step in the process.

exclusion of all others.[7] At the same time, the effective manager avoids the pitfall of stagnation.

A flexible, forward-looking stance for managers is an essential attribute for using the change model outlined in Figure 14–1. The model assumes that forces for change continually act upon the firm, reflecting the dynamic character of the modern world. At the same time, it is the manager's responsibility to sort out the information received from the firm's control system and other sources that reflect the magnitude of change forces (A). This information is the basis for recognizing the need for change; it is equally desirable to recognize when change is *not* needed. But once the problem is recognized, the manager must diagnose the problem (B) and identify relevant alternative change techniques (C). The change technique selected must be appropriate for solving the problem, as constrained by limiting conditions (D). One example of a limiting condition discussed in an earlier chapter is the prevailing character of group norms. A work group may support some of the change techniques but may sabotage others.

The fact that a change program can be thwarted underscores the fact that the choice of change *strategy* is as important as the change technique itself (E).

[7]See the range of change strategies in Wendell L. French, Cecil H. Bell, Jr., and Robert A. Zawacki, *Organization Development* (Plano, Tex.: Business Publications, 1987).

Finally, managers must implement the change and monitor the change process and change results (F). The model includes feedback to the selection-of-strategy phase and to the forces-for-change phase. These feedback loops (G and H) suggest that the change process itself must be monitored and evaluated. The implementation strategy may be faulty and lead to poor results, but prompt action could correct the situation. Moreover, the feedback loop to the initial step recognizes that *no* change is final. A new situation is created within which other problems and issues will emerge; a new setting is created that will itself become subject to change. The model suggests no final solution. Rather, it emphasizes that managers operate in a dynamic setting where the only certainty is change itself.

STEP 1: STIMULI—FORCES FOR CHANGE

The forces for change (stimuli) can be classified into two groups: external and internal forces. **External change forces** include changes in the marketplace, technology, and environment; they usually are beyond the control of the manager. **Internal change forces** operate inside the firm and are generally within the control of management.

EXTERNAL FORCES

Managers of business firms historically have been concerned with reacting to changes in the *marketplace*. Competitors introduce new products (Diet Pepsi versus Tab), increase advertising (General Motors versus Toyota), reduce prices (Delta Airlines versus United), or improve customer service (Apple versus IBM). In each case, a response is required unless the manager is content to permit the erosion of profit and market share. At the same time, changes occur in customer tastes and incomes. The firm's products may no longer have customer appeal; customers may be able to purchase less expensive, higher-quality forms of the same product.

The Coca-Cola Company instituted one of the major changes in a successful product when it introduced New Coke. The firm studied the competition (Pepsi), conducted over 190,000 taste tests around the United States, and decided to make a change. The original formula for Coca-Cola was dropped, and the sweeter and smoother New Coke went on the market.[8] Did external forces drive Coca-Cola to make the change, or was it a progressive management gamble or poor market research? The results indicated it was poor market research and a gamble. Sacks of mail and over 1,500 telephone calls a day registered the irate consumers' vote. A group called Old Cola Drinkers staged protests and even threatened to bring a class action suit.

---

[8]Philip Kotler and Gary Armstrong, *Principles of Marketing* (Englewood Cliffs, N.J.: Prentice-Hall, 1989), pp. 87–88.

The gasoline industry is one of many businesses that has responded to changes in external forces.

In a short two months, old Coke was back. It sold side by side with New Coke and outsold it two to one. External forces (consumers) actually indicated that Coca-Cola was a part of society that shouldn't be changed. The pressure of the "Pepsi Challenge" on Coca-Cola almost cost the company its lead as the number one seller in the $25 billion soft drink business.

Another source of external forces in the marketplace is that of the supply of resources to the firm. A change in the quality and quantity of human resources can dictate changes in the firm. For example, the adoption of automated processes can be stimulated by a decline in the supply of labor. The techniques of coal mining and tobacco farming have changed greatly because of labor shortages. We also can understand how changes in the supply of materials and energy can cause the firm to attempt to substitute one material for another. Rayon stockings and synthetic rubber tires are direct outgrowths of World War II–induced shortages of raw materials.

The second source of external change forces is *technology*. The knowledge explosion since World War II has introduced new technology for nearly every management function. Computers have made possible both high-speed data processing and the solution to complex production problems. New machines, new processes, and robots have revolutionized the way in which many products are manufactured and distributed.[9]

Finally, the third external force consists of *environmental changes*. Managers must be "tuned in" to great movements over which they have no control but that, in time, affect the firm's fate. Worldwide changes in international markets and competition are occurring rapidly. Japan, Korea, Taiwan, West Germany, and Hong Kong have become major economic forces. Within these countries are firms that are competing worldwide for human resource talent, market share, and technology. The great movement of the 1990s and beyond will be the continued internationalization of the business world, which will create intensified environmental forces for change.

---

[9]Leon Martel, *Mastering Change* (New York: Simon & Schuster, 1986).

INTERNAL FORCES

The forces for change occurring within the organization can be traced to *processes* and *people*. Process forces include decision making, communications, and interpersonal relations. Breakdowns or problems in any of these processes can create forces for change. Decisions either are not being made, are made too late, or are of poor quality. Communications are short-circuited, redundant, or simply inadequate. Tasks are not undertaken or not completed because the person responsible did not "get the word." Because of inadequate and nonexistent communications, a customer order is not filled, a grievance is not processed, an invoice is not filed, or a supplier is not paid. Interpersonal and interdepartmental conflicts reflect breakdown in the interaction between people.

Low levels of morale and high levels of absenteeism and turnover are symptoms of people problems that must be followed up. A wildcat strike or a walkout may be the most tangible sign of a problem; such tactics usually are employed because they arouse the management to action. There is in most organizations a certain level of employee discontent; a great danger is to ignore the complaints and suggestions. The spring 1989 machinists union strike at Eastern Air Lines illustrates what can occur when problems are not recognized.[10] The machinists refused to take the company-recommended 20 percent pay cut. And pilot complaints and requests for job security were not heeded by management.

In the five-step process of change, the first step is the *recognition* phase. It is at this point that management must decide to act or not to act.

STEP 1: REACTION—RECOGNITION OF THE NEED FOR CHANGE

Information helps managers comprehend the magnitude of the change forces. Some of the important sources of information were discussed above. Certainly, the most important information comes from the firm's preliminary, concurrent, and feedback control data. Indeed, the process of change can be viewed as a part of the control function, specifically the corrective action requirement. Financial statements, quality control data, budget, and standard cost information are important media through which both external and internal forces are revealed. Declining profit margins and market shares are tangible signs that the firm's competitive position is deteriorating and that change may be required. Spiraling hospital costs may be a sign of inefficient hospital management. Because of their crucial importance, these sources of feedback control information are highly developed in most organizations.

Intel microchips which power every IBM personal computer and most of the machines compatible with them are constantly being challenged.[11] A new

---

[10]"Lorenzo Is Running Out of Choices—and Time," *Business Week,* March 20, 1989, pp. 37–38.

[11]Carrie Gottlieb, "Intel's Plan for Staying on Top," *Fortune,* March 27, 1989, pp. 98–100.

technology has emerged that threatens Intel's dominance in the market. Recognizing the technology and deciding to produce the new technology itself, Intel is now in the business of producing ultrafast processors based on a design called RISC (reduced instruction set computing). Intel has recognized a need to change its product to stay on top and has taken action.

STEP 2: REACTION—DIAGNOSIS OF THE PROBLEM

Before appropriate action can be taken, the symptoms of the problem must be analyzed to discover the problem itself. Experience and judgment are critical to this phase unless the problem is readily apparent to all observers. However, managers often disagree as to the nature of the problem. There is no magic formula, but the objectives of this phase can be met by answering three questions:

1. What is the problem, as distinct from the symptoms of the problem?
2. What must be changed to resolve the problem?
3. What outcomes (objectives) are expected from the change, and how will such objectives be measured?

The answers to these questions can come from information ordinarily found in organizations, such as financial statements, department reports, or attitude surveys. Or it may be necessary to generate ad hoc information through the creation of committees or task forces. Meetings between managers and employees provide a variety of points of view that can be sifted through by a smaller group. Technical operational problems may be diagnosed easily, but more subtle human relations problems usually entail extensive analysis.

One approach to diagnosing the problem is the attitude survey. Attitude questionnaires such as shown in Figure 14–2 can be administered to the entire work force or to a sample of it. Such surveys permit the respondents to evaluate and rate (1) management, (2) pay and pay-related items, (3) working conditions, (4) equipment, and (5) other job-related items. The appropriate use of such surveys requires that the data be collected (usually by questionnaires) from members of an organization, analyzed in detail, and communicated to various organization members. The objective of the survey is to pinpoint the problem or problems as perceived by the members of the organization. Subsequent feedback discussions of the survey results at all levels of the organization can add additional insights into the nature of the problem.[12]

The approach management uses to diagnose the problem is a crucial part of the total strategy for a change. As will be seen in a later section, the manner in which the problem is diagnosed has clear implications for the final success of the proposed change.

Finally, the diagnostic step must specify *objectives* for change. Given the diagnosis of the problem, it is necessary to define objectives to guide as well as to evaluate the outcome of the change.

---

[12]Randall B. Dunham and Frank J. Smith, *Organizational Surveys* (Glenview, Ill.: Scott, Foresman, 1979).

FIGURE 14–2	Employee Attitude Survey (sample)*

INSTRUCTIONS

This is a survey of the ideas and opinions of Baker Company salaried employees. WHAT YOU SAY IN THIS QUESTION-NAIRE IS COMPLETELY CONFIDENTIAL. We do not want to know who you are. We do want to know, however, how employees with different interests and experience and doing different kinds of work feel about their jobs and Baker.

This is not a test. There are no right or wrong answers. Whether the results of this survey give a true picture of the Baker Company depends on whether you answer each of the questions in the way you really feel. The usefulness of this survey in making Baker a better place to work depends on the honesty and care with which you answer the questions.

Your answers will be compiled with many others and summarized to prepare a *report* for Baker. Your identity will always be protected. We do not need your name, only your impressions. Your written comments will be put in typewritten form so that your handwriting will not even be seen by anyone at Baker.

Please complete each part of the survey so that all of your impressions can be recorded. Remember, your honest impressions are all that we are asking for.

PART I: THE JOB AND CONDITIONS

The statements below are related to certain aspects of your job at Baker. Please circle the response number that best describes how you feel about each statement.

1—strongly disagree   2—disagree   3—undecided   4—agree   5—strongly agree

Pay

	Strongly Disagree	Disagree	Undecided	Agree	Strongly Agree
My pay is all right for the kind of work I do.	1	2	3	4	5
I make as much money as most of my friends.	1	2	3	4	5
My pay allows me to keep up with the cost of living.	1	2	3	4	5
I am satisfied with the pay I receive for my job.	1	2	3	4	5
Most employees at Baker get paid at least what they deserve.	1	2	3	4	5
I understand how my salary is determined.	1	2	3	4	5

What changes, if any, should be made with the Baker pay system?

Fringe Benefits

	Strongly Disagree	Disagree	Undecided	Agree	Strongly Agree
Our major fringe benefit plan provides excellent coverage.	1	2	3	4	5
I understand what our fringe benefits at Baker are.	1	2	3	4	5
I am satisfied with our fringe benefit plan.	1	2	3	4	5

What, if anything, should be done with the Baker fringe benefit plans?

---

*This is only a portion of an attitude survey used by John M. Ivancevich and Michael T. Matteson in a study conducted for an organization.

Attitude surveys can provide management with a wealth of information within a short period of time.

STEP 3: STIMULI—ALTERNATIVE CHANGE TECHNIQUES

The choice of the particular change technique depends on the nature of the problem management has diagnosed. Management must determine which alternative is most likely to produce the desired outcome. As we have noted above, diagnosis of the problem includes specification of the outcomes management desires from the change. In this section, we will describe a number of change techniques. They will be classified according to the major focus of the technique: structure, people, or technology.[13] This classification of organizational change techniques in no way implies a distinct division among the three types. On the contrary, the interrelationships of structure, people, and technology must be acknowledged and anticipated. The majority of literature on organizational change indicates the relative weakness of efforts to change only structure (e.g., job design), only people (e.g., sensitivity training), or only technology (e.g., introducing new equipment or a new computer).[14]

STRUCTURAL CHANGE

Changes in the structure of the organization ordinarily follow changes in strategy.[15] Logically, the organizing function follows the planning function since the structure is a means for achieving the goals established through planning. A publicly announced major structural change occurred at AT&T when six major businesses were restructured into 19 smaller units. Seven regional companies (e.g., Bell Atlantic, Pacific Telesis Group, Nynex) were created after Judge Harold Green ordered the structural breakup of AT&T.[16] General Electric cut the number of management layers from nine to four. To make the company feel small, McDonald's added a position in its structure called the vice president for individuality.[17]

Structural change in the context of organizational change refers to managerial action that attempts to improve performance by altering the formal structure of task and authority relationships. At the same time, we must recognize that the structure creates human and social relationships that gradually can become ends for the members of the organization. These relationships, when they have been defined and made legitimate by management, introduce an element of stability.[18] Members of the organization may resist efforts to disrupt these relationships.

Structural changes alter some aspect of the formal task and authority definitions. As we have seen, the design of an organization involves definition

[13]See Harold J. Leavitt, "Applied Organizational Change in Industry: Structural, Technological and Humanistic Approaches," in *Handbook of Organizations*, ed. James G. March (Skokie, Ill.: Rand McNally, 1965), pp. 1144–68.

[14]Clayton P. Alderfer, "Change Processes in Organization," in *Handbook of Industrial and Organizational Psychology*, ed. Marvin D. Dunnette (Skokie, Ill.: Rand McNally, 1976).

[15]Alfred Chandler, *Strategy and Structure* (Cambridge, Mass.: MIT Press, 1962).

[16]Kenneth Labich, "Was Breaking Up AT&T a Good Idea?" *Fortune*, January 2, 1989, pp. 82–86.

[17]"Is Your Company Too Big?" *Business Week*, March 27, 1989, pp. 84–94.

[18]R. K. Ready, *The Administrator's Job* (New York: McGraw-Hill, 1967), pp. 24–30.

The nature of jobs changes in response to technology.

and specification of job depth and range, grouping of jobs in departments, determination of the size of groups reporting to a single manager, and provision of staff assistance. Within this framework, the communication, decision-making, and human interaction processes occur.

Changes in the Nature of Jobs.   Changes in the nature of jobs originate with the implementation of new methods and new machines. Job enrichment, work simplification, and job enlargement are examples of methods changes. Scientific management introduced significant changes in the way work is done, through the use of motion and time studies. These methods tend to create highly specialized jobs. Job enrichment (see Chapter 10 for a discussion of motivation and job enrichment), however, moves in the opposite direction, toward despecialization.

An interesting example of attempted job enrichment took place in the stock transfer department of a large metropolitan bank.[19] The department was responsible for transferring the ownership of securities from one owner to another and recording the transfer. In order to remain competitive with other

---

[19]Linda L. Frank and J. Richard Hackman, "A Failure of Job Enrichment: The Case of the Change that Wasn't," *Journal of Applied Behavioral Science,* October 1975, pp. 413–36.

banks in the area, the entire stock transfer had to be completed within 48 hours. At the time of the study, 300 employees worked in the department.

Each employee reported to a "work coordinator," who was responsible for 8 to 12 employees performing the same function. A job enrichment plan was developed in which the work of the department was divided into 13 modules. The modules focused on total responsibility for a group of corporations whose stock was handled by the bank. Under the old arrangement, employees arbitrarily handled whatever work was assigned.

It was hoped that the assignment of a specific set of corporations to each group working on a module would increase the employees' identification with and commitment to the work. These feelings were to be strengthened by allowing the workers in the module to leave work together when the security transactions from their assigned companies had been completed.

Modules were scheduled to be introduced one at a time. The researchers collected data on the nature of the jobs themselves, employee performance, and the change process by use of questionnaires, interviews, company records, and actual observations.

Employees reported almost no impact from the changes in the characteristic of the jobs. Researchers concluded that the type of changes in structure that, if performed, should have increased performance and effectiveness were not initiated as planned. For example, it was planned that employees would experience more autonomy in the modules, because each module would be making its own decision. In fact, however, no structural changes were made to encourage the module members to take more responsibility. Moreover, managers continued to give orders and to supervise rather closely. In effect, management did not delegate as had been planned. And employees had the same feeling as before the modules were started—namely, that they had little autonomy.

This example illustrates the value of research even on unsuccessful job changes. In a "pure" sense, this change in the job did not occur. However, it provided a valuable lesson about the interrelationships between people and structure. It also indicated that job enrichment is not always a simple solution to managerial work-related problems.

Enlargement.   Job enlargement involves making a job "larger" by increasing the number of tasks to perform. A traditional assembly line can be converted to a line with enlarged jobs. The assembly line is created by breaking down the total product (a television set, an automobile, a clothes dryer) into specialized stations. Each station has tools and workers that do a specific job. Stations are connected to each other by a workflow plan. At a General Motors assembly plant in Lordstown, Ohio, the average time cycle that a worker performs on a job at a station is 36 seconds. Thus, a worker faced a new automobile part over 700 times in each eight-hour shift.

Saab Company in Sweden decided to build a new automobile engine assembly plant and considered alternative ways of setting up jobs on the assembly line.[20] The engineering team working on the problem decided that

[20]W. F. Dowling, "Job Design in the Assembly-Line: Farewell to the Blue Collar Blues?" *Organizational Dynamics,* Spring 1973, pp. 51–67; P. G. Gyllenhammer, *People at Work* (Reading, Mass.: Addison-Wesley Publishing, 1977).

FIGURE 14–3   Saab Engine Assembly Line before Enlarging Jobs

In Saab's traditional assembly line, an engine spent, on average, 1.8 minutes at each of seven workstations.

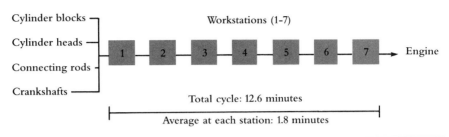

the typical system of assembly with a cycle of 12.6 minutes to put an engine together (1.8 minutes per station) at seven workstations could be improved. The traditional assembly system is presented in Figure 14–3.

Rather than have seven specialists (one at each workstation on the line), Saab management elected to have one person follow an engine from start to finish. The new arrangement is presented in Figure 14–4. The average time a worker spends on the assembly of an engine is about 30 minutes, as opposed to the 1.8 minutes spent at the old workstation. By assembling an entire engine, a worker might find the work more interesting and challenging. Of course, whether the work becomes more interesting and challenging depends on the person and the change. Adding tasks that are meaningless may be enlargement, but it may have negative effects on performance and morale.

Changes in Line–Staff Relationships.   The usual approach in changing line–staff relationships is to create staff assistance as either an ad hoc or permanent solution. An illustrative case is a company that had grown quite rapidly since its entry into the fast-food industry. Its basic sources of field control were area directors who supervised the operations of sales outlets of particular regions. During the growth period, the area directors had considerable autonomy in making the advertising decisions for their regions. They could select their own media, formats, and budgets within general guidelines. But as their markets became saturated and as competitors appeared, corporate officials decided to centralize the advertising function in a staff unit located at corporate headquarters. Consequently, the area directors' freedom was limited, and an essential job aspect was eliminated.[21]

A second illustration of changes in line–staff relationships is based on the case of a large insurance company that hired a management consulting firm to analyze the problem created by a deteriorating market position.[22] The consulting company recommended changing a staff position to a line manager.

---

[21]See Herbert A. Simon et al., *Centralization versus Decentralization in Organizing the Controller's Department* (New York: Controllership Foundation, 1954), for a classic discussion of the key issues to be resolved in deciding where to locate staff units—in this case, an accounting unit.

[22]Jeremiah J. O'Connell, *Managing Organizational Innovation* (Homewood, Ill.: Richard D. Irwin, 1968).

FIGURE 14-4   Saab Engine Assembly after Enlarging Jobs

In the new work flow at Saab, each worker has a total job.

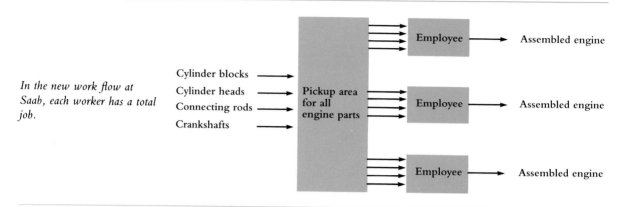

The consultants' belief was that the company must have its best personnel and resources available at the branch office level to increase premium income. Accordingly, the consultants recommended that assistant managers be converted to first-level supervisors reporting to branch managers. The transformation required a significant change in the work of both assistant managers and managers throughout the organization.

Changes in Sociotechnical Systems.   The term *sociotechnical systems* is identified with research originally done by the Tavistock Institute in Great Britain. Change efforts have attempted to develop a better fit between the technology, the structure, and the social interaction patterns of a unit, department, or office.[23]

While jobs, rewards, physical equipment, work schedules, and other factors may be altered in sociotechnical change, none of these is the central focus of the change activities. Instead, employees, union members, nonunion members, and managers examine all aspects of the work operation. Potential changes emerge from the collaboration and discussion of employees. A distinct feature of sociotechnical systems change is that groups of employees share the responsibility for initiating changes.

One of the earliest studies of sociotechnical change was in British coal mining. A team approach was used to develop enlarged jobs and team pay incentive plans. This study indicated improved productivity, safety, and morale after the team initiated changes.[24] Using the British results, a study was conducted at the Rushton Coal Mine in Phillipsburg, Pennsylvania. A steering committee comprising management and local union officials met to consider methods for improving mine safety. It was decided to train crew members in all jobs in a section, to train them in state and federal mine laws and in group

[23]Marvin R. Weisbord, "Participative Work Design: A Personal Odyssey," *Organization Dynamics*, Spring 1985, pp. 5–20; J. Richard Hackman and Greg R. Oldham, *Work Redesign* (Reading, Mass.: Addison-Wesley Publishing, 1980), p. 62.

[24]E. L. Trist et al., *Organization Choice* (London: Tavistock Publications, 1965).

problem solving, and to make them responsible for the production of coal and any initial handling of grievances.[25]

The results after one year indicated fewer violations of federal laws by the crews in the study, lower absenteeism, increased job satisfaction and cooperation, and generally better performance. The crews involved in recommending and initiating the sociotechnical changes were overall better performers and reported higher morale than counterparts not collaborating in changing the system.

Despite some reported successes with changes in sociotechnical systems, there are problems with the approach. Sociotechnical system change approaches have, in many cases, ignored individual differences in how people react to various changes. Some people do not want the sociotechnical aspects of their jobs or work environment altered. There also are union representatives who claim that collaborative efforts between management and operating employees undermine the union's influence on rank and file members. Likewise, some managers claim that collaborative efforts will permanently undermine management's right to manage. These types of problems will be addressed by managers and behavioral scientists who are learning more about the strengths, weaknesses, and future uses of changes in sociotechnical systems.

PEOPLE CHANGE

The early efforts to engage in people change date back to scientific management work improvement and employee training methods. These attempts were directed primarily at improving employee skills and knowledge bases. The employee counseling programs that grew out of the Hawthorne studies were (and remain) primarily directed at improving employee attitudes. In the Management Focus, Rosabeth Kanter outlines some important pointers for increasing the commitment of people to changes in the workplace. These pointers are guidelines that managers can use in introducing any form of change—structural, people, or technological.

Training and development programs for managers typically have emphasized supervisory relationships. These programs attempt to provide supervisors with basic technical and human relations skills. Since supervisors are primarily concerned with overseeing the work of others, the content of these traditional programs emphasizes techniques for dealing with people problems: how to handle the malcontent, the loafer, the troublemaker, the complainer. The programs also include conceptual material dealing with communications, leadership styles, and organizational relationships. The vehicles for training include role-playing, discussion groups, lectures, and organized courses offered by universities.[26]

Training continues to be an important technique for introducing people changes. Training has taken on quite a different form in some applications

[25]T. Mills, "Altering the Social Structure in Coal Mining: A Case Study," *Monthly Labor Review,* October 1976, pp. 3–10.

[26]Ernest Dale and L. C. Michelon, *Modern Management Methods* (New York: World Publishing, 1966), pp. 15–16.

MANAGEMENT FOCUS

How Managers Can Improve Commitment to Change

1. Allow room for participation in the planning of the change.
2. Leave choices within the overall decision to change.
3. Provide a clear picture of the change, a "vision" with details about the new state.
4. Share information about change plans to the fullest extent possible.
5. Divide a big change into more manageable and familiar steps; let people take a small step first.
6. Minimize surprises; give people advance warning about new requirements.
7. Allow for digestion of change requests—a chance to become accustomed to the idea of change before making a commitment.
8. Repeatedly demonstrate your own commitment to the change.
9. Make standards and requirements clear; tell exactly what is expected of people in the change.
10. Offer positive reinforcement for competence; let people know they can do it.
11. Look for and reward pioneers, innovators, and early successes to serve as models.
12. Help people find or feel compensated for the extra time and energy that change requires.
13. Avoid creating obvious "losers" from the change (but if there are some, be honest with them—early on).
14. Allow expressions of nostalgia and grief for the past; then create excitement about the future.

Source: Adapted from Rosabeth Moss Kanter, "Managing the Human Side of Change," *Management Review*, April 1985, pp. 52–56.

from that which developed in classical management theory.[27] Among some managers, a popular behavioral change approach is sensitivity training.

Sensitivity Training. This change technique attempts to make the participants more aware of themselves and of their impact on others. "Sensitivity" in this context means sensitivity to self and to relationships with others. An assumption of sensitivity training is that the causes of poor task performance are the emotional problems of people who collectively must achieve a goal. If these problems can be removed, a major impediment to task performance is eliminated. Sensitivity training stresses the "*process* rather than the *content* of training and . . . *emotional* rather than *conceptual* training."[28] We can see that this form of training is quite different from traditional forms stressing the acquisition of a predetermined body of concepts with immediate application to the workplace.

[27]A survey of alternative training methodologies is presented in Edward C. Ryterband and Bernard M. Bass, "Management Development," in *Contemporary Management*, ed. Joseph W. McGuire (Englewood Cliffs, N.J.: Prentice-Hall, 1974), pp. 579–609.

[28]L. This and G. L. Lippit, "Managerial Guidelines to Sensitivity Training," *Training and Development Journal*, June 1981, pp. 144–50; Henry C. Smith, *Sensitivity to People* (New York: McGraw-Hill, 1966), p. 197.

The process of sensitivity training includes a group of managers (training group or T group) that, in most cases, meets at some location other than their place of work. Under the direction of a trainer, the group usually engages in a dialogue with no agenda and no focus. The objective is to provide an environment that produces its own learning experiences.[29] The unstructured dialogue encourages one to learn about self in dealing with others. One's motives and feelings are revealed through behavior toward others in the group and through the behavior of others. The T group typically is unstructured. As Alfred Marrow points out in a report of his own sensitivity training, "It [sensitivity training] says, 'Open your eyes. Look at yourself. See how you look to others. Then decide what changes, if any, you want to make and in which direction you want to go.' "[30]

The role of the trainer in the T group is to facilitate the learning process. According to Joe Kelly, the trainer's mission is "to observe, record, interpret, sometimes to lead, and always to learn."[31] The artistry and style of the trainer are critical variables in determining the direction of the T group's sessions. The trainer must walk the uneasy path of unobtrusive leadership, able to interpret the roles of participants and encourage them to analyze their contributions without being perceived as a threat. Unlike the group therapist, the T-group trainer is dealing with people who are not having emotional problems but who have come together to learn. The ordinarily prescribed role of the trainer is that of "permissive, nonauthoritarian, sometimes almost nonparticipative" leadership.[32]

A critical test of sensitivity training is whether the experience itself is a factor leading to improvement in task performance. It is apparent that even if the training induces positive changes in the participant's sensitivity to self and others, such behavior may be either not possible or not permissible back in the workplace. The participant must deal with the same environment and the same people as before the training. The open, supportive, and permissive environment of the training sessions is not likely to be found on the job. Even so, proponents of sensitivity training would reply that it makes the participant better able to deal with the environment. We also should recognize that sensitivity training may well induce negative changes in the participant's ability to perform organizational tasks. The training sessions can be occasions of extreme stress and anxiety. The capacity to deal effectively with stress varies among individuals, and the outcome may be dysfunctional for some participants.

The research evidence to date suggests mixed results on the effectiveness of sensitivity training as a change technique.[33] A detailed review of 100 research studies found that sensitivity training was most effective at the personal level.[34] The studies compared the influence of 20 or more hours of training on

---

[29]L. P. Bradford, J. R. Gibb, and K. D. Benne, *T-Group Theory and Laboratory Method* (New York: John Wiley & Sons, 1964).

[30]Alfred J. Marrow, *Behind the Executive Mask* (New York: AMACOM, 1964), p. 51.

[31]Joe Kelly, *Organizational Behavior,* 3rd ed. (Homewood, Ill.: Richard D. Irwin, 1980), p. 569.

[32]Leavitt, "Applied Organizational Change," p. 1154.

[33]Robert Golembiewski and A. Blumberg, eds., *Sensitivity Training and the Laboratory Approach: Readings about Concepts and Applications* (Itasca, Ill.: F. E. Peacock Publishers, 1977).

[34]P. B. Smith, "Controlled Studies of the Outcome of Sensitivity Training," *Psychological Bulletin,* July 1975, pp. 597–622.

the participants' attitudes or behaviors. The review concluded that sensitivity training:

- Stimulated short-term improvement in communication skills.
- Encouraged trainees to believe that they controlled their behavior more than others.
- Was likely to increase the participative orientation of trainees in leadership positions.
- Improved the perceptions of others toward the trainee.

Managers should critically examine this technique in terms of the kinds of changes desired and those that are possible. Our model suggests the existence of conditions that limit the range of possible changes. In this light, managers must determine whether the changes induced by sensitivity training are instrumental for organizational purposes and whether the prospective participant is able to tolerate the potential anxiety of the training.

A major limitation of sensitivity training is the assumption that when people are aware of themselves, positive changes will be made. This assumption evolves from principles of psychotherapy, where individuals are encouraged to confront their emotions, values, and experiences. Of course, each person has a different capacity to confront values, emotions, and experiences, and some simply refuse.

Team Building.   Team building is a change technique that involves an entire group (e.g., a unit, a department) that works on a problem facing the members.[35] Figure 14–5 presents the events that typically occur in team building. First the problem is identified. Then the full group participates to diagnose the problem. The main contributing reasons to the problem are identified. After the problem and reasons are clarified, alternative solutions and their positive and negative features are discussed. A solution is selected and then implemented.

An important potential benefit of team building as an organizational change approach is that through interaction in solving problems, the group members become more familiar with each other and the solution. This results in an increased commitment to the solution and its implementation.

A number of barriers to effective team building have been concisely outlined for managers to consider before they adopt it as a change strategy. In order for team building to have a chance at being successful, it must meet four conditions:[36]

1. The group must have a natural reason (e.g., task completion) for existing.
2. Group members must be mutually dependent on one another in terms of task experience and abilities. If dependence is not present, there is less commitment.
3. Group members must have similar status.
4. Group communications must be open and trusting.

---

[35]S. Jay Liebowitz and Kenneth P. DeMeuse, "The Application of Team Building," *Human Relations,* January 1982, pp. 1–18.

[36]P. Palleschi and P. Heim, "The Hidden Barriers to Team Building," *Training and Development Journal,* July 1980, pp. 14–18.

FIGURE 14–5   Team Building: Sequence of Events

Team building places an entire group in close contact to work on solving a specific problem.

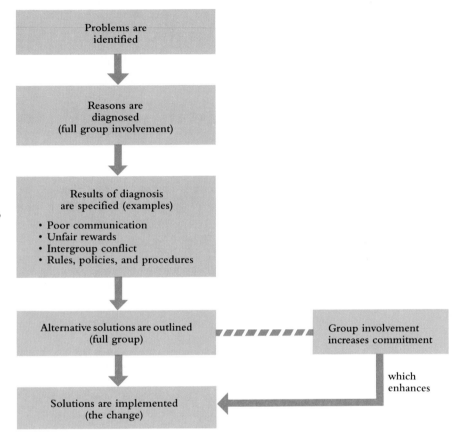

General Motors reopened a Fremont, California, plant as a joint venture with Toyota Motor Corporation. The company was called New United Motor Manufacturing, Inc. (NUMMI). Labor and management worked to develop a team approach at the plant, aiming at high productivity levels, low levels of defects, low absenteeism, and more satisfied employees. For four years, the results have looked excellent. But opponents of the labor-management team building approach claim that team building is a management device to substitute peer pressure for traditional management practice; a number of employees have criticized their union leadership as being too close to management. At NUMMI, the majority of employees appear to be pleased with the team concept. However, there are signals that dissension, disappointment, and jealousy are not eliminated by team building.[37]

[37]John Holersha, "Labor Pains in a U.S. Utopia," *Herald International Tribune,* February 1, 1989, pp. 9, 12.

Life and Career Planning.   Company-sponsored programs for life and career planning are growing in popularity. These programs use formal classroom or counseling settings. Participants are asked to focus on their past, present, and future[38] and to work out their life and career plans. Typically plans are developed after some self-assessment and self-study.[39] These plans may be discussed with colleagues, a human resource development specialist, or a manager. The objective is to have people look at their lives and career plans in a systematic and thorough manner.

The sequence of steps in many life and career planning programs is:

1.   Assess life and career paths up to now, noting highlights.
2.   Formulate objectives for both desired lifestyle and career path, and forecast the future.
3.   Develop a plan of action for achieving the goals and schedule target dates.

Generally life planning and career planning are done concurrently because career planning is but one subset of life planning. Whether life and career planning has any impact on individual attitudes and behaviors has not been scientifically determined at this time. Most of the support for this type of program is found in the form of testimonials of those who have participated in life and career planning. Those who complete such exercises enthusiastically claim that they understand themselves, their careers, and their lifestyles better. They also report less anxiety about the future.

TECHNOLOGICAL CHANGE

This category of change includes any application of new ways to transform resources into the product or service. In the usual sense of the word, technology means new machines—robots, lathes, presses, computers, and the like. But we expand the concept to include new techniques, with or without new machines. From this perspective, the work improvement methods of scientific management can be considered as technological breakthroughs.

Robots.   The word conjures visions of complex machines that both look and perform like human beings. R2D2 in the popular *Star Wars* movies helped create these viewpoints. In reality, robots are quite different; they scarcely resemble people and perform a limited range of job tasks.[40] However, robots are a technological force that is creating resistance and fears among many people—namely, workers in the automobile and electrical-component industries.

The Robotics Institute of America defines a robot as a "reprogrammable multifunctional manipulator designed to move material, parts, tools, or specialized devices through programmed motions for the performance of a

---

[38]Margaret Butteress and Karl Albrecht, *New Management Tools* (Englewood Cliffs, N.J.: Prentice-Hall, 1979), pp. 57–62.

[39]William F. Rothenback, "Career Development: Ask Your Employees for Their Opinions," *Personnel Administrator,* November 1982, pp. 43–51.

[40]Jeffrey G. Miller and Thomas E. Vallmann, "The Hidden Factory," *Harvard Business Review,* September–October 1985, pp. 142–50.

variety of tasks."[41] The more sophisticated robots are called intelligent, while their less sophisticated counterparts are labeled as dumb, slaves, grasshoppers (an automobile industry term), and CAM (computer-aided manufacturing).

Robot use is expected to continue to grow throughout the remainder of this century because of wage inflation and the development of the microprocessor, a computer small enough to use as the brains of a robot.[42] In the 1960s, a typical assembly-line robot cost $4.20 an hour (averaged over its lifetime), which was slightly higher than the average factory worker's wages and fringe benefits. Today, the robot can be operated for less than $4 an hour, while the employee now makes between $25 and $30 an hour.

One of the earliest countries to realize the economic benefits of robots was Japan. Although most of the original research and development on robotic technology occurred in the United States, Japan has over 40,000 of the world's 60,000 robots.

Some American firms realize that to be competitive in various manufacturing industries, robots are mandatory. General Motors has formed a joint-venture robotics company, GM Fanus Robotics Corp., which is the largest robotics manufacturer in the United States. At an engine plant in Romulus, Michigan, 40 percent more engines are produced per day than prior to the introduction of robots.[43]

The changes in organizational efficiency brought about by a new machine or robot are calculable in economic and engineering terms. Whether the robot or machine is a good investment is a matter of estimating its future profitability in relation to its present cost. These calculations are an important part of the managerial control function. Here, however, we are interested in the impact of the machine or robot on the structure of the organization and on the behavior of the people in the organization.

As some scholars have observed, technology is a key determinant of structure.[44] They tentatively conclude that firms with simple and stable technology should adopt a structure that tends toward classical organization, whereas firms with complex and dynamic technology ought to move toward the more open and flexible neoclassical structure.[45] Thus, it would appear that the adoption of new technology involves a concurrent decision to adapt the organizational structure to that technology.

The most recognizable impact of robot technology is likely to be on the behavior of groups and individuals. In the short run, robots have displaced some employees. This displacement creates feelings of insecurity, uncertainty,

---

[41]George L. Whaley, "The Impact of Robotics Technology upon Human Resource Management," *Personnel Administrator,* September 1982, p. 61.

[42]Robert A. Pierson, "Automation," *Management Review,* July 1985, pp. 33–35.

[43]*General Motors Public Interest Report,* 1988.

[44]For example, Joan Woodward, *Industrial Organization* (New York: Oxford University Press, 1967); Frank J. Jasinski, "Adapting Organization to New Technology," *Harvard Business Review,* January–February 1959, pp. 79–86.

[45]Tom Burns and G. M. Stalker make this point in their analysis of the ways Scottish electronics firms responded to technological change. They use the terms *mechanistic* to refer to relatively tight, highly structured organizations and *organic* to refer to relatively loose, flexibly structured organizations. Tom Burns and G. M. Stalker, *The Management of Innovation* (London: Tavistock Publications, 1961).

and fear, which lead to resistance on the part of workers.[46] Some organizations have attempted to minimize this type of resistance by having workers participate in planning the introduction of robots.

In order to catalog the impact of technological change on structure and behavior, Floyd C. Mann analyzed a number of actual cases and concluded that the adoption of new machines in the factory involves:[47]

1. Major changes in the division of labor and the content of jobs.
2. Changes in social relations among workers.
3. Improving working conditions.
4. The need for different supervisory skills.
5. Changes in career patterns, promotion procedures, and job security.
6. Generally higher wages.
7. Generally higher prestige for those who work.
8. Around-the-clock operations.

The degree and extent of these observed changes in structure and behavior depend upon the magnitude of the technological change. Obviously, the introduction of a new offset printing press will not cause the great dislocations and changes that Mann observes, but the introduction of robots on a previously human-paced manufacturing process would include many, if not all, of them.

Figure 14–6 portrays the three approaches to organizational change, the types of programs in each approach, and the anticipated outcomes. The potential and actual accomplishment of such outcomes is why managers search out, test, and evaluate various change techniques.

STEP 3: REACTION—RECOGNITION OF LIMITING CONDITIONS

The selection of the change technique is based on diagnosis of the problem. But the choice is tempered by certain conditions that exist at the time. Three sources of influence on the outcome of management development programs have been identified. They can be generalized to cover the entire range of organizational change efforts, whether structural, behavioral, or technological. They are leadership climate, formal organization, and organizational culture.

Leadership climate refers to the nature of the work environment resulting from the leadership style and administrative practices of superiors. Any change program that does not have the support and commitment of management has slim chance of success; managers must be at least neutral toward the change. The style of leadership itself may be the subject of change. For example, sensitivity training is a direct attempt to move managers toward a certain style—open, supportive, and group centered. But the participants may be unable to adopt styles that are not compatible with their own superiors' styles.

The *formal organization* must be compatible with the proposed change. This includes the effects on the environment that result from the philosophy and

[46]Vandra L. Huber and Geri Gay, "Channeling New Technology to Improve Training," *Personnel Administrator,* February 1985, pp. 49–57.

[47]Floyd C. Mann, "Psychological and Organizational Impacts," in *Automation and Technological Change,* ed. John T. Dunlop (Englewood Cliffs, N.J.: Prentice-Hall, 1962), pp. 50–55.

FIGURE 14–6   Selected Programs, Techniques, and Outcomes of
Organizational Change

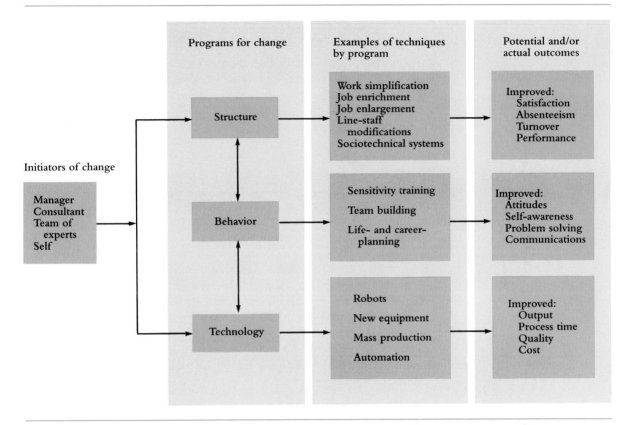

Managers seek change techniques in the hope of making improvements in many areas of production and performance.

policies of top management, as well as legal precedent, organizational structure, and the system of control. Of course, each of these sources of impact may be the focus of the change effort; the important point is that a change in one must be compatible with all others. For example, a change in technology that eliminates jobs contradicts a policy of guaranteed employment.

The *organizational culture* refers to the impact on the environment resulting from "group norms, values, philosophy, and informal activities."[48] The impact of traditional behavior, sanctioned by group norms but not formally acknowledged, was first documented in the Hawthorne studies. A proposed change in work methods or the installation of an automated device can run counter to the expectations and attitudes of work groups. The concept of culture is rooted in theories of group dynamics and group growth. Such being the case, the change strategist must anticipate the resulting resistance that can evolve from the group.[49]

[48]Edgar H. Schein, *Organizational Culture and Leadership* (San Francisco: Jossey-Bass, 1985).

[49]Lawrence A. Benningson, "Managing Corporate Cultures," *Management Review,* February 1985, pp. 31–32; Ralph H. Kilman, *Beyond the Quick Fix* (San Francisco: Jossey-Bass, 1984), pp. 21–124.

STEP 4: REACTION—THE STRATEGY FOR CHANGE

Selection of a strategy for implementing the change technique has consequences in the final outcome. Larry Greiner analyzes a number of organization changes to determine the relationship of various change strategies to the relative success of the change itself.[50] He identifies three approaches, located along a continuum, with unilateral authority at one extreme and delegated authority at the other extreme. In the middle of the continuum are approaches he calls shared authority.

Unilateral approaches can take the form of an edict from top management describing the change and the responsibilities of subordinates in implementing it.[51] *Shared approaches* involve lower-level groups in the process of either (1) defining the problem and alternative solutions or (2) defining solutions only after higher-level management has defined the problem. In either case, the process engages the talents and insights of all members at all levels. Finally, *delegated approaches* relinquish complete authority to subordinate groups. Through freewheeling discussions, the group ultimately is responsible for the analysis of the problem and proposed solutions. According to Greiner, the relatively more successful instances of organizational change are those that tend toward the shared position of the continuum.

Why would this be the case? As has been observed, most instances of organizational change are accompanied by resistance from those involved in the change. The actual form of resistance may range in extreme from passive resignation to deliberate sabotage. The objective of shared approaches is at least to minimize resistance and at most to maximize cooperation and support. The manner in which the change is managed from beginning to end is a key determinant of how employees and lower-echelon managers react.

STEP 5: REACTION—IMPLEMENTATION AND EVALUATION

The implementation of the proposed change has two dimensions: timing and scope. *Timing* is the selection of the appropriate time to initiate the change. *Scope* is the selection of the appropriate scale of the change. The matter of timing is strategic and depends on a number of factors, particularly the company's operating cycle and the groundwork preceding the change. Certainly, if a change is of considerable magnitude, it is desirable that it not compete with ordinary business operations. Thus, it might well be implemented during a slack period. On the other hand, if the problem is critical to the survival of the organization, immediate implementation is in order. The scope of the change depends on the strategy. The change may be implemented throughout the organization and become an established fact in a short period of time. Or it may be phased into the organization, level by level, department by department. The strategy of successful changes, according to Greiner,

---

[50]Larry E. Greiner, "Patterns of Organization Change," *Harvard Business Review,* May–June 1967, p. 119.

[51]Greiner identifies replacement of key personnel and structural changes as two other forms of unilateral change. For our purposes, personnel and structural changes are change techniques, not strategies for implementing change. Techniques specify *what* is to be done; strategies specify *how* it is to be done.

FIGURE 14–7   An Evaluation Matrix: Issues to Consider

Relevant Issues to Cover and Evaluate	Examples of What to Measure	Who or What to Examine for Answers	How to Collect Data to Answer Issue Questions
1. Are the employees learning, changing attitudes, and/or improving skills?	Employees' attitudes and/or skills before and after (even during) training or development sessions.	Comments. Method of participation. Co-workers. Superiors.	Interviews. Questionnaires. Records. Observation.
2. Are organizational change materials used on the job?	Employees' on-the-job performance, behavior, and style.	Subordinate performance, attitudes, and style.	Records. Interviews. Questionnaires. Critical incidents. Observation.
3. What are the costs of organizational change programs and techniques?	The fixed and variable costs of conducting the change programs.	Cost of consultants. Participant time. Travel expenses. Training aids. Rent. Utilities.	Budget records.
4. How long does the organizational change program have an effect on employees?	Employees' on-the-job performance, behavior, and style over an extended period of time.	Subordinate performance, attitudes, and style.	Records. Interviews. Questionnaires. Critical incidents. Observation (repeated).

Systematic evaluation programs enable managers to more accurately assess the costs and benefits of organizational change.

makes use of a phased approach, which limits the scope but provides feedback for each subsequent implementation.

Evaluation is an important and often overlooked step in organizational change programs. Essentially, evaluation should be made by comparing the results (the benefits) with the objectives of the organizational change program. It is difficult to evaluate the effectiveness of most change efforts. But it is crucial to know what has resulted in terms of attitudes, productivity, and behavior.

There are three types of criteria for evaluating organizational change programs: internal, external, and participant reaction. *Internal criteria* are directly associated with the basis of the program. For example, did the sociotechnical change result in increased frequency of employee exchange of job information, or did the employees in the job enrichment seminar learn the core dimensions of the job? *External criteria* are related to the effectiveness of employees before and after the change is implemented. Possible external criteria include increased number of units produced per work hour, increased sales volume, and better quality of workmanship. *Participant reaction criteria* attempt to determine how the individuals affected by the change feel about it.

One useful device encourages the use of multiple and systematic assessment. Figure 14–7 presents a guideline for managers to use. The costs and benefits of any organizational change effort can be determined only if evaluation programs are used. Simply asking individuals if they like the sensitivity training program or the job enlargement changes is not very thorough. It would be more systematic and thorough to monitor changes in structure, people, and technology over long periods of time.

SUMMARY OF KEY POINTS

- Organization development (OD) is a method for facilitating change and development in structures and processes (e.g., relationships, roles), people (e.g., styles, skills), and technology (e.g., more routineness, more challenge).

- Employees have numerous reasons for resisting change. Some of the most commonly cited are parochial self-interest, misunderstanding and lack of trust, different assessments, and a low tolerance for change.

- Managers can take some steps to minimize resistance: education and communication, participation and involvement, facilitation and support, negotiation and agreement, manipulation and co-optation, and explicit and implicit coercion.

- A five-part model presented in Figure 14–1 provides some order and a framework for the study of organizational change and development. Step 1 includes stimuli such as internal and external forces that trigger a reaction or recognition of the need for change. Step 2 involves the diagnosis for problem areas. Step 3 involves stimuli in the form of alternative change techniques that can be selected and a reaction by managers in that limiting conditions are recognized. In step 4, a decision is made on the strategy and the technique to use. Step 5

involves the implementation and evaluation of the change.

- The choice of a particular change technique depends upon the nature of the problem management has diagnosed. We classify them according to the major focus of the change technique: structure, people, or technology. Techniques to change structure include changes in the nature of jobs, job enlargement, changes in line-staff relationships, and changes in sociotechnical systems. Techniques to change people include sensitivity training, team building, and life and career planning. Techniques to change technology include any application of new ways to transform resources into the product or service, such as new technology (e.g., robots).

- Strategies for introducing change are *unilateral* (an edict for change from top management), *delegated* (control for the change is relinquished to those being affected by the change), and *shared* (participation between the initiators and recipients of change in deciding on the problem or solution).

- In many cases, not enough time and effort are spent on the evaluation of change. Evaluation of behavior, results, and attitudes is needed to examine the costs and benefits of any structural, people, or technological change effort.

DISCUSSION AND REVIEW QUESTIONS

1. How could team building enhance commitment to a structural change in an organization?

2. Why was Coca-Cola's change to New Coke resisted by many consumers?

3. The notion of planned change is assumed to be more effective than a nonplanned approach. In fact, some state that the federal government could benefit from a planned approach in efforts to bring about changes

in various agencies. Do you believe this is true? Why?

4. Can you present an example that you are familiar with in which a job can be enlarged? Use the Saab example to help you think through the necessary features for job enlargement.

5. It has been claimed that as the tasks performed by humans become more complex, the probability of

robots replacing human labor increases. Do you agree?

6. Would employees' resistance to change be more or less intense during times of high unemployment? Why?

7. International competition is a major change to which managers must adapt more in the future. Why?

8. Behavioral change is difficult to measure accurately. Some changes in employee behavior occur subtly, over time. Why would it be difficult to measure

subtle changes in behavior that may be occurring during a sensitivity training program? Should these changes, if they are occurring, be measured at all?

9. A model can serve as a guideline for someone actually managing employees. The model used can alert managers to various constraints or issues that may appear. Would there be any value for a manager in understanding the parts of the model represented in Figure 14–1? Explain.

10. What are some of the human costs of using robots in manufacturing plants?

ADDITIONAL REFERENCES

Boss, W. *Organizational Development and Health Care.* Reading, Mass.: Addison-Wesley Publishing, 1989.

Calvert, R., Jr. "Training America: The Numbers Add Up." *Training and Development Journal,* November 1985, pp. 35–37.

Eden, D. "Team Development: A True Field Experiment at Three Levels of Rigor." *Journal of Applied Psychology,* February 1985, pp. 94–100.

Gilmore, T. N. *Making a Leadership Change.* San Francisco: Jossey-Bass, 1988.

Gordon, J. "Games Managers Play." *Training/HRD,* July 1985, pp. 30–47.

Hage, J., ed. *Futures of Organizations: Innovating to Adapt Strategy and Human Resources to Rapid Technological Change.* Lexington, Mass.: Lexington Books, 1988.

Hatcher, L. L., and **T. L. Ross.** "Organization Development through Productivity Gainsharing." *Personnel,* October 1985, pp. 42–50.

Kimberly, J. R., and **R. E. Quinn.** *Managing Organizational Transitions.* Homewood, Ill.: Richard D. Irwin, 1984.

London, M. *Change Agents.* San Francisco: Jossey-Bass, 1988.

Magaziner, I., and **M. Patinkin.** *The Silent War.* New York: Random House, 1989.

Maxey, C., and **T. Cummings.** "Organization Development and Labor Law: Implications for Practice/Malpractice." Center for Effective Organizations Working Paper, University of Southern California, 1985.

Morgan, G. *Reading the Waves of Change.* San Francisco: Jossey-Bass, 1988.

Naisbitt, J., and **P. Aburdene.** *Re-Inventing the Corporation.* New York: Warner, 1985.

Sayles, L. R., and **V. L. Wright.** "The Use of Culture in Strategic Management." *Issues and Observations,* November 1985, pp. 1–9.

Seashore, S. E.; E. E. Lawler; P. H. Mirvis; and **C. Cammann.** *Assessing Organizational Change.* New York: John Wiley & Sons, 1983.

Simon. D. F. *Technological Innovation in China.* Cambridge, Mass.: Ballinger, 1988.

Sullivan, S. M. "Management a la Francais." *Management Review,* June 1985, pp. 11–14.

Vicars, W. M., and **D. D. Hartke.** "Evaluating OD Evaluations: A Status Report." *Groups and Organization Studies,* 1984, pp. 177–88.

Woodman, R. W., and **S. J. Wayne.** "An Investigation of Positive-Finding Bias in Evaluation of Organization Development Intervention." *Academy of Management Journal,* December 1985, pp. 889–913.

CASE 14–1   General Motors' Quality-of-Work-Life Survey

General Motors has decided to use a survey questionnaire called "The Quality of Your Work Life in General Motors" to learn about employee attitudes and to locate potential trouble spots. The survey is a part of the company's organizational development efforts. The dimensions of GM's

---

EXHIBIT 1   Dimensions of GM's Quality-of-Work-Life Survey Questionnaire*

Employee commitment: Feelings of loyalty to GM; a commitment to and concern for the future of the organization.

Absence of developing apathy: A measure of employees' concern and ambition regarding their work.

On-the-job development and utilization: Opportunity for the employees to learn and apply skills and abilities in a meaningful and challenging way.

Employee involvement and influence: The extent to which employees feel involved in decision making.

Advancement based on merit: The extent to which management is interested in the progress of individuals and rewards people on the basis of ability, performance, and experience.

Career goal progress: Making progress in the achievement of career objectives and the belief that there are opportunities for further progress.

Relations with supervisor: The working relationship with one's supervisor as reflected in fairness, honesty, and mutual respect.

Work group relations: The way employees in a work group provide mutual support and encouragement.

Respect for the individual: The feeling of being treated as an adult, with respect and dignity.

Confidence in management: Belief that management is aware of and concerned about employee problems and interests.

Physical working environment: Conditions affecting employees' health, comfort, and convenience.

Economic well-being: Receiving adequate financial rewards and having income protection.

Employee state of mind: Whether the employees feel upset or depressed while at work.

Absence of undue job stress: The relative absence of excessive work demands and pressures that might interfere with doing the job well.

Impact on personal life: The spillover effect of the job on employees' personal lives.

Union-management relations: The extent to which the union and management recognize mutual goals and are working together.

★The survey form has 90 items and uses a five-point scale to record employee responses. Additionally, there are 11 items for recording such information as sex, length of service, educational level, salary level, and kind of work performed. Space has also been provided so that local units can include up to 20 additional items.

---

quality-of-work-life survey questionnaire are presented in Exhibit 1, and the instructions and some sample questions are presented in Exhibit 2.

This type of survey can provide management with important information from employees. However, sole reliance on survey data is questioned by some who believe that honest responses are rarely provided by individuals because of an innate sense of insecurity. On the other hand, one of the most efficient ways to gather a general picture of what employees think in different units and locations is to ask them in a survey.

QUESTIONS FOR ANALYSIS

1. What is your opinion about the dimensions covered in the GM survey? Is it comprehensive?
2. Is the use of a survey worthwhile for diagnosing the attitudes in a large organization such as General Motors?
3. Why would some employees feel insecure about answering an attitude survey?

EXHIBIT 2	"The Quality of Your Work Life in General Motors" (instructions and sample questions from GM's questionnaire)

Instructions

This survey is aimed at getting your ideas about what it is like to work here. We are trying to learn more about the quality of work life where you work. The purpose of this survey is to measure the attitudes, opinions, and work climate of GM organizations from the employee's point of view.

You should answer each question as honestly as you can so your answers, along with those of other employees, will provide a good measure of the quality of work life at this location.

The best answer is *always* just what you think.

Your answers are completely confidential. Except for the survey administrator, no one in your organization will see your filled-out survey. The survey administrator will see to it that your survey, together with all others taken today, is sent to an independent company. The filled-out surveys will be processed by computers for groups of people, and your survey copy will be destroyed. To be sure that your answers will not be identified, please do *not* write your name on the form.

Sample Questions *

1. What happens to GM is really important to me. ① ② ③ ④ ⑤
2. I feel very little loyalty to this GM organization. ① ② ③ ④ ⑤
3. I could care less what happens to GM as long as I get my paycheck. ① ② ③ ④ ⑤
4. I often think of quitting. ① ② ③ ④ ⑤
5. I really care about the future of this GM organization. ① ② ③ ④ ⑤
6. I used to care about my work more than I do now. ① ② ③ ④ ⑤
7. I used to be more ambitious about my work than I am now. ① ② ③ ④ ⑤
8. Around here, I am asked for my ideas. ① ② ③ ④ ⑤
9. GM rewards those who do their jobs well. ① ② ③ ④ ⑤
10. People who get ahead in this part of GM deserve it. ① ② ③ ④ ⑤
11. In this part of GM, getting ahead is based on ability. ① ② ③ ④ ⑤
12. Job experience is financially rewarded in GM. ① ② ③ ④ ⑤
13. GM management is really interested in my getting ahead. ① ② ③ ④ ⑤
14. I think more job opportunities should be given to women and minorities around here. ① ② ③ ④ ⑤

*Meaning of ratings: 1—strongly disagree; 2—disagree; 3—neither agree nor disagree; 4—agree; and 5—strongly agree.

CASE 14–2   The International Arena: Changes in Management Understanding Are Needed

In this chapter, we have discussed change, resistance to change, and various alternatives for job, people, and structural change. One area in which each of these change-related factors plays a role is international banking. Bankers need to learn more about how to introduce change in the international arena so that resistance is minimized and profits are earned.

Source: Adapted from Kevin McLaughlin, "Going Overseas? Bank on It," *World Trade,* Spring 1989, pp. 40–54.

International banking is getting bigger each year, with estimates of a $2 trillion banking market in the United States alone. As we enter the 1990s, it appears that U.S. bankers must go overseas, to Africa, Latin America, Hong Kong, Korea, Singapore, Japan, and other locations. The development of large multinational institutions has changed how business is conducted. Today, 500 of the largest multinational firms control over half of the world's exchange of manufactured goods and services. Banking personnel have to be knowledgeable about how to do business in a world of trade, countertrade, joint ventures, and direct investments.

Bankers, treasurers, and financial analysts must be keenly aware of worldwide financial markets. Training programs, self-instruction, and working with experts are ways to acquire knowledge. Instead of simply worrying about what an appliance manufactured in Dayton is selling for in San Diego, the marketers, production experts, and money managers must consider what foreign competitors' appliances could sell for in San Diego. One area of concern is what the dollar will be worth in six months. For that matter, what will the deutsch mark or French franc be worth? International purchasing power influences customers' buying decisions, bankers' loan decisions, manufacturers' production lot size and inventory scheduling decisions, and a nation's balance of trade.

Examining a foreign exchange highlights the type of knowledge, skill, and expertise required in a changing international world. Assume it is March 1 and you are the treasurer of a small Canadian manufacturing firm in Toronto that has just sold goods to a U.S. firm (for delivery, versus payment of $5 million Canadian on July 1). The Canadian dollar spot rate is .8200 (82.00 U.S. cents per Canadian dollar). The July 1 Canadian dollars futures contract on the Chicago Mercantile Exchange is trading with a 30-point discount to spot at .8165. The treasurer has determined that the firm can meet its profit objectives as long as the Canadian dollar spot rate is .8350 or less on the payment date. Thus, a Canadian dollar rate greater than .8350 when the U.S. dollar is received represents the company's foreign exchange risk on this transaction.

The treasurer has to learn about exchange rates, how to hedge the exchange rate risk, and how to explain this in simple terms to decision makers. Is this a change in handling domestic transactions? Yes. A treasurer that only focused on domestic business but now has to focus on international business would be facing job enlargement and job enrichment. His or her job would have changed.

Let's return to the treasurer and her need to hedge the exchange rate risk. She would have to learn how to make assumptions. If she was 100 percent certain that on July 1, when the U.S. dollar payment is received, the Canadian dollar rate will have declined or remained stable, there would be no hedging. If she was completely confident that the Canadian dollar rate will be less favorable when the U.S. dollar payment is received, it would be best to lock in today's rate by buying July Canadian dollar futures. If this is done, the firm would not benefit from a decline in the Canadian dollar rate.

A third scenario might involve the use of exchange-traded options on currency futures. One way to do this is to use what is called an option fence. The firm could set the highest price it will have to pay for Canadian dollars at .8350 and be in position to benefit from any decrease in the Canadian dollar rate down to .8000. In order to implement the fence strategy, the manufacturer would purchase Canadian dollar call options with a set strike price and simultaneously sell July dollar futures contracts.

The specific mathematical calculations are not the point here. What we are attempting to convey is that (1) the treasurer in an internationally oriented job must change her knowledge base and job to be effective; (2) changes in the international arena will require that managers learn about foreign exchange risk, call options, and how business is conducted; and (3) money rates change more violently than structure, people, or technology in organizations.

Another example of change in international business involves countertrade. Countries that lack hard foreign currency swap products or other assets for needed imports. The early Egyptians are said to be the originators of countertrade, which is now used widely in Eastern Europe and China. In East–West business, it works like this: A Western seller (e.g., the United States, West Germany, France) delivers products to an Eastern buyer (e.g., the Soviet Union, Romania, Bulgaria), in return for agreeing to purchase Eastern products equivalent to a specified percentage of the export contract value. Pepsi-Cola exports to the Soviet Union and is paid back by being granted rights and given Stolichnaya vodka to sell in the United States. Instead of paying Pepsi in rubles, the Soviet Union provides the U.S. soft drink company with cases of Stolichnaya, which are sold in the United States for dollars.

Foreign exchange rates, countertrade, futures, and risk assessment are becoming a part of the business manager's vocabulary and need-to-know list. Powerful international external forces are requiring managers to change the way they think, conduct business, organize the work force, and view opportunities. The model displayed in Figure 14–1 can help the manager cope with the shifts in the international marketplace. Are you prepared for the worldwide changes in doing business and managing?

QUESTIONS FOR ANALYSIS

1. How could the change model in Figure 14–1 be used to emphasize why American managers must learn to deal with foreign exchange rate changes?
2. What type of people change approaches could be used to help managers such as the treasurer prepare for a changing international world?
3. Why is it likely that some managers will resist learning about international market conditions, requirements, and opportunities?

EXPERIENTIAL EXERCISE

ARE YOU RECEPTIVE TO CHANGE?

Purpose

The purpose of this exercise is to help students determine how open- or closed-minded they are to change.

Exhibit 1   Questionnaire: Are You Receptive to Change?

Statement	Agree Very Much	Agree in General	Agree Somewhat	Disagree Somewhat	Disagree in General	Disagree Very Much
1. The main thing in life is for a person to want to do something important.	1	2	3	4	5	6
2. Most people don't care about others.	1	2	3	4	5	6
3. Most ideas found in the press are worthless.	1	2	3	4	5	6
4. Compromising with the Soviet Union is dangerous.	1	2	3	4	5	6
5. Our way of living and doing business is proven and should be the world model.	1	2	3	4	5	6
6. I would love to become a famous person like Einstein.	1	2	3	4	5	6
7. The United States and the Soviet Union have nothing in common.	1	2	3	4	5	6
8. Freedom of speech is generally great, but some restrictions should be placed on radical groups.	1	2	3	4	5	6
9. I become very angry when a person refuses to admit he or she is wrong.	1	2	3	4	5	6
10. I would like to find someone to tell me how to solve my personal problems.	1	2	3	4	5	6
11. It is best to reserve judgment about what's going on until one hears the opinions of respected people.	1	2	3	4	5	6
12. Most people don't know what's good for them.	1	2	3	4	5	6

Source: Adapted from V. C. Troldahl and F. A. Powell, "A Short-Form Dogmatism Scale for Use in Field Studies," *Social Forces,* December 1965, p. 213.

The Exercise in Class

1.   Take a few minutes and complete the questionnaire in Exhibit 1. Circle one response for each question that best reflects your opinion. There are no right or wrong answers.
2.   Go to Exhibit 2 for the scoring format. Add your scores up and answer the question: Are you open- or closed-minded? Compare your scores with others in the class. How do your results match your self-image of how willing you are to accept change?

EXHIBIT 2   Scoring Format: Are You Receptive to Change?

Response	Number of Responses	× Weight	= Score
(1) Agree very much	————	+3	————
(2) Agree in general	————	+2	————
(3) Agree somewhat	————	+1	————
(4) Disagree somewhat	————	−1	————
(5) Disagree in general	————	−2	————
(6) Disagree very much	————	−3	————
Total score			═══════

Interpretation: A high score indicates a tendency to resist change because of fixed or rigid attitudes. A rigid person is called closed-minded. The most rigid person would have the highest score: +36. A totally open-minded person will score a −36.

The Learning Message

Resisting change is almost a fact of life. The way a person thinks indicates how resistant to change he or she will be when faced with changes in structure, technology, and personnel. This exercise will provide some insight into a person's openness toward change.

COMPREHENSIVE CASE PART III
MANAGING PEOPLE

NOTE: Do not read this case until directed to do so by your instructor. It has been set up as a prediction case so that you can test your analysis by answering questions before reading the entire case.

PART I

During the summer of my freshman year in college, I worked for a small private landscaping company planting shrubs, seeding new lawns, cutting grass, and tending flower gardens. The company was located in my hometown of Seaview, New Jersey, which is a rural community on the coast about 80 miles from Philadelphia. The company was owned and run by Joe Brewster, a 45-year-old man who had lived in Seaview all his life. He had started the company some years ago and not only handled the paperwork (payroll, bills, estimates, and so on) but also worked along with the crew six days a week.

The crew consisted of five guys ranging in age from 17 to 20 years. We all lived in towns around Seaview and had gone to the regional high school, which was physically located in Seaview. Only two of us were attending college, but all had been hired personally by Joe following a short, informal interview. I can't be completely certain about the others, but I think all of us and several others sought the job because we needed work, enjoyed the outdoors, and had heard that Joe paid well and was an OK guy to work for. Working hours were from 8 A.M. to 4:30 P.M. with an hour off for lunch, Monday through Saturday. Once in a while, we'd work overtime to help out some customer who had an urgent need. Each worker began at the same wage with the understanding that hard workers would be rehired the next summer at a higher wage. Several of the crew I was part of had been rehired under this policy.

Most of the customers we serviced lived in Seaview, knew Joe personally, and seemed to respect him.

Joe owned one truck, which he used to transport all of us and necessary supplies and equipment from job to job. Each morning he would read off a list of houses that had to be completed that day. He would then leave it up to us to decide among ourselves who would do what task while at a particular house. We also were the ones who determined by our work pace how long we would spend at each house.

In doing the work itself, we were able to use our own ideas and methods. If we did a good job, Joe would always compliment us. If we lacked the necessary know-how or did a poor job, Joe was right there willing to help us.

At each house, Joe worked along with us doing basically the same work we did. He dressed the same as we did and was always very open and friendly toward us. He seldom "showed his authority," and treated us as equals.

Source: Allan R. Cohen, Stephen L. Fink, Herman Gadon, and Robin D. Willits, *Effective Behavior in Organizations,* 3rd ed. (Homewood, Ill.: Richard D. Irwin, 1984), pp. 454–58.

Although our workday was scheduled to begin at 8, Joe never became upset nor penalized us if we were 10 to 15 minutes late. Our lunch hour was usually an hour long, starting anytime between 11:30 and 12:30 depending on what time we, the crew, felt like eating. Each member brought his own lunch to work and anytime during the day could take time off to go to the truck for a snack.

The crew itself became very well acquainted, and we were always free to talk and joke with each other at any time and did so. We enjoyed each other's company, although we did not socialize after hours.

We also became very friendly with the customers. They were always eager to talk to us as we worked, and Joe never objected. All in all, the job had a very relaxed, easygoing atmosphere. I for one felt little pressure to hurry and, like the others, respected and liked Joe very much.

PREDICTION QUESTION

1. What will be the productivity in terms of quantity and quality of the work crew? Why?

PART II

The attitude we had toward the job was very high. We sometimes talked among ourselves about how we felt a sense of responsibility toward the job. While we talked and joked a lot when working, little horseplay occurred; and the talking and joking did not interfere with the work. We were always working steadily and efficiently, seeking to keep ahead of schedule. The days seemed to go fairly quickly, and a lot seemed to get done. I know Joe said that our output was 15 percent above that which other landscaping companies experienced with summer crews.

We also took a lot of pride in our work. Feeling responsible for the job we did, we were constantly checking and rechecking every job to be sure it was perfect. We were always willing to work overtime for Joe when he needed us to do so.

CASE QUESTION

1. What elements in the situation contributed to these positive results? Can you think of things that, if present, might have led to very different results? Explain how.

PART III

I returned the following summer to work for Joe because of the strong satisfaction I had with the job the summer before. So did the others. However, we were in for a surprise. Many things had changed. Joe had increased the number of workers to 10, bought another truck, and hired two young college graduates from Philadelphia as crew supervisors. His plan was to concentrate on the paperwork and on lining up new customers, leaving the direct guidance of the two work crews to the new supervisors.

Joe had hired the two supervisors during the early spring after interviewing a number of applicants. Both were young (23 and 24), from the city, and had degrees in agricultural management from Penn State but had not known each other previously.

We "old-timers" were assigned to one crew, and five new workers were hired for the other crew. These new workers had little experience in landscaping. Except for the working hours, which were the same as during the previous summer, the two supervisors were told that they could run their crew in any manner they wished as long as they kept to the schedule prepared by Joe.

No one on the crew had known the supervisors before. Joe had found them through ads in the paper. The supervisors didn't dress quite as informally as Joe did, perhaps because they didn't do as much actual physical work, but they did dress casually in dungarees and shirts, the same as the crew. Though we called the supervisors by their first names, they did some nit-picky things. For example, Joe never cared who drove the truck or who did what job; sometimes a crew member would drive, and Joe would talk with the rest of us. But the supervisors always drove the truck and decided when we would eat. Nor did the supervisors help us unload the tools as Joe had done. They stood around and watched us.

Both supervisors refused to tolerate tardiness in the morning and immediately set up a scheduled lunch hour that would remain the same throughout the summer. We were no longer allowed to go to the truck for a snack during the day and were constantly being watched over by our supervisor. The supervisors assigned us to specific tasks to be done at each job and told us how "they" wanted them to be completed. They also told us how much time we were to spend doing each job. They refused to let us talk to each other or to the customers (except about business) saying that it "only wasted time and interfered with our work." It was a more structured, more formal atmosphere than the summer before.

Prediction Questions

1. What kind of issues or problems are likely to develop during the second summer? Why?
2. How will productivity compare with that of the previous summer in terms of quantity and quality? Why?
3. What would have been your advice to the two supervisors about how they could best approach their new role?

Part IV

I was disappointed at the new setup and a little bit surprised that Joe hadn't hired one of the more experienced members of the old crew as supervisor. But I figured it was necessary because of the increased volume of business, so I tried to make the best of it. However, very soon, my attitude and that of the rest of the old crew changed significantly. We began to hate the new supervisors and soon developed a great disinterest in the work itself. While I'm a person who usually is very conscientious and responsible, I have to admit that before long I along with the others began to put little care or concern into my work. The supervisors soon found it very difficult to get anyone to work overtime.

The new employees didn't react as strongly as we did, but I could tell that they weren't working with much enthusiasm either.

I thought about talking to the supervisors but didn't because I'd only worked there the one year and figured that it was not my place to. The others were older than I and had worked there longer, so I figured that they should, but no one did. Instead, we talked among ourselves and individually griped to Joe.

Joe didn't seem to know how to deal with our complaints. He passed them off by saying "Oh . . . I'll talk to the supervisors and straighten it out with them." But nothing changed, and in fact they seemed to clamp down more and push even harder. This only made us madder. Our work rate continued to fall.

Incidentally, throughout this period, we had little social interaction with the supervisors, but I noticed that they became more and more friendly with each other.

Meanwhile, the new crew's difficulties increased. Being new and inexperienced, they couldn't do the work as easily as we could. Also, the supervisors didn't, or couldn't, give them any adequate training. Their productivity went lower and lower. The supervisors were very upset and yelled at them, pushing them to get out their quota. We felt sorry for them and tried to help them; but we concentrated on reluctantly meeting our own quota.

I don't think Joe realized that the supervisors were not teaching the new crewmen. He was very busy and not around much, and I think he assumed that they were training the new men. I think he began to put pressure on the supervisors as the work rate fell, because things continued to get worse. We couldn't even accept drinks. Production lagged greatly as compared to the previous summer, and the two supervisors struggled to meet the schedule and deal with customer complaints about quality. By July 15, the overall productivity of the company was 5 percent below "normal" and way below the previous summer.

As Joe became aware of this huge decrease in production, he became very concerned and wondered what to do about it.

CASE QUESTIONS

1. What caused the poor production condition during the second summer?
2. How might this situation have been avoided from the beginning?
3. What should Joe do now?
4. Do you think the supervisors could have effectively adopted Joe's style of leadership? What kind of problems might they have had if they did? How should they have conducted themselves?

PART

IV

MANAGING PRODUCTION AND OPERATIONS

FOUNDATIONS OF MANAGING PRODUCTION
AND OPERATIONS

FOUNDATIONS OF MANAGING PRODUCTION AND OPERATIONS

Part IV explores the third major contribution to modern management theory and practice: the **management science approach.** The central theme of management science is *to provide managers with quantitative bases for decisions regarding the operations under their control.*[1] A more complete definition of the field is that it "is the science devoted to describing, understanding, and predicting the behavior of complicated systems of men and machines operating in natural environments."[2] The ideas and concepts of management science are, in fact, extensions of scientific management, which was a major part of the classical approach, even as the behavioral approach is an extension of earlier developments arising out of the Hawthorne studies and human relations. Thus, we can see the thread of continuity that runs through each of the three contributions to contemporary management.

DEVELOPMENT OF MANAGEMENT SCIENCE

The field of management science has formally existed only for approximately 40 years. During this period, individuals associated with the field began to have a noticeable impact on the solution of complex military and business problems through the use of engineering and mathematical skills. Also during this period, a new profession emerged: the management scientist.

The terms *management science* (MS) and *operations research* (OR) are synonymous. In recent years, the field is generally designated MS/OR. The use of different terms for essentially the same set of ideas is a characteristic of emerging bodies of knowledge; management science is no exception. But the reader should keep in mind that the aim of management science is *to provide managers with quantitative bases for decisions.*

The activities of management scientists have emphasized the mathematical modeling of systems. Applications of these models by operations research specialists, mostly confined to the production segment of business firms, began after World War II. During the war, operations researchers had successfully solved a number of military problems ranging from those of a logistical nature (equipment and troop movements) to developing strategy for submarine warfare. As a result, management science caught on in some of the larger firms in the United States after the war. Such companies as E. I. du Pont de Nemours and H. J. Heinz pioneered the use of early operations research applications. However, not until these bolder firms had tried it with success did civilian operations research make any major headway in the United States.

---

[1]This definition is based on an early and influential book in management science, Philip M. Morse and George E. Kimball, *Methods of Operations Research* (New York: John Wiley & Sons, 1951), p. 1.

[2]John C. Anderson and Thomas R. Hoffman, "A Perspective on the Implementation of Management Science," *Academy of Management Review,* July 1978, p. 564.

While it is difficult to place clear boundary lines around the management science process, it is possible to distinguish certain characteristics of its approach. It is generally agreed that most management science tools and techniques possess the following characteristics.[3]

1. *A primary focus on decision making.* The principal end result of the analysis must have direct implications for management action. Decision making is still the central activity for production and operations managers today, as will be illustrated in Chapter 16.

2. *An appraisal resting on economic effectiveness criteria.* A comparison of feasible actions must be based on measurable values that reflect the future well-being of the organization. Examples of such measured variables include costs, revenues, and rates of return on investment.

3. *Reliance on formal mathematical models.* These models, stated in mathematical form, are actually possible solutions to problems. The procedures for manipulating the data must be so explicit that another analyst can derive the same results from the same data. This *replicability* requirement is not new to the reader, who saw in the previous section that this was also a major requirement of the behavioral science approach to management. In fact, replication is the keynote of scientific analysis.

4. *Dependence on an electronic computer.* This requirement is necessitated by either the complexity of the mathematical model, the volume of data to be manipulated, or the magnitude of computations needed to implement the model.

Managers were faced with the problem of *planning, organizing, and controlling* their organizations' operations long before the advent of the electronic computer and management science models; they are still performing these functions. Mathematical models can be especially useful as an *aid* to the manager performing the functions of planning and controlling production and operations, as shown in Figure 1.

While management scientists were constructing sophisticated quantitative models and theories, managers in organizations were struggling to manage their day-to-day production and operations more efficiently. What has emerged from this partnership of managers and scientists is a distinct area of inquiry, analysis, and application that focuses on the management of production and operations in manufacturing and service industries. This area is known as production and operations management (P/OM).[4]

PRODUCTION AND OPERATIONS MANAGEMENT

The most widespread application of management science tools and techniques in modern organizations has been in the area of production and operations management.

The term **production** focuses on manufacturing technology and the flow of materials in a manufacturing plant. The production function in a business

[3]Efraim Turban and Jack R. Meredith, *Fundamentals of Management Science* (Plano, Tex.: Business Publications, 1981), pp. 15–23.

[4]Charles G. Andrew and George A. Johnson, "The Crucial Importance of Production and Operations Management," *Academy of Management Review*, January 1982, pp. 143–47.

FIGURE 1   Managing Production and Operations

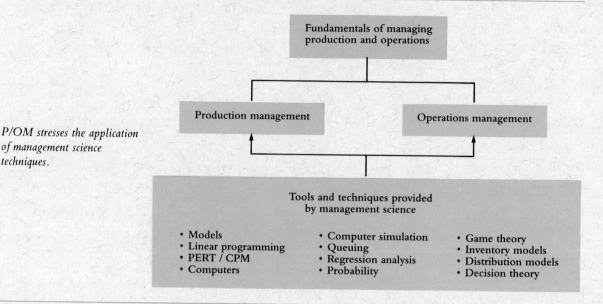

P/OM stresses the application of management science techniques.

organization is specifically concerned with the activity of producing goods—that is, the design, implementation, operation, and control of people, materials, equipment, money, and information to achieve specific production objectives. The term **operations** is broader in scope and refers to the goods- or service-producing activity in any organization—public, private, profit, or nonprofit. Thus, a bank and a hospital have operations functions although they have nothing to do with manufacturing technology, production assembly lines, and assembled products. Operations management, therefore, is similar to production management except that it focuses on a wider class of problems and includes organizations whose technologies may be quite different from those of a manufacturing organization. However, there are important similarities between the flow of materials in a manufacturing plant, customers waiting in line at a bank or supermarket, the processing of claims in an insurance company, student registration in a college or university, and the provision of health care in a hospital.

Production and operations management has management science as its foundation. To understand the P/OM approach, it is essential to understand the relationship between the two areas, graphically portrayed in Figure 1.

THE ROLE OF MATHEMATICAL MODELS

Mathematical models play a significant role in production and operations management. Before defining mathematical models, however, let us examine two points. First, in a previous section of the book, we saw that experimentation is an important part of the scientific approach. However, rarely if ever can a manager perform what would be considered a bona fide scientific experiment to test the feasibility of taking a particular action; the practicalities of the real world preclude this. In other words, a manager cannot usually experiment with inventory to determine which level minimizes carrying costs and ordering costs. However, an accurately constructed mathematical model enables the decision maker to experiment with possible solutions without interrupting the ongoing system. If the model accurately represents the ongoing system, it will provide the decision maker with the results of proposed solutions. In other words, it will react as the real system would react, enabling the decision maker to simulate the behavior of the real system. It is this experimental role of mathematical models that makes them useful to managers.

Second, while there are several different types of models used, the emphasis in P/OM is on mathematical models. Thus, the models examined in this section of the book are quantitative, or mathematical, in nature.

What do we mean by mathematical model? A **mathematical model** *is a simplified representation of the relevant aspects of an actual system or process.* The value of any model depends on how well it represents the system, or process, under consideration. A highly simplified model that accurately describes a system or process still provides a more clearly understood starting point than a vague conception. An accurate model forces the manager to consider systematically the variables in the problem and the relationships among the variables. And forcing the manager to formalize thinking reduces the possibility of overlooking important factors or giving too much weight to minor factors.

You are probably more familiar with models for decision making than you think. The accounting equation $A = L + C$ is a mathematical model. It is a mathematical model showing a simplified relationship between assets, liabilities, and capital. It does not resemble the actual system physically, but it does *behave as the real system behaves.* It is an abstraction of the financial condition of a particular enterprise at a given moment of time.

SOME USEFUL P/OM MODELS

ALLOCATION MODELS

Allocation models are used in a variety of situations in which numerous activities are all competing for limited resources. These models enable the decision maker to allocate scarce resources to maximize some given objective. In certain departments, the resources may include labor time that the production manager must allocate to several different products to maximize the objective of profit. One of the most widely used allocation models is the linear programming (LP) model. Linear programming, as discussed in Chapter 18, expresses the objective to be achieved in the form of a mathematical function, the value of which is to be maximized (e.g., profits) or minimized (e.g., costs).

Network Models

Network models are extremely useful in planning and controlling both simple and complex projects. Actually, network models are as old as scientific management. The Gantt chart is one of Henry Gantt's contributions to the managerial task of managing work and organizations. While network models are more sophisticated than the Gantt chart, both are based on the same philosophy. The basic type of network model is PERT (Program Evaluation and Review Technique). PERT (to be discussed further in Chapter 18) is a method of planning and controlling nonrepetitive projects—projects that have not been done before and will not be done again in the same exact manner (for example, the first space shuttle).

Inventory Models

Inventory models provide answers to two questions: how much, and when. Just as the business organization is concerned with obtaining goods to be sold at the most favorable price, it must also be concerned with the time at which orders are placed for repeat goods and the quantity of each order. On the one hand, enough inventory must be available at all times to ensure that there are no lost sales or loss of customer goodwill due to stock-outs; on the other hand, frequent orders result in increased costs, such as the storage costs from carrying an excessive inventory. The costs of ordering and carrying an inventory are inversely related: one increases while the other decreases. Inventory models enable the manager to compute the economic order quantity (EOQ) and the optimum reorder point. Because these models can be applied wherever inventories are kept, they have also found wide use in nonbusiness organizations. Chapter 19 will discuss inventory models.

Conclusion

The next five chapters give an introductory view of managing production and operations. Covering the entire production and operations field is beyond the scope of this book. Thus, we have selected an overview of production and operations management; decision making, decision support systems, production planning, and inventory planning and control as representative areas to highlight the fundamentals of managing production and operations.

PEOPLE IN MANAGEMENT

William H. Gates III

The opportunity to make personal computers (PCs) accessible to everyone had been there for years. But it was William H. Gates III, a Harvard dropout, who turned opportunity into reality. In 1980, Gates's company, Microsoft, won a coveted contract with IBM to make the operating software for IBM's personal computer. By 1984, Microsoft's software was being used with 2 million computers and had become an industry standard.

In 1976, at 20, Bill Gates founded Microsoft, the first personal computer software firm. Today, at 33, Gates is a billionaire, having made more money than anyone else his age, ever, in any business. In addition to making the basic operating software for all IBM and IBM-compatible PCs, Microsoft has developed a raft of other popular programs, including Excel, a spreadsheet product that earned $97 million in 1984, and Windows, a major breakthrough in PC user friendliness, which made $140 million in 1985.

Gates's vision for his young company remains the same today: "A computer on every desk and in every home, running Microsoft software." Microsoft is now the world's largest computer software company. It employs over 2,000 people, and its revenues are in the billions of dollars annually.

About 90 percent of Gates's employees are hired right out of college or graduate school. During the interview, prospective employees discuss projects which they've worked on. If they are unable to explain the entire project—even if they only worked on a segment of it—they are not hired.

Gates wants people to constantly prime their creative pumps. To this end, he holds weekend "innovation retreats" to bring marketing and software development people together for a free exchange of ideas, especially about new product development. After formal presentations, people break into small groups, then come back and present their ideas. Regular product reviews are held so employees can continuously refine their ideas on all aspects of a product's development.

Gates encourages the use of in-house computers at Microsoft. If employees have a sudden brainstorm, they send a computerized message to whomever they want to alert. If they read something they think will be of interest to others, they use the electronic mail system to disseminate the information. Electronic mail allows Gates to interact with people he would not otherwise have time to see.

Motivating people is high on Gates's list of managerial priorities. Thus, employees are promoted without necessarily becoming managers. These promotions take the form of handsome salary increases and stock options. Those who want to move up the job ladder can take the more traditional promotion to a bigger job title.

Gates says: "A lot of my role is about leadership. My strengths are things like: What are the products? Where are we going? Talking to people building the products and taking our vision outside the company."

Source: Anne R. Field, "Managing Creative People," *Success*, October 1985, pp. 85–87; Robert Slater, *Portraits in Silocon* (Cambridge, Mass.: MIT Press, 1987), pp. 263–71.

15

PRODUCTION AND OPERATIONS MANAGEMENT

LEARNING OBJECTIVES

After completing Chapter 15, you should be able to:

Define
the term *product (service) quality.*

Discuss
why the production process at Burger King is a worker-paced system.

Describe
the area of influence of production and operations management.

Identify
some of the main factors that affect quality.

Compare
the four specific functions: design, scheduling, operation, and transformation control.

American Businesses that Lead in the Quality Competition

Today, quality is central to world competitiveness. Throughout the world, however, many people remark that American goods are of throwaway quality. When asked once what was wrong with a garbage disposal, an oriental repairman responded, "It's American." One might ask: Does America make the best of anything?

To answer that question, *Fortune* surveyed quality experts, management consultants, securities analysts, industry representatives, academics, consumers, unions, and other informed observers of world commerce. *Fortune* established a stringent set of criteria to qualify a product as a world champ: The item had to be the most durable, the leader in innovation and technology, a value for the price, and a world market share leader.

Not surprisingly, *Fortune* found a wide mixture of high- and low-technology American products. In over 100 categories, American products lead the field. In aerospace (General Dynamics), agricultural equipment (John Deere), personal computers (Apple), pharmaceuticals (Genetek), and medical instrumentation (Medtronic), these and other U.S. companies produce products that are tops. The United States also gets superior marks for craftsmanship in dishwashers (General Electric), ballpoint pens (A. T. Cross), clothes dryers (Whirlpool), jeans (Levi Strauss), and hunting boots (L. L. Bean).

What formula do these firms follow? *Fortune* found that American quality leaders totally commit to meeting and exceeding standards for excellence year after year. In addition to surpassing customer expectations, the elite American products suit their function. The unequaled managers constantly improve their products and listen to anyone who has something to say about those products. The superior firms use grade A raw materials and the most dependable suppliers. American world product leaders also ride herd on their suppliers to improve the quality of the suppliers' parts. These firms' leaders have little tolerance for assembly-line rework. It simply costs less to make it right the first time.

Strangely, managers at world-leader companies view factory automation circumspectly. Automation simply produces more product; however, quality and world dominance come only through managing people, technology, and the managers themselves. Product excellence and world domination, in essence, result only from a total, coordinated commitment to a quality ethic, from top management all the way down to the lowest worker. The leaders admit, however, that no one has a monopoly on quality. Everyone who tries can learn how to do it. That is why a constant commitment to quality is imperative.

Source: "Victory in the Quality Crusade," *Fortune*, October 10, 1988, pp. 80–86; "What America Makes Best," *Fortune*, March 28, 1988, pp. 40–53.

The terms *manufacturing management, production management,* and *operations management* are used interchangeably to refer to the functional field of production and operations management (P/OM). Traditionally, the word *production* brings to mind smokestacks, assembly lines, and machine shops. P/OM, however, refers to a broader idea: the producing activities of all kinds of organizations—manufacturing or service, public or private, large or small, profit or nonprofit.[1]

P/OM as a field of study and practice uses concepts and principles from scientific management and management science. It also uses ideas from the behavioral sciences. As a part of management, P/OM is quite eclectic and application oriented.[2] As the opening Management in Action indicated, the achievement of high levels of productivity and quality depends on good management of people as well as machines. In this chapter, the nature and area of influence of P/OM will be surveyed. We will emphasize the analytical side of P/OM while acknowledging the importance of people-related issues.

The Nature of Production and Operations Management

P/OM goes well beyond manufacturing operations involving the assembly of products. It also covers the operation of banks, transportation companies, hospitals and clinics, school systems, insurance companies, and high-technology firms. Any system that generates tangible products (e.g., a Ford automobile, a Sunbeam shaver) or intangible services (e.g., a flight on American Airlines, advice on computer programming) is part of the P/OM domain.

A Systems View

P/OM practitioners view organizations in terms of systems. A **system** is a collection of objects united by some form of regular interaction and interdependence. We noted in Chapter 2 that organizations themselves are systems made up of interacting subsystems. One of the significant subsystems of many organizations is the production and operations management department. Figure 15–1 illustrates the organization as a system that takes in and transforms inputs and then provides outputs that are consumed or demanded. The transformation portion of Figure 15–1 is the point at which P/OM activities, or processes, are conducted. According to this representation, organizations can be thought of in terms of being productive transformation systems. The P/OM executive gives special attention to the creation of goods and services—that is, the productive transformation work that occurs within an organization.

[1]Christopher W. Hart and Gregory D. Casserly, "Quality: A Brand-New, Time-Tested Strategy," *Cornell Hotel and Restaurant Administration Quarterly,* November 1985, pp. 52–63.

[2]Numerous texts survey the P/OM field. See Richard B. Chase and Nicholas J. Aquilano, *Production and Operations Management: A Life-Cycle Approach,* 5th ed. (Homewood, Ill.: Richard D. Irwin, 1989); Elwood S. Buffa, *Production/Operations Management* (New York: John Wiley & Sons, 1983); Donald Del Mar, *Operations and Industrial Management: Designing and Managing for Productivity* (New York: McGraw-Hill, 1985).

FIGURE 15–1   Scope of Production and Operations Management

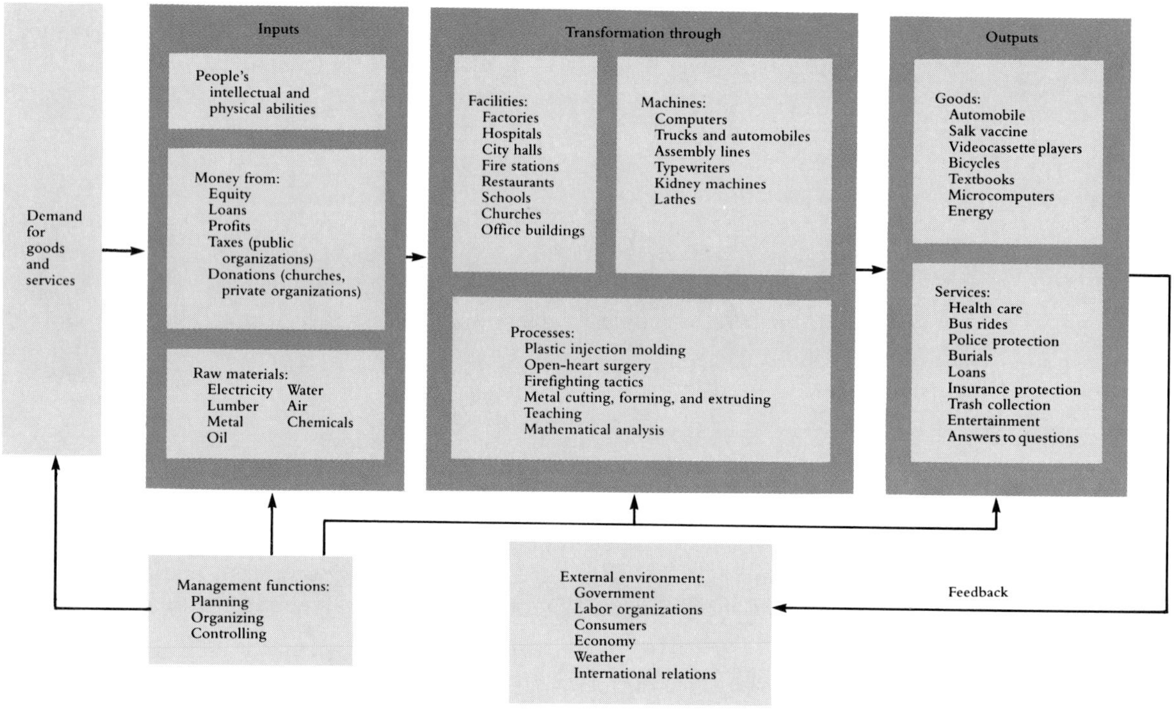

Source: Adapted from Franklin G. Moore and Thomas E. Hendrick, *Production/Operations Management*, 9th ed. (Homewood, Ill.: Richard D. Irwin, 1985), p. 11.

P/OM activities can be understood in the context of systems theory concepts such as inputs, outputs, transformation, and feedback.

P/OM is a specific function that affects the behavior and performance of other major functions, such as marketing and accounting. The interrelationships of these three main functions of any organization can be better understood by thinking of an organization as a system. The marketing subsystem deals primarily with the demand side of business; the accounting subsystem addresses the control side of business; the P/OM subsystem centers around converting inputs into outputs, or the supply side of business. No matter how great the demand is for a product or service, there must be a supply available. Producing enough goods and services to meet demand is, according to the P/OM viewpoint, the primary task of organizations.[3]

GOODS AND SERVICES

According to P/OM managers, the term *product* is a generic label for the output of a productive system. A product can be a good or a service. In economic terms, *goods* are defined as movable personal property; examples

[3]Vincent G. Reuter, "Trends in Production Management Education," *Industrial Management*, May–June 1983, pp. 1–3.

FIGURE 15–2   Transformation Process on a Farm

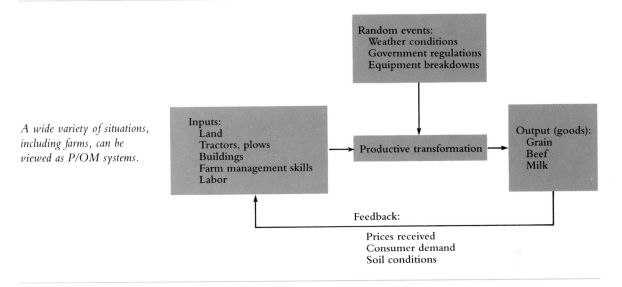

A wide variety of situations, including farms, can be viewed as P/OM systems.

include autos, home computers, desks, and microwave ovens. A *capital good* is immovable personal property, such as a house or factory. A *service*—an activity required by a customer or a client, or work done for another person—is another production output.

Economists refer to the transformation of inputs into goods and services as the *production function*. Managers are aware of the fact that simply moving goods and services from input to transformation to output is often affected by unpredictable or random events. For example, a farm manager takes land, equipment, livestock, labor, and skills and transforms them into goods such as grain, beef, and milk. However, the weather, government regulations, and equipment breakdowns affect the transformation or productive work activities. Figure 15–2 illustrates this example in terms of a systems framework. The framework reflects the P/OM viewpoint, paying particular attention to inputs, transformation, outputs, and feedback cycles. Table 15–1 highlights the variety of productive systems in society by examining a few of the various input transformations, random events, and outputs of some typical organizations.

MANAGING THE TRANSFORMATION PROCESS

When managing the transformation process, P/OM managers pay particular attention to four specific functions: design, scheduling, operation, and transformation control.[4] Table 15–2 categorizes major responsibilities of managers from a P/OM perspective.

[4]Richard Wild, "Survey Report—The Responsibilities and Activities of UK Production Managers," *International Journal of Operations and Production Management* 4, no. 1 (1984), pp. 69–74.

TABLE 15–1   Productive Systems and Their Characteristics

System	Main Inputs	Transformation Activities	Random Events	Main Outputs
Chrysler Motors	Steel, glass.	Assembly of autos.	New government regulation, new car of competitor.	Automobiles.
Methodist Hospital, Houston, Texas	Patients.	Diagnosis, surgery, rehabilitation.	Reduction in medicare payments.	Well patients.
Apple Computer	Electrical circuits, computer languages.	Assembly of personal computers and development of software.	Competitive product from IBM.	Computers and software.
Tadich's Grill, San Francisco, California	Lobsters, hungry patrons, waiters.	Preparation of food.	Price increase for lobsters, strike by waiters.	Satisfied patrons who want to come back.
College or university	High school graduates.	Classroom instruction, lecture enrichment, discussions with alumni who are brought back to the campus, use of library.	Missing books in library, cancellation of course with outstanding instructor.	Educated and employable graduates.

All organizations can in fact be viewed in terms of a production system.

1. *Design.*   Designing the transformation process involves making decisions on equipment selection, type of production process, and work flow patterns.[5] Transformation processes are usually either continuous, intermittent, or "one-shot" projects. Continuous processes are generally very specialized, producing one type of product (e.g., Oldsmobiles) or service (e.g., H & R Block tax services). Intermittent processes are more general and utilize a variety of equipment; for example, an intermittent process is used in a job shop (i.e., a shop that produces a product to meet a customer's specifications). The one-shot project is found in building, bridge, and highway construction. The decision on which process to utilize is based on economic considerations, volume required, and labor resources and skills available. Managers must design transformation systems to take advantage of all existing knowledge and technology. How to do that is often the compelling issue in the development of a new product. The Management Focus describes how a manager at Motorola gathered information that enabled him to design a top-notch production process.

2. *Scheduling.*   Once designed, the optimal process must be scheduled to produce the desired product or service at the right time. Scheduling, in P/OM terms, covers both long and short runs. In long-range scheduling, forecasts and estimates of product/service demand are developed so that labor, capacity, raw materials, and other input needs can be met. Scheduling also can involve

---

[5]R. P. Sadowski and N. J. Tracey, "Concepts to Increase Productivity Are Used in the Design of a Manufacturing Facility," *Industrial Engineering,* September 1982, pp. 61–65.

TABLE 15–2	**P/OM Responsibilities of Managers**

The P/OM manager is re-sponsible for one or all of the specific functions of a produc-tion system.

Design

1. Product design.
2. Job and process design.
3. Capital equipment selection.
4. Setting labor standards.
5. Developing labor skills.
6. Plant location and layout.

Operation

1. Purchasing.
2. Forecasting requirements.
3. Process redesign.
4. Operating transformation process.
5. Maintenance.

Scheduling

1. Aggregate planning.
2. Scheduling work force levels.
3. Project management.
4. Timing inventory replenishments.
5. Routing and sequencing.
6. Job shop scheduling.

Control

1. Quality control.
2. Inventory control policies.
3. Monitoring production processes.
4. Cost control.
5. Resource allocation.

Source: Adapted from Thomas M. Cook and Robert A. Russell, *Contemporary Operations Management: Text and Cases* (Englewood Cliffs, N.J.: Prentice-Hall), © 1980, p. 10. Reprinted by permission of Prentice-Hall, Inc.

the management of projects over time. Short-range scheduling involves employees' daily or weekly work activities: the sequencing of work flow, raw materials, patients, or other similar inputs.[6]

3. *Operation.* Operating the transformation process involves the actual implementation of P/OM procedures. The planning, organizing, and control-ling of operations directly affect the output of a productive system. The operating function also involves such activities as purchasing, redesigning the process (if necessary), and forecasting requirements.

4. *Control.* The transformation control function requires some method of measuring the product or service before it is sold or used. For example, computers are used to monitor sales in Kroger and Safeway stores. By using the computer, the store manager can monitor inventory levels so that stock reorders can be placed and outages minimized. Another means of control is inspection. For example, inspectors monitor the waterproof protection of upholstery in Ford automobiles in the Chicago assembly plant.

EFFECTIVE MANAGEMENT OF THE TRANSFORMATION PROCESS

What then are the key differences between good plants and poor plants? What distinguishes factories that year in and year out manufacture high-quality goods and services without sacrificing productivity, from factories that do not do as well? These questions and their answers are of great importance to the American economic system and to the managers of firms that make up that system. Remaining competitive in an increasingly international marketplace requires American managers to evaluate every avenue of potential productivity and quality gains. To obtain some answers to these questions, *Fortune*

[6]Richard Schonberger and Edward Knod, *Operations Management,* 3rd ed. (Plano, Tex.: Business Publications, 1988), pp. 200–241.

MANAGEMENT FOCUS

Designing a Production Process by Emulation

How does one design a manufacturing facility that will produce the highest-quality numeric display pager? Scott Shamlin at Motorola considered two approaches: start from the beginning or borrow ideas from successful producers all around the world. Shamlin called his design choice Operation Bandit. Guess which approach he took?

Shamlin traveled the world, viewing plants that, according to experts, had some superlative part of the production process. Shamlin visited over 60 separate facilities, many of which did not build electronic pagers. From Detroit's carmakers, Shamlin nabbed parts delivery. He commandeered robotics technology from Japanese watchmakers. He even pinched computer-integrated manufacturing from his own company.

The result is a marvelous manufacturing application. Humans never touch the pager assembly. 50 employees eyeball as 42 computers assemble and track each pager from start to finish. Computers even program each pager to one of 29 million unique signals. At their Boynton Beach plant in Florida, Motorola can assemble a pager in one and one-half hours, that competitors may take up to 27 days to build. According to Shamlin, "the workers are like airline pilots in computer-controlled jets, who only act when something goes wrong."

Have Scott Shamlin and Motorola made out like bandits? Motorola dominates the market for numeric display pagers in Japan. The Japanese want to form a joint venture; however, Motorola has no interest.

Source: Adapted from "Motorola Borrows the Best to Beat Rivals," *USA Today,* November 25, 1988, p. 6B.

magazine examined the 10 best factories in the United States to see what they have in common.[7] The plants were selected because of their record of high productivity, high product quality, or both. Included in the 10 were factories bearing logos of well-known firms: AT&T, GE, IBM, and Hewlett-Packard.

According to the author of the study, these 10 plants all made use of the most current production management methods for planning and controlling the process. But in addition to those technically oriented practices, these plants tended to do many other things the same way. They all began by reducing the barriers between product design and manufacturing. (In the typical plant, considerable friction and even hostility exist between the group that designs the product and the group that manufactures the product.) The most successful plants manage to design the product and the required manufacturing process concurrently rather than sequentially. This means merging the two groups into a single unit from the time of the initial idea for the product to the final production layout for the product.

Another characteristic of the 10 excellently managed factories is the ability to create working conditions that allow employees to make quality products. That includes enabling employees to stop the production line to correct defects and to continue to hold the line until the source of the product defect is discovered. In effect, these factories have turned every employee into a quality

[7]Gene Bylinsky, "America's Best-Managed Factories," *Fortune,* May 28, 1984, pp. 16–24.

inspector. To obtain employee commitment to quality, the competitors' products are displayed prominently on the factory floor to demonstrate what is at stake.

Excellently managed factories do things to help employees understand that their enemy is competition, not management. Not that these plants are free of employee complaints and union grievances, but their managers seem to do a better job of substituting trust and communication for strife and confrontation. The basic idea is to get managers and nonmanagers to think of themselves as teams with a common stake in the outcome of their daily work activities. With this kind of atmosphere in place, production management methods and techniques can be implemented to achieve their maximum potential.

Designing and managing these plants involves managers in many diverse issues. Table 15–3 presents questions that all production/operations managers must ask. The standard for judging whether they answer such questions effectively is found in the quality of the products and services they produce, the subject of the following section.

THE QUALITY CONCERN OF P/OM

The last set of questions presented in Table 15–3 addresses quality control—an extremely important responsibility of managers. But while the P/OM manager works very hard at improving quality control, other managers may emphasize quantity. Why? Outputs such as assembled autos, manufactured pipes, or tons of grain processed can be easily quantified by counting or weighing, but it is generally more difficult to evaluate their quality. And quality is often judged on subjective opinions rather than on objective data. Emphasizing quantity, however, may lead to lack of concern for quality.

Quality is important. Products of fine quality lead to customer goodwill and satisfaction that manifest themselves in the form of repeat sales, loyal customers and clients, and testimonials to prospective customers or clients. One of the Big Three automakers has a case on record where the irate owner of a luxury car cost the company no fewer than 100 lost sales in a single year.[8] To achieve total customer satisfaction not only would be cost prohibitive but also would lead to unrealistic expectations.[9] However, a reasonable record of quality must be established.

Quality has often been defined as the perception of excellence.[10] Although many may *evaluate* quality, the customer is the key *perceiver* of quality. His or her purchase decision determines the success of the organization's product or service and often the fate of the organization itself.

A consumer's perception of a product/service's excellence generally depends on how well the product or service meets his or her specifications and requirements. Specifically, a consumer perceives excellence by evaluating one or more dimensions of quality (see Table 15–4). In judging the quality of a

[8]Edward M. Stiles, *Handbook for Total Quality Assurance* (Englewood Cliffs, N.J.: Prentice-Hall, 1977), p. 3.

[9]Madhav Sinha and Walter O. Willborn, *The Management of Quality Assurance* (New York: John Wiley & Sons, 1985).

[10]Tom Peters, *Thriving on Chaos* (New York: Harper & Row, 1987), p. 10.

TABLE 15–3   Questions Asked by P/OM Managers

Subject	Questions
Capital investment analysis	When should new machinery be bought to replace old machines? When should investments be made in machines in order to economize on labor? What methods of analysis need to be used when making such decisions?
Design of products and services	Are our products safe for consumers to use? How long a life should our products have before they wear out or become obsolete? Are they energy efficient?
Facilities location and design	Where should facilities be located? What building and equipment design will allow work to be done in the most economical manner? What are the best ways to make products or to deliver services? What machines, labor skills, and processes are required?
Maintenance	How shall the organization's facilities be maintained and kept in repair? Should repairs be done on a preventive basis or confined to taking care of breakdowns? Which work should be done by inside crews, and which should be contracted to outsiders?
Energy management	Are we using energy efficiently in our processes? Can alternate energy sources be used?
Work measurement and standards	How much output can reasonably be expected from workers? How much is being turned out, and how can discrepancies between expected and actual output be corrected?
Safety	Are our facilities and machines safe for people to operate? Do the processes produce harmful fumes? Are machines too noisy? Are injuries more than rare? How and at what cost can we meet federal and state regulations in these areas?
Production scheduling and control	How should work priorities be determined? How should work be assigned to machines and labor so that the capacity is used effectively while, at the same time, customers get good service?
Inventory management	How much inventory of finished products should we carry in order to give good customer service? What raw material and work-in-process inventories should be carried? Should we make or buy component parts? How much should be ordered or produced at a time, and when should it be ordered so that materials are available as needed?
Purchasing	From whom should we buy our raw materials and component parts? How can we tell if their quality and delivery reliability will meet our needs?
Quality standards and control	How can the organization produce goods and services of the quality required by the marketing department? How can internal operations be controlled so that unacceptable deviations in quality can be detected, and how can they be remedied?

The work of production management can be understood in terms of the key questions that production managers ask or are asked.

Source: Adapted from Franklin G. Moore and Thomas E. Hendrick, *Production/Operations Management,* 9th ed. (Homewood, Ill.: Richard D. Irwin, 1985), p. 12.

Most of these items are high-quality goods, but ultimately the customer is the key perceiver of quality.

Sony television set, for example, a prospective buyer may examine performance, how well the TV set performs its primary function. (Is the picture sharp, the color vivid, the sound clear?) Extra features such as automatic fine-tuning may be evaluated. The rate of repair, or reliability, may be a factor as well as serviceability, the convenience and quality of repair should a breakdown occur. Conformance (e.g., the set's compatibility with a VCR of another brand) may be assessed. Durability, the typical life span of the set, may also be examined, as well as the visual appeal of its design (aesthetics). Sony's reputation for product quality may also influence the consumer's evaluation of the set's overall quality (perceived quality).[11]

Concerning a consumer's "perception" of excellence or quality, two points are noteworthy. First, consumers emphasize different dimensions of quality when judging a product or service. Some prospective car buyers value performance above all; others may be more influenced by the car's appearance (aesthetics). Because of such differences in consumer preferences, a company may choose to emphasize one or a few dimensions of quality rather than compete on all eight dimensions. For example, Tandem Computers emphasizes superior reliability in its computer systems. The company achieved exceptional reliability by designing and building dual processors into its computers. If one processor fails, which would shut down most computers,

[11]David A. Garvin, "Competing on the Eight Dimensions of Quality," *Harvard Business Review,* November–December 1987, pp. 101–9.

TABLE 15–4	Dimensions of Quality

	Dimension	**Example**
	Performance: Product/service's primary operating characteristics.	Sony TV's richness of color, clarity of sound.
	Features: Secondary, "extra" characteristics.	Hyatt Regency's complimentary breakfasts.
	Reliability: Consistent performance within a specific period.	Honda Acura's rate of repair in the first year of purchase.
Quality, a relatively abstract term, has some rather specific dimensions when we stop to consider it.	*Conformance:* Degree to which design and characteristics meet specific standards.	Apple computer's compatibility with IBM software.
	Durability: Length of a product/service's useful life.	Average 17-year life of Kirby vacuum cleaners.
	Serviceability: Speed, courtesy, competence, and ease of repair.	Caterpillar Tractor's worldwide guarantee of 48-hour delivery of replacement parts.
	Aesthetics: Looks, taste, feel, sound, smell of a product/service.	Flavor, texture of Baskin-Robbins ice cream.
	Perceived quality: Quality conveyed via marketing, brand name, reputation.	Bose's reputation in stereo speakers.

Source: David A. Garvin, "Competing on the Eight Dimensions of Quality," *Harvard Business Review,* November–December 1987, pp. 101–9.

work automatically shifts to the second processor, and no operation time is lost. This quality feature has provided tremendous sales growth for Tandem.[12] Second, perceptions of excellence can be highly subjective. Although some dimensions (e.g., reliability or durability) can be quantified by simply reviewing the product's records, other dimensions (e.g., aesthetics) depend on personal likes and dislikes, which are highly subjective. Differences in preferences and the subjectivity of perceptions underscore the need for organizations to obtain accurate market information about consumer perceptions and preferences.[13]

One other important element of the quality concept concerns the relationship between quality and price. In many cases, the relationship between a product's or service's quality and price is positive and linear, as shown in Figure 15–3.[14] If quality increases, so will the price (given that price reflects the cost of providing the product or service). This relationship is particularly strong when an organization produces a product or service that rates high on all eight dimensions of quality. Sometimes, however, a higher level of quality does not result in a higher price, because improving quality may actually reduce the cost of quality.

To understand this relationship, it is first necessary to understand the concept of cost of quality and its component parts. An organization's cost of quality is the total expense involved in ensuring that a product or service meets established quality standards. The cost of quality comprises three types of costs. *Prevention costs* are the costs of preventing product or service defects—

[12]Ibid., p. 108.

[13]Ibid., p. 107.

[14]Everett E. Adams, Jr., James C. Hershauer, and William A. Ruch, *Productivity and Quality* (Englewood Cliffs, N.J.: Prentice-Hall, 1981).

FIGURE 15-3   The Price–Quality Relationship in Airline Service

Generally, price and quality are directly related, as in airline service.

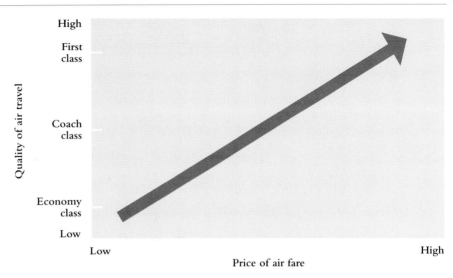

the precontrol aspect of quality control. Examples of prevention costs are the expenses of effective employee training, reengineering the product's manufacturing process, or working with suppliers to ensure that materials are of high quality. *Appraisal costs* are all expenses involved in directly evaluating quality, such as the costs of quality inspection and testing. *Failure costs* occur once a defect is identified. If a defect is found before the product leaves the plant, the failure costs are internal (e.g., the costs of scrap material or of reworking the defective part or product). If the defect is found by the customer, external failure costs are incurred (the costs of recalled products, customer complaints, and a damaged product image).[15]

These three components of cost make up different proportions of the total cost of quality, largely because they are incurred at different points of the production process. Figure 15–4 represents what is often referred to as the **quality funnel principle**. According to the principle, the nearer to the start of the production process, the lower the cost of quality. This is true because more resources, such as labor, time, and materials, are invested as the product or service progresses through the process. The greater the amount of resources invested, the higher the cost of rejection (and quality). Applying this principle, prevention costs are incurred primarily at the beginning of the production process and are the least expensive component (5 to 10 percent of total quality costs). Failure costs are incurred mostly at the end of the process and thereafter and are the most expensive component (65 to 75 percent). Appraisal costs (20 to 25 percent of total quality costs) are incurred primarily during the production process and are larger than prevention but smaller than failure costs.[16]

[15]Jack Campanella and Frank J. Corcoran, "Principles of Quality Control," *Quality Progress,* April 1983, pp. 16–22.

[16]A. V. Feigenbaum, *Total Quality Control* (New York: McGraw-Hill, 1983), pp. 112–13.

FIGURE 15–4 The Quality Funnel Principle

Managers need to identify poor quality before the product/service gets too far into the process, certainly before the customer receives it.

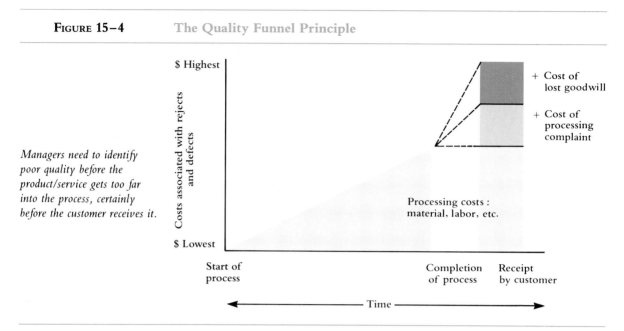

Source: Adapted from David Bain, *The Productivity Prescription: The Manager's Guide to Improving Productivity and Profits* (New York: McGraw-Hill, 1982), p. 120.

Many companies are shifting their quality control emphasis to prevention (precontrol). They are increasing prevention costs of quality by focusing more on such preventive mechanisms as employee training and the design of the manufacturing process. Over time, this increase in prevention costs produces larger returns. Quality is improved. Appraisal costs are reduced because improved prevention reduces the need for inspection and testing activities. Above all, failure costs—the most costly quality component—are reduced because the service or product is produced right the first time. Overall quality costs decline.

FACTORS THAT AFFECT QUALITY

Quality depends on a number of factors: policy, information, engineering and design, materials, equipment, people, and field support. An integrated quality control system must focus on all of these factors.

Policy. Management establishes policies concerning product quality. These policies specify the standards, or levels, of quality to be achieved in a product or service; they can be an important precontrol and concurrent control means for ensuring quality.

Management considers three factors in determining its quality policies: the product's or service's market, the competition, and image. Evaluating the market provides an indication of customers' expectations of quality and the price they are willing to pay for it. Quality and price expectations within the auto industry, for example, differ widely between the luxury car (Mercedes) and economy car markets. Quality levels provided by the competition also affect policies because products/services must be competitive to succeed in the marketplace.

Besides considering the market and competition, management must also consider the organization's image. Long-term interests may be damaged by making a product whose quality is inconsistent with the firm's image. For example, marketing a low-priced Porsche or a new, low-priced Baskin-Robbins ice cream flavor might create a backlash from regular customers. Consumers' images of these products (and their loyalty to the company) may be tarnished if they equate lower price with lower quality.

Information.   Information plays a vital role in setting policy and ensuring that quality standards are achieved. Accurate information must be obtained about customer preferences and expectations and about competitors' quality standards and costs. Competitive benchmarking is one effective approach to obtaining valuable information about a competitor's quality standards and costs.[17] Also, new computer technology is enabling organizations to quickly obtain and evaluate information about the quality of products while they are being produced.

Engineering and Design.   Once management has formulated a policy concerning quality, the engineer or designer must apply the policy to the actual product or service. The engineer/designer must create a product that will appeal to customers and that can be produced at a reasonable cost and provide competitive quality.

Materials.   A growing number of organizations realize that a finished product is only as good as the materials used in it. In this regard, many manufacturing companies are implementing a new precontrol strategy with material suppliers. They are reducing their number of suppliers, weeding out the lower-quality vendors, and focusing on developing effective, long-term relationships with the better ones. Ford, General Motors, and Chrysler use this approach. Chrysler, for example, which started with 2,700 parts and materials suppliers in 1985, set a goal of having under 1,500 by 1991. It has also set new standards for materials quality.[18]

Equipment.   The ability of equipment, tools, and machinery to accurately and reliably produce desired outputs is important, especially in manufacturing industries. If the equipment can meet the acceptable tolerances at competitive costs and quality, an organization has the opportunity to compete in the marketplace.

People.   Materials, design, and equipment are important ingredients in quality products. But people are the vital contributors. Working individually or in teams, employees take the ingredients and process them into the final product or service. Managers must therefore not only provide the proper training to produce quality but also enable people to develop attitudes that

[17]Bernard Taylor, "Corporate Planning for the 1990s: The New Frontiers," *Long Range Planning,* December 1986, pp. 13–18.

[18]Alex Taylor III, "Lee Iacocca's Production Whiz," *Fortune,* June 22, 1987, pp. 36ff.

Management Focus

A Novel Way to Involve Employees in Production Management

Cost cutting sometimes means quality gets slashed too, because worker morale or performance diminishes. Faced with the need to prune costs and maintain quality, Sundance Spas of Chino, California, decided to play a modified version of the game "The Price is Right." Ron Clark thought workers simply did not know what component parts for Sundance's hot tubs cost. In high-spirited sessions, employees consistently underestimated the cost of expensive components. For example, workers guessed that one part, which repeatedly broke in assembly, cost only $2; the actual cost was $32.40. After the games, the volume of worker suggestions for improvements and cost savings astonished Clark. (One even was a design that replaced the $32.40 item and only cost $2.) According to Clark, if you have to do some belt-tightening, the game approach is an alternative way to break the news. Simply handing out memos informing supervisors that their budgets will shrink can hurt in many unintended ways.

Source: Adapted from "Game Theory," *Inc.*, October 1988, p. 112.

---

value quality. One relatively small manufacturer achieved surprising results by involving employees in the important decisions relating to quality and costs. The Management Focus describes that approach.

Field Support. Often, the field support provided by the supplier determines a product's quality image (perceived quality). IBM, General Electric, and Sears Roebuck have reputations for providing strong field support for their products. This is not to say that the products of these firms are necessarily the best in their industries. Many customers select IBM computers, GE refrigerators, and Sears Roebuck dishwashers because the field support of these firms is considered excellent.

DEVELOPING A QUALITY CONTROL SYSTEM

A system to reduce the chances that poor-quality output will get to the customer involves the following steps (see Figure 15–5).[19]

STEP 1: DEFINE QUALITY CHARACTERISTICS

The first step in establishing a quality control system is to define the quality characteristics desired by the customer or client. Examining customer preferences, technical specifications, marketing department suggestions, and competitive products provides information about quality characteristics. As previously noted, the preferences of the customer—the key perceiver of quality—

---

[19]David Bain, *The Productivity Prescription: The Manager's Guide to Improving Productivity and Profits* (New York: McGraw-Hill, 1982), pp. 119–27.

FIGURE 15–5   Five Key Steps in Developing a Quality Control System

Action	Purpose
1. Develop quality characteristics	Quality control systems must ensure that products deliver what customers expect.
2. Establish quality standards	Standards of quality must pertain to customer-defined characteristics.
3. Develop quality review program	Quality control is realized only through the implementation of specific procedures.
4. Build commitment to quality	Employees make the product — their commitment is necessary to achieve quality standards.
5. Design reporting system	Product quality information must be channeled to employees who can take corrective action.

Managers who want to improve quality must take five specific, sequential actions.

are especially important. These preferences will greatly influence both the dimensions of quality an organization will choose to emphasize and the level of quality to be achieved for each dimension.

STEP 2: ESTABLISH QUALITY STANDARDS

Once quality characteristics have been defined, the next step is to determine the desired standards of quality. These standards quantify the specific quality requirements for the organization's output. Quality standards serve as the reference point for comparing the ideal to what actually is produced.

In many organizations, quality standards include cost objectives. Often, the objective is to reduce the failure costs (both internal and external) of quality. These costs constitute 15 to 40 percent of a company's sales.[20] Tennant Co., a Minneapolis business, confronted substantial quality problems in the maintenance equipment it produces for industrial floors. The company's failure costs of quality averaged 17 percent of sales. Tennant launched a companywide program to reduce the failure costs to less than 9 percent of sales in four years.[21] Du Pont's polymer products department once faced a similar problem. When internal and external failure costs were running $400 billion each year, about double the department's yearly profits, the department launched a quality campaign designed to reduce failure costs by 10 percent each year.[22]

STEP 3: DEVELOP A QUALITY REVIEW PROGRAM

Management must establish methods for quality review and decide where the reviews will be conducted, by whom, when they will occur, and how the

[20]Peters, *Thriving,* p. 74.

[21]Ed Bean, "Causes of Quality Control Problems Might Be the Managers—Not Workers," *The Wall Street Journal,* April 10, 1985, p. 31.

[22]Thomas C. Gibson, "The Total Quality Management Resource," *Quality Progress,* November 1987, pp. 62–66.

review will be reported and analyzed by managers.[23] One important decision involves determining how many products will be checked for quality. Will all products be inspected, or will there be representative sampling (inspecting only a sample, not every product)? Representative sampling is less costly but creates (1) the risk that a greater number of low-quality products will get into the hands of customers, (2) more likelihood that customer goodwill will be tarnished, and (3) the need to decide what constitutes an acceptable number of defects or low-quality products.

Representative sampling in manufacturing firms can take one of many forms. Some organizations use a random spot check. A number of products (e.g., cars, generators, computers) are randomly selected from a sample and are inspected for quality. When a formal random spot check is used, the results can be meaningful and can provide adequate control. Other forms of sampling plans using statistical analysis also are available.[24] In each case, the decision about which plan to use will involve making inferences about the entire production, based on samples. Representative sampling, however, means that defective products occasionally will slip through the quality control network.

STEP 4: BUILD QUALITY COMMITMENT

A commitment to quality by all employees is essential to an effective quality control system. Management can encourage this commitment through four actions:

Communicate the Need for Quality.   Effective quality control systems require a communication program designed to demonstrate to employees the importance of quality to the consumer, the company, and ultimately themselves.[25] Such programs use videotapes, seminars, and discussions to illustrate the impact of quality on organizational sales and profits and on compensation and benefits for the work force.

Train Employees in the Skills and Knowledge of Quality. Inadequate training can be a major barrier to quality. Tennant Co. found that poor training was a primary source of its quality problems. Management had not effectively trained assembly workers to correctly install certain product parts; the company's engineers were not instructed in the latest technology concerning relevant circuitry. To avoid such problems, companies focus training on providing the skills and abilities needed to achieve the organization's quality standards. And training is not limited to nonsupervisory employees. At Tennant Co., every manager completed at least five courses in quality control during the initial years of the company's quality campaign.

---

[23]J. M. Juran, Frank M. Gryna, and R. S. Bingham, Jr., eds., *Quality Control Handbook* (New York: McGraw-Hill, 1974).

[24]Sherie Posesorski, "Here's How to Put Statistical Process Control to Work for You," *Canadian Business,* December 1985, pp. 163ff.

[25]Allen E. Puckett, "People Are the Key to Productivity," *Industrial Management,* September–October 1985, pp. 12–15; Philip E. Atkinson and Brian W. Murray, "Managing Total Quality," *Management Services,* October 1985, pp. 18–21.

Secure Employee Involvement in Quality.   Some organizations such as Toyota and Du Pont train employees in problem-solving techniques and skills and encourage them to use what they've learned in identifying and solving quality-related problems. One indicator of employee involvement in quality at Toyota is the number of suggestions employees offer management concerning productivity and quality. Averaging about 5,000 ideas a year in the early 1960s, Toyota employees now provide about 1.9 million ideas each year.[26]

Reward for Quality.   Management boosts employee motivation and involvement in the quality effort by rewarding them for their contributions to meeting and especially surpassing quality standards. To motivate managers, Ford Motor Co. includes quality objectives as part of its executive compensation plan. In 1986, for example, Ford based 40 to 65 percent of a manager's annual bonus on contributions to quality. IBM rewards its suppliers for quality. The company pays premiums for materials that exceed a certain quality standard; it also penalizes suppliers for materials of lesser quality via reductions in the prices it pays for those materials.[27]

STEP 5:   DESIGN AND USE A QUALITY MEASUREMENT AND REPORTING SYSTEM

To control and improve product or service quality, management requires information in the form of quality measurements and progress reports. *Measures of inputs* entering the process are important indicators of how good, questionable, or poor these inputs are. Input measures prepare management for possible process and output problems. *Measures of quality during processing* are also valuable. Concurrent control information can indicate the need to alter, regulate, or shut down the process. And making these changes or decisions could prevent faulty outputs from reaching customers or clients. *Measures of final outputs* must be taken and the results reported. Checking output prior to shipment can result in last-minute corrections. Measures and reports from customers or clients also can provide crucial data.

Without a measurement and reporting system, critical quality problems can be overlooked. The consequence of such faulty control can be the loss of customers or clients. Conversely, when customers or clients perceive that quality meets their expectations, the image of the product or service is enhanced. It is these perceptions that the five-step quality program attempts to influence.

TOTAL QUALITY CONTROL

In response to competitive pressures, a growing number of organizations are adopting a unique quality philosophy, termed **total quality control (TQC).** Hewlett-Packard, IBM, Milliken & Co., and other companies who

[26]Benjamin Tregoe, "Productivity in America: How to Get It Back," *Management Review,* February 1983, pp. 23–28, 41–45.

[27]Peters, *Thriving,* p. 75.

have adopted this philosophy generally follow three principles in their quest for quality: (1) The objective of quality control is to achieve a constant and continual improvement in quality. Meeting the same quality standards year after year is not sufficient. Instead, the goal is to provide more and better quality for customers. (2) The focus of quality improvement and quality control extends beyond the actual product or service that an organization provides. The focus of quality is on every process in the organization. Accounting systems, product promotion activities, R&D processes, and virtually all other activities in the organization are the target of quality improvement. (3) Employees bear the major responsibility for quality improvement, as quality is an integral element of every job in the organization.

Implementing total quality control involves the same five-step approach used to establish a quality control system. However, the breadth of the quality focus and the challenge of continual improvement require extra effort. For example, an integral part of the TQC system is the *quality audit,* a careful study of every factor that affects quality in an activity or process. Audits are conducted in every department and division to identify existing and potential contributors to quality problems and to discover new ways to further improve quality.[28]

As in the traditional quality control system, employee training is emphasized. However, because employees are key participants in quality improvement efforts, training focuses on problem-solving skills and techniques such as data collection methods, statistical analysis, and group brainstorming. The chief executive officer (CEO) and the top management team are often the first to receive training in quality concepts and quality control. Employees put their newly acquired skills to work in project teams in their divisions. These teams tackle specific assignments such as improving customer service and the manufacturing work flow or making the performance of a certain job more efficient. Team members come from the division's various departments. Projects of wider scope are handled by cross-functional teams with representatives from the organization's different divisions.[29]

To help implement and maintain total quality control, an organization often creates a staff of managers trained in TQC principles and techniques. Staff members direct employee training in problem-solving techniques, coordinate quality audits, assist in the development of quality standards and measurements, and perform other functions in the TQC effort. TQC councils or committees are also often created at the division and top management level to oversee the organization-wide TQC effort.

Corning Glass Works, an industrial glass manufacturer, has successfully implemented a total quality control system. In the mid-1980s, Corning's international competitors were making substantial gains in product quality. To keep its competitive edge, Corning launched a total quality management

---

[28]John H. Farrow, "Quality Audits: An Invitation to Management," *Quality Progress,* January 1987, pp. 11–13.

[29]Harry W. Kenworthy, "Total Quality Concept: A Proven Path to Success," *Quality Progress,* July 1986, pp. 21–24.

system to improve quality in every company operation and to involve all of its 28,000 employees in the effort.[30]

Among Corning's objectives in the TQC effort were (1) to identify the key quality "errors" in every department and reduce those errors by 90 percent, (2) to manufacture new products that equal or beat the competition in quality, and (3) to substantially reduce the company's failure cost of quality (at the time, its total cost was estimated to be 20 to 30 percent of sales). The deadline for these objectives was set at 1991.

Employee training has been a major element of Corning's system. To provide effective training, the company established the Corning Quality Institute, which is staffed by 10 veteran employees specially trained in quality concepts and techniques. Every salaried employee has completed courses in quality awareness and skills at the institute. Corning also trained 150 local line employees as instructors. These trainers have provided quality training to more than 12,000 production and maintenance people in Corning's plants worldwide. Training has focused on overall quality awareness and on statistics, problem-solving skills, communications, and group dynamics.

To provide employees with opportunities to use the skills they've acquired, Corning organized quality improvement teams in every department. Some of the teams are cross-functional; for example, the customer financial services and information services departments formed a joint corrective action team to find ways to reduce computer-processing costs of accounts receivable. These efforts help to achieve quality implementation goals. All departments—and all employees—have quality goals. Corning also received valuable ideas and suggestions from responses to "99 Questions," Corning's worldwide employee survey conducted to identify barriers to total quality.

To head the quality system, Corning appointed a top-level executive as director of quality and created a quality council staffed by representatives from each division to monitor the overall effort. To date, Corning has substantially reduced its cost of quality and boosted product quality.

P/OM: A Visit to Burger King

To portray P/OM management, nothing serves better than to see it in a real-world setting. Burger King, an organization that most readers know about and have probably visited, provides an example of managing a production and operation system in the real world. As you read, relate the concepts and techniques of P/OM discussed above to the management of Burger King.

On the Assembly Line

Burger King Corporation is a wholly owned subsidiary of the Pillsbury Company.[31] Today, over 5,800 Burger King fast-food restaurants are produc-

---

[30]William W. Wagel, "Corning Zeros In on Total Quality," *Personnel,* July 1987, pp. 4–9.

[31]The discussion is based on Roger W. Schmenner, *Production/Operations Management: Concepts and Situations* (Chicago: Science Research Associates, 1981), pp. 97–109.

The internal and external design of Burger King restaurants has changed in response to market and production demands. Here, a Burger King of the 1950s is contrasted with a Burger King of the 1990s.

ing a wide selection of hamburger, ham and cheese, and fish sandwiches, salads, french fries, onion rings, soft drinks, shakes, pies, and a frozen dessert. In general, the Burger King restaurant is square in design, stands on about one acre of land, and is constructed largely of brick and glass. The restaurant seats about 100 customers.

Making sandwiches and filling orders at Burger King is viewed as an assembly-line operation. All burgers follow a straight path from the back of the kitchen to the front (order) counter; along this assembly line are a series of workstations. At Burger King a "board" is used as one workstation. The board is where buns and meat (inputs) are transformed into Whoppers and other sandwiches and products. The board is a long table on which pickles, onions, cheese slices, plastic squeeze bottles of ketchup and mustard, sliced tomatoes, shredded lettuce, mayonnaise, and tartar sauce are kept.

Each Burger King workstation is staffed differently, depending on the pace of demand at the restaurant. At any time, the preferred ratio of front-counter hostesses to back-room production workers (cooks, preparers) is about 1 to 1.5. During a peak period, the crew in a Burger King often increases to 12 to 15 workers.

The typical Burger King employee works part-time and is a high school student. Wages are paid for hours worked. The days and hours to be worked are scheduled in advance. The use of high school labor permits day-to-day and peak- to slow-time adjustments.

MANAGEMENT SYSTEM

Most Burger King restaurants have a manager and two assistant managers. Since the week contains 14 shifts and each manager works about 5 shifts a week, one of the three is always present in the restaurant.

Management's primary responsibility is to ensure that a quality product is promptly served in a clean environment. Quality is stressed in every part of the production process. While management's abilities to control costs are valued,

FIGURE 15–7   Information Flow Diagram at a Burger King Restaurant
(nonpeak period)

*The Burger King system
requires accurate and timely
information flows to achieve
its high-quality outputs.*

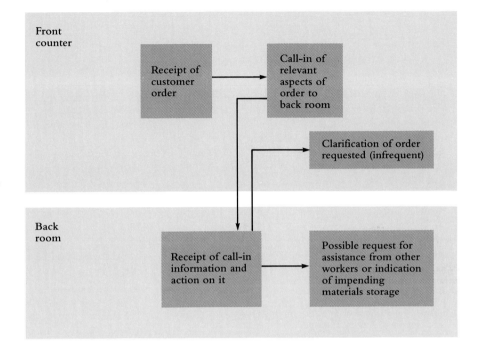

Source: From *Production/Operations Management: Concepts and Situations* by Roger W. Schmenner, p. 107. ©
1980, Science Research Associates, Inc. Reprinted by permission of the publisher.

■ Management can, through the development of a quality control program, improve quality. A five-step program to achieve quality improvement includes (1) defining quality characteristics, (2) establishing quality standards, (3) developing the quality review program, (4) building quality commitment, and (5) designing and using quality measurements and a reporting system.

DISCUSSION AND REVIEW QUESTIONS

1. How important is worker cohesiveness in a worker-paced service operation such as a Burger King restaurant?

2. How could international politics affect the inputs required for a production process? Provide some recent examples of this in American organizations.

3. What production activities are involved in a Kroger or Safeway supermarket?

4. Does a city like Lincoln, Nebraska, have a production system? What is produced?

5. Pick a specific organization (other than a fast-food restaurant) and identify its inputs, transformation processes, and outputs.

6. Some quality specialists say that quality control starts right on the drawing board. What do they mean?

7. If maintaining quality is so important to the success of an organization, why isn't a 100 percent inspection always used?

8. Folklore says that you should not buy a car assembled on a Monday, Friday, or during hunting season. Why?

9. How does the design of services differ from the design of products?

10. How does P/OM generally fit in with other functional areas of business, such as marketing and accounting?

ADDITIONAL REFERENCES

Adams, F. P., and **J. F. Cox.** "Manufacturing Resource Planning: An Information System Model." *Long Range Planning,* April 1985, pp. 86–92.

Andrew, C. G., and **G. A. Johnson.** "The Crucial Importance of Production and Operations Management." *Academy of Management Review,* January 1982, pp. 143–47.

Bhada, Y. K. "A Framework for Productivity Measurement." *Business,* January–February–March 1984, pp. 27–33.

Brown, R. M., and **K. F. Murrmann.** "Productivity Measurement in Manufacturing Firms." *Cost and Management,* January–February 1984, pp. 25–29.

Ettlie, J. E. *Taking Charge in Manufacturing.* San Francisco: Jossey-Bass, 1988.

Gaither, N. *Production and Operations Management.* Hinsdale, Ill.: Dryden Press, 1984.

Garvin, D. A. *Managing Quality: The Strategic and Competitive Edge.* New York: Free Press, 1988.

Gold, B. "Foundations of Strategic Planning for Productivity Improvement." *Interfaces,* May–June 1985, pp. 15–20.

Greene, J. H. *Production and Inventory Control Handbook.* New York: McGraw-Hill, 1987.

Hendrick, T. D., and **F. G. Moore.** *Production/Operations Management,* 9th ed. Homewood, Ill.: Richard D. Irwin, 1985.

Juran, J. M. *Juran on Planning for Quality.* New York: Free Press, 1988.

Kearns, D. T. "Xerox's Productivity Plan Is Worth Copying." *Planning Review,* May 1985, pp. 14–17.

Ross, J. E., and **Y. K. Shetty.** "Making Quality a Fundamental Part of Strategy." *Long Range Planning,* February 1985, pp. 53–58.

Shetty, Y. K. "Corporate Responses to the Productivity Challenge." *National Productivity Review,* Winter 1984–1985, pp. 7–14.

Steck, R. N. "Strategies for Boosting Productivity." *D & B Reports,* January–February 1985, pp. 44–46.

Weeks, J. K. "Stochastic Dominance: A Methodological Approach to Enhancing the Conceptual Foundations of Operations Management Theory." *Academy of Management Review,* January 1985, pp. 31–38.

Weisbord, M. R. *Productive Workplaces.* San Francisco: Jossey-Bass, 1987.

Williams, J. L. "Microcomputing: Production Planning's Liaison." *Production and Inventory Management Review,* April 1984, pp. 54–56.

Young, J. A. "The Quality Focus at Hewlett-Packard." *Journal of Business Strategy,* Winter 1985, pp. 6–14.

CASE 15–1 Ford Uses a Dr. Quincy Type of Autopsy

Engineering/design work is an extremely important function in P/OM. Robert Camron does engineering-design work with a small staff at Ford Motor Co.'s research center in Dearborn, Michigan.

In a sense, Camron is Ford's chief "pathologist." As the "Dr. Quincy" of Ford Motor Co., he dismantles or dissects automobiles to find out what the competition is up to. As soon as rival competitors introduce a car, Camron and his team go to work, systematically disassembling, cataloging, and examining

Source: Adapted from Kevin Totlis, "Auto Makers Look for Ideas in Rivals' Cars," *The Wall Street Journal,* July 20, 1982, p. 1.

each of its 30,000 or so parts. In the process, they look for production, safety, or any other ideas that might be applied to Ford's own cars.

The job of Camron and his team is extremely important, according to Ford. Scrambling to improve quality and cut costs, Ford is hungry for innovations that can help its products work better and can save money. The engineering/design team's philosophy is that when someone has a better idea, use it.

To keep posted on models that are nearing public introduction, Camron constantly reads trade magazines, travels to auto shows, and evaluates companies that supply the industry. When a car is introduced, he buys it through a local dealer. His current inventory that is ready for disassembly includes two J-cars built by General Motors, a Nissan Stanza, a Toyota Supra, and the engine from a Chevrolet Chevette.

Before he recommends a competitor's idea to management, Camron often puts it through a series of torture tests, using machines that spray parts with salt, roll windows up and down, and turn electrical equipment on and off. One machine pounds the heel of a woman's shoe into the carpet to test durability.

Because both GM and Chrysler Corporation have operations similar to Camron's at Ford, the companies sometimes wind up reimproving one another's innovations. This practice raises the issue of patent infringements, which must be carefully handled to avoid legal suits.

Of course, not everything Camron uncovers is usable in Ford products. He also finds competitors' mistakes and helps Ford avoid such problems. He found that a plastic strip window regulator in the door of a Chevrolet didn't stand up well to wear and tear. Ford decided to use metal rods to avoid the problems with plastic rods.

When Camron finishes one of his autopsies, he mounts all of the parts on long white boards to display for Ford executives. They visit, look over the display, and experiment with their own approaches to products and parts.

QUESTIONS FOR ANALYSIS

1. What is your opinion of the engineering/design work done by Robert Camron at Ford? Do you consider it ethical to conduct such work?
2. If Ford relies solely on Camron to improve engineering/design work, would this effort be sufficient to compete with firms like Toyota, Nissan, and Honda? Why?
3. Some might claim that Camron's work affects all phases of the production process—inputs, transformation, and outputs—as well as quality. Do you agree? Why?

CASE 15–2   Production Management at Mrs. Fields' Cookies

Nowadays, the cookie business is big business. David's Cookies, Blue Chip Cookies, The Original Great Chocolate Chip Cookie, and dozens of regional

Source: This case is adapted from Tom Richman, "Mrs. Fields' Secret Ingredient," *Inc.,* October 1987, pp. 64ff.

and local cookie shops are hotly competing for a share of the growing retail cookie market. Currently, the leader of the pack is Mrs. Fields' Cookies of Park City, Utah. The company is owned and operated by a young husband and wife team, Debbi and Randy Fields.

Sample some cookies at a Mrs. Fields' store, and you'll see one obvious reason why the shops are tops. The cookies are always fresh, warm, and tasty, and the service is friendly. The company sells a "feel-good feeling," says Debbi Fields, the company's CEO.

However, successfully producing and selling this feeling with a consistent-quality product and service can be very difficult—especially when your 500 stores and about 4,500 employees are located in 37 states and five foreign countries. An effective control system is a must. The Fieldses have developed a unique computerized approach to management and operations control. At the core of the control system is a computer network that links every store with corporate headquarters.

To illustrate how the control system works, consider Richard Lui, manager of the Pier 39 shop in San Francisco. Each morning, Richard begins his day at the shop by calling up the Day Planner program on his personal computer terminal. The computer asks for the day of the week, the type of day (holiday, school day, sale day), and the day's sales projection, which is based on last year's sales adjusted for growth. Richard inputs the information (it's a Thursday holiday, for example) and the computer responds by telling what must be done *hour by hour* to meet the sales goal: how many customers are needed every hour, how much must be sold by the hour, how many batches of cookie mix must be made, and so on. The computer's advice is generated from an analysis of the sales levels and hour-by-hour fluctuations that the shop experienced on the three previous Thursday holidays.

Richard will input sales information each hour into the computer system; in many Mrs. Fields' stores, cash registers automatically do the task. The computer uses the information to update its early morning suggestions. For example, the computer may detect that while the customer count is fine, the per-sales amount is a bit low. The computer will then offer some suggestions such as having the sales crew boost its suggestive selling.

The computer is a control tool in other areas. For instance, it helps schedule the store's staff. Richard inputs the projected sales levels for the coming two weeks, and the computer responds with a work schedule showing Richard how many employees with what type of skills will be needed to work at what hours. The schedule is calculated using the performance time standards set by Debbi Fields for tasks (e.g., mixing, baking). Mrs. Fields uses her past experience in running her first shop to set the standards. If she took an average five minutes to prepare the cookie dough, for example, then five minutes becomes the standard.

The computer also helps Richard interview job applicants. When a prospect comes in for an interview, Richard sits the candidate down by the computer and calls up the interview program. He asks the applicant questions provided by the computer and inputs the responses. The computer then projects how well the applicant will perform on the job. The computer makes its prediction based on answers given by past applicants who were hired and their subsequent job performance.

The computer helps with other tasks such as personnel administration (the personnel manual is available on the computer) and equipment maintenance. If a machine isn't working, the computer will offer several suggestions on how to fix it before calling the repairman. When service is needed, the computer processes the work order to headquarters. The computer also generates the inventory supply orders, which are based on sales projections and weekly inventory reports. Richard only checks the orders to be sure they're correct before sending them electronically to headquarters.

The computer is especially useful in one key area: communications between the 500 store managers and Debbi Fields. Whenever Richard Lui has a message for Debbi, he calls up the FormMail program on his computer, types the communication, and sends it electronically to headquarters. It reaches Debbi's desk by the next morning; she or her staff will be in personal contact with him within 48 hours. Richard also telephones headquarters every day for any recorded messages from Debbi.

Although the computer system sounds intimidatingly high tech, it isn't. All of the shop computers are basic PCs, and the software is menu driven and quite simple to run.

All information provided hourly by shop managers is fed into the company's data base at headquarters. There, the controller staff checks how the shops are doing. Did they meet their daily sales goals last week, or are there any inventory discrepancies? The controllers handle any problems by working directly with the shop manager.

Debbi and Randy Fields believe that the computerized control system provides several advantages. The system provides the Fieldses with direct control of the 500 stores and 4,500 employees. The Fieldses believe that close contact with store managers is essential to maintaining the company's high quality standards. Debbi's presence is felt in each shop via her frequent computer and telephone communications with shop management and in the computer-provided goals, scheduling, and suggestions that all reflect her experience and preferences.

By computerizing many administrative tasks, the system has kept the size of the corporate staff to a minimum; it also frees store managers from much time-consuming paperwork and administrative tasks. In Randy Fields' view, if a computer can conceivably perform a task, it should—which frees managers to manage people, not paperwork. His plan is to continue to computerize as many such tasks as possible.

QUESTIONS FOR ANALYSIS

1. Besides the advantages, do you see any shortcomings in the Fieldses' computerized approach to control? If so, what are they?
2. Is one type of control emphasized in the computerized control system? Explain in terms of preliminary, concurrent, and feedback control.
3. Would this approach to control be useful in all types of companies and industries? Explain.

EXPERIENTIAL EXERCISE

UNDERSTANDING THE DIVERSITY OF QUALITY CONTROL SYSTEMS

Purpose

This exercise enhances the students' understanding of actual quality control systems in different organizations.

The Exercise in Class

The instructor will divide the class into groups of four to six students each. Each group will complete the following steps:

1. Select a quality control system in a particular organization that you would like to learn more about. The choices are numerous, including the control of student quality, faculty quality, instructional quality, graduate quality, and administrative quality at any college; the control of materials quality, employee quality, process quality, output quality at any local business; the control of treatment quality, care quality, and physician and nurse quality at any local hospital; or any other organization that interests you.

2. Interview the individual who manages the respective control system. Your objective is to develop a written profile of the system. The interview should last approximately 30 minutes. Some suggested questions:

   a. What are the objectives of the control system?
   b. How are standards set and information collected to determine whether standards have been met?
   c. How has the control system changed over the years? What factors led to the changes?
   d. In what ways have you fine-tuned the system to meet your organization's particular needs and constraints?
   e. What are the challenges in implementing and managing the system?

3. Prepare a five-page written report on your findings. The paper should focus on presenting an overall profile of the objectives, makeup, and function of the system. You should also address how the system has evolved over the years and how the system is designed to meet the organization's particular needs. Be sure to include any system problems you identified and to suggest solutions.

The Learning Message

This exercise illustrates that quality control systems differ widely across organizations, even when the same variable, such as input, is the focus of the system.

16

MANAGEMENT DECISION MAKING

LEARNING OBJECTIVES

After completing Chapter 16, you should be able to:

Define
programmed and nonprogrammed decisions.

Describe
how the types of decisions managers make are related to their level in the organization.

Discuss
the process of decision making.

Compare
decision making under conditions of certainty, risk, and uncertainty.

Identify
the major sources for locating problems that require management decisions.

Using Decision Theory to Manage Unemployment Funds

Managers who oversee a state's unemployment insurance benefit fund have a legal and moral obligation to provide unemployment benefits. This commitment holds regardless of how well or how badly a state's economy performs. However, maintaining an acceptable unemployment insurance fund balance is a stiff challenge. Uncontrollable and volatile international, national, and state conditions directly influence the tax receipts and the unemployment benefits a state must pay. Unless administered properly, state funds for unemployment benefits may simply run out, or fund levels may be perilously subnormal for a long time.

The Virginia Unemployment Commission (VUC) faced the latter situation in the late 1970s. From 1975 to 1980, the unemployment trust fund plunged precipitously, due to changing international and domestic economic conditions. Sparked by definitive state legislation in 1981, VUC adopted a payoff decision approach to resolve its problem. Now VUC systematically evaluates the impact of differing tax benefit strategies and differing potential economic scenarios on trust fund balances.

VUC first formulates best case, most likely, and worse case assessments of Virginia's economic climate. The international strength of the U.S. dollar in world economic markets, federal monetary and fiscal policies, worker productivity, and inflation pressures are the basis of this climate. Next, under each case assessment, VUC projects trust fund balances that should result from differing tax benefit strategies. VUC then focuses on the minimum projected fund balance of each tax benefit strategy. (State law now demands that the fund be capable of comfortably paying benefits under 18 months of heavy demand for unemployment benefits.) If any of the alternative tax benefit strategies projects a more positive impact than does present state law, VUC recommends the package that has the maximum overall impact on trust fund balances.

How has it worked? From a deficit of $45 million in 1983, the fund reached 90 percent solvency in 1986. According to the state unemployment commissioner, "this model is one of the agency's most valuable tools, and there can be no doubt that its impact on unemployment insurance policy and use for . . . planning have been profound."

Source: "Risk Funding of Unemployment Insurance: An Econometric Approach," *Interfaces,*
March–April 1988, pp. 64–71.

Managers at all levels in an organization make decisions. The ultimate influence of these decisions may extend to the survival of the organization or only to the starting salary of a new college trainee. All decisions, however, have some influence—large or small—on performance. Thus, it is important for managers to develop decision-making skills. The quality of the decisions they reach is the yardstick of their effectiveness and of their value to the organization. Like it or not, managers are evaluated and rewarded on the basis of the importance, number, and results of their decisions.

TYPES OF MANAGERIAL DECISIONS

Although managers in large business organizations, government offices, hospitals, and schools may be separated by background, lifestyle, and distance, they must all make decisions involving several alternatives and outcomes. In this section, we will discuss various types of decisions.[1]

PROGRAMMED AND NONPROGRAMMED DECISIONS

If a particular problem occurs often, managers will develop a routine procedure for solving it. The decision as to how to handle it is essentially "programmed." Thus, **programmed decisions** have repetitive and routine solutions. The managers of most organizations face great numbers of programmed decisions in their daily operations. Such decisions should be made without expending unnecessary time and effort on them. When a problem has elements that are different from previous occurrences or is complex or extremely important, it will require a different unique decision. **Nonprogrammed decisions** are solutions for novel and unstructured problems. The two classifications are broad, but the distinction is important.[2] Table 16–1 presents examples of programmed and nonprogrammed decisions in different types of organizations.

Managers can usually handle programmed decisions through rules, standard operating procedures, and the development of specific policies. In this section of our book, we shall see that through the development of mathematical models the management science approach has made a great contribution to handling these types of decisions.

Nonprogrammed decisions, however, need to be properly identified. On the basis of this type of decision making, billions of dollars in resources are allocated in our nation every year. Government organizations make decisions that influence the lives of every citizen; business organizations make decisions to manufacture new products; hospitals and schools make decisions that influence patients and students years later.

Unfortunately, very little is known about the nonprogrammed type of human decision making.[3] Such decisions have traditionally been handled by

[1]Bernard M. Bass, *Organizational Decision Making* (Homewood, Ill.: Richard D. Irwin, 1983).

[2]Herbert Simon, *The New Science of Management Decision* (New York: Harper & Row, 1960), pp. 5–6.

[3]Neil M. Agnew and John L. Brown, "Executive Judgment: The Intuition/Rational Ration," *Personnel*, December 1985, pp. 48–54.

	Type of Decision	Type of Problem	Procedures	Examples
	Programmed	Repetitive, routine.	Rules. Standard operating procedures. Policies.	Business: Processing payroll vouchers. College: Processing admission applications. Hospital: Preparing patient for surgery. Government: Using state-owned motor vehicle.
	Nonprogrammed	Complex, novel.	Creative problem solving.	Business: Introducing a new product. College: Constructing new classroom facilities. Hospital: Reacting to regional disease epidemic. Government: Solving spiraling inflation problem.

Table 16–1   Types of Managerial Decisions

Programmed and nonprogrammed decisions result from different types of problems and use different types of procedures.

problem-solving processes, judgment, intuition, and creativity.[4] But although some managers are uncomfortable with basing decisions on intuition, modern management techniques have not made the same advances in improving managerial performance in nonprogrammed decision making as they have in programmed decision making.[5]

Coping with nonprogrammable decisions, always a formidable task, is especially so in small firms. The small business manager just may not have the managerial and financial resources to deal with difficult situations when they arise. Such managers must consider the possibility of hiring someone else to make the decision. Rather than hire a permanent senior-level manager to deal with a weighty problem, many small firms hire temporary senior executives. The Management Focus describes how one small firm handled the nonprogrammable decision of devising a strategic plan.

Types of Decisions and Level of Management

Problems that come up frequently and have a great deal of uncertainty surrounding them are often of a strategic nature and should be the concern of top management. Problems that occur frequently and have fairly certain outcomes should be the concern of lower levels of management.[6]

Middle managers in most organizations concentrate mostly on programmed decisions. As Figure 16–1 indicates, the nature of the problem, how

[4]Paul C. Nutt, "Types of Organizational Decision Processes," *Administrative Science Quarterly,* September 1984, pp. 414–50.

[5]Weston Agor, "The Logic of Intuition: How Top Executives Make Important Decisions," *Organizational Dynamics,* Winter 1986, pp. 5–18.

[6]Anna Gandori, "A Prescriptive Contingency View of Organizational Decision Making," *Administrative Science Quarterly,* June 1984, pp. 192–209.

MANAGEMENT FOCUS

Coping with a Nonprogrammable Decision in a Small Firm

Joe Marinello, president of Homecraft Industries in Newington, Connecticut, needed help to develop a strategic plan for his collection of start-up companies. Although Marinello wanted a coherent marketing and advertising plan to unify his splintered collection of business interests, he simply could not afford an experienced marketing professional on a full-time basis. Enter Richard Haumann—a veteran General Electric marketing manager. Haumann put together a complete plan that even included brochures and press releases. After business picked up, he left for another assignment as quickly as he came. Because Haumann's plans worked so well for Homecraft, Marinello now can afford to hire a permanent marketing executive.

According to Donald Hambrick, a Columbia University business professor, temporary execu-

tives may not always be a great idea. When the temporary manager's actions negatively impact workers, problem solving may damage social cohesion and company loyalty. Workers may even defy the temporary's authority. When their lives are adversely influenced, workers commonly view executive temporaries as quick fixes. To workers in these situations, temporaries represent remote-control management, cowardice, and a lack of leadership.

Homecraft's Marinello refuses to use a temporary executive to solve a production problem. In a production situation, he feels, a temporary would be too much of an unknown.

Source: "And Now, Temp Managers," *Newsweek,* September 26, 1988, pp. 53–54.

FIGURE 16–1   Types of Problems, Types of Decisions, and Management Level in the Organization

Programmed decisions are made at lower levels of management; nonprogrammed decisions are made at higher levels of management.

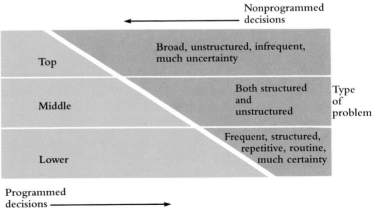

Decision making takes place in different ways in different settings.

frequently it arises, and the degree of certainty surrounding it should dictate the appropriate level of management for making the decision.

THE PROCESS OF DECISION MAKING

There are numerous approaches to decision making. Which is best will depend on the nature of the problem, the time available, the costs of individual strategies, and the mental skills of the decision maker.

Decisions are means rather than ends. They are mechanisms by which a manager seeks to achieve some desired state. They are the manager's (and hence the organization's) responses to problems. Every decision is the outcome of a dynamic process influenced by many forces. Thus, decision making is the process of thought and deliberation that results in a decision; the process influences how good the decision is likely to be.

Decision making is not a fixed procedure, but it is a sequential process.[7] In most decision situations, managers go through a number of stages that help them think through the problem and develop alternative strategies. The stages need not be rigidly applied; their value lies in their ability to force the decision maker to structure the problem in a meaningful way. Figure 16–2 enables us to identify each stage in the normal progression that leads to a decision. You may find it helpful to develop your own list of stages for the decision-making process.

The process represented in Figure 16–2 applies more to nonprogrammed than to programmed decisions. Problems that occur infrequently with a great deal of uncertainty surrounding the outcome require the manager to utilize the entire process.[8] In contrast, problems that occur frequently are often handled

---

[7]James E. Hopper and Kenneth J. Euske, "Facilitating the Identification and Evaluation of Decision Objectives," *Cost and Management*, July–August 1985, pp. 36–40.

[8]Jane M. Booker and Maurice C. Bryson, "Decision Analysis in Project Management: An Overview," *IEEE Transactions on Engineering Management*, February 1985, pp. 3–9.

FIGURE 16–2   The Process of Decision Making

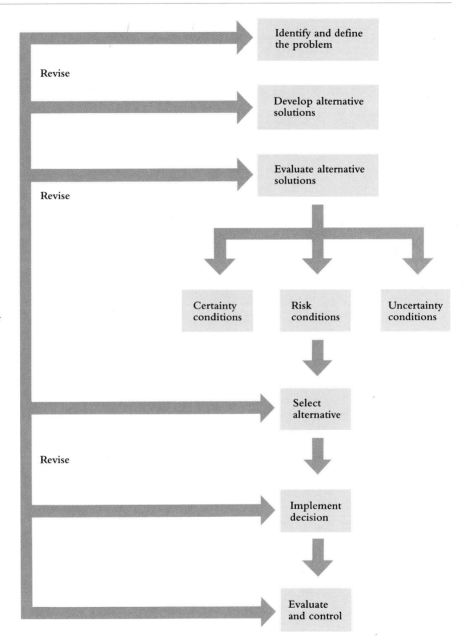

In the decision-making process, taking certain specific steps will contribute to high-quality decisions.

by policies or rules, so it is not necessary to develop and evaluate alternatives each time these problems arise.[9]

PROBLEM IDENTIFICATION

Identifying problems is not as easy as it may seem. If the problem is incorrectly identified or defined, any decisions made will be directed toward solving the wrong problem.[10]

Warning Signals.   To locate problems, managers rely on several different indicators:

1. *Deviation from past performance.*   A sudden change in some established pattern of performance often indicates that a problem has developed. When employee turnover increases, sales decline, student enrollments decline, selling expenses increase, or more defective units are produced, a problem usually exists. If, for example, the error rate among tellers has always been below the standard until this year, this departure from the historical pattern could signal a problem.

2. *Deviation from the plan.*   When results do not meet planned objectives, a problem is likely. For example, a new product fails to meet its market share objective, profit levels are lower than planned, the production department is exceeding its budget, or the teller error rate exceeds the performance objective. These occurrences signal that some plan is off course.

3. *Outside criticism.*   The actions of outsiders may indicate problems. Customers may be dissatisfied with a new product or with their delivery schedules; a labor union may present a grievance; investment firms may not recommend the organization as a good investment opportunity; alumni may withdraw their support from an athletic program.

Sources of Difficulties in Problem Identification.   It is easy to recognize that some problems exist when a gap occurs between desired results and actual results. However, identifying the exact problem is often made more difficult by one or more factors:[11]

Perceptual problems.   Our individual perceptions may protect or defend us from unpleasant realities. Thus, negative information may be selectively perceived in order to distort its true meaning. It may also be totally ignored. For example, a college dean may fail to identify increasing class sizes as a problem while at the same time being sensitive to problems faced by the president of the university in raising funds for the school.

---

[9]J. W. Boudreau, "Decision Theory Contributions to HRM Research and Practice," *Industrial Relations,* Spring 1984, pp. 198–217.

[10]David A. Cowan, "Developing a Process Model of Problem Recognition," *Academy of Management Review,* October 1986, pp. 763–77.

[11]George P. Huber, *Managerial Decision Making* (Glenview, Ill.: Scott, Foresman, 1980).

Defining problems in terms of solutions.   This is really a form of jumping to conclusions. For example, a sales manager may say, "The decrease in profits is due to our poor product quality." The sales manager's definition of the problem suggests a particular solution: the improvement of product quality in the production department. Certainly, other definitions—and solutions—may be possible. Perhaps the sales force has been inadequately selected or trained. Perhaps competitors have a less expensive product.

Identifying symptoms as problems.   "Our problem is a 32 percent decline in orders." While it is certainly true that orders have declined, the decline is actually only a symptom of the real problem. Not until the manager identifies the real problem will the cause of the decline in orders be found.

Types of Problems.   Problems are usually of three types: opportunity, crisis, or routine. Crisis and routine problems present themselves and must be attended to by the managers.[12] Opportunities, in contrast, must usually be found; they wait to be discovered. Often they go unnoticed and are eventually lost by an inattentive manager. Because, by their very nature, most crises and routine problems demand immediate attention, a manager may spend a great deal of time in handling minor crises and solving routine problems and may not have time to pursue important new opportunities. Many well-managed organizations try to draw attention away from crises and routine problems and toward longer-range issues through planning activities and goal-setting programs.

DEVELOPING ALTERNATIVES

Once the problem is defined, feasible alternatives (actually, potential solutions) to the problem should be developed, and the potential consequences of each alternative should be considered. This is really a search process in which the relevant internal and external environments of the organization are investigated to provide information that can be developed into possible alternatives.[13] Obviously, this search for solutions is conducted within certain time and cost constraints, since only so much effort can be devoted to developing alternatives.[14]

For example, a sales manager may identify an inadequately trained sales force as the cause of declining sales. The sales manager would then identify possible alternatives for solving the problem, such as (1) a sales training program conducted at the home office by management, (2) a sales training program conducted by a professional training organization at a site away from the home office, and (3) more intense on-the-job training.

---

[12]Dean Tjosvold, "Effects of Crisis Orientation on Managers' Approaches to Controversy in Decision Making," *Academy of Management Journal,* March 1984, pp. 130–38.

[13]David B. Jamison, "The Importance of Boundary Spanning Roles in Strategic Decision Making," *Journal of Management Studies,* April 1984, pp. 131–52.

[14]Paul Shrivastava, "Knowledge Systems for Strategic Decision Making," *Journal of Applied Behavioral Science,* Winter 1985, pp. 95–108.

Some decisons are made with a lot of information on what happens "on average."

EVALUATING ALTERNATIVES

Alternatives, once developed, must be evaluated and compared. In every decision situation, the objective is to select the alternative that will produce the most favorable outcomes and the least unfavorable outcomes. In selecting among alternatives, the decision maker should be guided by the previously established goals and objectives; this again points up the necessity for objectives and goals. The alternative-outcome relationship is based on three possible conditions:

1. **Certainty.** The decision maker has complete knowledge of the outcome of each alternative.
2. **Uncertainty.** The decision maker has absolutely no knowledge of the probability of the outcome of each alternative.
3. **Risk.** The decision maker has some probabilistic estimate of the outcomes of each alternative.

Decision making under **conditions of risk** is probably the most common situation.[15] It is in evaluating alternatives under these conditions that statisticians and operations researchers have made important contributions to decision making. Their methods have proved especially useful in the analysis and ranking of alternatives.

CHOOSING AN ALTERNATIVE

The purpose of selecting an alternative is to solve a problem so as to achieve a predetermined objective. This point is an important one. It means that a decision is not an end in itself but only a means to an end; the decision maker's

---

[15]J. E. Hodder and H. E. Riggs, "Pitfalls in Evaluating Risky Projects," *Harvard Business Review*, January–February 1985, pp. 128–35.

choice should not be an isolated act. If it is, the factors that led to and lead from the decision are likely to be excluded from consideration, and the chosen alternative may not be the best way to solve the problem. Specifically, the steps following the decision should include implementation, control, and evaluation. The critical point is that decision making is more than an act of choosing; it is a dynamic process.

Unfortunately for most managers, it is a rare situation in which one alternative achieves the desired objective without having some positive or negative impact on another objective. Often, two objectives cannot be optimized simultaneously. If one objective is fully achieved, achievement of the other suffers. In a business organization, for example, if production is optimized, employee morale may be lowered, or vice versa. Or a hospital superintendent may optimize a short-run objective such as maintenance costs at the expense of a long-run objective such as high-quality patient care. Thus, the multiplicity of organizational objectives complicates the real world of the decision maker.

Sometimes, attainment of an organizational objective would be at the expense of a societal objective. The reality of such situations is clearly seen in the rise of ecology groups, environmentalists, and the consumerist movement. Apparently, these groups question the priorities (organizational versus societal) of certain organizational decision makers. In any case, whether an organizational objective conflicts with another organizational objective or with a societal objective, the values of the decision maker strongly influence the alternative chosen. Individual values were discussed in Chapter 3, and their influence on the decision-making process should be clear.

For all of these reasons, optimal solutions are often impossible in managerial decision making. The decision maker cannot possibly know all of the available alternatives, the consequences of each alternative, and the probability of occurrence of these consequences.[16] Thus, rather than being an optimizer, the decision maker is a satisfier, selecting the alternative that meets an acceptable (satisfactory) standard.

IMPLEMENTING THE DECISION

A decision that is not implemented is little more than an abstraction. In other words, a decision must be effectively implemented to achieve the objective for which it was made. It is entirely possible for a "good" decision to be hurt by poor implementation. In this sense, implementation may be equally important as the actual choice of the alternative.[17]

In most situations, implementing decisions involves people. And people cannot be manipulated in the same manner as other resources. A technically sound decision can easily be undermined by dissatisfied subordinates. Thus, a manager's job is not only to choose good solutions but also to transform such solutions into behavior in the organization. This is done by effectively

---

[16]Paul Shrivastava and I. I. Mitroff, "Enhancing Organizational Research Utilization: The Role of Decision Makers' Assumptions," *Academy of Management Review,* January 1984, pp. 18–26.

[17]Paul C. Nutt, "Tactics of Implementation," *Academy of Management Journal,* June 1986, pp. 232–61.

communicating with the appropriate individuals and groups. The test of the soundness of a decision is the behavior of the people affected by the decision.[18]

CONTROL AND EVALUATION

Effective management involves periodic measurements of results. Actual results are compared with planned results (the objective); if deviations exist, changes must be made. Here again we see the importance of measurable objectives. If such objectives do not exist, then there is no way to judge performance. If actual results do not match planned results, then changes must be made in the solution chosen, in its implementation, or in the original objective if it is deemed unattainable. If the original objective must be revised, then the entire decision-making process is reactivated. The important point is that once a decision is implemented, a manager cannot assume that the outcome will meet the original objective. Some system of control and evaluation is necessary to make sure the actual results are consistent with the results planned for when the decision was made.

BEHAVIORAL INFLUENCES ON MANAGERIAL DECISION MAKING

Several factors influence the decision-making process. Some of these factors affect only certain aspects of the process, while others affect the entire process. However, each may have an impact and must therefore be understood in order for us to fully appreciate decision making as a process in organizations. In this section, we discuss four individual behavioral factors: values, personality, propensity for risk, and potential for dissonance. Each has a significant impact on the decision-making process.

VALUES

In the context of decision making, *values* are the guidelines that a person uses when confronted with a situation in which a choice must be made. Values are acquired early in life and are a basic (often taken for granted) part of an individual's thoughts. The influence of values on the decision-making process is profound:[19]

- In establishing objectives, it is necessary to make value judgments regarding the selection of opportunities and the assignment of priorities.
- In developing alternatives, it is necessary to make value judgments about the various possibilities.
- In choosing an alternative, the values of the decision maker influence which alternative is chosen.
- In implementing a decision, value judgments are necessary in choosing the means for implementation.

[18]William Taggart, Daniel Robey, and Galen Krocek, "Managerial Decision Styles and General Dominance: An Empirical Study," *Journal of Management Studies,* April 1985, pp. 175–92.

[19]E. Frank Harrison, *The Managerial Decision Making Process* (Boston: Houghton Mifflin, 1975), p. 42.

■ In the evaluation and control phase, value judgments cannot be avoided when corrective action is taken.

Clearly, values pervade the decision-making process. They are reflected in the decision maker's behavior before making the decision, in making the decision, and in putting the decision into effect.[20]

Personality

Decision makers are influenced by many psychological forces, both conscious and subconscious. One of the most important of these forces is personality.[21] Decision makers' personalities are strongly reflected in the choices they make. Studies examining the effect of personality on the process of decision making have generally focused on the following sets of variables:

1. *Personality variables.* These include the attitudes, beliefs, and needs of the individual.
2. *Situational variables.* These pertain to the external, observable situations in which individuals find themselves.
3. *Interactional variables.* These pertain to the momentary state of the individual as a result of the interaction of a specific situation with characteristics of an individual's personality.

The most important conclusions concerning the influence of personality on the decision-making process are:

1. It is unlikely that one person can be equally proficient in all aspects of the decision-making process. The results suggest that some people do better in one part of the process, while others do better in another part.
2. Such characteristics as intelligence are associated with different phases of the decision-making process.
3. The relationship of personality to the decision-making process may vary for different groups on the basis of such factors as sex and social status.

This research determined that the personality traits of the decision maker combine with certain situational and interactional variables to influence the decision-making process

Propensity for Risk

From personal experience, the reader is undoubtedly aware that decision makers vary greatly in their *propensity for taking risks*. This one specific aspect of personality strongly influences the decision-making process.

In a given situation a decision maker who has a low aversion to risk establishes different objectives, evaluates alternatives differently, and selects different alternatives than a decision maker with a high aversion to risk. The latter attempts to make choices where the risk or uncertainty is low or where the certainty of the outcome is high. Many people are bolder and more

[20]Linda K. Trevino, "Ethical Decision Making in Organizations: A Person–Situation Interaction Model," *Academy of Management Review,* July 1986, pp. 601–17.

[21]P. A. Renwick and Henry Tosi, "The Effects of Sex, Marital Status, and Educational Background on Selected Decisions," *Academy of Management Journal,* March 1978, pp. 93–103.

innovative and advocate greater risk-taking in groups than as individuals. Apparently, such people are more willing to accept risk as members of a group.

POTENTIAL FOR DISSONANCE

Much attention has focused on the forces and influences on the decision maker before a decision is made and on the decision itself. Only recently, however, has attention been given to what happens after a decision has been made. Specifically, behavioral scientists have focused attention on the occurrence of postdecision anxiety, or **cognitive dissonance.**

Such anxiety is related to a lack of consistency or harmony among an individual's various cognitions (attitudes, beliefs, etc.) after a decision has been made.[22] When this state exists, the decision maker has doubts and second thoughts about the choice that was made. In addition, the intensity of the anxiety is likely to be greater when any of the following conditions exist:

1. The decision is psychologically or financially important.
2. There are a number of forgone alternatives.
3. The forgone alternatives have many favorable features.

Dissonance can, of course, be reduced by the decision maker admitting that a mistake has been made. Unfortunately, many individuals are reluctant to admit that they have made a wrong decision. These individuals are more likely to use one or more of the following methods to reduce their dissonance:

1. Seek information that supports the wisdom of their decisions.
2. Selectively perceive (distort) information in a way that supports their decisions.
3. Adopt a less favorable view of the forgone alternatives.
4. Minimize the importance of the negative aspects of the decisions and exaggerate the importance of the positive aspects.

While each of us may resort to some of this behavior in our personal decision making, a great deal of it could be extremely harmful in terms of organizational effectiveness. The potential for dissonance is influenced heavily by personality, specifically the level of self-confidence and persuadability. In fact, all of the behavioral influences are closely interrelated and are only isolated here for purposes of discussion.[23]

DECISION MAKING IN PRODUCTION AND OPERATIONS

To illustrate the use of decision making in production and operations, we will develop an example that highlights the compelling issue in production/operations management: how many units should be produced. The example will focus on the production decision of a publisher of specialty books. If the publisher knows exactly how many books will be demanded at each possible

---

[22]Leon Festinger, *A Theory of Cognitive Dissonance* (New York: Harper & Row, 1957).

[23]J. Richard Harrison and James G. March, "Decision Making and Postdecision Surprises," *Administrative Science Quarterly*, March 1984, pp. 26–42.

TABLE 16–2 Conditional-Value Payoff Table for Production Decision

A conditional-value table relates payoffs, strategies, and states of nature.

Strategies: Books Printed	*States of Nature: Number of Books Demanded*			
	5,000	**10,000**	**15,000**	**20,000**
5,000	$ 3,750	$ 3,750	$ 3,750	$ 3,750
10,000	−1,250	7,500	7,500	7,500
15,000	−6,250	2,500	11,250	11,250
20,000	−11,250	−2,500	6,250	15,000

and feasible price, then the number of books to produce is obvious. However, perfect knowledge of demand is seldom, if ever, the case, particularly for a publisher of commemorative books. Often, a book will commemorate a special event such as the nation's bicentennial celebration. Since the book is unique, the publisher may have only sketchy information about its potential sales.

Let us assume that the publisher has established the price of the book at $1.75 and that the incremental cost of each book is $1.00. Thus, each book that is sold will contribute 75 cents to overhead and profit. Assume also that there is no secondary market for the book. If it is not sold by the end of the bicentennial celebration period, there will be no market for it. Such production and operations decisions are characteristic of situations having perishable products. With that in mind, we can understand that if the publisher prints one book and one book is demanded (sold at a price of $1.75), then the contribution is 75 cents; if two books are printed and two are demanded, the contribution is $1.50. But if two books are printed and three are demanded, the contribution remains $1.50, and the publisher has no more books to sell. By the same reasoning, if the publisher prints three books and two are demanded, the contribution is 50 cents: The revenue is $3.50 (2 × $1.75), the incremental cost is $3.00 (3 × $1.00), and $3.50 − $3.00 = $.50. The contribution for any combination of production and demand can be calculated in this manner.

For simplicity of explanation, assume that the publisher decides it is only necessary to investigate four levels of possible demand, in 5,000-unit intervals (that is, rather than dealing with the infinite range of production and demand combinations, we will illustrate only four): 5,000, 10,000, 15,000, and 20,000 books. With this information, we can determine the contribution for each of the four levels of sales and each of the four production levels. In the terminology of decision theory, each level of sales is called a *state of nature,* and each production level is a *strategy.* The contribution associated with each state of nature and strategy is a *conditional value.* The conditional values, or *payoffs,* for each of the 16 possible combinations of production and demand are presented in Table 16–2.

In the present example, the payoffs associated with each possible strategy and state of nature are based on the previously presented price ($1.75) and cost

($1.00). Thus, the payoff (Revenue − Cost = Payoff) associated with producing 5,000 books and selling 5,000 books is:

Revenue (5,000 × $1.75)	$8,750
Cost (5,000 × $1.00)	5,000
Payoff	$3,750

If, however, the publisher prints 15,000 books and only 10,000 are demanded, the payoff is:

Revenue (10,000 × $1.75)	$17,500
Cost (15,000 × $1.00)	15,000
Payoff	$ 2,500

Each payoff in Table 16–2 is calculated in the above manner. The fact that some of the values are negative reflects the cost of overproducing.

The payoff table is useful, but it does not make the decision; it simply organizes the important information on which to base the decision. But how can the publisher make such a decision? Let's examine the three different conditions the publisher might face: certainty, risk, and uncertainty.

CONDITIONS OF CERTAINTY

If a manager knew exactly which state of nature would occur (e.g., knowing that on April 15 income taxes are due), the decision could be made with certainty. A certainty situation means that a perfectly accurate decision will be made time after time. Of course, decision making under certainty is rare.

For illustrative purposes, however, assume that the publisher knows with certainty that 10,000 books will be demanded. The maximum payoff associated with this state of nature is to produce 10,000 units: The payoff of $7,500 associated with the joint occurrence of 10,000 books produced and demanded is greater than any other payoff associated with that state of nature.

The publisher in this situation is fortunate to have perfect information about future states of nature (our example simply assumes that certainty exists). In fact, relative certainty can exist in real organizations. The Management Focus describes some interesting examples of firms that enjoy the benefits of decision making under relative certainty. In other instances, decision making involves uncertainty to some degree, and our discussion of risk conditions identifies one such instance.

CONDITIONS OF RISK

Probabilities fall into two categories. *Objective* probability is based on historical evidence. For example, the probability of obtaining either heads or tails on the toss of a fair coin is .50 (50 percent); the coin is equally likely to come up a head or a tail. In many cases, however, historical evidence is not

---

MANAGEMENT FOCUS

Some Relatively Small Firms Face Relatively Certain Conditions

People say that the only certain things in life are death and taxes. If you have a good accountant, then only death is certain. What if your firm produces wooden view cameras, wooden airplane propellers, or glass vacuum tubes? Is there any certainty in these businesses?

L. F. Deardorf of Chicago, Illinois, makes cured mahogany wooden box cameras held together with brass screws. He makes them today the same way his grandfather did in 1893. Photographers today use some of his cameras with hand-held bulbs, mounted shutters, and 8- by 10-inch sheet negatives. Despite the German and Japanese advances over the years, expert photographers in aircraft reconnaissance and high fashion cataloging prefer a huge Deardorf. Why does Deardorf regularly sell 300 cameras a year at a price around $3,000? No competing format controls focus and perspective as accurately as the design Deardorf's grandfather perfected decades ago.

Air pockets of revenues often result if you stick it out while everyone else leaves a business. Sensensich Corporation of Lancaster, Pennsylvania, is the last surviving domestic maker of wooden airplane propellers. Despite the jet age's heavy independence on light metals, Gary Sensensich has survived by repairing and replacing wooden propellers on old airplanes. Long ago, Sensensich discovered that one does not ditch an entire aircraft just because the propeller

develops a disgusting nick in one of the blades. Sometimes, also, serendipity comes along in an old business when technology takes a giant leap backward. Sensensich sells several of his propellers to the defense department. They prefer his radar-insensitive propellers on their new midget spy planes.

Richardson Electronics of LaFox, Illinois, is the largest and almost the last supplier of vacuum tubes in America. Edward Richardson stocks over 10,000 different tubes. He survives because the industrial world still uses a considerable quantity of old electronic equipment that would be expensive to replace with solid state. Richardson knows that $350 for a $10 tube is a bargain for a manufacturer who is facing $50,000 worth of downtime. Richardson also knows that even Star Wars technology cannot replace some vacuum tube technology. In certain radar and welding applications, no semiconductor or computer developed to this point in time can outperform tubes.

Is there any certainty in the business world other than death? If you are the last producer (or one of the last) of an item that still has a moderately stable yearly demand, the product cannot be outperformanced by any competing technology, and no sane person would ever think of going into this business, well, you decide.

Source: "Endgame Strategy," *Forbes*, July 13, 1987, pp. 181–204.

---

available, so a manager must rely on a personal estimate, or *subjective* probability, of the situation outcome.

Even a manager who is able to estimate the likelihood that the various states of nature will occur faces risk conditions. A risk situation requires the use of probability estimates. The ability to estimate may be due to experience, incomplete but reliable information, or intelligence.[24]

[24]Hal R. Arkes and Kenneth R. Hammond, *Judgment and Decision Making: An Interdisciplinary Reader* (New York: Cambridge University Press, 1986).

Decision making under risk conditions also necessitates the use of expected values. (Recall that the payoffs listed in Table 16–2 are conditional values because they will occur only if a specific state of nature occurs and a specific strategy is chosen.) The expected value of an alternative is the long-run average return; in other words, you would obtain the same results, on average, if you made the same decision in the same situation over and over again. In decision making, the average return, or *expected value,* is found by taking the value of an outcome if it should occur (the conditional value) and multiplying that value by the probability that the outcome will occur. This is a standard and acceptable procedure. Remember that:

$$\text{Expected value} = \text{Conditional value} \times \text{Probability}$$

If the book publisher is able to estimate subjectively the probabilities associated with each of the four levels of demand (states of nature), these estimates can be used to construct a table of expected values. Suppose, for example, that the publisher estimates the following probabilities:[25]

Demand	Probabilities
5,000 books	.20
10,000	.40
15,000	.30
20,000	.10

Table 16–3 presents the expected values for each of the four strategies. For example, the expected value for the strategy of printing 10,000 books (refer to row 2 in Table 16–1) is computed as follows:

$$(.2 \times -\$1,250) + (.4 \times \$7,500) + (.3 \times \$7,500) + (.1 \times \$7,500) = \$5,750$$

The proper decision for the book publisher is to print 10,000 books. The expected value of that strategy exceeds the expected value of any alternative strategy. When given the probabilities of different states of nature, decision theory can aid managers make decisions that maximize the value of some outcome.

What if the decision maker has absolutely no basis for estimating probabilities of future states of nature? As we have seen, probabilities are necessary if one is to calculate expected values. But in many instances, decision makers confront problems that do not lend themselves to the application of expected-value methods. The next section presents some ways that decision theory can assist decision makers with such problems.

CONDITIONS OF UNCERTAINTY

When no historical data exist concerning the probabilities for the occurrence of the states of nature, the manager faces conditions of uncertainty. The

---

[25]The calculation of such probabilities involves mathematical computations beyond the scope of this book. Interested readers may wish to consult a basic text on statistics or economics.

TABLE 16–3   Expected-Value Table for Production Decision

An expected-value table relates expected (average) payoffs to strategies and states of nature.

Strategies: Books Printed	States of Nature: Number of Books Demanded				Expected Value
	5,000 (.20)*	10,000 (.40)*	15,000 (.30)*	20,000 (.10)*	
5,000	$750 +	$1,500 +	$1,125 +	$375 =	$3,750
10,000	−250 +	3,000 +	2,250 +	750 =	5,750
15,000	−1,250 +	1,000 +	3,375 +	1,125 =	4,250
20,000	−2,250 −	1,000 +	1,875 +	1,500 =	125

*Estimated probability.

management science approach focuses on improving the decision-making process under such conditions.[26] A number of different decision criteria have been proposed as possible bases for decisions under uncertainty, including:

1. Maximax criterion (optimistic): maximizing the maximum possible payoff.
2. Maximin criterion (pessimistic): maximizing the minimum possible payoff.
3. Minimax criterion (regret): minimizing the maximum possible regret to the decision maker.
4. Insufficient-reason criterion: assuming equally likely probabilities for the occurrence of each possible state of nature.

As with conditions of certainty and risk, the first step in making decisions under conditions of uncertainty is to construct a conditional-value payoff table. The next step is to select and apply one of the above decision criteria. Using the conditional-value payoffs in Table 16–2, we will illustrate the four criteria for decision making under conditions of uncertainty.

Maximax Criterion.   Some decision makers think optimistically about the occurrence of events influencing a decision. A manager with this attitude will examine the conditional-value table and select the strategy allowing the most favorable payoff. But this criterion is dangerous to employ, because it ignores possible losses and the chances of making or not making a profit.

Using a maximax criterion, the publisher would assume that no matter what strategy is selected, the best possible state of nature will occur. Therefore, the publisher should print 20,000 books because that strategy is associated with the maximum payoff of $15,000 (see Table 16–2).

Maximin Criterion.   Some managers act on the belief that only the worst possible outcome can occur. This pessimism results in the selection of the

[26]Jatikumar Sengupta, *Optimal Decisions under Uncertainty* (New York: Springer-Verlag, 1981).

TABLE 16–4   Regret Table for Production Decision

A regret table relates quantitative estimates of regret to strategies and states of nature.

Strategies: Books Printed	States of Nature: Number of Books Demanded			
	5,000	10,000	15,000	20,000
5,000	$ 0	$ 3,750	$7,500	$11,250
10,000	5,000	0	3,750	7,500
15,000	10,000	5,000	0	3,750
20,000	15,000	10,000	5,000	0

strategy that maximizes the least favorable payoff. Using this criterion, the publisher would locate the worst possible outcome associated with each alternative. Table 16–2 indicates that the worst possible payoffs associated with each strategy and state of nature are as follows:

Strategy	Worst Outcome
Print 5,000 books	$ 3,750
Print 10,000 books	−1,250
Print 15,000 books	−6,250
Print 20,000 books	−11,250

The publisher will minimize the worst possible outcome by selecting the strategy of printing 5,000 books. Of the four worst possible outcomes, that one is the least—the maximum of the minimums.

Minimax Criterion.   If a manager selects a strategy and if a state of nature occurs that does not result in the most favorable payoff, regret occurs. The manager is regretful that the strategy selected did not lead to the best payoff.

A manager who does not know and does not want to guess which state of nature will occur selects a regret strategy. Managerial regret is the payoff for each strategy under every state of nature, subtracted from the most favorable payoff that is possible with the occurrence of the particular event. For example, if the publisher prints 5,000 books and the demand is for 10,000, the publisher will experience regret of $3,750 (the difference between the realized payoff for that strategy and the potential payoff associated with printing 10,000 books). The regret for any particular strategy is the difference between the best possible outcome and the actual outcome.

Applying the minimax criterion requires the development of regret tables. These tables indicate the amount of regret associated with each strategy and state of nature. Table 16–4 presents the amounts of regret associated with the book publisher's production decisions.

Next the maximum regret value for each of the four strategies is identified:

Strategy	Regret
Print 5,000 books	$ 11,250
Print 10,000 books	7,500
Print 15,000 books	10,000
Print 20,000 books	15,000

The minimax criterion indicates that the publisher should print 10,000 books because that strategy produces the minimum regret.

Insufficient-Reason Criterion. The three preceding decision criteria assume that without any previous experience, it is not worthwhile to assign probabilities to the states of nature. The insufficient-reason criterion, however, states that if managers do not know the probabilities of occurrence for the various states of nature, they should assume that all are equally likely to occur. In other words, managers should assign equal probabilities to each state of nature.

Using the insufficient-reason criterion, the publisher would assign a one-in-four (¼) probability to each of the four states of nature (see Table 16–5). Based on those probabilities, the publisher should print 10,000 books.

Reviewing the Choices. The application of the four criteria to the decision faced by the book publisher results in different choices, depending on the orientation of the decision maker:

1. The optimist would print 20,000 books.
2. The pessimist would print 5,000 books.
3. The regretter would print 10,000 books.
4. The insufficient-reasoner would print 10,000 books.

Different criteria result in different decisions. Each decision problem has unique data that lead to unique situations.

One point should be clear. The greater the amount of reliable information, the more likely it is that the manager will make a good decision. Making sure

---

TABLE 16–5   Expected Values, Using Insufficient-Reason Criterion

Expected values can be calculated and related to strategies and states of nature under conditions of insufficient reason.

Strategies: Books Printed	Calculation									Expected Value
5,000	¼ ($3,750	+	$3,750	+	$ 3,750	+	$ 3,750)	=		$3,750.00
10,000	¼ (−1,250	+	7,500	+	7,500	+	7,500)	=		5,312.50
15,000	¼ (−6,250	+	2,500	+	11,250	+	11,250)	=		4,687.50
20,000	¼ (−11,250	−	2,500	+	6,250	+	15,000)	=		1,875.00

Management Focus

Hallmark Uses Payoff Matrixes

Hallmark Cards Corporation and the local newsstand have at least one management problem in common: No one wants to buy leftover inventory. On December 26, there is likely to be scant demand for Christmas cards or December 25 newspapers. Managers at Hallmark Cards and newsstands must somehow produce and order just enough product to satisfy demand without running either short or over. To run short means lost sales; to run over means excessive inventory costs.

Hallmark's production managers face many such decisions each year. The company produces numerous special theme cards and promotional materials that have never before been made. Consequently, they have little basis for deciding how many to produce. Prior to 1982, production managers decided how many first-time and specialty cards to produce by applying the "similar experience" approach, a method by which one looks for the most similar past experience and projects that experience to the new one. Thus, the production run for a specialty card featuring a Walt Disney character could be determined by

consulting the sales experience of a previously issued Disney character card. These past experiences enabled production managers to obtain "best estimates" as the basis for their production decisions.

Beginning in 1982, Hallmark began to apply somewhat more sophisticated decision-making techniques to their production problems. The new techniques enable production managers to use their judgment to make probabilistic estimates (e.g., the chance that something will happen) of the effects of different production runs. Each level of production has an associated revenue and cost that can be combined to obtain a "payoff." When the managers apply probabilistic estimates to each level of production, they can calculate expected payoffs. Such estimates of expected sales and costs enable the managers to take into account all their collective information about an essentially uncertain future event—expected sales—to make a production decision.

Source: Based on F. Hutton Barron, "Payoff Matrices Pay Off at Hallmark," *Interfaces*, July–August 1985, pp. 20–25.

---

the right information is available at the right time to the right decision maker is the function of a decision support system, the topic of the next chapter.

Decision theory has many applications in production and operations when managers have some bases for making estimates of the relevant probabilities.[27] The Management Focus illustrates how Hallmark follows many of the same procedures we have described in our example.

Hallmark's experience illustrates the applicability of decision theory in production/operations management, the focus of this part of the book. But as we indicated at the beginning of this chapter, decision making is a pervasive aspect of management and pertains to all management functions.

---

[27]Karl Aiginger, *Production and Decision Theory under Uncertainty* (New York: Basil Blackwell, 1987).

SUMMARY OF KEY POINTS

■ Managers make both programmed and nonprogrammed decisions. Programmed decisions are responses to repetitive and routine problems. Nonprogrammed decisions are responses to novel and unstructured problems. Top management should focus on nonprogrammed decisions. Middle and first-level managers in most organizations concentrate mostly on programmed decisions.

■ Decisions are means rather than ends. They are mechanisms through which a manager seeks to achieve some desired state. They are the manager's (and hence the organization's) responses to problems. Problems must exist in order for decisions to be necessary. Managers use the following warning signals to locate problems: (1) deviation from past performance, (2) deviation from the plan, and (3) outside criticism.

■ The approach to decision making suggested in this chapter encourages the manager to discover and enumerate potential strategies and possible states of nature. In addition, it (1) encourages logical definition of objectives and assumptions, (2) encourages precise definition of problems, (3) facilitates systematic consideration of a large number of factors, (4) facilitates the identification of alternative strategies, and (5) facilitates the prediction of outcomes.

■ While a manager may not actually construct payoff tables, the disciplined process of specifying possible states of nature enables the manager to add some clarity to a situation where none existed previously.

DISCUSSION AND REVIEW QUESTIONS

1. Interview managers in one or more organizations where you are employed or have some other connection. Attempt through your questioning to identify the programmed and nonprogrammed decisions of the organization(s). List them and compare the ways in which the organization goes about deciding among alternatives for both types of decisions.

2. Review your understanding of the differences between classical and neoclassical organization designs as we described them in Chapter 7. Explain how the distinction between programmed and nonprogrammed decision making helps you to understand how managers make decisions in these two types of organizations.

3. Use the process of decision making as depicted in Figure 16–2 to describe how a personnel manager would decide whom to hire, how a production manager would decide how many units to produce, how a marketing manager would decide which salesperson to assign to which territories, and how a financial manager would decide between debt and equity as sources of additional funds.

4. The Ace Music Company is considering two strategies for promoting the records of a new recording artist: (1) concentrate entirely on television advertising; (2) concentrate entirely on newspaper advertising. In the past, the company's profits have been influenced by general economic conditions. The profit payoffs for each strategy depend on future economic conditions, as noted:

	States of Nature: Economy		
Strategies	**Downturn**	**Stable**	**Upturn**
1. Television advertising	$ 4,000	$40,000	$60,000
2. Newspaper advertising	10,000	20,000	30,000

a. What would the maximax choice be?
b. What would the minimax choice be?
c. What would the maximin choice be?
d. What would the insufficient-reason choice be?

5. A dairy store manager observes the daily sales of skim milk for a 100-day period and develops this table of sales:

Quantities Purchased	**Number of Days**
40	20
50	15
70	15
100	30
120	20

The milk sells for 30 cents a quart, and the store manager's cost of securing the milk from the dairy is 20 cents.

  a. If 70 units are stocked every day, what will be the firm's expected profit per day over the long run?

  b. Using the data presented in the table, what quantity (40, 50, 70, 100, or 120) should be purchased every day to maximize long-run profits?

6. Distinguish between decisions under conditions of risk and those under uncertainty. Under what circumstances can a manager convert an uncertain decision to a risky decision?

7. Explain in ordinary language the meaning of the term *expected value*. With this meaning in mind, how useful is the term for reaching solutions to nonprogrammed decisions?

8. An analysis and forecast of next year's sales results in the following probability distribution:

Total Demand	Probability
1,000 units	.20
1,200	.20
1,400	.40
1,600	.20

The price per unit is $58. The cost of the product is $38. If the product is not sold during the year, it is worthless.

  a. Prepare a table of conditional values.

  b. Prepare a table of expected values and indicate the optimum choice if management is attempting to optimize profits.

9. What kinds of managers would most likely use the maximax criterion as the basis for deciding among alternatives? Would these managers be likely to have a record of good decisions?

10. Explain why decisions under uncertainty depend so much on factors unrelated to the nature of the decision itself. For example, why is the decision maker's personality such a key factor in these decisions?

ADDITIONAL REFERENCES

Archer, E. R. "How to Make a Business Decision: An Analysis of Theory and Practice." *Management Review*, February 1980, pp. 54–61.

Bass, B. M. *Organizational Decision Making.* Homewood, Ill.: Richard D. Irwin, 1983.

Bell, D. E. "Disappointment in Decision Making under Certainty." *Operations Research*, January–February 1985, pp. 1–27.

Booker, J. M., and **M. C. Bryson.** "Decision Analysis in Project Management: An Overview." *IEEE Transactions on Engineering Management,* February 1985, pp. 3–9.

Chao, H. P.; B. R. Judd; P. A. Morris; and **S. C. Peck.** "Analyzing Complex Decisions for Electric Companies." *Long Range Planning,* April 1985, pp. 46–55.

Churchman, C. W. *Challenge to Reason.* New York: McGraw-Hill, 1968.

Clough, D. B. *Decisions in Public and Private Sectors.* Englewood Cliffs, N.J.: Prentice-Hall, 1984.

Davis, D., and **R. M. Cosenza.** *Business Research for Decision Making.* Boston: Kent Publishing, 1985.

Dixson, D. N. *Using Logical Techniques for Making Better Decisions.* New York: John Wiley & Sons, 1983.

Donaldson, G., and **J. W. Lorsch.** *Decision Making at the Top: The Shaping of Strategic Direction.* New York: Basic Books, 1983.

Dung, N. "An Analysis of Optimal Advertising under Uncertainty." *Management Science,* May 1985, pp. 622–33.

Eppen, G. D., and **F. J. Gould.** *Introduction to Management Science.* Englewood Cliffs, N.J.: Prentice-Hall, 1984.

Fallon, R. *Subjective Assessment of Uncertainty.* Santa Monica, Calif.: Rand Corporation, 1976.

Harrison, F. L. "Decision Making in Conditions of Extreme Uncertainty." *Journal of Management Studies.* May 1977, pp. 169–78.

Hertz, D. B., and **H. Thomas.** *Risk Analysis and Its Applications.* New York: John Wiley & Sons, 1983.

Hunsaker, P. L., and **J. S. Hunsaker.** "Decision Styles in Theory and in Practice." *Organizational Dynamics,* Autumn 1981, pp. 23–36.

McCall, M. W., and **R. E. Kaplan.** *Whatever It Takes: Decision Makers at Work.* Englewood Cliffs, N.J.: Prentice-Hall, 1985.

Menzefricke, U. "Using Decision Theory for Planning Audit Sample Size with Dollar Unit Sampling." *Journal of Accounting Research,* Autumn 1984, pp. 570–87.

Moody, P. *Decision Making: Proven Methods for Better Decisions.* New York: McGraw-Hill, 1983.

Nigro, L. G., ed. *Decision Making in the Public Sector.* New York: Marcel Dekker, 1984.

Pennings, J. M., ed. *Decision Making: An Organizational Behavior Approach.* Bridgeport, Conn.: Wiener, 1983.

CASE 16–1   General Instrument Corporation: Lucky or Smart?

General Instrument Corporation (GI) was at one time a rather lackluster and heavily in debt maker of $375 million worth of electronic and electromechanical products annually. Then something very nice happened. The company caught a fast ride on two rising stars. The first was the video games market, to which it supplies specialized semiconductor chips, including those that run Mattel, Inc.'s Intellivision and Atari, Inc.'s Pac Man. The second is cable TV, for which General Instrument builds distribution gear and converter boxes, products that generate 43 percent of the company's revenues and 70 percent of its operating profits.

In the mid-1980s, the company experienced six consecutive years of growth despite a recession and reached $1 billion in annual sales. But some observers agreed with one of the firm's competitors, who said: "GI didn't create the demand for game chips. And they didn't create the cable business. They just got lucky."

Executives at GI agreed with that observation but only up to a point. They believed, like many others, that the company also got smart. For example, Chief Executive Officer Frank G. Hickey cut GI's long-term debt from nearly 36 percent of equity to less than 8 percent. He also mapped out a growth plan to put the company in other selected communications markets and invested in outside companies to acquire the remaining technology GI needed to compete in those markets. Mr. Hickey believed that the company could parlay its position in targeted markets into 25 percent annual growth. At the time, he stated: "We're beginning another era. We've got a vision of the portfolio of our businesses again. We're going to become a $3 billion communications company in five years."

In an even more aggressive decision, GI moved into the risky but highly visible business of direct satellite-to-home television broadcasting. Through its part ownership of—and exclusive supply contract with—United Satellite Television Corp., GI expected to sell at least $1.5 billion worth of direct broadcast satellite (DBS) gear to some of the 30 million homes in rural and other areas that will not be supplied by cable systems.

Such decisions have given GI a new popularity as a high-technology stock on Wall Street. The company is on the "buy lists" of most brokerages. One broker said, "Hickey has done an absolutely incredible job. GI has a shot at

Source: Adapted from "Mixing Luck and Knowhow," *Business Week,* October 18, 1982, pp. 118, 120–21.

becoming the hottest technology stock on the Big Board over the next three years. It's a combination of being lucky and being good."

Mr. Hickey observed that the DBS decision had resulted in "the single largest growth opportunity ever available to our company." This decision apparently underscores the company's strategy. As Hickey said, "The strength of our business mix is such that we don't have to rely only on the semiconductor industry or only on telecommunications or anything else."

To a large number of observers, GI's plan was more than just luck. One commented, "They did get lucky, but they have exploited their position to the hilt."

Questions for Analysis

1. Do you believe GI was lucky? Why?
2. What does this case indicate to you about decision making? Be specific.

Case 16–2   The "Old Man"

Ted Gray smiled as he carried some of his belongings into the huge, oak-paneled office that would be his on Monday. At the relatively young age of 46, he had been appointed president of Newtown Developers (the nation's largest developer of planned model cities) three months ago when Don Stevens announced his retirement.

Stevens, or the "Old Man" as he was affectionately known in the organization, had been the only other president Newtown ever had. Most agreed he was responsible for the tremendous growth and success the company had achieved in the last two decades. Ted had worked closely with the Old Man for the past seven years and was his choice to succeed him.

Ted had learned all he could from Stevens. The two were very close and had spent much time together discussing management philosophies, decision making, and human relations. While they sometimes differed in opinion, the discussions were always helpful to Ted.

When he opened the top drawer in his new desk, Ted was surprised to find two old and worn pieces of paper that Don had apparently left behind. Both contained statements from Clarence Randall, head of the Inland Steel Company during the 1950s. The first read as follows:

> Decision making is a lonely business, and the greater the degree of responsibility, the more intense the loneliness. It is human to wish to share the risk of error and to feel the comforting strength of outside support, like the flying buttresses along the wall of a medieval cathedral. But the strong man, the one who gives free enterprise its vitality, is the man who weighs thoughtfully the entire range of available opinion and then determines policy by relying solely on his own judgment.

The second piece of paper contained Randall's response to the question "What, then, are the outward attributes displayed by a man who comes to be regarded by his associates as one who may be highly trusted with the authority to say yes or no?" It read as follows:

> The instinct for recognizing when a problem exists.
> The ability to articulate the problem with clarity.
> The ability to saturate himself with pertinent data.
> The ability to maintain an open mind until the evidence is in.
> A sense of urgency that forces him to work as rapidly as possible.
> The courage not to look back after a decision is made.

Ted put the pieces of paper in his briefcase to give to Stevens the next time he saw him. Then he thought, "I'm still learning from that old goat. I bet he left them here for me."

As Ted left the building on his way home, he thought, "On Monday, I'll be the Old Man." He wasn't sure now if he was glad or scared.

QUESTIONS FOR ANALYSIS

1. Given today's technology, rapidly changing environment, and the increased complexities facing managers, what should Ted Gray do with the two pieces of paper? In other words, would they be of any use to him as he begins his term as president? Discuss in detail.

2. In the statements about decision making, is there anything that has changed in the past 30 years?

EXPERIENTIAL EXERCISE

LOST-AT-SEA DECISION MAKING

Purpose

The purpose of this exercise is to offer students the opportunity to compare individual versus group decision making.

The Exercise in Class

Scenario.   You are adrift on a private yacht in the South Pacific. As a consequence of a fire of unknown origin, much of the yacht and its contents have been destroyed. The yacht is now slowly sinking. Your location is unclear because of the destruction of critical navigational equipment and because you and the crew were distracted trying to bring the fire under control. Your best estimate is that you are approximately 1,000 miles south-southwest of the nearest land.

Exhibit 1 contains a list of 15 items that are intact and undamaged after the fire. In addition to these articles, you have a serviceable rubber life raft with oars, large enough to carry yourself, the crew, and all the items listed here. The total contents of all survivors' pockets are a package of cigarettes, several books of matches, and five $1 bills.

EXHIBIT 1   Worksheet

Items	(1) Individual Ranking	(2) Group Ranking	(3) Ranking Key
Sextant	_____	_____	_____
Shaving mirror	_____	_____	_____
Five-gallon can of water	_____	_____	_____
Mosquito netting	_____	_____	_____
One case of U.S. Army C rations	_____	_____	_____
Maps of the Pacific Ocean	_____	_____	_____
Seat cushion (flotation device approved by the coast guard)	_____	_____	_____
Two-gallon can of oil-gas mixture	_____	_____	_____
Small transistor radio	_____	_____	_____
Shark repellent	_____	_____	_____
Twenty square feet of opaque plastic	_____	_____	_____
One quart of 160-proof Puerto Rican rum	_____	_____	_____
Fifteen feet of nylon rope	_____	_____	_____
Two boxes of chocolate bars	_____	_____	_____
Fishing kit	_____	_____	_____

Individual accuracy index	_____
Group accuracy index	_____
Average of group's individual accuracy indexes	_____
Lowest individual accuracy index (correct ranking)	_____

Activity. After reading the above scenario, you and your classmates should complete the following steps:

1. Working independently and without discussing the problem or the merits of any of the items, rank the 15 items in terms of their importance to your survival. Under column 1, place the number 1 by the most important item, the number 2 by the second most important, and so on through number 15, the least important. When you are through, *do not discuss* the problem or rankings of items with anyone.

2. Your instructor will establish teams of four to six students. The task for your team is to rank the 15 items, according to the group's consensus, in the order of importance to your survival. Do not vote or average team members' rankings; try to reach agreement on each item. Base your decision on knowledge, logic, or the experiences of group members. Try to avoid basing the decision on personal preference. Enter the group's ranking in column 2. This process should take between 20 and 30 minutes, or as the instructor designates.

3. When everyone has finished, your instructor will read the correct ranking, as provided by officers of the U.S. Merchant Marine. Enter the correct rankings in column 3.

4. Compute the accuracy of your individual ranking. For each item, use the absolute value (ignore plus and minus signs) of the difference between column 1 and column 3. Add up these absolute values to get your *individual accuracy index*. Enter it on the worksheet.

5. Perform the same operation as in step 4, but use columns 2 and 3 for your group ranking. Adding up the absolute values yields your *group accuracy index*. Enter it on the worksheet.

6. Compute the *average* of your group's individual accuracy indexes. Do this by adding up each member's individual accuracy index and dividing the result by the number of group members. Enter it.

7. Identify the *lowest* individual accuracy index in your group. This is the most correct ranking in your group. Enter it on the worksheet.

The Learning Message

This exercise is designed to let you experience group decision making. Think about how discussion, reflection, and the exchange of opinions influenced your final decision.

17

DECISION SUPPORT SYSTEMS

LEARNING OBJECTIVES

After completing Chapter 17, you should be able to:

Define
decision support systems and their increasing importance.

Describe
how the types of decisions a manager makes relate to the types of information a manager needs.

Discuss
the organization of decision support systems.

Compare
decision support systems and management information systems.

Identify
the major functions performed by a decision support system.

Big Business Discovers Small Business's Need for Decision Support Systems

The prevailing attitude among the giants of the computer software industry has been that small business applications of decision support systems are limited. Firms such as Lotus Development Corporation have viewed the "small business" market as being fragmented and dominated by specialized software companies. Big firms have distrusted their ability to develop and distribute products to small business firms. But as the evidence began to come in that the big business market for software has been saturated, Lotus and other firms started to look for opportunities in the small business sector. The room for expansion is indicated by market research which finds that only about 50 percent of the 5 million small firms (fewer than 100 employees) are computerized.

Developing products that persuade mom-and-pop businesses to trade paper and pencils for PCs and spreadsheets requires different approaches from those that have been successful in big business applications. The biggest problem is the existence of computer fear. Small business owners and managers are not typically as comfortable with computers as are their big business counterparts. Nevertheless, it is nearly impossible to find a small businessperson who does not have the attitude that now is the time to develop computer-assisted decision-making skills. It is also nearly impossible to find a developer of software products who is not interested in helping to overcome that fear.

The compelling fact of contemporary business, whether large or small, is the increasing importance of managing information. Information is the basis for decision making at all levels in organizations. The small business uses of computers to assist in information management are increasing as the applications are made more user-friendly and relevant to the small business environment. Traditionally, software companies have been reluctant to make concessions to small business users of products developed for big business applications. But as software developers have discovered the profit potential in small business applications, they have begun to develop products that meet the specific needs of small businesspeople.

Thus, the small business sector has now been brought into the computer age. We can expect to see small business owners and managers make greater use of computers in a wide range of applications. Decision support systems depend on computers, and as computer literacy spreads among small business managers, so too will they come to depend on decision support systems.

Source: "Software's Big Guns Take Aim at Small Business," *Business Week*, September 25, 1989, pp. 216–18.

The Management in Action touches on the compelling management issue that we will address in this chapter: What information does a manager need to make a decision, and how can that information be obtained? As organizations grow in complexity, managers depend more heavily on various internal and external sources of information. Growing complexity also increases the number of points at which decisions must be made, ranging from individual decision makers at the lowest operating levels to strategic decision makers at the top. *Management information systems* (MIS's), designed to provide information to these decision makers, are certainly not new. Many firms have accounting information systems, marketing information systems, customer information files, warehouse information systems, and others. But one very important idea moves beyond the management information system: the *decision support system* (DSS).[1]

THE NEED FOR DECISION SUPPORT SYSTEMS

You know from the last chapter that the quality of a decision greatly depends on understanding the circumstances surrounding an issue and knowing the available alternatives and states of nature. The better the information, the better the resulting decision, because there is less risk and uncertainty. If new, advanced information technology is to support management decision making, organizations must plan now. The need for comprehensive decision support systems has resulted from three factors: (1) the importance of information in decision making,[2] (2) mismanagement of current information,[3] and (3) the increased use of personal computers by individual decision makers.[4]

IMPORTANCE OF INFORMATION IN DECISION MAKING

Information is really a fuel that drives organizations. A major purpose of a manager is to convert information into action through the process of decision making. Therefore, a manager and an organization act as an information-decision system.

Information-decision systems should be considered in conjunction with the fundamental managerial functions: planning, organizing, and controlling. If organization is to implement planning and control, if organization is tied to communication, and if communication is represented by an information-decision system, then the key to success in

---

[1]Guisseppi A. Forgionne, "Building Effective Decision Support Systems," *Business,* January–February–March 1988, pp. 19–30.

[2]Cornelius H. Sullivan, Jr., "Systems Planning in the Information Age," *Sloan Management Review,* Winter 1985, pp. 3–12.

[3]C. Wood, "Countering Unauthorized Systems Accesses," *Journal of Systems Management,* April 1984, pp. 26–28.

[4]E. W. Robak, "Toward a Microcomputer-Based DSS for Planning Forest Operations," *Interfaces,* September–October 1984, pp. 105–11; W. L. Fuerst and M. P. Martin, "Effective Design and Use of Computer Decision Models," *MIS Quarterly,* March 1984, pp. 17–26.

planning and controlling any operation lies in the information-decision system.[5]

Viewing an organization as an information-decision system points out the importance of only generating information that is necessary for effective decisions. If management converts information into action, then how effective the action is depends on how complete, relevant, and reliable the information is. The effectiveness of an organization is more often than not at the mercy of the information available to its managers.[6]

MISMANAGEMENT OF CURRENT INFORMATION

The ability of organizations to generate information is really not a problem, since most are capable of producing massive amounts of information and data. In fact, the last decade has often been described as the Age of Information. Why then do so many managers complain that they have insufficient or irrelevant information on which to base their everyday decisions? Specifically, most managers' complaints fall into the following categories:

1. There is too much of the wrong kind of information and not enough of the right kind.
2. Information is so scattered throughout the organization that it is difficult to locate answers to simple questions.
3. Vital information is sometimes suppressed by subordinates or by managers in other functional areas.
4. Vital information often arrives long after it is needed.

Historically, managers did not have to deal with an overabundance of information. Instead, they gathered a bare minimum of information and hoped that their decisions would be reasonably good. In some business organizations, in fact, marketing research came to be recognized as an extremely valuable staff function during the 1930s and 1940s because it provided information for marketing decisions when previously there had been little or none.

Today, by contrast, managers often feel buried by the deluge of information and data that comes across their desks. This deluge of information, much of which is not useful, has led to the mismanagement of current information. More is not always better.

INCREASED USE OF PERSONAL COMPUTERS

Personal computers have the capability of increasing both the productivity of managers and the quality of their decisions. First, the capacity of computers to extract, process, and analyze data swiftly and accurately is awesome. Second, computers have gotten smaller, faster, and smarter in a shorter period of time than has any other technological innovation in history. A common

---

[5]Richard A. Johnson, Fremont E. Kast, and James E. Rosenzweig, *The Theory and Management of Systems* (New York: McGraw-Hill, 1978), p. 108.

[6]D. Lynch, "MIS: Conceptual Framework, Criticism, and Major Requirements for Success," *Journal of Business Communication,* Winter 1984, pp. 19–31; Michael Davis and Joseph L. Sardinas, Jr., "Creating the Right Decision Support System—Pitfalls," *Management Accounting,* June 1985, pp. 12, 69.

Personal computers have accelerated the development of decision support systems.

desktop personal computer can solve ordinary arithmetic problems 18 times faster than the world's first large-scale computer (weighing 30 tons) built years ago. Present-day computers have become extremely inexpensive compared to earlier models. Just 30 years ago, a medium-sized computer cost a quarter of a million dollars. A firm can now buy a desktop computer with three times the memory capacity for less than $2,000. Consequently, many firms are now making personal computers widely available to their employees.

The computer has changed the ways information is utilized. Through computer networks, managers can instantly access information sources and communicate directly with other managers who have appropriate information. Westinghouse has made considerable progress in the development of systems to facilitate information utilization, as described in the Management Focus on that company.

The means necessary to produce information are available. Still, managers complain of information losses, delays, and distortions. Apparently, many managers have been so concerned about advancing technology and the ready availability of computers that they have overlooked the planning necessary for effective use.[7] To enable managers to make swift and effective decisions, however, present management information systems must be developed into more effective decision support systems.

MIS and DSS

Decision support systems have one primary purpose: to provide the manager with the necessary information for making intelligent decisions. The

[7]Raul Espejo and John Watt, "Information Management, Organization, and Managerial Effectiveness," *Journal of the Operations Research Society,* January 1988, pp. 7–14.

MANAGEMENT FOCUS

Westinghouse Uses Computers to Link Managers and Information

In order to improve management productivity, Westinghouse Electric Corporation decided to electrify its executives. No, they did not install electrodes in every manager's chair and threaten to jolt managers who did not increase productivity. Rather, Westinghouse adopted advanced electronic mail and voice message systems to facilitate greater output. Westinghouse's centerpiece of management productivity is its electronic mail (E-mail) system: 6,000 personal computers link 10,700 managers and over 1,000 top customers. Today, managers can exchange and store ideas and information far more rapidly than before. Message exchanges that heretofore took days now consume only minutes.

Westinghouse Electric's president, Paul Lego, is a strong believer in E-mail. Because Lego can connect his home IBM personal computer AT to the system at Westinghouse's Pittsburgh, Pennsylvania, headquarters, Lego can send or respond at home to anyone in the 38-country network.

Lego says, "It makes it possible both at home and at work for me to have continuous access to important information." Lego recently purchased a laptop computer. Now, wherever he treks in the world, he can stay in constant contact with Pittsburgh as well as the rest of the world.

The E-mail system has generated some shocking results. Westinghouse presently has a permanent and secure record of who said what to whom and when. Telephone tag is a thing of the past. Overseas E-mail is 90 percent less expensive than a personal call. E-mail is 75 percent less costly than a telex letter and far more time effective. Lego credits management's productivity increase of over 2 percent annually since 1980 solely to E-mail. Lego feels that E-mail gives Westinghouse Electric a competitive edge.

Source: "At Westinghouse, 'E-Mail' Makes the World Go Round," *Business Week*, October 10, 1988, p. 110.

---

critical point here is that not just any information will do. A system is needed that converts raw data into information that management can actually use in the decision-making process. Such systems, decision support systems, can be differentiated from MIS's as:

> a wide variety of systems which have the direct objective of supporting managerial decision making. Thus, a management information system (MIS) is a DSS if, and only if, it is designed with the primary objective of managerial decision support. A computerized data processing system is not a DSS—despite that it may, as a by-product, produce aggregated operating data that are useful to management in making decisions. Only those systems that have the direct and primary objective of supporting managerial decision making are considered DSS's.[8]

Thus, a DSS is a specialized MIS designed to support a manager's skills at all stages of decision making: identifying the problem, choosing the relevant

---

[8]William R. King, "Developing Useful Management Decision Support Systems," *Management Decision*, Fall 1978, pp. 262–73; R. W. Blanning, "What Is Happening in DSS?" *Interfaces*, October 1983, pp. 71–80.

Table 17–1   Looking at MIS and DSS in Four Organizations

Organization	Type of System	Description
United Services Automobile Association	MIS	Nation's eighth-largest insurer of passenger cars purchased $4 million information system that now contains virtually all of company's written records. When customer reports an accident, adjustor can call up customer's file, check coverage, and keep track of all paperwork through final settlement of claim. Company figures that one person now handles in 20 minutes what used to take five people a day and a half to perform.
Savin Corporation	MIS	Computer terminal in each warehouse keeps track of every item in inventory. System identifies quantity on hand, location and movement of stock, and status of all orders. Major purposes of this system are to plan shipments, locate single items in inventory, and locate customer records.
Crocker National Bank	DSS	Has desktop terminals for most of its top-level executives. Each terminal is tapped into huge computers that record all bank transactions. Executives are able to make comparisons, analyze problems, and prepare charts and tables in response to simple commands (e.g., analyze emerging trends in deposits and loans; monitor influence of various interest rates and loan maturities on the bank.
Gould, Inc.	DSS	System developed to help managers retrieve, manipulate, and display information needed for making decisions. System combines large visual display and video terminals with computerized information system. Designed solely to help managers make comparisons and analyze problems for decision-making purposes, DSS instantly prepares tables and color charts in response to simple commands.

MIS's capture and retrieve information for the entire organization and for a variety of purposes; DSS's capture and retrieve information for managers and for specific purposes.

data, picking the approach to be used in making the decision, and evaluating the alternative courses of action. A DSS must produce information in a form that managers understand and at a time when such information is needed, and it must place the information under the managers' direct control. Thus, a DSS is an MIS, but an MIS is not always a DSS; their purposes are different, as shown in Table 17–1, which describes the two systems, as used in four different organizations.

In short, an MIS provides information, but a DSS shapes that information to the needs of management. A DSS provides support for the types of decisions—programmable and nonprogrammable—discussed in the previous chapter as well as for decision making under conditions of certainty, risk, and uncertainty.

PROVIDING THE RIGHT INFORMATION FOR THE RIGHT DECISIONS

The preceding chapter discussed how the types of problems faced and the procedures used for dealing with them vary according to a manager's level in the organization. The same factors—level in the organization and type of decision being made—also affect managerial information requirements. To ensure that the types of information match the types of decisions being made, appropriate information must be directed to the proper decision points.

The types of information needed are classified by the types of decisions being made: planning decisions, control decisions, and operations decisions. Decision support systems must generate the right types of information for particular types of decisions.[9] Planning, control, and operations decisions require planning, control, and operations information.

PLANNING DECISIONS

These decisions, made by top managers, involve formulating objectives for the organization, the amounts and kinds of resources necessary to attain these objectives, and the policies that govern the use of the resources. Much of this planning information comes from external sources and relates to such factors as the present and predicted state of the economy, the availability of resources (nonhuman as well as human), and the political and regulatory environment. Effective planning is crucial for effective performance in public as well as private organizations.[10] Planning information forms the input for nonprogrammed types of decisions made at this top level in the organization.[11]

CONTROL DECISIONS

Middle management makes control decisions to ensure that the organization's performance is consistent with its objectives. Control information comes mainly from internal sources (often interdepartmental) and involves such problems as developing budgets and measuring performance of first-line supervisors. The nature of problems faced may be either programmable or nonprogrammable.[12]

Control decisions take on many forms and in some instances involve providing information to the company's customers. Manufacturers of chemicals, for example, must be concerned with how customers use their products; in a sense, the manufacturer must control the customers' usage of the chemical. To accomplish this purpose, organizations must provide customers with information that enables them to make informed decisions about the product.

[9]L. Mann, "User Profiles for Systems Planning and Development," *Journal of Systems Management,* April 1984, pp. 38–40.

[10]Robert R. McGowan and Gary A. Lombardo, "Decision Support Systems in State Government," *Public Administration Review,* Winter 1986, pp. 579–83.

[11]Robert Fildes, "Quantitative Forecasting—the State of the Arts," *Journal of the Operations Research Society,* July 1985, pp. 549–80; Kelvin Cross, "Manufacturing Planning with Computers at Honeywell," *Long Range Planning,* December 1984, pp. 64–75.

[12]John Murdoch, "Forecasting and Inventory Control on Micros," *Journal of the Operations Research Society,* July 1985, pp. 607–8.

MANAGEMENT FOCUS

Information to Control Material Safety

Imagine this nightmare. You are a diversified company that produces enormous quantities of toxic chemicals at 18 separate plants. You employ 6,000 workers and have thousands of customers worldwide. Congress passes the Superfund Amendment and Reorganization Act. Now you must prepare and maintain detailed technical descriptions on how to handle each of your thousands of chemicals under normal as well as adverse situations. These detailed material safety data sheets (MSDS's) cost between $10,000 and $20,000 per chemical to prepare. Not only must you compile these MSDS's, you must make them available to every production employee, common carrier, warehouse, state chemical disposal agency, and local fire department that might come in contact with each chemical. The nightmare gets worse. You have just acquired several companies. Each has its way of interpreting and meeting these new government standards. You discover six separate groups simultaneously undertaking this expensive nonrevenue task.

Ross Ahntholz, Olin Chemical's chief information officer, faced this situation. Rather than capitulate to the problem, Ahntholz confronted the challenge head-on. Ahntholz first established a four-person task force to oversee the creation and maintenance of an MSDS system. Next, he and his task force created what has to be one of the greater composition undertakings on record. Through Olin's computerized mail system, Ahntholz simultaneously linked technical service people in Kentucky, Tennessee, Louisiana, and Connecticut; environmental engineers and transit authorities in New Jersey, Kansas, and Connecticut; and medical technicians from five different cities. Together, these persons wrote, edited, verified, and centrally stored in one database detailed MSDS's for all of Olin's toxic chemicals.

Once positioned, Ahntholz linked the MSDS database to Olin's order system. First, all persons and agencies who had recently come in contact with each of Olin's chemicals or anyone who needed an initial MSDS received one through a mass mailing. Next, Ahntholz attached the database to new orders. Today, when an order leaves Olin, appropriate MSDS's shadow Olin's toxic chemicals wherever they go.

Source: "Olin Computerizes Safety Data," *Management Review*, October 1988, pp. 60–61.

The Management Focus describes an information system that Olin developed to control product usage.

OPERATIONS DECISIONS

These decisions focus on the day-to-day activities of the organization and how efficiently its resources are being used. Operations information comes from routine and necessary sources, such as financial accounting, inventory control, and production scheduling.[13] This information is generated internally; and because it usually relates to specific tasks, it often comes from one designated department. First-level supervisors are the primary users. Since

---

[13]H. G. Heymann and Robert Bloom, *Decision Support Systems in Finance and Accounting* (Westport, Conn.: Quorum Books, 1988).

Information must be distributed to be utilized.

decision making at this level in the organization usually involves programmed types of problems, many problems at the operations level are stated as mathematical models.[14] Examples of such models and the information they require are presented in the next two chapters.

DESIGNING A DECISION SUPPORT SYSTEM

The first step in designing a DSS is to develop a clear understanding of the various information flows that must be dealt with.

UNDERSTANDING INFORMATION FLOWS

An organization must deal with two broad types of information flows (see Figure 17–1):

External Information Flows.   These proceed from the organization to its environment and/or from the environment to the organization. The inward flow is referred to as intelligence information and the outward flow as organizational communications.

Intelligence information includes data on the various elements of the organization's operating environment (e.g., clients, patients, customers, competitors, suppliers, creditors, and the government) for use in evaluating short-run, strategic planning information on the economic environment (e.g., consumer income trends and spending patterns for a business organization) as well as tracing developments in the social and cultural environment in which the organization operates. This type of information has long-run significance to the organization and aids in long-range strategic planning.

[14]John Bowers, "Network Analysis on a Micro," *Journal of the Operations Research Society,* July 1985, pp. 609–12; A. C. McKay, "Linear Programming Applications on Microcomputers," *Journal of the Operations Research Society,* July 1985, pp. 633–36.

FIGURE 17–1   Information Flows and Types of Information

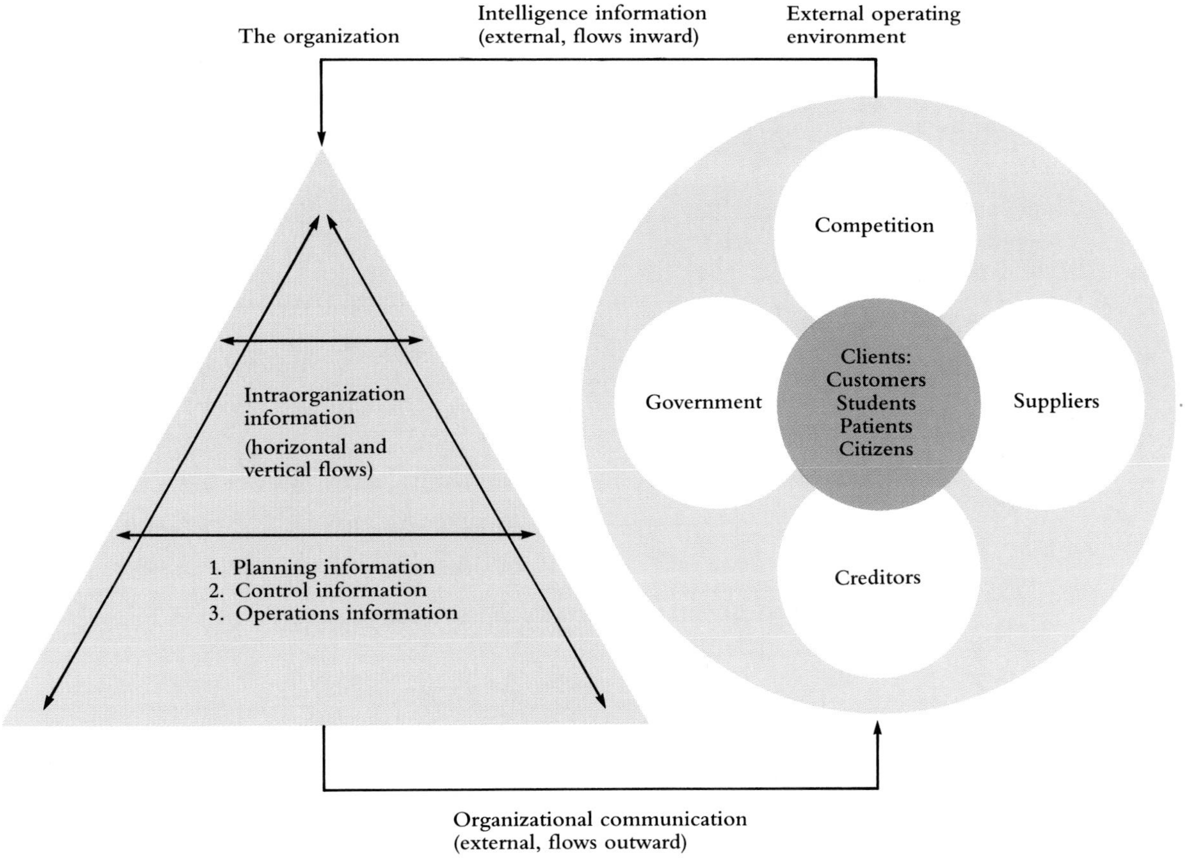

Intelligence information
(external, flows inward)

The organization   External operating
                          environment

Competition

Intraorganization
information
(horizontal and
vertical flows)

Government   Clients: Suppliers
                    Customers
                    Students
                    Patients
                    Citizens

1. Planning information   Creditors
2. Control information
3. Operations information

Organizational communication
(external, flows outward)

Information flows both to and from the organization; once inside the organization, it moves both vertically and horizontally.

Organizational communications flow outward from the organization to the various components of its external operating environment. Advertising and other promotional efforts are considered organizational communications. Whatever the type of organization, the content of this information flow is controlled by the organization. Although important, it nevertheless is an outward flow, one with which we will not be concerned in this book.

Intraorganization Flows.   This term means exactly what the name says: information flowing within an organization. To be useful, intelligence information must, along with internally generated information, reach the right manager at the right time. Within every organization, there are vertical (both upward and downward) as well as horizontal information flows.[15] The rationale of a DSS is that all information flows must become part of a master plan and not be allowed to function without a formal scheme and direction.

[15]Lawrence W. Foster and David M. Flynn, "Management Information Technology: Its Effects on Organizational Form and Function," *MIS Quarterly,* December 1984, pp. 229–36.

FIGURE 17–2   The Functions of a Decision Support System

The outcomes from decisions based on DSS information become inputs in the system to determine future informational needs.

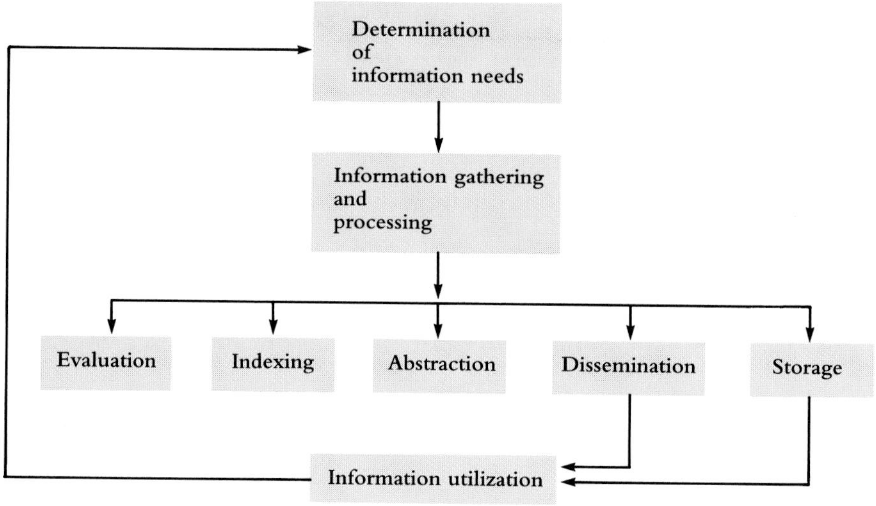

The objective of the master plan is to circulate information to the proper person at the right time.

THE FUNCTIONS OF A DECISION SUPPORT SYSTEM

An effective DSS should provide managers with four major services: determination of information needs, information gathering, information processing, and utilization (see Figure 17–2).

Determination of Information Needs. At the start, the manager must attempt to answer such questions as: How much information is needed? How, when, and by whom will it be used? In what form is it needed? In other words, the manager begins with an examination of the output requirements. Questions helpful for identifying a manager's information needs appear in Table 17–2.

As discussed throughout this book, research and practical experience have demonstrated the need to involve people in changes that affect them. No less is true if a decision support system is being installed: Managers expected to use it should be involved in implementing it.[16] Thus, output requirements are based on answers to such questions as: What information is necessary for planning and controlling operations at different organizational levels? What information is needed to allocate resources? What information is needed to evaluate performance? These types of questions recognize that a different kind of information is needed for formulating organizational objectives than for

[16]William J. Doll, "Avenues for Top Management Involvement in Successful MIS Development," *MIS Quarterly,* March 1985, pp. 17–36; Robert I. Mann and Hugh J. Watson, "A Contingency Model for User Involvement in DSS Development," *MIS Quarterly,* March 1984, pp. 27–36.

TABLE 17–2	Checklist for Manager's Information Needs

Knowing the right questions can assist the design of an information system.

1. What types of decisions do you make regularly?
2. What types of information do you need to make these decisions?
3. What types of information do you regularly get?
4. What types of information would you like to get that you are not now getting?
5. What information would you want daily? Weekly? Monthly? Yearly?
6. What types of data analysis programs would you like to see made available?

Source: Adapted from Philip Kotler, *Principles of Marketing*, 3rd ed. (Englewood Cliffs, N.J.: Prentice-Hall, 1986).

scheduling production. They also recognize that too much information may actually hinder a manager's performance. The manager must distinguish between "need to know" types of information and "nice to know" types of information. Remember the point made at the beginning of this chapter: More information does not always mean better decisions.

Determining what information a manager needs for decision making is a useless exercise unless that information can be obtained. For example, any production manager would like to know exactly how many employees are going to show up each day. With that information, the production manager could always schedule the use of part-time and temporary employees. But such information is seldom available. Other information that a manager might need is likely to be found in the minds of experts who have done a particular task for many years but are unable to articulate what it is that they do.[17] For example, Campbell Soup Company recently faced the problem of replacing an employee who was retiring after 44 years with the company. This particular employee knew more about operating the company's huge soup kettles than anyone in the organization. To replace him was next to impossible.[18]

In response to the problem of obtaining information about the kettle operation, Campbell developed an *expert-decision system*.[19] The system incorporates the latest in decision system technology and includes computer software that simulates the thought processes that the retired employee used when running the kettles. Other companies are engaged in the development of these systems for application in production management.[20] The field of artificial intelligence, as it is developing,[21] promises to be an exciting extension of decision support systems.[22]

[17]Ashrok R. Nadkarni and Graham Kenny, "Expert Systems and Organizational Decision-Making," *Journal of General Management*, Autumn 1987, pp. 60–68.

[18]Emily T. Smith, "Turning an Expert's Skill into Computer Software," *Business Week*, October 7, 1985, pp. 104, 108.

[19]Richard Vedder and Chadwick H. Nestman, "Understanding Expert Systems: A Comparison of DSS and MIS," *Industrial Management*, March–April 1985, pp. 1–8.

[20]Keith Denton, "Decision-Making Technology," *Production and Inventory Management Review*, January 1988, pp. 35–37.

[21]Alec Chang, Michael Leonard, and Jay Goldman, "Artificial Intelligence: An Overview of Research and Application," *Industrial Management*, November–December 1986, pp. 14–19.

[22]Ramesh Sharda, Steve H. Barr, and James C. McDonnell, "Decision Support System Effectiveness: A Review and an Empirical Test," *Management Science*, February 1988, pp. 139–59.

Information Gathering and Processing.   The purpose of processing is to improve the overall quality of the information. Processing includes five component services:

1. *Evaluation* involves determining how much confidence can be placed in a particular piece of information. Such factors as the credibility of the source and reliability of the data must be determined.
2. *Indexing* provides classification for storage and retrieval purposes once information has been gathered.
3. *Abstraction* involves editing and reducing incoming information in order to provide the managers with only information relevant to their particular task.
4. *Dissemination* entails getting the right information to the right manager at the right time; indeed, this is the overriding purpose of a DSS.
5. *Storage* is the final information-processing service. As noted earlier, an organization has no natural memory, so every DSS must provide for storage of information so that it can be used again if needed. Modern electronic information storage equipment has greatly improved the "memory" capabilities of organizations.

Information Utilization.   How information is used depends greatly on its quality (accuracy), presentation (form), and timeliness. Effective utilization is only possible if the right questions to determine information needs are asked in the beginning and if the system is planned carefully. The major goal of a DSS is to provide the right information to the right decision maker at the right time. To this end, timeliness may take precedence over accuracy.[23] If information is not available when needed, then its accuracy is not important. In most cases, however, both accuracy and timeliness are critical.

Timeliness is not the same for every manager; it is determined by the nature of the decisions that must be made. For example, a sales manager may find accurate weekly reports of sales for each company product to be adequate, while an investment manager may need accurate information every few minutes.

Organizing a Decision Support System

Most organizations utilize many different independent information systems for different organizational functions. Along with the development of accounting information systems, other line and staff groups in businesses have developed management information systems uniquely suited to their own needs. While management information systems are critical for effective performance within functional areas, what happens when a decision maker requires information from other functional areas? Designing a DSS requires a system perspective.[24] The system perspective means developing a central databank and an information center, plus viewing information as an important organizational resource.

[23]Kenneth M. Drange, "Information Systems: Does Efficiency Mean Better Performance?" *Journal of Systems Management,* April 1985, pp. 22–29.

[24]Charles R. Necco, Carl L. Gordon, and Nancy W. Tsai, "Systems Analysis and Design: Current Practices," *MIS Quarterly,* December 1987, pp. 461–78.

FIGURE 17–3   The Central Databank in a DSS, and Two Component Management Information Systems

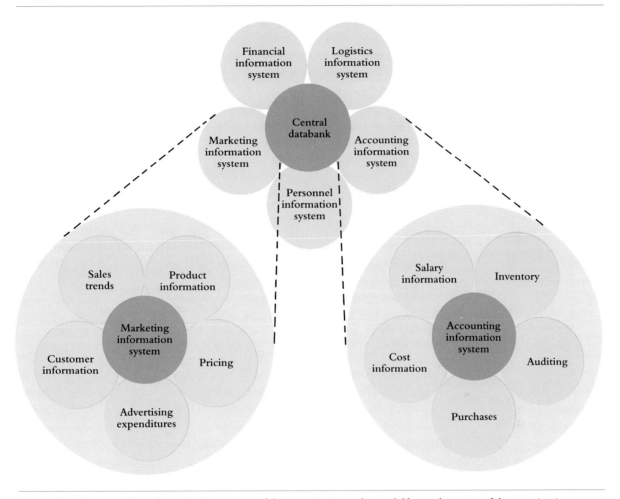

A central databank enables information in one area of the organization to be available to other areas of the organization.

CENTRAL DATABANK

Through the use of a central databank, the core of a decision support system, information in one area of an organization is made readily available for decision making in other areas. Developments in computer and communications technology have made such decision support systems both possible and affordable. And the idea is simple: Centralizing information means that sales data would not have to be stored in accounting, marketing, and production but would be available in one central databank. Since its data can be accessed at will by any decision maker needing them, the central databank increases both the quality and timeliness of decisions. Figure 17–3 presents the central databank concept, illustrating two subsystems in more detail.

INFORMATION CENTER

The information requirements of most managers have greatly changed in the past decade, while the information arrangements within most organizations have remained essentially the same. Because both users and suppliers of information are scattered throughout an organization, some unit is needed to oversee the operation of the central databank. In fact, a basic weakness in most organizations has been the absence of a central entity—known as the information center—for the gathering and processing of information.

To develop an information center, three steps are necessary:

1. Dispersed information activities must be identified throughout the organization.
2. These activities must be viewed as parts of a whole.
3. These activities must be brought under the management of a separate, centralized information center.

The information center is a consultant, coordinator, and controller for the DSS functions: determination of information needs, information gathering and processing, and information utilization. In order to justify its existence, the center must facilitate improved managerial performance through more as well as better information availability and use.[25]

Many information-oriented organizations have developed a separate, centralized, companywide information office. The use of such an office is probably more widespread in highly competitive, volatile consumer goods industries; however, the need is increasing in both private industry and the public sector.[26] This organizational arrangement offers several advantages (such as increased efficiency and more effective use of information) because all computer facilities, knowledge, and storage and retrieval facilities become available to all other functions in the organization.

INFORMATION AS AN ORGANIZATIONAL RESOURCE

Developing a central databank and an information center does not guarantee that information will be used wisely. A frequent problem in many organizations is that a great deal of information is generated for no real purpose and should be eliminated. The tendency to generate large quantities of information is based on the assumption that a direct relationship exists between the amount of information and the quality of decisions. But as we have seen, the quality rather than the quantity of information is more important for decision making.[27] To promote effective utilization of a DSS is to see information as a basic resource of the organization, just as we do money, materials, personnel, and plant and equipment. Thus, as a basic resource, information:

---

[25]Clinton E. White, Jr., and David P. Christy, "The Information Center Concept: A Normative Model and a Study of Six Installations," *MIS Quarterly,* December 1987, pp. 451–60.

[26]John C. Henderson and David A. Schilling, "Design and Implementation of Decision Support Systems in the Public Sector," *MIS Quarterly,* June 1985, pp. 157–70.

[27]T. Hirouchi and T. Kosaka, "An Effective Database Foundation for Decision Support Systems," *Information and Management,* August 1984, pp. 183–95.

MANAGEMENT FOCUS

Decision Support Systems at IBM

International Business Machines Corp. (IBM) operates a manufacturing facility in Poughkeepsie, New York. The plant develops and manufactures processors for the highly competitive international market. The plant's 150-person purchasing department is responsible for procurement of all production and nonproduction parts from outside vendors. These parts range from relatively expensive frames to inexpensive screws. Because the cost of purchased parts is a large percentage of total product cost, the procurement manager constantly seeks ways to attain cost savings.

The purchasing decision at IBM involves selecting specific vendors to supply specific parts in specific quantities to arrive at specified times. The decision is extremely complex and involves a great number of considerations. For example, several different vendors can supply several different parts, and the prices they charge for the parts will depend on how many IBM orders from them. Seldom will a single vendor specialize in supplying IBM with only one kind or type of part. Thus, the decision involves selecting a particular combination of vendors, parts, quantities, and times that minimizes the sum of purchasing, transportation, and inventory costs over multiple time periods. The constraints that must be observed include the expected usage of the parts and the ability of the vendors to supply the parts within their own capacity limitations.

IBM began its effort to achieve minimum costs by realizing that the solution required a *model* that simulates the relationships among the vendors, parts, quantities, and time; *data* that specify the relationships; and information that portrays the relationships according to the model. After investing considerable time and money, the Poughkeepsie procurement department developed a system that enabled it to make the optimal decision. The system is termed a vendor selection system (VSS) because it enables the decision maker to specify the decision variables and constraints and select the optimal combination of vendors. The system is no more complicated to use than an electronic spreadsheet routine such as VisiCalc® or Lotus® and is an excellent example of how management science analysis can be combined with computer capability to produce an information system dedicated to the production of decision-relevant information: a decision support system.

Source: Based on Paul S. Bender, Richard W. Brown, Michael H. Issac, and Jeremy F. Shapiro, "Improving Purchasing Productivity at IBM with a Normative Decision Support System," *Interfaces,* May–June 1985, pp. 106–15.

1. Is vital to the survival of the organization.
2. Can only be used at a cost.
3. Must be at the right place at the right time.
4. Must be used efficiently for an optimal return on its cost to the organization.

Each user of information should consider the cost of the information relative to its utility for decision making. For example, the cost of compiling complete information for a decision must be weighed against the expected value of a decision made with incomplete information.

While the concept of a DSS is relatively new, we have seen in this chapter that it is a reality in both small[28] and large[29] organizations. Certainly, one of the major reasons for the increased interest in and the development of DSS has been the growth in information technology. However, the development of DSS is more than technology; its purpose is more effective management decision making, as noted in the final Management Focus for this chapter (p. 579).

SUMMARY OF KEY POINTS

- More comprehensive decision support systems are necessary because of the importance of information in decision making, mismanagement of current information, and the increased use of personal computers by decision makers.

- A management information system is a decision support system if, and only if, it is designed with the primary objective of managerial decision support. Thus, a DSS is an MIS, but an MIS is not necessarily a DSS.

- A DSS must be designed to support a manager's skills at all stages of the decision-making process—from identifying and defining problems to evaluating alternative courses of action.

- The types as well as sources of information required for management decisions will vary by level in the organization. We identify three types of information—planning, control, and operations—based on the types of decisions made.

- Designing a DSS involves understanding information flows as well as the functions of such a system. The functions of a DSS are determination of information needs, information gathering, information processing, and information utilization.

- Organizing a DSS involves developing a central databank and an information center, plus viewing information as an important organizational resource.

DISCUSSION AND REVIEW QUESTIONS

1. What accounts for the growing importance of information in management decision making? Can a manager make a decision without information? Explain.

2. Do you believe that it is easy to mismanage information in contemporary organizations? Why? What personal experiences have you had with organizations that mismanaged information?

3. What are the key differences between management information systems and decision support systems?

4. What kinds of information would a manager need to make the following decisions?
   a. Hiring a new employee.
   b. Promoting an employee.
   c. Purchasing a computer system.
   d. Assigning salespersons to regions.
   e. Assigning shelf space to a product.

5. Provide examples of decisions other than the ones listed in question 4 to illustrate the differences between planning, control, and operations decisions.

6. What are the different external and internal information flows that the college or university you attend must deal with? If possible, interview campus administrators and determine which of these flows they consider most critical for the effectiveness of their decisions.

7. What are the different functions of a decision support system? How do these functions differ in manufacturing as compared to service organizations?

8. Explain how a manager could make sure that the centralized information center does not become

---

[28]Stewart C. Malone, "Computerizing Small Business Information Systems," *Journal of Small Business Management,* April 1985, pp. 10–16.

[29]G. Nigel Gilbert, "Decision Support in Large Organizations," *Data Processing,* May 1985, pp. 28–30.

overly powerful in the organization by virtue of its position as monopolist of information.

9. If information is a resource, as suggested by the chapter discussion, should it be valued in the balance sheet like other assets? Why or why not?

10. In the modern age of information, is the study of information little more than the study of computer technology, including hardware and software? Explain your answer.

ADDITIONAL REFERENCES

Ayers, A. F. "Decision Support System—New Tool for Manufacturing." *Computerworld,* June 1985, pp. 35–38.

Bahl, H. C., and **R. G. Hunt.** "Problem-Solving Strategies for DSS Design." *Information and Management,* February 1985, pp. 81–88.

Brophy, P. *Management Information and Decision Support Systems in Libraries.* Brookfield, Vt.: Gower, 1986.

Brown, D. C. "The Anatomy of a Decision Support System: How Abbott Labs Puts DSS to Work for 2,000 Products." *Business Marketing,* June 1985, pp. 80–86.

Chan, K. H. "Decision Support Systems for Human Resource Management." *Journal of Systems Management,* April 1984, pp. 17–25.

Emery, J. C. *Management Information Systems: The Strategic Imperative.* New York: Oxford University Press, 1987.

Ford, F. N. "Decision Support Systems and Expert Systems: A Comparison." *Information and Management,* January 1985, pp. 21–26.

Gilbert, G. N. "Decision Support in Large Organizations," *Data Processing,* May 1985, pp. 28–30.

Hollingum, J. *Implementing an Information Strategy in Manufacturing: A Practical Approach.* Bedford, Conn.: IFS Publications, 1987.

Holsapple, C. W., and **A. B. Whinston.** *Decision Support Systems: Theory and Application.* New York: Springer-Verlag, 1987.

Horn, S. "Managers Analyze Data with DSS, Make Future Planning Decisions." *Bank Systems and Equipment,* April 1984, pp. 66–69.

Kroeber, D. W. *Management Information Systems.* New York: Free Press, 1982.

McLeod, R. *Management Information Systems.* Chicago: Science Research Associates, 1986.

Meador, C. L., P. G. Keen; and **M. J. Guyote.** "Setting Priorities for DSS Development." *MIS Quarterly,* June 1984, pp. 117–29.

Taylor, T. C. "Honeywell's Computer Makes Managers Out of Salespeople." *Sales and Marketing Management,* May 14, 1984, pp. 59–61.

Vedder, R., and **C. H. Nestman.** "Understanding Expert Systems: Companion to DSS and MIS." *Industrial Management,* March–April 1985, pp. 1–8.

Wedley, W. C., and **R. H. G. Field.** "A Predecision Support System." *Academy of Management Review,* October 1984, pp. 696–703.

CASE 17–1   Stealing Electronic Information

A deputy sheriff resigned from the Los Angeles County Sheriff's Department to become a private investigator, but he continued to use the department's files. The sheriff's department discovered that the man made 286 unauthorized phone calls in one year for his own investigations to check criminal histories, automobile registrations, and outstanding warrants. He was, in effect, stealing information.

This example is only one of a growing number of information crimes. This kind of crime is increasing for a variety of reasons. First, storing information electronically in a centralized place makes it more available than when it was printed and stored on paper. It is faster and easier to steal important

Source: Adapted from "Locking the Electronic File Cabinet," *Business Week,* October 18, 1982, pp. 123–24.

information stored in a computer rather than in individual departments. Second, electronic equipment facilitates crime. For example, two securities salesmen who were about to resign their jobs with one firm did not have to spend any time and effort copying customer names and addresses; they simply ordered a computer printout, which they took with them to their jobs at a competitor. Third, information stored on magnetic disks or tapes is far less bulky than the same amount of information printed on paper, making the information easier to steal. Finally, information can be changed in a computer without leaving any trace.

The problem is complicated by the difficulty in prosecuting information crime. Larceny is defined as depriving someone of their possessions permanently. But when someone steals information, it is still left in the computer.

In response to the growing crime rate, more and more corporations are increasing their information security. Most companies have always carefully guarded their market data, product designs, and other secrets. However, few of them have bothered to update their security practices for the new electronic equipment.

For the growing problem of information crime, however, experience is still the best teacher. One expert notes: "The places doing the best jobs of protecting their information are those that have had previous problems."

Questions for Analysis

1. As a student and a customer, you are probably part of numerous information systems. Can information crime have any impact on you? Discuss.
2. With the rapid growth in technology, are there any ethical concerns associated with information systems? How would you deal with these concerns?

Case 17–2   How Do We Ever Make a Decision?

Return on investment for Lobo Enterprises had not been over 7 percent for the last five years. Late last year, when it became apparent that it would not reach 5 percent for the year, top management finally decided that something needed to be done. One of the nation's largest management consulting firms was contracted to examine the company's operations from top to bottom.

Seven weeks later, the consultants submitted their report with numerous suggestions and recommendations. One of the strongest recommendations read as follows:

Decision makers at the present time are relying on an inefficient, ineffective information system. In fact, Lobo Enterprises does not have anything that resembles an information system. We strongly recommend the design of an information system to include all levels of the organization. Its major goal should be to provide decision makers with relevant, accurate, and timely information for use in making decisions in their specific areas of responsibility.

The top management agreed with the recommendation and ordered the EDP (electronic data processing) department to work with the consultants in designing a DSS. As part of the initial phase of the project, all decision makers in the organization were asked to think carefully about the information needed and used in making decisions related to their area of responsibility. Each manager was asked to submit a report within three weeks, relating information needs and the specific types and sources of information utilized on a regular basis.

Two weeks later, Ralph Reeves, the chief purchasing agent for Lobo, had just completed a rough draft of his report. He called in one of his purchasing agents, Scott Reed, and asked him to take the report home for the weekend, read it, and be prepared to comment on it and make recommendations for changes on Monday. Here is Reeves' report:

Information Needs and Sources of Information for Purchasing Function

In order to make effective purchasing decisions, an industrial buyer needs a certain amount and quality of information. Primarily, our information needs are related to the following:

1. Price of the items.
2. Quantities to be purchased.
3. Number of sources of supply.
4. Urgency of the buy.
5. Complexity of the items.
6. Current market situation relative to the items.
7. Authority over details of the purchase decision.

The specific informational needs will, for the most part, be of two types: technical or quantitative. The technical needs relate to such things as dimensional prints, engineering specifications, and quality requirements. The quantitative requirements are things such as lot size, estimated prices, and terms of shipment.

A careful analysis of the purchasing task reveals numerous and diverse sources of information. Some of our most important and widely used sources are the following:

1. Engineering department.
2. Research and development department.
3. Production control.
4. Supplier literature.
5. Trade papers and magazines.
6. Supplier salespersons.
7. Accounting department.
8. Receiving department.
9. Competitors.
10. Other buyers in the department.
11. Production department.
12. Legal department.

Exhibit 1   Sources of Information Used by an Industrial Buyer at Lobo Enterprises

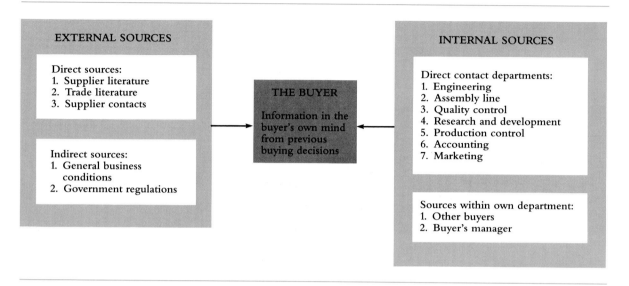

Exhibit 1 illustrates more completely the sources of information used by a buyer prior to most procurement decisions. We in the purchasing department believe it clearly illustrates the need for some type of formal systemization of information.

On Monday, Scott Reed brought the report in to Ralph Reeves. "What do you think?" asked Reeves.

"Ralph, it's excellent. I believe you have accurately detailed the information needs and sources for most purchasing decisions. I have no suggestions or recommendations for changes. One thing did cross my mind as I saw all of our information needs and numerous sources all laid out before my eyes."

"What's that?" asked Reeves.

There was a slight pause before Reed said, "How do we ever make a decision?"

Questions for Analysis

1. What would be your answer to Scott Reed's question?
2. Could Figure 17–3 be of use to Lobo Enterprises? How?
3. Could the concept of a central databank be of use to Lobo Enterprises? Why? Illustrate, using specific examples.

EXPERIENTIAL EXERCISE

DSS DESIGN IN A CAMPUS BOOKSTORE

Purpose

This exercise enables students to experience the difficulty of developing an information system that provides pertinent and timely data for decision making.

The Exercise in Class

Scenario. The manager of the campus bookstore has requested that the class determine the essential features of a decision support system that would enable its book buyers to do their jobs, specifically how much these employees should pay for used books brought in by the students at the end of a particular semester, how many of each book they should buy at different prices, and what price they should charge students who purchase the books for use in subsequent semesters. The manager indicates that the system should be compatible with the store's personal computer system, which enables each of the six book buyers to have access to a common database through the network. The manager envisions a system that would enable the book buyer to call up all the pertinent information on the personal computer whenever an individual comes into the store with a book to sell.

Activity. The instructor will divide the class into groups of 8 to 10 students. Each group will complete the following steps:

1. Consider the problem as outlined in the scenario.
2. Develop ideas for the design of a decision support system to meet the bookstore manager's needs.
3. Present to the class a report that outlines:
    a. The specific informational needs of the book buyers, as well as the needs of other jobs in the bookstore that the group believes can be satisfied by its decision support system.
    b. Internal and external sources of pertinent information.
    c. The means by which the system will be updated.

The Learning Message

The exercise will reinforce the students' understanding of decision making and decision support systems in the context of an organization that they know very well, since they all will likely have bought and sold books at the campus bookstore.

18

PRODUCTION PLANNING

LEARNING OBJECTIVES

After completing Chapter 18, you should be able to:

Define
the concept of production planning in terms of competing products and activities.

Describe
the differences between types of production planning settings for which linear programming (LP) and program evaluation review techniques (PERT) are applicable.

Discuss
the concepts and assumptions that are the bases for linear programming and program evaluation review techniques.

Compare
the informational requirements of linear programming and program evaluation review techniques.

Identify
the optimal production plan for a two-product, three-process firm, given the required information.

Computer Developments Enhance the
Application of PERT

Granite Construction Corporation in California used to prepare manual project analyses for all road construction projects. For each job, a project manager would tape large sheets of paper together, enter a time line, note the activities along the line, and mark the critical path. This process crudely monitored things. Minor changes, however, meant the estimator had to spend hours redrawing the charts and conveying the changes to everyone.

The advent of microcomputers and microcomputer project management software has changed all of this for Granite. Now, at the start of each job, the project manager only has to outline the beginning date of each activity, its expected duration, and any contingencies. A keyboardist enters this into the computer in 15 minutes. The micro quickly checks to make sure that the activities relate and there are no timing errors. The micro also identifies the impact of weekends and holidays on the schedule. If timing is critical, the project manager can add workers or a longer workweek to hurry the project along. After completing the initial PERT charts, Granite sends copies to subcontractors with highlighted colors to show the exact day-by-day role of each subcontractor in the job.

Jim Roberts, manager of Granite, can now monitor progress weekly. If a project gets bottlenecked, Roberts knows what he can juggle to meet completion. If a project changes, he can update everybody in two hours instead of two days. Roberts figures that his engineers save up to 10 hours per week on each project. Now Granite can handle more construction projects without additional stress.

The development of computer software has greatly expanded the range and types of applications. In this chapter, we will describe two of the more widely used techniques: linear programming and the program evaluation review technique. These two are representative of the vast array of techniques available to managers who must confront the production and operations planning issue. Our presentation will emphasize the applications of these two techniques.

Source: "Critical Path Management Speeds Road Reconstruction," *Highway and Heavy Construction*, July 1986, p. 52.

Production planning is a key recurring issue in production/operations management. Production planning requires managers to decide what products and services to produce as well as when, where, and how to produce those products and services. The management of Granite Construction Corporation (in the Management in Action) had to decide not only what road contracts to bid on but also what and how much resources to allocate among all the activities necessary to construct a highway. A manufacturer must make similar decisions: what products to produce and what and how much resources to allocate to each product.

In this chapter, production planning will be presented in the context of two situations. The first situation is that of a manufacturer with multiple products that are demanded by large numbers of consumers willing to buy them at particular prices. Manufacturers of autos, home products, appliances, and textiles are representative of this first situation. The production planning decision requires managers to determine the specific number of each product to produce, given the resource constraints of the firm and the relative profitability of each product.

The second situation to be dealt with in this chapter is the firm that takes on few, but large-scale, construction or product development projects. Sometimes, these projects are one of a kind; the firm may never again produce an identical or even similar product. Builders of roads (such as Granite), buildings, ships, missiles, spacecrafts, and dams are but a few examples of firms that produce under these circumstances. In this scenario, the production planning decision requires managers to determine the combination and sequence of activities to complete the project, given the cost and time constraints of each activity.

These two situations depict a range of typical production planning possibilities. The management science approach offers numerous techniques applicable to each. As indicated in the Management in Action, computerization and software development have had a tremendous effect on the usefulness of management science techniques. In fact, in the absence of computer technology, the management science approach could not have attained and sustained its importance in production and operations management. To represent the many techniques available, we will focus on linear programming and the program evaluation review technique.

PLANNING REPETITIVE PRODUCTION: LINEAR PROGRAMMING

Determining which specific combination of products to manufacture during a time period becomes more complex as the number of products increases. To assist management in making this decision, a class of techniques called "programming methods" is available. The simplest of these methods is linear programming (LP). Since World War II, linear programming models increasingly have been used to solve management problems. With the growth of the electronic computer, complex linear programming models are now being utilized on a wide scale.[1]

---

[1]H. O. Guenther, "Comparison of Two Classes of Aggregate Production Planning Models under Stochastic Demand," *Engineering Cost and Production Economics*, April 1982, pp. 89–97.

The model is called linear because the mathematical equations employed to describe the particular system under study and the objective to be achieved are in the form of linear relations between the variables. A linear relationship between two or more variables is directly and precisely proportional.

A linear programming model enables managers to maximize an objective (such as profits) or minimize an objective (such as costs) by determining the future value of certain variables affecting the outcome. These variables are ones that the manager can control.

SPECIFIC APPLICATIONS OF LINEAR PROGRAMMING

Linear programming has been applied to a number of specific management problems:

1. *Production planning.* In production planning (the specific interest of this chapter), a manager must determine the levels of a number of production activities for the planning period. If a firm manufactures two products, both of which must go through the same three production processes, the manager faces a problem of this nature. The two products compete for time in the three production processes, and the task of the linear programming model would be to allocate the limited resources (available time in the three processes) in such a way as to produce the number of each product that will maximize the firm's profit. Linear programming is a general tool of analysis that managers have adapted to numerous production problems, such as inventory problems,[2] and to work force allocation decisions.[3]

Applications also have few geographical boundaries. Textile mills in India use linear programming to allocate loom time to alternative fabric types.[4] A number of improvements in productivity have resulted. For example, the linear programming method identified fabric styles that were unprofitable and subsequently have been dropped from the production plan. More important, the profitability of each loom increased because each was used to produce an optimal quantity of the most profitable fabrics. These positive results demonstrate the superiority of linear programming over the more traditional manual planning systems that dominate the Indian textile industry. Moreover, the social and economic consequences of increasing productivity in developing countries cannot be overestimated. Improved production planning can contribute to productivity gains that can, in turn, improve a country's standard of living, as reflected in India's experience.

2. *Feed mix.* Large farming organizations purchase and mix together several types of grains for different purposes. For one situation, the production manager must mix the different grains to produce feed for livestock. Each grain contains different amounts of several nutritional elements. The mixture must meet minimal nutritional requirements at the lowest cost. Linear programming is used to allocate the various grains so that the resulting

[2]Gabriel R. Bitran and Li Chang, "A Mathematical Programming Approach to a Deterministic Kanban System," *Management Science,* April 1987, pp. 427–41.

[3]Robert P. Crum and Mohammad Namazi, "Multi-Objective Linear Programming Techniques in Manpower Staff Assignments," *Akron Business and Economic Review,* September 1987, pp. 95–109.

[4]S. C. Bhatnagar, "Implementing Linear Programming in a Textile Unit: Some Problems and a Solution," *Interfaces,* April 1981, pp. 87–93.

mixture meets both nutritional and dietary specifications at the minimum cost. A number of different problems in agriculture lend themselves to application of linear programming.[5]

3. *Fluid blending.* This variation of the feed-mix problem requires the manager to blend fluids such as molten metals, chemicals, and crude oil into a finished product. Steel, chemical, and oil companies make wide use of linear programming models for problems of this type. Computing the right mixture of octane requirements in the blending of different gasolines is an example of such a problem in the oil industry.[6]

4. *Transportation.* The managers at many manufacturers and large retail chains must select transportation routes that minimize total shipping costs, given a number of supply sources (e.g., warehouses) and destinations (e.g., customers) and the cost of shipping a product from the source to each destination. This problem becomes even more complex if the firm has many warehouses and thousands of customers in different parts of the country. Other interesting transportation-related applications of linear programming include scheduling ports of call for oceangoing tankers[7] and scheduling optimal routes for school buses.[8]

5. *Advertising media mix.* In most organizations, a manager must sooner or later face a media mix problem. Given an advertising budget, how can the funds be allocated over the various advertising media to achieve maximum exposure of the product or service? Linear programming enables the manager to make these decisions regarding a number of media (e.g., five magazines) all competing for limited resources (the advertising budget). In fact, many advertising agencies use linear programming for problems of this type.

Although the above examples represent the most common applications, linear programming has proven its worth in handling many other practical problems. For example, Grant Hospital in Chicago uses linear programming to determine the optimal schedule for its staff of 300 nurses. Before the hospital adopted the technique, the scheduling task required over 20 hours of work each month. The job of ensuring that the schedule placed the right number of nurses with the right abilities in every ward and on every shift was complicated, especially when vacations and unexpected absences must be considered. Linear programming provides a solution in four hours and saves the hospital $80,000 a month because of improved scheduling efficiency. The hospital no longer needs to hire temporary nurses and schedule overtime.[9]

In British Columbia, water resource experts use linear programming to regulate water levels of lakes controlled by dams. The experts found that more electricity is generated by a dam when the lake behind it is full; however, when the lake overflows due to rain, much generating power is lost. Linear

---

[5]Keith Butterworth, "Practical Applications of Linear Programming in U.S. and Canadian Agriculture," *Journal of the Operations Research Society,* January 1985, pp. 99–108.

[6]Thomas E. Baker and Leon S. Lasdon, "Successive Linear Programming at Exxon," *Management Science,* March 1985, pp. 264–74.

[7]Raymond F. Boykin and Reuven R. Levary, "An Interactive Decision Support System for Analyzing Ship Voyage Alternatives," *Interfaces,* March–April 1985, pp. 81–84.

[8]A. J. Swersey and W. Ballard, "Scheduling School Buses," *Management Science,* July 1984, pp. 844–53.

[9]William M. Buckley, "The Right Mix: New Software Makes the Choice Much Easier," *The Wall Street Journal,* March 27, 1987, p. 24.

programming boosted electricity generation from dams by 5 percent by telling when and how to open and close the walls of the dam.[10] In other applications, linear programming has aided allocation of tax dollars to public projects,[11] space and time to tree development,[12] credit to customers,[13] dollars to investments,[14] and hospital resources to patients.[15]

AN EXAMPLE OF PRODUCTION PLANNING WITH LP

To illustrate the application of LP to production planning, assume that Apex Corporation manufactures two products, both of which must go through the same three production processes. The firm's manager, using linear programming, must decide on the optimal allocation of limited resources to produce the number of each product that will maximize profits. (This production and operations decision recurs frequently in repetitive manufacturing settings, such as textile manufacturing.)

The manager of the Apex Corporation has the choice of producing two different products, A and B. Furthermore, both products must go through three departments—X, Y, and Z—to be completed. Assume that department X is production, department Y is assembling, and department Z is packaging. Both products require the same amount of time in department X. Because of special features, however, product B requires twice as much time in department Y as product A does but less time in department Z. Product A contributes $10 per unit to profits, and product B contributes $12 per unit. Given these facts, the manager must determine a production program for the two products.

Key Elements of LP. In this particular problem, products A and B are the competing users; the available time in the three processes (production, assembling, and packaging) represents the limited resource. The capacity of this resource is limited because there is only so much time per day available in each of the three departments. If we assume that no expansion plans are called for, then this limitation is expressed as a set of constraints on the values that can be assigned to the competing products.

Apex Corporation's desired outcome is maximum profit. In linear programming, the desired outcome is formulated as a mathematical expression termed an *objective function*. The value of the objective function depends on the values of all other variables.

[10]Ibid.

[11]Colin O. Benjamin, "A Linear Goal Programming Model for Public-Sector Project Selection," *Journal of the Operations Research Society*, January 1985, pp. 13–24.

[12]T. H. Mattheiss and S. B. Land, "A Tree Breeding Strategy Based on Multiple Objective Linear Programming," *Interfaces*, September–October 1984, pp. 96–104.

[13]John D. Stowe, "An Integer Programming Solution for the Optimal Credit Investigation-Credit Granting Sequence," *Financial Management*, Summer 1985, pp. 66–76.

[14]Gordon J. Alexander and Bruce G. Resnick, "Using Linear and Goal Programming to Immunize Bond Portfolios," *Journal of Banking and Finance*, March 1985, pp. 35–54.

[15]William L. Hughes and Soliman Y. Soliman, "Short-Term Case Mix Management with Linear Programming," *Hospital and Health Services Administration*, January–February 1985, pp. 52–60; Eugene W. Grant, Jr., and Fred N. Hendron, Jr., "An Application of Linear Programming to Hospital Resource Allocation," *Journal of Health Care Marketing*, September 1987, pp. 69–72.

TABLE 18–1	**Apex Corporation's Resource Requirements and Constraints**

Linear programming depends on accurate assessment of available resources, product requirements for those resources, and capacity for each resource.

Department	Minutes Required per Unit		Capacity per Day in Minutes
	Product A	**Product B**	
X (production)	6	6	300
Y (assembling)	4	8	320
Z (packaging)	5	3	310
Profit contribution per unit	$10	$12	

The linear programming model selects the best alternative to optimize some objective (profit in this case), and all variables are assumed to be known with certainty. Also, in order to utilize the linear programming model, it is necessary to *assume certainty* (all factors are exact quantities) and to *simplify relationships* (assume linear relationships among variables) in the problem. These simplifying assumptions limit the application of LP to relatively certain environments. Table 18–1 depicts numerical values for the Apex Corporation example.

The LP Solution.   To begin solving this problem by means of linear programming, we must restate it in mathematical form. Since the goal is to maximize profit (P), the objective function can be stated:

$$\text{Objective function} = P = \$10A + \$12B$$

This equation is read: Profit equals $10 multiplied by the number of product A produced plus $12 multiplied by the number of product B produced. Assuming we produced and sold 20 of each, profit would equal $10 (20) plus $12 (20), or $440.

The next step is to express the constraints in mathematical form. The time used in the three departments cannot exceed the total time available per day in each of the departments. For example, the time needed to produce one product A times the number produced *plus* the time needed to produce one product B times the number produced must be equal to or less than the 300 minutes available each day in the production department (department X). Using the values from Table 18–1, the constraints for all three departments can be expressed as follows:

$$6A + 6B \leq 300 \text{ minutes in department X (production)}$$
$$4A + 8B \leq 320 \text{ minutes in department Y (assembling)}$$
$$5A + 3B \leq 310 \text{ minutes in department Z (packaging)}$$

Finally, every linear programming problem has a set of *nonnegativity* constraints. These are imposed to ensure that any derived values for A and B are positive since we cannot produce a minus quantity of a product. Thus, the optimal solution must have nonnegative values for A and B; expressed mathematically, $A \geq 0$ and $B \geq 0$.

Summarizing the problem in mathematical form yields:

$$\text{Maximum profit } (P) = \$10A + \$12B$$

subject to the following constraints:

$$6A + 6B \leq 300$$
$$4A + 8B \leq 320$$
$$5A + 3B \leq 310$$

and

$$A \geq 0$$
$$B \geq 0$$

After stating the problem mathematically, the next step is to construct a two-dimensional graph. With product A on the horizontal axis and product B on the vertical axis, plot each of the three constraint equations.

Figure 18–1 illustrates the inequalities (constraints) for each department on a separate graph and all together on a composite graph. The arrow associated with each line shows the direction indicated by the inequality signs (less than or equal to) in the constraint equations. Any combination of products A and B that lies in that area can be produced, assembled, or packaged without exceeding the available time in the particular department. Note that the nonnegativity constraints $A \geq 0$, $B \geq 0$ restrict us to zero or more units of products A and B.

All values for products A and B satisfying all three constraints are shown in the shaded region in Figure 18–1. In this particular problem, any pair of values for products A and B that satisfies the constraints in departments X and Y also satisfies department Z. To complete one unit of product A or B, work must be done in all three departments. Therefore, the best combination of products A and B falls within the shaded area in Figure 18–1. Any combination in this *feasibility space* will not exceed the maximum time in either department X, Y, or Z.

The construction of Figure 18–1 is the first step in solving the problem by the graphical method. The goal is to locate at least one point from the shaded area in the figure that will maximize the objective function.

Finding the Optimal Solution.   The problem can be solved by selecting any arbitrary profit figure and determining how many units of product A alone or product B alone would be needed to earn such a profit. Any profit figure will suffice, but common sense tells us to select a point within the feasibility space in Figure 18–1. Let us assume a profit figure of $300. Since product A contributes $10, we would need 30 units in order to earn a profit of $300. If we manufacture only product B, we would need 25 units in order to earn a $300 profit, since product B contributes a profit of $12. If we locate these two points in the feasibility space and join them, we obtain what is known as a $300 equal-profit line, which is nothing more than the locus of all points (all combinations of products A and B) that will yield a profit of $300. This is illustrated in Figure 18–2 as the dotted line between 30 on the A axis and 25 on the B axis.

We can continue to construct these lines for higher and higher profit figures, illustrated in Figure 18–2 by dotted lines, as long as we remain within the feasibility space. We are forced to stop when we reach a boundary line or

FIGURE 18–1   Constraint Equations

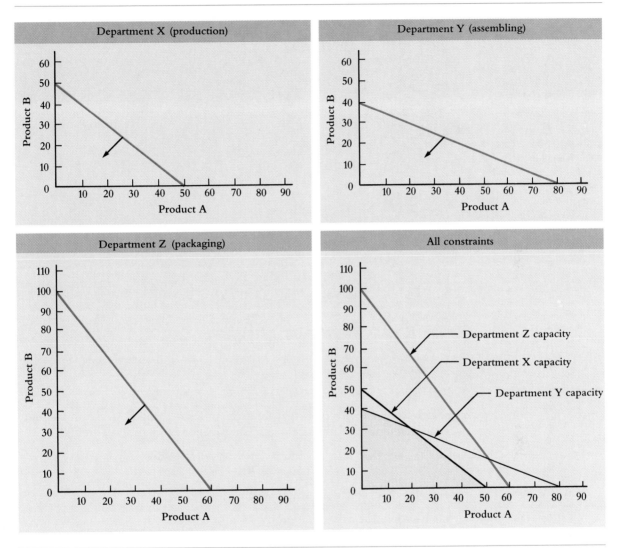

Once the production planning problem is expressed in mathematical terms, the equations can be plotted to reach a solution.

corner point of the feasibility space. The highest combination still having a point in the feasibility space provides the optimal value of the objective function.

The equal-profit line farthest from the origin and still within the feasibility space occurs at the intersection of the department X and department Y constraints—at point *H* in Figure 18–2. Although there are an infinite number of solutions within the feasibility space, point *H* provides the optimal solution.

The coordinates of point *H* can be read directly from the graph if it is constructed perfectly, but they are usually found by solving simultaneously the

FIGURE 18–2   Equal-Profit Lines

Equal-profit lines reflect the total value of the objective function for each feasible combination of the two products. Only one of the equal-profit lines provides the maximum value for the objective function.

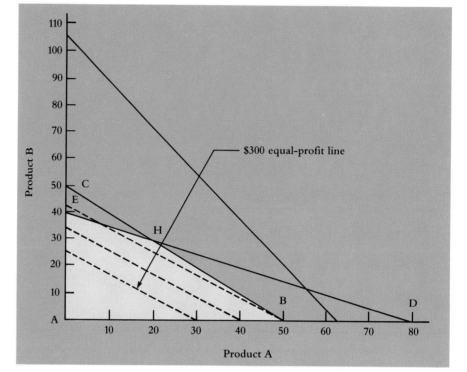

equations of the two lines that intersect to form point *H,* which is the only point common to both equations. The equations to be solved are:

$$\text{Line } BC: 6A + 6B = 300$$
$$\text{Line } DE: 4A + 8B = 320$$

To solve these equations simultaneously,

a. Multiply the first equation by 4.
b. Multiply the second equation by -3.
c. Add the results.

$$
\begin{array}{r}
4(6A + 6B = 300) = \quad 24A + \quad 24B = 1{,}200 \\
-3(4A + 8B = 320) = -12A + (-24B) = -960 \\
\hline
12A \qquad\qquad = \quad 240 \\
A \qquad\qquad = \quad 20
\end{array}
$$

d. Substitute 20 for *A* in the second equation:

$$
\begin{array}{r}
4A + 8B = 320 \\
4(20) + 8B = 320 \\
80 + 8B = 320 \\
8B = 240 \\
B = 30
\end{array}
$$

Point *H* therefore, is, (20, 30).

We can test the four points that delineate the feasibility space in order to determine the highest dollar profit.

$$
\begin{aligned}
\text{Point } A \ (0,0) \quad &= 10(0) \ + 12(0) \ = \$0 \\
\text{Point } B \ (50,0) \quad &= 10(50) + 12(0) \ = \$500 \\
\text{Point } E \ (0,40) \quad &= 10(0) \ + 12(40) = \$480 \\
\text{Point } H \ (20, 30) &= 10(20) + 12(30) = \$560
\end{aligned}
$$

The point that provides the most profit is point *H,* where we manufacture 20 units of product *A* and 30 units of product *B* for a profit of $560.

THE VALUE OF LINEAR PROGRAMMING

Properly constructed linear programming models provide managers with three specific benefits:

1. *Improved planning.* Linear programming can, with the aid of a computer, quickly solve a problem containing over 500 equations and 1,000 variables. This incredible capability means that linear programming can expand the analytic ability, and therefore the planning ability, of a manager. It permits an exhaustive search of numerous alternative solutions and systematically searches for the optimum one. Previously, time constraints might have permitted examination of only a few possible alternative solutions when numerous potential solutions actually existed.

The production planning decision is crucial in manufacturing. The outcome of the decision determines how the scarce resources are to be allocated to the alternative products. The LP method is a very flexible method that has general applicability. As the service sector of the American economy becomes more important, managers of service organizations have discovered LP as a way to improve efficiency. The banking industry in particular has found LP to be especially useful.[16] For example, Central Carolina Bank and Trust Company (CCB) uses a linear programming model for financial planning. The model determines the optimal bank "inventory" of assets (sources of bank earnings) and liabilities and equities (sources of bank costs). The model generates target balance sheets and rank orderings of the relative profitability of the bank's services. With this information, bank executives make decisions that maximize the difference between total yields on all assets and total costs of all liabilities. In order to maximize the difference between yields and costs, it is necessary to specify the constraints that must be observed. Banking is subject to many operational, legal, and policy constraints. Examples of constraints include (1) existing demand for bank services, (2) policies that reflect prudent bank practices (e.g., limits on how much the bank will invest in relatively risky securities), (3) legal and regulatory constraints, such as legal reserve requirements, and (4) necessity of maintaining a level of liquidity to meet short-run cash requirements. These constraints limit the distribution of funds in the cash and liability categories.[17]

[16]Thomas O. Davenport and H. David Sherman, "Measuring Branch Profitability," *Bankers Magazine,* September–October 1987, pp. 34–38.

[17]Sheldon D. Balbirer and David Shaw, "An Application of Linear Programming to Bank Financial Planning," *Interfaces,* October 1981, pp. 77–83; Sheldon D. Balbirer and David Shaw, "The Evolution of Financial Planning Models at a Commercial Bank," *Interfaces,* November–December 1984, pp. 67–69.

MANAGEMENT FOCUS

Linear Programming Applications in a Small Manufacturing Firm

Producing a fine American wooden cabinet is very much a challenge today. Because foreign competition is fierce, it is imperative that domestic producers minimize costs, yet not reduce quality. Wellborn Cabinets of Ashland, Alabama, recently employed linear programming to achieve these goals. Before, Wellborn purchased a mixture of 65 percent expensive, high-grade and 35 percent cheaper, low-grade logs. However, after subjecting procurement costs, lumber yields, and processing costs to an LP analysis, Wellborn made a discovery. Wellborn could lower material costs by 32 percent, expand its raw material market area, and sustain quality by only using lower-grade logs. The $412,000 annual savings definitely did not go against the grain.

The use of linear programming reduced material costs by 32 percent at Wellborn Cabinets.

Source: Honorio F. Carino and Clinton H. LeNoir, Jr., "Optimizing Wood Procurement in Cabinet Manufacturing," *Interfaces*, March–April 1988, pp. 10–19.

The Management Focus describes the application of linear programming to planning in a relatively small manufacturing firm.

2. *Improved decisions.* Linear programming models can also improve management decisions by quickly finding the optimal solution for a problem under a variety of conditions. For example, after a solution has been selected using an LP model, the manager may alter or add a constraint or change the objective. The computer can quickly provide a new solution under the revised set of conditions. Only a manager, however, can determine which of the two solutions is better.

3. *Improved understanding of problems.* Since linear programming models are highly efficient ways of analyzing very complex problems, they also improve a manager's comprehension and an appreciation of these complex problems. By structuring a problem, LP models enable the manager to comprehend more easily the effects of alternative assumptions. They not only provide a solution but also enable the manager to understand the problem.

PLANNING NONREPETITIVE PRODUCTION: PERT

Techniques used to combine resources or to control activities so that plans are carried out as stated are called *network models.* Such models are especially suited for projects that are not of a routine or repetitive nature. Coordination is needed for these projects, to ensure that prerequisite tasks are completed before subsequent tasks are started. For nonrepetitive projects, some method is needed to avoid unnecessary conflicts and delays by keeping track of all events and activities—and their interrelationships. Network models provide the means to achieve these purposes. As such, they are valuable aids in managerial planning and controlling.

Program evaluation and review technique (PERT) is a type of network model that minimizes conflicts, delays, and interruptions in a project by coordinating the various parts of the overall job. PERT's goal is to complete the job on schedule. It does not solve a manager's problems, but it does help identify what the problems are and what solutions are realistic, as well as aid in anticipating problems.

PERT is especially useful for nonrepetitive projects—ones that the manager has not previously encountered and is not likely to encounter again. Nonrepetitive projects pose a special problem: How can the manager learn to manage work that is done only once? Such projects have two major characteristics. First, they are extremely complex in that hundreds or thousands of interdependent tasks must be accomplished; second, most of the tasks are single-occurrence tasks that are not likely to be repeated. In contrast to repetitive processes (such as the mass production of a product or the periodic reorders of inventory for which management has past experience, standards, and costs), historical data is not available for nonrepetitive projects. However, each task in a one-of-a-kind program must be performed on time and be of the necessary quality, just as with routine work. In other words, management must still plan and control nonroutine operations. PERT is extremely helpful in such situations because it enables a manager to think through a project in its entirety. As such, it usually results in a more optimum utilization of resources.

SPECIFIC APPLICATIONS OF PERT

PERT (and variations of it) is probably one of the most widely used production planning models. It was developed through the cooperation of the U.S. Navy and the management consulting firm of Booz Allen & Hamilton Inc. Introduced by the Special Projects Office of the U.S. Navy in 1958 on the Polaris missile project, PERT was widely credited with helping to reduce by two years the time originally estimated for the completion of the engineering and development programs for the missile. By identifying the longest paths through all of the tasks necessary to complete the project, it enabled the program managers to concentrate efforts on those tasks that vitally affected the total project time. PERT has spread rapidly throughout the defense and space industries. Today, almost every major government agency involved in the space program utilizes PERT. In fact, many government agencies require contractors to use PERT and other network models in planning and controlling their work on government contracts.

While the areospace business faces peculiar problems, one-of-a-kind development work is also an important element in many other kinds of organiza-

---

MANAGEMENT FOCUS

PERT Goes to the International Olympics

History does not record much about the first Olympiad. However, if Hercules had attempted to coordinate over 30,000 activities—food, security, transportation, assistants, and medical backup for thousands of competitors—relating to the 1988 Winter Games in Calgary, Canada, he might have cried uncle. A company named Project Software and Development, however, rose to the Olympian task. Employing PERT-based software developed for the space shuttle, PSD broke down the games into 15-minute segments. PSD also developed an integrated computer network to monitor the Olympic activities. Although a few glitches occurred, the games were completed in a manner that would have pleased Hercules.

Source: Nell Margolis, "Software Firm Tackles Olympian Project Management Task," *Computerworld*, February 22, 1988, pp. 85ff.

---

tions and industries. In addition to developing space vehicles and putting a man on the moon, PERT has also been utilized successfully in:

1. Constructing new plants, buildings, and hospitals.
2. Designing new automobiles.
3. Coordinating the numerous activities (production, marketing, and so forth) involved in managing a new product or project.[18]
4. Planning and scheduling space probes.[19]
5. Managing accounts receivable.[20]
6. Coordinating the installation of large-scale computer systems.
7. Coordinating ship construction and aircraft repairs.

In addition to engineering-oriented applications, PERT has been used to coordinate the numerous activities associated with mergers and acquisitions and with economic planning in underdeveloped countries. The technique has also contributed to planning large conventions and meetings. The Management Focus describes PERT's application to a special type of a convention: the Olympics.

---

[18]Gary L. Wolf and Warren C. Hauck, "PERT/CPM: A Tool for Managing Projects," *Industrial Management,* January–February 1985, pp. 22–25; James A. G. Krupp, "Project Plan Charting: An Effective Alternative," *Production and Inventory Management,* First Quarter 1984, pp. 31–47.

[19]James E. Zerega, "Down and Up with PERT at Goddard," *Astronautics and Aeronautics,* February 1976, p. 65.

[20]Ann Wiles and Ronald M. Horowitz, "PERT Charts Pinpoint Problems in Accounts Receivable Management," *Healthcare and Financial Management,* September 1984, pp. 38–40.

FIGURE 18–3

FIGURE 18–3   Two Events and One Activity

The basic building blocks of PERT are events (circles 1 and 2) and activities (arrow).

EXAMPLES OF PRODUCTION PLANNING WITH PERT

Using PERT and other network models involves two fundamental steps: (1) constructing the network and (2) estimating activity time requirements.

Constructing the Network.   PERT networks are developed around two key concepts: activities and events. An **activity** is the work necessary to complete a particular event. An **event** is an accomplishment at a particular point in time and consumes no time. In PERT diagrams, an event is designated with a circle and an activity as an arrow connecting two circles. These two concepts are shown in Figure 18–3.

Before a PERT network can be constructed, the activities and events that will be represented on the diagram must be identified. Table 18–2 describes the activities and events required to manufacture a prototype aircraft engine.

The information from Table 18–2 is represented by the network model shown in Figure 18–4. Examination indicates that event 1 is the network

TABLE 18–2   Description of PERT Activities and Events for Manufacturing of Prototype Aircraft Engine

The effectiveness of PERT depends on accurate determination of all events and activities.

Activity		Event		
Arrow	Description	Prerequisite	Circle	Description
1–2	Develop engineering specifications.		2	Specifications completed.
2–3	Obtain test models.	1–2	3	Test models obtained.
2–4	Locate suppliers of component parts.	1–2	4	Suppliers located.
3–5	Develop production plans.	2–3	5	Plans completed.
5–6	Begin subassembly 1.	3–5	6	Subassembly 1 completed.
4–6	Place orders for component parts and await receipt.	2–4	6	Component parts received.
6–7	Begin subassembly 2.	5–6 and 4–6	7	Subassembly 2 completed.
7–8	Begin final assembly.	6–7	8	Engine completed.

FIGURE **18–4**   PERT Network for Information in Table 18–2

A PERT network chart enables managers to perceive complex problems in relatively simple graphic form.

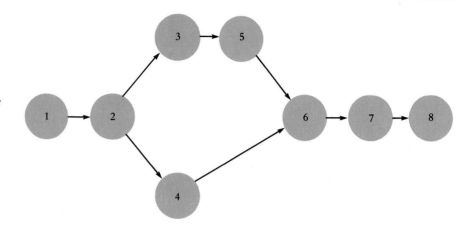

beginning event since there are no activities leading to it and event 8 is the network ending event since there are no activities leading away from it. Note also that event 2 is the beginning event for two activities and event 6 is the ending event for two activities as well as the beginning event for one activity.

PERT emphasizes identifying events and activities with enough precision so that it is possible to monitor accomplishment as the project proceeds. There are four basic phases in constructing a PERT network:

1. Define each necessary activity.
2. Estimate how long each activity will take.
3. Construct the network.
4. Find the **critical path**—that is, the longest path, in time, from the beginning event to the ending event.

All events and activities must be sequenced in the network under a strict set of logical rules (e.g., no event can be considered complete until all predecessor events have been completed) that allows for the determination of the critical path.[21]

The paramount variable in a PERT network is time.[22] Estimating how long each activity will take is extremely difficult, since the manager may have no experience to rely on.

---

[21]For complex projects, networking is a difficult task better left to trained individuals. The reader interested in networking principles should consult Louis R. Shaffer, J. B. Ritter, and W. L. Meyer, *Critical Path Method* (New York: McGraw-Hill, 1965); Jerome D. Wiest and Ferdinand K. Levy, *Management Guide to PERT/CPM* (Englewood Cliffs, N.J.: Prentice-Hall, 1977).

[22]D. Sculli, "The Completion Time of PERT Networks," *Journal of the Operations Research Society,* February 1983, p. 155.

Time to complete an activity is the critical variable in the PERT technique.

Estimating Activity Time Requirements.   Since PERT projects are usually unique, they are subject to a great deal of uncertainty. PERT is designed to deal specifically with the problem of determining time estimates.

For example, assume you are trying to estimate how long it will take to complete a term project for your management class. You know that one activity will be to collect certain information. If all goes well, you believe that you could complete this one activity in eight weeks. However, if you encounter numerous obstacles (dates, parties, illness, material not available in the library), this one activity will take much longer to complete. Estimating the time needed to complete your term project becomes a complex process when you try to account for the delays that might occur.

For PERT projects, *three time estimates are required for each activity.* The individual or group chosen to make each time estimate should be that individual or group most closely connected with and responsible for the particular activity under consideration. The three time estimates needed are:

Optimistic time *(a):* The time in which the activity can be completed if everything goes exceptionally well and no obstacles or problems are encountered.

Most likely time *(m):* The most realistic estimate of how long an activity might take. If the activity were repeated, most likely time would equal the average completion time.

Pessimistic time *(b):* The time that would be required if everything goes wrong and numerous obstacles and problems are encountered.

It is extremely difficult to deal simultaneously with the optimistic time, the most likely time, and the pessimistic time. Fortunately a way has been developed to arrive at one time estimate. An **expected time** (t_e) can be estimated satisfactorily for each activity by using the following formula:

$$t_e = \frac{a + 4m + b}{6}$$

Note that in the formula for computing the expected time (t_e), the weight that is given to the most likely time (m) is much greater than the weight given to the optimistic and pessimistic times, since each of them has only a small chance of occurring. Also note that optimistic and pessimistic time each receive the same weight.

To illustrate the use of this formula, recall the prototype-engine project described in Table 18–2. Suppose you estimate that three weeks is the most likely completion time (m) for the activity of developing engineering specifications. However, you feel that there is a small chance that the activity might be completed in one week. Therefore, the optimistic time (a) is 1. You also feel there is a slight chance things could go wrong and it would take eight weeks to develop specifications. Therefore, the pessimistic time (b) is 8.

In order to compute the expected time from the three time estimates, we must determine at what time there is a 50–50 chance of completing the activity. The expected time formula provides that figure. The time estimates are as follows:

> Optimistic time *(a)*   = 1 week
> Most likely time *(m)* = 3 weeks
> Pessimistic time *(b)*   = 8 weeks

Substituting these time estimates into the formula yields:

$$\text{Expected time} = t_e = \frac{1 + 4(3) + 8}{6} = 3.5$$

Thus, there is a 50–50 chance that the information will be collected in 3.5 weeks.

The expected time may be either longer or shorter than the most likely time, depending on the three time estimates. To illustrate an expected time shorter than the most likely time, assume the following three time estimates for developing engineering specifications:

> Optimistic time *(a)*   = 2 weeks
> Most likely time *(m)* = 4 weeks
> Pessimistic time *(b)*   = 5 weeks

Substituting these values into the formula yields:

$$\text{Expected time} = t_e = \frac{2 + 4(4) + 5}{6} = 3.83$$

In this case, the expected time of 3.83 weeks is shorter than the most likely time of 4 weeks.

FIGURE 18–5   PERT Network: Time Estimates for Each Activity

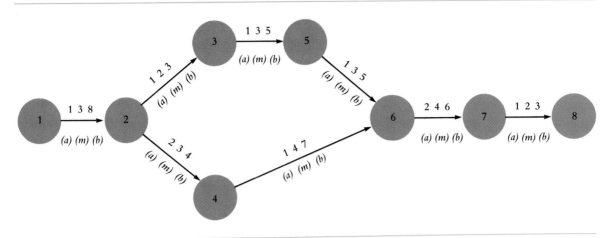

PERT networks become more complicated when time estimates are included.

When there is a great uncertainty in a project, this three-way time estimate is an important advantage of PERT. While it does introduce a complicating feature, it recognizes realities that can cause problems in planning for the future. The three-way time estimate usually results in a greater degree of honesty and accuracy in forecasting time. If nothing else, it provides the manager with the opportunity to be aware of and to evaluate the degree of uncertainty involved, especially along the critical path.

The completed PERT networks for the aircraft engine prototype project are shown in Figures 18–5 and 18–6. Figure 18–5 shows the three time estimates for each of the eight activities. Figure 18–6A shows the expected time for each activity. Obviously, expected times are only estimations. But if carefully constructed, they form a solid base for subsequent management decisions.

Critical Path.   The critical path is the most time-consuming sequence of activities from the beginning event to the ending event.[23] Therefore, the most crucial calculation in a PERT network is for the critical path.[24] Using two steps, we can calculate the critical path for the network shown in Figure 18–6A. First, we must identify each discrete path from beginning to end. In Figure 18–6B, two paths are shown. Second, we must sum the expected times for each discrete path. Path 1 is expected to be completed in 17.5 weeks (3.5 + 2 + 3 + 3 + 4 + 2); path 2 is expected to be completed in 16.5 weeks (3.5 + 3 + 4 + 4 + 2). Path 1, which takes 17.5 weeks, is the critical path.

Path 1 is "critical" because any delay in the completion of its activities will delay the total project. Yet, a delay of up to one week can occur on path 2, and

[23]Bajis M. Dodin and Salah E. Elmaghraby, "Approximating the Criticality Indices in the Activities in PERT Networks," *Management Science,* February 1985, pp. 207–23.

[24]Richard J. Schonberger, "Why Projects Are 'Always' Late: A Rationale Based on Manual Simulation of a PERT/CPM Network," *Interfaces,* October 1981, pp. 66–70, notes the problems associated with assuming that time estimates for each activity are independent of all other activities.

FIGURE 18–6   Expected Time (t_e) for Each Activity

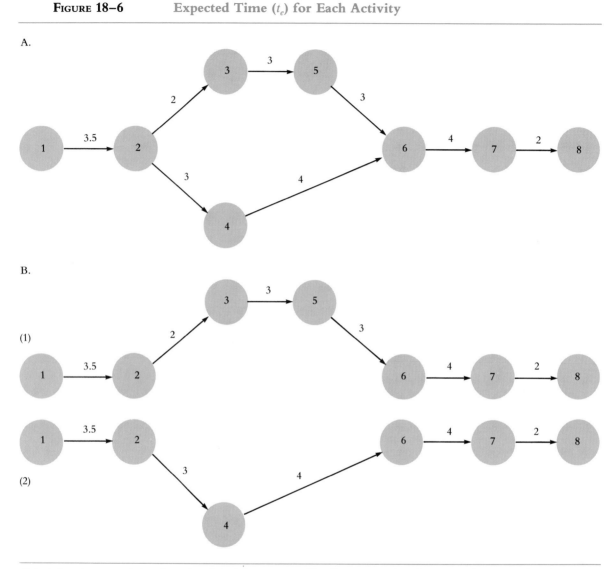

A.

B.

(1)

(2)

Calculating the expected time for each activity helps managers identify ways to reduce the time it takes to complete the project.

project will still be completed in 17.5 weeks. Path 1 is critical for another reason. If the project must be completed sooner than the expected 17.5 weeks, management can see that additional resources must be allocated to it rather than to path 2.

In this example, the project network is rather simple; it has only two paths, and the critical path is readily identifiable. Real-world problems are seldom so simple.[25] As projects become more complex, the development of PERT

[25]Bajis M. Dodin, "Determining the K Most Critical Paths in PERT Networks," *Operations Research,* July–August 1984, pp. 859–77.

networks also becomes more complex. In fact, were it not for developments in computer programming, the use of PERT would be seriously hampered.[26]

THE VALUE OF PERT

Properly constructed, PERT and other network models provide direct aid to managers in two important areas.[27]

Improved Planning.   Network models help managers handle the uncertainties involved in projects where no standard cost and time data are available. Because it shows the manager the interconnections of tasks and provides estimated times, PERT increases the manager's ability to plan an optimum schedule before starting work.[28] In other words, while a project is still in the planning stage, management can take a number of steps to reduce the total time needed to complete the project. Time reductions can be brought about in a number of ways:

1.   By reducing the expected time on the longest path through the network (the critical path) by transferring resources or additional funds from those activities that can afford it since they do not take as long to complete.
2.   By eliminating some part of the project that previously might have been considered desirable but not necessary.
3.   By adding more resources—men or machines.
4.   By purchasing a component if the time required to produce the component is too long.
5.   By changing some work to parallel activities that had previously been planned in a series.

Better Control—A Major Advantage.   The planning necessary to construct the network contributes significantly to the definition and ultimate *concurrent control* of the project. In the case of PERT, the construction of the network is a very demanding task that forces the planner to visualize the number, different kinds, and sequence of all the necessary activities. This kind of thinking cannot help but be a benefit in and of itself in most cases.

Throughout the early days of space exploration, Goddard Space Flight Center (GSFC) made extensive use of PERT as its principal schedule planning and control tool in flight projects.[29] Each project was assigned a schedule team of from two to four PERT analysts to draft and update PERT networks. However, budget and manpower reductions forced Goddard to reduce the size of schedule teams and the use of PERT. Goddard was forced to substitute less detailed methods of schedule planning and control. One result was a loss of monitoring information necessary for controlling key activities in a project.

[26]Mickey Williamson, "Project Management Software," *Computerworld,* December 8, 1986, pp. 55ff.

[27]D. M. Dougherty and D. B. Stephens, "The Lasting Qualities of PERT," *R&D Management,* January 1984, pp. 47–56.

[28]Mitchell H. Goldstein, "Project Management Systems," *National Productivity Review,* Summer 1986, pp. 290–92.

[29]Zerega, "Down and Up with PERT at Goddard."

In the early 1970s, a number of computer graphic programs became available. These programs have the capability of producing high-quality and accurate PERT network drawings in a few hours. PERT analysts simply sketch out a network, put the information in a proper format, submit the data for computer processing, and in a few hours receive a complete, finished network. The critical paths are identified and highlighted in the computer-produced network, and any subsequent updates or corrections can be quickly processed.

Since the adoption of the computer graphic program, the use of PERT has increased to a point exceeding the use in the early 1960s. The time and manpower-consuming aspects of PERT have been virtually eliminated. A PERT analyst can now handle five times more PERT networks than was possible using manual methods.

Used effectively, PERT can be valuable as both an internal and external control device. For internal control, it provides time schedules for each activity. Networks can therefore be revised if unforeseen difficulties arise. Resources can be shifted and activities rescheduled with minimal delay in the outcome of the project.

Financial controllers in a variety of organizational settings have applied PERT to their operations problems. Hospitals, in particular, have found PERT a useful technique for controlling costs[30] because the rising cost of health care encourages health care managers to search for ways and means to manage resources more efficiently. The more efficiently they manage resources, the more competitive they are in obtaining clients for their hospitals and clinics. One opportunity for efficient management of resources is the collection of patients' accounts receivable. The sooner an account is collected, the sooner the cash is available for other uses. Hospital managers have discovered that PERT enables them to identify the events and activities related to accounts receivable collection cycles for different types of patients. The PERT network for the cycle begins when the patient is physician-referred or self-referred and ends when the bill for services rendered is collected. Between the beginning and ending events are other events and activities for which critical times can be estimated.

Most hospitals require three distinct networks for each of three distinct patient types: inpatients, outpatients, and emergency room patients. Because each of these three types utilizes different hospital services, each requires its own PERT network. Nevertheless, the analysis for each is the same: Managers identify the critical path and then search for ways to reduce the times along the critical paths. Any reduction in time in the critical path from referral to collection represents a cost saving in that the hospital has cash rather than a promise to pay cash.

For external control, in projects where subcontractors are used, the necessity for meeting scheduled dates can be stressed by showing the subcontractor the negative effects a delay will have on the entire project. In projects involving subcontractors, it is vital that these firms meet their scheduled delivery dates. For example, the Polaris project involved some 250 prime contractors and almost 10,000 subcontractors. The failure of any one of these

---

[30]Wiles and Horowitz, "PERT Charts Pinpoint Problems."

subcontractors to deliver a piece of hardware on schedule could have stalled the entire project.

Program evaluation review technique is a powerful technique that has numerous applications in production/operations management. It and linear programming are the bases for more sophisticated techniques that have enabled managers to deal with the complex issues associated with the production/operations function in business. This chapter has briefly surveyed these issues to introduce the reader to the possibilities of modern management science.

SUMMARY OF KEY POINTS

- Production planning involves determining the quantity of each product to manufacture, given the relative *profitability* of each product and the availability of scarce resources. It is a recurring decision that managers make with the aid of information, knowledge, and methods such as linear programming and program evaluation review technique.

- Linear programming (LP) is widely used to determine optimal production schedules when management must allocate scarce resources to alternative products. Each product competes, in a sense, with other products for the productive resources of the firm.

- Linear programmming has applications for a variety of settings in which resources must be allocated. Production planning is the focus of this chapter, but LP can be applied to decisions involving optimal feed mixes, fuel blendings, transportation routes, and an advertising media mix.

- Management can determine an optimal production schedule if the decision support system provides (1) the profit contribution of each product, (2) the resource requirements of each product, and (3) the availability of resources to be allocated to the products. In addition, the LP method is most applicable if the relationships among the different variables are linear and if the required data are fairly certain.

- The value of linear programming is to improve managerial decisions, plans, and understanding of the problem. The process of setting up LP solutions requires the manager to thoroughly analyze the elements of the problem under study.

- Many firms produce a single, nonrepetitive product or project. Unlike the multiproduct firm, the single, nonrepetitive product firm must find the optimal allocation of resources to activities that are necessary to complete the product or project.

- A class of management science techniques termed network models is applicable to nonrepetitive production planning. Of this class of models, program evaluation review technique (PERT) has enjoyed the greatest popularity among production planners.

- PERT has been a useful aid in planning new plants, building dams, and other large-scale construction projects. It is also useful for planning new product developments, sales campaigns, computer installations, and other projects that involve sequences of activities.

- To implement a PERT solution, the decision support system must provide data that enable managers to define the network of activities and the time required to complete those activities. Management can then determine the critical path—the longest path, in terms in time, through the network. Resources can be allocated to the critical path to expedite completion of the project.

- The value of PERT is that it assists management in planning and controlling large-scale projects. A completed network of activities enables management to know better how resources should be allocated among the activities. The network also provides standards for gauging progress toward project completion.

DISCUSSION AND REVIEW QUESTIONS

1. Explain the two general types of production systems and give examples of each one.
2. Why is it useful to think of production planning as a problem that involves the allocation of scarce resources to alternative products or services?
3. The text discusses a number of different production planning problems for which linear programming solutions are available. Describe what these problems have in common that makes them amenable to linear programming.
4. Illustrate the practical value of linear programming by relating the benefits to the planning and controlling functions of management.

5. Helene Manufacturers, Inc. produces two different models of professional hair dryers. Dryer A contributes $20 profit, and dryer B contributes $10. In order to be completed, each dryer must go through three manufacturing processes, as shown in Exhibit 1. Using the graphic method, find the optimum combination of the products that would maximize total profit. Suppose the company could concentrate all its efforts on one model. Would this change the solution?

EXHIBIT 1   Hair Dryers' Manufacturing Processes: Time Requirements

Department	Time Required		Available Time
	Dryer A	Dryer B	
Department X	4	9	180
Department Y	5	6	150
Department Z	5	14	175

---

6. What are the specific characteristics of production problems for which PERT is an applicable technique?
7. Cite some nonrepetitive problems, other than those discussed in the chapter, for which PERT would be useful as a planning and control tool. Use your personal experiences if necessary. Which of these problems would cause you the greatest difficulty in determining expected times of completion?
8. Assume that you have been assigned a term project in one of your management courses. It is your task to collect data for the report from both library sources and personal interviews with local business-people. You have a total of 10 weeks in which to complete the assignment. List the activities and their optimistic, most likely, and pessimistic times and construct a PERT network for the project.

9. Place the following activities in the form of a PERT network:

    a. Remove carburetor.
    b. Rotate tires.
    c. Put on snow tires.
    d. Tune motor.
    e. Clean and replace air filter.
    f. Test drive car.
    g. Remove air filter.
    h. Complete tune-up.

10. Assume that you have just received word to begin production on a special device that your company will make for the government. You have developed the PERT network for the project and the time estimates for each activity (Exhibit 2). Determine the critical path.

EXHIBIT 2   PERT Network for Government Project

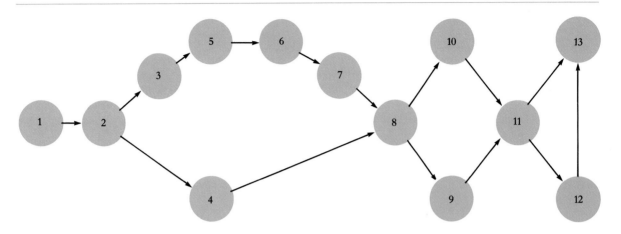

	Time Estimates (Weeks)		
		Most	
Activity	Optimistic	Likely	Pessimistic
1–2	1	2	3
2–3	2	4	6
2–4	2	4	6
3–5	1	3	5
4–8	2	4	6
5–6	4	7	10
6–7	1	2	3
7–8	1	2	3
8–9	1	2	3
8–10	1	2	3
9–11	2	3	4
10–11	3	4	5
11–12	1	2	3
11–13	4	6	8
12–13	1	1	1

ADDITIONAL REFERENCES

Aronofsky, J. S.; J. M. Dutton; and **M. T. Tay-yabkhan.** *Managerial Planning with Linear Programming.* New York: John Wiley & Sons, 1978.

Arranovich, D.; T. M. Cook; G. D. Langston; and **F. Sutherland.** "A Decision Support System for Fleet Management." *Interfaces,* June 1982, pp. 1–6.

Bazaraa, M. S., and **J. J. Jarvis.** *Linear Programming and Network Analysis.* New York: John Wiley & Sons, 1977.

Beale, E. M. L. "The Evolution of Mathematical Programming Systems." *Journal of the Operations Research Society,* May 1985, pp. 357–66.

Best, M. J. *Linear Programming.* Englewood Cliffs, N.J.: Prentice-Hall, 1985.

Boesch, F. T., ed. *Large-Scale Networks: Theory and Design.* New York: IEEE Press, 1976.

Borgwardt, K. M. *The Simplex Method: A Probabilistic Analysis.* New York: Springer-Verlag, 1987.

Feiring, B. R. *Linear Programming: An Introduction.* Beverly Hills, Calif.: Sage Publications, 1986.

Hilal, S. S., and **W. Erikson.** "Matching Supplies to Save Lives: Linear Programming the Production of Heart Valves." *Interfaces,* December 1981, pp. 48–55.

Kao, E. P. C., and **M. Queyranne.** "Budgeting Costs of Nursing in a Hospital." *Management Science,* May 1985, pp. 608–21.

Lester, A. *Project Planning and Control.* London: Butterworth Scientific Press, 1982.

Luh, J. Y. S., and **C. S. Lin.** "Scheduling Parallel Operations in Automation for Minimum Execution Time Based on PERT." *Computers and Industrial Engineering 9,* no. 2 (1985), pp. 149–64.

Ozan, T. *Applied Mathematical Programming for Engineering and Production Management.* Englewood Cliffs, N.J.: Prentice-Hall, 1986.

Park, K. S., and **D. K. Yun.** "Optimal Scheduling of Periodic Activities." *Operations Research,* May–June 1985, pp. 690–95.

Patel, H. M. "The Transportation Technique Solves Linear Programming Problem." *Industrial Engineering,* March 1988, pp. 16–23.

Randolph, P. H., and **H. D. Meeks.** *Applied Linear Optimization.* Columbus, Ohio: Grid Publishing, 1978.

Rothenberg, R. I. *Linear Programming.* New York: Elsevier–North Holland Publishing, 1980.

Schriver, A. *Theory of Linear and Integer Programming.* New York: John Wiley & Sons, 1986.

Wendell, R. E. "The Tolerance Approach to Sensitivity Analysis in Linear Programming." *Management Science,* May 1985, pp. 564–78.

CASE 18–1 Linear Programming in Furniture Production

A furniture manufacturer had recently developed and marketed a line of self-assembly furniture. Each item (chair, table, sofa) in the line consisted of a set of rectangular, laminated plywood panels, along with the required metal fittings and hardware. The customer purchased the furniture unassembled and unfinished, but no special carpentry skills were required to assemble and finish the items.

The relatively low price, low margin, and initially low sales volume dictated high concern for cost savings at the manufacturer's sites. A major expense factor, in relation to other costs, was found to be in the panel-cutting operation. Specifically, production management believed that there was excessive waste associated with cutting the plywood panels required for each item in the line.

The complete line required 20 different panel sizes, each cut from a larger sheet of plywood. The lamination process was such that only one size of the larger plywood sheet could be used. Thus, the production problem was to determine the most efficient cutting patterns for producing the 20 different panel sizes from the laminated plywood sheets. The most efficient patterns would be ones in which there were no leftover, unusable pieces of plywood.

Of course, production management recognized that these patterns were unattainable. Nevertheless, they believed that the present cutting patterns produced excessive scrap. The basis for that belief was rather subjective. Management had had little experience in the production of such furniture under these conditions. Obviously the cutting of panels, spindels, legs, arms, and other parts of furniture from stock lumber was as old as the craft of carpentry itself. Yet the production of furniture in a manner roughly equivalent to an assembly-line process was new to the company's experience. Its managers recognized that a vast number of cutting patterns existed, but they were skeptical that the ones devised by a veteran employee in the cutting room were optimal.

The company contacted a group of production management professors at a nearby university and requested a review of the cutting patterns. The group arrived on the scene and immediately recognized that the problem could be set up in a linear programming format, with the objective function stated in terms of minimizing the quantity of scrap material.

The group constructed a linear programming model and then compared the results obtained from it to those obtained by the veteran employee. The comparison indicated that waste could be reduced by some 2 percent at a net cost saving of $6,000 per year through use of the linear programming solutions. These figures were not impressive, as the total annual production costs of this company were in the millions of dollars. The production manager expressed the view that the cutting patterns the company had been using were quite satisfactory, given the cost of the more sophisticated ones generated by the professors.

QUESTIONS FOR ANALYSIS

1. What general principles, if any, regarding the application of linear programming models are suggested by this case?
2. How would you, as production manager, explain to the veteran employee your decision to engage the college professors? How would you avoid giving the impression that your decision expressed lack of confidence in the employee's work?
3. In addition to the problem of defining efficient cutting patterns, what are some of the other problems to which linear programming can be applied in furniture manufacturing?

CASE 18–2   PERT at Westinghouse Electric

When Westinghouse Electric picked Harry Butler to head up purchasing for its plant being erected in South Boston, Virginia, he recognized immediately the enormity of the assignment. The new plant was expected to cost $20 million when fully built and equipped to produce power transformers. Butler's responsibilities included arranging for capital equipment purchases, scheduling machinery deliveries, contracting for interior designers, and buying furniture. These responsibilities were to be coordinated with the construction of the plant itself, so that the project would be completed without undue delay.

The relationships among purchasing and installing capital equipment and constructing the building are illustrated by Butler's experience with a punch press that cost over $250,000. To get the machine into the plant, the completion of one wall of the building had to be delayed. Because the machine was being shipped by rail, it was necessary to have the rail siding laid prior to its arrival. Moreover, the concrete footing for the press had to be poured in time; the electrical crew had to be available to install the machine; and power had to be available. Installing the punch press, however, was only one of the instances in which Butler was required to sort out interrelationships.

Butler and his associates decided that the nature of their job necessitated a procedure to schedule and control the various sequence of events and activities involved in equipping the plant. They selected PERT as the primary method to assist them in scheduling the logical sequence and in identifying the critical paths. With the network drawn, Butler was able to anticipate problems and bottlenecks and to deal with them before they became major obstacles. The PERT network enabled the Westinghouse management team to contact suppliers to expedite delivery dates. The team also found it useful to hold review sessions with major suppliers to go over the PERT network from the perspective of their commitments for timely delivery of equipment. One result of the use of the PERT method was to minimize "crash program" expediting.

As Butler stated, "A PERT diagram is extremely helpful because it indicates the way all the activities can best be coordinated. If something along the critical path fails, the network shows which other events must be either speeded up or delayed."

Questions for Analysis

1. What characteristics of the Westinghouse project made PERT a useful method for scheduling and controlling it?
2. In addition to those activities for which Butler was responsible, what other activities associated with constructing and opening a new manufacturing facility might be aided by PERT?
3. What would be the effects of unexpected bad weather, labor disputes, and other unforeseen circumstances on the PERT diagram?

Experiential Exercise

Constructing a PERT Network for a Project

Purpose

This exercise provides hands-on experience with the use of PERT to construct a network for a typical student project: writing a term paper. The exercise also demonstrates the judgmental and subjective nature of the decisions that go into constructing the network.

The Exercise in Class

Each student will come to class with a solution already worked out for question 8 at the end of this chapter. The question requires the construction of a network for the completion of a term paper with a directed completion time of 10 weeks. (If time is available, this part of the exercise could also be done in class.) When every student has completed the requirements of question 8, the instructor will assign each student to a group consisting of no more than five students.

Each group is allowed 20 minutes to prepare a complete PERT network for the term paper assignment. Then, each group will present its network to the class and justify the inclusion of particular activities and time estimates. Class discussion should focus on the process by which the groups arrived at their networks, including consideration of the extent to which the networks reflect subjective opinion and compromise within the group.

The Learning Message

The exercise calls attention to the element of subjectivity that goes into the construction of the PERT network even when the group members have considerable experience with writing term papers. The discussion of the effects of group decision making on the final outcome will also reinforce the students' understanding of group decision making.

19

INVENTORY PLANNING AND CONTROLLING

LEARNING OBJECTIVES

After completing Chapter 19, you should be able to:

Define
the concept of inventory control in the context of strategic and production planning.

Describe
the types and purposes of inventory found in manufacturing firms.

Discuss
the importance of inventory control.

Compare
the components and behavior of ordering and carrying costs.

Identify
the characteristics of inventories for which economic order quantity and material requirements planning are applicable.

Inventory Control Has International Implications

Apparel industry inventory planning and control is not easy. Fashion is so trendy. If correct, you profit handsomely. If wrong, you lose your shirt.

Fifteen years ago, many American apparel makers opted to move production overseas. Labor was so cheap that profits were possible even if predictions were wildly wrong. Recently, several U.S. producers have opted to bring home some production in order to control quality, inventory costs, and lead times (competitive pressures now make speed of delivery critical). The return to America comes because:

1. *Cost differentials are narrowing.* Korean and Taiwanese workers are getting higher wages. A weaker dollar makes the cheapest Chinese imports more expensive.
2. *Computers boost productivity.* Greif Companies of Allentown, Pennsylvania, utilizes computerized design and automated sewing machines to increase productivity by 30 percent.
3. *Telecommunications have become more advanced.* They instantaneously link retailers with designers. Presently, Arrow Shirts can domestically produce and ship orders on Tuesday that were electronically placed on Sunday. Stores base Sunday orders on computerized inventory/sales analyses of last week's business.
4. *Quality control and travel containment are better.* Seminole Manufacturing does not have to rework as much of its domestic production. Seminole also fills orders from its Evergreen, Alabama, plant in one fourth the time it takes from Jamaica.
5. *Mergers have left some domestic producers highly leveraged.* Manhattan Industries (the Perry Ellis label) avoids cash commitments to big inventories, long lead times, markdowns, and shipping delays.
6. *Import quotas have constrained Asian imports.*

Will this domesticating thread weave into a protective blanket for American producers? Foreign giants like Italy's Benneton and Hong Kong's Goetz Trading plan to open U.S. plants soon. Federal law still grants import advantages to Mexico, the Caribbean Islands, and Canada. Only time will tell if this emphasis on domestic output is a long-term trend or just another fad.

Source: "Why Made-in-America Is Back in Style," *Business Week,* November 7, 1988, pp. 116ff.

Rising energy costs, increasing foreign competition, and declining productivity are only a few of the factors that have caused managers to renew their interest in production and operations activities. The development of sophisticated managerial techniques in inventory and production planning and scheduling, along with the availability of advanced computerized systems, enables production managers to become more adept at cost control. These new developments include automated and computerized methods to handle orders, manage materials, control production inventories, manage shop floor operations, and measure product and order costs.

Both the pace of competition and international commercial rivalry demand that manufacturing activities be turned into a strategic weapon.[1] As such, production and operations must be integrated into the overall strategic plan of the organization, thus achieving a coordinated effort with marketing and financial strategies. Manufacturing activities are strategically important for both large and small businesses: No sector of American industry is insulated from the effects of competition.[2]

An important, and indeed crucial, aspect of production and operations management (P/OM) is the utilization of appropriate methods such as economic order quantity (EOQ), material requirements planning (MRP), linear programming, simulation, and networks. But without consideration of the broader, strategic implications of production and operations, management can still fail to achieve the most efficient and effective use of the firm's resources.

A key factor in P/OM is inventory control. In its broadest sense, inventory control implies securing and maintaining the optimal quantities and types of physical resources required by the organization's strategic plan. The importance of inventory is underscored when we visualize the manufacturing process as a flow of materials through a process that changes the form of those materials into finished goods. Thus, inventory control is at the heart of production control, and some experts make no distinction between the two.[3]

Organizations such as Black & Decker (BD) fully realize the relationships among inventory, production, and profit.[4] This international corporation, with annual sales in excess of $1 billion, is the world's largest manufacturer of power tools. Its product line includes drills, saws, sanders, grinders, hedge trimmers, and lawn mowers. (If it is powered by an electric motor, chances are that BD makes it.) The largest BD plant, located in Hampstead, Maryland, assembles some 120 major product groups requiring 20,000 inventory items. Because of the large required investment in inventory and the costs associated with such a large inventory, managers at the Hampstead plant are especially alert for ways to control inventory.

[1]Steven A. Melnyk and Richard F. Gonzalez, "MRP II: The Early Returns Are In," *Production and Inventory Management*, First Quarter 1985, pp. 124–36.

[2]John H. Blackstone and James F. Cox, "Inventory Management Techniques," *Journal of Small Business Management*, April 1985, pp. 27–33; "Material Requirement Planning—Overcoming the Biggest Obstacle to Productivity," *Small Business Reports*, June 1985, pp. 37–40.

[3]Thomas E. Hendrick and Franklin G. Moore, *Production/Operations Management: Fundamental Concepts and Methods* (Homewood, Ill.: Richard D. Irwin, 1981), p. 63.

[4]John J. Kanet, "Inventory Planning at Black & Decker," *Production and Inventory Management*, Third Quarter 1984, pp. 9–21.

Over time, BD management has developed an effective inventory control system that has attracted much industry attention. The system, which combines the latest computer technology and control techniques, has four essential features:

1. *A sound materials plan* that controls quantities ordered, order dates, and reorder dates in coordination with changes in specifications due to product or production changes. This materials plan is the foundation of the entire system, and the other three elements build on it.

2. *A commitment to executing the plan,* which in turn requires adherence to the specified order dates and lead times. Through faithfulness to the discipline of the plan, BD seeks to avoid unnecessary inventory costs associated with administrative mistakes.

3. *Constant evaluation* of ways to reduce inventory levels commits BD managers to continuous review of the inventory system. Through this commitment, the company instills the attitude that proactive attention to potential problems is preferable to reaction to actual problems.

4. *Insistence on maintaining accurate records* of inventory levels and characteristics reflects BD understanding that keeping accurate records is a major concern in any inventory control system. That the Hampstead plant must keep records on some 20,000 different inventory items indicates the importance of this part of the plan.

These four elements come together in a unified system that Black & Decker managers believe to be an effective inventory control system. The acronym that describes the system is PACE: planned action and constant evaluation. It aptly expresses the philosophy of inventory management at this important international corporation.

The development of PACE required BD managers to consider all of the issues that we address in this chapter: What are the types and purposes of inventory? How much of each is required? When should inventory be acquired? How can we control inventory cost?

TYPES OF INVENTORIES

The particular inventories that must be managed depend on the nature of the particular business. But the following inventory types are generally found in all businesses.[5]

RAW MATERIALS

Raw materials are the ingredients that go into the final product. Raw materials are the adhesive, gauze, and paper required to make sanitary bandages; the grains, sweeteners, preservatives, paper, and adhesive required to make and box breakfast cereals; the paper, ink, and binding required to make books. The exact form of the raw material depends on the manufacturing process.

Some manufacturers take nature's own resources and convert them to a product. Steel-making firms must have iron ore and coal to produce steel,

[5]Hendrick and Moore, *Production/Operations Management*, pp. 68–69.

which is then sold to auto manufacturers. For them, steel becomes a raw material. Other manufacturers assemble component parts into a final product. Their raw materials inventory consists of many different components supplied by other manufacturers. Corning Incorporated makes more than 60,000 different products, but its largest facility doesn't manufacture a thing. The company's Greencastle, Pennsylvania, facility packages, warehouses, and distributes some 1,250 finished goods items from eight different manufacturing plants.[6] Despite the fact that the Greencastle plant doesn't manufacture a product, it has a considerable inventory of raw materials.

SUPPLIES

Every business requires materials that do not become part of the final product. These materials, termed MRO (maintenance, repair, and operating) items, are usually small in number and expense, compared to other inventories. Nevertheless, they are essential to the operation of the plant. Examples of MRO items include stationery and other office-related materials, repair tools and parts, lubricants, and cleaning supplies.

WORK IN PROCESS

Raw materials moving through the stages of production are termed work in process. Depending on the length and complexity of the production process, work-in-process inventory can be relatively large or small. Westinghouse Electric estimates that work in process accounts for 80 percent of its inventory investment.[7] Controlling work-in-process inventory is an important element of scheduling goods through the various stages of production as rapidly as possible but also in order of priority. Multiproduct manufacturers must determine not only how many of each product to make but also when to produce each product.

FINISHED GOODS

Finished goods inventory consists of final, unsold products. Finished goods are stored at the manufacturing facilities itself or at some point in the distribution channel—at warehouses or retailers, for example. Job order manufacturers carry little, if any, finished goods inventory, since their products are made to customer specifications. Process and assembly manufacturers typically carry large finished goods inventory. Automobile manufacturers, for example, must produce large quantities in anticipation *of* rather than in response *to* customer demand.

The relative size of the inventory depends on the relative certainty of customer demand. Firms in the fortunate position of having unmet demand will have no finished goods inventory except that being transported to customers. When electronic games first appeared on the market, manufactur-

[6]Bruce Horovitz, "Why Corning Is Sticking with MRP," *Industry Week,* January 25, 1982, p. 46.

[7]Hendrick and Moore, *Production/Operations Management,* p. 68.

ers such as Atari and Coleco experienced demand beyond their ability to supply. Consequently, their investment in finished goods was minimal.

Manufacturing firms have experienced the effects of inventory costs on their profitability. Blue Bell, Inc. manufactures apparel, including Wrangler jeans, Red Kap work clothing and uniforms, and Jantzen sportswear.[8] From 1979 to 1982, the company experienced hard times as the cost of carrying inventory soared to 20 percent, sending interest expense from $1.1 million to $21.9 million. Management recognized that extreme measures were called for to bring this cost down. The focus of the control measures was materials and finished goods inventories. These two inventories together made up more than 50 percent of the company's asset base, and in 1982 they were running an average of $371 million!

Controlling inventory cost required concerted effort, including production planning that took into account the complexities of a vast product line, more demanding customers, and sophisticated computer technology. A task force undertook the job of cutting inventories through the application of inventory control models. A key part of the overall plan was a model that forecasts sales on monthly and annual bases. These forecasts became the foundation for determining production volumes and safety stocks. The completely revised inventory control system took some 21 months to develop and install, but the results appeared to justify the effort: By mid-1984, inventory had dropped to an average of $256 million for a savings of $16 million in interest expense.

Thus, when we recognize the extent of inventories, the importance of inventory control is apparent. In 1981, for the economy as a whole, the cost of carrying all the various inventories was $110 billion, almost 15 percent of the total value of the inventory itself.[9] Many factors contribute to the cost of carrying inventory; a significant one is the interest rate. For example, the prime interest rate in 1974 was below 10 percent. Other carrying costs such as storage, insurance, theft, and obsolescence were between 5 and 10 percent for all companies. For the economy as a whole, the cost of carrying a $324 billion inventory was less than $10 billion (after adjusting for the effects of inflation). In the early 1980s, the higher interest rates caused the cost of carrying inventory to increase to $110 billion, while the inventory value had only increased to $710 billion. Thus, for the economy as a whole, the cost of carrying inventory increased tenfold, whereas the value of the inventory only doubled.

The effect of interest rates in inventory costs is not lost on company managers. The management of PPG Industries found ways to reduce its inventory holding by means of a computer-based control system.[10] The company's inventory includes over 5,000 different raw materials and 10,000 finished goods. The computer-based system integrates information from purchasing, shipping, sales, manufacturing, and warehousing to arrive at optimal quantities, order points, and inventory sizes. The system has resulted in considerable efficiencies and cost savings for the company.

[8]Jerry R. Edwards, Harvey M. Wagner, and William P. Wood, "Blue Bell Trims Its Inventory," *Interfaces*, January–February 1985, pp. 34–52.

[9]Lewis Berman, "A Big Payoff from Inventory Controls," *Fortune*, July 27, 1981, p. 77.

[10]Ibid., pp. 76–80.

An inventory control system is often computer based.

PURPOSES OF INVENTORIES

In one form or another, inventory exists in all organizations, whether business or nonbusiness. Although we usually think of inventory in the context of manufacturing and distribution firms, other types of businesses have inventory. Banks, for example, must maintain an inventory of cash to meet customer demand. Nonbusiness organizations have inventories. Hospitals have inventories of medicine, surgical supplies, and all kinds of house-keeping items; schools have instructional supplies; and government agencies have inventories of office supplies (and red tape, some would say).

Inventory is costly. the organization must store it, move it from place to place, and safeguard it. The organization also incurs the opportunity cost of having funds tied up in inventory and therefore unavailable for other, profit-making investments. We will have more to say about inventory costs later. The point is that inventory is costly and organizations would prefer to do other things with their funds. Because the costs of carrying inventories are significant, they must serve some purpose; otherwise, why would organizations carry them? Here are the most important purposes.[11]

To Promote Customer Service

Inventory on hand means the product is available when customers are ready to buy it. Obviously, if it is not on hand, customers are not served, and the firm loses that sale and future ones as well. If the firm knew with certainty when customers would be ready to buy, it could have just enough inventory on hand to meet the demand. But such is not the case.

---

[11]The following discussion is based on Gordon K. C. Chen and Robert E. McGarrah, *Productivity Management* (Hinsdale, Ill.: Dryden Press, 1982), pp. 74–76.

Manufacturers, wholesalers, and retailers all face the problem of deciding how many of what kinds of products to have available. This decision involves balancing the costs of having too little inventory versus having too much. Even firms that manufacture to customer specifications must maintain an inventory of materials. Job order printing firms, which keep no finished goods because each product is produced only after the customer orders it, must have an inventory of paper, ink, and supplies to meet uncertain customer demand.

Customers usually must be convinced that a product has three attributes before they buy it: the "right" price, quality appropriate to the price, and delivery service. Inventory contributes to customer service by providing delivery service—the product is available when demanded. Thus, having inventory is vital to keeping customers.

Service providers are no less concerned with controlling inventory, as noted in the Management Focus on that topic.

To Promote Manufacturing Flexibility

Most manufacturing firms produce more than one product with the same machines in the same facility. The flexibility of being able to shift back and forth from one product to another is possible only because of inventory. Inventory promotes the use of multiproduct manufacturing in two ways. First, the inventory of raw materials enables the manufacturer to produce the specific product on schedule. Unless there are raw materials and components on hand, the changeover is impossible. Second, any demand for the product not presently being produced can be satisfied by selling the finished goods inventory.[12] Gains in productivity can be achieved to the extent that managers can use manufacturing equipment in flexible ways.

To Promote Certainty in Production/Operations

In nearly every aspect of business, decision making takes place in conditions of uncertainty. The demand for the final product is typically uncertain; the supply of materials to produce the product is uncertain. The amount of uncertainty varies from business to business. A provider of electricity for residential consumption operates under more certain demand than the manufacturer of electronic games. But uncertainty exists to some degree in both instances.

Inventories serve as a hedge against the effects of uncertainty. The greater the uncertainty, the greater the need for hedging against its effects. Consequently, firms will keep a reserve of raw materials, components, and other inventories on hand as **safety stocks.** Safety stocks safeguard the firm against lost production or sales due to unforeseen shortages and forecasting errors.

To Promote Production Smoothing

Manufacturing firms prefer smooth (i.e., relatively consistent) rates of production over time. Smooth production enables the firm to retain a stable,

[12]P. P. Kleutghen and J. C. McGee, "Development and Implementation of an Integrated Inventory Management Program at Pfizer Pharmaceutical," *Interfaces,* January–February 1985, pp. 69–87.

MANAGEMENT FOCUS

Inventory Control in a Service Firm

R. L. Waltrip of Service Corporation watched firms such as McDonald's and Holiday Inns become giants through inventory planning and control. Could their tactics help him become a leader in funeral service and cemetery management? Employing inventory planning principles similar to those followed by big corporations, Waltrip focused on areas where he could buy, or form a cooperative network of, high-volume funeral homes located near each other. Before, each funeral home kept parlor, casket, hearse, and personnel levels capable of sustaining peak demand. Waltrip streamlined each parlor to the bare bones. Now, when business picks up at one location, other parlors lend personnel, fixtures, and vehicles to meet the demand. Where possible, Waltrip centralizes embalming and cremations at one location. This focus lowered fixed costs from the industry's standard 75 percent of total costs.

Waltrip's applications produced lively results. From 1982 to 1987, revenues doubled, and profits grew at a spirited 20 percent increase per year.

Source: "R. L. Waltrip Livens Up a Growing Industry," *Management Review*, September 1988, pp. 15–16; "Bob Waltrip Is Making Big Noises in a Quiet Industry," *Business Week*, August 25, 1986, pp. 66–67.

trained work force. It also avoids the costs of sustained downtime or the opposite, the costs of extra-capacity production. Production smoothing involves leveling manufacturing during seasonal fluctuations. Thus, the purpose of inventory is to meet demand during periods of peak sales without having to increase the rate of production.

TO PROMOTE PROFITS THROUGH PRICE SPECULATION

A final, secondary purpose of inventory is that, during periods of inflation, a firm can profit by buying inventory at the lower price, holding it until prices increase, and selling it at a profit. Inventory speculation is not the primary purpose of manufacturing concerns. But other organizations, such as those that trade and process farm products, could well argue that speculation in farm commodities is part of their business. Inventory in such firms can become a major source of profit.

In most instances, however, firms consider inventory a major source of cost. Managers in these firms seek approaches to controlling inventory cost. One of the most widely used approaches is the economic order quantity (EOQ) model.[13]

[13]Richard R. Jesse, Jr., Amitava Mitra, and James F. Cox, "EOQ Formula: Is It Valid under Inflationary Conditions?" *Decision Sciences*, July 1983, pp. 370–74; James A. G. Krupp, "Deterministic EOQ in a Production Environment," *Journal of Purchasing and Materials Management*, Summer 1984, pp. 24–30.

FIGURE 19–1   Ordering and Carrying Cost Relationship

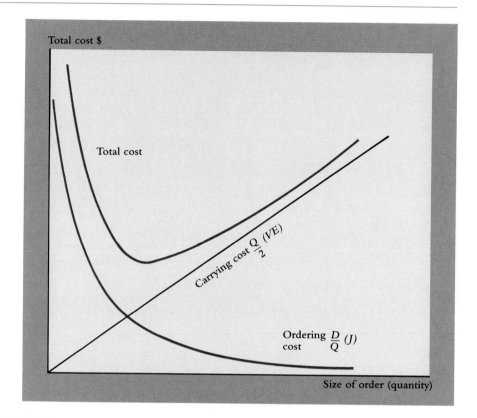

As the size of the order increases, carrying costs increase and ordering costs decrease.

EOQ METHOD

The **economic order quantity (EOQ) model** enables managers to make a number of key inventory decisions. Managers who order goods from a supplier can use EOQ to decide how many units to order and how often to order them. When used to determine the size of batches to produce and when, the method is called the economic lot size (ELS) model. The principles of the model are the same whether the goods are ordered or produced. Here, we will emphasize the EOQ variation. EOQ involves balancing the costs of having too much inventory and the costs of having too little inventory.

COST FACTORS IN INVENTORY CONTROL

To effectively control inventory, the manager must initially identify cost factors. First, there are the **ordering costs** of getting a particular item into the actual inventory. These costs are incurred each time an order is placed. They are the clerical and administrative costs per order, which also include the cost of receiving the goods and placing them into inventory.

TABLE 19–1   Average-Inventory Analysis

	Week	Inventory at Midpoint of Week
Average inventory, an	1	450
important measure, can be	2	350
calculated if inventory usage	3	250
is constant over time.	4	150
	5	50
		1,250

Second, there are the **carrying costs.** These include the interest on money invested in inventory; the cost of storage space, rent, obsolescence, and taxes; and the cost of insurance on losses due to theft, fire, and deterioration. Carrying costs are usually expressed as an annual figure and as a percentage of the average inventory.

To reduce inventory costs, a manager must minimize both ordering and carrying costs. Unfortunately, these two costs are related to each other in opposing directions, as shown in Figure 19–1. As the size of each order increases, the number and cost of orders decrease; but since larger quantities are being ordered and placed in inventory, the cost of carrying the inventory increases. (The total cost curve, which is the summation of the other two curves, is discussed in a later section.)

Computing ordering costs is relatively simple. The number of orders for a given period of time is equal to demand (D) for the period divided by the size of each order quantity (Q). The total ordering cost per period (week, month, or year) is equal to the cost of placing each order (J), multiplied by the number of orders per period. Thus, the formula for computing ordering costs reads $(D/Q)J$. As the order size increases, fewer orders are required to meet the demand for a period; consequently, ordering costs decrease, illustrated by the downward sloping order-cost curve in Figure 19–1.

Carrying costs for one item in inventory are calculated by multiplying the value of the item (V) by a percentage figure (E), which is management's estimate of taxes, insurance, and so forth, per period as a percentage of the value of inventory. Total carrying costs are equal to the cost of carrying one item (VE) multiplied by the average inventory $Q/2$. Thus, the formula for calculating total costs is $(Q/2)VE$. For the sake of simplicity, carrying cost is shown as a straight line in Figure 19–1.

An example will illustrate why average inventory equals $Q/2$. Assume that an organization orders 500 items and uses 100 of them each week; at the midpoint of the first week, it has 450 on hand. Table 19–1 lists the number in inventory at the midpoint of each week over a period of five weeks. The average inventory is found by dividing total inventory (1,250) by the number of weeks (5), yielding an average of 250. The average can also be found by utilizing the $Q/2$ formula; that is, $500 \div 2 = 250$.

Figure 19–2   Constant Inventory Usage

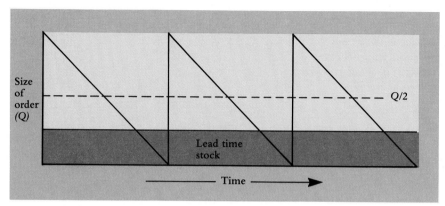

Average inventory can also be illustrated in a simple graph that shows inventory declining at a constant rate only to be replenished by the order placed and received during the use of lead-time stock.

Trial-and-Error Methodology

With ordering and carrying costs calculated, a manager can use trial and error to determine what size of order to place. However, attempting to select the optimal size of inventory from a cost standpoint usually involves a number of assumptions:

1. That the demand for the item over the period is known with certainty. Thus, we are developing the economic order quantity (EOQ) model under conditions of certainty.
2. That the rate at which the inventory of the item is depleted is constant. Figure 19–2 illustrates depletion at a constant rate. The average inventory is found under conditions of constant usage (e.g., selling the same amount monthly for the year).
3. That the lead time—the time between the placement of an order and the actual delivery of that order—is exactly known.

These assumptions are not completely realistic, but they allow us to study the development of the EOQ model in an uncomplicated manner. Further sophistication of the basic model can occur only if the simplified form is clearly understood.[14]

Suppose that a production manager is attempting to solve a lot size problem involving a component part that is purchased from a supplier. The yearly demand for the part, which is constant, is estimated to be 1,000. The administrative and clerical cost of placing an order is $40. The manager estimates insurance and taxes to be 10 percent per year. The value of a single part is $20. Thus, the variables involved are:

Demand (D) = 1,000 units.
Ordering costs (J) = $40.

TABLE 19–2   Trial-and-Error Method

The trial-and-error method is a cumbersome way of calculating inventory costs associated with different order sizes.

Number of Orders	Size of Order Q	Ordering Cost D/Q(J)		Carrying Cost Q/2 (VE)	=	Total Cost
1	1,000	$ 40	+	$1,000	=	$1,040
2	500	80	+	500	=	580
4	250	160	+	250	=	410
10	100	400	+	100	=	500
20	50	800	+	50	=	850

Insurance and taxes $(E) = 10$ percent.
Value of the item $(V) = \$20$.

The manager could use this data to calculate total inventory costs by randomly choosing the size of the order to place. By compiling a table that summarizes the size of inventory order and cost relationships as shown in Table 19–2, the manager could decide at a glance how many orders to place to minimize total inventory costs.

A review of the total-cost data in Table 19–2 indicates that placing four orders of 250 each yields the lowest cost ($410). However, note that the trial-and-error method could be tedious, so management scientists have developed a formula for the economic order quantity model.

THE EOQ FORMULA

Looking back to Figure 19–1, we see that the minimum total inventory cost is at the point directly above the intersection of carrying cost and ordering cost. Thus, the EOQ formula may be derived by utilizing this relationship. It should be noted that, for simplicity, the relationship shown is linear. The first step in algebraic derivation is to set carrying and ordering costs equal to each other.

$$\frac{Q}{2}(VE) = \frac{D}{Q}\ (J)$$

Solving for Q yields:

$$Q(VE) = \frac{2DJ}{Q}$$

$$Q^2\ (VE) = 2DJ$$

$$Q^2 = \frac{2DJ}{(VE)}$$

$$Q = \sqrt{\frac{2DJ}{(VE)}}$$

The final equation is commonly referred to as the *economic order quantity formula* and can be used to solve the inventory problem we have outlined.

Using the data in our problem ($D = 1,000$, $J = \$40$, $E = 10$ percent, and $V = \$20$), we can determine the economic order size:

$$Q = \sqrt{\frac{2(1,000)(\$40)}{(\$20)(.10)}}$$

$$Q = \sqrt{\frac{\$80,000}{\$2.00}}$$

$$Q = \sqrt{40,000}$$

$$Q = 200$$

For this problem, the trial-and-error method indicates that the least costly alternative is to place four orders to satisfy the overall demand of 1,000. However, utilization of the more exact EOQ formula suggests that placing five orders of 200 each will be least costly. Since the five-order alternative was not considered in the trial-and-error solution, the manager was not able to really minimize inventory costs.

The EOQ model can also be used to consider changes in demand for a product. Assume that demand is 1,000 for the first 10 months of the year and 2,000 for the last 2 months of the year. For the January–October period, the EOQ calculations would be as follows: $D = 1,000$; $J = \$40$; $E = 10$ percent; and $V = \$20$ for 10 out of 12 months. Thus,

$$EOQ = \sqrt{\frac{2(1,000)(\$40)}{(\$20)(.10)(10/12)}}$$

$$EOQ \cong \sqrt{48,000}$$

$$EOQ \cong 219 \text{ units}$$

The November–December inventory strategy would be determined as follows: $D = 2,000$; $J = \$40$; $E = 10$ percent; and $V = \$20$ for 2 months out of 12. Thus,

$$EOQ = \sqrt{\frac{2(2,000)(\$40)}{(\$20)(.10)(2/12)}}$$

$$EOQ = \sqrt{484,848}$$

$$EOQ \cong 696$$

The EOQ decision for January–December is relatively clear-cut in that the demand of 1,000 can be satisfied with five orders of 200 each. Because the EOQ during the November–December peak period is approximately 696, however, the manager must decide whether two or three orders are appropriate. The human element is essential, since $2 \times 696 = 1,392$ and $3 \times 696 = 2,088$, and the exact demand is 2,000. The above example shows that, despite the use of mathematical formulas, human judgment is still an important factor in many inventory control decisions.

LIMITATIONS OF THE EOQ MODEL

The most obvious limitation of the EOQ model is that conditions of certainty rarely exist in the real world. In our problem, we have assumed that the correct time to order is known. But transportation problems, order requisition difficulties, and other related problems will often make the lead time a highly unpredictable phenomenon.[15]

Estimating demand is another problem. Throughout our discussion, demand is known with certainty. But the demand for any item in the real world can at best only be roughly estimated. Many variables—competitors' prices, economic conditions, social conditions, and substitutable items—can influence demand.

A final limitation of the EOQ model is that it is most useful for controlling inventory that has independent demand. That is, the demand is unrelated to the sale or usage of other items. Finished goods and supplies are examples of inventories that have independent demand. Inventory errors for these items are isolated and have no cumulative effects. Therefore, the EOQ model can be applied to these inventories, given its inherent limitations.

MATERIAL REQUIREMENTS PLANNING

Raw material, component, subassembly, and work-in-process inventories have dependent demand. The demand for these inventories depends on the demand for the finished goods. The EOQ model is much less applicable to these inventories because errors, such as shortage, compound forward. In recent years, an inventory control method termed **material requirements planning (MRP)** has been developed to control inventories with dependent demand. MRP uses sophisticated computer software to plan and control inventory costs. This method enables management to combine a vast number of interlocking decisions related to ordering, scheduling, handling, and using inventories of parts and supplies that are components of the final product. MRP, certainly a contemporary production/operations technique, applies advances in decision support systems, materials-handling technology, and decision making to the difficult problem of planning and controlling.

The popularity of MRP has increased significantly since the early 1970s. The firms that have been quickest to adopt MRP are in the transportation equipment, instruments, and electrical machinery industries. Firms in these industries must carry a complex and expensive array of materials and components. At the other extreme, firms in continuous-process industries (e.g., paper, petroleum, lumber and wood) have not rushed to adopt MRP. Generally, MRP is more applicable in firms that manufacture to order and whose manufacturing process includes both assembly and fabrication.[16] But what is MRP and how does it work?

THE BASICS OF MRP

Material requirements planning involves breaking down a product into its components and subassemblies. Management can then coordinate the ordering

---

[15]Alvin C. Adkins, Jr., "EOQ in the Real World," *Production and Inventory Management,* Fourth Quarter 1984, pp. 50–54.

[16]John C. Anderson, Roger G. Schroeder, Sharon E. Tupy, and Edna M. White, "Material Requirements Planning Systems: The State of the Art," *Production and Inventory Management,* Fourth Quarter 1982, pp. 51–66; R. Dave Garwood, "Explaining JIT, MRP II and Kanban," *Production and Inventory Management Review,* October 1984, pp. 72–74.

An item as simple as a baby stroller must be assembled from scores of individual parts.

and delivery of components and the production start date of all subassemblies.[17] MRP is applicable to a wide range of problems related to producing an end product with numerous components. For example, the method has been successfully applied to the management of NASA's space operations.[18]

The basic tools of MRP are the master production schedule, the bill of materials, and inventory records. Although most manufacturing firms have some form of these schedules and records, MRP requires greater detail and sophistication than is usually present in a manual system.

Master Production Schedule.   The **master production schedule** details the planned quantities of finished goods to be produced during a particular time period. The master production schedule is based on (1) the company's strategic plan and (2) the production plan.[19] The strategic plan identifies the product market strategies that will propel the firm toward its long-run objectives. The production plan details the production volume of each product or class of products. The optimum product mix must reflect product demand, resources, and overall profitability. Linear programming or more complex programming models can assist managers in determining what combination of products is optimal. (If only one product is produced, the ELS model is

[17]Charles J. Anton and Charles J. Malmborg, "The Integration of Inventory Modeling and MRP Processing: A Case Study," *Production and Inventory Management,* Second Quarter 1985, pp. 79–90.

[18]Earl Steinberg, William B. Lee, and Basheer M. Khumawala, "MRP Applications in the Space Program," *Production and Inventory Management,* Second Quarter 1982, pp. 65–77.

[19]Gerald R. Gallagher, "How to Develop a Realistic Master Schedule," *Management Review,* April 1980, pp. 19–25.

FIGURE 19–3   The Relationship between the Master Schedule and Bills of Materials

Bills of materials and master schedules enable managers to see the types and amounts of inventory required to produce a particular volume of output for a specified time period.

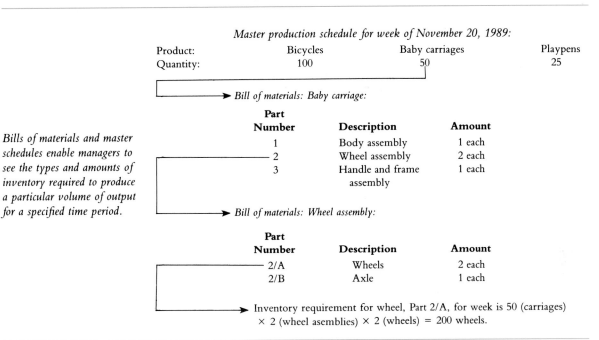

Master production schedule for week of November 20, 1989:

Product:	Bicycles	Baby carriages	Playpens
Quantity:	100	50	25

Bill of materials: Baby carriage:

Part Number	Description	Amount
1	Body assembly	1 each
2	Wheel assembly	2 each
3	Handle and frame assembly	1 each

Bill of materials: Wheel assembly:

Part Number	Description	Amount
2/A	Wheels	2 each
2/B	Axle	1 each

Inventory requirement for wheel, Part 2/A, for week is 50 (carriages) × 2 (wheel asemblies) × 2 (wheels) = 200 wheels.

applicable.) In any case, the master schedule depends on prior determination of a production plan.

The master schedule takes the information from the production schedule and adds the timing element; it details what will be produced and when it will be produced. Thus, the master schedule provides the bases for controlling the amount and type of work-in-process inventory during a specified period of time.

Bill of Materials.   The **bill of materials** defines the required components—those items of inventory that have dependent demand—for each subassembly and finished good. The required quantity, quality, and timing of components depend on the production schedule for the final products.

Figure 19–3 shows the relationship between the master production schedule and bills of materials. In MRP terms, the bill of materials is the result of "exploding" each final product into its subassemblies and components. As shown in the figure, the requirement for wheels depends on the production schedule for baby carriages. The material requirements are determined by "exploding" the bill of materials for 50 baby carriages into subassemblies and components. The information could be expanded to include the bills of materials for the subassemblies and components of bicycles and playpens.

It should be obvious that the master schedule and supporting bills of materials become considerably more complex as the number of products increases. To control the scheduling by manual and intuitive means becomes unwieldy and unproductive.

Inventory Records. The current status of each component subassembly and finished good item must be available. This information requirement necessitates developing and maintaining records that are updated to reflect current usage and replenishment. Thus, perpetual rather than periodic **inventory records** are parts of an MRP system.

THE MRP SYSTEM

In practice, the MRP system involves complex calculations and administrative routines. The intent of MRP is to coordinate all activities required to produce the final product(s) or service(s) sustaining the organization. We can sense the complexity by outlining the basic decisions that managers must make to operate MRP.[20]

Determination of Gross Requirements. Managers must determine the gross requirements for all dependent demand items, based on a production plan that specifies how many end products are to be produced. Gross requirements must be determined in terms of both quantity required and delivery dates. The key to successful MRP is to have just the right amount of inventory available at just the right time.

Determination of Net Requirements. The calculation of net requirements is inventory on hand plus quantity on order, minus the safety stock. The difference, net requirements, must be ordered from suppliers, or produced if the firm makes rather than buys the item. The purpose of net requirement calculations is to set the replenishment process in motion.

Determination of Safety Stocks and Lead Times. Safety stocks enable managers to meet unexpected demand for the product; they are a hedge against the costs of being out of stock, a lost sale, and a disappointed customer. MRP requires that safety stocks be decided for finished goods only and be included in the production schedule. The calculation of gross requirements will automatically take into account safety stocks for dependent demand items. Calculating lead time enables managers to obtain components at the time they are needed. The idea is to keep to a minimum the quantity of component items carried, so as to reduce carrying cost. By coordinating calculations of time required and lead time, managers can keep the size of component inventory at a low level.

Determination of Order Quantities. The determination of net requirements necessitates deciding how many components should be ordered each time—the order quantity. Ordinarily, orders are planned in exact amounts, and timing is determined in the net calculation. The EOQ method can be used to determine order size if the sources and lead times for all components can be coordinated. Otherwise, there would be as many different order quantities as there are components, and the opportunities for stockouts and averages would increase.

---

[20]Gabriel R. Bitran, David M. Marieni, Hirofumi Matsuo, and James W. Noonan, "Multiplant MRP," *Journal of Operations Management,* February 1985, pp. 183–203.

Determination of Order Release.   Order release time, when the order is placed with the supplier, is calculated by subtracting lead time from the date the item is required for production. Order release calculations become as complex as PERT networks when a finished good has a lengthy bill of materials involving many assemblies and subassemblies. General Motors, Ford, and Chrysler face bills of materials of staggering complexity. In other instances, order release calculations can be quite simple.

Determination of Aggregate Requirements.   Planned orders and release dates for all components are aggregated in a master schedule. The complexity of the schedule is directly related to the number of products and the required components for those products. The aggregate requirements data are the basic outputs of an MRP system. Their accuracy depends on the quality of information and of management decision making that went into them.

THE COMPLETE MRP SYSTEM

A complete MRP system is diagrammed in Figure 19–4. The simplicity of the diagram should not disguise the complexity of the system. To fully implement the system requires managerial commitment, adequate decision support systems, and computer facilities.[21]

One apparently successful MRP system is operating at the IPE–Cheston Company, which has integrated inventory control with computer capability.[22] The company produces equipment used for heat treating steel, aluminum, copper, and other metals. The company's customers are firms in the forging and metalworking industries. The company experienced rapid growth from 1976 into the early 80s; one effect of that growth was that the number of items in inventory increased from 3,000 to 6,000.

The company's method of inventory control was unable to deal with the increased complexity. The old method, primarily a manually operated reorder point and tracking system, permitted numerous errors; inventory on hand and production orders became badly imbalanced. A change was required.

Under the direction of John W. Stoll, director of materials, IPE–Cheston switched to an MRP inventory control system. The switch was greatly facilitated by the use of existing computer hardware, a Wang VS80. The MRP system (produced by Computer Technology Inc.) that IPE–Cheston adopted is compatible with the Wang. The new system increased customer service and reduced inventory by 34 to 40 percent (about $500,000). If carrying costs are 2 percent per month, the savings represents a profit increase of $120,000 per year. "A good investment," states Mr. Stoll.

The MRP system at IPE–Cheston contributes to productivity increases because it is adaptable to unexpected changes. For example, bills of materials change as a consequence of engineering and technical improvements. The development of a welding technique can make obsolete a bill of materials that includes bolts and nuts that previously attached the components. Lead times

[21]James F. Cox, Robert W. Zmud, and Steven J. Clark, "Auditing an MRP System," *Academy of Management Journal,* June 1981, pp. 386–402.

[22]"MRP System Cuts Inventory, Improves Service, Productivity," *Industrial Engineering,* July 1982, p. 80.

FIGURE 19–4   Elements of an MRP System

The master production schedule, the key element of the MRP system, integrates information from all other elements of the system.

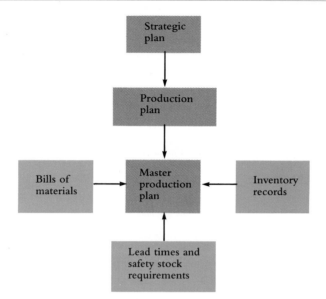

and safety stock determinations can be altered by changing supplier capabilities. A key supplier may suffer a work stoppage that upsets the entire ordering schedule. The ability to adapt to these changes depends on accessing and quickly entering the required data. Thus, the importance of computer capability is underscored.

Another example of inventory control underscores the plantwide effort required to make a system effective. Norton Company's Construction Products Division in Gainesville, Georgia, has been a case study in the successful application of a manufacturing resource planning system.[23] The division's managers implemented a broad-based effort to reverse the upward trend of costs due to late deliveries, downtime, excessive inventory, and record-keeping. Implementation involved the application of computers, the education of employees, and the commitment of top management—the usual three ingredients in successful efforts to implement new systems of inventory control.

MRP, when fully operational, is more than a method for managing inventory. Because of its integrative nature, a newer term—resource requirements planning (RRP)—has been adopted to describe more accurately the breadth of its application. RRP expands the concept of bills of materials to include all resources required of a product. Such a bill of resources would specify required materials and labor, machines, capacity, managerial and technical skills, energy, capital, and cash. Thus, planning and controlling

[23]Richard L. Thompson, "How to Achieve and Maintain Inventory Accuracy," *Production and Inventory Management*, First Quarter 1985, pp. 38–44.

inventory is, in the final analysis, planning and controlling the organization itself.

JUST-IN-TIME INVENTORY CONTROL

An advanced version of MRP is termed **just-in-time (JIT).** As its name implies, JIT inventory control attempts to provide the raw material or component part on the very last day, or even hour, before it is needed.[24] It attempts to eliminate the need for inventory by altering some of the basic conditions of manufacturing. The JIT approach originated in Japan and is one of the keys to that country's manufacturing success. The Japanese believed that if the underlying reason for inventory could be eliminated, inventory could be eliminated. American industry soon discovered the advantages of JIT, and countless firms have adopted it.[25]

The underlying reason for inventory is the existence of uncertainty in the production system. Rather than being a smooth-flowing integrated process, production systems are loosely coupled subsystems that produce component parts at different rates. The component parts do not arrive at assembly points at reliable, predictable times. Thus, it is necessary for faster-moving subsystems to have inventories of slower-moving subsystems' outputs so that production proceeds without interruption. The mismatch in the production rates of interdependent production units combines with other factors to create uncertainty, which management usually copes with by investing in inventory.

The other important factors contributing to production uncertainty include unreliable deliveries of acceptable materials from vendors. If a vendor's shipment contains unacceptable units or if it is not on time, production will come to a halt unless there is an inventory on hand, a safety stock. Equipment breakdowns and insufficiently skilled or trained employees can also contribute to production uncertainty and the need for inventory. The flow of components is interrupted by unacceptable quality or quantity of components, whether internally produced or externally supplied. But even the most reliable vendors, maintained equipment, and skilled employees cannot overcome poorly designed production layouts or incompetently drawn production plans. Management also can contribute to the necessity to maintain inventory. But when everything is done competently, JIT produces significant results, as noted in the Management Focus on JIT in the automobile industry.

Japanese and American manufacturers who have successfully implemented JIT did so by eliminating both the human and technical reasons for inventory. The Japanese are notable for their success in developing cooperation among interdependent groups. Japanese managers, as discussed in previous chapters, use participative management and quality circles to encourage communication among groups connected in the workflow; they also invest heavily in

[24]Richard J. Schonberger, "The Transfer of Japanese Manufacturing Management Approaches to U.S. Industry," *Academy of Management Review,* July 1982, p. 480; Richard J. Schonberger, "Just-in-Time Systems Focus on Simplicity," *Industrial Engineering,* October 1984, pp. 52–63.

[25]Steven P. Galante, "Small Manufacturers Shifting to Just-in-Time Techniques," *The Wall Street Journal,* December 21, 1987, p. 21.

MANAGEMENT FOCUS

Just-in-Time Saves Time in Auto Manufacturing

Just-in-time (JIT) delivery has revolutionized the seating business in the American automotive industry. Before JIT, automakers would maintain a cushion room next to the assembly line. In this room were stored foam, fabric, nuts and bolts, frames, and motors supplied by up to 20 separate vendors. With JIT, this entire inventory and assembly does not exist in many plants.

Today, at General Motors' Willow Run plant in Michigan, a single supplier, Lear Siegler, located in Romulus (15 miles away), makes the seats in the same sequence as GM assembles its cars. Three to four hours before assembly, GM electronically notifies Lear Siegler of not only the number, color, style, and options needed on each seat but also the sequence in which GM will need the seats. Lear Siegler then assembles the seats that hour and loads them in reverse order on special trucks. Every hour, a truck leaves Romulus for Willow Run. When the truck arrives, robots assist in unloading the seats as needed on GM's line.

Both firms benefit from the arrangement. For GM, seating inventories at Willow Run are minimal; GM has a reliable supplier almost at its back door. Because GM commits to a steady order schedule, Lear Siegler's inventory is one fifth of pre-JIT levels. Despite the tight delivery schedules, GM and Lear Siegler have not experienced a single delay. The closest instance came when police seized a truck for a short time to block off traffic. Even under JIT, one cannot guard against all contingencies.

Source: "JIT in Detroit," *Purchasing,* September 15, 1988, pp. 68–77.

employee training and development, including management. American firms such as General Electric, Goodyear, Ford, Chrysler, and General Motors have had some success with JIT.[26] It is no coincidence that these same firms face the stiffest competition from the Japanese.

On the technical side, a full-scale and encompassing evaluation of the production system must precede the installation of JIT inventory control. JIT requires effective quality control, preventive maintenance, and vendor relations programs. Many American companies have found that developing effective supplier relationships under JIT requirements is the most challenging aspect of JIT implementation. Demands on suppliers are considerable; they must make frequent deliveries of high-quality materials and make them on time. Daily, even hourly deliveries are not uncommon. Under the JIT concept, late or defective materials can shut down the production process, as there are no safety stocks to cushion the effects of such problems.

In developing JIT-based supplier relationships, companies such as Xerox and Harley-Davidson have initially made the mistake of viewing JIT as a way to push their inventory onto the supplier. The supplier holds the manufacturer's raw materials and incurs the carrying costs. However, this strategy fails

[26]Richard J. Schonberger and Marc J. Schniederjans, "Reinventing Inventory Control," *Interfaces,* May–June 1984, pp. 76–83; Mehran Sepehri, "Kanban and JIT: American Style," *Manufacturing Systems,* June 1985, pp. 49–50.

over the long term, because the vendor simply increases materials costs to cover the extra carrying charges.[27]

Successful implementers of JIT usually follow three steps in developing relationships with suppliers. They first communicate the technique's benefits for themselves and the supplier (who benefits from a stable, long-term purchasing relationship). They train the supplier in JIT concepts; many companies encourage suppliers to adopt JIT in their own operations and help them implement the concept to reap the same benefits in productivity, costs, and quality. They also help the supplier find ways to simplify its own production process to make frequent deliveries easier.[28]

Omark Industries is one company that has successfully implemented JIT.[29] The firm manufactures equipment for the forest products industry. In 1981, Omark's president observed the concept at work in one of Japan's auto manufacturing plants and, on returning to Omark, headed a corporate team that presented two-day seminars on JIT at each of the company's 21 plants. From there, small groups of managers and employees were formed at each plant to read, study, and discuss Toyota's manual on JIT, chapter by chapter.

Once the study period was completed, Omark's Zero Inventory Production System (ZIPS) was launched. ZIPS teams were established in each plant to devise ways to implement JIT concepts. In Omark's chain saw manufacturing plant in Portland, Oregon, teams were staffed with employees having a week of training in ZIPS and quality control. They were further cross-trained in several jobs to boost the flexibility of the production process. These teams worked on ways to lower inventory. Machine tooling was changed, some machines were redesigned, and the plant's layout was altered to speed the setup and production process. In the early stages of ZIPS, the plant arbitrarily took one week's supply of safety stock off the factory floor and found that the production process ran more smoothly. With little inventory to cushion the effects of production problems and employees trained in quality inspection, quality problems in materials and the production process became very evident; employees found defects that had previously gone undetected.

Special efforts were made to share production information with suppliers and help them implement ZIPS in their materials production plants. After one year of ZIPS management, the Portland plant had cut finished goods inventory by 50 percent, reduced work-in-process inventory by 50 percent, and reduced manufacturing costs by 6 percent. About one third of the plant's floor space was cleared of inventory, along with half of the 100,000 square feet of space in the materials warehouse. Overall, Omark invested $200,000 to implement ZIPS across its plants. In return, the company saves $7 million annually in inventory carrying costs.[30]

[27]Dexter Hutchins, "Having a Hard Time with Just-in-Time," *Fortune,* June 9, 1986, pp. 64ff.

[28]Nicholas J. Pennucci, "Just-in-Time for a Change," *Quality Progress,* November 1987, pp. 67–68.

[29]For other descriptions of successful JIT implementation, see Ira P. Krepchin, "How One Company Is Approaching JIT," *Modern Materials Handling,* January 1988, pp. 101–4; Elisabeth Ryan Sullivan, "AT&T Invests in Training Factory Workers," *Manufacturing Week,* January 11, 1988.

[30]Craig R. Waters, "Why Everybody Is Talking about Just-in-Time," *Inc.,* March 1984, pp. 77ff.

JIT is a powerful tool for lowering inventory costs and investment, cutting labor costs, and boosting product quality and plant capacity/productivity. By eliminating delays in the production process, JIT makes a company's production more flexible. Because the process is quicker, the company can more swiftly respond to customer demand for product variations.[31] However, because it is a challenging concept to implement, many companies first establish JIT on a small scale before making a plantwide commitment to the concept. For example, Hewlett-Packard's Computer Systems Division first implemented JIT in the last two steps of the production process before implementing the concept back through the factory to the first step in the process.[32] JIT works best in companies where inventory and product demand can be accurately forecast, the production processes are repetitive, and high-quality suppliers are located nearby.[33]

EOQ and MRP: A Comparison

EOQ and MRP systems are usually mutually exclusive but can be combined in some instances.[34] The EOQ model is intended for use in process manufacturing settings, where the usage of inventory is likely to be continuous and constant—a key requirement for effective use of EOQ. If demand and usage are not constant over time or known with some certainty, then inventory shortages and overages will disrupt production schedules. Total inventory costs will be far from minimized.

MRP is ideally suited for firms that manufacture in job-lot or batch processing technology. In such firms, production is discontinuous, varied, and dependent upon relatively uncertain customer demand. MRP systems pay special attention to each component and subassembly item, using the master production schedule, bills of materials, and inventory records. Successful applications of MRP result in synchronized orders of all inventories, based on safety stocks and lead times.

The two methods can be used simultaneously in firms that have both types of products and production. Items with constant and relatively certain demand can be controlled by EOQ; items with discontinuous, batch-type, and relatively uncertain demand can be controlled by MRP.

Finally, it must be understood that MRP can be a fully integrated production/operations system. In its most complete form, MRP (or RRP, as referred to earlier) is used for capacity planning and for establishing production priorities. Top management uses it to "run the business." One survey of MRP estimated that this level of sophistication is attained by less than 10 percent of its users.[35] Why? The very process of being controlled is so complex as to defy even the most rigorous management science approaches.

[31]Bruce D. Henderson, "The Logic of Kanban," *Journal of Business Strategy,* Winter 1986, pp. 6–12.

[32]Richard C. Walleigh, "What's Your Excuse for Not Using JIT?" *Harvard Business Review,* March–April 1986, pp. 38ff.

[33]Waters, "Why Everybody Is Talking"; Walleigh, "What's Your Excuse?"

[34]Norman Gaither, "An Improved Lot-Sizing Model of MRP Systems," *Production and Inventory Management,* Third Quarter 1983, pp. 10–20.

[35]Anderson et al., "Materials Requirements Planning Systems," p. 59.

SUMMARY OF KEY POINTS

■ A key to increased productivity in P/OM is inventory control. Inventory control methods attempt to reduce the costs of inventory by maintaining a balance between the cost of having too much inventory and the cost of having too little.

■ The management science approach has long recognized the importance of inventory control. That recognition has resulted in an impressive array of ideas, theories, and methods of inventory management. Economic order quantity (EOQ) methods and material requirements planning (MRP) systems are the most widely used.

■ A typical manufacturing firm must manage several different inventories: raw materials, supplies, work in process, and finished goods. In recent years, the annual cost of carrying these inventories has exceeded $100 billion for the economy as a whole. The staggering level of inventory costs testifies to the importance of improving inventory management.

■ Effective management of inventory requires a distinction between independent and dependent demand for inventory. Independent demand inventory is unrelated to the demand or usage of other items. Finished goods (end products) are subject to independent demand. Dependent demand inventory is related to demand or usage of other items. Raw materials and work in process (components and subassemblies) are subject to dependent demand.

■ The economic order quantity (EOQ) method is appropriate for controlling independent demand inventories, whose demand is relatively constant over time and known with certainty. EOQ controls inventory cost by determining the size of an order (or lot size, if manufactured rather than bought) that minimizes the total inventory cost.

■ EOQ is based on the idea that the optimal order quantity equates carrying cost and ordering cost. The logic is that as order size increases, carrying costs increase (average inventory increases) but ordering costs decrease (the number of orders decreases). But at some point, the increase in carrying cost equals the decrease in ordering costs, and no further cost reductions can be obtained by increasing the size of the order.

■ EOQ is most applicable in organizations whose product or service is consumed in fairly constant rates and has relatively few dependent items in the bills of materials.

■ Material requirements planning (MRP) is applicable for dependent demand inventory, in which the demand or usage of inventory is discontinuous, such as job-lot or batch manufacturing. MRP stresses the control of the dependent inventory through computer-based ordering and scheduling.

■ The key elements of MRP are the master production schedule, the bills of materials, and inventory records. In most instances, MRP also requires computer capability. Through successive steps, the gross requirements are "exploded" into constituent items and summarized in an aggregate requirements schedule of what items are needed when.

■ In its most fully developed state, MRP has evolved into a general P/OM technique: resource requirements planning (RRP). At this point, MRP is a way of "managing the business."

DISCUSSION AND REVIEW QUESTIONS

1. Why is it necessary for firms to carry inventories of finished goods? What purposes are served by such inventories?

2. Discuss how a firm could go about developing and implementing a strategic inventory control system.

3. Explain the relationship between the various inventories and the systems theory explanation of a firm's activities.

4. Why do production managers prefer relatively smooth production rates? How do inventories help them achieve this kind of production?

5. Explain why the total inventory costs of ordering and carrying move in opposite directions as the size of the inventory increases.

6. The Slag Valley Construction Corporation uses 5,000 pressure valves annually. The cost accountants

ascertain that the ordering cost for securing the valves from suppliers is $60. Each valve costs $10. The carrying charge for the valves is estimated to be 20 percent per year of the average inventory.

  a. Utilize the trial-and-error method to derive the economic order quantity for the number of valves to order, using the following possibilities: 500, 1,000, 2,500, 5,000.

  b. Utilize the EOQ formula to determine the economic order size.

7. How would you redefine the variables in the EOQ formula to make it applicable to determining the lot size in the case of making rather than buying the part? What costs would have to be taken into account if you were attempting to determine the optimal number of items to produce?

8. Under what circumstances is MRP preferable to EOQ as an inventory control method? Are EOQ and MRP mutually exclusive? That is, must a firm use one or the other for all inventory items? Explain.

9. Define the basic tools and decisions that make up an MRP system. Which decisions are pivotal for determining the relative effectiveness of an MRP system?

10. Explain why MRP usually requires computer utilization. Does the computer requirement place limits on the kinds of firms for which MRP is applicable? Explain.

11. Describe and illustrate the application of MRP in managing the university cafeterias. Assume that the menu plan for the semester is the master production schedule. What then are the bills of materials? The inventory records? How would order points and lead times be determined? How would aggregate requirements be determined?

ADDITIONAL REFERENCES

Ackerman, K. "Just-in-Time American Practitioners." *Management Review,* June 1988, pp. 55ff.

Adkins, J., and **R. Tieken.** "MRP Keeps Production on Schedule." *Production Engineering,* July 1985, pp. 22–23.

Anderson, J. C. *Material Requirements Planning: A Study of Implementation and Practice.* Falls Church, Va.: American Production and Inventory Control Society, 1981.

Axsater, S.; C. Schneeweiss; and **E. Silver, eds.** *Multi-Stage Production Planning and Inventory Control.* New York: Springer-Verlag, 1986.

Bemelmans, R. *The Capacity Aspect of Inventories.* New York: Springer-Verlag, 1986.

Bose, G. J., and **A. Rao.** "JIT with MRPII Creates Hybrid Environment." *Industrial Engineering,* September 1988, pp. 42–48.

Byrd, J., and **D. M. Carter.** "A Just-in-Time Implementation Strategy at Work." *Industrial Management,* March–April 1988, pp. 8–10.

Davis, D. J. "Transportation and Inventory Management." *Distribution,* June 1985, pp. 10–16.

Goyal, S. K. "Economic Order Quantity under Conditions of Permissible Delay in Payments." *Journal of the Operations Research Society,* April 1985, pp. 335–38.

Greene, J. H., ed. *Production and Inventory Control Handbook.* New York: McGraw-Hill, 1987.

Hall, R. W. *Attaining Manufacturing Excellence: Just-in-Time, Total Quality, Total People Involvement.* Homewood, Ill.: Dow Jones–Irwin, 1987.

Hay, E. J. *The Just-in-Time Breakthrough: Implementing the New Manufacturing Basics.* New York: John Wiley & Sons, 1988.

Herrington, D. L. "Customized Hands-On Training Removes the Barriers to Implementing MRP II." *Production and Inventory Management Review,* August 1987, pp. 43–45.

Kelly, D. A. "The Principle of Complex Demand." *Production and Inventory Management,* Second Quarter 1985, pp. 115–20.

Lawler, W. "EOQ, MRP, JIT: Inventory's Alphabet Soup." *Massachusetts CPA Review,* Summer 1984, pp. 10–15.

Mather, H. *Bills of Material.* Homewood, Ill.: Dow Jones–Irwin, 1987.

Monden, Y. *Applying Just-in-Time: The American-Japanese Experience.* Norcross, Ga.: Industrial Engineering and Management Press, 1986.

Musselwhite, W. C. "The Just-in-Time Production Challenge." *Training and Development Journal,* February 1987, pp. 30–33.

Myers, W. S. "Let Just-in-Time Mend Your Split Culture." *Industrial Management,* March–April 1988, pp. 11–18.

Savage-Moore, W. "Creating a JIT Environment at a Customer Service Center." *Industrial Engineering,* September 1988, pp. 60ff.

Savaiano, R. A. "MRP for Small Manufacturers: Keys to Success." *Production and Inventory Management Review,* December 1987, pp. 31ff.

Schlaegel, J. T., and **J. Petrucci.** "Case Study: Working Together to Solve MRPII Problems." *Production and Inventory Management Review,* October 1987, pp. 38–47.

Sepehri, M. "Case in Point: Buick City—Genuine Just-in-Time Delivery." *Production and Inventory Management Review,* March 1988, pp. 34–35.

CASE 19–1   Inventory Control at Corning

Corning Incorporated (formerly Corning Glass Works) is a major U.S. corporation operating in a multinational market. The company makes 60,000 products, employs some 29,000 people in 63 plants located throughout the world, and does business in more than 90 countries. Its record of product success and reliability accounted in large measure for its $1.6 billion in sales in 1981. But Corning had inventory control problems that it was just beginning to deal with.

During the mid-1970s, Corning executives had been disturbed to find that the company's reputation for prompt and reliable shipment of orders was being threatened. Plants were unable to complete products on time because required inventory was not on hand. For example, they could not coordinate the availability of bowls made in a Pennsylvania plant with lids for those bowls made in a West Virginia plant. When the manufacture of these two parts is not synchronized, Corning Ware cannot be shipped. Executives correctly identified the problem as inventory control and, more broadly, as production management. But they had to find a solution that could apply to this broad area.

The magnitude and complexity of Corning are suggested by the fact that it manufactures 60,000 items of great variety. Everyone is familiar with its baking dishes and coffeepots. But nearly two thirds of its business is in technical, scientific, medical, and industrial products. It makes components for computers, lenses for eyewear, glass products for autos and TVs, and even supplies for the space industry. Corning's major competitors include many of the most progressive and productive Japanese and European firms. Efficiency in production can reap big dividends. Therefore, production management at Corning takes in a lot of ground.

So, where to begin? The executives decided that to solve the inventory problems by improving production management would require a company-wide effort. Every functional area from marketing to finance to purchasing would have to be involved in the solution. The technique that appealed most to the managers was material requirements planning, and they began to implement it. Since MRP implementation would affect all parts of the company, they had to design the implementation process as carefully as they designed the technique itself.

To begin the changeover to MRP, management selected three plants that had already made considerable progress toward managing inventories. Corning believed that these plants would develop and adopt MRP and become examples for the rest of the company. The plants selected are located in Greencastle, Pennsylvania, Harrodsburg, Kentucky, and Martinsburg, West Virginia. In short order, each facility implemented MRP, and plant managers were able to document productivity gains that resulted.

Source: Based on Bruce Horovitz, "Why Corning Is Sticking with MRP," *Industry Week,* January 25, 1982, pp. 44–48; Myron Magnet, "Corning Glass Shapes Up," *Fortune,* December 13, 1982, pp. 90–96, 102, 104, 108–9.

Dick Sphon, plant manager of the Harrodsburg facility at that time, was an enthusiastic supporter of MRP. The system went on line in 1979, and by 1981 the plant was saving $500,000 per year. These savings resulted from elimination of the need to take physical inventory, inventory accuracy of 90 percent, and balanced production. "The system and its computer do the busywork," said production supervisor Al Webber, "and we manage the plant instead of fire fighting."

Success stories were told at the other two sites as well, and these stories spread throughout the organization. The plant managers became featured speakers at the semiannual get-togethers of Corning's plant managers. As a result of these success stories, more and more plants began the conversion.

According to some executives, MRP can create ego problems. Its computerized scheduling enables headquarters officials to make decisions that plant managers once made. So, many managers view the system as a threat to their authority and prerogatives as plant managers. Proponents of MRP respond by noting that MRP eliminates minor problems and permits the manager to spend time on important decisions.

QUESTIONS FOR ANALYSIS

1. Evaluate the manner in which Corning implemented the MRP system.
2. Explain fully why plant managers would resist the installation of MRP at their locations.
3. Explain the productivity implications of reducing inventory levels and lowering breakdown points.

CASE 19–2   Just-in-Time Inventory Control at the Toyota Truck Plant

Long Beach, California, is the site of a truck bed manufacturing facility owned and operated by Toyota Motor Company. The plant has attracted considerable attention because of its successful application of Japanese-style inventory control procedures. The Long Beach plant fabricates, assembles, and paints four models of truck beds for Toyota light trucks. It has a capacity of 150,000 units per year and an annual payroll of $10 million. The plant is a significant economic factor in the Long Beach community, as well as an enlightened user of modern inventory control methods.

The Long Beach plant's mission is to supply truck beds of appropriate style, size, and color to each of the eight ports of entry receiving truck cabs from Toyota plants in Japan. The cabs are shipped from Japan without beds, which are added upon arrival. Close coordination is required to ensure that cabs and beds match at the eight ports. The system puts a high premium on production

Source: Mehran Sepehri, "How Kanban System Is Used in an American Toyota Motor Facility," *Industrial Engineering,* February 1985, pp. 50–56.

scheduling, inventory management, and shipping. At the heart of the Long Beach system is a practice and philosophy termed just-in-time (JIT) inventory control.

JIT involves a complete commitment to the idea that whatever is being done now can be done in a better way. Consequently, there is never a sense of acceptance of the status quo. As soon as a practice or procedure is implemented in response to a problem, it itself becomes the focus of scrutiny. This critical attitude is necessary in order to attain the ideal inventory situation: lot sizes of one unit and zero work in process. At that point, the cost of raw materials and work-in-process inventories is at its absolute minimum.

The JIT system takes its name from the idea that a required inventory part or unit should arrive at the point where it is needed at the split second before it is needed. Thus, a brace for a truck bed would arrive on the assembly line at the precise moment when the worker is ready to weld it in place. As we move on down the line, we can see that the truck bed is completed at the precise instant when it is to be painted; it comes off the line at the precise moment when it is to be loaded and shipped to one of the eight ports of entry; it arrives at the port of entry precisely on time to coincide with the arrival of the cabs from Japan.

The ultimate purpose of JIT is to eliminate the need for inventory. But that requires the elimination of defects, late arrivals of component parts from outside vendors, assembly-line breakdowns, and work stoppages in general. The focus of JIT, then, is more than inventory; the focus is the entire manufacturing process from beginning to end.

The managers of the Long Beach plant had the advantage of knowing what to expect when they decided to adopt JIT. Toyota plants in Japan had adopted the method. The difference at Long Beach was that American, not Japanese, workers and managers would be responsible for planning, implementing, and operating the system. Could Americans do the job as well as the Japanese? Could Americans be retrained to expect perfect quality rather than acceptable quality? Could they be motivated to accept the idea that nothing is perfect, that anything can be improved? Could they be expected to develop and implement procedures that would mean the elimination of their jobs, if the company promised to relocate them to other jobs? Could they work effectively in problem-solving groups, called *quality circles,* rather than working as individuals to solve knotty problems?

Apparently they not only could, they did. Some of the early performance improvements included a reduction by 45 percent of the work-in-process inventory and a reduction of 24 percent in raw materials inventory in the first year. The warehousing costs of material were reduced by 30 percent. In the production area, the labor cost savings were 20 percent and productivity increased by 40 percent, absenteeism and turnover decreased, and interdepartmental conflicts went down.

These gains stirred considerable pride of accomplishment among the employees of the plant. Their successes were publicized throughout the Toyota organization and the community. The company believes that JIT is no longer a Japanese management tool. JIT is as American as management by objectives and could be adopted by any American manufacturing plant that seeks productivity improvements in manufacturing.

1. Do you believe that JIT can be applied in plants that do not have a "Japanese connection"? What, if anything, is there about JIT that is peculiarly Japanese?
2. Why is it necessary to consider the entire manufacturing process in order to make improvements in inventory control?
3. What feature of the JIT approach can apply in organizations that do not have inventories, such as banks, professional firms, and the like?

EXPERIENTIAL EXERCISE

UNDERSTANDING INVENTORY CONTROL

Purpose

This exercise reinforces students' understanding of the technical aspects of inventory control, as well as their appreciation of information and assumptions as vital parts of inventory control.

The Exercise in Class

The instructor will divide the class into groups of four to six students in order for each group to consider a hypothetical firm in a specific industry. The choice of firms is at the instructor's discretion. (The exercise works best when the firms chosen relate to those in the surrounding community.) Assigning the same firm to more than one group will facilitate useful comparisons, during class discussion, of the underlying assumptions and knowledge used by each group as bases for its report. After receiving its assigned business, each group will:

1. Evaluate the applicability of inventory control in the hypothetical firm.
2. Prepare a report that describes the features of the system, including the underlying technique (EOQ, MRP, JIT, etc.) and the expected costs of the system (e.g., record-keeping and administration).
3. Present the report to the rest of the class, and answer questions about its content.

The Learning Message

Inventory systems are technical applications, but they also depend on the knowledge base of those who develop them. In the absence of knowledge, assumptions become even more important.

COMPREHENSIVE CASE PART **IV**
MANAGING PRODUCTION AND OPERATIONS

McCall Diesel Motor Works

McCall Diesel Motor Works has been a pioneer in the manufacture of diesel internal-combustion engines. The plant is located on tidewater in the state of New Jersey, a site dictated originally by the fact that the company built engines for the marine field, chiefly fishing boats and pleasure craft. Later, its production was extended to include stationary types of engines. They are used essentially for the production of power in small communities, in manufacturing plants, or on farms.

During the earlier years of the company's operation, its engines were largely special-order jobs; even at the present time, about 60 percent of the output is made to order. In recent years, however, there has been a trend toward standardization, particularly in component parts but also in lines of engines. The engineering department has followed the principle of simplification and standardization in the case of minor parts such as studs, bolts, and springs, giving a degree of interchangeability to these components among the various sizes and types of engines. Sizes of marine engines have also been standardized to some extent, although customer requirements still necessitate special designs. In the small engines for agricultural use, there has been a genuine effort to concentrate sales on a standard line of engines of three sizes—20, 40, and 60 horsepower.

The company has always been advanced in its engineering development and design. The production phase, on the other hand, has not been progressive. The heritage of job-shop operation persists. Despite the definite trend toward standardization, production continues largely on a made-to-order basis. But the increasing popularity of diesel engines has brought many new companies into the field, tightening the competitive situation.

High manufacturing costs and poor service have been reflected in the loss of orders. Customer complaints, together with pressure from the sales department, prompted management to call in a consulting engineer to make a survey of the manufacturing department and recommend what action should be taken. The engineer submitted the following findings:

1. *Manufacturing methods,* while still largely of the job-shop character, are in the main good, and no wholesale change should be made. As production is still 60 percent special, a complete shift to line manufacture or departmentalization by product is not feasible.

2. *Machinery and equipment* is for the most part general-purpose, in line with manufacturing requirements. Some machine tools are approaching obsolescence; high-production, single-purpose machines would be advisable and for certain operations. Extensive replacement of machine tools is not a pressing need, but an increased use of jigs and fixtures should be undertaken

Source: Prepared by Frank K. Shallenberger, Stanford University. Used with permission.

immediately. Many bottlenecks exist in the plant; but contrary to your belief as well as that of your superintendant and other shop executives, there is no serious lack of productive equipment. The trouble lies in the improper utilization of the machine time available.

3. *Production control* is the major element of operating weakness, and improvement is imperative. The lack of proper control over production is evidenced by the following:

a. In-process inventory is too high, as indicated by piles of partially completed parts over the entire manufacturing floor area.

b. There are no records concerning the whereabouts of orders in process from their initiation to delivery at assembly.

c. The number of rush orders is inordinately high, particularly in assembly but also in parts manufacture.

d. Too many parts chasers must be used to force orders through the shops by pressure methods.

e. Piecemeal manufacture—a lot of 20 parts usually is broken up into four or five lots before it is finished—is a problem. Not infrequently the last sublot remains on the shop floor for months and, in a number of instances, is lost so far as records are concerned. Subsequent orders for the same part are issued and new lots pass through to completion while the remains of the old lot lie in a partially fabricated condition.

f. Setup costs are excessive, resulting from the piecemeal methods mentioned in *e* as well as the failure to use proper lot sizes, even when lots are not broken up during manufacture.

g. All the necessary component parts fail to reach assembly at approximately the same time. The floor of the assembly department is cluttered with piles of parts awaiting receipt of one or more components before engines can be assembled.

h. The department lacks a definite sequence of manufacturing operations for a given part. Reliance as to the exact way by which a part is to be made rests entirely on the various departmental supervisors. These people are able machinists, but they are burdened with detail and their memories cannot be relied on to ensure that parts will always be manufactured in the best, or even the same, sequence of operations. Moreover, they have undue responsibility for determining the department to which a lot of parts should be sent when it has been completed in their department.

i. In the case of certain small standard parts, shop orders have been issued as many as six or eight times in a single month.

j. Information is lacking from which to estimate, with any degree of close approximation, the overall manufacturing time for an engine. The result is failure to meet delivery promises or high production cost due to rush or overtime work.

k. Parts in process or in storage and destined for imminent assembly are frequently taken by the service department to supply an emergency repair order. The question here is not the academic determination of priority between the customer whose boat may be lying idle due to a broken part and the customer who has not yet received his engine. The question is why there should be any habitual difficulty in rendering adequate repair service and, at the same time, meeting delivery promises.

l. Virtually all basic manufacturing data reside in the heads of the superintendent, departmental supervisors, assistant supervisors, and setup workers.

m. Delivery dates are set by the sales department and generally are dates that customers arbitrarily stipulate.

n. The general superintendent shows little enthusiasm for the idea of a system of production control. In fact, he is opposed to such an installation. He is of the opinion that reasonably satisfactory results are now being obtained by placing responsibility in the supervisors and maintaining contact between them and the parts chasers, who in turn are held responsible for meeting delivery promises. He believes that no system can be substituted for the supervisors' knowledge of the workers' ability. He feels that operation of a production control system requires time studies of all jobs; this, he points out, is difficult because of the many operations involved, the high degree of special work, the probable resistance of the workers, and the cost which would be incurred. He states further that emergencies and rush orders would upset any rigid scheduling of work through the plant. Finally, he is convinced that any system of production control involves an excessive amount of clerical detail to which the supervisors, who are practical shop men, object. The state of affairs found by the consultant was, he realized, due to two main causes: (1) the strong influence of the original job-shop character of manufacture and the very slow evolution to large-scale operations, and (2) the fact that top management of the company was essentially salesminded.

The engineer's recommendations, therefore, had to be made with the idea of presenting a simple, straightforward program to provide adequate control over production and to enable this control to be instituted gradually and logically.

QUESTIONS FOR ANALYSIS

1. Outline the essential features of a production control system for this company, giving sufficient detail to make clear how the system will function.
2. Indicate what part of your procedure should be centralized and what part decentralized. That is, what functions should be handled by a central production control office, and what functions should be carried out in the various production and assembly departments?
3. What data must be compiled before your system can become fully effective?
4. List the benefits that the company will derive when your production control system is in operation.

PART

V

EMERGING
MANAGEMENT ISSUES

FOUNDATIONS OF EMERGING
MANAGEMENT ISSUES

20
ENTREPRENEURSHIP

21
MANAGING IN A MULTINATIONAL ENVIRONMENT

22
MANAGEMENT CAREERS

Foundations of Emerging Management Issues

Management is one of the most dynamic and demanding endeavors today. Managers must perform a wide variety of work: planning, organizing, controlling, and leading people—tasks that, as you have learned, are in themselves quite challenging. However, managers must do more. They must also address an ever changing variety of issues and trends that significantly affect the work and well-being of organizations.

For example, managers in the 1970s dealt with energy crises that significantly affected costs of operation and required that organizations perform work in new ways that conserve energy. The trend of increasing government regulation in such areas as industrial pollution, employee safety, and personnel practices also required major changes in the work of management. In the early 1980s, a severe recession and intensifying competition dealt managers the tasks of restructuring their organizations and finding new ways to strengthen the competitiveness of their companies.

As management enters the 1990s, we believe that three emerging issues will greatly influence the work of organizations. In some ways, these issues will also affect you as a member of an organization, whether you are an employee or a manager. Because of their importance, we devote a chapter in Part V to each of the following issues.

Entrepreneurship

Today, an unprecedented number of people are putting their personal resources (money, skills, time, and energy) into the task of creating a small business. However, the risk of failure is high because the task is so challenging. One individual must plan, organize, control, and lead an enterprise in which resources are limited and the room for mistakes small. Yet, despite the risks, America is experiencing a boom in entrepreneurship that will continue in the 1990s. This trend is strengthening the already considerable impact of small business on America's economic well-being. The boom has also raised a key issue: how to effectively create and manage small businesses to reduce the risk of failure and increase the chances of entrepreneurial rewards and success. Chapter 20 discusses this question.

Globalization of Business

The 1990s will be the decade of internationalization. Organizations, from small shops to Fortune 500–sized corporations, will venture outside their domestic boundaries and manufacture and/or sell their products and services in markets worldwide. In doing so, these organizations will deal with an entirely new set of challenges. They will confront the task of managing in new

environments where consumer preferences, government relationships, employees, and societal cultures differ greatly from those at home. The globalization of business raises the important question of how to effectively manage in a multinational environment. This issue is the focus of Chapter 21.

MANAGEMENT CAREERS

In times past, an implicit contract existed between managers and their organizations: do good work and your job is secure. Today, however, regular corporate restructurings have severed this agreement in many organizations, and this trend of corporate downsizing is expected to continue through the 1990s. As a result, the nature of management careers is changing. Building a career in management today often means assuming more personal responsibility for developing the career and working for several organizations across the span of a career, instead of only one or two. Many managers in the 1990s will also deal with the problem of limited opportunities for advancement, because restructurings have reduced the number of positions in the middle and upper levels of the organizational hierarchy.

In turn, organizations face several challenges concerning management careers in the 1990s. They must find new ways to develop, retain, and motivate good managers when promotion opportunities are limited. Given the projected huge influx of women into the managerial ranks in the 1990s, organizations must also find ways to help women balance work and family demands. These challenges, focal concerns of both managers and organizations in the 1990s, are addressed in the coverage of management careers in Chapter 22.

As you read these concluding chapters in your study of management, keep in mind that you will probably be affected by the issues of entrepreneurship, globalization, and management careers at some point in your future. Consider that you will likely observe and experience the challenges of entrepreneurship by working in a small business; you could well become an entrepreneur yourself. It is very likely that at some time during the 1990s you will join an international business and your work will in some way be affected by the company's international concerns and activities. And if you choose a career in management, proactively managing your career, balancing family and work responsibilities, and dealing constructively with obstacles to upward advancement will all, at some time, be primary concerns.

People in Management

Barbara Nyden Rodstein

Business acumen, a highly developed ethical sense, determination, and empathy are among the traits that characterize Barbara Nyden Rodstein, president and cofounder of Harden Industries, a Los Angeles–based manufacturer of unique and high-priced designer faucets for kitchens and bathrooms.

Nyden Rodstein is the only female business head in the male-dominated plumbing industry. She and her late husband founded the company in 1982. After an initial burst of success, Harden floundered when a Japanese company began offering faucets for less than the Nyden Rodsteins' manufacturing costs. In response, the entrepreneurial couple rethought their business plan and defined their goal: "To produce an American-made product made and sold with American dollars." They then pressed forward.

After Harry Rodstein died in 1987, Barbara became determined to expand the company. At the end of its first year of operation, Harden Industries had grossed $3 million. By the close of 1988, the company had grossed approximately $25 million, generated by a possible 1.6 million combinations of 68 different product lines. Nyden Rodstein also increased output at Harden so that employees were turning out a new product, on average, every two weeks.

Today Harden employs 300 people, has sales offices operating in London and Tokyo, and recently started construction on a large manufacturing facility in the Philippines. The company has developed a new manufacturing process by which fixtures are machined and welded by hand, piece by piece, in brass. This means that a basic lavatory faucet set can retail for $1,100, the most expensive pricing on the market.

Nyden Rodstein's management style is open and generous. Asked about her hiring practices, Nyden Rodstein says, "I put golden handcuffs on people," meaning that she pays higher salaries than her competitors. In addition, at Harden, people are encouraged to speak openly. Nyden Rodstein takes frequent tours of her factory, where virtually every employee knows her personally. Impromptu meetings are often held on the factory floor, including factory workers as well as Harden's three-person management team.

Nyden Rodstein's door is always open. If employees spot a problem in manufacturing, sales, or another area, she encourages them to come in and spell it out for her. Says Nyden Rodstein, "The worst sins are sins of omission. I understand . . . when people make mistakes, but I'm not so understanding when they fail to report a problem."

Harden employs members of at least 12 ethnic and racial groups. Nyden Rodstein sees minority growth in the United States as positive and inevitable and is committed to "bringing minorities into the mainstream, letting them see the system work, and giving them a chance." To this end, Harden pays the college tuition for all employees' children, with a special emphasis on those for whom English is a second language.

Nyden Rodstein describes the philosophy by which she operates as "those four-letter words: *hard work*." She is the driving force behind Harden Industries, setting policy, interacting with and motivating employees, and pushing ahead toward bigger sales and new product lines. She typifies the entrepreneurial spirit that is making successful business people of women throughout the country.

Source: J. A. Dunnington, "Instincts, Ethics, and 4-Letter Words," *Woman's Enterprise*, June 1989, pp. 62–65; personal interview.

20

ENTREPRENEURSHIP

LEARNING OBJECTIVES

After completing Chapter 20, you should be able to:

Define
the term *entrepreneur.*

Describe
the characteristics and motivations of entrepreneurs.

Discuss
the primary tasks of the entrepreneur in terms of the planning, organizing, and controlling functions.

Compare
the managerial tasks of the entrepreneur with those of the nonfounder CEO of a large, ongoing corporation.

Identify
the three major challenges facing many entrepreneurs today.

Contact Lenses for Chickens (and Other Entrepreneurial Ideas)

It seemed a silly, even nonsensical idea—rose-colored contact lenses for chickens who populate poultry farms. However, this entrepreneurial brainstorm has generated sizable profits for Randall Wise, founder of Animalens, Inc., because the lenses alleviate a very costly consequence of chickens' instinctive behavior.

Chickens instinctively peck each other on the head to establish a social hierarchy in the coop. The stronger chickens affirm their dominant status in the group by pecking smaller chickens into submission. Thereafter, the weaker chickens walk with their heads bowed submissively to escape injury. However, establishing the "pecking order" within the coop is very costly to the poultry farmer; on average, about 25 percent of the birds are pecked to death.

Mr. Wise found that, with rose-tinted lenses in their eyes, chickens pecked less; with their blurred vision, they could not see their potential victims. On average, the lenses reduce fatalities in a coop to 5 to 7 percent. They also provide other benefits. Because the rose color has a calming effect on the birds, they are less active and eat less, which lowers feed costs. The lenses also reduce feed waste caused by "billing"—the chicken spewing feed from their beaks onto the ground. The birds' lens-blurred vision forces them to lower their heads into the feed bins to see what they are eating, which reduces the amount of feed lost from billing. Although initially skeptical, many farmers are now convinced that the lenses, at a only few cents a pair, are an effective way to lower expenses. Sales at Animalens are doing very well.

Each year, many thousands of energetic and ambitious individuals like Randall Wise create business enterprises founded on unique ideas. Some have achieved success: Laura Newman sells audio tapes of background office sounds to at-home entrepreneurs who want phoning clients to hear telephones ringing and typewriters clicking instead of children yelling and the television blasting. Ronald Bayles designs and markets Naughty checks, bank checks with tasteless designs for those who want their creditors to know what they think of them.

However, translating an innovative idea into a successful enterprise requires that an entrepreneur incur substantial risks and effectively overcome often significant obstacles. The risks, tasks, and challenges of entrepreneurship are among the topics of this chapter.

Source: Adapted from Dyan Machan, "How Gus Blythe Smelled Opportunity," *Forbes,* October 3, 1988, pp. 104ff; Robin Kamen, "Office Chatter," *Venture,* January 1989, p. 10; Robin Kamen, "Pay It with Feeling," *Venture,* August 1988, p. 10.

Peruse the latest issues of *The Wall Street Journal, Fortune, Business Week,* and other major business periodicals; watch the evening's national news broadcast. The impression is clear: Big businesses provide the foundation of the U.S. economy. Exxon, IBM, Citicorp, R. J. Reynolds–Nabisco, and other huge corporations generate the jobs, revenues, and financial strength central to our economic well-being.

However, this "clear" impression is misleading and woefully incomplete. The vital, missing contributor is small business. The gas stations, corner grocery stores, hobby shops, medical clinics, and any number of other small businesses you see in a given day produce about half of the nation's gross national product.

Because the vast majority of these mostly privately owned companies publish little information about their activities and they are rarely covered by the business press, we are often unaware of the size and power of small businesses. From 1980 to 1987, America's "hidden economy" created 17 million new jobs.[1] Each year, these small companies, some 14 million of them, generate over 80 percent of the new jobs in the United States. Altogether, America's small business community is the world's fourth greatest economic power, behind the economies of the United States, Japan, and the Soviet Union.[2]

At the helm of many, if not most, of these companies is the **entrepreneur:** the individual who, propelled by an idea, personal goals, and ambition, brings together the financial capital, people, equipment, and facilities to establish and manage a business enterprise. As the creators and navigators of small business, entrepreneurs are a dominant force in the U.S. economy.

In starting and managing a business, entrepreneurs face challenges unique from those of their big business counterpart, the nonfounder chief executive officer (CEO) of a large, ongoing corporation. Unlike the corporate CEO, entrepreneurs are deeply and personally involved in every aspect of the enterprise, at least in the early stages of the business. They apply the management functions in creating, building, and shaping the business. As a result, the organization significantly reflects the entrepreneur's needs, goals, and values.[3] Entrepreneurs also cope with far greater personal and professional risk. In most cases, personal financial resources will be lost if the business fails. Unlike large corporations, there are no resources to cushion the effects of mistakes or unexpected developments. Most small businesses are initially run on a shoestring budget that heightens the importance and stresses of the entrepreneur's decision making. Entrepreneurs are also strictly and singularly

---

[1]David L. Birch, "The Hidden Economy," *The Wall Street Journal Reports on Small Business (Special Section),* June 10, 1988, p. 25R.

[2]George Melloan, "Small Firms Brace for Legislative Attack," *The Wall Street Journal,* May 5, 1987, p. 37; "Millions of New Jobs to Be Created in '86, Survey Shows," *Mobile Register,* March 31, 1986, p. 3A.

[3]Several studies have examined the impact of an entrepreneur's personal characteristics on the firm (e.g., firm growth, structure, flexibility). For two insightful examples, see Norman R. Smith and John B. Miner, "Type of Entrepreneur, Type of Firm and Managerial Motivation: Applications for Organizational Life Cycle Theory," *Strategic Management Journal* 4 (1983), pp. 325–40; Graeme Salaman, "An Historical Discontinuity: From Charisma to Routinization," *Human Relations* 30, no. 4 (1977), pp. 373–88.

accountable for their businesses' success or failure. There is usually no board of directors to share the burden of responsibility.

This chapter's discussion of entrepreneurship focuses specifically on the entrepreneur. We devote much of the chapter to the tasks of entrepreneurship, which are presented in terms of the three functions of managing work and organizations (planning, organizing, and controlling) and the entrepreneur's activities involved in managing people, specifically leadership. We will also discuss three special challenges that confront many entrepreneurs today.

We devote a chapter to this topic because of the entrepreneur's considerable economic and social importance in the United States and because of the growing prevalence of entrepreneurship. Every year, about 1.3 million individuals assume the challenge and risks of creating a business in the United States.[4] At some point in your career, you may well become one of them.

THE ENTREPRENEUR

Management scholars and observers have differed in their definition of an entrepreneur. Many view an entrepreneur as the creator, owner, and chief executive of a business enterprise. Some have emphasized financial risk as a key characteristic of the entrepreneur. A more recent perspective distinguishes between the small business owner and the entrepreneur. The small business owner establishes and manages a business to attain personal objectives. The business is an extension of the owner's needs, goals, and personality, and growth may not be a primary objective. In contrast, entrepreneurs create a business to build the enterprise for growth and profit. They use a deliberate, planned approach that applies strategic management concepts and techniques. The entrepreneur is also highly innovative, creating new products and markets and applying creative strategies and ways of managing.[5]

Our perspective assumes the more general definition of the entrepreneur as the creator and manager of a business. However, this discussion will emphasize the innovative, growth-oriented entrepreneur. Tom Monaghan, founder and chief executive of Domino's Pizza, is an example of this type of entrepreneur. He is profiled in the Management Focus.

RISKS

At least during the early stages of the enterprise, the entrepreneur works in the domain of a small business. Combining definitions provided by the Small Business Administration and the Committee for Economic Development, a small business is an organization that is privately owned (usually by top management), is not dominant in its market, maintains local operations (though it may serve a much larger market), and employs less than 500 people.[6] Half of

---

[4]Walter Kiechel III, "The Microbusiness Alternative," *Fortune,* October 24, 1988, p. 219.

[5]James W. Carland, Frank Hoy, William R. Boulton, and Jo Ann C. Carland, "Differentiating Entrepreneurs from Small Business Owners: A Conceptualization," *Academy of Management Review,* April 1984, pp. 354–59.

[6]*Meeting the Special Problems of Small Business* (New York: Committee for Economic Development, 1974), p. 14; *The State of Small Business: A Report to the President* (Washington, D.C.: U.S. Government Printing Office, March 1983), p. 28.

TABLE 20–1	Business Failure Rates in Nine Industries			
		Age of Company When It Failed		
	Industry	**5 Years or Less**	**6 to 10 Years**	**More than 10 Years**
	Agriculture, forestry, and fishing	29.1%	23.0%	47.9%
	Mining	49.1	28.7	22.2
	Construction	43.6	30.0	26.4
	Manufacturing	51.5	23.7	24.8
	Transportation and public utilities	53.1	23.4	23.5
	Wholesale trade	51.2	24.5	24.3
	Retail trade	61.5	22.3	16.2
	Finance, insurance, and real estate	52.3	25.3	22.4
	Services	60.6	22.0	17.4
	Total	54.5%	24.1%	21.4%

The failure rate of new businesses indicates that the entrepreneur must take great risks to start a business.

Source: 1986 data from Dun & Bradstreet's "Business Failures Record." Table reprinted from "Down to Earth Advice for Angels," *Changing Times,* January 1988, p. 72. Reprinted with permission.

the small businesses in the United States have annual sales of less than $500,000 and employ 10 or fewer individuals.

In launching a small business, the entrepreneur usually faces substantial *business risk.* Although well over 1 million new businesses are started each year (an estimated 1.3 million in 1988), the failure rate of young companies is disturbingly high.[7] According to research by the Small Business Administration, from 25 to 33 percent of all independent small businesses fail during the first two years of operation.[8] Eight of every 10 businesses end within 10 years.[9] Table 20–1 shows the failure rates of businesses in nine industries during 1986. Besides considerable business risk, entrepreneurs face significant *financial risk,* as they typically invest most if not all of their financial resources in the business. They take a *career risk* when leaving a secure job for a venture with a highly uncertain future. They incur *family and social risks* because the demands of starting and running a young business consume 60- to 80-hour workweeks that leave little time for attention to family and friends. The demands of entrepreneurship often strain marriages and friendships. They also assume a *psychological risk*—the risk of a deep sense of personal failure if the business does not beat the odds and succeed.[10] One highly successful entrepreneur succinctly summed up the considerable personal risks of entrepreneurship by describing the emotions of launching a business as "entrepreneurial terror."[11]

[7]David L. Birch, "The Truth about Start-Ups," *Inc.,* January 1988, pp. 14–15.

[8]Jeremy Main, "Breaking Out of the Company," *Fortune,* May 25, 1987, p. 83.

[9]Richard Greene, "Do You Really Want to Be Your Own Boss?" *Forbes,* October 21, 1985, pp. 86–87.

[10]Patrick R. Liles, *New Business Ventures and the Entrepreneur* (Homewood, Ill.: Richard D. Irwin, 1974), pp. 14–15.

[11]Wilson Harrell, "Entrepreneurial Terror," *Inc.,* February 1987, pp. 74–76.

MANAGEMENT FOCUS

Tom Monaghan: Prince of Pizza

Times were not always so enjoyable for Tom Monaghan, founder of Domino's Pizza. When he launched his business on a $900 investment in 1960 near Eastern Michigan University, college students would play pranks. Everyone in a dorm would order pizzas at the same time. Often, while Monaghan was making deliveries in a dorm, students would steal the pizzas still in his delivery truck. To stop the problem, the former marine would hide in the truck and ambush the robbers with a mallet or a Coke bottle. "It made me so mad," he recalls. "People were threatening my livelihood, and it was a campus sport."

However, Monaghan's tenacity paid off. After years of steady expansion (and a comeback from near-bankruptcy in 1970), Domino's Pizza is today the world's largest home delivery pizza chain. The company maintains 4,300 outlets, of which two thirds are franchises. Many observers credit the company's success to several factors, notably Monaghan's unrelenting energy and optimism and a keen understanding of what it takes

to deliver a hot, good-tasting pizza and make a profit.

During his 30 years in business, Monaghan has maintained a simple business concept, selling only one basic pizza (three sizes with up to 11 toppings) and Pepsi. The company has no sit-down service and guarantees a 30-minute delivery or provides a discount on the pizza (drivers meet the guarantee on 90 percent of the orders).

The company works to keep its franchises efficiently run and the franchise owners, store managers, and employees well trained. Only store managers may apply for a franchise; if they qualify, they are rigorously trained in all aspects of franchise management at one of Domino's Pizza's regional training centers. Employees are trained on the job by store managers equipped with a variety of training aids provided by the corporate training staff, including videocassette training tapes that are upbeat and musical (MTV style). Performance standards are demanding (e.g., the order taker must answer a call within three rings and take the order within 45 seconds;

MOTIVATIONS

Given the sizable risks, time, and energy requirements of entrepreneurship, why do so many individuals take the entrepreneurial plunge every year? Entrepreneurs are motivated to launch businesses for a number of reasons. While the potential costs are high, the rewards can also be substantial.

Independence. "Being my own boss" is a powerful motivator for many entrepreneurs, who seek the freedom to act independently in their work. As heads of business, they enjoy the autonomy of making their own decisions, setting their own work hours, and determining what they will do and when they will do it.

Personal and Professional Growth. The challenges of building a business innately involve individual growth. To be successful, an entrepreneur must be able to cope with risk, uncertainty, and stress, handle many different interpersonal relationships, and manage a business with limited resources.

the oven tender must cut and box one pizza by the count of 15).

Monaghan also rewards his managers well. Senior executives drive company-provided BMWs; top-performing store managers and franchise owners take weekend cruises on the company's million-dollar yacht, receive trips to Hawaii, or spend time at the company's plush corporate retreat. Any manager who exceeds the company's weekly sales record (currently about $62,000) receives a $12,000 Swiss gold wrist-watch, the same style that the CEO wears. Monaghan once bet an overweight vice president that the man could not run a marathon by the end of the year. The CEO lost the wager—and paid the runner $50,000.

At 52, Monaghan is a bit of a maverick. Once a child who spent many years in an orphanage or foster homes, he spends his money rather than accumulating it. In 1983, he bought the Detroit Tigers baseball team. He maintains an $18 million collection of classic cars, and once threw a $1 million, three-day Halloween party for friends and associates. He also generously donates to charity. One of his several projects is the development of a small community in the mountains of Honduras. Monaghan has funded a Catholic mission, medical clinic, and factory there—and opened a Domino's Pizza outlet.

Last year, Monaghan complicated his simple, 30-year-old business concept. He added deep-dish pizza to Domino's menu to respond to consumer demands for variety and to more effectively compete against Pizza Inn (hundreds of small single-shop operations) and Pizza Hut, which leads with 20.7 percent (to Domino's 17 percent) of the eat-in and take-out pizza market. Domino's was one of the last large pizza chains to add pan pizza to the menu. Only time will tell whether the company's success will continue in the very tough pizza industry.

Source: Adapted from Wendy Zellner, "Tom Monaghan: The Fun-Loving Prince of Pizza," *Business Week,* February 8, 1988, pp. 90ff; Bradley A. Stertz, "Domino's Beefs Up Menu to Keep Pace with Rivals," *The Wall Street Journal,* April 21, 1989, p. B1.

Many individuals become entrepreneurs to experience this growth and the fulfillment gained from building a business into a purposeful, productive entity.

A Superior Alternative to a Dissatisfying Job.   Many entrepreneurs are former executives and employees of larger corporations who were highly dissatisfied with their jobs. Some were bored with their work and frustrated with the corporation's disinterest in their ideas.[12] Others were frustrated by the slow decision making, the bureaucracy, and their limited autonomy as managers in larger companies. Among surveyed CEOs of the Inc. 500 (the 500 fastest-growing private companies in the United States), such dissatisfaction was the primary motivator for starting a business.[13]

Other executives, plateaued in their jobs, have launched businesses as a second career, contributing to a growing number of "late bloomer"

[12]Kiechel, "The Microbusiness Alternative," p. 220.

[13]Curtis Hartman, "Main Street, Inc.," *Inc.,* June 1986, p. 52.

entrepreneurs.[14] These entrepreneurs bring to their ventures years of business experience and professional contacts. In the period of major organizational downsizing in the 1980s, many of these employees took early retirement and used the income from severance packages to launch their businesses.[15]

Many female entrepreneurs report poor advancement opportunities as their major reason for launching a business.[16] One third of the female members of the Inc. 500 (twice the percentage of male members) cite their inability to move up as a major motivator for becoming an entrepreneur.[17] Other women have tired of the "corporate grind," which can be exceptionally difficult for women with children. They view running a business as ultimately providing the needed flexibility for having both a professional career and children. These trends have contributed to a boom in female entrepreneurship; today, women own 28 percent of all U.S. businesses and account for one third of all start-ups each year.[18]

Income.   Many entrepreneurs are enticed by the hefty profits of a highly successful business, although the odds in favor of such considerable success are slim. Others are motivated by making their own money in business. Surprisingly, however, many entrepreneurs do not rate money as a primary motivator for starting a business. The surveyed Inc. 500 entrepreneurs, for example, ranked money fourth in importance (behind frustration, independence, and controlling one's life). However, money is a major factor among part-time entrepreneurs, those who work full-time for a company and maintain a one-person business during off-hours. According to recent statistics, the number of these "microbusiness" entrepreneurs is increasing significantly.[19]

Security.   Given the substantial risks and uncertainty of entrepreneurship, personal security may seem an unlikely motivator. However, in a time of much corporate downsizing and layoffs, some entrepreneurs view running their own business as a more secure alternative, especially those in the middle and latter stages of their corporate careers.

Characteristics

A number of studies have been conducted to determine whether entrepreneurs distinctly differ from managers and the public at large in personality and other characteristics. Drawing generalizations from this body of research is difficult because studies differ in their definitions of an entrepreneur. However,

---

[14]Main, "Breaking Out," p. 83. See also Faye Rice, "Lessons from Late Bloomers," *Fortune,* August 31, 1987, pp. 87–91; Harry Bacas, "Leaving the Corporate Nest," *Nation's Business,* March 1987, pp. 14ff.

[15]Roger Ricklefs, "Making the Transition to Small Business," *The Wall Street Journal,* February 28, 1989, p. B1.

[16]See Susan Fraker, "Why Women Aren't Getting to the Top," *Fortune,* April 16, 1984, pp. 40–44; Alex Taylor III, "Why Women Managers Are Bailing Out," *Fortune,* August 18, 1986, pp. 16–23.

[17]Hartman, "Main Street, Inc.," p. 54.

[18]"Starting Their Own," *Nation's Business,* May 1987, pp. 23–24. Also see "Women-Owned Companies," *Inc.,* January 1987, p. 11.

[19]Kiechel, "The Microbusiness Alternative," p. 220.

FIGURE 20–1   Personal Characteristics: Comparing Entrepreneurs with
Corporate Executives

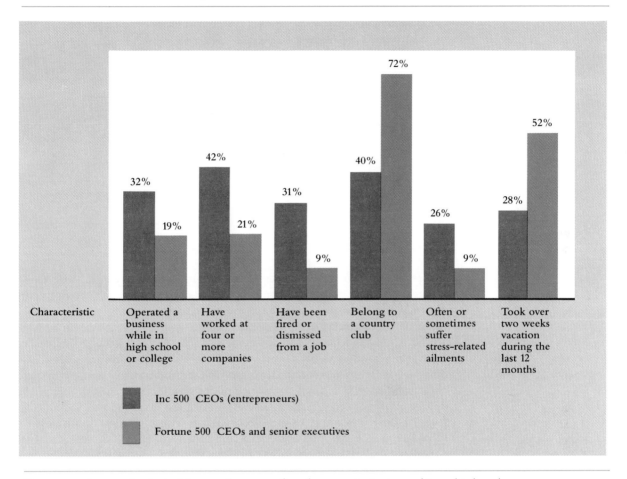

Inc 500 CEOs (entrepreneurs)

Fortune 500 CEOs and senior executives

Entrepreneurs' personal traits tend to move them away from the corporate structure and toward independence.

assuming a general definition of the term, some research support exists for a number of characteristics.[20]

Studies have found that entrepreneurs possess a significantly greater need for independence and autonomy, compared to managers. Other studies picture the entrepreneur as having a substantial need to achieve and a tolerance of ambiguity—the ability to handle uncertain and ambiguous situations. Many entrepreneurs also have high energy and endurance, substantial self-esteem, and strong dominance; that is, a need to take charge, control, and direct others. Several studies also find that the entrepreneur has a lower need for social support, compared to managers. He or she is not a team player or joiner. Figure 20–1 shows some distinct differences in the characteristics of Inc. 500 CEOs and the CEOs and senior executives of Fortune 500 companies.

[20]The discussion that follows is drawn primarily from Donald L. Sexton and Nancy Bowman, "The Entrepreneur: A Capable Executive and More," *Journal of Business Venturing* 1, no. 1 (1985), pp. 129–40.

TABLE 20–2   Assessing Your Entrepreneurial Potential

	Yes	No
1. Are you a self-starter?	_____	_____
2. Do you have a positive, friendly interest in others?	_____	_____
3. Are you a leader (do you inspire confidence and loyalty)?	_____	_____
4. Can you handle responsibility (do you enjoy taking charge)?	_____	_____
5. Are you a good organizer?	_____	_____
6. Are you prepared to put in long hours?	_____	_____
7. Do you make up your mind quickly?	_____	_____
8. Can people rely on you?	_____	_____
9. Can you withstand setbacks without quitting?	_____	_____
10. Can you adapt to changing situations?	_____	_____

If you hesitate to answer yes to many of these questions, think hard before becoming an entrepreneur.

Source: S. Norman Feingold and Leonard G. Perlman, "A Quiz for Would-Be Entrepreneurs," *Nation's Business,* March 1986, pp. 26–27.

THE ENTREPRENEUR'S TASKS

Creating and building a successful enterprise requires, above all, effectively managing work, the organization, people, and production/operations. As research clearly indicates, both poor and inexperienced management primarily cause new venture failure.[21] In 1986 alone, 9 of every 10 closings were attributed to inadequate management.[22] Thus, knowing the principles of management and applying them well are critical to new venture success. By now, you are well versed in the three primary functions in managing work and organizations (which apply in managing production/operations) and in the dynamics of managing people. Therefore, our discussion in this section will focus on how they apply to the special task of launching a small business.

Before we begin, however, it is important to briefly discuss the first entrepreneurial task—the critical first step that precedes planning. The first step is the *entrepreneur decision:* specifically deciding whether to become an entrepreneur. Making the right decision requires a clear understanding of entrepreneurship and the requirements for success. Above all, the decision should be based on an accurate self-assessment of individual skills, abilities, and shortcomings, because initially the entrepreneur *is* the business. He or she makes all the decisions, initiates critical business relationships, and performs the management functions. The entrepreneur's strengths and limitations will directly and profoundly affect the enterprise. Take a minute and answer the questions in Table 20–2 for a brief self-assessment of your entrepreneurial potential.

Many management observers agree that success requires certain entrepreneurial attributes. The entrepreneur must be motivated to make a profit, because profitability (not self-fulfillment, independence, or other motivations) is essential for survival. The entrepreneur must be an effective planner,

---

[21]For example, see *USA Today,* March 13, 1987, p. 13.

[22]Business Economics Department, Dun & Bradstreet, *Business Failures Record* (New York: Dun & Bradstreet, 1986).

MANAGEMENT FOCUS

Entrepreneurship 101

Can an individual acquire the special talents and abilities that make an entrepreneur successful? Many organizations think so; a growing number of universities, colleges, and companies are offering special courses designed to prepare aspiring students for the risks, rigors, and demands of entrepreneurship. Although these courses focus on teaching the technical side of managing a new business (e.g., preparing a business plan, balancing accounts, managing inventory), many of them also emphasize developing such nontechnical abilities as perseverance, unrelenting self-confidence, and interpersonal skills.

At the University of Michigan, for example, Jack Matson teaches a graduate business course called "Innovative Entrepreneurship." However, the semester-long course is more commonly known as "Failure 101" because of Mr. Matson's emphasis on teaching students to face failure (a frequent reality of entrepreneurship) and to learn to overcome it. He teaches lessons in failure in various ways. For example, students in one class were given a weekend assignment of creating something of value with popsicle sticks, pricing the product, and developing a marketing pitch for it.

In class on the following Monday, students presented their creations (e.g., a jewelry box, a hat that repels pesky birds), which were evaluated by the class in a "boo-off." Mr. Matson then had the students take to the streets and sell their creations. More than a few failed, and class discussions then focused on the roots of entrepreneurial failure. Later in the course, students create legitimate, ongoing ventures, and they must generate their own funding.

Kwik Kopy, the nationwide printing chain, credits its franchisee training program for at least part of the company's success (over 1,200 franchises that produce $225 million a year in sales). Each new franchisee attends Kwik Kopy University, a 23-acre pastoral campus outside Houston in Cyprus, Texas. For three weeks, students live and work at the university. Although they learn the how-to elements of printing (job scheduling, press upkeep), most of the training focuses on developing interpersonal and speaking skills in dealing with clients and on role-playing. For example, the trainees role-play sales calls, practicing how to sidestep prospective customers' secretaries to get to the boss. They also practice "cold calls" in nearby Cyprus.

Overall, Kwik Kopy University focuses on developing enthusiastic franchisees, ones with the perseverance, sense of team spirit, and skills to make their printshop franchises a success.

Source: John H. Sheridan, "Failure 101," *Industry Week,* January 2, 1989, pp. 20–21; Thomas Petzinger, Jr., "Kwik Kopy College," *The Wall Street Journal Reports on Small Business (Special Section),* June 10, 1988, p. 27R.

organizer, problem solver, and decision maker and be able to manage people well. Experience in the business is a virtual must, as are a talent for getting along with people and the ability to handle stress. The entrepreneur must have nerve, be prepared to bounce back from inevitable setbacks, and be willing to devote long hours to the business.[23] Now, count the number of your affirmative answers to the self-assessment quiz. If you gave six or more unconditional yes responses, you have definite entrepreneurial potential.

[23]Harry Bacas and Nancy L. Croft, "Go Out on Your Own?" *Nation's Business,* March 1986, pp. 18–21.

Whether an individual can acquire the skills and talents necessary to succeed as an entrepreneur is an important question. This issue is discussed in the Management Focus entitled "Entrepreneurship 101."

PLANNING

Of the three functions of managing, planning probably contributes the most to new venture performance. Planning provides a well-thought-out blueprint of action for the critical first months of the new business. This activity is vital because mistakes can be costly, even fatal, when resources are so slim in the early days of the business. Careful planning reduces the chances of major mistakes; it also forces the entrepreneur to examine the business's external environment, competition, potential customers, and the strengths and limitations of the new business.[24] However, despite the importance of planning, many entrepreneurs don't like to plan because they believe planning hinders their flexibility.[25]

The entrepreneur performs two types of planning. *Start-up planning* occurs before the enterprise opens for business. Thereafter, the entrepreneur performs *ongoing planning,* which provides further strategic and operational direction for the established business. Chapters 4 and 5 address this latter type of planning, which will not be discussed here.

Start-up planning essentially involves providing comprehensive, carefully thought-out answers to the following five questions:

1. What product or service will the business provide?
2. What market will be served?
3. How will the business be established?
4. How will the business be operated?
5. How will the business be financed?

What Product or Service Will the Business Provide? What Market Will Be Served? These two questions are addressed jointly because answering one requires consideration of the other. Doing so also avoids a classic flaw of many new product entrepreneurs: the assumption that a good product will automatically sell itself and that a ready-made market exists. The entrepreneurial graveyard is filled with unique, creative products that died for lack of customers.[26]

Many entrepreneurs address the product question by first conducting a widespread information search to identify opportunities. Numerous resources exist for this task: the business section of the newspaper, business magazines, and trade journals that focus on one industry are a few published sources of ideas. The Small Business Administration provides free, informative publications on many types of businesses.[27] Trade shows and discussions with bankers, business consultants, and large businesses can also provide direction.

[24]See Erik Larson, "The Best-Laid Plans," *Inc.,* February 1987, pp. 60–64; Bruce G. Posner, "Real Entrepreneurs Don't Plan," *Inc.,* November 1985, pp. 129–35.

[25]Richard L. Osborne, "Planning: The Entrepreneurial Ego at Work," *Business Horizons,* January–February 1987, pp. 20–24.

[26]Larson, "The Best-Laid Plans," p 63.

[27]The Small Business Administration (SBA) publishes a *Starting Out* series on many types of businesses and a *Management Aids* series of booklets on marketing and all aspects of small business management. These booklets are available free at your regional SBA field office.

At Kwik Kopy, a franchisee training program has been an important part of the company's success. Pictured here is the campus of Kwik Kopy University.

Once a large list of prospective businesses is developed, the list is reduced by considering each business's feasibility and compatibility with the entrepreneur's goals and strengths. For instance, does the entrepreneur want a business that is relatively easy to establish, one with few barriers to entry? Or is stability (long-term survival) or profit growth the primary objective? These considerations are critical because few businesses satisfy all three criteria. In a study of 1.4 million ventures (236 types of businesses), researchers found that, as shown in Table 20–3, businesses with relatively easy start-up ranked low on long-term survival; those with high survival rates were the ones that were less frequently launched. High-growth ventures (such as basic steel and electronic component manufacturers) ranked low on both stability and ease of start-up.[28]

Concerning personal strengths, the entrepreneur compares each prospect's key ability requirements with his or her own strengths. For example, people skills are essential in a clothing retail store, while technical abilities are vital in a computer repair service.

Effectively answering these two questions requires an analysis of each business's market, assessing four factors: (1) the market's size—assessing past and projected sales trends, the life-cycle stage of the product/service, and business survival rates; (2) the competition—determining the bases of competition (price, quality, image, customer service) and the strengths and limitations of competitors; (3) customers—assessing average income; and (4) market share—determining the share of the market that a new business can reasonably obtain.[29]

Many free sources of information exist for this analytical task. For example, the Chamber(s) of Commerce in the prospective market area can provide data;

[28]Birch, "The Truth about Start-Ups," pp. 14–15.

[29]Leon C. Megginson, Charles R. Scott, Jr., Lyle R. Trueblood, and William L. Megginson, *Successful Small Business Management* (Plano, Tex.: Business Publications, 1988), pp. 87–88.

TABLE 20–3	Start-Up Statistics	

Ten Most Frequently Started Businesses	Survival Rank*
1. Miscellaneous business services	132
2. Eating and drinking places	161
3. Miscellaneous shopping goods	159
4. Automotive repair shops	78
5. Residential construction	141
6. Machinery and equipment wholesalers	138
7. Real estate operators	38
8. Miscellaneous retail stores	100
9. Furniture and furnishings retailers	206
10. Computers and data processing services	163

Ten Businesses Most Likely to Survive	Start-Up Rank*
1. Veterinary services	125
2. Funeral services	158
3. Dentists' offices	108
4. Commercial savings banks	93
5. Hotels and motels	27
6. Campground and trailer parks	166
7. Physicians' offices	35
8. Barbershops	151
9. Bowling and billiards places	118
10. Cash grain crops	197

The inverse relationship of start-up ease and survival signals that the entrepreneur should not expect an easy ride on the entrepreneurial journey.

*Based on rankings of 236 types of businesses (approximately 1.4 million firms in the United States from 1978 to 1987).

Source: Reprinted from David L. Birch, "The Truth about Start-ups," *Inc.,* January 1988, p. 14. Reprinted with permission.

other census and market information is available in the local library. To gain an in-depth understanding of the competition, some prospective entrepreneurs scan trade journals, newspaper articles, and government filings for information on their prospective competitors. Because business computer databases are also becoming cheaper and easier to use, many prospective entrepreneurs are tapping these bases for competitors' annual reports, financial statements, patent information, and even in-depth profiles of corporate managers.[30]

Most entrepreneurs launch a business that offers a product or service already available in the market. However, some businesses are based on a totally new product or service idea. These ideas sometimes produce the largest business successes; consider, for example, the weed-eater, personal computer, garage door opener, and microwave oven. (Some other successful new product/service ideas are summarized in Table 20–4.) Market analysis is more challenging in this case. Because the product or service is new, there is no market data on demand or pricing. The entrepreneur must determine whether demand exists and, if so, what customers would pay. Market surveys are essential to answer

[30]Mark Robichaux, " 'Competitor Intelligence': A Grapevine to Rivals' Secrets," *The Wall Street Journal,* April 12, 1989, p. B2.

TABLE 20-4   Successful New Product/Service Ideas

Area	Idea
Health/fitness	An exercise studio for large women. Women at Large Systems Inc. (Yakima, Washington) found a successful market niche—overweight women who feel uncomfortable at regular aerobics classes. The company also offers fashion shows, makeup, and hair design. National franchise is coming soon.
Special occasions	An 8-foot personalized card (for birthdays, anniversaries, etc.) placed in the front yard at night, removed 24 hours later. The cost is $35. Yard Cards (Belleville, Illinois).
Evening wear	Evening gown rentals for big occasions. Gowns priced at $500 to $5,000 rent for $75 and up, plus a $200 minimum deposit (three-day rental). One Night Stand (New York City) carries 600 gowns, sizes 4–18.
Baby products	Toddler Casseroles—microwave dinners for children, ages nine months to three years. Kid-sized servings in beef, turkey, and chicken with grains and vegetables. Cost: $2.50 each. Growing Gourmet Inc. (Walnut Creek, California).
Auto parts	An Alter-Break device to automatically adjust an auto carburetor. About the size of a cigarette package, it attaches to the carburetor. A microchip inside detects when to make the adjustment. Cost is about $50. Nutronics Corp. (Longmont, Colorado).
Paintings	Custom ceiling designs. Using phosphorescent paint, Stellar Vision (Portland, Oregon) paints star constellations on bedroom ceilings. Sleep under the stars for a cost of $49.95 per ceiling. Service in seven states.
Portable cold drinks	A five-gallon backpack and uniform, worn by vendors at sports stadiums and concert halls, keeps drinks frosty while vendors work the aisles. A backpack stores up to 100 drinks that lose only 1 degree of temperature per hour. Manufactured by Thirstenders International Corp. (Houston, Texas).
Scuba diving equipment	Wearing a mouthpiece made by Aqua Vox Inc. (Cape Canaveral, Florida), scuba divers can hold underwater conversations and clearly understand each other.
What-if hairdos	The New Image Salon System allows customers to "try on" new hairstyles or hair colors by using a computer, camera, and interactive video with a memory of hundreds of cuts and colors. A stylist takes a "before" photo of the customer, superimposes the suggested hairstyle, and projects the results on the monitor.

Source: Adapted from "100 Ideas for New Businesses," *Venture*, November 1988, pp. 35ff, and December 1987, pp. 35ff; "The Franchisor 50," *Venture*, February 1987, pp. 39ff; "Exercise Studios—and More for Larger Women," *Venture*, March 1988, pp. 40, 41; "Yard Cards Inc: A Giant Surprise for All Occasions," *Venture*, April 1988, p. 11; "Dresses Perfect for a One Night Stand," *Venture*, May 1988, p. 14; "Dialing for Diapers," *Venture*, May 1988, p. 15.

these questions.[31] (Entrepreneurs of new ideas must also realize that marketing a new product or service requires additional spending just to explain what the new product or service is.)[32]

Regardless of whether the product or service is new or already exists, the entrepreneur should select a business that has a healthy market, is financially feasible, and matches his or her own objectives and abilities.

How Will the Business Be Established?   In other words, how will the entrepreneur enter the business? Three strategies are available: buyout, start-up, and franchise.[33]

The entrepreneur may *buy out* and acquire an existing company in the chosen business and market. This strategy affords a speedy entry into a business and market; the staff, facilities, and supplier and distribution networks are immediately provided, once the buyout contract is signed. A company with a solid track record and consumer image provides advantages that normally require years to develop. However, companies for sale can possess major, sometimes hidden problems. Entrepreneurs must deal with what they have purchased; they can't develop all aspects of the business exactly as they prefer. An effective buyout requires careful selection of a company, a thorough evaluation of the company's strengths and weaknesses, and obtaining a fair price for the business.

In the *start-up,* the entrepreneur creates the business from scratch. He or she has the freedom to define and build the business largely according to preference. However, as previously discussed, the time, effort, requirements, and risks of start-ups are usually high.

In the *franchise,* the entrepreneur (franchisee) provides a product or service under a legal contract with the franchise owner (franchisor). The franchisor provides the distinctive elements of the business (the name, image, signs, facility design, patents), an operating system, and other services. To obtain a franchise, the entrepreneur pays an initial fee and thereafter a percentage royalty on sales. The entrepreneur operates under the rights and restrictions of the contract.

Franchises are an increasingly popular form of new business. Over 500,000 franchise outlets currently operate in the United States.[34] Table 20–5 shows the top 10 franchises in the United States. Franchises are popular because they are less risky than start-ups or buyouts. During the first five years of operation, about 65 percent of all start-ups fail; only 5 percent of franchises close, according to the SBA.[35] This lower failure rate is primarily due to the support the franchisor provides—usually management and employee training,

---

[31]For an excellent, down-to-earth approach for assessing the feasibility of a new product/service idea, see Wilson Harrell, "But Will It Fly?" *Inc.,* January 1987, pp. 85ff. Also, some insightful perspectives on the pitfalls of bringing a new idea to market (and suggested strategies) are provided in Doug Garr, "The Practical Inventor," *Venture,* October 1988, pp. 35ff.

[32]Paul B. Brown, "Mission Impossible?" *Inc.,* January 1989, pp. 109–10.

[33]This discussion is based primarily on Megginson et al., *Successful Small Business Management,* pp. 88–95, 130–44; John G. Burch, *Entrepreneurship* (New York: John Wiley & Sons, 1986), pp. 101–26, 130–37.

[34]Dennis Holder, "Franchise Fever Catches On," *Working Woman,* July 1986, pp. 35–36.

[35]Ibid.

TABLE 20–5	Top 10 Franchises in the United States

	Franchise	Parent Company	Industry
Fast food and maintenance/cleaning franchises top the increasingly popular franchise market in the United States.	1. Subway Sandwiches & Salads	Doctor's Associates Inc.	Fast food
	2. Domino's Pizza	Domino's Pizza Inc.	Fast food
	3. Chem-Dry	Harris Research Inc.	Maintenance/cleaning
	4. Little Caesar's Pizza	Little Caesar Enterprises	Fast food
	5. Coverall	Coverall North America	Maintenance/cleaning
	6. Novus Windshield Repair	Novus Franchising Inc.	Auto maintenance
	7. "TCBY"—The Country's Best Yogurt	TCBY Enterprises	Ice cream/yogurt
	8. Jani-King	Jani-King International	Maintenance/cleaning
	9. United Package Mailing Service	Senpax Inc.	Packaging/shipping
	10. McDonald's	McDonald's Corp.	Fast food

Source: "The Franchise 100," *Venture,* December 1988, p. 36.

operations and accounting systems, a recognized brand name, reputation, and financial, marketing, and management assistance.

Although a franchise can provide substantial benefits, the strategy is not fault free. Major problems can arise when the franchisor does not provide the necessary guidance, reputation, and support. Consider, for example, the 130,000 franchisees of Burger King, a unit of Pillsbury Co. For the last several years, franchisees have been greatly troubled by Pillsbury's continual management turnover and its weak Burger King promotional campaigns. Burger King's demand for fast returns on investment from its franchisees in the early 1980s also prohibited new franchisees from locating their outlets in prime locations. Pillsbury's limited investment in Burger King also reduced the structural quality and appearance of its Burger King outlets. All of these factors have significantly contributed to franchisees' declining sales. In 1983, each Burger King franchise averaged about $100,000 less in sales than McDonald's. By 1989, the gap had widened to $500,000 less in annual sales.[36] Inadequate franchisor support has led other franchisees to band together and buy out the franchisor.[37]

Beyond inadequate franchisor support, the entrepreneur's creative freedom is usually inhibited by the franchise contract. The franchisor usually decides what to sell, the sales price, and many other aspects of the business.

Ensuring a successful franchise requires carefully evaluating the prospective franchisor (growth rates, performance, reputation, degree of support) and the franchise contract. Many entrepreneurs obtain franchisor evaluations from the company's other franchisees and examine the franchisor's depth of management (e.g., McDonald's maintains one manager for every 20 franchisees).[38] Many entrepreneurs also conduct their own market analysis in addition to reviewing the franchisor's assessment.

[36]Mike Connelly, "Pillsbury Feels Fury of Franchisees Scorned," *The Wall Street Journal,* November 11, 1988, p. B2; Joanne Lipman, "More Turmoil at Burger King as Chain Fires Its Ad Agency," *The Wall Street Journal,* April 24, 1989, pp. B1, 3.

[37]Buck Brown, "Believing They Can Do Better, Franchisees Are Seizing the Reins of Their Companies," *The Wall Street Journal,* March 7, 1989, pp. B1–2.

[38]Jeannie Ralston, "Promises, Promises," *Venture,* March 1988, pp. 55–57.

How Will the Business Be Operated?   The entrepreneur answers this question by planning the business's various functions such as production, marketing, personnel, and research and development. Concerning production, for example, the entrepreneur determines who will supply materials and plans the layout of the production facilities. In marketing, the entrepreneur plans how the product will be distributed to retailers and promoted. Planning for operations also involves the other management functions (organizing and controlling).

How Will the Business Be Financed?   Successfully funding a new business requires financial planning, which comprises three steps: (1) estimating the business's projected income and expenses; (2) estimating the required initial investment; and (3) locating sources of funding.[39] In estimating the new venture's income and expenses, the entrepreneur uses sales projections from the market analysis and approximates cost of production and other operating expenses, drawing from past experience and industry research. These projections are typically done for at least the first year of business.

The start-up costs are also calculated. These expenses are one-time-only costs of establishing the business (e.g., installation of equipment, beginning inventory, licenses and permits). Estimates of start-up costs and ongoing income and expenses provide a projection of the amount of funding needed to launch the business and cover costs until the business is profitable.

Many entrepreneurs rely substantially on their own personal savings to launch their businesses. As shown in Figure 20–2, personal finances were used by almost three out of four founders of the Inc. 500 companies. Other funding alternatives are often available. Commercial and investment banks, savings and loan associations, and the Small Business Administration are all frequently used sources of new venture funding. Venture capitalists, groups of investors who provide funding in exchange for a share of ownership in the company, are a possibility for ventures with substantial profit potential.[40] And a number of communities provide loans to businesses they believe will boost the area's employment and contribute to the local economy.[41]

When approaching a prospective investor, the entrepreneur's chances of obtaining funding are enhanced by presenting a formal **business plan.** This document presents an overall analysis of the proposed business. It contains a description of the product/service, a thorough analysis of the market, the entrepreneur's strategic objectives, the plans for each of the business's functional areas, a profile of the firm's management team, and most important, the company's projected financial position and funding needs. Answers to the five questions of start-up planning provide the plan's content. A basic outline for a business plan is shown in Table 20–6.

[39]Megginson et al., *Successful Small Business Management*, pp. 112–14.

[40]For an insightful look at sources and requirements of venture funding, see Marj Charlier, "Patient Money," *The Wall Street Journal Reports on Small Business (Special Section)*, February 24, 1989, p. R22; Jose De Cordoba, "Wanted: Good Managers," *The Wall Street Journal Reports on Small Business (Special Section)*, February 24, 1989, p. R16; Marie-Jeanne Juilland, "Alternatives to a Rich Uncle," *Venture*, May 1988, pp. 62ff.

[41]Minneapolis is one community that provides substantial assistance for new businesses. A profile of the city's efforts is provided by Curtis Hartman, "Is It Easier than Ever to Start a Business?" *Inc.*, March 1987, pp. 69ff.

FIGURE 20–2   Sources of Funding for New Venture Start-Ups

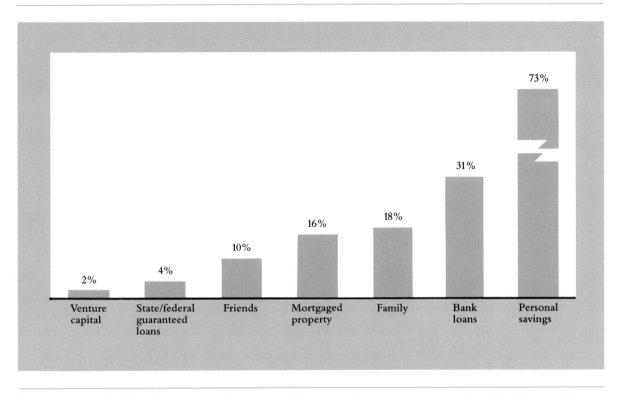

Source: Reported by the CEOs of the 1986 Inc. 500 firms. Some CEOs gave more than one response. Reprinted from Curtis Hartman, "Main Street, Inc," *Inc.,* June 1986, p. 52. Reprinted with permission.

Most entrepreneurs risk their own savings on new ventures; however, others are sometimes willing to invest also.

TABLE 20–6   Basic Outline for a Business Plan

I.   *Executive summary:* Presents a believable snapshot of the problem, the market, and the solution and a candid assessment of the risks and rewards of the proposed business.
II. *General company description:* Profiles the overall company, location, and goals.
III. *Products and services:* Describes the products or services the business will provide and how they will differ from those currently in the market.
IV. *Marketing plan:* Contains an assessment of product or service demand and an overview of how the company will develop a competitive advantage and sell and promote its product/service.
V.   *Management plan:* Explains who will manage the company, how they will be paid, and how the company will be structured.
VI. *Operational plan:* Defines manufacturing and labor requirements and how supplies will be obtained.
VII. *Financial plan:* Summarizes in detail the company's financial needs and how they will be met.
VIII. *Appendixes:* Contains key managers' résumés, product information, and market research and technical reports.

Source: Adapted from "What's in a Business Plan?" *Nation's Business,* August 1988, p. 20.

Many successful entrepreneurs consider the business plan for launching a business the most important document an entrepreneur will ever write.[42] It is the formal blueprint for the development of the new venture. Prospective investors will scrutinize it closely before making a funding decision. Other important parties (e.g., suppliers and prospective major customers) often will ask to see the plan before establishing a relationship with the new business. The entrepreneur can also use the plan as a tool for communicating to employees his or her vision and concept of the company. The business plan is also an important guide for ongoing decision making as the company develops.[43]

ORGANIZING

As we discussed in Chapters 6 and 7, the organizing function involves developing an organizational structure via job design, departmentation, determining span of control, and delegating authority. Ideally, these tasks provide a structure of relationships and authority that effectively coordinates the organization's efforts.

Organizing activities, obviously important, are often neglected by entrepreneurs in the early stages of the start-up. With limited resources and personnel, entrepreneurs focus on the immediate demands of generating sales and producing the product/service to meet the demand and to earn income. Organizational issues seem less important, especially when the business is so small.

When entrepreneurs do explicitly address organizing tasks, the results are often more informal and flexible than in larger organizations. This informality is often intentional. One study of successful growth-oriented entrepreneurs found that most of the founders intentionally avoided developing written job descriptions for their employees in the early stages of the firm's development; in more than two thirds of the cases, oral descriptions were maintained through the company's first major expansion.[44] Written job descriptions were avoided because the entrepreneurs felt they would constrain the potential contributions and growth of employees while the firm was still small. None of the entrepreneurs wanted an employee's motivation and development to be hemmed in by the boundaries of a written description. The strategy also enabled the entrepreneurs to quickly change major job responsibilities when needed, which happens frequently when the organization is still taking shape.

Many of the entrepreneurs in the sample prepared an organization chart; however, the chart was viewed as a dynamic, continually changing picture of the company's structure. The chart also served an important purpose as a tool for continually assessing and reevaluating the company. The study's researcher summed up the entrepreneurs' use of the organization chart: "It was more a means of thinking through key activities . . . a way to identify gaps and new needs—a tool for *thought*."[45]

[42]For excellent, in-depth advice on how to prepare and present a business plan, see Burch, *Entrepreneurship,* pp. 367–477.

[43]Charles J. Bodenstab, "Directional Signals," *Inc.,* March 1989, pp. 139ff; Roger Thompson, "Business Plans: Myth and Reality," *Nation's Business,* August 1988, pp. 16ff.

[44]Thomas F. Jones, *Entrepreneurism* (New York: Donald I. Fine, 1987).

[45]Ibid.

As the firm grows in the number of employees, functions, and size of work groups and departments, job design, descriptions, and the overall structure of the business gradually become more formalized. However, the emphasis of organizing initially is on informality and flexibility to accommodate the dynamic change and adjustments that usually occur in the early stages of a new enterprise.

CONTROLLING

As we discussed in Chapter 8, the controlling function involves establishing standards, obtaining information that provides a comparison of actual with desired results, and taking actions to correct any adverse deviations from standards. In the small business, the controlling activities are particularly important because, in the initial stages of the venture, every aspect of the business is newly established. Given the newness of the business and its operations, mistakes are bound to be made. Because the business's resources are limited, it is essential that the entrepreneur detect and correct problems as quickly as possible. Effective controlling activities enable the entrepreneur to do so.

In the early stages of business, control systems are usually basic rather than sophisticated. However, most entrepreneurs develop financial, production, and inventory control systems that provide key indicators that they monitor weekly, even daily. These indicators include sales, production rates, inventory, accounts receivable, accounts payable, and, most important, cash flow and the cash flow outlook.[46] Ensuring that funds are on hand to pay immediate expenses is a particularly troublesome task, according to a survey of small business owners, as shown in Figure 20–3.[47]

A growing number of entrepreneurs are installing computerized control information systems to assist them in monitoring aspects of the company's performance and in conducting financial and production analysis. Many software firms are developing programs specifically designed for a small business's control needs; this development along with the decreasing costs of computer hardware are making computerized control information systems a reality for small businesses.

Pacific Smelting, a manufacturer of zinc products based in Torrance, California, is one small business that has abandoned its manual record-keeping for a computerized system. The manual system severely hindered the company's ability to determine which of its products were profitable, which customers were most important, and whether product pricing was accurate from a cost perspective. With its computer system, the company now can instantly obtain a broad range of control-related analyses, including profit margins per sale and trend analysis of long-term changes in sales and profits across its product line. System analysis has led to the elimination of one product and revised product pricing to meet sales and profit objectives.[48]

---

[46]Dan Steinhoff and John F. Burgess, *Small Business Management Fundamentals* (New York: McGraw-Hill, 1986), p. 339.

[47]*The Wall Street Journal,* November 2, 1986, p. 35.

[48]Mark Stevens, "Computerizing Your Business," *Working Woman,* September 1987, pp. 33ff.

FIGURE 20–3   Most Important Entrepreneurial Problems Faced by Small Business Owners

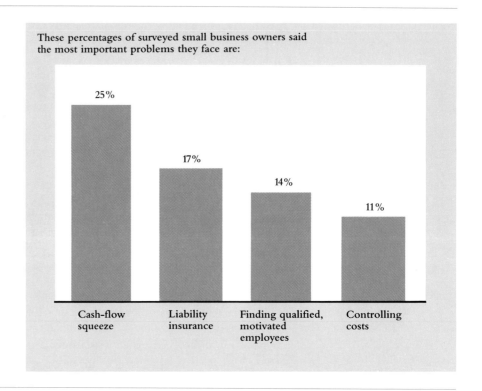

Source: Reprinted from L. C. Megginson, C. R. Scott, Jr., L. R. Trueblood, and W. L. Megginson. *Successful Small Business Management* (Plano, Tex.: Business Publications, 1988), p. 581. Used with permission.

MANAGING PEOPLE IN THE SMALL BUSINESS

Effectively managing and motivating employees is a critical ingredient of effective entrepreneurship. These activities make up the leadership function—encouraging employees to work to achieve the business's goals by effectively communicating the tasks to be done, rewarding good performance, and creating an environment that supports the employees' efforts and individual needs.

Significant differences exist between the small business entrepreneur and the corporate CEO in performing the leadership function. First, in the newly launched business, the entrepreneur is solely responsible for effective leadership. There is no cadre of managers who share leadership responsibilities. Usually, the entrepreneur is the organization's single boss. Leadership—effective or not—depends totally on the entrepreneur.

Second, although leadership is a critical activity of the corporate CEO, quality of leadership is even more vital for the entrepreneur because there are no extra resources to compensate for the adverse effects (employee absenteeism, poor workmanship) of poor leadership. Moreover, the entrepreneur's relationship with each employee has a considerable impact on the firm. Consider that in a 10-employee company, each employee proportionately provides 10 percent of the firm's output. Therefore, the quality of the entrepreneur's personal or business relationship with an employee can have a major effect on the overall venture. Every individual's effort is critical to the firm.

In performing the leadership function, entrepreneurs usually must deal with one primary disadvantage. Given the firm's very limited financial resources, they usually cannot offer employees the salary and benefits that larger, more established firms can provide. Given the uncertainty of any new business, neither is long-term job security assured. These disadvantages may prevent entrepreneurs from obtaining the quality of employees they prefer.

However, entrepreneurs often possess two important advantages. First, they are in a unique position to create an atmosphere in the company that promotes effective performance. Unlike the corporate CEO, the entrepreneur does not have to deal with prior company traditions and policies that may hamper motivation and performance. There are no established traditions, practices, or preexisting norms of behavior. The venture is new, and the entrepreneur is the firm's creator and—if he or she chooses—promoter and nurturer of employee excellence.

A second factor facilitates the entrepreneur's efforts in this regard. In the early days of a new, small business, the venture's employees often are a small group. Especially when the company's product is new and promising, a camaraderie and cohesiveness develop among members. Under a strong leader, the company's purpose is clearly communicated: make the product a success and put the venture on the map. In this type of highly challenging, stressful, and familial environment, employees can become highly motivated, driven by the sense that "anything is possible." Such is particularly the case when part of the employee's income is tied to company profits. Perhaps this is one reason why 96 percent of the Inc. 500 companies include some sort of profit sharing as part of employee compensation.

The entrepreneur can create a climate of excellence and productivity in large part by setting a personal example in the ways he works and approaches the business, customers, and employees. Tom Watson of IBM, James Lincoln of Lincoln Electric, and Steven Jobs, cofounder of Apple Computer, are among those who utilized daily personal example as one way to motivate employees.

Although resources are limited, some entrepreneurs are creating innovative ways to facilitate effective leadership and motivation. Original Copy Centers Inc., a reproduction service in Cleveland, Ohio, assessed the needs of its 76 employees, who are mostly under 30 years of age and single. The company established a laundromat, exercise room, game room, and kitchen in its facility and provided employees with free coffee and private use of the company's personal computers. Although the company's compensation is no higher than the industry average, the work force is productive and the quality of work is exceptional. During the business's first 12 years of operation, only three employees quit.[49]

Smith & Hawken, an importer of garden tools, uses a technique called the "5–15 report" for maintaining open communication with employees (5–15

---

[49]Robert A. Mamis, "Details, Details," *Inc.,* March 1988, pp. 96–98.

stands for 15 minutes to write and 5 minutes to read). Each week, every employee completes the three-part report by telling what he did during the week, describing his morale and that of his department, and providing one idea for bettering his job, department, or company. Management takes no longer than one week to respond to each idea. The technique is one way that Smith & Hawken keeps tabs on each employee's development, finds ways to improve the business, and provides needed support for the employees to do their jobs.[50]

SPECIAL CHALLENGES OF ENTREPRENEURSHIP

At some point in their careers, entrepreneurs encounter major challenges that test their abilities and character. Three particular challenges merit special mention at this point.

GROWTH OF THE ENTERPRISE

Successful entrepreneurs who create a business for growth and profit inevitably discover that the business they are running is dramatically different from the one they created. Because of growth, the company is no longer a shop with a handful of employees, a one-page customer list, and a single supplier and distributor. Rather, the company now employs several hundred workers in many departments. There are networks of suppliers and distributors, and operations run on a much larger scale.

Successfully managing a company with this type of growth requires a transition in management tasks and focus. Because of the company's greater size and complexity, coordination and control must be emphasized. Professional managers must be hired, and more sophisticated and formal control systems and procedures must be developed and managed.[51]

The company's transition from a small shop to complex corporation also requires a major change in the entrepreneur's task and management style. To effectively lead the company, the entrepreneur can no longer make all decisions and maintain a hands-on involvement in all aspects of the business; the company is simply too big. Instead, he or she must delegate authority to subordinate managers and focus on coordinating their efforts. In this situation, many entrepreneurs find that the very skills that brought the company its early success are no longer effective. The company requires a new set of abilities from its CEO.

Do entrepreneurs effectively make this transition? Some, like Bill Gates of Microsoft, do. However, others have major difficulties in managing a much larger and more complex company.[52] Many have particular problems with delegating authority. As the creators of the business, they have a strong need to control its operations and find it extremely difficult to relinquish any

---

[50]Paul Hawken, "The Employee as Customer," *Inc.,* November 1987, pp. 21–22.

[51]See Neil C. Churchill and Virginia L. Lewis, "The Five Stages of Small Business Growth," *Harvard Business Review,* May–June 1983, pp. 30ff.

[52]For some interesting profiles, see Lucien Rhodes, "At the Crossroads," *Inc.,* February 1988, pp. 66ff; Lucien Rhodes, "Kuolt's Complex," *Inc.,* April 1986, pp. 72ff.

decision making. ("It's my baby," said one entrepreneur.) Others find that they simply lack the professional management skills needed to run a complex business.

Some entrepreneurs, like Mitch Kapor, are uncomfortable with the environment of a big business. As founder of Lotus Development Corp., Kapor saw his computer software firm quickly grow from a small shop operation to a diversified, international corporation with more than 1,300 employees and $275 million in sales. Kapor found that "leading by coordinating" poorly matched his management skills, his desire to work with people in small groups, and his penchant for perfectionism.[53] Joseph Solomon, founder of Vidal Sassoon Hair Products, had similar problems when his company boomed in size. Solomon became frustrated because he missed the fast-moving, flexible, more spirited small group environment that his smaller company had provided.[54]

Entrepreneurs resolve this dilemma in several ways. Many learn to delegate, often by being careful in selecting those to whom they delegate and by delegating gradually. Some, like Mitch Kapor, resign from their company or, like Joseph Solomon, sell their firm and start all over, launching a new venture. Other entrepreneurs avoid the dilemma entirely by deliberately restricting the size of their companies.[55]

ENTREPRENEURIAL STRESS

All CEOs experience stress due to the burden of responsibility for managing a business. However, entrepreneurs, especially those who run small businesses, often experience particularly high levels of stress. The stress is partly caused by the risks the entrepreneur incurs in launching a business and his sense of total accountability for its success or failure.

According to a study of 210 small business owners, other factors contribute to entrepreneurial stress.[56] Loneliness is a major source (over half of the entrepreneurs reported they "frequently feel a sense of loneliness"); there is no one in the business or among friends or family with whom the entrepreneur can openly talk about the business and its problems and seek advice, especially in the early days of the company. No one is experiencing the same or even similar work activities or problems.[57]

Total immersion in the business, frustration with employee problems, and an overly high need for achievement can also contribute to entrepreneurial stress. Some entrepreneurs set unreasonable goals for themselves, push

[53]Keith H. Hammonds, "Mitch Kapor's Well-Greased Dream Machine," *Business Week,* May 30, 1988, pp. 92–93; Michael W. Miller, "Starting Over: High-Tech Entrepreneurs Who Have Left Their Old Firms Ponder Next Moves," *The Wall Street Journal,* September 8, 1987, p. 33.

[54]Jones, *Entrepreneurism,* pp. 248–50.

[55]For an interesting perspective from an entrepreneur who maintains a limited growth strategy, see Robert Mulder, "Sole Proprietor," *Inc.,* November 1986, pp. 96–98.

[56]See David E. Gumpert and David P. Boyd, "The Loneliness of the Small-Business Owner," *Harvard Business Review,* November–December 1984, pp. 18ff; David P. Boyd and David E. Gumpert, "Coping with Entrepreneurial Stress," *Harvard Business Review,* March–April 1983, pp. 44ff.

[57]Ibid.

themselves too hard, and experience great frustration when they fall short of their expectations.[58]

There is no perfect cure for entrepreneurial stress. Indeed, many entrepreneurs believe that high stress is an inherent element of entrepreneurship, and many cope with and even thrive on it. However, entrepreneurs who do view stress as a problem have alleviated it with a number of strategies, such as making changes in their business routine (e.g., scheduling more time between meeting appointments and taking time off for exercise), setting time aside for social activities, and creating more opportunities for interacting with employees. Some entrepreneurs participate in local business organizations (such as the Rotary Club) that provide an opportunity to talk with other CEOs of noncompeting companies about their businesses.[59]

SELLING THE COMPANY

Most U.S. businesses acquired today are not large corporations; they are small, independent businesses, many of which were owned by entrepreneurs who were ready to sell their companies. Entrepreneurs decide to sell their businesses for several reasons. They may sell the company to retire and enjoy the financial returns the sale provides them or to use the profits to launch yet another company. Entrepreneurs may sell their firm because, on the verge of retirement, they realize that no qualified successor is available to assume leadership. (This problem often arises among family owned and managed entrepreneurships.[60]) Or they may sell because the buyer can provide much-needed additional cash and other resources to fund the company's growth.[61]

Regardless of the motivation, the decision to sell the business introduces a complex acquisition process and concerns. Most entrepreneurs want their businesses to continue to thrive after the sale, and many are well aware of the poor performance record of acquisitions: From one half to two thirds of all acquisitions ultimately fail.[62]

Entrepreneurs approach selling their companies with many objectives; three are particularly important:

1. *Locate the right buyer.* For entrepreneurs concerned about the company's future, this task involves finding a buyer whose objectives for the firm are compatible with those of the entrepreneur. Compatibility is particularly

[58]Ibid.

[59]For insightful profiles of how four founders dealt with stress by changing their managerial lifestyles, see Joshua Hyatt, "All Stressed-Up and Nowhere to Go," *Inc.*, January 1987, pp. 74ff; John Grossman, "Burnout," *Inc.*, September 1987, pp. 89ff.

[60]For a look at the special problems (and some solutions) common in family entrepreneurships, see Patricia W. Hamilton, "The Special Problems of Family Businesses," *D & B Reports*, July–August 1986, pp. 18–21; Curtis Hartman, "Taking the 'Family' Out of Family Business," *Inc.*, September 1986, pp. 70ff; Sharon Nelton, "Strategies for Family Firms," *Nation's Business*, June 1986, pp. 20ff.

[61]See Suzanne Woolley, "Rule No. 1 for Selling Your Company: Don't Rush," *Business Week*, April 3, 1989, pp. 114–15; Beatrice H. Mitchell and Michael S. Sperry, "Selling Out," *Venture*, January 1988, pp. 25–26; Sandra Salmans, "Cutting the Deal," *Venture*, January 1988, pp. 27ff.

[62]See S. E. Prokesch and W. J. Powell, Jr., "Do Mergers Really Work?" *Business Week*, June 3, 1985, pp. 88–94; Amanda Bennett, "After the Merger, More CEOs Left in Uneasy Spot: Looking for Work," *The Wall Street Journal*, August 27, 1986, p. 15.

important for entrepreneurs who want to continue to head the company after the sale.

2. *Secure satisfactory terms of the sale.*   These terms focus on price for the company, payment, and special conditions concerning the company's employees and other aspects of the business. An entrepreneur's bargaining position is strengthened if the company possesses valuable resources such as an impressive record of financial performance, a strong reputation with customers, and difficult-to-replace assets (such as exceptionally talented management and strong, specialized research and development capabilities).

3. *Obtain satisfactory autonomy.*   Entrepreneurs who stay with the acquired firm usually seek to maintain as much autonomy as possible in managing the company after its sale. For those who continue with the acquired company, managing the firm after the acquisition requires major adjustments. The entrepreneur must cope with less independence in running the business. Regardless of the amount of autonomy promised by the new owners, the entrepreneur must still report to a senior manager in the parent company, provide ongoing, detailed reports of the business, and account for its performance. This is often a difficult adjustment for entrepreneurs, who previously only answered to themselves.[63] Also, the entrepreneur's salary is also often reduced.[64] Many entrepreneurs have problems making these adjustments; consequently, many leave the acquired firm sooner than they expected.[65]

THE FUTURE OF ENTREPRENEURSHIP

The trend toward new business creation will likely continue in the 1990s as more people assume the risks in order to achieve the personal and professional rewards of running a small business. Success requires the ability to effectively implement the important principles and functions of management—especially during the early stages of the new venture, when mistakes can be costly. Success also requires that the entrepreneur take to heart the valuable lessons learned by others and avoid the mistakes that are so common to many new ventures. Some of these are summarized in the Management Focus on a "fallen" business.

Perhaps above all, successful entrepreneurship requires a keen understanding of personal assets and limitations and a strong commitment to the challenge. The adage "know thyself" aptly applies to anyone contemplating launching a business. If one day you seriously consider this important step, thoroughly examine your motivations for starting a business, and the personal strengths and shortcomings you would bring to the enterprise. Self-understanding greatly improves the odds of building a productive company and reaping the substantial rewards of entrepreneurship.

[63]R. H. Hayes and G. H. Hoag, "Post-Acquisition Retention of Top Management," *Mergers and Acquisitions,* Summer 1974, pp. 8–18.

[64]See Sanford L. Jacobs, "Unrealistic Expectations Pose Problems for Sellers of Firms," *The Wall Street Journal,* August 20, 1984, p. 17.

[65]Hayes and Hoag, "Post-Acquisition Retention," p. 10.

MANAGEMENT FOCUS

Lessons from a Fallen Business

As with many entrepreneurs, James Dunnigan's business was an extension of a beloved hobby—military games. Dunnigan gained experience in war games while serving in the U.S. Army. His company, Simulations Publications Inc. (SPI), designed and produced military board games and published *Strategy & Tactics,* a military history magazine that also contained a sophisticated, ongoing game for readers to play.

At the company's peak in the late 1970s, SPI sold hundreds of thousands of military board games each year, along with thousands of military books and magazines. Annual sales averaged over $2 million for SPI and its 50 employees, who set their own hours and often worked long into the night. However, by the early 1980s, the company had failed, the victim of problems and miscalculations that often beset many young ventures. The firm's major problems and Dunnigan's mistakes included:

1. *Hiring the wrong people.* Although he was seeking synergy from his team of employees, Dunnigan committed a common entrepreneurial mistake: hiring people who were all like himself. Said he, "I'm a go-getter, and I hired lots of go-getters—when what I really needed were some drones and drudges who could do the details. Much to my chagrin, I found out that most people are either idea people or detail people, but not both." Dunnigan also hired a few ineffective managers ("who couldn't hack it"), which in a very small company created major headaches.

2. *Managerial conflicts.* Dunnigan's best managers were female; however, he found they couldn't deal effectively with the male employees. "The guys would outshout them. . . . [They] would turn into killing machines. Guys would lie, run roughshod" over the women managers.

3. *Expanding too fast in attempting to sell games in retail outlets.* Before the expansion, SPI sold games through mail orders, which gave them a direct link to their customers and more control over the customer relationship. However, they lost much of that control when they sold through others' retail stores, and their inexperience led to costly mistakes. As losses began to mount, SPI continued to expand. "When you're losing money, you don't expand. You retrench," Dunnigan said.

Dunnigan is now a prominent military writer, lecturer, and adviser to military groups. His advice for prospective entrepreneurs: Make decisions based on market research, stay in close touch with customers, fire poor performers fast, and "instill a fear of failure" among employees. "You've got to run scared . . . to be hungry," he advises. "I made sure everyone got credit for what they did, and this helped make everybody afraid of failure. You have to have that fear to make things work."

Source: Tom Herman, "Running Aground," *The Wall Street Journal Reports on Small Business (Special Section),* June 10, 1988, p. 17R.

SUMMARY OF KEY POINTS

- An entrepreneur is the creator and chief executive of a business enterprise. Entrepreneurs lead over 14 million U.S. businesses, which provide about half the nation's gross national product and over 80 percent of all new jobs.

- Despite the risks, many individuals launch new businesses each year for a number of reasons: to attain independence, personal and professional growth, income, and security or to achieve an alternative career which they view is superior to a dissatisfying job.

■ Success in entrepreneurship requires careful start-up planning. This activity involves determining the product or service to be provided, the market to be served, and how the business will be established, financed, and operated.

■ Although many entrepreneurs perform organizing activities in the early stages of their businesses, they often keep job descriptions and other organizational aspects of the firm flexible because of the dynamic change that the firm frequently experiences.

■ Although often financially unable to provide compensation packages strongly competitive with larger, more established firms, the entre-preneur often has a special opportunity to develop an organizational culture that promotes employee productivity and excellence.

■ Much of an entrepreneur's efforts in performing the controlling function centers on financial control, particularly ensuring that enough cash is on hand to cover immediate expenses.

■ At some point in their careers, many entrepreneurs face the challenges of coping with entrepreneurial stress, making the transition from small business manager to large-company CEO, and dealing with the tasks and concerns that surround selling the company.

DISCUSSION AND REVIEW QUESTIONS

1. Several studies have found that many entrepreneurs were the first-born child of their parents. Can you explain this relationship between birth order and entrepreneurship?

2. In your opinion, can an individual acquire, via training, the talents and skills essential for entrepreneurial success? Discuss.

3. In your opinion, which entrepreneurship task in the start-up phase of the business is the most difficult to complete successfully? Explain.

4. Hewlett-Packard, Lands' End, David's Cookies, and Cuisinart are all highly successful businesses that had no formal business plan when they were established. Does their success diminish the importance of a formal plan? Discuss.

5. In your view, what special problems face "late bloomer" entrepreneurs? What unique advantages do they bring to their businesses?

6. What are the drawbacks of maintaining orally communicated and flexible job descriptions in the early stages of a new business?

7. Suppose you are the head of a young, fast-growing computer software manufacturer. You are experiencing considerable stress from your job. What changes would you make to alleviate the problem?

8. Beyond those noted in the chapter, identify other strengths and shortcomings of the franchising strategy for starting a new business. In your view, which strength is the most valuable; which shortcoming is the most costly for a franchisee?

9. What special problems face the entrepreneur who needs highly skilled employees but lacks the financial resources to fund a strongly competitive compensation program? How can an entrepreneur deal with this problem?

10. Many acquisition observers assert that one reason so many acquisitions fail is that the acquired company is so much smaller than the buyer and the practices of the two firms are so distinctly different. Explain.

ADDITIONAL REFERENCES

Ballas, G. *The Making of an Entrepreneur—Keys to Your Success.* Englewood Cliffs, N.J.: Prentice-Hall, 1980.

Bird, B. "Implementing Entrepreneurial Ideas: The Case for Intention." *Academy of Management Review,* July 1988, pp. 442–53.

Carsrud, A. L.; C. M. Gaglio; and **K. W. Olm.** "Entrepreneurs—Mentors, Networks, and Successful New Venture Development: An Exploratory Study." *American Journal of Small Business,* Fall 1987, pp. 13–18.

Covin, J. G., and **D. P. Slevin.** "Strategic Management of Small Firms in Hostile and Benign Environments." *Strategic Management Journal,* January–February 1989, pp. 75–87.

"Digging for Dollars: The Successful Entrepreneur Has Persistence for a Partner." *The Wall Street Journal Reports on Small Business (Special Section),* February 24, 1989, section R.

Fells, G. "Venture Capital and the New Entrepeneurial Society." *Business Quarterly,* Winter 1989, pp. 22–27.

Gendron, G., and **B. Burlingham.** "The Entrepreneur of the Decade: An Interview with Steve Jobs." *Inc.,* April 1989, pp. 114ff.

Gerber, M. E. *The E-Myth.* Cambridge, Mass.: Ballinger, 1986.

"Going for It: The Rewards and Risks of the Entrepreneurial Life." *The Wall Street Journal Reports on Small Business (Special Section),* June 10, 1988, section 3.

Hawken, P. *Growing a Business.* New York: Simon & Schuster, 1987.

Hisrich, R. D. *Entrepreneurship, Intrapreneurship, and Venture Capital.* Lexington, Mass.: Lexington Books, 1986.

Justis, R. T., and **R. J. Judd.** *Franchising.* Cincinnati: South-Western Publishing, 1988.

Kinkead, G. "The New Independents." *Fortune,* April 25, 1988, pp. 66ff.

Kuratco, D. F. *Entrepreneurship: A Contemporary Approach.* Hinsdale, Ill.: Dryden Press, 1988.

Longenecker, J. G.; J. A. McKinney; and **C. W. Moore.** "Egoism and Independence: Entrepreneurial Ethics." *Organizational Dynamics,* Winter 1988, pp. 64–72.

McWhinney, W. "Entrepreneurs, Owners, and Stewards: The Conduct of a Family Business." *New Management,* Summer 1988, pp. 4–11.

McWhinney, W. "The Family Business: American Dream or Medieval Serfdom?" *New Management,* Fall 1988, pp. 61–64.

Perry, L. T. "The Capital Connection: How Relationships between Founders and Venture Capitalists Affect Innovation in New Ventures." *Academy of Management Executive,* August 1988, pp. 205–12.

Prescott, E. "How a One-Woman Show Becomes a Big-Bucks Business." *Working Woman,* March 1989, pp. 51–56.

Sandberg, W. R. *New Venture Performance.* Lexington, Mass.: Lexington Books, 1986.

Scarborough, N. M., and **T. W. Zimmerer.** *Effective Small Business Management.* Columbus, Ohio: Merrill Publishing, 1988.

Scott, M. G., and **D. F. Twomey.** "The Long-Term Supply of Entrepreneurs: Students' Career Aspirations in Relation to Entrepreneurship." *Journal of Small Business Management,* October 1988, pp. 5–13.

Siropolis, N. C. *Small Business Management: A Guide to Entrepreneurship.* Boston: Houghton Mifflin, 1988.

Steiner, M. P., and **O. Solem.** "Factors for Success in Small Manufacturing Firms." *Journal of Small Business Management,* January 1988, pp. 51–57.

Walters, K., ed. *Entrepreneurial Management: New Technology and New Market Development.* Cambridge, Mass.: Ballinger, 1988.

Welsch, J. A., and **J. F. White.** *The Entrepreneur's Master Planning Guide.* Englewood Cliffs, N.J.: Prentice-Hall, 1983.

CASE 20–1 Hairdressing with a Twist

Hair salons are not a glamorous business. Although growing (revenues have tripled in the last 10 years), the industry is dominated by small, single shops that are poorly managed and marketed, with hairdressers that are inadequately trained and very underpaid. A few large chains exist, but none has captured more than 2 percent of industry sales.

However, one company, Visible Changes Inc., is fast emerging as a comer in the industry, with a sales performance unprecedented in the industry. While the average salon grossed $168,108 in revenues during 1986, the typical Visible Changes salon attained $885,387 in sales. Three of its 16 salons took in over $1.5 million. The company outshines the industry by every performance yardstick, including average sales per customer (about twice the industry average).

Source: Adapted from Bruce G. Posner and Bo Burlingham, "The Hottest Entrepreneur in America," *Inc.,* January 1988, pp. 44ff.

Visible Changes was founded in 1978 by John McCormack (chairman) and his wife Maryanne. McCormack attributes his company's exceptional success partly to professional management. The salons are clean and classic looking; operations are streamlined and smoothly run. An advanced computerized information system keeps McCormack informed of the latest performance figures—for instance, yesterday's sales per salon, per hairdresser, per product. Even a profile of yesterday's customers is available by age, gender, and birthday and how all this compares with any previous days, weeks, or months.

However, that's not the real key to McCormack's success. The core is his hairdressers and a motivation/compensation program that directly links pay to performance. Every hairdresser earns everything he receives. All income—salary, commissions, even benefits—depends on performance. For example, each of the company's 300 hairdressers is paid a commission of 25 percent on all walk-in customers (the basic haircut costs $19). But McCormack believes that the key to an effective salon is excellent customer service by highly trained hairdressers. So he boosts the commission rates for customer requests: A hairdresser requested by a customer earns a 35 percent commission on the fee. If requested more than 75 percent of the time, the hairdresser can charge a higher price, which by all indications the customers are willing to pay. Thus, the hairdresser receives a higher income per customer.

Visible Changes hairdressers also sell hair products. They earn 15 percent commission on sales (the first $120 earned pays for health insurance). Each year, each hairdresser's performance is evaluated on a 10-point scale. Those who receive a top score receive a bonus of 10 percent of their total pay for the year. Those among the company's 50 top product sellers or 50 most requested hairdressers receive a "superbonus." All employees receive profit sharing, which amounts to 15 percent of everyone's gross pay for the year. The more business everyone brings in, the more everyone makes.

This system results in large incomes for hairdressers (and also the hair salon managers and receptionists, whose pay is performance based). While the typical hairdresser in the industry earns $12,000 a year, a Visible Changes hairdresser earns about $33,000 a year. Some superstars like Tony Hatty, who works at one of the company's salons in Houston, Texas (its home base), earn, with a 99 percent request rate, over $50,000 a year. Overall, the program is designed to attract and keep strong performers. Turnover is under 10 percent (the industry averages 30 percent).

McCormack, a former stockbroker and New York City police officer, believes the system emphasizes employee growth and development and a focused attention to the customer. However, although the pay can be lucrative, performance standards are high. Employees must earn everything, even the right to attend the company's advanced training sessions (earned by achieving performance goals for two consecutive months). His current projects: Wisp International, which is marketing the company's computer system to other hair salons, and expansion. McCormack is giving his hairdressers the opportunity to open their own Visible Changes salons.

QUESTIONS FOR ANALYSIS

1. What entrepreneurial characteristics are needed to achieve the type of success Visible Changes is experiencing?

2. Based on your own knowledge of hair salons (and Visible Changes), are hair salons a high-risk industry? Why or why not?

3. In your opinion, which management function (planning, organizing, leading, controlling) has played a primary role in Visible Changes' development?

CASE 20–2   Will This Business Succeed?

Todd LeRoy and Michael Atkinson have launched a franchise business that they are certain will be a sure winner. The business, Associated Video Hut Inc., franchises drive-through video rental outlets.

Each "Video's 1st" outlet is a small Fotomat-type kiosk that a franchise owner buys and can place in a small shopping mall parking lot or in some other suburban, high-traffic area. There, customers can drive up to the kiosk window, review the list of titles shown on the promo board, pay the rental fee, and obtain a videocassette without leaving their cars. The outlet specializes in hit movies, carrying only the current top titles (10 to 25 copies of each title, for a total inventory of 300 to 750 tapes). Because several copies of each title are available, customers are assured of obtaining the hit film they want.

Each film rents for $2.95 a day, more than the industry's average $2-a-day rental. The two founders believe that customers will pay more for the time-saving convenience (just as people do at convenience food stores) and for the selection (hit films are difficult to rent at other video stores that carry only one or two copies). The kiosks are portable so that, if one location doesn't net much business, the franchise owner can easily move the shop to another site.

LeRoy and Atkinson believe their venture will succeed for the following reasons:

1. *The market is there.* In 1987, consumers nationwide spent more than $4 billion in videocassette rentals; in 1988, the rental revenues continued to climb for the several thousand video rental businesses in the industry. By 1995, an estimated 90 percent of all homes with TVs will also have a videocassette recorder. The founders believe that the rental industry should eventually top $15 billion in sales annually.

2. *Low overhead.* LeRoy and Atkinson believe that most video rental stores incur unnecessary costs because they carry tapes that aren't rented. As shown in the competitive analysis in Exhibit 1, the average video rental store carries 3,478 tapes but only rents 5.3 percent of its inventory each day. The remaining tapes are unused, incurring high inventory costs as well as costs of the storage space (rent, utilities). The Video's 1st concept eliminates this problem by keeping a limited inventory (300 to 750 cassettes) of high-volume

Source: Adapted from Tom Richman, "Drive-In Movies," *Inc.* February 1988, pp. 42ff.

(*Note:* Your instructor will provide a summary of the critiques of Associated Video Hut made by the expert panel.)

EXHIBIT 1	Competitive Analysis		
		Industry Average Performance for Video Retailer	**Video's 1st Performance Assumptions**
Store size		2,089 square feet*	48 square feet
Tapes stocked		3,478* tapes	300 tapes
Individual titles stocked		2,417* titles	30 titles
Tapes rented daily		185† tapes	120 tapes
Percent of stock rented daily		5.3%†	40%
Rental price		$ 1.80†	$ 2.95
Wholesale tape cost (new releases)		$50†	$60
Resale price of used tapes		$16†	$20
Full-time employees		3*	1
Part-time employees		4*	4

*Source of statistics: Video Software Dealers Association.
†Source of Statistics: The Fairfield Group Inc.
Source: Tom Richman, "Drive-In Movies," *Inc.,* February 1988, p. 43. Reprinted with permission.

tapes. Overhead is much lower. The two founders believe that their top competition is provided by the video superstores, which carry virtually all titles, and the "rack jobbers," which maintain limited inventory at gas stations, convenience stores, and other locations.

3. *Franchise support.*   The two entrepreneurs estimate that each kiosk will be highly profitable for a franchise owner (the pro forma statement is shown in Exhibit 2). These figures are estimates of an average month and annual totals for a kiosk's second year of operation. Given the pro forma projections, a franchise owner will earn $33,807, a pretax return on assets of at least 40 percent each year per kiosk if about 40 percent of a 300-tape inventory is rented every day. Franchise costs (which include a kiosk, initial inventory, training, a grand opening, and sufficient working capital) will run about $88,000. The company will provide promotion materials (such as ads, four-color newsletters for the franchisee's customers, and a list of movie titles for insertion into local newspapers). The founders will realize a profit of $23,500 per kiosk franchise, excluding royalties.

Associated Video Hut has already opened two pilot stores and sold their first franchise to a group of investors in New York. They are negotiating with a Burger King multifranchise owner who wants to provide drive-through video rentals along with drive-through burgers. The founders' goal is to sell 5,000 kiosk franchises by the mid-1990s. To meet this objective, they are targeting individuals who want to set up at least three kiosks.

LeRoy and Atkinson recently presented their business plan to a group of experts on new ventures. "We keep asking people to shoot holes in the concept," asserted Atkinson, "and they can't do it." Some of the experts disagree.

EXHIBIT 2   Video's 1st Pro Forma Operating Statement per Kiosk*

	Monthly Average	Yearly Total
Revenues:		
Tape rental fees (116 rentals per day @ $2.95)	$10,260	$123,117
Used tape sales (55 tapes per month @ $20)	1,100	13,200
Popcorn	150	1,800
Other	100	1,200
Total revenues	11,610	139,317
Cost of sales:		
Prerecorded tapes (55 tapes per month @ $60)	3,300	39,600
Popcorn	93	1,116
Other	50	600
Total cost of sales	3,443	41,316
Gross profit	8,167	98,001
Operating expenses:		
Rent	500	6,000
Payroll (12 hours per day, seven days per week)	1,950	23,400
Payroll taxes	234	2,808
General (insurance, supplies, utilities, miscellaneous)	505	6,055
Royalty payment (7% gross receipts)	813	9,752
Local advertising (2% gross receipts)	232	2,786
Corporate advertising (1% gross receipts)	116	1,393
Note payable, principal, and interest ($45,000 note @ 12%, five-year term)	1,000	12,000
Total operating expenses	5,350	64,194
Net income before taxes	$2,817	$33,807

*Depreciation and amortization not included.

Source: Tom Richman, "Drive-In Movies," *Inc.*, February 1988, p. 43. Reprinted with permission.

QUESTIONS FOR ANALYSIS

1. Identify and assess the strengths and shortcomings of the concept behind Associated Video Hut.
2. Would you buy a "Video's 1st" franchise? Why or why not?
3. What suggestions can you provide to improve the business concept and operations?

EXPERIENTIAL EXERCISE

PORTRAIT OF AN ENTREPRENEUR

Purpose

This activity is designed to enhance students' understanding of the entrepreneurial personality and the motivations, challenges, and rewards of entrepreneurship.

The Exercise in Class

The instructor will divide the class into groups of up to four students each. Each group should complete the following assignment:

1. Identify a successful entrepreneur in your community that you can interview. Concentrate on identifying a successful small business that is directed by its founder. The business section of recent issues of your community's newspaper(s) and/or the local Chamber of Commerce should be helpful in locating an entrepreneur.

2. Interview the entrepreneur. Don't underestimate your chances of obtaining an entrepreneur's cooperation. Entrepreneurs typically enjoy talking about themselves and their businesses. The interview should take from 30 minutes to one hour. Here are some suggested questions:

   a. What motivated you to start your own business?

   b. How would you describe yourself to a stranger? Are you self-confident, energetic, independent? Are you an optimist, a realist, a pessimist?

   c. In your opinion, what personality characteristics and abilities are essential for success as an entrepreneur?

   d. How would you describe your leadership style?

   e. Describe a typical workday.

   f. What aspects of your work do you find the most satisfying? The most frustrating?

   g. Which aspects of your work are the easiest for you? The most difficult?

   h. In which of your business's activities (operations, finance, marketing, personnel) are you most involved?

   i. How much emphasis do you place on motivating employees?

   j. What important lessons have you learned from your experience in creating and running your own business?

   k. What advice would you offer to a young, prospective entrepreneur?

3. After completing the interview, develop an oral report that profiles the entrepreneur.

4. Elect a spokesperson, who will present your group's findings to the class.

The instructor will lead an open discussion that draws together general, common characteristics of entrepreneurs, based on the interviews.

The Learning Message

This exercise should illustrate the common characteristics possessed by entrepreneurs, including substantial energy, optimism, a practical, nuts-and-bolts approach to business, and ambition. Among the profiles, entrepreneurial differences should also emerge, especially between the entrepreneur(s) driven by growth objectives and those with other goals.

21

Managing in a Multinational Environment

Learning Objectives

After completing Chapter 21, you should be able to:

Define
culture and the ways in which cultures can differ across nations.

Describe
the three primary issues that encompass an organization's decision to become a multinational company.

Discuss
the economic and political influences in a host country environment and how they affect the performance of a multinational company.

Compare
the functions of management in a domestic company with those in a multinational company.

Identify
the major challenges facing expatriate managers in their overseas assignments.

The China Challenge

For decades, China stood beyond the boundaries of international business. Staunchly communist and led by a government that viewed free enterprise with contempt, China remained a less developed country in need of technological, economic, educational, and other development.

In recent years, however, China has experienced economic reforms resulting in a growing acceptance of free enterprise, imports, and direct investment by foreign companies. With 1 billion consumers (a quarter of the world's population) and a wide variety of needs, China is an enticing and very feasible market for many international businesses. As a result, U.S. companies are investing $3 billion in the task of establishing ventures in China—an amount that far exceeds American investment in the Soviet Union.

Companies working to pry open China's door to foreign business are finding that success requires overcoming some serious challenges. Because of the government's erratic transportation and production systems, raw materials and parts shortages are common. This problem has continually plagued H. J. Heinz Co. since 1986, when it established facilities to make baby food and cereal in China. Shortages in rice and wheat flour occur regularly, which shuts down production.

To establish a venture in China, a U.S. business must obtain a Chinese partner; the company must also bring into China as much foreign currency as it takes out. PepsiCo deals with this latter requirement by maintaining joint ventures that export Chinese toys and spices out of China. The Chinese also frequently demand that a U.S. company share its technology with its Chinese partner and provide production and managerial skills to Chinese employees via training. In its $1 billion contract with the Chinese government, McDonnell-Douglas is jointly building aircraft with Shanghai Aviation in China. McDonnell-Douglas is providing the technological and managerial know-how.

Although the obstacles are many, China offers plentiful rewards, which some companies are reaping. Procter & Gamble has scored a big success with its Head & Shoulders shampoo (which translates as "Sea Flying Silk" in Chinese). On a sunny afternoon, hundreds of Chinese wait patiently in line at the year-old Kentucky Fried Chicken outlet in Beijing.

The Chinese economy continues to grow by at least 20 percent each year. Experts estimate that in the 1990s an unprecedented number of U.S. businesses will brave the obstacles and enter China.

Source: Adapted from Ford S. Worthy, "Why There's Still Promise in China," *Fortune*, February 27, 1989, pp. 95ff; Louis Kraar, "How One Man Landed China's $1 Billion Order," *Fortune*, August 18, 1986, pp. 46ff.

Table 21–1	Examples of Various Types of Multinational Companies

MNCs fall under several different categories.

American-Owned MNCs

General Motors	Ford Motor
IBM	Pan Am
General Electric	American Express
F. W. Woolworth	Bank America
Sears Roebuck	Eastman Kodak
Mobil Oil	Procter & Gamble
ITT	Gulf & Western

Foreign-Owned MNCs

Unilever	Toyota Motors
Royal Dutch/Shell	Sony
Nestlé	Volkswagen
Datsun (Nissan)	Perrier
Honda	Norelco

Nonprofit MNCs

Red Cross (Swiss)
Roman Catholic Church (Italy)
U.S. Army (U.S.)

American Firms Owned by Foreign MNCs

Magnavox	Bantam Books
Gimbel's Department Store	Baskin-Robbins
Libby, McNeill & Libby	Capitol Records
Stouffer Foods	Kiwi Shoe Polish
Saks-Fifth Avenue	Lipton

Products or Services to Be Marketed

What products or services should an organization establish in an international market? In answering this question, many firms opt for the *shot-in-the-dark* method: They simply select one or more of their products (or services) that have done well in their domestic market and introduce it into the chosen international market. Kellogg's Corn Flakes, Coca-Cola, and McDonald's hamburgers were introduced in this manner.[7]

A growing number of companies are utilizing more analytical and deliberate approaches to product or service selection. Some firms utilize a *phased internationalization* approach. They travel to the selected host country and conduct product market research to determine consumer needs in the overall product area in which the company does business. Then the company returns home with the research and designs a product that fits the consumers' needs. The new product (often some variation of the company's product line) is then

[7]Martin Van Mesdag, "Winging It in Foreign Markets," *Harvard Business Review,* January–February 1987, pp. 71, 73.

MANAGEMENT FOCUS

International Winners

A growing number of U.S. companies are succeeding in international markets, earning profits overseas that substantially contribute to the company's overall financial performance. One analysis by *Fortune* magazine has found that these international winners utilize a surprisingly similar formula in establishing business overseas. In *Fortune's* view, this formula involves a number of rules:

1. *Be patient*. Regardless of the mode of market entry, profits are usually long in coming in different countries because of differences in culture, employment practices, and consumers— in short, usually very unfamiliar ways of doing business. In Japan, a U.S. operation requires 10 years or more before becoming profitable. Many international winners initially lost money but continued on because of the often substantial profits to be made.

2. *Don't rush into an overseas market*. Most winners were painstakingly careful before establishing a business overseas. Many managers first visited the host country several times, talked with potential suppliers, and analyzed market demand and cultural differences. In short, they studied every aspect of business before taking the plunge.

3. *Hire host country citizens to manage the business*. This practice provides a company with managers who thoroughly understand the market and prevailing business practices. It also eases government concern about foreign intrusion into the country's business community. Many companies emphasize hiring talent overseas. IBM, for example, has vigorously recruited at Japanese universities for years. Engineering students rate IBM among the three best employers in Japan. IBM also focuses on hiring women for management positions in Japan, where few women are

introduced into the host country. Ferrero's Tic Tac breath mints and IDV's Bailey's Irish Cream liqueur are products specifically developed and marketed on the basis of research of multiple international markets.[8]

Regardless of the approach taken by an organization, a successful international product or service requires primary attention to the needs, preferences, and idiosyncrasies of the consumers in the selected host country. Many hugely successful American products have failed abysmally in international markets because U.S. companies simply ignored international consumer differences.

Other products that failed initially found success once the manufacturer made some seemingly slight though important changes. Consider S. C. Johnson & Son's Lemon Pledge furniture polish. After the product sold poorly in Japan among older consumers, the company conducted marketing research and found that the polish smelled like a latrine disinfectant used throughout Japan during World War II. Johnson & Son reduced the lemon scent in the polish, and sales boomed.

Mattel's Barbie doll was another faltering product in Japan until marketing research determined that few Japanese identified with the Americanized doll.

[8]Ibid.

permitted to become managers. There, women rate IBM as the best place to work.

4. *Thoroughly educate these managers about the company's culture.* Many successful companies have established training centers for their expatriate managers. Hewlett-Packard brings its recruits to corporate headquarters in Silicon Valley for education in the company's management principles.

5. *Alter products and marketing to fit the market.* Many U.S. companies have experienced the failure of marketing an American product in a country where customs find the product utterly foreign and unacceptable. International winners accommodate the international consumer's needs. Hewlett-Packard, for example, manufactures computer keyboards that accommodate European traditions. Kellogg found that Japanese consumers had problems speaking the Japanese translation of the famous "snap, krackle, and

pop" slogan for Rice Krispies; in Japan, Rice Krispies now go "patchy, pitchy, putchy." Boeing scored a major success with its marketing of the Boeing 737 plane in undeveloped countries. Boeing analyzed the runways in these countries and found they were too short and soft to accommodate the 737 and most other U.S. commercial jets. They also studied the flying techniques of Third World pilots (e.g., the tendency to land hard, bounce the plane, and land off the runway). Boeing responded by redesigning the wings to allow shorter landings, more powerful engines for faster takeoffs, and low-pressure tires so the plane wouldn't bounce on hard landings. The Boeing 737 is now the world's best-selling commercial jet in aviation history.

Source: Adapted from Andrew Kupfer, "How to Be a Global Manager," *Fortune*, March 14, 1988, pp. 52ff; Kenneth Labich, "America's International Winners," *Fortune*, April 14, 1986, pp. 34ff.

For the Japanese, Barbie was too tall, too long-legged, and her blue eyes were the wrong color. Mattel produced a Japanized Barbie—shorter, with brown eyes and a more Asian figure. Thereafter, 2 million Barbies were sold in two years.

Even name changes can produce positive results. Pillsbury changed its "Jolly Green Giant" name in Saudi Arabia once it found that the name translated to "intimidating green ogre"; in China, Coca-Cola instituted a name change after it found that, in Chinese, "Coca-Cola" means "bite the wax tadpole."[9]

Adapting products to international consumer tastes is one characteristic of businesses that have achieved substantial success in international markets. Their approach to business abroad is discussed in the Management Focus on "International Winners."

[9]John Thackray, "Much Ado about Marketing," *Across the Board,* April 1985, pp. 39–46; Vernon R. Alden, "Who Says You Can't Crack Japanese Markets?" *Harvard Business Review,* January–February 1987, pp. 53–56; John S. Hill and Richard R. Hill, "Adapting Products to LDC Tastes," *Harvard Business Review,* March–April 1984, pp. 92–101.

FIGURE 21–1   Evolution of a Multinational Corporation

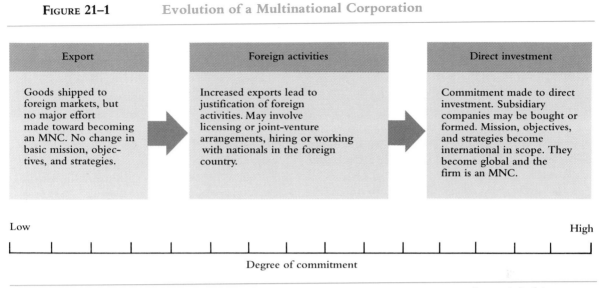

Export	Foreign activities	Direct investment
Goods shipped to foreign markets, but no major effort made toward becoming an MNC. No change in basic mission, objectives, and strategies.	Increased exports lead to justification of foreign activities. May involve licensing or joint-venture arrangements, hiring or working with nationals in the foreign country.	Commitment made to direct investment. Subsidiary companies may be bought or formed. Mission, objectives, and strategies become international in scope. They become global and the firm is an MNC.

Low   High

Degree of commitment

Most organizations gradually evolve into a multinational corporation rather than becoming one in a short period of time.

MODE OF ENTRY

Once the market and product/service for international expansion have been selected, an organization must decide specifically how it will enter its selected market. The three basic, sequential strategies involved in market entry are illustrated in Figure 21–1. Each strategy increases commitment to the international venture.

Export.   Exporting involves selling a product in the international market without establishing manufacturing facilities there. Exporting encompasses promotion to stimulate demand for the product, collecting revenues, making credit arrangements for sales, and shipping the product to the market.

Most companies utilize an *agent* to perform some or all of these tasks.[10] The agent may be sales representatives who obtain sales for a commission while the home company handles the shipping and required paperwork. Or an agent may be an export management company that performs all the exporting tasks (e.g., obtaining import licenses, making sales calls, handling shipping documents) for a larger commission fee.[11] However, once a home company becomes accustomed to the exporting business, it may assume most or all of these tasks, often establishing a staff in the host country.

The United States is currently experiencing an upsurge in exporting by American businesses. In 1987 and 1988, the volume of exports increased by almost 30 percent annually.[12] Surprisingly, the bulk of this growth is not coming from America's 25 largest MNCs, which account for over 85 percent

---

[10]James M. Livingstone, *The International Enterprise* (New York: John Wiley & Sons, 1975).

[11]Robert W. Casey, "Should You Be Competing in the Global Marketplace?" *Working Woman,* October 1988, pp. 58ff.

[12]Ibid.

Small to medium-sized companies venture into exporting because it is the least complicated and least risky strategy for entering a foreign market.

of U.S. exports.[13] Instead, novices in exporting—small to medium-sized companies with under $400 million in yearly sales—account for much of the export boom. These companies have launched exporting activities largely because of the declining value of the U.S. dollar relative to foreign currencies. Between 1985 and 1988 the dollar's value dropped by about 50 percent.[14] As the dollar declines, American exports become less expensive and thus more attractive to buyers in other countries.

Smaller companies venture into exporting for another important reason. Exporting is the least complicated and least risky strategy for entering a foreign market. The strategy involves little or no change in the organization's basic mission, objectives, and strategies, since all production occurs at home. If problems arise in the host country, an exporting organization can easily leave the market. The simplicity of exporting, relative to other strategies for market entry, is more compatible with smaller companies that have less resources.

However, exporting is still a challenging undertaking. When an agent is used to handle the exporting tasks, the organization has little control over the overall exporting situation (such factors as product price, advertising, and distribution). If the company handles many of the exporting tasks, it must contend with language differences, taxes, regulations, customs inspections, differing transportation systems, and time zones.

---

[13]See Hilary Stout, "Export Davids Sling Some Shots at Trade-Gap Goliath," *The Wall Street Journal*, March 8, 1989, p. B2; William J. Holstein, "The Little Guys Are Making It Big Overseas," *Business Week*, February 27, 1989, pp. 94–96; William J. Hampton, "The Long Arm of Small Business," *Business Week*, February 29, 1988, pp. 63–66; Christopher Knowlton, "The New Export Entrepreneurs," *Fortune*, June 6, 1988, pp. 87ff. Although most U.S. exporters ship their goods to Europe, the Far East is playing an increasingly powerful role in world trade. For an excellent discussion of this trend, see Joel Kotkin and Yoriko Kishimoto, "Winning in the Asian Era," *Inc.*, September 1988, pp. 71ff.

[14]William J. Holstein, "Made in the USA," *Business Week*, February 29, 1988, p. 60.

Export barriers are also a troublesome reality. The most common barrier is the export tariff, a tax levied by a foreign government on imported goods. However, since the 1970s, the use of tariffs has declined, and nontariff barriers have multiplied. For example, the European Economic Community (composed of 10 European countries) recently developed standards for postal and telecommunications equipment that were more compatible with the production processes of European manufacturers than with U.S. competitors.

An exporter may be required to subsidize domestic competitors. For instance, to export videocassettes in Brazil, a foreign distributor must buy Brazilian films, copy the films, and market them in Brazil. MNCs that operate movie theaters in Brazil must set aside 140 days for Brazilian films and pay a percentage of their gross profits to Brazilian filmmakers.

Poor patent protection is another common barrier. In the United States, a company with a patented invention (e.g., software or a pharmaceutical formula) has the exclusive rights to use the invention for a number of years; patent violators are prosecuted. However, some countries are negligent in enforcing these patents or ignore them totally. As a result, the foreign country's businesses can freely pirate the invention. U.S. pharmaceutical exporters lose over $110 million each year in Argentina and Brazil alone due to patent negligence.[15] Before exporting in a targeted international market, a prospective exporter must identify all export barriers that exist and assess the barriers' impact on costs, profits, and competitive advantage.

Foreign Activities.   As the importance of exports increases, the firm may decide that it now can justify its own foreign subsidiary. This decision usually involves establishing production and/or marketing facilities in the host country. This strategy differs from *direct investment* because it entails some type of association with a local firm or individual. This type of association usually takes the form of *licensing* or a *joint venture*.

When a firm negotiates a licensing agreement, it is granting the right to produce the firm's product to an outside company in the host country. A firm may also grant an outside company the right to use the firm's intangible assets such as patents or technology. In the 1950s, many U.S. firms transferred technology to Japanese companies via licensing agreements. The licensing firm usually receives a flat payment plus royalties from the sale of the goods that are produced using the licensed technology.

Licensing can be an effective way to obtain profits from product sales without establishing and managing facilities in the host country. However, in licensing, a firm loses some control over the asset that is licensed. The company also runs the risk of the outside licensee eventually becoming a competitor.

In the joint venture arrangement, a business joins with local investors to create and operate a business in the host country. Each investor is a partner and shares the ownership of the new venture. Joint ventures are a quite popular strategy for launching a business abroad; over 40 percent of America's largest industrial corporations maintain international joint ventures.[16] They are

---

[15]Rahul Jacob, "Export Barriers the U.S. Hates Most," *Fortune,* February 27, 1989, pp. 88–89.

[16]A. K. Janger, *Organization of International Joint Ventures* (New York: Conference Board, 1980).

especially popular with U.S. investors in countries, such as China and Japan, where the business and cultural environment is quite unique from that of the United States.[17] In recent years, the joint venture has become the cornerstone of McDonald's global expansion. The company has found the approach ideal for maintaining some 2,000 outlets outside the United States. McDonald's requires that its overseas partners adhere to the company's strict production standards, while providing them the freedom to be creative in marketing, new products, and aspects of the outlet's decor. Such autonomy enables the partner to develop an outlet that caters to local tastes and culture.[18]

The popularity of joint ventures is largely due to the substantial advantages the strategy can provide. A joint venture is a lower-cost and less-risky approach to establishing production and marketing operations abroad, compared to direct foreign investment. Substantial gains can be reaped when partners with complementary abilities pool their skills and resources in making and selling a product. For example, several U.S. companies such as Kentucky Fried Chicken have achieved success in the challenging Japanese markets via joint ventures. These companies provide financing and technology while the Japanese partner provides the personnel and knowledge of the Japanese markets and business practices.[19]

However, the failure rates of joint ventures are disturbingly high. Approximately 40 percent of these international arrangements fail; most ventures last only from three to four years.[20] At the core of the arrangement's problems are the difficulties of joint ownership and management. Usually, two partners from different countries and cultures must work together in setting venture objectives and strategy and in operating the new business. Emerging differences in management and cultural styles can create major conflicts between the parties, as can differing objectives for the venture. Several U.S.–Japanese joint ventures failed because of conflicting objectives. America's business culture tends to emphasize profitability as a key objective; in Japan, the overriding business objective is growth in market share. Thus, conflict emerges when a U.S. partner wants to take its share of venture profits back to corporate headquarters in the United States while the Japanese partner wants to reinvest profits for growth.[21] There is also the ever present danger of, in time, a joint venture partner using the licensed technology to become a powerful compet-

---

[17]For an excellent study and discussion of the motives and use of joint ventures in China, see John D. Daniels, Jeffrey Krug, and Douglas Nigh, "U.S. Joint Ventures in China: Motivation and Management of Political Risk," *California Management Review,* Summer 1985, pp. 46–58.

[18]Kathleen Deveny, "McWorld?" *Business Week,* October 13, 1986, pp. 78ff.

[19]Several excellent articles are available on the advantages, problems, and shortcomings of joint ventures. Among the more noteworthy are Carmela E. Schillaci, "Designing Successful Joint Ventures," *Journal of Business Strategy,* Fall 1987, pp. 59–63; Marjorie A. Lyles, "Common Mistakes of Joint Venture Experienced Firms," *Columbia Journal of World Business,* Summer 1987, pp. 79–84; F. Kingston Berlew, "The Joint Venture—A Way into Foreign Markets," *Harvard Business Review,* July–August 1984, pp. 48ff; Oded Shenkar and Yoram Zeira, "Human Resources Management in International Joint Ventures," *Academy of Management Review,* July 1987, pp. 546–57.

[20]Kathryn R. Harrigan, "Joint Ventures that Endure," *Industry Week,* April 20, 1987, p. 14. Also see L. G. Franko, *Joint Venture Survival in Multinational Corporations* (New York: Praeger Publishers, 1971).

[21]Schillaci, "Designing Successful Joint Ventures," p. 61; Lyles, "Common Mistakes of Joint Venture Experienced Firms," p. 80; Berlew, "The Joint Venture," p. 48.

	1960	1970	1980	1986
TABLE 21–2				

TABLE 21–2   Direct Investment in Other Countries (in millions of dollars)

Direct investment in foreign countries has grown enormously in the last 30 years.

	1960	1970	1980	1986
United States	$2,940	$7,589	$19,220	$28,050
Japan	79	355	2,385	14,480
West Germany	139	876	4,180	8,999
Great Britain	700	1,308	11,360	16,691
Canada	52	302	2,694	3,254
France	347	374	3,138	5,230
Italy	17	111	754	2,661

Source: "Entering a New Age of Boundless Competition," *Fortune*, March 14, 1988, p. 46. Copyright 1988 by Time, Inc. Used with permission of the publisher. All rights reserved.

itor. Ampex Corp., a Silicon Valley–based firm, fell victim to this pitfall of joint venturing. It licensed videotape patents that Japanese companies later utilized as the foundation of Japan's leadership in VCR technology.[22]

Given the inherent difficulties of joint ventures, a company must thoroughly evaluate and carefully select a joint venture partner. Selection should be based on such factors as compatibility of venture objectives, similar value systems, and mutual respect. Partners should reach agreements concerning mechanisms for resolving disputes and the specific roles of each partner in managing the venture.[23]

Direct Investment. The strongest commitment to becoming a global enterprise is a management decision to begin producing the firm's products abroad with no association with a host country investor. This entry strategy is booming in international business; Table 21–2 depicts its growth among seven countries over 36 years. The United States currently accounts for about 40 percent of all direct investment worldwide.

Businesses build and/or buy manufacturing facilities abroad for a number of reasons. In some cases, direct investment reduces manufacturing expenses, due to lower labor and other costs. This benefit triggered the booming growth of the maquiladoras industry along the Mexican border (profiled in Case 21–1, at the end of this chapter). Direct investment also enables a business to avoid the tariff and other government-imposed costs associated with exporting. The strategy is an effective means for building major national markets and for maintaining total control over international operations. Also, larger benefits can be gained by establishing a local presence via direct investment. By paying taxes in the host country and providing local employment, a foreign business can build confidence among consumers and receive more equitable treatment from the host government.[24] However, direct investment entails a full commitment to an international venture. When problems arise in the host

[22]Joel Kotkin, "Do the Japanese Make Good Partners?" *Inc.*, March 1987, p. 27.

[23]John S. McClenahen, "Alliances for Competitive Advantage," *Industry Week*, August 24, 1987, pp. 33–36; J. Peter Killing, "How to Make a Joint Venture Work," *Harvard Business Review*, May–June 1982, pp. 120–27.

[24]Robert Grosse and Duane Kujawa, *International Business: Theory and Managerial Applications* (Homewood, Ill.: Richard D. Irwin, 1988), pp. 91–93.

country (e.g., market decline, economic depression, government instability), leaving the country is often quite difficult and costly.

In summary, the exporting, foreign activities, and direct investment strategies for market entry offer different strengths and shortcomings. As one moves along the continuum from exporting to direct investment (depicted in Figure 21–1), commitment to the venture and control over international operations increase. However, risk due to this greater commitment also increases.

ENVIRONMENT OF THE MULTINATIONAL MANAGER

Future managers might wonder if multinational enterprises involve unique requirements for effective performance of the managerial functions. Planning, organizing, and controlling are required regardless of the business setting. However, differences between cultures may require multinational managers to learn about special environmental factors and institutions. They also may have to change some of their basic assumptions concerning people, organizations, and the role of the manager.

In the opening section of our book, we discussed the importance of environmental factors in managerial performance. Their importance is magnified many times in an international setting, where effective management requires careful consideration and appreciation of potential differences in *culture, economics, politics,* and *technology.*

CULTURE

Culture is a very complex environmental influence, encompassing knowledge, beliefs, values, laws, morals, customs, and other habits and capabilities an individual acquires as a member of society. These elements of culture can all vary a great deal across societies. If an MNC is global in nature, management must adapt its managerial practices to the specific and unique aspects of culture in each host country. An MNC's management must be culturally sensitive in its business practices and learn to bridge the cultural gap that exists between its ways of management and business and those of the host country. In making these adjustments, management must be aware that cultures are *learned,* cultures *vary,* and cultures *influence behavior.*

Cultures Are Learned. Cultures include all types of learning and behavior, the customs that people have developed for living together, their values, and their beliefs of right and wrong. A culture is the sum of what humans learn in common with other members of the society to which they belong.

Cultures Vary. Different societies have different cultures. Different objectives are prized, and behavior valued in one society may be much less important in another. This cultural diversity affects individual perception and, therefore, individual behavior.

Two examples illustrate the substantial differences in Eastern and Western cultures. In Asian countries, a major cultural rule of behavior in society is to

An MNC's management must be sensitive to cultural diversity.

maintain and "save face," essentially to preserve an individual's self-respect, pride, and dignity. This principle governs the ways that Asians communicate and interact with other people. For example, if a Taiwanese is asked for the location of a particular restaurant by an American business owner and does not know, he or she will lie rather than admit ignorance. Conceding ignorance causes embarrassment and loss of face. Also, while American culture prizes individuality and frankness, the Asian culture emphasizes conforming to society. Individualism is shunned because, by disagreeing with others' behavior, individualism insults others and causes them to lose face. Frank criticism is avoided because criticizing others causes a loss of face. Asians avoid demonstrations of anger because it is viewed as a humiliating loss of dignity.[25]

In Japan and other Asian countries, the culture emphasizes the social relationship as the foundation of business. Consequently, an American business executive who negotiates a joint venture with a prospective Japanese partner will discover that the Japanese will spend much time asking questions about the American's family and other subjects that seemingly have nothing to do with the joint venture. The American executive seeks to obtain a legal contract, which American culture views as the foundation of the business relationship. However, the Japanese attempt to establish some foundation of a mutual relationship of personal trust and understanding, which they view as the core of the business relationship. The time-consuming questions are an attempt to do so.

There are other distinct differences between American and other cultures. For example, in the American culture, time is valued as a precious commodity; therefore, punctuality is emphasized, especially in organizations. However, some other cultures value a more relaxed lifestyle; consequently, arriving late

[25]John A. Reeder, "When West Meets East: Cultural Aspects of Doing Business in Asia," *Business Horizons,* January–February 1987, pp. 69–74.

for business appointments is not considered rude. In America's culture, success is often equated with material possessions. Some other cultures view material wealth as unimportant; success is measured by the quality of relationships and the time one spends with family. Exhibiting one's material wealth is seen as disrespectful, greedy, and even vulgar.[26]

Cultures Influence Behavior. Diversity in human behavior can be found in almost every human activity. Religious ceremonies, beliefs, values, work habits, food habits, and social activities vary endlessly with culture environment. Behavioral differences between peoples of different countries arise from differences in culture rather than differences in people.

Culture can affect behavior in many ways. For example, although human needs may be inherently similar, the cultural environment determines the relative importance of needs and the means through which they are satisfied.[27] Recall for a moment the different needs in Maslow's hierarchy of needs discussed in Chapter 10. A study of 116,000 employees in one U.S. MNC with locations across 50 countries found that employees differed in need importance in different countries. Employees in the Netherlands and Scandinavian countries, for example, valued social needs more highly than self-actualization needs (which contradicts Maslow's theory).[28] An individual's need for achievement has also been found to differ among cultures.

Culture also influences attitudes of individuals concerning the importance of work, authority, material possessions, competition, time, profit, risk-taking, and decision making. Many employees in Israel, Austria, New Zealand, and Scandinavian countries, for example, prefer consultative over unilateral decision making. In some cultures, time is measured in days and years rather than hours, which can substantially affect work scheduling and control. In some countries, especially Muslim societies, the culture does not emphasize self-determination, which is a strong cultural norm in the United States. People believe that fate rather than self-initiative determines the future. This belief has a major impact on business planning, objectives, and work.[29]

Economics

The *economic influences* of a host country substantially affect MNC performance. Its income levels, economic growth, inflation rates, and balance of payments can significantly affect an MNC's sales, earnings, and business practices. The MNC must constantly be aware of each host country's

[26]Rose Knotts, "Cross-Cultural Management: Transformations and Adaptations," *Business Horizons*, January–February 1989, pp. 29–33.

[27]George W. England, *The Manager and His Values* (Cambridge, Mass.: Ballinger/Lippincott, 1975); John Fayerweather, *International Business Strategy and Administration* (Cambridge, Mass.: Ballinger/Lippincott, 1978), pp. 449–57.

[28]Geert Hofstede, "National Cultures in Four Dimensions," *International Studies of Management and Organization*, Spring–Summer 1983, p. 68, as cited in Daniels and Radebaugh, *International Business*, p. 99.

[29]Endel-Jakob Kolde, *Environment of International Business* (Boston: Kent Publishing, 1982), pp. 29–32; Daniels and Radebaugh, *International Business*, pp. 93–102; Stephan H. Robock, Kenneth Simmonds, and Jack Zwick, *International Business and Multinational Enterprises* (Homewood, Ill.: Richard D. Irwin, 1977), pp. 309–40.

MANAGEMENT FOCUS

The Costs of Manufacturing Overseas

An increasing number of companies are looking overseas for the manufacturing components of the products they sell. They obtain parts or whole products from makers in countries with low labor costs, in order to capitalize on the lower total manufacturing costs of the product. Many of these companies become "hollow"—they maintain marketing, financial, and other activities in the United States but with reduced or nonexistent U.S. manufacturing activities.

Some examples: Virtually all of General Electric's consumer electronics products are made in Asia. Once the largest buyer of American-made steel, Caterpillar Tractor now looks overseas for much of its steel. Nike's U.S. manufacturing activities are limited, with only 100 manufacturing people among its 3,500-member work force. Liz Claiborne has 250 among its 3,000 employees. And in Louisiana, at its only U.S. telephone manufacturing plant, AT&T has shut down the

production of residential telephones and transferred production to Singapore.

This "outsourcing" strategy is profitable for the company. However, some observers believe it is damaging to the United States. They assert that outsourcing robs America of the strong industrial base it needs in order to prosper. For example, manufacturing activities provide business for many service companies (e.g., insurance, transportation, and even communications). Transfer manufacturing abroad and with it goes demand for many service activities. This type of deindustrialization, critics assert, will weaken America's productivity and standard of living. According to productivity statistics, most gains in productivity and thus in standard of living come from the manufacturing, not the service, sector. If America outsources its manufacturing, it will also lose the ability to innovate. If companies don't manufacture, they will lose techno-

economic stability. The rate of inflation and currency stability must be closely monitored.

In terms of economic and overall development, countries are classified either as a *developed country (DC)* or a **less developed country (LDC),** which has a lower level of economic development than a developed country. It usually has a low gross national product, little industry, and underdeveloped educational, distribution, and communication systems. Making up 80 percent of the world's population, LDCs have an unequal distribution of income that keeps many of their people in deep poverty.

Although LDCs include most of the world's population, only about 25 percent of the world's international business activity occurs in these countries.[30] However, the amount of international activity is increasing. In particular, a growing number of American companies are establishing direct investments in LDCs to obtain the advantages of much lower labor costs. This trend and the debate it has triggered are discussed in the Management Focus on overseas manufacturing costs.

Economic relations between MNCs and LDCs have often been the subject of controversy. Many LDCs have strong feelings of nationalism. During the

[30]Grosse and Kujawa, *International Business,* pp. 606–7.

logical know-how and understanding of how new technology can be developed. The best ideas come from manufacturing experience, not from the laboratory.

Other observers disagree with this position, stating that while U.S. manufacturers are outsourcing, foreign countries are building manufacturing facilities in the United States. Further, the number of small manufacturing businesses is booming in this country.

However, critics respond, if the Japanese and other foreign businesses with manufacturing facilities in the United States can compete, why can't American companies, especially when outsourcing provides other disadvantages for its practitioners? Because, for example, it takes more time to transport parts or goods from overseas, an outsourcing company must maintain larger inventories at home. And the company's fast response to changing market de-

mands in the United States is diminished. Moreover, savings from outsourcing are often less than expected, because in many industries labor is no longer a substantial portion of total production costs. Instead of resorting to this "quick fix" strategy, companies should work to improve their competitive position at home by such actions as reducing overhead, restructuring, and boosting production efficiency.

Regardless of the impact of outsourcing on the U.S. economy and industry, the trend is likely to continue unabated. It is difficult for many large U.S. companies to resist, given that in China, for example, workers are making exceptionally high quality products at a wage of $1 a day.

Source: Constantinos C. Markides and Norman Berg, "Manufacturing Offshore Is Bad Business," *Harvard Business Review*, September–October 1988, pp. 113–20; a special report, "The Hollow Corporation," *Business Week*, March 3, 1986, pp. 57ff; Susan Lee and Christie Brown, "The Protean Corporation," *Forbes*, August 24, 1987, pp. 76–79.

last 30 years, in their drives for political independence and freedom from foreign domination, many developing nations have felt the need to consolidate control of their economies by altering the past pattern of relationships with foreign firms. In some LDCs, extensive government regulations have been adopted with the ultimate purpose of limiting the growth of MNCs. More recently, however, there has been a movement away from this trend. The reasons for the shift are *changing attitudes* and *rising direct investment*.[31]

Changing Attitudes.   Although charges of exploitation by MNCs still are made quite frequently, attitudes of both host governments and MNCs have changed. This has led to greater mutual understanding and accommodation in relations. Although host country fear of foreign domination still exists, it has eased substantially. Apparently, foreign governments realize that the relationship with MNCs need not be a no-win situation but rather one of mutual gain.

Rising Direct Investment.   Improved relations have given rise to a doubling of direct investment, compared to the early 1960s. Apparently, many

[31]This section is based on *Transnational Corporations and Developing Countries: New Policies for a Changing World Economy* (New York: Committee for Economic Development, 1981), pp. 1–3.

MNCs believe the possible returns are worth the risk. Also, these direct investments do not reflect the flow of other resources—such as managerial skills, technology, and marketing skills—which may overshadow the monetary contribution.

Despite greater mutual trust and a greater volume of investment, it would be wrong to assume that MNCs and developing countries have achieved total agreement on the questions of exploitation of resources and threats to sovereignty. These issues have divided them for years, and even today opinions still diverge widely within each group.

At the heart of the controversy is a basic difference in perceptions and objectives. The MNCs, though they now are more willing to recognize their social responsibilities, still tend to concentrate on short-run performance criteria. Efficient and profitable operation is regarded as benefiting workers, customers, and suppliers directly, while the rest of the host country benefits indirectly through taxes. Critics in the host country, on the other hand, point to undesirable political, social, and economic consequences. They charge that MNCs create many problems in developing countries struggling to achieve political and economic autonomy. In fact, similar arguments are made in discussions of the social responsibilities of business firms in the United States.

In response to these concerns, a number of large MNCs have launched efforts to aid in the development of the LDCs where they conduct international business. Ford Motor Co.'s South American subsidiary, for example, has constructed 128 schools in Mexico over the last 20-plus years. These schools educate about 170,000 children each year. Champion International Corp. subsidizes 13,000 meals each day for its Brazilian employees. Warner-Lambert's Tropicare Inc. provides training in primary health care in the four West African countries where it operates (Cameroon, Ivory Coast, Senegal, and Zaire). These efforts are not totally selfless; the MNCs realize that helping to solve the host country's developmental problems serves both the LDC's and the MNC's interests.[32]

Politics

The political influences in a host country environment can substantially affect all of the managerial functions of an MNC and can frequently determine the ultimate success of an MNC's international operations. Our discussion of the political environment will focus on two topics: the *characteristics* of the host country government that most affect an MNC and the concept of *political risk,* including how MNCs forecast and cope with political uncertainty in their international settings. Concerning the host government, three factors most significantly influence an MNC's operations and performance:

Governmental Attitudes. Host country governments express their attitudes concerning international imports and investments with actions that can greatly help or hinder an MNC. Governments that encourage investment often provide incentives to persuade foreign companies to establish manufacturing facilities there. Such incentives are often provided by LDCs who want

---

[32]Ann McKinstry Micou, "The Invisible Hand at Work in Developing Countries," *Across the Board,* March 1985, pp. 8–15.

access to the technology, capital, jobs, and educational and managerial skills that an MNC can provide. Singapore, for example, offers low-interest government loans, tax holidays, and accelerated depreciation to foreign investors from certain industries. India provides capital grants to companies that will build manufacturing facilities in certain depressed areas of the country. Malaysia waives taxes for as long as 10 years for companies who also locate in certain areas.[33]

Although LDC governments are often eager to attract certain foreign investors, they will also set requirements that seek to obtain as much value as possible from the MNC while not compromising the country's sovereignty. These requirements take a variety of forms. Many LDCs, for example, require a "fadeout," where the majority ownership of the MNC's facility in the host country is transferred to a host country investor within a certain number of years. Other LDCs, such as India, set a strict limit on foreign ownership of an MNC facility. India limits foreign ownership of a local facility to 40 percent and must approve the operation's production capacity and entry into new markets. IBM left India after the government refused to agree to IBM's worldwide policy of total ownership of its subsidiaries. Coca-Cola left India because it refused to comply with the government's requirement that the company disclose its Coke formula to its Indian partners.[34]

LDCs may also require that an MNC hire a specified number of local citizens for employee and management positions to boost the area's employment. Other LDCs require that the MNC sell its technology to local businesses. Many host countries restrict the amount of funds that an MNC can transfer out of the country. To obtain access to markets in developed countries, some LDCs (e.g., Colombia) require that for every good imported by a resident MNC, the MNC must export a Colombian good of equal or higher value.[35]

Both LDC and DC governments often seek to restrict the import of certain goods that compete with host country businesses. In these cases, barriers are established to discourage imports. On certain imported goods, a government may impose a tariff, which is a tax calculated as a percentage of the product's value. These tariffs raise the import's sales price, which provides domestic competitors with a competitive advantage. In Japan, for example, imported cookies, crackers, and baked goods are taxed in the amount of 20 percent of their value; a tariff of 25 percent of value is applied to imported ham and bacon.[36]

To further aid domestic competitors, a government may provide them with subsidies such as low-cost loans and tax breaks, or a quota may be set on a product to limit the number of goods that can be imported. Another barrier is to require inspection standards that are cost prohibitive for potential imports.

[33]Robert Weigand, "International Investments: Weighing the Incentives," *Harvard Business Review,* July–August 1983, pp. 146–52.

[34]Dennis J. Encarnation and Sushil Vachani, "Foreign Ownership: When Hosts Change the Rules," *Harvard Business Review,* September–October 1985, pp. 152–60.

[35]Grosse and Kujawa, *International Business,* pp. 219–27.

[36]David Gerstenhaber, "Japan's Markets Are Ripe for U.S. Exports," *The Wall Street Journal,* September 14, 1987, p. 21.

Efficiency of Government.   Many American business executives become disillusioned with the inefficient bureaucracies they must deal with in many countries. Often, little assistance is provided by foreign governments to American businesspeople. Customs handling procedures are inefficient and burdensome, and market information is nonexistent. Systems of law in each country also can be quite different. For example, the United States has developed its legal system by means of English *common law:* The courts are guided by principles derived from previous cases. In much of Europe and Asia, however, the legal system is one of *civil law.* In such systems, judges are less important, and the bureaucrat (civil servant) is extremely important. Unfortunately, American managers have found that many of the inefficiencies and obstacles in local governments tend to disappear when a suitable payment is made to some civil servant. Such bribes are considered a part of doing business in many nations. For example, during the late 1970s, Northrop Corporation was accused of spending a substantial part of $30 million over approximately five years for bribes and kickbacks. One factor that emerged during congressional hearings was that such payments were considered in the Middle East to be traditional peculiarities of business practice.[37]

Out of the above and some 400 other cases came the Foreign Corrupt Practices Act, which was passed into law in 1977. For the first time in U.S. history, it became a crime for corporations to bribe an official of a foreign government in order to obtain or retain business in another country. More specifically, the law requires publicly held companies to institute internal accounting controls to ensure that all transactions are made in accordance with management's specific authorization and are fairly recorded. Meanwhile, in West Germany, France, and Great Britain, payments of bribes abroad in business dealings remain not only legal but tax deductible. This practice obviously places the United States at a disadvantage in certain areas.

Government Stability.   The stability of the host country government is perhaps the characteristic that has the greatest impact on an MNC. Highly unstable governments that are subject to volatile change can upend an MNC's operations. The most extreme impact of government instability can occur when an unstable government changes hands. In such cases, the MNC may face *expropriation,* where the new leaders in power seize the MNC's facility without compensation. *Nationalization* may occur, where the government forces the MNC to sell its facility to local buyers. Since World War II, most takeovers of MNC facilities have occurred in LDCs, particularly in Latin America. Since the early 1970s, manufacturing facilities have been the most susceptible to government takeover.[38] Beyond these more dramatic events, government instability can render substantial changes in MNC taxation, product pricing, employment of managers from the MNC's corporate headquarters, and other important aspects of doing business.[39]

---

[37]For an excellent account, see "Northrop Corporation: Development of a Policy on International Sales Commissions," in *Marketing and Society,* ed. R. D. Adler, L. M. Robinson, and J. E. Carlson (Englewood Cliffs, N.J.: Prentice-Hall, 1981), pp. 329–51.

[38]Daniels and Radebaugh, *International Business,* p. 552.

[39]See Thomas A. Cook, "Political Risk: Not for the Fainthearted," *Best's Review (Property/Casualty),* February 1989, pp. 44–47.

TABLE 21–3   Terrorism against Business (during first three quarters of 1985)

	Latin America	Europe	Asia	Mideast	Africa	North America
Bombings	443	101	76	29	20	2
Kidnappings	12	2	2	1	1	0
Attacks on installations	56	6	8	3	5	0
Assassinations	7	10	1	0	0	0
Hijackings	0	2	1	3	0	0
Total	518	121	88	36	26	2

Source: "Business Copes with Terrorism," *Fortune*, January 6, 1986, p. 48. Copyright 1986 by Time, Inc. Used with permission of the publisher. All rights reserved.

Government instability and the uncertainty of other elements of the political environment introduce a degree of *political risk* into an MNC's operations in a respective host country. Political risk refers to unanticipated changes in the host country's political environment that affect MNC operations. *Macro risk* involves political changes that affect all multinational corporations operating in a host country; *micro risk* is changes that affect certain industries or firms. Saudi Arabia's nationalization of all foreign operations in the country's oil industry in 1974 is one example of micro political change.[40]

Terrorism is an increasingly important element of political risk abroad. Terrorism can be defined as "the use, or threat of use, of anxiety-inducing . . . violence for political purposes."[41] International terrorism has assumed many forms, such as attacks on military bases, airplane hijackings, the bombing of foreign embassies, and the kidnapping of political officials and business executives.

Although acts of terrorism are usually highly publicized, the actual number of terrorist incidents worldwide is not substantial. In 1986, for example, 3,000 terrorist acts occurred worldwide, including 763 against businesses (mostly in Latin America). Sixty-seven incidents were targeted at U.S. businesses abroad.[42] Table 21–3 provides a summary of terrorist incidents across continents for the first three quarters of 1985.

However, two developments in terrorism are causes of concern for many U.S. MNCs. First, terrorist incidents are increasing by 12 to 15 percent each year, and the numbers are expected to continue to climb.[43] Terrorism is becoming more popular because it is a relatively low-risk and profitable activity. In over 70 percent of the cases of terrorism, the terrorists' demands are met—ransom is paid or political prisoners are freed. About 80 percent of all terrorists overseas escape execution or capture. Over half of those who are

[40]Robock, Simmonds, and Zwick, *International Business*, pp. 292–94.

[41]Edward F. Micklous, "Tracking the Growth and Prevalence of International Terrorism," in *Managing Terrorism: Strategies for the Corporate Executive*, ed. Patrick J. Montana and George S. Roukis (Westport, Conn.: Quorum Books, 1983), p. 3.

[42]Lennie Copeland, "Terrorism: The Mouse that Roared," *Personnel Administrator*, September 1987, p. 71.

[43]Ibid., pp. 70, 71.

arrested never go to jail.[44] Second, terrorists are becoming more professional and skilled in their trade, and their tactics are becoming much more deadly.[45] These developments concern MNCs, especially given that many companies are ill equipped to handle a terrorist incident when one occurs. Moreover, when terrorism strikes an MNC, neither the host country nor the U.S. government is likely to intervene and provide assistance. The MNC's management is on its own.

In deciding whether to establish operation in a country, few MNCs neglect to consider political risk. Rather, most conduct *political risk analysis,* which involves identifying and assessing the sources of risk and the probabilities that adverse political change will occur in the prospective host country. Several methods of analysis are available. Some MNCs visit the prospective host country and meet with government officials, business executives, and other nationals to obtain their own first-hand assessment of the political environment. Some MNCs employ panels of individuals who are experts on the country. They rate the country on a given number of political risk factors (such as the history of government stability, the role of the military in the host government, and the government's attitude toward foreign investors). Some businesses also produce and publish risk ratings on nations. Business International (BI), for example, rates 70 countries on 55 political risk factors. The ratings are provided by BI specialists who live in the countries they assess. The ratings are published for BI's subscribers.[46]

Rather than hire external experts or rely solely on published risk ratings, a growing number of companies are designing political risk analysis programs that meet the MNC's specific needs. Dow Chemical, for example, maintains its own economic, social, and political risk program (ESP). Six to eight line managers trained in political and economic analysis, along with executives from the respective country, provide specific risk analyses of a country. Xerox maintains its Issues Monitoring System, which regularly identifies the 10 most important political issues for each host country where Xerox operates. Xerox's managers in the respective country assess the issues, evaluate their potential impact on Xerox, and then offer strategies for dealing with the issues. Using these strategies, "external relations" objectives are then set for each local manager. Part of the manager's yearly bonus is based on the accomplishment of the objectives.[47]

Regardless of the method of analysis used, the findings are incorporated into the MNC's decision making about operating in the host country. Beyond this analysis, MNCs also take actions to hedge against political risk. Some MNCs restrict operations to joint ventures, where a local partner shares the risk. They may develop the operation by local borrowing, which builds alliances with local banks. MNCs may spread the risk by locating plants in

---

[44]Don R. Beeman, Thomas W. Sharkey, and Sharon L. Magill, "Will You Return from Your Next Business Trip?" *Business Horizons,* July–August 1988, p. 59.

[45]Ibid., p. 62.

[46]William D. Guth, *Handbook of Business Strategy* (Boston: Warren, Gorham, & Lamont, 1983), p. 136.

[47]Thomas W. Shreeve, "Be Prepared for Political Changes Abroad," *Harvard Business Review,* July–August 1984, pp. 111–18.

several countries, reducing their dependence on one host country. Many MNCs also obtain insurance policies (available from Lloyd's of London and other companies) that provide coverage against expropriation, damages due to war or terrorism, and other politically related losses.

Companies are also developing strategies for coping with the threat of terrorism. Some MNCs (e.g., IBM and Exxon) maintain low profiles and develop a benevolent image in high-risk countries. These MNCs make contributions to the local community to develop goodwill and popular support. They minimize publicity in the host country about their business activities and even reduce the size of corporate signs displayed at their company sites.[48] More companies are boosting security measures at their MNC facilities and hiring counterterrorism consulting firms to train employees in how to deal with a terrorist attack when it occurs. Given the vulnerability of U.S. airlines to terrorist attacks, some large companies such as IBM and General Dynamics periodically advise their employees to avoid U.S. airlines when flying overseas.[49]

In many MNCs, top-level management is establishing crisis management teams to deal with terrorist incidents. Company plans consider the patterns of terrorism, which are surprisingly consistent in different areas of the world. For example, airplane hijackings are the most popular terrorist technique in the Middle East; in Western Europe, U.S. banks and computer companies are popular targets, and the bomb is a favorite terrorist weapon. Kidnappings are popular in Latin America, where terrorists kidnap for money to finance political activities. In the Mideast, terrorists (usually well funded by local governments) kidnap foreigners to obtain release of political prisoners.[50]

High-level executives who are potential kidnapping targets are receiving special training in a growing number of large, visible U.S. MNCs. Companies are also sending to counterterrorism schools the drivers who chauffeur their executives. There they learn such techniques as escape tactics and battering through blockades (many terrorist experts believe that executives are most vulnerable to attack when driving to and from work).[51]

TECHNOLOGY

Technology influences productivity, jobs, interpersonal relationships, and the structure of organizations. And it has obvious impacts on multinational companies. A company's technological superiority in multinational operations often is the major reason for its direct foreign investment and commitment to multinational business. But some nations have an abundance of technological capacity, while others virtually have none. International managers must determine how the levels of technology in foreign countries might affect their operations and sources of raw materials, energy, and transportation.

---

[48]Brian O'Reilly, "Business Copes with Terrorism," *Fortune,* January 6, 1986, p. 48.

[49]Jonathan Dahl, "Firms Warn Workers Traveling Abroad," *The Wall Street Journal,* April 10, 1989, p. B1.

[50]O'Reilly, "Business Copes with Terrorism," pp. 48, 50.

[51]"Multinational Firms Act to Protect Overseas Workers from Terrorism," *The Wall Street Journal,* April 29, 1986, p. 33.

TABLE 21–4	The Planning Environment in Domestic versus Global Settings

The management function of planning takes on greater complexity in an international environment.

Domestic Setting	**Global Setting**
Similar culture.	Diverse cultures.
Limited language differences.	Multilingual.
One economic system.	Multiple economic systems.
One political system.	Numerous political systems.
One basic legal system.	Diverse legal approaches.
One monetary system.	Multiple monetary systems.
Similar markets.	Diverse markets.

MANAGEMENT IN A MULTINATIONAL CORPORATION

PLANNING FUNCTION

The objectives of a multinational company cannot be the same as if it were operating only in the United States. There is too much potential for conflict between corporate objectives and the economic and political objectives of the countries in which the firm operates.[52] In many nations, the role played by government in planning helps heighten the possibility of conflicts with the MNC. For example, Japan's Ministry of International Trade and Industry plans the nation's economy to the point of specifying five-year percentage growth rates in exports of specific products.

In certain situations, a country may have objectives—such as a favorable balance of payments or an improved standard of living for its citizens—that do not coincide with the corporate objectives of the MNC. A common source of conflict is that in order to achieve a profitable objective, some of the earnings of the foreign subsidiary must be returned to the MNC's headquarters. This outward flow of earnings could have a negative impact on the host country's balance of payments. For this reason and similar ones, some nations place restrictions on multinational companies.

Civil servants hold influential positions in foreign bureaucracies. Thus, they often dominate the planning functions of many countries. Managers of multinational companies must become acquainted with the attitudes and practices of these individuals, for an important reason: The civil servants often establish the conditions under which the managers must do their planning.

Table 21–4 presents some factors that can complicate the planning environment for a multinational manager. The greater the number of differing factors, the more complex the planning environment.

ORGANIZING FUNCTION

After a company decides to go multinational and its planning function is well along, an organization structure must be devised to provide a structure of

---

[52]Gary Hamel and C. K. Prahalad, "Do You Really Have a Global Strategy?" *Harvard Business Review,* July–August 1985, pp. 139–48.

FIGURE 21–2   Product Organization Design

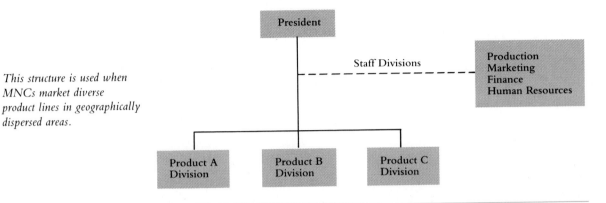

This structure is used when MNCs market diverse product lines in geographically dispersed areas.

jobs and authority for achieving the organizational objectives.[53] As with planning in international management, organization structures often must be adapted to local conditions. Organizational effectiveness depends greatly on flows of information. And these flows become more difficult to maintain as geographically dispersed decision centers are established. Consequently, an MNC must have an effective worldwide communication system for transmitting information throughout the organization.

Multinational companies usually employ the three basic organizational structures discussed in this textbook:

1. *Product design.*   An MNC following the product design structure assigns to a single unit the operational responsibilities for a product or product line. Product design structure is widely used in multinational companies with diverse product lines that are being marketed in geographically dispersed areas. Such multinationals as Sperry Rand and Clark Equipment Company use this design, illustrated in Figure 21–2.

2. *Geographic design.*   With this design, a multinational company groups all functional and operational responsibilities into specific geographical areas. The geographic design is used widely and by such organizations as International Telephone and Telegraph and Pfizer, which do not have highly diversified product lines. The area managers are given decentralized decision-making authority. And they coordinate practically all of the operations within their geographic areas. The geographic design is illustrated in Figure 21–3.

3. *Functional design.*   For an MNC using the functional design, managers at the corporate headquarters, who report to the chief executive, are given global responsibilities for such functions as production, marketing, and financing. Each manager has the authority to plan and control worldwide operations within the function he or she manages. The functional design is

[53]Theodore Herbert, "Strategy and Multinational Organization Structure: An Interorganizational Relationships Perspective," *Academy of Management Review,* April 1984, pp. 259–70.

FIGURE 21-3   Geographic Organization Design

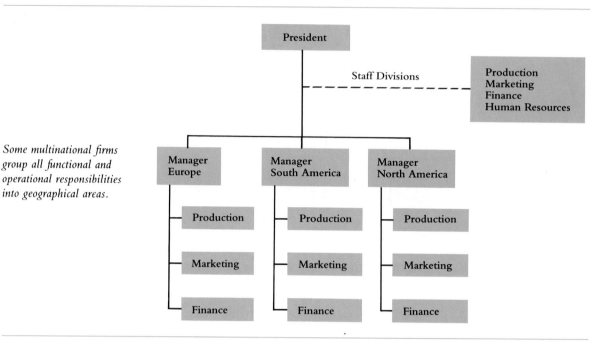

Some multinational firms group all functional and operational responsibilities into geographical areas.

useful for an MNC with a very limited product line, because duplication of effort can be avoided. Extractive industries such as oil and gas often use this design, illustrated in Figure 21-4.

No organization structure is suitable in all cases for either multinationals or companies that operate only at home. We saw in Chapter 7 that organization design is affected by numerous factors. A multinational company in a high-technology industry probably would not organize around geographic regions. More likely, it would use a functional design. A company with relatively inexperienced managers probably would not use a product design.[54]

Another factor that influences the organizing function of a multinational company is the degree to which management is home country oriented, host country oriented, or world oriented. How management views itself and the organization will affect how it organizes the firm in foreign countries.[55] Table 21-5 shows how management's particular orientation can influence the organizational design. The figure also demonstrates the impact the orientation can have on decision making, control, performance evaluation, communication, and staffing.

[54]See J. D. Daniels, R. A. Pitts, and M. J. Tretter, "Organizing for Dual Strategies of Product Diversity and International Expansion," *Strategic Management Journal,* July–September 1985, pp. 223–39, for a study of organizational structures of 37 large U.S. multinationals.

[55]J. D. Daniels, R. A. Pitts, and M. J. Tretter, "Strategy and Structure of U.S. Multinationals: An Exploratory Study," *Academy of Management Journal,* June 1984, pp. 292–307.

FIGURE 21-4   Functional Organization Design

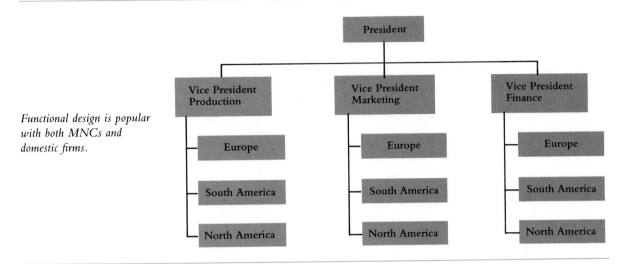

Functional design is popular with both MNCs and domestic firms.

CONTROLLING FUNCTION

Effective performance of the controlling function is extremely important in a multinational company. The more global the operation, the more difficult effective management control becomes. The concepts of preliminary control, concurrent control, and feedback control also are applicable in controlling multinational companies. However, because of cultural differences, the controlling function may not be used in some countries to the same degree it is used in the United States. For example, such things as performance appraisals and quality controls may have little meaning in certain countries. Nevertheless, the implementation of control in the international environment requires the same three basic conditions needed domestically: standards, information, and action.

In establishing *standards* for an MNC, consideration must be given both to overall corporate objectives and to local conditions. This often involves bringing local managers into the planning process. As citizens of the country in which they work, the local managers can provide input useful in establishing standards that contribute to organizational objectives without causing intercultural conflicts.

Information must be provided that reports actual performance and permits appraisal of that performance against standards. Problems can occur here that may not appear in domestic organizations. For example, should profitability be measured in local currency or the home currency? The value of different currencies may cause headquarters to arrive at performance measures that differ from those of the local managers. Finally, the long distances between subsidiaries and headquarters can help cause too much information—or too much irrelevant information—to be fed into the MNC's communications system. Decision support systems must be designed or altered to optimize the amount of information necessary for control.

| **TABLE 21–5** | Management Orientation and Impact on the Organizational Design |

	Orientation		
Organizational Design Factors	**Home Country**	**Host Country**	**World**
Complexity of organization	Complex in home country, simple in subsidiaries.	Varied and independent.	Increasingly complex and interdependent.
Authority; decision making	High in headquarters.	Relatively low in headquarters.	Aim for a collaborative approach between headquarters and subsidiaries.
Evaluation and control	Home standards applied for persons and performance.	Determined locally.	Find standards that are universal and local.
Rewards and punishments; incentives	High in headquarters, low in subsidiaries.	Wide variations; can be high or low rewards for subsidiary performance.	International and local executives rewarded for reaching local and worldwide objectives.
Communication; information flow	High volume to subsidiaries; orders, commands, advice.	Little to and from headquarters, little between subsidiaries.	Both ways and between subsidiaries; heads of subsidiaries part of management team.
Staffing, recruiting, development	Recruit and develop people of home country for key positions everywhere in the world.	Develop people of local nationality for key positions in their own country.	Develop best people everywhere in the world for key positions everywhere in the world.

Source: Adapted from Howard V. Perlmutter, "The Tortuous Evolution of the Multinational Corporation," *Columbia Journal of World Business,* January–February 1969, p. 12.

Management's orientation also affects how a firm is organized in a foreign country.

Managerial *action* to correct deviations is the final step of the controlling function. The possible actions range from total centralization of decisions—where all operating decisions are made at corporate headquarters—to a situation where international units are independent and autonomous. In the majority of cases, most actions are taken by international managers with specific guidelines from corporate headquarters. Effective managerial control of a global enterprise is extremely complex but vital to the firm's survival.

MANAGING PEOPLE IN A MULTINATIONAL CORPORATION

Effectiveness in managing people can vary from nation to nation because motivational incentives and styles of leadership are influenced by a variety of factors. As with domestic organizations, effective management of a multinational company requires managers who understand the needs, values, and expectations of people in the nations in which the MNC operates. As we noted earlier, attitudes toward work, competition in the marketplace, and authority vary greatly across cultures. Thus, leadership styles and motivational techniques that may be effective in the United States, Canada, and Great Britain probably would not work well in Mexico, Africa, Taiwan, or South America.

TABLE 21–6   Should Expatriate or Local Managers Staff a Host Country Facility? Factors to Consider

Staffing decisions for foreign facilities involve the consideration of many factors.

In Favor of Expatriates

Expatriates possess technical and managerial skills.

Using expatriates enhances communications between parent and subsidiary.

Presence of expatriates promotes foreign, or MNC, image.

Parent/subsidiary relations are facilitated by presence of expatriates familiar with corporate culture.

Assignment of expatriates is part of their professional development program, and it improves senior management's decision making.

In Favor of Locals

Total compensation paid to locals is usually considerably less than that paid to expatriates.

No host country cultural adaptation is necessary when locals are used.

Using locals is consistent with a promote-from-within policy.

No work permits are needed with locals.

Using locals promotes a local image.

Using expatriates with special employment contracts rather than local nationals may violate local equal employment opportunity regulations.

Source: Adapted from Robert Grosse and Duane Kujawa, *International Business: Theory and Managerial Applications* (Homewood, Ill.: Richard D. Irwin, 1988), p. 480.

Not only do cultures differ greatly; so may the dominant needs of the people in different countries.

Because substantial differences can exist between the leadership styles and ways of doing business in many countries, an important issue in managing the MNC's facility in a host country is whether local or expatriate managers should staff the facility. An *expatriate* is an MNC employee transferred to the facility from the MNC's home base or from a facility in some other country. Well over 250,000 U.S. citizens work as expatriates in MNC facilities abroad.

This decision requires evaluating many factors that both favor and disfavor the use of expatriates abroad. A number of these factors are shown in Table 21–6. For example, the use of expatriates ensures that the MNC facility has the necessary managerial skills to oversee the operations, a key advantage in LDCs where there exists a shortage of managerial skills. However, an expatriate policy is much more costly than hiring local managers; many MNCs estimate that expatriates are three times more expensive than are locals. The high costs are due to the double-taxing of an expatriate's compensation and the extra costs such as educational and family-related expenses.[56]

Although many MNCs utilize expatriates, the failure rate of U.S. expatriate managers overseas is significant. Experts estimate that, on average, 30 percent of all expatriate assignments end in failure, often with the manager returning home sooner than expected.[57] Two main reasons account for such disappoint-

[56]Grosse and Kujawa, *International Business,* pp. 480–81.

[57]See Rosalie L. Tung, "Expatriate Assignments: Enhancing Success and Minimizing Failure," *Academy of Management Executive,* May 1987, pp. 117–26.

MANAGEMENT FOCUS

Japanese Expatriates in America: A Challenging Assignment

Currently, over 200,000 Japanese managers and professionals work in Japanese-owned companies in the United States. As expatriates, their assignment in America brings some substantial financial benefits. Spacious housing is available at a small fraction of the cost in Japan; food is much cheaper (in Japan, a T-bone steak can cost $40; a cantaloupe, $10); And recreational activities are more plentiful and less costly. In Japan, where golf is immensely popular, it costs $800 for a group of four to play one 18-hole round.

However, the Japanese expatriate also encounters major challenges. The English language is often a significant barrier. As youngsters, the Japanese spend years learning the language; however, because their training focuses on reading and writing English rather than speaking it, the Japanese have problems expressing themselves clearly. These problems are worsened by the heavy reliance by the Japanese on nonverbal communication (e.g., facial expressions, body movements). For these reasons, Americans often have problems understanding what the Japanese are saying—verbally and nonverbally.

Differences in Japanese and American management styles and practices can also create problems. The Japanese culture greatly discourages interpersonal confrontation and conflict; therefore, Japanese managers will not openly debate or disagree with their employees, and they rarely provide critical feedback to subordinates. They also utilize the Japanese-styled, group-based decision making, where consensus agreement from many participants is sought. These practices contrast sharply with American managers' tendency to take the initiative and make decisions on their own and to frequently debate and disagree with their subordinates, peers, and bosses. Many Japanese managers are uncomfortable with this type of confrontation.

ing performance: (1) The expatriate often has problems adjusting to the cultural, social, and business environment in the host country, frequently because the MNC has not adequately prepared the manager for the significant cultural differences that will be encountered. (A recent survey of MNCs found that less than 12 percent of the firms provide formal training on the cross-cultural aspects of managing in a foreign country.[58]) (2) Some expatriate managers also lack the special characteristics and abilities that an overseas assignment requires, such as communication skills, flexibility, adaptability to change, emotional maturity, and the ability to work with people with different backgrounds, perspectives, and cultures. These human skills (discussed in Chapter 2) are not emphasized by many MNCs in the selection of individuals for expatriate assignments overseas.[59]

A growing number of MNCs are taking steps to boost the effectiveness of their expatriate managers. Some companies are sending their prospective expatriates to *culture camps* run by consultants who specialize in cross-cultural training. At these off-site programs, managers spend several days, even weeks,

[58]Madelyn R. Callahan, "Preparing the New Global Manager," *Training and Development Journal,* March 1989, p. 30.

[59]See John S. McClenahen, "Why U.S. Managers Fail Overseas," *Industry Week,* November 16, 1987, pp. 71ff; Tung, "Expatriate Assignments."

They must also deal with being perceived by their American employees as indecisive and weak because they do not openly disagree or make decisions on their own.

While in the United States, parent expatriates must prepare their children for Japan's rigorous entrance exams that alone determine whether a youngster is admitted to a Japanese university. In Japan, children begin studying for these critical exams in kindergarten. Because U.S. schools are typically a year or two behind Japanese primary and secondary schools, many expatriates are concerned about their children's education. Some have their children tutored while in the United States. In some cases, the children remain behind in Japan to continue their preparatory education there.

Despite these and other challenges, many expatriates enjoy the greater individual freedom and emphasis on family life in the United States.

(In Japan, managers return home weekdays after 11 P.M.; they see their families only on Sundays.) About 5 percent of the expatriates remain in the United States after their four-year assignment ends. The remaining 95 percent return to Japan, where Japanese society is extremely homogeneous and quick to ostracize any Japanese who shows signs of being "Americanized." A manager who shows Western ways (a bit of impatience, for example, with the slowness of consensus decision making) may well be sent to a remote office until he reforms. His children may be shunned at school; a Westernized Japanese daughter may have problems finding a Japanese husband. In sum, an American assignment can be difficult, both during and after the fact.

Source: Brian O'Reilly, "Japan's Uneasy Managers," *Fortune*, April 25, 1988, pp. 245ff.

being immersed in the culture, traditions, and customs they will encounter in their new locale.[60]

Some MNCs also carefully screen employees for expatriate assignments. McDonnell-Douglas's selection program involves close questioning about personal habits, religious and political beliefs, medical histories, and family situations. The company looks for any situation that may cause problems for the individual or the company once the expatriate is working abroad. McDonnell-Douglas also encourages each of its expatriate managers to return home at least once a year (the company pays the round-trip air fare) to relieve two potential expatriate problems: homesickness and the "out of sight, out of mind" syndrome. Many expatriates fear that once away from the home office they will be forgotten by the company and that no opportunities will be available for them at the MNC home base when they return.[61]

Regardless of the degree of preparation for the assignment, many expatriates believe that managing overseas (and returning home) presents many challenges. The Focus discusses some that face Japanese expatriate managers.

[60]Dyan Machan, "Ici On Parle Bottom-Line Responsibility," *Forbes*, February 8, 1988, p. 140.

[61]Eileen Daspin, "Managing Expatriate Employees," *Trends, Tactics and Techniques for Today's Manager*, 1987, pp. 47–49.

SUMMARY OF KEY POINTS

- The multinational corporation (MNC) presents a critical challenge to future managers—the challenge of managing organizations, people, and operations in an international environment.

- The decision to become an MNC involves determining the international market to be served, the products or services to be produced and marketed, and the strategy for entering the selected market.

- The environment of a multinational manager will differ in many respects from the domestic environment. The culture, economics, politics, and technology of the international environment are among the most important differences.

- Cultural differences can result in differing attitudes toward the importance of work, authority, competition, material possessions, time, risk-taking, profits, and other factors.

- Economic differences in income levels, growth trends, inflation rates, balance of payments, and the stability of the currency and overall economy can significantly affect MNC performance.

- It is difficult to separate politics and the MNC. The attitudes in host countries toward imports and direct investment, the stability of government, and the efficiency of government vary widely between nations. Each may change rapidly in those nations where governments change rapidly.

- Technology has affected and will continue to affect multinational companies. Often a company's technological superiority in multinational operations is the major reason for its commitment to multinational business. Technology levels also influence the sources of raw materials, energy, and transportation in a particular area.

- The management function of planning can be more complex in an MNC. The greater the cultural and language differences, the more diverse the economic, political, and legal systems. Also, the greater the number of markets and monetary systems it faces, the more complex the planning environment for an MNC.

- MNCs employ the basic organizational structures of domestic organizations: product design, geographic design, and functional design.

- Effective performance of the controlling function is extremely important in MNCs. Because of cultural differences, the controlling function may not be used in some countries to the same degree that it is used in the United States. Such techniques as performance appraisals and quality control may have little meaning in some cultures. However, the conditions for effective control—standards, information, and corrective action—are still required.

- Managing people will vary across nations because styles of leadership and motivational techniques are influenced by the needs, values, and expectations of the people in the nations in which the MNC operates. Thus, leadership styles and motivation techniques that might be effective in America may not be in other parts of the world.

- An important decision for MNCs is whether to utilize expatriate managers for overseas assignments. To date, the effectiveness of U.S. expatriate managers has been limited by such problems as difficulties in adjusting to environmental differences in the host country, and the lack of human relations skills required for effectively managing abroad.

DISCUSSION AND REVIEW QUESTIONS

1. Culture, economics, politics, and technology are environmental factors that greatly influence managerial performance in an MNC. Briefly discuss the role of each.

2. In your opinion, is the practice of establishing manufacturing facilities in countries having low labor costs a constructive strategy for U.S. businesses? Discuss.

3. Do you believe that you would be an effective expatriate manager? Explain why or why not.

4. Many U.S. MNCs are calling for the repeal of the Foreign Corrupt Practices Act, charging that the law greatly diminishes their competitiveness abroad. In your view, should the law be repealed? Discuss.

5. Discuss the management function of planning in a domestic versus a global setting.

6. "How effective an individual is in international management will be determined by how well he or she can adjust to local conditions." Discuss.

7. Suppose you were the CEO of a computer manufacturing company with plans to establish a production facility in Japan. You want to transfer some of your managers to the Japanese facility. What steps

would you take to ensure that your expatriate managers are effective in their new assignments?

8. Some management observers assert that terrorism will forever remain a substantial risk in MNC operations, because terrorism is low risk and profitable. Do you agree? What, if any, strategies could be implemented to reduce terrorism against MNCs?

9. Would the social responsibility aspects of managerial actions differ between domestic and international managers? Discuss.

10. Of the economic, cultural, political, and technological factors in the international environment, which factor do you believe most impacts MNC performance? Explain.

ADDITIONAL REFERENCES

Baker, J. C., and **M. A. Hashmi.** "Political Risk Management: Steering Clear of Risky Business." *Risk Management,* October 1988, pp. 40–47.

Bassing, G. R., and **R. H. Dekmejian.** "MNCs and the Iranian Revolution: An Empirical Study." *International Management Review* 25, no. 2 (1985), pp. 67–75.

Fleck, J. D., and **J. R. D'Cruz.** "The CEO's Guide to Strategy under Free Trade." *Business Quarterly,* Spring 1988, pp. 43–47.

Galbraith, J. K. "The Defense of the Multinational Company." *Harvard Business Review,* March–April 1978, pp. 83–93.

Ghoshal, S. "Global Strategy: An Organizing Framework." *Strategic Management Journal,* September–October 1987, pp. 425–40.

Gill, S. *The Global Political Economy: Perspectives, Problems, and Policies.* Baltimore: The Johns Hopkins Press, 1988.

Jelinek, M., and **N. J. Adler.** "Women: World-Class Managers for Global Competition." *Academy of Management Executive,* February 1988, pp. 11–19.

Kedia, B. L., and **R. S. Bhagat.** "Cultural Constraints on Transfer of Technology across Nations: Implications for Research in International and Comparative Management." *Academy of Management Review,* October 1988, pp. 559–71.

Kennedy, C. R., Jr. "Political Risk Management: A Portfolio Planning Model." *Business Horizons,* November–December 1988, pp. 26–33.

Kim, L., and **L. Yooncheol.** "Environment, Generic Strategies, and Performance in a Rapidly Developing Country: A Taxonomic Approach." *Academy of Management Journal,* December 1988, pp. 802–27.

Kirk, W. Q., and **R. C. Maddox.** "International Management: The New Frontier for Women." *Personnel,* March 1988, pp. 46–49.

Kobrin, S. J. "Expatriate Reduction and Strategic Control in American Multinational Corporations." *Human Resource Management,* Spring 1988, pp. 63–75.

Milner, H. V. *Resisting Protectionism: Global Industries and the Politics of International Trade.* Princeton, N.J.: Princeton University Press, 1988.

O'Hagan, J. P., and **M. S. Allen.** "Expatriate Compensation: An Alternative Approach." *Benefits and Compensation International,* March 1988, pp. 14–16.

Rice, F. "Should You Work for a Foreigner?" *Fortune,* August 1, 1988, pp. 123ff.

Ricks, D. A. *Big Business Blunders: Mistakes in Multinational Marketing.* Homewood, Ill.: Dow Jones–Irwin, 1983.

Savich, R. S., and **W. Rodgers.** "Assignment Overseas: Easing the Transition Before and After." *Personnel,* August 1988, pp. 44ff.

Tung, R. L. "Career Issues in International Assignments." *Academy of Management Executive,* August 1988, pp. 241–44.

Weekly, J. K. *International Business: Operating in the Global Economy.* Hinsdale, Ill.: Dryden Press, 1987.

CASE 21–1   The Maquiladoras

Located in four Mexican towns along the 2,000-mile Mexico–U.S. border are what Texas governor Bill Clements asserts is "the best-kept industrial secret in the United States." The secret is the maquiladoras, foreign (mostly U.S.) owned and managed factories that take parts transported across the border and assemble them into products. Once assembled, the products are shipped back to the United States for sale.

In a few years, this maquila industry along Mexico's border has grown to over 1,000 maquiladoras in Tijuana, Nogales, Juarez, and Matomoros. (*Maquiladora* is "handwork" in Spanish.) The plants employ over 350,000 Mexicans, over 10 percent of Mexico's work force.

The reason for this booming industry: astoundingly low labor costs. Mexico is a less developed country, and its peso has been devalued several times. As a result, the country's minimum *daily* wage is less than $3, and a weekly paycheck is less than $15. These labor costs are less than half of the prevailing wages in Hong Kong, Singapore, South Korea, and other low-labor-cost countries where U.S. companies have constructed assembly plants. The U.S. manufacturers pay no tariffs on the parts shipped into Mexico as long as the assembled products are reimported to the United States. Duties on reimported parts are very low.

In short, the maquiladoras are enabling U.S. manufacturers to substantially reduce their production costs. As a result, literally hundreds of U.S. companies have set up assembly shops in Mexico. For example, General Motors has established 17 plants for its labor-intensive assembly work, such as cutting and sewing car seats.

Asian and especially Japanese companies are also fast establishing maquiladoras in the border towns. Over 30 Japanese manufacturers already assemble there. Hitachi, for example, assembles about 100,000 color TV chassis in its Tijuana maquiladora each year. The chassis are then transported to Hitachi's plant in Anaheim, California, for final assembly. Matsushita has a plant in Tijuana where 1,600 Mexican workers assemble TV chassis. Sony, Sanyo, and 100 other Japanese manufacturers are expected to either build more or expand their maquiladoras in the next few years.

The maquiladoras have likewise provided benefits for the Mexican economy. They are transforming the four Mexican communities, which were once tourist towns, into industrial centers. The maquiladoras also provide badly needed employment for Mexican workers. In Mexico, earning $15 a week provides a middle-class existence for many citizens who otherwise would remain unemployed. The output from the maquiladoras is second only to oil as Mexico's top foreign exchange earner.

Source: Adapted from Stephen Baker and Todd Vogel, "Will the New Maquiladoras Build a Better Mañana?" *Business Week,* November 14, 1988, pp. 120ff; Brian O'Reilly, "Business Makes a Run for the Border," *Fortune,* August 18, 1986, pp. 70ff; Eugene Carlson, "Japanese Companies Increase Presence Near Mexico Border," *The Wall Street Journal,* December 22, 1987, p. 19; Kathleen K. Wiegner, "How to Mix Sake and Tequila," *Forbes,* March 23, 1987, pp. 48ff.

However, the work is long and demanding for the $15 weekly paycheck. Employees work about 49 hours a week in a factory that is typically a one-story, windowless, concrete building. Inside, the surroundings are clean but spare, often containing long tables, chairs, and parts bins. In such plants, employees assemble a wide array of products: computer keyboards, toys, carburetors, refrigerators, garage door openers, and even water beds. A few plants sort coupons; one plant even sorts walnuts. Over one third of the assembly work in the maquiladoras involves the production of clothing.

Operating the maquiladoras, while profitable, can also be challenging. Most of the American managers live in the United States just across the border. Each of the major Mexican maquiladoras communities is located less than an hour's driving time from a large U.S. community. Tijuana, for example, is about a half hour's drive from San Diego. Each day, the managers commute; the drive back often requires hours due to the customs inspection of cars traveling from Mexico into the United States. Electrical blackouts are also common, and telephoning a Mexican border town from the United States often requires 15 to 20 attempts.

Turnover at the maquiladoras is also a problem, often running from 70 to 100 percent each year. Younger, unskilled employees continually seek better working conditions and a shorter distance from their home (often in the mountains) to work. The companies won't increase the minimum wage to attract recruits; rather, they will offer extras such as inexpensive food in the factory cafeteria, attendance bonuses, discounts on bus rides to work, and Michael Jackson records.

Beyond these problems, a growing number of Mexicans are becoming dissatisfied with the operations. They charge that the maquiladoras transfer little technology or employee training into Mexico, as the plants' operations and jobs are at a low skill level. Partly as a result of these criticisms, a new type of inner maquiladoras, fully integrated manufacturing facilities, is being built by international companies in the interior of Mexico. These plants do transfer technology and provide high-skill jobs and higher wages. The plants also use Mexican-made parts, which provides Mexican companies with much-needed business.

The maquiladoras industry will continue to grow at a projected rate of over 12 percent each year. However, concern is mounting among the AFL–CIO union organization and other U.S. groups that the establishment of maquiladoras by U.S. companies is contributing to unemployment in the United States. Said one union official, "The more maquiladoras the companies build, the more layoffs and the fewer jobs there are for Americans."

QUESTIONS FOR ANALYSIS

1. From an international management perspective, what other challenges are involved in managing a maquiladora?
2. In your opinion, is the union concern about maquiladoras merited? Explain.
3. Some observers respond to the union concern by asserting that maquiladoras actually help employment in the United States. Do you agree? If so, how?

CASE 21–2   Federal Express's International Gamble

In 1989, Federal Express made a daring move in international business. Breaking its long-held tradition of growing only through internal expansion, Federal paid $880 million to buy Tiger International Inc., the world's largest heavy-cargo airline. Created in the 1940s by some members of the Flying Tigers, a group of daring World War II fighter pilots, Tiger International is best known for its worldwide Flying Tiger airfreight service.

Federal Express bought Tiger International to boost Federal's flagging performance in its overseas markets. Although it has worked hard to become the leader in international delivery, the company's efforts have been hindered by well-established competitors in foreign markets and by tedious and time-consuming government regulations. Overseas, for example, Federal Express must negotiate with the government to obtain flight approvals and landing rights in each of the countries in which it operates. Federal lost $74 million on its international business between 1985 and 1989.

Tiger International has what Federal sorely needs overseas—a network of approved delivery routes that will give Federal speedy entry into the Far East, South America, and Australia and will greatly strengthen its routes in Europe. Tiger's routes and fleet of huge planes will boost Federal's overseas express delivery services and provide entry into the heavy-cargo freight business.

Federal must strengthen its international business because of intensifying competition in the U.S. overnight delivery market. Although Federal has 45 percent of the U.S. market, price wars with United Parcel Service and other competitors have reduced revenues per package by 15 percent since 1984. An even more troubling factor is the surging sales of facsimile machines that can send a letter from one location to another in seconds. Experts expect fax machines to cut Federal's overnight letter business by at least 30 percent in the next few years.

While Federal Express looks abroad for new growth and profits, the Tiger International acquisition presents major challenges. First, Federal must cope with an awkward reality: Many of Tiger's biggest customers are Federal's competitors. These companies (such as UPS) pay Tiger to ship packages to countries where they have no landing rights. It is expected that a number of these companies will stop using Tiger rather than put money into Federal's pockets. Said one industry analyst, "(They) would rather use a barge than Flying Tiger."

Second, Federal must merge two organizations with distinctly different cultures. Tiger International has 6,500 unionized employees and a conservative culture. Federal's workers are nonunionized, and the company's culture is highly entrepreneurial and competitive, one that supports risk-taking and expects high performance. Federal's CEO Fred Smith, a Vietnam veteran, rewards exceptional performers with Bravo Zulu stickers—two Naval signal

Source: Adapted from Dean Foust, "Mr. Smith Goes Global," *Business Week*, February 13, 1989, pp. 66ff; Resa W. King, "UPS Isn't about to Be Left Holding the Parcel," *Business Week*, February 13, 1989, p. 69.

flags that mean "job well done." Observers wonder whether the merger will weaken Federal's valuable entrepreneurial culture and spirit.

Third, acquisition costs and Tiger's existing debt have increased Federal's total debt load to $2.1 billion, well over twice Federal's preacquisition amount. Such heavy debt will make the company more vulnerable to shifts in the economy, and the heavy-cargo business is much more cyclical and requires far more capital than does the small-package market.

If Federal can keep Tiger's customers, successfully integrate the two companies, and manage its debt, the company must still contend with formidable overseas competition. In the Far East, Federal must battle Japan Air Lines and Nippon Cargo; in Europe, DHL carries 40 percent of all air delivery packages and 60 percent of all packages flown to the United States.

However, Federal's toughest domestic competitor—United Parcel Service— will likely be its chief international rival. Like Federal, UPS has also set its sights on dominating worldwide package delivery. Since launching international service three years ago, UPS or its partners have established operations in Europe, West Africa, Asia, and the Middle East.

UPS had several opportunities to buy Tiger International but declined. It believed that cultural differences and union problems would outweigh Tiger's advantages. Instead, UPS bought Alimondo, its partner in Italy, and is using the operation as a base for building ground transport service throughout Europe. UPS is also buying small European courier companies to build and expand its overseas air delivery service.

UPS has been dealt a major blow by Federal's acquisition, as it uses Tiger planes for servicing the Far East. However, with huge assets and cash and very little debt, the company can afford the years of high costs and financial losses it takes to establish effective worldwide operations. UPS lost $20 million on its international air service last year.

QUESTIONS FOR ANALYSIS

1. In your opinion, what is the most difficult challenge facing Federal Express in its efforts to strengthen and expand its international operations?
2. What are the advantages and shortcomings of entering international markets by acquiring competitors rather than by expanding internally?
3. In your view, how does Federal Express's move into international markets alter its planning, organizing, leading, and controlling tasks?

EXPERIENTIAL EXERCISE

LAUNCHING AN INTERNATIONAL BUSINESS

Purpose

This activity is designed to enhance students' understanding of the key elements of the international environment and their impact on expanding a business internationally.

The Exercise in Class

The instructor will divide the class into groups of four students each. Each group should complete the following project:

1. Assume that your group is the top-management team of a manufacturing company. Your team's first task is to select a product that your company manufactures. Once you've selected the product, assume that your company makes the product domestically and wants to expand production overseas. Specifically, your company seeks to produce and sell the product in a Latin American, European, or Asian country.

2. Select a country for your international expansion. Once you've identified the nation, conduct an assessment of the country as an international market for your product:
   a. Conduct library research on the cultural, economic, and political aspects of the country's environment.
   b. Review your research, answering the following questions:
      (1) What is the level of demand for your product in this potential market?
      (2) In what ways do the cultural, economic, and political aspects of the country's environment facilitate the success of your product in the market?
      (3) In what ways do these environmental aspects hinder the success of your product?
      (4) In your team's opinion, what are the primary challenges in establishing manufacturing facilities and launching your product in this market?

3. Prepare a five- to seven-page typed report that provides an overall profile of your selected market, including your responses to these questions. Be prepared to defend your findings in class discussion.

The Learning Message

This exercise effectively illustrates the importance of the international environment in launching manufacturing and marketing activities in an international market. Students should quickly realize the complexities involved in expanding business abroad, which is one major reason why a number of overseas ventures fail.

22

MANAGEMENT CAREERS

LEARNING OBJECTIVES

After completing Chapter 22, you should be able to:

Define
the concept of career effectiveness and the criteria that determine career effectiveness.

Describe
the relationship between career stages and career paths.

Discuss
the positions supporting and opposing the creation of "mommy track" career paths in organizations.

Compare
the needs of individuals and organizations in career planning.

Identify
the potential benefits and pitfalls of mentoring relationships.

The Baby Busters

A new generation of young adults is assuming management positions in U.S. organizations today. Labeled "the baby busters" by the business media, these young men and women were born after 1964, when the birth rate in the United States began to decline. Although they are as individualistic as any other generation, observers assert that many baby busters appear to share some values and opinions that differ from previous generations, especially the "baby boomers," individuals born after the end of World War II and through the early 1960s.

By reports, baby busters are just as hardworking in their management jobs as were their baby-boomer predecessors. However, they appear to be less motivated by money. Surveys of managers in their early 20s find that money is far less valued than are the goals of self- and career development and a satisfying and challenging work environment that gives them access to upper-level managers.

Perhaps because they and their parents grew up during times of prosperity, baby busters are less concerned about job security than are baby boomers. Less patient about paying their dues as young managers, baby busters are not as tied to their jobs and are more willing to leave an organization for a job that provides greater opportunities for professional and career growth. Many baby busters seek self- and career development via part-time studies in business education programs, such as working toward a master's degree in business administration.

Many baby busters are committed to developing a fuller life outside work, which differs from the early, dues-paying years of young baby-boomer managers, many of whom devoted their waking hours almost exclusively to their jobs. The baby busters place more emphasis on sports, family, and leisure activities; and many expect their employers to provide a fitness center, assistance with day care, and other support that facilitates a more multidimensional life.

Some older observers of the workplace view baby busters as a demanding bunch. However, their independent-mindedness is welcomed by many organizations that today can no longer ensure long-term employment but rather encourage employees to rely on themselves rather than the company for job security. Much fewer in number than was the baby-boomer generation in its early 20s, baby busters are also much in demand to fill lower-level management positions. To secure and keep baby busters, organizations are expected to be more attentive to their requirements for challenging jobs, professional growth, and other needs.

Source: Adapted from Amanda Bennett, "New Generation Asks More than Its Elders of Corporate World," *The Wall Street Journal*, October 26, 1988, pp. 1, 6.

The distinction between careers *in* management and management *as* a career is more than a play on words. A career in management implies *descriptions* of *what* constitutes such careers and *where* such careers are acted out. Management as a career implies somewhat more personal issues, such as *why* one should pursue such a career, *who* should attempt such careers, and *how* an individual can increase the odds of having a successful and fulfilling career in management. This chapter explores both careers in management and management as a career.

CAREERS IN MANAGEMENT

The idea of **career** connotes a profession that requires training and is undertaken for life. It also brings to mind the idea of moving upward in one's chosen line of work: commanding larger salaries, assuming more responsibility, and acquiring more status, prestige, and power.

For our purposes, *"The career is the individually perceived sequence of attitudes and behaviors associated with work-related experiences and activities over the span of the person's life."*[1] This definition implies that (1) a career consists of both attitudes and behaviors, (2) it is an ongoing sequence of work-related activities, and (3) it is clearly work related. Nevertheless, a person's nonwork life and roles play significant parts in it. For example, a midcareer manager, 50 years old, can have quite different attitudes about a job advancement involving greater responsibilities than a manager nearing retirement. A bachelor's reaction to a promotion involving relocation is likely to be different from that of a father of school-age children.

CAREER EFFECTIVENESS

Career effectiveness in organizational settings is judged not only by the individual but by the organization itself. But what is meant by career effectiveness? Under what circumstances will individuals state that they have had "successful" or "satisfying" careers? And will the organization share the individuals' views about their careers? Of the numerous criteria of career effectiveness, the four most often cited are performance, attitude, adaptability, and identity.[2]

Performance. Salary and position are the usual indicators of career performance. Specifically, the more rapidly one's salary increases and one advances up the hierarchy, the higher the level of career performance. As one advances (is promoted), responsibilities become greater in terms of employees supervised, budget allocated, and revenue generated. The organization is vitally interested in career performance, since it relates directly to goal attainment. That is, salary and position in most instances reflect the extent of an individual's contribution to attainment of the organization's objectives.

---

[1]Douglas T. Hall, *Careers in Organizations* (Santa Monica, Calif.: Goodyear Publishing, 1976), p. 4.

[2]Ibid., pp. 93–96, is the basis for our discussion of these criteria.

As the Management Focus titled "Toil and Tarry" indicates, people are working longer hours on the job, at least partly to boost their career performance. But do longer hours equate with higher performance?

Two obstacles sometimes hinder accurate appraisal of career effectiveness. First, an organization may fail to recognize performance fully. Thus, employees may not be rewarded with salary increases and promotions. Second, the organization's expectations for an individual may not match the individual's goals or abilities. The organization may accurately assess the individual's potential for greater performance, yet the individual's noncareer interests, such as family, community, or religion, might prevent optimal job performance. In such instances, the individual may be satisfied with career performance, yet the organization is disappointed. This mismatch results from the individual's *attitudes* toward the career.

Attitudes.   This aspect of career effectiveness refers to the way individuals perceive and evaluate their careers. The more positive these perceptions and evaluations are, the more effective the careers are. Individuals with positive attitudes are more likely to be committed to the organization and interested in their jobs.

Adaptability.   Few professions are stagnant. On the contrary, change and development are much more common in contemporary professions, and change requires new knowledge and skills. For example, medicine and engineering have and will continue to use new information and technology. Individuals unable to *adapt* to these changes and to *adopt* them in their careers run the risk of early obsolescence. Career adaptability, therefore, means application of the latest knowledge, skill, and technology in a career.

Identity.   Two important components make up career identity: (1) the extent to which individuals are aware of their interests, values, and expectations; (2) the manner in which individuals view their lives, the extent to which they see themselves as extensions of their pasts. The important question is, "What do I want to be, and what do I have to do to become what I want to be?"[3] Individuals who find satisfactory answers to this question are likely to have effective careers and to make effective contributions to their organizations.

Effective careers in management are likely for individuals with high levels of performance, positive attitudes, adaptiveness, and identity resolution. These criteria are not unique to management. They apply to all careers.

Career Stages

Individuals go through distinct but interrelated stages in their careers. The simplest version would include four stages:

1. Prework stage: attending school.
2. Initial work stage: moving from job to job.

[3] Erik H. Erikson, "The Concept of Identity in Race Relations: Notes and Queries," *Daedalus* 95 (1966), p. 148, as cited in Hall, *Careers*, p. 95.

MANAGEMENT FOCUS

Toil and Tarry

American adults are working harder than ever before in their careers, according to researchers. In the last 15 years, the average adult's leisure time has declined 40 percent—from 26.6 to 16.6 hours a week. Those at the upper levels of the career ladder devote the longest hours to their careers, dispelling the belief that employees at lower levels of the organization must work longer hours to advance up the organizational hierarchy. While the average adult spends about 47 hours a week working, studying, and commuting (compared to 41 hours in 1973), professionals log over 52 hours a week.

Probably few individuals spend more time on the job than senior-level executives, especially at large companies. A survey of upper-level managers among Fortune 1,000 companies found that executives work an average 56 hours a week. About 60 percent of the chief executive officers (CEOs) work at least 60 hours a week (compared to 40 percent in 1980). Overall, several studies have found that the larger the company, the longer the hours logged by managers.

Clearly, many people are working longer hours. But do longer hours mean better performance? No, according to researchers, who have found that performance plummets after a certain number of hours on the job. The exact number varies by occupation and individual, but many researchers agree that any manager who works over 50 hours a week is performing at less than his or her best.

Many career counselors advise that managers should work smarter, not harder, by adopting such strategies as scheduling the day's most difficult work during your peak productivity time, those hours when you're sharpest and at your best. It's also useful to complete tasks in one sitting, so time isn't wasted refocusing on the task after each interruption. It is important to know your limits—the point where your performance begins to decline—and to pace your work accordingly.

These and other strategies can enable a manager to do 60 hours of work in a 40-hour week. However, be aware that many companies want workaholics—individuals who labor evenings and weekends on the job. If two individuals are up for a major promotion and are equally talented, many career advisers assert that 9 out of 10 companies will hire the employee who toils 80 hours on the job each week over the one who can do the same job in 40 hours. Why? Because the 80-hour toiler sets an example of "brute force of effort" that other employees see. The long hours communicate great commitment and loyalty to the company. In sum, the toiler sets a style that subordinates will likely follow.

If you don't want to put in 80 hours a week, career counselors advise that you stay away from workaholic companies, those that maintain a culture of long hours at the job, whether those hours are spent working or are simply "face time"—staying around after hours so those above you see you on the job. Some companies do frown on workaholism. To prevent employees from overworking, one Chicago insurance company locks all doors after 7 P.M. each weekday evening and for all but four hours on the weekends. To work other afterhours, an employee must obtain a pass from the boss—good for one time only.

Source: Adapted from Ford S. Worthy, "You're Probably Working Too Hard," *Fortune,* April 27, 1987, pp. 133ff; "Work Smarter, Not Harder," *Psychology Today,* March 1989, pp. 33–34.

This student is in the prework stage of his career.

3. Stable work stage: maintaining one job.
4. Retirement stage: leaving active employment.

Most working people prepare for their occupation by undergoing some form of organized education in high school, trade school, vocational school, or college. They take a first job, but chances are they will move to other jobs in the same or other organizations. Eventually, they settle into a position in which they remain until retirement. The duration of each stage varies among individuals, but everyone generally goes through them.

Studies have found that needs and expectations change as the individual moves through the career stages.[4] Managers in American Telephone & Telegraph (AT&T) expressed considerable concern for security needs during the first years on their jobs. This stage, called the *establishment* stage, ordinarily lasts during the first five years of employment. Next, the *advancement* stage occurs, approximately between age 30 and age 45. During this period, the AT&T managers expressed considerably less concern for security

[4]Douglas T. Hall and Khalil Nougaim, "An Examination of Maslow's Need Hierarchy in an Organizational Setting," *Organizational Behavior and Human Performance* 3 (1968), pp. 12–35; Raymond E. Hill and Edwin L. Miller, "Job Change and the Middle Seasons of a Man's Life," *Academy of Management Journal,* March 1981, pp. 114–27.

needs satisfaction and more concern for achievement, esteem, and autonomy. Promotions and advancement to jobs with responsibility and opportunity to exercise independent judgment are characteristics of this stage.

After the advancement stage comes the *maintenance* phase, a period marked by efforts to stabilize the gains of the past. In some respects, this stage is a plateau—no new gains are made. Yet it can be a period of creativity, since the individual has satisfied many of the earlier psychological and financial needs. Although individuals and careers vary, esteem and self-actualization tend to be the most important needs in the maintenance stage. Many people experience a midcareer crisis during this stage, which signals problems encountered in achieving satisfaction from their work.[5]

The maintenance stage is followed by the *retirement* stage. The individual has completed one career and may move on to another one. A retiree experiences self-actualization through activities that were impossible to pursue while working. Painting, gardening, volunteer service, and quiet reflection are some of the many possibilities. But, depending on the individual's financial and health status, the retirement years can be spent satisfying security and physiological needs.

These four, generally applicable career stages have been studied in a variety of settings. One recent study of "knowledge" workers raised some interesting issues about career stages and career effectiveness.[6]

The fastest growing segment of the work force is knowledge workers—professionals such as accountants, scientists, and engineers. These professionals spend their careers in large, complex organizations after having spent several years obtaining advanced training and degrees. Organizations that employ them expect them to provide the innovativeness and creativity necessary to survive in dynamic and competitive environments. Obviously, the performance levels of professional employees must be of the utmost concern for the organizations' leaders.

Effective management of professionals begins with understanding the crucial characteristics of the four stages of professional careers. Professional employees could avoid some disappointments and anxieties if they also understood more about their career stages:

Stage I.   Young professionals enter an organization with technical knowledge but not with understanding of the organization's demands and expectations. Consequently, they must work closely with more experienced persons. The relationship that develops between the young professionals and their supervisors is an *apprenticeship*. The central activities expected of apprentices include *learning* and *following directions*. To move successfully and effectively through stage I, professionals must be able to accept the *psychological state of*

---

[5]Abraham K. Korman, Ursula Wittig-Berman, and Dorothy Lang, "Career Success and Personal Failure: Alienation in Professionals and Managers," *Academy of Management Journal,* June 1981, pp. 342–60; John Veiga, "Plateaued versus Non-Plateaued Managers: Career Patterns, Attitudes and Path Potential," *Academy of Management Journal,* September 1981, pp. 566–78.

[6]The following discussion is primary based on Gene W. Dalton, Paul H. Thompson, and Raymond L. Price, "The Four Stages of Professional Careers—A New Look at Performance by Professionals," *Organizational Dynamics,* Summer 1977, pp. 19–42.

dependence. Some professionals cannot cope with a situation similar to school; and during apprenticeship, they are directed by an authority figure, just as they were in school. Often, people anticipate considerably more freedom from their first job. Those who do not cope successfully can compromise their careers.

Stage II.   Once through the dependency of stage I, the professional employee moves into a stage that calls for working independently. Passage to this stage depends on proven competence in some specific technical area. The technical expertise may be in a content area such as taxation, product testing, or quality assurance, or it may be in a skill area such as computer applications. The professional's primary activity in stage II is to be an *independent contributor* of ideas in the chosen area. The professional is expected to rely much less on direction from others. The *psychological state of independence* may pose some problems because it is in such stark contrast to the dependence required in stage I. Stage II is extremely important for the professional's future career growth. Those who fail do so because they either do not have the requisite technical skill to perform independently or lack the self-confidence to do so.

Stage III.   Professionals in stage III are expected to become mentors of those in stage I. They also tend to broaden their interests and to deal more and more with people outside the organization. Thus, the central activities of professionals in this stage are *training* and *interacting* with others. They assume *responsibility for the work of others,* a characteristic of stage III that can cause considerable psychological stress. An individual who cannot cope with this new and different requirement may decide to return to stage II. Others may be satisfied seeing some of their peers move on to bigger and better jobs. They are content to remain in stage III until their retirement.

As mentors, stage III professionals can make an important contribution to the career development of their protégés. The mentor can help the protégé by sponsoring (recommending the protégé for promotion), providing visibility (creating opportunities for the protégé to demonstrate special skills and talents), coaching (suggesting ways to handle demanding and difficult tasks and situations), and protecting (steering the protégé away from controversial situations). Overall, the mentor counsels, guides, supports, and protects the less experienced protégé.[7]

Stage III professionals can mentor one or multiple protégés, and the mentor relationship can develop informally (initiated by the mentor or prospective protégé) or formally. In formal mentor programs, the organization matches mentors with protégés. At BankAmerica Corporation, for example, a stage III manager may be asked to mentor three of four junior managers for one year at a time.[8] In a growing number of companies, formal mentor programs are being established to provide mentors for promising minority and female managers. Research indicates that these employees are often less likely to obtain an informal mentor.[9] General Aluminum's successful formal mentoring program is profiled in the Management Focus.

[7]Raymond A. Noe, "Women and Mentoring: A Review and Research Agenda," *Academy of Management Review,* January 1988, p. 66.

[8]Selwyn Feinstein, "Women and Minority Workers in Business Find a Mentor Can Be a Rare Commodity," *The Wall Street Journal,* November 10, 1987, p. 31.

[9]Ibid.

MANAGEMENT FOCUS

Mentoring at General Aluminum & Chemical Corp.

When Jim Poure bought General Aluminum & Chemical Corp. in 1978 and merged it with his chemical distributorship, he immediately faced two problems. To remain competitive, the company had to immediately build a second production facility. And General Aluminum's management team lacked depth and experience. The team possessed great potential; but at an average age of 28, they lacked the expertise and seasoning that comes with experience.

Poure needed more help than he could get from his young managers and realized that he could not carry the ball totally on his own. He could quickly hire experienced executives from other companies. However, he felt that often those with a long record of experience come with preconceived ideas of how the company should be run.

Poure's preference: Work with talented, energetic people who will "get in on the ground floor and roll up their sleeves, with the understanding that the rewards will come later." Poure's solution: He looked to three friends and business associates who possessed career-long expertise in finance, marketing, and research and development. All three men had recently retired and were willing to work part-time for General Aluminum. Poure hired them as advisers and utilized their expertise in building a second and, later, a third production plant and in managing the company. He found that the arrangement gave his company the expertise it needed, while providing his three advisers with the flexibility to enjoy their retirement.

Then, in late 1984, Poure paired each adviser with one of the company's up-and-coming managers. For example, John Berger, the 64-year-old research and development (R&D) scientist, was teamed with Mike Feehan, 23, the company's production manager. Hap Murphy, 65, was paired with Poure's 22-year-old son Tim, a marketing manager. And Poure himself focused on the career development of Barbara Lehman, 29, his administrative assistant.

To date, each of the advisers has mentored his young protégé, providing counsel when the young manager encounters new management situations and challenges. For example, Hap Murphy provided valuable guidance in helping Tim Poure prepare for a major sales pitch to a team of paper company executives who were in their 40s and 50s. Murphy's counsel helped the 22-year-old to establish credibility with his much older audience. The two teamed together and beat out two other competitors for the contract.

Says Murphy, "Our role is to critique them if we think they are doing wrong." The managers are free to follow their own instincts, against their mentors' advice, which occasionally happens.

To date, the mentor system that pairs retiree with protégé has worked exceptionally well. Poure estimates that the young managers are "two to three years ahead of their time." Sales and profits have climbed steadily. And the advisers and the mentor system have given Poure the time to deal with long-term tasks such as strategic planning.

Source: Lisa R. Sheeran and Donna Fenn, "The Mentor System," *Inc.*, June 1988, pp. 138ff.

Successful mentor relationships can advance a stage I manager's career in the organization. In a study of 1,300 senior executives, mentors were ranked second only to education in terms of positive impact on the executives' careers.[10] Some studies have found that managers with mentors earn more, are

[10]Ibid.

more likely to follow a career plan, and are more satisfied with their careers than are managers without mentors.[11]

However, the mentor relationship has potential pitfalls. A 25-year study of 3,000 mentor-protégé pairs found that many of the studied relationships were hindered by several problems. Protégés often resented their mentors and believed that they were overworked, too heavily scrutinized by the mentors, and too closely identified with them. Protégés also were frustrated when their mentors publicly reprimanded them for performance mistakes. The mentors, in turn, believed that heavy workloads and public criticism were necessary to avoid the criticism of playing favorites.[12] In sum, mentor relationships, while potentially beneficial for both mentor and protégé, can be delicate relationships to manage and maintain.[13]

Besides mentoring, the stage III professional can enhance his or her career development by developing peer relationships. Kathy Kram and Lynn Isabella examined the nature of supportive and significant peer relationships at early, middle, and late career stages in a large manufacturing company.[14] The researchers interviewed managers and peers. Analysis of the interview data indicated that a continuum of peer relationships exists. The relationships were classified as information peer (information sharing), collegial peer (job-related feedback, friendship), and special peer (emotional support, confirmation).

The three types of peer relationships seem to be perceived somewhat differently by individuals at different career stages. For example, concerns about competence and professional identity often characterize the developmental needs of a person such as an engineer or an accountant at the initial, or establishment, stage. Individuals in their 20s use information peers to learn the ropes on how to get the job done, they use collegial peers to help define their professional role, and they use special peers to acquire a sense of competence and to help manage the stresses and anxieties of work and developing families.

Kram and Isabella's interesting study suggests that peer relationships can be an adjunct to or used instead of a mentor relationship to support individual career development. For individuals without a mentor, peers can be a valuable source of help, support, and encouragement. It would be interesting to examine peer relationships in other than manufacturing settings. Would such relationships be able to mature in rapidly changing environments, such as those found in high-tech industries?

Stage IV.   Some professional employees remain in stage III, while others progress to stage IV, which involves *shaping the direction of the organization itself.* Although we usually think of this as the job of one individual (the chief

---

[11]See Gerald R. Roche, "Much Ado about Mentors," *Harvard Business Review,* January–February 1979, pp. 14ff.

[12]Srully Blotnick, "With Friends like These," *Savvy,* October 1984, pp. 42ff. Also see Donald W. Myers and Neil J. Humphreys, "The Caveats in Mentorship," *Business Horizons,* July–August 1985, pp. 9–14.

[13]Some spouses in a dual career relationship look to each other for mentorlike support and guidance. For a look at these relationships and their benefits, see Anita Shreve, "Mutual Mentors," *Working Woman,* September 1988, pp. 128ff.

[14]Kathy E. Kram and Lynn A. Isabella, "Mentoring Alternatives: The Role of Peer Relationships in Career Development," *Academy of Management Journal,* March 1985, pp. 110–32.

executive), it may in fact be undertaken by many others. For example, key personnel in product development, process manufacturing, or technological research may be stage IV types. As a consequence of their performance in stage III of their careers, stage IV professionals direct their attention to strategic planning. In doing so, they play the roles of manager, entrepreneur, and idea generator. Their primary duties are to *identify* and *sponsor* the careers of their successors and to interact with key people outside the organization. The most significant shift for a person in stage IV is to accept the decisions of subordinates without second-guessing them. Stage IV professionals must learn to influence (that is, practice leadership) through such indirect methods as idea planting, personnel selection, and organization design. These shifts can be difficult for one who has relied upon direct supervision in the past.[15]

CAREER PATHS

A **career path** is the sequence of jobs a person holds during a career. To the organization, career paths are important for human resource planning. An organization's future human resource needs depend on the projected passage of individuals along the paths. From the individual's perspective, a career path is the sequence of jobs that can lead to achieving personal and career goals. It is virtually impossible to integrate completely the needs of both the organization and the individual in the design of career paths, yet systematic career planning has the potential for closing the gap.

In the traditional sense, career paths emphasize upward mobility in a single occupation or functional area. When recruiting personnel, the organization's representative will speak of engineering, accounting, or sales career paths. In these contexts, the recruiter will describe the different jobs typical individuals will hold as they work progressively upward in an organization. Each job, or rung, is reached when the individual has accumulated the necessary experience and ability and has demonstrated a readinesss for promotion.

An example of a career path for general management in a telephone company is depicted in Figure 22–1. According to the path, the average duration of a first-level management assignment is four years. It consists of two and a half years as a staff assistant in the home office and one and a half years as the manager of a district office in a small city. By the 14th year, the average manager should have reached the fourth level of management. At this level, the assignment might be that of division manager of the commercial sales and operations division. Obviously, few managers reach the fifth level, much less the seventh (president). The number of openings declines, and the number of candidates increases as one nears the top of the organization.

The performance of businesses, universities, hospitals, indeed all organizations depends on the effectiveness of managers. Their careers, similar to those in any occupation, follow the same general stages along appropriate career paths, although there is no single correct path to a successful management career.

Implicit in Figure 22–1 and indeed in the concept of the career path is that career progress occurs when you move up the organizational hierarchy to positions with progressively more responsibility, challenge, and rewards.

---

[15]For insight into the changing skills, perspectives, and motivations as a manager ages, see Walter Kiechel III, "The Ages of a Manager," *Fortune,* May 11, 1987, pp. 170ff.

FIGURE 22–1   Career Path, General Management

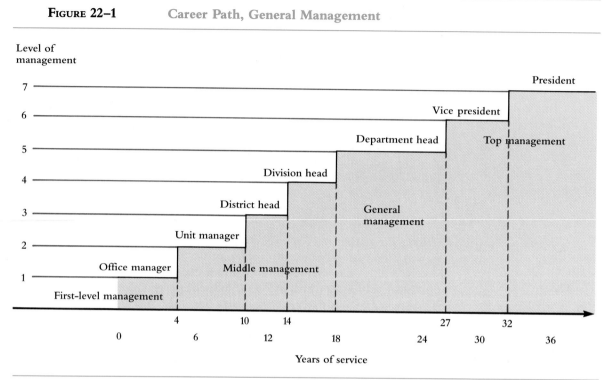

Most jobs are stepping stones to other, more demanding positions.

Today, however, moving upward is becoming increasingly difficult for many employees, especially those in large organizations. During the 1980s, a wave of mergers and intensely competitive environments led to the major reorganization of many companies. These restructurings eliminated many management jobs (some 1 million jobs from 1980 to 1990).[16] Typically, the number of levels in the organizational structure was also reduced.

These moves made organizations leaner and more flexible. They also changed the nature of the traditional, upward career path. Today, there are simply fewer positions in the middle and upper levels of organizations for individuals who want to move upward, even if they are highly qualified to do so. This reality will continue in the 1990s, given plans in many organizations to further restructure and reduce the size of their management work forces.[17] (The impact of these moves on employees' perceptions concerning opportunities for advancement is shown in Figure 22–2.)

Plateaus.   As a result of current trends, more employees are reaching a plateau in their career paths—the point in a career where the likelihood of further movement up the hierarchy is very low.[18] The plateau becomes the

[16]Paul Hirsch, "The Management Purges," *Business Month,* November 1988, pp. 39–42.

[17]Rosabeth Moss Kanter, "The Contingent Job and the Post-Entrepreneurial Career," *Management Review,* April 1989, pp. 22–27.

[18]Douglas T. Hall, "Career Plateauing and Subidentity Change in Midcareer," *Organizational Career Development,* ed. Douglas T. Hall (San Francisco: Jossey-Bass, 1986).

FIGURE 22–2   A Limited Future: How Middle Managers View Their Chances
for Advancement*

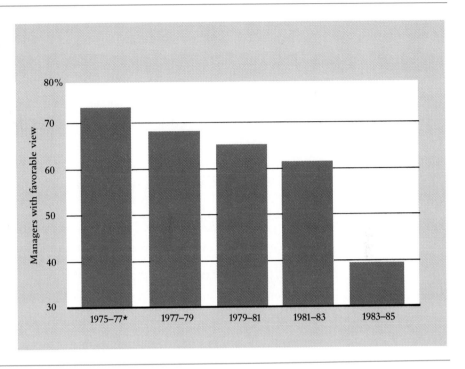

*Based on a survey of 1,600 companies and organizations.

Source: Data from Hay Research for Management Database. Adapted from "More Executives
Finding Changes in Traditional Corporate Ladder," *The Wall Street Journal,* November 14, 1986,
p. 25. Copyright © 1986 by Dow Jones & Co. Used with permission.

final point of ascent in a person's career. Employees are also reaching the
plateau sooner. One career management expert estimates that the average
white male manager plateaus by age 40 to 42; minorities and women plateau
at about age 38.[19] A career plateau is a frustrating dilemma for many
employees, who feel their careers are at a dead end; many also experience a
sense of personal failure.[20]

Zigzag Career Paths.   Some employees respond by adopting a *zigzag
career path*; they leave the organization and try to move upward by switching
from company to company, sometimes from industry to industry.[21] For
example, Jon Rotensteitch first worked 18 years for Salomon Brothers, where

[19]Walter Kiechel III, "High Up and Nowhere to Go," *Fortune,* August 1, 1988, pp. 229ff.

[20]See Lester Korn, "Plotting Your Next Career Move," *Working Woman,* January 1988, pp.
66ff.

[21]See James Braham, "Managers on the Move," *Industry Week,* January 2, 1989, pp. 11–12;
Neal E. Boudette, "Jumping into Smaller Ponds," *Industry Week,* January 2, 1989, pp. 15ff.

he reached the position of managing director. Feeling stymied, Rotensteitch left his prestigious position and accepted the position of treasurer at IBM. In sharp contrast to most IBMers, Rotensteitch stayed only three years. He moved on to become president of Torchmark Corp., an insurance and financial services company. A zigzag career path (especially one across industries) involves risk because, with each job, the employee must learn a new culture and ways of doing business. However, its increasing popularity indicates that more managers are willing to take the risk for potentially greater professional growth and career rewards.[22]

Plateaued employees who remain with a company may accept a lateral transfer to broaden their managerial skills and to assume new challenges. Sometimes, a lateral transfer can open a new path upward. Some employees become more involved in training younger managers in their areas of expertise. Others focus more on improving their marketability by obtaining more education and on further developing their lives outside the job. For their part, more and more companies are developing career training and seminars that focus on improving a manager's satisfaction with his or her present job, in part by better matching of aspects of the job to the manager's likes and talents and by giving the manager more responsibility.[23]

Dual Career Paths.   Companies are also rejuvenating the *dual career path,* a concept first introduced in the mid-1970s. Dual career paths were designed to provide nonmanagerial professionals (e.g., scientists, engineers, R&D specialists) with the opportunity to progress up a career ladder, receiving the same rewards and prestige as their managerial counterparts while still working in their professional fields. The dual career path was intended to retain talented professionals who were frustrated by the lack of advancement opportunities in the organization unless they went into management (which many did not want to do).

However, with few exceptions, the dual career paths created in the mid-70s were ineffective. According to many management observers, the management path to achievement is so ingrained in organizational cultures that the dual career paths were not viewed as legitimate by either management or professionals in many organizations. Often, the dual ladders were poorly maintained; the rewards were not commensurate with those provided for employees on managerial career paths. However, in the late 1980s, a growing number of organizations began developing dual career paths for many types of professional employees (e.g., salespeople, bank loan officers, service representatives) and are taking greater care to communicate the path options to professional employees and to ensure that the path's rewards correspond to those in managerial career ladders. In some organizations, plateaued managers with strong professional backgrounds are being given the opportunity to change to a dual career path. From that point, they resume their professional

---

[22] Carol Hymowitz, "More Executives Finding Changes in Traditional Corporate Ladder," *The Wall Street Journal,* November 14, 1986, p. 25.

[23] Larry Reibstein, "As Firms Try to Refocus Workers' Career Prospects," *The Wall Street Journal,* November 14, 1986, p. 25.

work and are no longer managers; however, opportunities exist for upward advancement.[24]

The "Mommy Track."   In 1989, Felice Schwartz, president of Catalyst, a national research and advisory group on women's leadership, proposed the creation of a different type of career path for women managers and professionals in organizations. She suggested that organizations:

1. Identify two separate groups of women employees. One group, "career-primary" women, are individuals, most of whom are childless, who have made their careers their top priority. The second group, "career-and-family" women, are working mothers and mothers-to-be who want to combine family and career but require flexibility in work hours and responsibilities in order to do so.
2. Provide career-primary women with the same career paths and opportunities as their male counterparts.
3. For career-and-family women, create a separate career path that enables them to take time off or to work part-time during critical child-rearing years. In either case, the rate of advancement and pay will be lower for those on the mommy track until they resume full-time work and responsibilities.[25]

Schwartz's proposal has stirred a storm of controversy. Proponents assert that the mommy track provides substantial benefits for both the organization and its female managers and professionals. The mommy track enables a company to keep many talented career-and-family women who otherwise would leave because of family demands. (According to one study, turnover among top-performing women managers occurs at over twice the rate of male managers; in many cases, the turnover occurs when a woman does not return to the company after maternity leave or returns and then leaves later.) By being flexible, the organization retains the contributions of these employees over the long term and avoids the substantial investment in training and development that is lost if they resign.[26]

For women, the mommy track provides the needed time to devote to family and the opportunity to later resume their careers with the company. It gives more women the flexibility to have children, an option many executive women have not taken because of the price they pay in their careers. According to one major study, 61 percent of female executives are childless, compared to less than 5 percent of male executives.[27]

However, critics respond that the mommy track legitimizes the view that women alone should bear the major responsibilities and make the professional sacrifices for bearing and raising children. Such, they argue, contradicts the

[24]Mark L. Goldstein, "Dual-Career Ladders: Still Shaky but Getting Better," *Industry Week,* January 4, 1988, pp. 57ff.

[25]Felice N. Schwartz, "Management Women and the New Facts of Life," *Harvard Business Review,* January–February 1989, pp. 65–76.

[26]Ibid.

[27]Elizabeth Ehrlich, "The Mommy Track," *Business Week,* March 20, 1989, pp. 126ff.

growing trend of fathers assuming a greater role in raising their children. Second, the mommy track may legitimize the status of women as second-class employees and permanently derail women's careers. Once they're on the track, they may be on a slow track for the rest of their careers. Instead of implementing the mommy track, critics argue, organizations should provide parental support for both male and female employees, in terms of day care support, parental leave, and other programs.[28]

Mommy track programs currently exist in some organizations. For example, Katie Glockner, a brands manager for Quaker Oats Co., switched to part-time work soon after the birth of her son. She manages fewer brands and earns less income in exchange for Mondays and Fridays off. She will soon resume her full-time career at Quaker Oats.[29]

Whether the mommy track will proliferate in organizations remains to be seen. However, the controversial career path is another example of attempts by organizations to help employees balance the demands of family and career.

MANAGEMENT AS A CAREER

An individual striking out on a career has a vital interest in doing everything possible to make an informed job decision. Initial choices are reversible but not without some costs—lost time being the most obvious.[30] Although it is impossible to know at age 20 or so what one's interests, values, abilities, and needs will be when age 40, there are some things to consider. For example, the reader should have a general idea at this point of what managers do and are expected to do.

We know that managers are called upon to manage work, people, and operations. They are expected to plan, organize, and control individuals, groups, and organizations. They are expected to motivate people and groups, to provide leadership, and to sense, recognize, and provide for change. They are expected to use information to make decisions that either directly or indirectly affect efficient production and operations.

1. *Managing work and organizations*:   The managerial issues associated with managing work and organizations are the focus of the classical approach. Planning, organizing, and controlling organizations were the first issues examined by management theorists and practitioners. Scientific management and classical organization theory made significant contributions that are now taken for granted in management practice, such as the principles of work measurement and simplification, principles of planning and organization, and basic control techniques.

2. *Managing people*:   The behavioral approach unites the ideas of the social and behavioral sciences and tests their applicability to management. Managing people to achieve effective levels of individual and group performance demands knowledge of individual differences, motivation, leadership, and group dynamics. Managing people is the most challenging and difficult aspect

---

[28] Ibid.; Janice Castro, "Rolling along the Mommy Track," *Time*, March 27, 1989, p. 72.

[29] Ehrlich, "The Mommy Track," p. 128.

[30] Meryl Reis Louis, "Managing Career Transitions: A Missing Link in Career Development," *Organizational Dynamics*, Spring 1982, pp. 68–77.

of the manager's job. People are unique; and while theories of motivation may be able to predict the behavior of most of the people most of the time, they cannot be counted on to predict what an individual will do in a specific situation. The art of management is to know the limitations of theory and to modify predictions when necessary.

3. *Managing production and operations*: All organizations exist to achieve results, whether producing goods or providing services. The process of acquiring and combining the physical and human resources to achieve the intended results is the production and operations function. The management science approach—with the aid of mathematics, statistics, and computers—has made great strides in providing models that achieve effective and efficient performance of the production and operations function.

Management is an applied discipline. Unlike medicine and engineering, there is no science of management per se. Instead management takes theories and concepts from all relevant sciences. Thus, effective managerial performance results from choosing appropriate theory and technique for a particular problem or situation that arises in the manager's job.

Understanding the job of a manager, we can attempt to answer some questions about careers in management. Who should pursue a career in management? What are the characteristics needed to achieve career effectiveness as managers? How does one who has these characteristics plan a management career?

WHO SHOULD PURSUE MANAGEMENT AS A CAREER?

The trait theory of leadership does not provide precise answers to the question of who will become a leader. The same can be said of the question, "Who will achieve a successful career in management?" Predicting success is difficult because many factors play a role in an individual's management career.

Some factors, such as effective career planning and a strong educational background, are within a manager's control. However, other factors are often beyond an individual's influence. For example, a faltering organization may undergo a reorganization that eliminates a manager's job, thus prohibiting him or her from acquiring further management experience that contributes to improved skills. Or, as research has found, luck can substantially influence an individual's career. Luck—mere happenstance—is, of course, beyond a person's control.[31] However, we do know that certain individual characteristics significantly enhance a manager's probability of becoming an effective manager.

WHAT ARE THE CHARACTERISTICS OF EFFECTIVE MANAGERS?

Although many characteristics contribute to managerial effectiveness, three are particularly important.

The Will to Manage. The desire or need to influence the performance of others and the satisfaction derived from doing so is termed the "will to

---

[31]For an insightful perspective of the impact of luck on careers (and some interesting examples of its effect), see Daniel Seligman, "Luck and Careers," *Fortune,* November 16, 1981, pp. 60ff.

manage."[32] The fundamental characteristic of management is that managers achieve results through other people and that the setting for managerial work is an organization. Those who have studied the will to manage correlate it with several attitudes:[33] favorable attitude toward authority, desire to compete, assertiveness, desire to exercise power, desire to stand out from others in the group, and sense of responsibility.

John Miner devised questionnaires that measure the strength of these attitudes and found that individuals who score relatively high on each item are likely to select management as a career and are likely to achieve career effectiveness. One of his more important findings was that students' will to manage (as measured by the questionnaire) declined throughout the 1970s from the level of the 1960s. Miner predicted that this shift would contribute to the shortage of managerial talent during the 1980s. If Miner's ideas were correct, an individual with a strong will to manage should have had a competitive edge in pursuing a managerial career during those years.

Some evidence suggests that the will to manage can be strengthened through training. In a study of 116 college leaders at a major university, scores on the will-to-manage questionnaire increased in one group that underwent training. Scores of the comparison group, student leaders who did not take the training courses, remained unchanged during the study.[34] Similar studies of practicing managers also indicate that the will to manage can be developed.[35]

Supervisory Ability. Supervisory ability is an important variable that distinguishes effective from ineffective managers.[36] Effective management involves utilizing the correct supervisory tactics required in a particular situation. The ability to use appropriate supervisory practices implies a contingency orientation toward management. Effective managers recognize and apply the relevant elements from each of the approaches of management, are responsive to changing social and economic conditions, and can motivate people.[37] As we have noted through this text, each approach to management contributes to the body of management thought and practice. Effective careers in management are related to the ability to select the appropriate idea for the situation.

Ability to Assess Potential for Effective Management Career.
Individuals can use personal initiative to discern whether they really want and are suited for a career in management. Both Miner and Edwin Ghiselli have devised measurements of will to manage and supervisory ability. With the

[32]Sterling Livingston, "Myth of the Well-Educated Manager," *Harvard Business Review,* January–February 1971, pp. 79–89; John B. Miner, *The Challenge of Managing* (Philadelphia: W. B. Saunders, 1975), p. 276.

[33]Miner, *The Challenge,* pp. 220–23.

[34]Timothy M. Singleton, "Managerial Motivation Development: A Study of College Student Leaders," *Academy of Management Journal,* September 1978, pp. 493–98.

[35]Miner, *The Challenge,* p. 296.

[36]Edwin E. Ghiselli, *Exploration in Managerial Talent* (Santa Monica, Calif.: Goodyear Publishing, 1971).

[37]Lawrence A. Armour, ed., *Managing to Succeed: Stories from The Wall Street Journal* (Homewood, Ill.: Dow Jones-Irwin, 1979).

FIGURE 22–3   A Career Planning Process

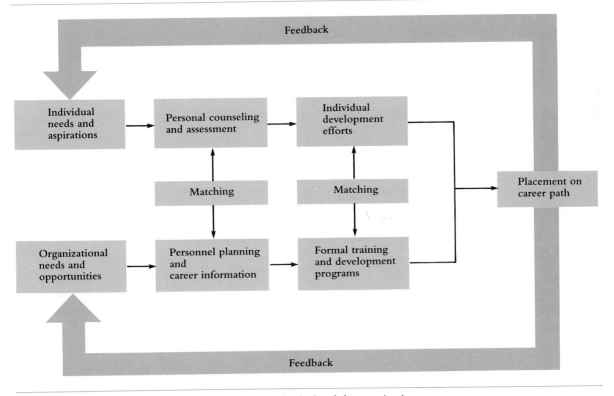

Effective career planning satisfies the needs of both the individual and the organization.

assistance of a counseling professional, individuals can reach some tentative understanding of their potential. However, our knowledge of which variables predict managerial success is quite incomplete. Moreover, the measurements of those variables are not totally valid. The emphasis should be on *tentative* understanding of whether one wants to manage and has or can develop the ability to manage. Confronting these two issues is a first step in career planning.

HOW DOES ONE PLAN A MANAGEMENT CAREER?

Career planning involves matching an individual's career aspirations with the opportunities available in an organization. **Career pathing** is the sequencing of specific jobs associated with those opportunities. The two processes are intertwined. Planning a career requires identifying the activities and experiences needed to accomplish career goals. Career path considerations include the sequence of jobs that results in reaching these career goals. Although still a relatively new practice, many organizations are turning to career planning as a way to be *proactive* about, rather than *reactive* to, problems associated with ineffective managerial careers.

The career planning and pathing process is described in Figure 22–3. Successful practice places equal responsibility on the individual and the organization. Individuals must identify their aspirations and abilities and, through counseling, recognize the training and development required for a particular career path. Organizations must identify their needs and opportunities and, through personnel planning, provide career information and training to their employees. Career planning cannot proceed unless information about career paths, expected vacancies, and position requirements is available to employees.[38]

Companies such as Weyerhaeuser, Gulf Oil, Exxon, and Eaton use career development programs to identify a broad pool of talent available for promotion and transfer opportunities. Career counseling is often restricted to managerial and professional staff, but IBM, General Electric, TRW, and Gulf provide career counseling for blue-collar as well as managerial personnel.

Matching individual and organizational needs can be done through a variety of personnel practices. A recent American Management Association survey revealed that the most widely used practices are informal counseling by the personnel staff and career counseling by supervisors. These two approaches are often quite informal. Less common, somewhat more formal practices involve workshops, seminars, and self-assessment centers.

Informal Counseling.

The personnel departments of organizations often include counseling services for employees who wish to assess their abilities and interests. Counseling that moves into personal matters is acceptable if these matters are important in determining career effectiveness. In this context, organizations tend to view career counseling as a service to employees, but not a primary one.

Career counseling by supervisors is usually included in performance appraisals. The question of where the employee is going in the organization quite naturally comes up in this setting. In fact, the inclusion of career information in performance appraisal predates the current interest in career planning. Effective performance evaluation, by definition, lets the employees know how well they have done and what the future holds. Thus, supervisors must be able to counsel employees in terms of organizational needs and opportunities both in a specific department and throughout the organization.

Formal Counseling.

Since supervisors usually have limited information about the overall organization, more formal, systematic counseling approaches are often adopted. Workshops, assessment centers, and career development centers are increasingly used. Such formal practices typically are designed to serve specific employee groups. To date, management trainees and "high potential" or "fast track" management candidates have received most of the attention. However, women and minority employees are increasingly benefiting from programs, a trend that reflects organizations' commitment to affirmative action.

An example of how one organization has implemented a formal career planning system is Syntex Corporation's Career Development Center. The center's staff first assesses the individual's strengths and weaknesses in the eight skills Syntex believes are most related to effective management: (1) problem

---

[38]Kenneth B. McRae, "Career-Management Planning: A Boon to Managers and Employees," *Personnel,* May 1985, pp. 56–60.

Getting help with one's career plan can enlarge the possibilities.

analysis; (2) communication; (3) setting objectives; (4) decision making and handling conflict; (5) selecting, training, and motivating employees; (6) controlling employees; (7) interpersonal competence; and (8) use of time. On the basis of scores in the eight areas, each manager sets career and personal goals with assistance from the center's staff.

Each manager's career planning effort is highlighted by a weeklong seminar. Usually attended by 24 managers, the seminar places each manager in simulated situations that require applications of the eight skill areas. Candidates participate in the simulations, then review their own career plans; the seminar encourages realistic self-appraisal. Afterward, participants meet with their immediate supervisors to set up their career development plans.[39]

There are also professional career counselors outside the organization. The Management Focus on professional counseling discusses this.

Other Personnel Practices.   Organizations can use a variety of personnel practices to facilitate their employees' career plans. One of the oldest, most widely used methods is some form of the *tuition aid program*. Employees can enroll in educational and training courses available at nearby schools, and the organization pays all or part of the tuition. J. I. Case, a Tenneco company with corporate offices in Racine, Wisconsin, is one of many organizations that provide in-house courses and seminars, plus tuition reimbursement for courses related to the individual's job.

Another practice is *job posting*. The organization publicizes job openings to employees. This requires more than simply placing a notice on the company's

---

[39] For other examples of career development programs, see Lorraine M. Carulli, Cheryl L. Noroian, and Cindy Levine, "Employee-Driven Career Development," *Personnel Administrator,* March 1989, pp. 67ff.

MANAGEMENT FOCUS

Getting Professional Career Counseling Help

Life used to be simpler. People picked the careers their parents expected them to or went to whatever job was available. Once employed, most people stuck to their careers; in fact, few had the luxury of considering a change. They patiently waited for a few moves up the corporate ladder, supported their families, and collected a gold watch upon retirement. Many people still follow this career course. But for millions of others, life is more complex.

Many people decide that they may be in the wrong career—that they would be better satisfied or more creative in a different one. When people become euphoric at 4 P.M. on Friday and depressed because it's Sunday evening and they have to go to work tomorrow, it says something about their feelings about the job. To help these people, there are professional career counselors, who charge fees that can range from less than $100 to several thousand dollars. The career counseling field, because of the demand for the service, has attracted some excellent professionals but has drawn others who have dubious credentials.

People in their 40s become conscious that all of their young dreams are not going to come true. Career counselors seem to be seeing an increasing number of clients of that age who are troubled by what is called "midlife crisis." Some want to confirm that they are in the right field;

others believe that a career shift will solve their problems. For any person to try a new career at 30 or 40 is a difficult task. It takes a lot of courage to look at yourself, your career, dreams, and goals and decide to make a shift. It is a lot easier to stay put and do the best you can.

Cindy Erb of Catalyst, a nonprofit career counseling and information agency in New York, states that career counseling is not a magical process where perfect solutions to problems are hatched at every session. Instead she asks clients to remember that career counseling is a guidance process that asks clients to look at their lives and goals, then to find out how their particular skill strengths fit into accomplishing their goals.

Most qualified professional career counselors use discussions, tests, surveys, life inventories, and other assessment tools to get people to look at themselves and to indicate strengths and weaknesses. Then comes the process of offering interpretation of results, a guiding hand, and support to clients.

If individuals prefer to not have management know that they are questioning present career situations, then a reputable outside professional career counselor may be a good idea.

Source: Adapted from Berkeley Rice, "Why Am I in This Job?" *Psychology Today,* January 1985, pp. 54–59.

bulletin board. At minimum, effective job posting should meet the following conditions:[40]

1. Posting should include promotions and transfers as well as permanent vacancies.
2. Available jobs should be posted at least three to six weeks prior to external recruiting.
3. Eligibility rules should be explicit and straightforward.

[40]David R. Dahl and Patrick R. Pinto, "Job Posting: An Industry Survey," *Personnel Journal,* January 1977, pp. 40–42.

4.   Selection standards and bidding instructions should be stated clearly.
5.   Vacationing employees should be given the opportunity to apply ahead of time.
6.   Employees who apply but are rejected should be notified in writing, and a record of the reason should be placed in their personnel files.

Whatever counseling approach is used, the crucial element of its success will be the extent to which *individual and organizational* needs are satisfied.

Career Planning Benefits.   Career planning is becoming more widespread in organizations. Individuals who wish to make formal career plans should seek out those organizations that have demonstrated a commitment to career planning.

From the organization's perspective, who is most likely to benefit from career planning? Although this question has only recently been raised, it appears that some individuals gain little from the process. Recent studies, for example, indicate that career planning is most effective for people who have relatively high needs for growth and achievement, the skill to carry out their career plans, and a past history of career successes.[41] These results should not be interpreted to mean that career planning is for the select few; much more needs to be known about the issue before conclusions are drawn. But the findings do indicate that organizations should try to identify people who are most likely to take advantage of career planning programs.[42]

Individuals need not rely on company-sponsored programs, however. Nothing except lack of initiative prevents any of us from using our own resources to answer the key questions:

1.   Do I want to be a manager?
2.   Do I have the ability to be a manager?
3.   How do I go about having an effective career in management?

SUMMARY OF KEY POINTS

- Management can be a challenging, rewarding career for those who have the knowledge, skills, attitudes, values, and opportunity to pursue it. Career effectiveness implies that one's performance, attitude, adaptability, and identity resolution are satisfying to both the organization and the individual.

- As a career, management progresses through stages that are more or less typical of all occupations. Career paths tend to be specific to individual organizations.

- Each career stage involves both career and personal demands. Both opportunities and problems arise when one's career and one's personal life conflict.

- In the 1980s, organizational mergers and restructurings have reduced the number of upper- and middle-level management positions available for

[41]Sam Gould, "Characteristics of Career Planners in Upwardly Mobile Occupations," *Academy of Management Journal,* September 1979, pp. 539–50; John B. Miner and Donald P. Crane, "Motivation to Manage and the Manifestation of a Managerial Orientation in Career Planning," *Academy of Management Journal,* September 1981, pp. 626–33.

[42]Mary Ann Von Glinow, Michael J. Driver, Kenneth Brousseau, and J. Bruce Prince, "The Design of a Career-Oriented Human Resource System," *Academy of Management Review,* January 1983, pp. 23–32.

ambitious and qualified employees. As a result, many managers are experiencing career plateaus. They are responding in a number of ways, such as becoming more mobile, improving their marketability via education, and further developing their lives outside of work. Some companies are responding by developing dual career paths.

■ Some organizations have "mommy track" career paths for female managers and professionals. These paths enable a woman with young children to take time off or work part-time during critical child-rearing years. She later resumes her full-time career with the company. The mommy track is a controversial strategy for helping women balance career and family demands.

■ Individuals desiring a career in management should be encouraged to plan their careers.

Career plans are tentative by nature, but they force individuals to consider their own strengths and weaknesses.

■ Two factors are essential in management: Does one really want to manage (will to manage), and does the person have or can the person develop the ability to manage (supervisory ability)?

■ More and more organizations are providing some form of career counseling and development for their employees.

■ The potential for effective managerial careers is crucial. Failure to recognize and develop managerial talent will almost certainly affect an organization's performance adversely throughout the 1990s.

DISCUSSION AND REVIEW QUESTIONS

1. Define and explain your personal concept of *career.* Is the concept, as you define it, applicable only to those who are gainfully employed? In the explanation, compare your concept of career with the one used in the chapter discussion.

2. Explain the interrelationships between life and career stages. If there are interrelationships, do they imply that we cannot or should not attempt to compartmentalize our lives into career and noncareer purposes and activities? Explain.

3. What information would you like to have if a prospective employer asked you to prepare a brief statement of career aims? What are the sources of such information? Do you presently have this information? Why or why not?

4. In your opinion, what are the advantages and shortcomings of being a mobile manager (changing jobs frequently throughout a managerial career)? Discuss.

5. Of what value to an organization is the mentor relationship?

6. How can you discover career paths in a particular organization? Is this the kind of information you would want to receive when you interview for a job? What questions would you ask to get this information?

7. As the CEO of a large company, would you implement a "mommy track" program in your firm? Why or why not? As a young female executive who plans to have a family, would you support a mommy track? Explain.

8. Is it important that the first organization you work for have a career counseling program? Why?

9. How would you know that your career had plateaued in an organization? If you were frustrated by being plateaued, what actions would you take to alleviate your dissatisfaction?

10. In your opinion, what personal characteristic is most important for achieving success as a manager? Explain.

ADDITIONAL REFERENCES

Bass, B. *Leadership and Performance beyond Expectations.* New York: Free Press, 1985.

Byrne, J. A. "Caught in the Middle: Six Managers Speak Out on Corporate Life." *Business Week,* September 12, 1988, pp. 80ff.

Clance, P. R. *The Imposter Phenomenon.* New York: Peachtree Publishers, 1985.

Fagenson, E. A. "The Power of a Mentor: Proteges' and Non-Proteges' Perceptions of their Own Power in

Organizations." *Group and Organization Studies,* June 1988, pp. 182–94.

Feldman, D. C. *Managing Careers in Organizations.* Glenview, Ill.: Scott, Foresman, 1988.

Fitzgerald, T. H. "The Loss of Work: Notes from Retirement." *Harvard Business Review,* March–April 1988, pp. 99–103.

Gaertner, K. N. "Managers' Careers and Organizational Change." *Academy of Management Executive,* November 1988, pp. 311–18.

Hauze, W. C. *Career Veer: How to Position Yourself for a Prosperous Future.* New York: McGraw-Hill, 1985.

Howard, A., and D. W. Bray. *Managerial Lives in Transition: Advancing Age and Changing Times.* New York: Guilford Press, 1988.

Jaffe, B. "The Career Audit." *Training and Development,* March 1989, pp. 45–47.

Josefowitz, N., and H. Gadon. *Fitting In: How to Get a Good Start in Your New Job.* Reading, Mass.: Addison-Wesley Publishing, 1988.

Kelley, R. E. *The Gold Collar Worker.* Reading, Mass.: Addison-Wesley Publishing, 1985.

London, M. *Managing Careers.* Reading, Mass.: Addison-Wesley Publishing, 1982.

Louchheim, F., and V. Lord. "Who Is Taking Care of Your Career?" *Personnel Administrator,* April 1988, pp. 46–51.

Luthans, F.; R. M. Hodgetts; and S. A. Rosenkrantz. *Real Managers.* Cambridge, Mass.: Ballinger, 1988.

Machlowitz, M. *Whiz Kids: Success at an Early Age.* New York: Arbor House, 1985.

McCall, M. W., Jr.; M. M. Lombardo; and A. M. Morrison. "Great Leaps in Career Development." *Across the Board,* March 1989, pp. 54–61.

Pines, A., and E. Aronson. *Career Burnout: Causes and Cures.* New York: Free Press, 1988.

Powell, G. N. *Women and Men in Management.* Newbury Park, Calif.: Sage Publications, 1988.

Ritti, R. R., and G. R. Funkhouser. *The Ropes to Skip and the Ropes to Know.* Columbus, Ohio: Grid, 1977.

Sekaran, U. *Dual-Career Families.* San Francisco: Jossey-Bass, 1986.

Sheehy, G. *Passages: Predictable Crises of Adult Life.* New York: E. P. Dutton, 1976.

"Worldwide Executive Mobility, 1988." Special study. *Harvard Business Review,* July–August 1988, pp. 105–23.

CASE 22–1   The Dual Career Couple

Until recently, America's work force largely consisted of the heads of traditional families—the husbands who work as the employed breadwinner while the wives remain home to raise the children. Today, however, the traditional family makes up less than 10 percent of all households. Increasingly, both spouses are launching careers and earning incomes. These dual career couples now account for 40 percent of the work force (over 47 million employees), and their numbers will substantially increase.

The advent of the dual career couple poses challenges for the working spouses and for business. According to a Catalyst survey of over 800 dual career couples, they experience myriad problems, most notably difficulties with allocating time (the top-ranked complaint), finances, poor communication, and conflicts over housework. For couples with children, meeting the demands of career and family usually becomes the top concern. Recent studies

Source: Adapted from Veronica J. Schmidt and Norman A. Scott, "Work and Family Life: A Delicate Balance," *Personnel Administrator,* August 1987, pp. 40–46; Fern Schumer Chapman, "Executive Guilt: Who's Taking Care of the Children?" *Fortune,* February 16, 1987, pp. 30–37; Susan Schiffer Stautberg, "Corporate Baby Sitting," *The Wall Street Journal,* February 8, 1988, p. 20; Jaclyn Fierman, "Child Care: What Works—and Doesn't," *Fortune,* November 21, 1988, pp. 164ff; Anastasia Toufexis, "Dual Careers, Doleful Dilemmas," *Time,* November 16, 1987, p. 90; Irene Pave, "Move Me, Move My Spouse," *Business Week,* December 16, 1985, pp. 57ff; Ronald F. Ribaric, "Mission Possible: Meeting Family Demands," *Personnel Administrator,* August 1987, pp. 70–79.

indicate that dual career families need (1) benefit plans that enable couples to have children without jeopardizing careers, (2) more flexible work arrangements to help balance family and career demands, (3) freedom from anxieties about child care while at work, and (4) employer assistance in finding the spouse employment when the employee relocates (a need of both parents and childless couples).

For businesses, the challenge lies in helping to ease the problems of dual career couples, especially those with children. According to a 1987 study commissioned by *Fortune,* organizations are losing productivity and employees due to the demands of family life. The study found that, among the 400 working parents surveyed, problems with child care were the most significant predictors of absenteeism and low productivity. For example, 41 percent of those surveyed took at least one day in the three months preceding the survey to handle family matters; 10 percent took from three to five days. (On a national scale, these figures amount to hundreds of millions of dollars in lost productivity.) About 60 percent of the parents polled expressed concerns about time and attention given to their children, and these anxieties were linked to lower productivity.

Overall, many experts advise that companies that ignore the problems of dual career couples (and working parents per se) stand to lose output and even valued employees. Companies are beginning to respond to these needs in a number of ways:

Hiring Spouses of Employees or Helping Them Find Jobs.

Studies indicate that more employees are refusing relocation assignments if their working spouses cannot find acceptable jobs. This has been a growing concern of business, given earlier predictions that, by 1990, 75 percent of all corporate moves would involve dual career couples. In response, many companies have recently begun to offer services for "trailing spouses." These services include arranging interviews with prospective employers; providing instruction in résumé writing, interviewing, and contract negotiation; and even paying plane fares for job-hunting trips. Some companies (General Mills, 3M, American Express) use outside placement services to find jobs for trailing spouses. Over 150 northern New Jersey companies created and use a job bank that provides leads for job-hunting spouses.

A small and growing number of companies (e.g., Chase Manhattan Bank; O'Melveny & Myers, one of the nation's largest law firms) are breaking tradition and hiring two-career couples. Martin Marietta maintains an affirmative hire-a-couple policy and hires about 100 couples a year in its Denver division. Proponents assert that couples who work for the same company share the same goals, are often more committed to the company, and are more willing to work longer hours. Hiring couples helps attract and keep top employees, and relocations are also easier for the couple and the company.

However, many companies still shun the practice, asserting that problems outweigh advantages. Often cited problems include the consequences of unequal performance—jealousy when one spouse is promoted faster than the other, or difficulties in firing one spouse while retaining the other. Forced competition can also be problematic: "You always . . . have a built-in tension with couples comparing job assignments, salary levels and so forth," said one personnel manager at Price Waterhouse & Co, which opposes the practice.

"Pillow talk" (couples exchanging confidential information) and problems inherent in the marriage going sour are also potential liabilities. A number of companies with policies of hiring couples do not allow spouses to supervise each other.

Providing Day Care Assistance.   About 3,500 companies (a 50 percent increase since 1984) now provide day care services and financial assistance or referral services for child care. Many experts predict that child care will become the fringe benefit of the 1990s.

About 150 companies currently operate on-site or near-site day care centers. For example, American Savings and Loan Association established the Little Mavericks School of Learning in 1983 for 150 children of employees on a site within walking distance of several of its satellite branch locations. Established as a for-profit subsidiary and with a staff of 35, the center's services include regular day care, holiday care, sick child care, scouting programs, a kindergarten program, and after-school classes. Service fees range from $135 to $235 a month, depending on the type of service, and parents pay via payroll deductions. Company officials report that the center has substantially reduced employee absenteeism and personal phone calls and has been a substantial boon to recruitment and retention. However, as many companies have found, limited openings prohibit serving all parent employees, and certain employees—sometimes those who can afford external day care services—get preferential treatment.

Many companies contract outside day care services run by professional groups, which relieves the company of the headaches of running a center. For example, IBM contracted the Work/Family Directions child care consulting group to establish 16,000 home-based family centers and to open 3,000 day care centers for IBM employees and other families throughout the United States. About 80 companies have created programs to help parents of sick children. If a child of an employee of First Bank System (Minneapolis) becomes ill, the company will pay 75 percent of the bill for the child's stay at Chicken Soup, a sick-child day care center. The policy enables the parent to still work and saves the company money. A growing number of companies have arranged to send trained nurses to the sick child's home.

Other companies are providing partial reimbursement for child care services. Zayre Corporation pays up to $20 a week for day care services used by employees who work at corporate headquarters. A growing number of cafeteria fringe benefit programs enable employees to allocate a portion of fringe benefits to pay for day care services. Chemical Bank pays these benefits quarterly in pretax dollars.

Many observers believe that consortiums may soon become the most popular type of day care available to employees. Twenty companies recently contributed $100,000 to start a day care center for their employees. The major reason: Every employee with a preschool child was costing the company $1,800 each year for the parent's time on the phone or time away from the job to handle child care–related problems. To raise the $100,000, each company paid $1,500 for each reservation for an employee's child; the remaining openings were made available to the public. An independent child care services company contracted by the group of firms hired the teachers and runs the center. Consortiums are particularly attractive for small businesses that individually lack the resources to substantially help employees with day care needs.

Providing Flexible Time Off.   A number of companies are combining vacation and sick leave to increase the amount of time off for family life. At Hewlett-Packard, for example, employees receive their regular vacation days plus five additional days of unused sick leave. Employees can take the time off in any increments at any time. Employees can carry a number of unused days over to the next year (the number is determined by tenure), and employees who leave the company receive cash value for their unused days (at current salary level).

Providing Job Sharing.   This program, which enables two people to share the same job on a part-time basis, is a major boon to spouses who want to continue their careers while raising children. The program was first established by Steelcase Inc., in Grand Rapids, Michigan, where company officials assert that the program has reduced turnover and absenteeism, boosted morale, and helped achieve the company's affirmative action objectives. However, job sharing can be difficult to implement. The program requires that a job can be divided into two related but separate assignments, that job sharers are compatible, and that the supervisor can provide task continuity between the two job sharers.

Questions for Analysis

1. Beyond those noted in the case, what are the advantages and potential problems of hiring two-career couples?
2. Many of the services for dual career couples and parent employees are provided by large corporations that have far greater financial resources than do smaller companies. Identify and discuss ways in which a small company might alleviate the challenges facing parent employees and employees with working spouses.
3. Suppose a dual career couple involves spouses who are each in a different career stage. Does this situation pose problems for the couple? For their employer(s)? Discuss.

Case 22–2   Career Development at the U.S. General Accounting Office

The U.S. General Accounting Office (GAO) recently devised a career development program whose primary purpose is to help employees make appropriate career decisions. Their experience indicates that an organization

Source: Adapted from I. Marlene Thorn, Francis X. Fee, and Jane O'Hara Carter, "Career Development: A Collaborative Approach," *Management Review,* September 1982, pp. 27–28, 38–41.

must first develop the ability of managers to "do" career development. GAO's managers are no different from those in other organizations. They tend to get caught up in the day-to-day routine and fail to budget time to consider long-run issues such as their subordinates' futures, yet GAO emphasizes career development of subordinates as an important managerial responsibility.

The first step in implementing the program was to assess the needs of managers. The following needs were identified:

1. To know more about the theory and practice of career development.
2. To know about opportunities throughout GAO, not just in that part where they presently work.
3. Access to career development information that exists in both line and staff units.
4. To take a more active role in career counseling and to recognize both nontraditional and traditional career paths.
5. Assurance that top management is committed to organizationwide career development and that time devoted to it is considered worthwhile.

GAO met these needs in a variety of ways. Chief among them was a new workshop called Career Development Orientation for Managers. The workshop consists of three parts: (1) philosophy, concepts, and overview, (2) individual career planning process, and (3) organizational career development process. Each of these parts draws on materials widely available in the career development literature, but the specific circumstances and experiences of GAO are highlighted.

For example, part 1 emphasizes the philosophy of career development at GAO rather than dealing with issues at an abstract level. Some of the questions raised include:

1. What is career development?
2. Who should be responsible for it?
3. Should career development address individual or organizational needs?
4. Do career development programs raise false expectations?
5. What are the characteristics of individuals who can make effective use of career development programs?

Admittedly, these questions are difficult to answer, but GAO believes that they must be addressed before proceeding to the next two parts.

Part 2 informs managers about the content of career counseling exercises provided by GAO's counseling and career development staff. Managers completed the exercise to learn what their subordinates would experience. Exercises consisted of four widely used career counseling steps:

1. Understanding self, including one's values, needs, skills, and abilities.
2. Understanding one's environment, including job options, educational and training options, financial considerations, and projected skill needs.
3. Planning the future course of events related to development of self, and taking advantage of opportunities.
4. Life management, including the whole range of nonwork-related events, activities, and experiences of individuals.

The activities of part 2 are person oriented. Doing them effectively requires expertise and training in psychology. GAO does not ask managers to lead subordinates through all four steps. The manager's role is that of a referral agent who assures that individuals who desire counseling receive it.

Part 3 emphasizes GAO's stake in employee career development. Mirroring part 2, it consists of four steps:

1. Understanding organizational needs, including identification of specific deficiencies within GAO.
2. Understanding organizational environment, including present and potential job opportunities and career paths within GAO.
3. Organizational action planning, which requires managers to identify the specific steps they will take to implement career development in their own units.
4. Problem recognition and referral, which requires managers to be alert and sensitive to employees' psychological well-being.

Managers' completion of the workshop signaled the implementation of career development in GAO. Management considers the program to be very timely. Since growth at GAO is limited, so are the number of career advancement opportunities. Therefore, matching individual and career needs is especially important.

QUESTIONS FOR ANALYSIS

1. Evaluate the GAO career development program.
2. What would be your answers to the five questions raised in part 1 of their training program?
3. What should the policy of organizations in mature and declining industries be toward career development?

EXPERIENTIAL EXERCISE

CAREER PLANNING

Purpose

The purpose of this exercise is to provide students with experience in thinking about what is important in their lives and careers.

The Exercise in Class

Each student should complete the following steps:

1. Draw a horizontal line that depicts the past, present, and future of your career. On that line, mark an X where you are now.
2. To the left of the X, on the part of the line that represents your past, identify events in your life that provided real and genuine feelings of fulfillment and satisfaction.

3. Examine these historical events and determine the specific causes of your feelings. Does a pattern emerge? Write as much as you can about the events and your reactions to them.

4. To the right of the X, on the part of the line that represents your future, identify career-related events that you expect to provide real and genuine feelings of fulfillment and satisfaction. You should be as explicit as possible when describing these events. If you are only able to write such statements as, "Get a job" or "Get a big raise," your career expectations are probably vaguely defined.

5. After you have identified future career-related events, rank them from high to low according to how much fulfillment and satisfaction you expect from each.

6. Now go back to step 3 and rank those historical events from high to low according to how much fulfillment and satisfaction each provided. Compare the two sets of ranked events. Are they consistent? Are you expecting the future to be the same or different from the past in terms of sources of feelings of fulfillment and satisfaction? If the future, expected sources are quite different from the past, actual sources, are you being totally realistic about the future and what you want from your career?

After completing the above steps, each individual should answer the following questions and share answers with others in open discussion:

1. Which one of the six steps was most difficult to complete? Why?

2. What are the principal categories of sources of fulfillment and satisfaction? Can all these sources be realized in a career? Which ones are most likely to go unrealized in the career of your choice?

3. Do you desire a career in management? Is your answer based on consideration of the potential sources of fulfillment and satisfaction that you value? Explain.

The Learning Message

This exercise will demonstrate the difficulties of identifying what we want from our careers. Most of us have vague and ill-formed notions of what careers are all about until we actually begin on a career path. Discussions with others about sources of career satisfactions can be very helpful.

INTEGRATIVE CASES

CASE ONE

SOUTHERN FEDERAL SAVINGS AND LOAN ASSOCIATION

Southern Federal Savings and Loan Association's offices were gearing up to offer consumer loans, NOW accounts, and renegotiable rate mortgages (RRMs), which were allowed by the Depository Institutions Deregulation and Monetary Control Act of 1980. By July 1980, steps to introduce these new products were well under way. Mr. Knight, the chief executive officer, explained:

> We'll get into consumer loans as early as September 1st or 15th—whenever we can gear up and get in. We're trying hard to get in just as soon as possible because we know it will affect all our branch offices—all branch managers and at least one other person have got to be trained and familiar with them. That's a big job. But we need to get on with it just as quickly as possible because NOW accounts are coming January 1st, and we don't want two things of this magnitude slapping us at the same time. If we can get into consumer lending in September, then we'll have a little bit of time to get feeling comfortable with that before starting to feel uncomfortable when NOW accounts go.

Southern Federal's Management

Mr. Knight was in his 16th year as president of Southern Federal. He had not grown up in this business but had become president of Southern Federal after selling his poultry business. In describing how he became involved, Knight explained:

> I sold out my interests in the poultry business on February 1, 1962, became mayor of the city on January 1, 1964, and came over here in December 1964. My predecessor had reached retirement age, but they didn't give him until the first of January as was customary. There was some internal conflict. I replaced him on the 11th of December. That didn't set well with him, but I didn't have anything to do with it.
>
> I didn't seek the job and didn't particularly want it, but one of the directors came by and asked me if I'd consider filling in for an interim time. I assumed he was talking from January on. I said, "Well, I hadn't

Source: This case was prepared by William R. Boulton and James A. Verbrugge, University of Georgia. Permission to publish granted by the authors and the Case Research Association.

thought about it, but I might be interested," because the position as mayor was supposed to be a part-time job. After that, four directors fell in behind me; they said, "We'd just like to have you fill in." So I've been filling in since 1964, but my filling-in time is about up, because I turned 65 on June 17. I don't know what my relationship will be after January 1.

James Redding, Southern Federal's second in command, also came from the outside in 1960. Prior to joining Southern Federal, he had been in the real estate and insurance business and had been helping the association part-time. He explained:

I was helping them out part-time with problems they were having in the appraising and construction end of the business and decided to try it full-time. I did the appraising and developed inspection sheets for builders to use in drawing money for construction loans. I worked on that end of it and later just sort of became general flunky around here.

Knight commented on the development of the organization:

There was no organization 16 years ago. We were small by comparison. But we are a whole lot larger, so we have had to departmentalize. We had to gear up for that. We had to employ people. Besides Redding and Billings, assistant in mortgage loans, I've employed everyone in frontline management. They are more or less the type of people that I like on my side.

In discussing the actual structure of Southern Federal, Knight continued:

The direct line is myself, James Redding, and Jack Pope. After that you break down into various departments. Bob Thompson is mortgage loan officer. Jim Heart is controller.

I'm the managing officer and the president and the chairman of the board. But after January 1, if I stay, I'd probably like to take a little different role—back off just a little bit—and let James and Jack and those folks really run the association, and I would act more in a policy and advisory capacity. If the board is willing to do that, I'd like to do it, because I'm not a retirement-type person.

A copy of Southern Federal's current organizational structure was not readily available to Vice President Jack Pope, the one to develop such charts. He explained:

I've done some sketches of the organization chart but passed them on to Redding and didn't keep a copy. We've talked about it. We know how it works, or at least the department heads know.

Exhibit 1 shows the organization chart which Pope drafted.

We regard to the key positions at Southern Federal, Jack Pope explained the concept:

I took an ideal S&L organization chart and tried to compare it to what we once had. I think that may have assisted in the decision to reorganize our loan department and put someone in control. The loan department had been split up between Thompson, Billings, and Heart into loan originations, loan processing, and taxes and insurance. . . . Now Bob

EXHIBIT 1 Southern Federal Savings and Loan Association Organization Chart—
August 4, 1980

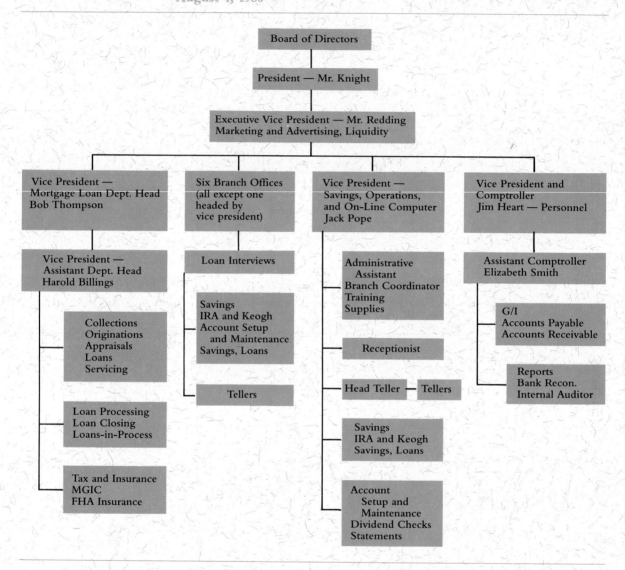

Thompson is department head. Harold Billings is responsible for closings and handling loans in process.

Jim Heart was put in charge of accounting. Elizabeth Smith had reported to me in accounting. Jim didn't have any training as controller, but it was felt he could do the job, and he has. I didn't think Elizabeth was particularly pleased at first, but it has worked out well. Jim is also responsible for new employee and personnel interviews and keeps EEOC and affirmative action records in order. He has little to do with daily personnel operations except in his own department.

My duties are in operations. I have responsibility for tellers and savings counselors. I have a branch coordinator working for me now. I'm responsible for the on-line computer service, so I write the procedures or make any changes when we change the system. Supplies and purchases also come under my jurisdiction. Someone else is responsible for custodial services.

The new branch coordinator position has responsibility for branch communication and training. Knight explained the branch coordinator's role:

We just promoted one of the girls who has a lot of talent and ability to branch coordinator. From that respect, she has no supervisory jurisdiction over a branch manager, but she is really coordinating personnel. If someone doesn't show and the manager doesn't think he can operate, he calls her and we get somebody on the road to help out. The same for supplies. When you get six branches, you just can't do it from your hip pocket. You have to have some plan of handling things.

The Board of Directors

Southern Federal's board of directors significantly changed after Knight joined the association. He explained the early structure:

When I came over here, the average age of the board was about 70. We had one that was 90. Another that was 80. Several were in their 70s—they were the young guys. I was just a babe in the woods. That had to be changed. You may think that's no trouble, but it is.

We set limits of 70. When I reach 70, I'm off the board, and that's the way it ought to be. We finally agreed that if they served three years from the time we made that agreement, that was fair, and they would become emeritus members and leave the board. It just takes time to do those things.

In describing the current membership of the board, Knight continued:

We have the director of campus planning, who has been here a long time. The university football coach also represents another area of thinking as a director. We also have the owner of a downtown retail men's store and a fine doctor and surgeon who has a good financial mind. We have the controller for a local textile plant and an ex-government official that now heads up the university research lab. We then have myself, Redding, the president of North County S&L, and one of our retired executives that knows the business.

Southern Federal's board of directors holds meetings on the second Tuesday of every month. Knight explained the role of his board members:

We have an agenda which includes basic items that are required, then gets into new business and things that need to be brought to the board's attention.

Two of the members, Redding and myself, serve as members of the Loan Committee. We provide a written report from the Loan Committee, and the board acts on that. The director of campus planning is a good board member who takes the time to read the information we send him.

So I usually ask if he has any comments on the Loan Committee's minutes. If he sees one he doesn't understand, he'll ask a question. We may give our reasons for that particular loan and the interest rate charged, or whatever attracted his attention.

The controller over at the textile mill has a really good financial mind. I usually ask him for comments on the financial statement that's prepared by Jim Heart. He's sharp enough that if he sees an unusual figure, it flags him and he'll put a circle around it. So we get into things that he doesn't understand or that need clarification. Sometimes, he'll understand it, but he'll do it for the benefit of the other board members. That kind of takes care of the nuts and bolts.

Redding commented further on their board's involvement:

Our board is made up of a pretty knowledgeable group of folks here in town. They set the policy and the tone of what we're going to do. For what services we offer, I think they take most of the recommendations that management makes.

They turned us down on a logo one time. We've got to get us a logo. I was talking to our advertising man the other day about getting one. We had about three logos, and they turned them all down. You have to get some uniformity in advertising as you get bigger. We're working on that in sort of a hit-and-miss way.

They were quite active in designing and planning the North Highway branch. Quite active. But they're not like down at South Bank and Trust—they're down there all the time. Of course, South Bank and Trust almost lost all the money they had down there, too.

They weren't active in the North County merger but, of course, participated in some group meetings and gave the green light to see if we could go ahead and effect it. That was a chore, and we don't have all the strings tied together yet.

They had a discussion of consumer loans last meeting. Bob Thompson was also at the last meeting talking about the rollover rate mortgage, explaining that. We had one meeting on NOW accounts; they said go ahead on those two things.

Southern Federal's Management Philosophy

Southern Federal has become a leading institution in the community. This has not always been the case, as Knight explained:

When I came here, we had several problems that I perceived. One was that we were really an organization that survived or prospered or declined based on its participation in the community. If you don't participate in the community, I don't know how the community is going to participate with you. The way that they participate with us is to put their savings and their loans here. But the association was really just withdrawn. It wasn't outgoing. It took no real part, for instance, in the United Way or in supporting those things that make a good community. It did not suggest that the officers of the association join the civic clubs and take part. These are things that I believe you've got to do if you're going to be successful in your operation and have the name and image out there all the time.

We gave just a little token to financial drives. Today, we are the largest financial institution in South County, given the fact that Republic is a branch and the chain could swallow us up many times; but one on one, we're larger. We try to give a leading gift. I think we have to.

Besides attempting to have a meaningful leadership role in the community, Southern Federal also attempts to maintain a good working environment for its employees, as Jack Pope explained:

We have a good working environment—somewhat relaxed. We don't push people. We assign a job and expect it to be completed in a reasonable period of time. Most people like that.

This atmosphere does not mean that employees live a "life of ease," as Knight pointed out:

One thing that Jack Pope places a lot of emphasis on is encouraging employees to take advantage of the courses that we pay for, which are furnished by the U.S. League's financial education section. They are constantly involved in courses.

This is part of our merit program—to be qualified for a position, you must have passed satisfactorily those courses to make you qualified for that position. Now if it comes down to two people going for the same position, the one who had qualified him or herself in the best manner— and, if it came down to a fine line, had the best grades—would probably be the one to get that position, everything else being equal. Most of these people will make As and A + s. When these girls go after something, they usually work at it and do a good job.

Southern Federal also has been able to attract and keep good people. With regard to their low employee turnover, Knight explained:

Generally speaking, we don't have much turnover. We have always had a great esprit de corps. We have tried to encourage that with fringe benefits, uniforms, family get-togethers, etc. So far we've screened our employees pretty darn well. We've been lucky. We've had some misfits, but I think they realized they were and eventually worked out.

Now, First National Bank works on a different concept. They employ a lot of students and have a lot of turnover. They kind of accept that turnover, and I think it costs them, too. We'd rather have continuity and have you see the same person when you come in here—if it's possible.

Commenting on the loss of several employees earlier in the year, Knight explained:

Gosh, we took a siege here about three months ago, and we lost them, bam, bam, bam, just like that. And we're losing another next Tuesday. You just can't help it—she used to work for this dentist in another town. That joker is now going to also have an office here; he remembered her and made an offer she couldn't turn down. He offered her $2,500 more than we are paying here. She's a good employee, and we hate to lose her; but there is no way we can keep her without destroying the whole scale. You lose some like that, reluctantly.

Redding also expressed his feelings about the recent turnover:

We had the quitting bug come through here about a year ago, and everyone got to quitting. And then we'll have the baby bug come by here, and it'll bite a bunch of them.

Employee Compensation and Incentives

Along with having a good work environment, Southern Federal has also attempted to provide competitive salary and benefits for its employees. Pope explained:

We try to be competitive on salary with the banks around here, and benefits are on top of that. We have not had a great deal of turnover except for earlier this year. Usually the bank people come to us for jobs because they hear good things about us.

All employees who have been with the company at least six months participate in Southern Federal's profit sharing. Knight explained the system:

We have profit sharing—I guess you would call it that. There is no setting aside and waiting 10 years. We have a little formula—Redding worked it up—that for the last two years has, generally speaking, amounted to between 10 and 14 percent of salary. How long you have been here and how much you are making is all tied into it. If you've been here over six months, you're gonna get a ham. If you've been here over six months, you're gonna get your pro rata.

We take a fixed percentage of income, which we're adding to net worth. It's about a 50 percent deal. I believe it behooves us to treat the employees well and try to have people who are willing and ready to wait on people when they come through our doors, and make the person want to come back. Most of our people go out of their way.

Southern Federal also provides employee uniforms and other benefits, as Redding explained:

Many years ago, we put in a dress code. We give the ladies dresses. They got to squabbling about the thing here the other day; so we put it to a vote, and they voted 34 to 4 to keep the dresses.

We also furnish meals here. We have a dining room downstairs. The branch personnel get $1.75 a day to buy their cokes and soup. Here, it's free cokes, free coffee, free doughnuts, free lunch, free uniforms. Whether we should put that in a paycheck and forget about it, I don't know; but I like it this way.

We provide hospital insurance, retirement, all of that—but not for the dependents—we have life insurance tied in with their retirement and hospitalization.

Southern Federal's Management Control and Information Systems

Southern Federal does not set formal goals and objectives for itself. Knight explained about the absence of objectives:

> We just haven't set any objective over here that we're trying to reach. I'll tell you, we would have missed them so far. I told the board at the first of the year that we would be lucky if we were in the black for the year. Well, we made so much money in the first four months on penalties that they said, "What are you talking about?" I said, "Just wait. It's coming." It came, but now, again, we're turning it back the other way. Our projections don't look all that bad for the rest of the year, if we can hold it. It's very upsetting. There is no real way to keep up with it.
>
> There just doesn't seem to be any way to cope with some of the things we encounter. Suppose that last January we had set up some goals and objectives. We would have missed them for various reasons. We would have missed it on income for four months. We had the best income we've ever had because we were collecting penalties. I wasn't smart enough to look ahead and say we were going to collect penalties, because I didn't even know we were going to be levying penalties. It's not from lack of thought or desire to do it that way; it just seems beyond our control. Everybody else seems to be controlling what you can do. The only thing we can do is operate as best we can with what they give us to operate with and try to better our performance. This is what we tell our employees, "We have to do better than we did last year," and we try to tell them various ways to do it.
>
> No, we don't set goals, except that we try to do better each year than we did the year before. It's a relative thing. We're working against ourselves to do better. I don't know how you can set goals with the Federal Home Loan Board and with policies, now, of the DIDC committee. You could set some goals, but you don't have the ability to meet them. They're changing things so fast. Now, if they ever settle down, it may be different.

Redding commented further:

> We don't have any formal goals. We don't belong to the Rotary Club. I guess subconsciously we'd like to be the biggest one in the state, try to build up our deposits, get savings. We look at it and, if it looks like the loan volume is off and we have money and feel the economy is better, we'll have our advertising man go after the loans, start working with the real estate people, try to be competitive with rates, and scheme as best we can. We would like to get one percent net, but we haven't done it. We're on profit sharing here, and everyone participates—it's not going to be as good a year as it has been.

Southern Federal's savings operations have been installed on NCR's time-sharing system, which allows management to trace savings throughout the day. Jack Pope explained:

When we first started using the NCR system, Redding used to come in every hour to find out how savings and withdrawals were coming. We found that you couldn't tell how you were doing until late afternoon because it fluctuates so much from hour to hour.

Besides tracking their savings operations, management also tracks the firm's overall performance. Knight, as he picked up a summary of branch profit performance, explained:

I can show you expenses and income from each branch. Of course, some of it's hard to come by exactly, but we can come within sight of it, and that's all you really need to know. The total accounting picture is accurate. River County, for instance, has a little branch out there. It's not a profitable situation. It's slowly growing.

We keep strict accounting on each branch. We separate them so I can look at my records and tell you how each one of them is doing. I can look at my daily record and tell you what each one of them is doing in savings. It is good to know how much you're receiving. You certainly don't want to put more money into an area than you're taking in. It varies. This month, Lakeview's having a real good month on savings. North Highway is the leading branch on savings and has been ever since Mary Defoe went out there. That's the way I knew it would happen, because she really has a good rapport with people that save with us.

Redding further explained:

We have an annual budget—keep up with it and track variances monthly. It's done by hand. We have a Wang upstairs but don't use it. The damn thing takes a chauffeur, and we don't have one.

Jack Pope commented on the reason Southern Federal has the Wang computer:

We bought the Wang because we were going to put our loan-processing records on the computer. We bought that system because we thought it would be easy to adapt the software—but then we got our lawyers involved and we couldn't decide what format was legal, etc. It's been a year and a half, and we still don't use it.

Management had also planned to have a more extensive computer facility in the future. Knight explained:

I was ready to buy a computer about two years ago, but Jack Pope, the operations officer, and Jim Heart, the controller, both felt like it would be money that could be better spent somewhere else. They felt we could stay on NCR until we reached about $250 million. Well, with NOW accounts coming in, I think that timetable is going to be changed.

The North Highway office was designed—the floor, wiring, and everything is ready to go—to set the computer and everything that goes with it in there. That will go into the basement out there—it's a good place because the temperature won't change as much and it's easy to keep it cool, which is better for the computer.

Pope also commented on their planning system:

> We have looked at several models but haven't decided on one yet. We do some hand calculations, or what-ifs, of existing figures. But it isn't done with much depth.

With regard to keeping in touch with the critical operations of the association, Redding looked at the papers covering his desk and responded:

> Gosh, I don't know. You see how tidy my desk is! I guess Knight and I talk, and we talk with the other people in the departments, listen to all sorts of rumors, talk to other people in the business—other associations. We watch our profit picture—it looks gloomy right now though. The money market rates being what they are, it'll be October before we really get rid of the bad stuff.
>
> I think we've done a pretty good job in spite of the fact that we're not organized. We're not highly structured. I'm just now getting around, after 20 years, to getting some little plan for the janitor. This has become a problem, now, on how to keep the darn branches cleaned up. That thing out on North Highway has weeds everywhere. We have about three acres out there. We ought to have had better sense. We had to paint the Eastside Mall Branch because it wasn't quite so clear—you see we throw a little competition in there. Get them competing with each other. South Rim and Lakeview, they're about the same size—I pick on them to ask them why they're not doing so well.

With Southern Federal's first priority being entrance into the consumer loan business, there is a need to recruit a new manager. James Redding, executive vice president, is concerned about the kind of person they are going to need. He explained:

> Now facing us is the consumer loan, which we'll be getting into by September. That will entail adding someone who is knowledgeable of consumer lending, which will include automobile loans, signature loans, 90-day loans, or anything oriented to family financing. We want someone who will charge enough. We might get someone from one of these short-loan places. I used to be in the short-loan business. I'm the secretary and treasurer for Equitable's loan company. We took it over. We had a manager, and I supervised it from afar. Our motto was "Consolidate all your little bills into one huge staggering debt." That's from the lending end.

With the rapid introduction of consumer lending activities, Southern Federal also has to prepare employees to handle them. Redding continued:

> That's a problem in going into consumer lending. You're going to have to do it in the branches. And what do they know about consumer lending? Nothing! So you're going to have to get them trained. Whether they do one automobile a day, a week, or an hour, we're going to have to give them responsibility and work from there. Jack Pope is reviewing that.

Of course, with consumer lending, you're going to have to be able to give customers answers in 10 minutes or an hour—so we're also going to have to change our approval process.

QUESTIONS FOR ANALYSIS

1. In response to environmental and competitive pressures, Southern Federal's management made several changes in the organizational structure. Describe and evaluate these changes.
2. Evaluate the management philosophy at Southern Federal. What are the central ideas of the philosophy? Are these central ideas consistent with the demands of the business?
3. Evaluate Southern Federal's planning and controlling methods and practices. What could be done to improve them?
4. What seems to be the prevalent leadership style at Southern Federal? Is this style appropriate for the situation? Explain.
5. What operations management methods appear useful in managing savings and loan companies? Are there, for example, applications of PERT, linear programming, and inventory control that Southern Federal's management should investigate?

CASE TWO

NATIONAL MOTOR PARTS COMPANY

The National Motor Parts Company is one of the five largest firms in the basic auto parts industry. It has nine operating divisions and a total work force of over 80,000 employees. Its extensive staff organization provides specialized skills at the corporate, divisional, and plant level. At each of these levels, the cost accounting and industrial engineering groups exert a considerable amount of influence over the development and execution of corporate policy. Though individual divisions are operationally autonomous, division officials generally follow the policy suggestions made by the cost accounting and industrial engineering staffs. A partial organization chart is shown in Exhibit 1.

One program recently advocated by Phil King, corporate director of industrial engineering, was a review of work standards on all jobs which had not been checked or audited within the previous two years. King's request arose from the fact that he had seen several instances of what appeared to him to be goldbricking during a tour of plants in several of National's operating divisions. Upon his return to the central office, King met with two of his staff engineers, and after careful deliberation, an audit plan was drawn up. This plan was subsequently approved by the executive vice president in charge of manufacturing operations.

The audit plan suggested by King used a technique known as work sampling to check on the idle time present in individual job standards. In essence, the approach taken relied on the fact that a series of short, random observations, if taken often enough over an appropriate time period, could

Source: Copyright 1977, by John G. Hutchinson and Charles E. Summer.

EXHIBIT 1 Partial Organization Chart

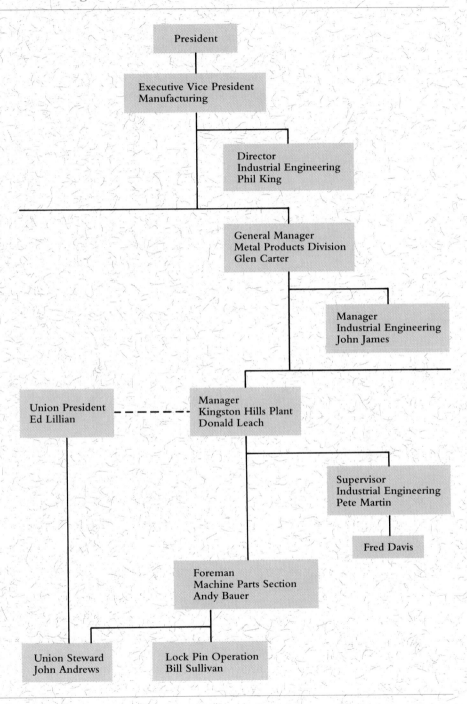

give an accurate picture of the operations performed in each job. The work-sampling results would be used to determine which jobs were not requiring the employees to work for an entire day to meet their stated output standards. By the same token, those jobs which were demanding a full day's work to meet existing standards would also be recognized. Though work sampling was to be used to identify standards which were loose (i.e., standards which did not require a full day's work to meet output requirements for that day), King's proposal included the further suggestion that looseness, when detected, should be checked in detail by the use of stopwatch time study and a thorough motion study of the job in question.

To launch his program, King held a series of meetings with the heads of divisional industrial engineering groups. Though objections were raised about the cost and time considerations inherent in the proposal, the division engineering managers agreed that the plan was technically sound and agreed to put it into effect as soon as possible.

One of the more receptive listeners to King's audit procedure was John James, manager of industrial engineering in National's Metal Products Division. This division employs 21,000 people in five plants. James, who holds degrees in both industrial engineering and mathematics, thought that King's plan was both technically sound and eminently practical. He returned to division headquarters in Kingston, Michigan, and drew up procedures to implement the plan in the Metal Products Division's five plants.

Within a month after the corporate staff meeting, James offered his own version of the audit plan to Glenn Carter, the division manager. Carter, who had come to respect James's technical ability and practical know-how, accepted the plan readily and agreed to present it at the next weekly meeting of his plant managers. Carter suggested that he should merely outline the plan to his plant managers and that James should be available to fill in details and to answer questions.

In the subsequent meeting, each of the plant managers agreed that such an audit was sound, and each in turn suggested that James contact the heads of their plant industrial engineering departments to explain the details of his plan. Three plant managers who had formerly been in charge of industrial engineering groups in the National hierarchy offered to provide additional clerical and engineering help on a temporary basis in order to get the program moving quickly.

After gaining the support of Carter and the five plant managers, James met with the heads of industrial engineering in each of the division's five plants. Though the familiar objections were raised about the time and cost of such a program, all five men stated that the audit procedure was practical, and they agreed to put it into effect immediately. Within this group, the plan was embraced most enthusiastically by Pete Martin, the industrial engineer in charge of the Kingston Hills plant.

The Kingston Hills plant shares the same plot of land as the headquarters of the Metal Products Division. It employs more than 5,000 workers and is generally considered to be the most modern and most efficient of the division's plants. Donald Leach, the plant manager, is one of the three men in the division who rose to his present position from a supervisory job in the industrial engineering hierarchy. Leach's plant is equipped with the latest advances in automated equipment; and it is, according to division records, the most profitable plant in the division. Leach prides himself on his ability to attract and retain good managerial talent, and he is particularly proud of the work done by Pete Martin in developing new methods of work and in adapting mathematical techniques and procedures to fit the needs of the operations at the Kingston Hills plant. Thus, when Martin suggested the adoption of an audit program, Leach agreed readily and offered Martin additional clerical help to work on the details of setting up the program.

Pete Martin went to work on the program immediately, and within a week the first audit reports were completed. After one month, audits had been completed on 17 operations. Sixteen of these audits indicated that very little idle time was evident in the operations studied, but the audit performed on one job, the production of a tiny metal lock pin used in automatic transmission units, seemed to show an unusual amount of idle time. The job in question was performed by Bill Sullivan, an experienced, long-service employee. Sullivan set up, tended, and performed certain minor maintenance tasks on an automatic screw machine. Because the products he worked on were varied, the original standards had been measured quite carefully.[1] Since the time when the original standards were set, changes had occurred which caused the standards to become loose. Materials changes, changes in tolerance limits on the various machined parts, the time and methods used to set up the various runs, the actual length of machine runs, and the adoption of a more standardized parts line had all occurred in recent years; and since several of these changes had apparently not been reflected in adjustments in the affected output standards, it was a rare day when Sullivan failed to obtain his expected or standard output.

The looseness of Sullivan's standards was no revelation to several of his immediate co-workers. One worker, for example, when conversing with Pete Martin about the audit, stated, "If your audit doesn't pick up that soft touch Sullivan's got, you'd better toss the whole thing down the drain." Few of the workers were bitter about Sullivan's "gravy train" job, however, since the looseness of his standards gave him no wage advantages over his fellow workers. In other National plants where payment is tied directly to output through the use of incentive payment plans, the relative looseness of standards had frequently caused bitter disputes because of the wage inequities it generated. In the Kingston Hills plant, the failure of management to detect a loose standard means that workers accrue leisure-time benefits, not higher wages. Though workers objected to such unfair workloads, no grievance had ever been filed to ask management to correct such inequities.

The second phase of the audit procedure entailed a review of Sullivan's job by Fred Davis, one of Martin's most competent engineers. In this study, Davis compared the previously set standard with the newly calculated time required to perform the operation under changed conditions. This, in turn, showed a tentative idle time of four hours per shift.[2] Davis's stopwatch time study of the

---

[1] Sullivan's standard at this time was .33734 minutes per piece, or approximately 180 units of output per hour.

[2] Though a four-hour idle time may seem to be so high as to be almost unbelievable, engineering studies performed elsewhere in National Motors uncovered similar looseness. Experts in the industrial engineering field concede that this situation can arise in even the best-managed plants.

screw-machine operation confirmed the results of the initial audit, and a detailed methods study of the job turned up substantial changes in the original working conditions, including changes in materials and methods of operation. Leach, when confronted with this information by Martin and Davis, ordered them to take steps to correct what he believed was an inequity in the basic workload structure.

After several weeks of study, Davis devised a plan where, with certain layout changes and some methods improvements, Sullivan would operate not one, but two machines. Davis's methods study showed that the time allowances were adequate enough to allow Sullivan to complete the requirements of the revised job if he worked a full eight-hour day. Davis showed his plan to Pete Martin, and together they presented it to Leach. Leach approved the plan and directed the Purchasing Department to acquire another automatic screw machine. He thereupon called in Andy Bauer, Sullivan's immediate supervisor and informed him that Sullivan should be told of the impending change.[3] Bauer, who had worked with Davis on the methods study, agreed to tell Sullivan that management intended to exercise its contractual right "to make changes in methods, equipment, materials, and conditions of work in order to obtain greater efficiency and to adjust existing work standards to reflect such changes." The labor contract further stated that "in case of such methods change, only those elements of the standard will be changed which are affected by the change in methods, etc." One other section of the contract spelled out the fact that "standards will be set on the basis of fairness and equity and that they shall be consistent with the quality of workmanship, efficiency of operation, and reasonable working capacities of normal operations." In the National Motors contract, as in most others in the basic auto industry, the resolution of work standards disputes can be solved only by dealings between management and the labor union. Arbitration is specifically prohibited as a means of settling disputes over work standards.

Two months later, the new machine was installed at the workplace along with several minor changes in layout and work flow. Foreman Bauer instructed Sullivan in his new duties, and Sullivan, though he was unhappy about the new layout, started to work with the two machines. During the day, John Andrews, the union steward, stopped by to check on the new job.[4] Sullivan complained violently that he was the victim of a "speedup." Andrews, after listening to the details of the shift from one to two machines, suggested that Sullivan file a grievance.

That evening Sullivan wrote a grievance and, shortly before starting work the next morning, turned it over to John Andrews. Andrews, following the normal procedure for processing such grievances, presented it to Andy Bauer for discussion and possible solution. Because of the technical nature of the grievance, Bauer called upon Pete Martin and Fred Davis to explain the nature of the change to Andrews. When Martin and Davis showed their detailed

---

[3]The new standard called for a time of .1664 minutes per piece, or approximately 360 units per hour.

[4]One of the main duties of a union steward is to represent the worker in presenting grievances to management. This person is usually elected to this office by fellow workers. Stewards hold regular jobs in the plants where they perform their duties, and they receive no extra pay for their union activities.

methods studies to Andrews, he stated, "What you guys have done here is to blow up a big smoke screen to hide the fact that you're pulling a speedup on Sullivan's job." The net result of the meeting was that the grievance, still unsettled, moved to the second step in grievance procedure. This step involved discussion between the head of the local union, Ed Lillian, and Donald Leach, the plant manager.

Leach, when presented with Bill Sullivan's grievance, immediately called Pete Martin into his office to discuss the problem. Together they reviewed the methods study and the subsequent standards revisions. The approaches and the figures shown by Martin seemed correct and reasonable to Leach, and he believed that the contractual clause allowing him "to make changes in methods, equipment, materials, and conditions of work in order to obtain greater efficiency and to adjust existing work standards to reflect such changes" justified the introduction of the second machine. He stated, "It's my duty to my work force to maintain an efficient operation so that the job security of all the workers will be protected." Leach also said, "The only way we can continue to grow and prosper and provide steady employment for our workers is to push for more efficiency in all of our plant activities." In his upcoming meeting with Ed Lillian, Leach planned to use this reasoning as the basis for his insistence on the introduction of the second machine. He also intended to allow Lillian to review any and all of the data used as the basis of changes made on the disputed job.

Ed Lillian, on the other hand, expected to rely heavily on John Andrews to present the union side of the dispute. Lillian told Andrews that he would support him fully if the company's actions were in violation of the labor contract.

The feelings of the parties prior to the grievance meeting are summarized below:

Bill Sullivan: All of a sudden I'm expected to turn out 3,000 pieces per day where I used to have to do 1,400.[5] If this isn't a speedup, I don't know what the hell it is. I've got rights, and I expect the union to protect them.

John Andrews: The company hasn't done a thing to change methods here. They've just come in and made changes to correct their mistakes from the past. Their actions violate the fairness and equity clauses relating to revision of work standards which exist in the labor contract.

Pete Martin: We've made good studies of Sullivan's job, and we know that the lock-pin standard is loose. It's not unfair to ask him to put in a fair day's work in order to earn a fair day's pay.

Ed Lillian: Even though Don Leach is sometimes tough in his dealings with us, he's been fair and consistent. On this issue, however, I'm not sure he's really right.

Donald Leach: I believe that I'm both contractually and economically correct when I take the stand that the second machine should be maintained on this operation. After all, if we don't have efficiency in this plant, the workers won't have any job security.

Glenn Carter: The real issue here is whether or not managers have the right to run their own plants. If we have to subsidize inefficiency in our operations, we won't be in business very long.

[5]In actuality, Sullivan was required to turn out 1,440 pieces per day before the audit. After the methods change and subsequent standards revision, Sullivan's quota rose to 2,880.

The grievance meeting scheduled to resolve this dispute was affected by at least two other factors:

1.   Strikes over production standards are legal during the life of the labor contract. Though other issues (wages, hours, working conditions, etc.) can be grieved, no strikes can be called legally on these matters until the existing contract expires.

2.   Though one more step remained in the division's grievance procedure, Carter had written a note to Ed Lillian which stated that he "would not, under any circumstances, alter the stand taken by Leach in the plant-level negotiations." Since the dispute cannot be arbitrated, the parties are faced with the problem of devising some other strategy to solve (or to "win") the disagreement.

In a front-page editorial on the day before the grievance meeting, the local *Kingston Daily Record* asked the disputants to act with "caution and care." The *Record's* editorial recalled that "the steel industry became embroiled in a similar issue which evolved into a strike lasting six months."

QUESTIONS FOR ANALYSIS

1.   Each of the parties to the disagreement has feelings about the causes of the dispute. Analyze the bases for each person's feelings in terms of unstated assumptions and values.

2.   Which people appear to be analyzing the causes of the dispute in terms of *work-related,* as distinct from *person-related,* management activities? Explain.

3.   What, in your judgment, are the underlying causes of this dispute? What do you believe should be the solution to the dispute? How can similar disputes be avoided in the future?

4.   What solution would a manager propose who understands principles and methods of only classical and management science approaches? What solution would be proposed by a manager who understands only behavioral approach principles and methods?

5.   Analyze the dispute in terms of the causes of intergroup conflict. What would be the appropriate strategy for managing the conflict during the grievance meeting?

GLOSSARY

Acceptance Theory of Authority A theory of authority, proposed by Barnard, according to which the ultimate source of authority is the decision of the subordinate to accept the superior's orders.

Accountability The process by which a subordinate reports the use of assigned resources to a designated superior.

Activity The work necessary to complete a particular event in a PERT network. An activity consumes time, which is the paramount variable in a PERT system. In PERT networks, three time estimates are used for each activity: an optimistic time, a pessimistic time, and a most likely time.

Administrative Duties The 16 guidelines that Fayol believed should direct the manager in carrying out the organizing function. There is considerable overlap between his 16 administrative duties and his 14 management principles.

Affective Attitude The part of attitude that involves a person's emotions or feelings.

Affirmative Action Program A program in which an employer specifies how the company plans to increase the number of minority and female employees.

Allocation Model This type of management science model is used in a situation where several candidates or activities all compete for limited resources. It enables the user to allocate scarce resources in order to maximize some predetermined objective.

Altruism An ethical standard which places highest value on behavior that is pleasurable and rewarding to society.

Anthropology The behavioral science that studies learned behaviors of individuals and groups. It seeks general laws which explain intercultural and extracultural behavior. This includes social, technical, and family behaviors. It is often defined as the study of man and his works.

Attitude A person's tendency to feel and behave toward some object in some way.

Attribution An inference made about one's own feelings or another person's feelings, based on observed behavior.

Authority The legitimate right to use assigned resources to accomplish a delegated task or objective; the right to give orders and to exact obedience. The legal bases for formal authority are private property, the state, or a Supreme Being.

Behavior Any observable response given by a person.

Behavioral Approach to Management A body of literature characterized by its concern for human behavior in the work environment. The school's primary means for acquiring knowledge is the scientific method, with emphasis upon research. Chronologically, the behavioral approach to management thought followed the classical approach. Its first phase was identified with "human relations" theory, popular in the 1940s and early 1950s. Its second phase was the "behavioral science" approach, which came into popular use in the early 1950s.

Behavioral Approach to Organizational Design A design approach that emphasizes people and how the structure of an organization affects their behavior and performance. The advocates of a people orientation to design believe that the classical approach suppresses personal development because it is so rigid and restrictive.

Behavioral Change Planned change in the attitudes, skills, and knowledge of organizational personnel.

Behaviorally Anchored Rating Scales (BARS) A set of rating scales developed by raters and/or ratees that uses critical behavioral incidents as interval anchors on each scale. About 6 to 10 scales with behavioral incidents are used to derive the evaluation.

Behavioral Motivation Theory The behavioral approach to management advocates the pluralistic view of motivation, which emphasizes that many different types of needs influence behavior and that man is motivated by the desire to satisfy many needs.

Behavioral Science Approach This approach to the study of management can be thought of as the study of observable and verifiable human behavior in organizations, using scientific procedures. It draws especially from psychology, sociology, and anthropology.

Behavior Modification An approach to motivation that uses operant conditioning: operant behavior is learned on the basis of consequences. In management, if a behavior causes a desired outcome (for managers), then it is reinforced (positively rewarded); and because of its consequences, it is likely to be repeated. Thus, behavior is conditioned by adjusting its consequences.

Benefits Financial payments (e.g., insurance premiums) made by an employer over and above the base wages and salary.

Bill of Materials A document that details the required components of each subassembly and finished good. The "demand" for components is derived from the demand for the subassemblies and finished goods.

Biofeedback A technique, usually involving the use of some kind of instrumentation, in which the user attempts to learn to control various bodily functions such as heart rate and blood pressure.

Bureaucracy An organizational design that relies on specialization of labor, a specific authority hierarchy, a formal set of rules and procedures, and rigid promotion and selection criteria.

Business Plan A written report that provides an overview and analysis of a proposed business. The plan is the basis for presentations to prospective investors in the business.

Career An individually perceived sequence of attitudes and behaviors associated with work-related experiences and activities over the span of a person's life.

Career Path Beginning with a particular job, the sequence of jobs involved in promotion and advancement.

Career Planning The process of systematically matching an individual's career aspirations with opportunities for achieving them.

Career Plateau The point or stage of a career at which the individual has no opportunity for further promotion or advancement.

Career Stages Distinct but interrelated steps or phases of a career, including the prework stage, the initial work stage, the stable work stage, and the retirement stage.

Carrying Costs The costs incurred by carrying an inventory. They include such costs as the taxes and insurance on the goods in inventory, interest on money invested in inventory and storage space, and the costs incurred because of the obsolescence of the inventory.

Case Study A type of research design that attempts to examine numerous characteristics of a person or group over an extended period of time. Since the results achieved by a case study are usually based on a sample of one, the user cannot be certain as to their generality. Most case studies raise questions for future research.

Categorical Imperative An ethical standard that judges behavior in terms of its consistency with the principle: "Act as if the maxim of your action were to become a general law binding on everyone."

Central Tendency Errors The appraiser tends to rate appraisees around the midpoint, in essence indicating that every subordinate is about average.

Certainty Decision A decision in which the manager is certain about the state of nature or competitor action that will occur. Thus, the probability that a particular event will occur is 1.00.

Civil Rights Act of 1964 An act that makes various forms of discrimination illegal. Title VII of the act spells out the forms of illegal discrimination.

Classical Approach to Management A body of literature that represents the earliest attempts to define and describe the field of management. The approach's main focus is on formally prescribed relationships. Its primary means for acquiring knowledge are personal observation and case studies.

Classical Approach to Organizational Design Relies on such management principles as unity of command, a balance between authority and responsibility, division of labor, and delegation to establish relationships between managers and subordinates.

Classical Management Motivation Theory The classical approach to motivation emphasized monetary incentives as prime means for motivating the individual. This approach was undoubtedly strongly influenced by the classical economists, who emphasized man's rational pursuit of economic objectives.

Closed System An approach that generally ignores environmental forces and conditions.

Coercive Power The power of a leader that is derived from fear. The follower perceives the leader as a person who can punish deviant behavior and actions.

Cognitive Attitude The part of attitude that involves a person's perceptions, beliefs, and ideas.

Cognitive Dissonance A state in which there is a discrepancy between a person's attitude and behavior.

Command Group The group of employees who report to a single manager, as shown on an organization chart.

Communication The transmission of information and understanding through the use of common symbols.

Conceptual Management Skill The ability to coordinate and integrate ideas, concepts, and practices. Such skill is most important to top-level managers.

Concurrent Control The techniques and methods that focus on the actual, ongoing activity of the organization.

Consideration Acts by a leader that imply supportive concern for the followers in a group.

Contingency Approach to Organization Design A set of ideas which concludes that there exists an effective organization design for a specific organization depending on factors in the setting.

Continuous Reinforcement A reinforcement schedule that involves administering a reward each time a desired behavior occurs.

Controlling Function All managerial activity undertaken to assure that actual operations go according to plan.

Core Job Dimensions As proposed by Hackman and others, the five core job dimensions that, if present, provide enrichment for jobs. The dimensions are variety, task identity, task significance, autonomy, and feedback.

Cost-Benefit Analysis A technique for evaluating individual projects and deciding among alternatives. This technique is being adapted to the needs of public sector organizations to aid them in improving their performance.

Cost Leadership Strategy An overall corporate strategy that involves being the lowest-cost producer in the industry.

Criterion A standard by which success in an activity may be measured.

Critical Incident Method A method by which the appraiser uses a log of positive and negative critical incidents to assess the performance of appraisees.

Critical Path The longest path in a PERT network, from the network beginning event to the network ending event.

Culture Culture is a very complex environmental influence that includes knowledge, beliefs, law, morals, art, customs, and any other habits and capabilities an individual acquires as a member of society. It is important to be aware that cultures are *learned,* cultures *vary,* and culture *influences behavior.*

Decentralization The pushing downward of the appropriate amount of decision-making authority. All organizations practice a certain degree of decentralization.

Decision Making The process of thought and deliberation that results in a decision. Decisions, the output of the decision-making process, are means through which a manager seeks to achieve some desired state.

Decoding The mental procedure that the receiver of a message uses to decipher the message.

Defensive Behavior Behavior (e.g., aggression, withdrawal, and repression) that is resorted to by an individual who is blocked in attempts to satisfy needs.

Delegation The process by which authority is distributed downward in an organization.

Departmentalization The process of grouping jobs together on the basis of some common characteristic, such as product, client, location, or function.

Descriptive Model A type of model that describes how a system works. It describes things as they are and makes no value judgments about the particular thing being studied. It may display the alternative choices available to the decision maker, but it does not select the best alternative.

Determinants of Personality The many factors that interact in the formation of the human personality. Four general classifications of factors must be considered: constitutional determinants, group membership determinants, role determinants, and situational determinants.

Deterministic Model A model in which the law of chance plays no role. The word *deterministic* refers to the type of variables included in the model. All the factors taken into account in the model are assumed to be exact or determinate quantities.

Diagnosis The use of data collected by interviews, surveys, observations, and records to learn and draw conclusions about people or organizations.

Differentiation Strategy An overall corporate strategy that involves creating real and perceived differences between the firm's products/services and those of competitors.

Direct Investment Entry Strategy The strongest commitment to becoming an MNC, when management decides to begin producing the firm's products abroad. This strategy enables the firm to maintain partial to full control over production, marketing, and other key functions.

Direction A method of concurrent control that refers to the manager's acts of communicating orders to subordinates and overseeing their work.

Discounted Rate of Return The rate of return that equates future cash proceeds with the initial cost of an investment.

Distinctive Competence A factor that gives the organization an advantage over similar organizations. Distinctive competencies are what the organization does best.

Downward Communication Communication that flows from individuals at higher levels of an organization structure to individuals at lower levels. The most common type of downward communica-

tion is job instructions transmitted from the superior to the subordinate.

Dual Careers A situation in which both the husband and the wife are pursuing careers.

Egoism An ethical standard that places highest value on behavior that is pleasurable and rewarding to the individual.

Emergent Leader A person from within the group who comes to lead or influence its members.

Encoding The converting of a communication into an understandable message by a communicator.

Entrepreneur An individual who establishes and manages a business.

EOQ Model The economic order quantity model, which is used to resolve problems regarding the size of orders. A manager concerned with minimizing inventory costs could utilize the model to study the relationships between carrying costs, ordering costs, and usage.

Equal Employment Opportunity Act of 1972 A law that has specific provisions about equal opportunities for employment.

Equal Employment Opportunity Commission A government commission that enforces laws that attempt to provide equal opportunities for employment without regard to race, religion, age, creed, sex, national origin, or disability.

Esteem Needs The needs both for awareness of importance to others and of the regard accorded by others.

Ethics Principles that distinguish right from wrong behavior.

Event An accomplishment at a particular point in time on a PERT network. An event consumes no time.

Expectancy Motivation Model Views motivation as a process governing choices. In this model, a person who has a goal weighs the likelihood that various behaviors will achieve that goal and is likely to select the behavior he or she expects to be most successful.

Expected Time *(t_e)* A time estimate for each activity that is calculated by using the formula:

$$t_e = \frac{a + 4m + b}{6}$$

where a = optimistic time, m = most likely time, and b = pessimistic time.

Expected Value The average return of a particular decision in the long run if the decision maker makes the same decision in the same situation over and over again. The expected value is found by taking the value of an outcome if it should occur and multiplying that value by the probability that the outcome will occur.

Experiment A type of research design that contains two key elements: manipulation of some variable by the researcher and observation or measurement of the results.

Expert Power The power that individuals possess because followers perceive them to have special skills, special knowledge, or special expertise.

Export Entry Strategy The simplest way for a firm to enter a foreign market is by exporting. This strategy involves little or no change in the basic mission, objectives, and strategies, since the organization continues to produce all of its products at home. The firm will usually secure an *agent* in the particular foreign market who facilitates the transactions with foreign buyers.

External Change Forces Forces for change outside the organization, such as the pricing strategies of competitors, the available supply of resources, and government regulations.

Extinction A behavior modification practice which involves withholding positive rewards to change behavior.

Feedback Control Techniques and methods that analyze historical data to correct future events.

Final Performance Review The last step in the MBO process, a final meeting between the manager and the subordinate. The meeting, which focuses on performance over an entire period, must accomplish two important purposes: (1) an evaluation of the objectives achieved and the relating of these accomplishments to rewards such as salary increments and promotion and (2) an evaluation of performance, intended to aid the subordinate in self-development and to set the stage for the next period.

First-Level Management The lowest level of the hierarchy. A manager at this level coordinates the work of nonmanagers but reports to a manager.

Focus Strategy An overall corporate strategy that involves developing either a cost leadership or differentiation strategy in a specific market segment of an industry.

Forecasting An important element of the planning function that must make two basic determinations: (1) what level of activity can be expected during the planning period and (2) what level of resources will be available to support the projected activity. In a business organization, the critical forecast is the sales forecast.

Foreign Activities Entry Strategy As exports increase in importance to the firm, it may decide that it can justify its own foreign activities. This decision usually involves joining with nationals in the foreign country to establish product and/or marketing facilities. It differs from direct investment in that some type of association is formed with a local firm or individual, usually in the form of licensing or joint venture arrangements. *Licensing* is granting the right to produce and/or market the firm's product in another country to an outside firm. *Joint venture* arrangements involve foreign investors forming a group with local investors to begin a local business, with each group sharing ownership.

Formal Groups The established departments, units, and terms created by the managers in an organization.

Friendship Group An informal group that evolves because of some common characteristic such as age, political sentiment, or background.

Frustration An emotion that occurs when individuals are unable to satisfy their needs. Frustration may result in constructive problem-solving behavior or in defensive behavior.

Generativity An individual's concern for actions and achievements that will benefit future generations.

Goal Participation The amount of involvement a person has in setting task and personal development goals.

Grapevine An informal communication network in organizations that short-circuits the formal channels.

Graphic Rating Scales A printed form with various job dimensions used by an appraiser to provide a rating for each appraisee.

Grid Training A leadership development method proposed by Blake and Mouton that emphasizes the necessary balance between production orientation and person orientation.

Group Assets The advantages derived from the increase in knowledge that is brought to bear on a problem when a group examines it.

Group Cohesiveness The attraction of individual members to a group in terms of the strength of the forces that impel them to remain active in the group and to resist leaving it.

Group Development The phases or sequences through which a group passes: mutual acceptance, decision making, motivation, and control.

Group Liabilities The negative features of groups, such as the group pressure that is expected to bring dissident members into line, the takeover by a dominant member, and the reduced creativity that results from the embarrassment of members about expressing themselves.

Group Norm Agreement among a group's members about how they should behave.

Group Politics The use of self-serving tactics to improve a group's position relative to that of other groups.

Groupthink A phenomenon that occurs when a group believes that it is invincible, turns off criticism, attempts to bring noncomplying members into line, and feels that everyone is in agreement.

Halo Effect The forming of general impressions (positive or negative) about a person, based on an impression formed from performance in one area.

Halo Error A positive or negative aura around a ratee that influences a rater's evaluation.

Hawthorne Effect The tendency of people who are being observed or involved in a research effort to react differently than they would otherwise.

Hawthorne Studies Management studies conducted at the Western Electric Hawthorne plant in a suburb of Chicago. These are the most famous studies ever conducted in the field of management.

Hierarchy of Needs A widely adopted pluralistic framework of motivation developed by psychologist A. H. Maslow. The theory stresses two ideas: (1) only needs not yet satisfied can influence behavior; and (2) human needs are arranged in a hierarchy of importance. When one level has been satisfied, a higher-level need emerges and demands satisfaction. Maslow distinguishes five general classes of needs: physiological, safety, social, esteem, and self-actualization.

Horizontal Communication Occurs when the communicator and the receiver are at the same level in the organization.

Horizontal Specialization of Management The process by which the natural sequence of a task is broken down into specialized subgroups and a manager is assigned the authority and responsibility for coordinating the subgroups.

Human Management Skill The ability to work with, motivate, and counsel people who need help and guidance. Most important to first-level managers.

Human Relations Approach An approach to management that emphasizes the important role that individuals play in determining the success or failure of an organization. It embarked on the critical task of compensating for some of the deficiencies in classical theory. Basically, it took the premises of the classical approach as given, but showed how these premises were modified as a result of individual behavior and the influence of the work group.

Human Resource Management The process of accomplishing organizational objectives by acquiring, retaining, terminating, developing, and properly using the human resources in an organization.

Human Resource Planning The steps taken in estimating the size and makeup of the future work force.

Immediate Performance Measures Measures of results that are monitored over short periods of time, such as a day, a week, a month, or a year. These include measures of output, quality, time, cost, and profit. Immediate performance measures are not always easy to obtain.

Incremental Influence This concept refers to the influence of a leader over and above the influence base best owed by position in the organization.

Informal Groups   Natural groupings of people in response to some need.

Initiating Structure   Leadership acts that develop job tasks and responsibilities for followers.

Insufficient-Reason Criterion   Assumes that if a manager is operating under conditions of uncertainty, there is an equal probability that each of the possible states of nature or competitive actions may occur.

Integration   The degree to which members of various departments work together effectively.

Intelligence Information   Data on elements of the organization's operating environment (e.g., clients, competitors, suppliers, creditors, and the government) for use in short-run planning, and data on developments in the economic environment (e.g., consumer income trends and spending patterns) and in the social and cultural environment for use in long-run strategic planning.

Interest Group   A group formed to achieve some job-related but personal objective.

Intergroup Conflict   The disagreements, hostile emotions, and problems that exist among groups. These conflicts emerge because of limited resources, communication problems, differences in perceptions and attitudes, and a lack of clarity.

Intermediate Performance Reviews   In the MBO process, periodic reviews of performance that monitor progress toward achieving the objectives that have been established and the action plans that have been developed. These reviews are an important element of control in management by objectives.

Intermittent Reinforcement   A reinforcement schedule that involves rewarding desired behavior only periodically.

Internal Change Forces   Forces for change that occur within the organization, such as communication problems, morale problems, and decision-making breakdowns.

Inventory Models   A type of production control model that answers two questions relating to inventory management: "How much?" and "When?" An inventory model tells the manager when goods should be reordered and what quantity should be purchased.

Job Analysis   The procedures for determining the tasks that make up a job, and the skills, abilities, and responsibilities an employee needs to do the job.

Job Depth   The relative freedom that a jobholder has in the performance of assigned duties.

Job Description   A statement that furnishes information about a job's duties, technology, conditions, and hazards. Data for preparing the description come from the job and analysis.

Job Enlargement   A form of despecialization in that the number of tasks performed by the employees is increased. The increase in tasks theoretically makes the job more interesting and challenging. Consequently, work becomes more psychologically rewarding.

Job Enrichment   Suggested formally by Herzberg, this involves building into individual jobs greater scope for personal achievement, recognition, and responsibility. It is concerned with strengthening the motivational factors and only incidentally with maintenance.

Job Evaluation   Attaching a dollar value to a job so that comparisons of jobs on the basis of value can be made.

Job Range   The relative complexity of the assigned task as reflected by its cycle time.

Job Rotation   The procedure of moving a worker from one workstation to another to minimize boredom.

Job Specification   A statement, derived from the job analysis, about the human qualifications needed to perform the job.

Just-in-Time (JIT) Inventory Control   A refined application of MRP that results in components becoming available at the precise moment in time when they are required. The effect of JIT is to reduce to a minimum the carrying cost of component parts.

Leader-Member Relations   In the Fiedler situational model of leadership, a factor that refers to the degree of confidence, trust, and respect that followers have in the leader.

Leadership   In the context of management theory, the ability of a person to influence the activities of followers in an organizational setting.

Lead Time   The length of time between ordering and receiving an item of inventory. Inventory on hand must be sufficient to meet demand during the lead-time period.

Legitimate Power   The power that rank gives to a leader in the managerial hierarchy. For example, the department manager possesses more legitimate power than the supervisor because the department manager is ranked higher than the supervisor.

Less Developed Country (LDC)   A country with a very low gross national product, very little industry, or a vastly unequal distribution of income, with a very large number of poor.

Linear Programming   A production planning technique with widespread applicability in organizations that produce repetitive and routine products and services. The technique enables management to make the optimal allocation of resources to alternative products and services.

Line Functions   Activities that contribute directly to the creation of the organization's output. In manufacturing, the line functions are production, marketing, and finance.

Maintenance Factors   Distinguished by Herzberg in his "two-factor" theory of motivation, those conditions of the job that operate primarily to dissatisfy employees when they are not present. However, their presence does not build strong motivation among employees. Herzberg distinguished 16 of these factors (e.g., salary, job security, work conditions).

Management by Objectives (MBO)   A planning and controlling method that comprises these major elements: (1) the superior and the subordinate meet to discuss goals and to jointly establish attainable goals for the subordinate; (2) the superior and the subordinate meet again afterward to evaluate the subordinate's performance in terms of the goals that have been set.

Management Development   The process of educating and developing selected personnel so that they have the knowledge, skills, attitudes, and understanding needed to manage in the future.

Management Science Approach   A body of literature characterized by its use of mathematical and statistical techniques to build models for the solution of production and operations problems. The approach's primary means for acquiring knowledge is mathematical deduction.

Managerial Roles   The organized sets of behavior that belong to the manager's job. The three main types of managerial roles discovered by such researchers as Mintzberg are interpersonal, informational, and decisional roles.

Master Production Schedule   A document that details the planned production of all finished goods for a particular time period. The master production schedule is based on the strategic plan and the production plan.

Material Requirements Planning (MRP)   An inventory planning and controlling technique that involves identifying each component and subassembly of a complete product and then coordinating the ordering and delivering of those components and subassemblies. The technique usually requires a computer to deal with the mass of required information.

Mathematical Models   A simplified representation of the relevant aspects of an actual system or process.

Matrix Organizational Design   A design in which a project-type structure is superimposed on a functional structure.

Maturity   As used in leadership theory, the term refers to the willingness of individuals and groups to take responsibility for directing their own jobs. The two dimensions of maturity are job maturity (ability to do the job) and psychological maturity (willingness to do the job).

Maximax Criterion   Criterion used by the optimistic manager, who believes that only the most favorable result will occur and decides to maximize the maximum payoff.

Maximin Criterion   Criterion used by the pessimistic manager, who believes that only the least favorable result will occur and therefore decides to maximize the minimum payoff.

Mechanistic System   An organizational design in which there is differentiation of job tasks, rigid rules, and a reliance on top-management objectives.

Mentor   A relationship that exists when an older employee helps a younger person learn the job, the systems procedures, and the rituals of the organization.

Middle Management   The middle level of an administrative hierarchy. Managers at this level coordinate the work of managers and report to a manager.

Minimax Criterion   Criterion used by the manager who believes that once a decision is made and an outcome occurs, there will be some regret and who selects the strategy that results in the least regret.

Mission   A long-term vision of what an organization is trying to become. The mission is the unique aim that differentiates an organization from similar organizations. The basic questions that must be answered in order to determine an organization's mission are, "What is our business? What should it be?"

Motion Study   The process of analyzing work in order to determine the most efficient motions for performing tasks. Motion study, a major contribution of scientific management, was developed principally through the efforts of Frederick Taylor and Frank and Lillian Gilbreth.

Motivation   The inner strivings that initiate a person's actions.

Motivational Factors   Distinguished by Herzberg in his two-factor theory of motivation, those job conditions that, if present, operate to build high levels of motivation and job satisfaction. However, their absence does not prove highly dissatisfying. Herzberg distinguished six of these factors (e.g., achievement, recognition, advancement).

Moving Budget   A form of budgeting that involves periodic updating; for example, a 12-month budget will be updated each month and projected for the following 12 months.

Multinational Company (MNC)   An MNC is a business firm doing business in two or more countries.

Negative Reinforcement   Removing a disliked event immediately after response occurs, in order to bring about an increase in the response's frequency.

Noise   Any interference with the flow of a message from a sender to a receiver.

Nonprogrammed Decisions   Decisions for novel and unstructured problems or for complex or extremely important problems. Nonprogrammed decisions deserve special attention of top management.

Nonverbal Communication   A form of communication that takes place without the use of words. Typical nonverbal communications include body language and gestures.

Normative Model   This type of model is specifically constructed to select from among alternatives the best one based on some previously determined criteria, which are also included in the model. It tells how the system should be in order to achieve a particular objective.

Norms   Standards of behavior agreed upon by members of a group, either formal or informal.

Occupational Safety and Health Act (OSHA)   An act to protect the health and safety of employees. Employers must furnish workplaces free from recognized hazards to life and health.

Operant Conditioning   An approach to behavior modification which involves manipulating the consequences of behavior to change behavior.

Operating Management   Manages the implementation of programs and projects in each area of performance, measures and evaluates results, and compares results with objectives.

Operations   A broad term used to describe the activities and flow of work, resources, and materials in goods- or service-producing organizations.

Ordering Cost   An element in inventory control models that comprises clerical, administrative, and labor costs; a major cost component that is considered in inventory control decisions. Each time a firm orders items for inventory, some clerical and administrative work is usually required to place the order and some labor is required to put the items in inventory.

Organic System   An organizational design with a behavioral orientation, participation from all employees, and communication flowing in all directions.

Organizational Change   The intentional attempt by management to improve the overall performance of individuals, groups, and the organization as a whole by altering the organization's structure, behavior, and technology.

Organizational Communications   Information that flows outward from the organization to the various components of its external operating environment. Whatever the type of organization, the content of this information flow is controlled by the organization (e.g., advertising).

Organizational Objectives The broad continuing aims that serve as guides for action and as the starting point for more specific and detailed operating objectives at lower levels in the organization. This book classifies organizational objectives into four categories: profitability, competitiveness, efficiency, and flexibility.

Organizational Performance The extent to which an organization achieves the results that society expects of it. Organizational performance is affected in part by managerial performance.

Organizational Psychology The study of behavior and attitudes within an organization, including the effect of the organization upon the individual and the individual's effect on the organization.

Organizational Strategies The general approaches that are utilized by the organization to achieve its organizational objectives. These approaches include market penetration, market development, product development, and diversification strategies.

Organizational Structure The formally defined framework of task and authority relationships. The organization structure is analogous to the biological concept of the skeleton.

Organizing Function All managerial activity that results in the design of a formal structure of tasks and authority.

Participative Approach A technique advocated by behavioralists that stresses the idea that employees throughout the firm should be allowed to participate in decision making.

Path-Goal Leadership An approach to leadership in which the leader indicates to followers the "paths" to accomplish their goals.

Payback Period The length of time that it takes for an investment to pay for itself out of future funds.

Peer Relationship A relationship between peers that provides support, feedback, information, and/or friendship.

Perception The process by which individuals organize and interpret their impressions of the environment around them.

Performance Appraisal A procedure used by managers to assess performance and inform the employee of their expectations and opinions.

Performance Evaluation A feedback control technique that focuses on the extent to which employees have achieved expected levels of work during a specified time period.

Personal-Behavioral Leadership Theories A group of theories based primarily on the personal and behavioral characteristics of leaders. These theories focus on *what* leaders do and/or *how* leaders behave in carrying out the leadership function.

Personality The sum of an individual's traits or characteristics. These traits interact to create personality patterns.

Physiological (Basic) Needs Needs of the human body, such as food, water, and sex.

Planning Function All managerial activities that lead to the definition of objectives and to the determination of appropriate means to achieve those objectives.

Policies Guidelines for managerial action that must be adhered to at all times. Policymaking is an important management planning element for assuring that action is oriented toward objectives. The purpose of policies is to achieve consistency and direction and to protect the reputation of the organization.

Position Power A factor in the Fiedler theory of leadership that refers to the power inherent in the leadership position.

Positive Reinforcement A reward (e.g., praise, recognition, bonus) that results in an increase in the frequency of the rewarded response.

Power The ability to influence another person's behavior.

Preliminary Control Techniques and methods that attempt to maintain the quality and quantity of resources.

Principle of Management A generally accepted tenet that guides the thinking and on-the-job practices of managers.

Private Sector Organizations Profit-making organizations in the U.S. economy.

Probabilistic Model Model based on the mathematics of statistics. Conditions of uncertainty are introduced in the model, often based on observations of real-world events.

Production A term used to address manufacturing technology and the flow of materials in a manufacturing facility.

Productivity Any ratio of output to one or more corresponding units.

Profitability Measures Mathematical measures that provide an indication of profitability. They include the ratio of net profit to capital, to total assets, and to sales.

Program Evaluation and Review Technique (PERT) A production planning technique with widespread applicability in organizations that produce large-scale, nonroutine products. The technique enables management to make the optimal allocation of resources to the activities that lead to completion of the product.

Programmed Decisions Responses to repetitive and routine problems, which are handled by a standard procedure that has been developed by management.

Projection The tendency of people to attribute to someone else the traits that they feel are negative aspects of their own personality.

Psychology The behavioral science that studies human behavior. It seeks general laws which explain individual and interpersonal behavior.

Punishment The introduction of something disliked or the removal of something liked following a particular response, in order to decrease the frequency of that response.

Quality Circles A small group from the work unit, ranging in size from 4 to 15, who voluntarily meet on a regular basis to study quality-control and productivity improvement techniques to identify and solve work problems.

Quality Funnel Principle A principle in quality control which states that the cost of poor quality increases as the output passes progressively farther through the transformation process. The implication is that the cost of poor quality is minimized if detected and corrected in the input stage.

Realistic Job Previews (RJP) The practice of providing realistic information to new employees. The recruiter "tells it like it is" to avoid creating expectations that cannot be realized.

Recruitment Steps taken to staff an organization with the best-qualified people.

Recycling The process by which one MBO cycle gives way to another. The final performance evaluation session of one MBO leads directly into the establishment of objectives for the next cycle. Divisional or departmental objectives are established, individual objective-setting sessions are conducted, and the MBO process recycles.

Referent Power The power of a leader that is based on the leader's attractiveness. The leader is admired because of certain personal qualities, and the follower identifies closely with those qualities.

Relationship Behavior The extent to which leaders maintain personal relationships with members of their group through supportive, sensitive, and facilitative behavior.

Resource Requirements Planning (RRP) An advanced application of MRP that includes all the resources required to produce a product or service. Bills of resources identify required materials and labor, machines, capital, cash, and any and all other resources.

Reward Power The power generated by followers' perception that compliance with the wishes of leaders can lead to positive rewards (e.g., promotion).

Risk Decisions Decision situations in which managers do not know for certain the probability of occurrence of the state of nature or competitive actions. However, they have some past experience and/or data upon which they can rely to develop probabilities. These probabilities are used with conditional values to determine expected values.

Robot A reprogrammable, multifunctional manipulator designed to move material, parts, tools, or specialized devices through programmed motions.

Safety Stock The quantity of materials that management decides is necessary to have on hand at all times to guard against stock-outs due to unforeseen circumstances.

Salaries Compensation based on time. The unit of time is a week, a month, or longer.

Sample Survey Collection of data from a limited number of units that are assumed to be representative of the entire group.

Scalar Chain The graded chain of authority through which all organizational communications flow.

Scientific Management The practices introduced by Frederick W. Taylor to accomplish the management job. Taylor advocated the use of scientific procedures to find the one best way to do a job.

Self-Actualization Needs The need to fully realize one's potential.

Self-Fulfilling Prophecy The notion that what a leader expects of someone else and the way the leader treats the other person will result in the expectation coming true. For example, if a manager treats a subordinate as if he or she is lazy, the subordinate will behave in a manner to support the treatment.

Sensitivity Training An organizational change approach that focuses on the emotions and processes of interacting with people.

Services Nonmonetary programs provided by companies to employees (e.g., gymnasium facilities).

Simulation Model A model that replicates some aspect of the firm's operation. By performing step-by-step computations with the model, one duplicates the manner in which the actual system might perform.

Situational Favorableness The degree to which a (work) situation enables a leader to exert influence over a group. This concept is associated with Fiedler's theory of leadership.

Situational Theory of Leadership An approach that advocates that leaders understand their own behavior, the behavior of their subordinates, and the situation before they utilize a particular leadership style. The application of this approach requires the leader to have diagnostic skills in human behavior.

Social Loafing The tendency of a member in a group to not work hard or carry a fair share of the work, by hiding within the group structure.

Social Needs Needs for social interaction and companionship.

Social Obligation The viewpoint that business social responsibility is satisfied when profit is pursued within the constraints of appropriate law.

Social Psychology Branch of psychology dealing with the behavior of individuals as they relate to other individuals.

Social Reaction The viewpoint that business social responsibility is satisfied when business pursues profit legally and reacts to demands for correction of past wrongs.

Social Responsiveness The viewpoint that business social responsibility is satisfied when business pursues profit legally, reacts to demands, and acts to prevent future wrongs and problems.

Sociology The behavioral science that studies group behavior. It seeks general laws which explain intergroup and intragroup behavior.

Span of Control The number of subordinates who report to a superior. The span of control is a factor that affects the shape and height of an organization structure.

Stable External Environment An environment in which there is little unpredictable change.

Staff Functions Activities that contribute indirectly to the creation of the organization's output. Ordinarily, staff personnel advise line personnel.

Staffing A process that includes the forecasting of personnel needs and the recruitment, selection, placement, and training and development of employees.

Status Consensus The agreement of group members about the relative status of members of the group.

Status Hierarchy The ranking of group members within the group; that is, the prestige rank order of group members.

Stereotyping The attribution of a whole set of traits to persons on the basis of their membership in particular groups.

Strategic Business Unit (SBU) A division or product line of an organization that can be considered a "business"; an important part of the organization's portfolio plan in the strategic planning process. Management must decide which business to build, maintain, or eliminate.

Strategic Management Develops the mission, objectives, and strategies of the entire organization; the top-level decision makers in the organization.

Strategic Planning A planning process that deals with long-range goals, selection of activities to achieve those goals, and the allocation of resources to those activities.

Stress The consequence of the interaction between an event or situation and the individual, as modified by individual differences.

Strictness or Leniency Rater Errors Ratings that are lower or higher than the average ratings usually given, because of the strictness or the leniency of the rater.

Structural Change A planned change of the formally prescribed task and authority relationships in an organization's design.

Supervision A subfunction of control that refers to the oversight of subordinates' work activity.

Supportive Relations The consideration and interest displayed by a manager toward subordinates.

System An entity consisting of several interrelated parts acting interdependently. The basic parts of any system are input, transformation, and output.

System 4 Likert's people-oriented organization design, which emphasized open communication, supportiveness, inputs from employees to managers, and general supervision. The extreme opposite of System 4 is System 1 organization design.

Tall Pyramid Structure A structure that fosters narrow spans of control, a large number of management levels, and more centralized decision making.

Task Group A formal group of individuals working as a unit to complete a task.

Task Structure The degree of structure imposed on a job. The job may be routine or nonroutine. If the job is routine, it will be spelled out in detail. An inspector on the assembly line has a structured task, while the job of the research scientist has relatively little task structure.

Team Building A change technique that focuses on the interaction within a group to identify and solve problems and implement changes.

Technical Management Skill The skill of working with the resources and knowledge in a specific area. Such skill is important to first-level and middle managers.

Technological Change A planned change in the machinery, equipment, or techniques that are used to accomplish organizational goals.

Technology The types and patterns of activity, equipment, and material and the knowledge or experience used to perform tasks. Technology is an important contingency variable in organization design theory.

Theory X and Theory Y McGregor's theory that behind every management decision is a set of assumptions that a manager makes about human behavior. The Theory X manager assumes that people are lazy, dislike work, want no responsibility, and prefer to be closely directed. The Theory Y manager assumes that people seek responsibility, like to work, and are committed to doing good work if rewards are received for achievement.

Time Series Analysis A statistical technique for analyzing the relationship between a specified variable and time.

Time Study The process of determining the appropriate elapsed time for the completion of a task or job. This process was developed as part of Frederick W. Taylor's effort to determine a fair day's work.

Top Management The top level of an administrative hierarchy. Managers at this level coordinate the work of other managers but do not report to a manager.

Total Quality Control An approach to quality in organizations that seeks to achieve continual quality improvements through the involvement and commitment of all employees.

Training A continual process of helping employees to perform at a high level. Training may occur on the job or at a special training facility.

Trait Theory Attempts to specify which personal characteristics (physical, personality, mental) are associated with leadership effectiveness. Trait theory relies on research that relates various traits to effectiveness criteria.

Transactional Analysis A behavioral change approach designed to give individuals insight into their impact on others and their interpersonal communication style.

Uncertainty Decisions Decision situations in which no past experiences or historical data are available. Any one of a number of criteria is employed, depending upon the personality of the manager.

Unity of Command A management principle that states that each subordinate should report to only one superior.

Unity of Direction The process of grouping all related activities under one superior.

Universalistic Approach to Organization Design A set of ideas which concludes that there exists only one effective design for all organizations regardless of setting.

Unsatisfied Need The starting point in the process of motivation. It is a deficiency of something within the individual that provides the spark that leads to behavior.

Upward Communication Communication that flows from individuals at lower levels of an organization structure to those at higher levels. Some of the most common upward communication flows are suggestion boxes, group meetings, and appeal or grievance procedures.

Value Set A lasting set of convictions held by a person, an accompanying mode of conduct, and the importance of the convictions to the person.

Variable Budgeting A form of budgeting that targets expected costs at various potential output levels.

Variable Costs Costs that vary with changes in production. For example, as the number of units produced increases, the amount of material used also increases. Thus, the cost of material used to produce a product would be an example of variable costs.

Vertical Specialization of Management The process by which the right to command is delegated downward so as to create a hierarchy of positions graded by degrees of assigned authority.

Vroom–Yetton Theory A situational theory of leadership that attempts to identify the appropriate leadership style for a given set of circumstances or situations. The leadership styles are defined in terms of the extent to which the subordinates participate in decision making.

Wages Compensations based on the time an employee works or the number of units produced.

Waiting-Line Models Waiting-line models enable the manager to reach optimal decisions in facilities planning. They help in striking a balance between the cost of additional facilities and some other factor such as idle time or customer ill will.

Weighted Checklist A rating system consisting of statements that describe various types and levels of behavior for a particular job. Each of the statements is weighted according to its importance.

Work Overload Two types of overload: *quantitative*—when a person has too many different things to do or an insufficient amount of time to do the job; *qualitative*—when a person feels a lack of ability to do a part of the job.

Photo Credits

Part I

Page 2: Background photo courtesy of IBM, Inc.; inset photo courtesy of The Library of Congress.

Chapter 1

Page 4: Courtesy of IBM, Inc. Page 8: Courtesy of Texaco. Page 11: Courtesy of Honeywell. Page 12: Courtesy of Hewlett-Packard.

Chapter 2

Page 24: Courtesy of Hewlett-Packard. Page 37: Courtesy of Erica Lauf. Page 52: Courtesy of Delta Air Lines.

Chapter 3

Page 62: Courtesy of The Convention and Visitors Bureau of Greater Cleveland (Nesnadny & Schwartz). Page 67: Courtesy of Stew Leonard's/ Dave LaBianca. Page 70: Courtesy of Erica Lauf. Page 79: Courtesy of Honeywell.

Part II

Page 96: Background photo courtesy of IBM, Inc.; inset photo courtesy of IBM, Inc.

Chapter 4

Page 108: Courtesy of IBM, Inc. Page 115: Courtesy of the Illinois Department of Transportation. Page 123: Courtesy of Erica Lauf. Page 127: Courtesy of Amoco Oil Company.

Chapter 5

Page 136: Courtesy of Hewlett-Packard. Page 149: Courtesy of Gillette.

Chapter 6

Page 162: Courtesy of Texaco, Inc. Page 166: Courtesy of IBM, Inc. Page 182: Courtesy of the U.S. Army.

Chapter 7

Page 192: Courtesy of IBM, Inc. Page 197: Courtesy of the District of Columbia Department of Tourism. Page 202: Courtesy of General Motors Corp.

Chapter 8

Page 222: Courtesy of General Motors Corp. Page 227: Courtesy of NASA. Page 236: Courtesy of Erica Lauf.

Chapter 9

Page 252: Courtesy of Woodhead Industries, Inc. Page 259: Courtesy of the U.S. Army. Page 270: Courtesy of Amoco Oil Company.

Part III

Page 290: Background photo courtesy of Texas Instruments; inset photo courtesy of the Library of Congress.

Chapter 10

Page 300: Courtesy of Woodhead Industries, Inc. Page 305: Courtesy of the New York State Commerce Department. Page 306: Courtesy of Erica Lauf.

Chapter 11

Page 338: Courtesy of Hewlett-Packard. Page 354: Courtesy of the New York State Commerce Department. Page 362: Courtesy of Xerox Corporation.

Chapter 12

Page 378: Courtesy of Hewlett-Packard. Page 383: Courtesy of The Library of Congress. Page 389: Courtesy of IBM, Inc. Page 406: Courtesy of Erica Lauf.

Chapter 13

Page 418: Courtesy of IBM, Inc. Page 430: Courtesy of Erica Lauf. Page 432: Courtesy of Erica Lauf.

Chapter 14

Page 450: Courtesy of Toyota. Page 460: Courtesy of Amoco Oil Company. Page 465: Courtesy of IBM, Inc.

Part IV

Page 492: Background photo courtesy of General Motors Corp.; inset photo courtesy of General Motors Corp.

Chapter 15

Page 500: Courtesy of Sunoco. Page 511: Courtesy of Erica Lauf. Page 522: Courtesy of Burger King.

Chapter 16

Page 532: Courtesy of General Motors Corp. Page 538 (left): Courtesy of Honeywell; Page 538 (right): Courtesy of IBM, Inc. Page 542: Courtesy of Erica Lauf.

Chapter 17

Page 562: Courtesy of Hewlett-Packard. Page 567: Courtesy of IBM, Inc. Page 572: Courtesy of Erica Lauf.

Chapter 18

Page 586: Courtesy of IBM, Inc. Page 598: Courtesy of Wellborn Cabinets, Inc./C. Akers. Page 603: Courtesy of Erica Lauf.

Chapter 19

Page 616: Courtesy of IBM, Inc. Page 623: Courtesy of Honeywell. Page 632: Courtesy of Erica Lauf.

Part V

Page 650: Background photo courtesy of The Federal Reserve Bank of Chicago; inset photo courtesy of The Federal Reserve Bank of Chicago.

Chapter 20

Page 656: Courtesy of Domino's Pizza, Inc. Page 669: Courtesy of Kwik Kopy.

Chapter 21

Page 692: Courtesy of Kentucky Fried Chicken, Inc. Page 701: Courtesy of the New York State Commerce Department. Page 706: Courtesy of IBM, Inc.

Chapter 22

Page 732: Courtesy of Toyota. Page 738: Courtesy of Erica Lauf. Page 753: Courtesy of Erica Lauf.

Name Index

Company Index

SUBJECT INDEX